The Kerr/Haslam Inquiry

Volume 1 of 2

**Presented to Parliament by
the Secretary of State for Health
by Command of Her Majesty**

July 2005

Cm 6640 – I   £97.50

Contents

Section Three: The Michael Haslam Story

Section Four: The response of the GPs

Section Five: Barriers to making complaints

Volume 2 contains the following material

Section Six: Problematic activities

Section Seven: New developments that need monitoring

Section Eight: Some answers

Foreword
by the Chairman of the Inquiry

It is my privilege to present this Report, as Chairman of the Inquiry. I do so in the hope that it will assist in understanding the problem of the sexual abuse of psychiatric patients, and in the expectation that our recommendations, if taken up, will enable the National Health Service to respond more effectively to the needs of those of us who use mental health services.

The Secretary of State for Health set up my Inquiry as one of three Inquiries looking at how the National Health Service dealt with concerns and complaints against four named doctors. It has surprised those of us working on the Kerr/Haslam Inquiry that it has taken so long to send our Report to the current Secretary of State, the third to occupy that post since the Inquiry was originally commissioned.

A private Inquiry is a time-consuming process. We detail in our Report some of the reasons for that. We started of course with the disadvantage that we were enquiring into concerns and complaints relating to two clinicians running more or less consecutively for over 20 years.

We also found that patients came forward to us in greater numbers than to either the Ayling or the Neale Inquiry, together with which we formed "The Three Inquiries". We again give reasons in our Report on why this should be so. One common theme across all three Reports is that it was only through feeling that they were not alone in making complaints, and doing so with the support of others, that patients were able to explain why they believed the NHS had failed them. I place on record my thanks to all those former patients who gave evidence to the Inquiry. I fully appreciate how, for many of them, it was a difficult and distressing experience. I hope they will be able to feel that they have achieved some sort of "closure" with the Report's publication. I also extend my appreciation to the present and former staff of the local NHS authorities – including clinicians, nurses, GPs, administrators and managers. Almost without exception they came forward, provided detailed evidence and offered helpful information; and they did so knowing that they would be subjected to close examination and possible criticism. I, and the members of my Panel, were extremely impressed by the level of willing cooperation we received. It does credit to the NHS, and causes us to be optimistic that existing structural and cultural problems identified in the Report can be rectified.

Another reason for the time taken, and the fact that we had to consider much more information than our sister Inquiries, was perhaps that our field of concern may also have been wider. The former patients of William Kerr and Michael Haslam raised issues involving both primary and secondary care providers perhaps in equal measure. Unique difficulties were presented by the problems of psychiatric treatment.

All of these and other issues meant that it took longer to ensure that we got things right. Where we have failed to do so, it is not through lack of effort. We have tried to keep any mistakes of fact or attribution out of this Report; if, despite our best efforts, they have crept in, they are mistakes honestly made.

I record here that the support of the Secretariat and Legal teams has served us well. Bruce Carr, ably supported by the skill and hard work of Clare Brown, is a first rate Counsel who tested the evidence presented to the Inquiry thoroughly and fairly. Michael Fitzgerald and Duncan Henderson got through a huge amount of work that sadly has become the lot of solicitors to Inquiries. Stephen Taylor, Tom Brennan, Karoon Akoon and David Altberg all provided us, and them, with paralegal support that could be relied upon.

The Secretariat was led by Colin Phillips, supported by his team of John Miller, Kypros Menicou, Emily Frost, Philip Otton, Virginia Berkholz and Gurjeev Johal. They all worked tirelessly to ensure that our procedures were followed, and the Inquiry was kept operating at full stretch. Dr Ruth Chadwick ensured that the team of Experts we consulted provided us with the most relevant, up-to-date and useful information and advice. They were enormously helpful, and their work was of the highest standards. All of this team, together with Dr Kathryn Ehrich, contributed greatly to our Part Two Seminars that looked at the wider issues raised during the earlier stage of the Inquiry's deliberations.

I am grateful to all those mentioned above for their hard work, professionalism and dedication. This leads me on to thanking my colleagues Ros Alstead and Ruth Lesirge, my fellow Panel members, for their huge contribution in considering all the issues, information and evidence before us and producing the Report that I have today been able to pass over to the Secretary of State for Health for consideration. They have been supportive throughout, providing constant assistance, analysis and insights. The recommendations made today owe much to their input. I am extremely grateful for their advice and support.

Finally, as noted above, I hope that the recommendations we have made will be taken up by those responsible for their implementation. We acknowledge in the Report that much progress has been made in many areas since the time that the incidents happened. Only when a system is in place that enables the voices of psychiatric patients and concerned NHS staff to be heard, and appropriate action to be taken, can we be confident that the situations described in our Report will not be repeated. That is the aspiration for us all.

Executive summary and Recommendations

General

1   This Inquiry begins in many ways at the end of the factual story. That end was the conviction in 2000 and 2003 respectively of two consultant psychiatrists both working during the 1970s and 1980s in the same psychiatric hospital in York, North Yorkshire. William Kerr was convicted (in his absence, on a Trial of the Facts) of one count of indecent assault, and Michael Haslam of four counts of indecent assault (a conviction of rape was quashed on appeal). The victims in all these cases were vulnerable female psychiatric patients, who had gone to their consultants for treatment, seeking help. In most if not all cases, the effect upon the women of the breach of trust that occurred has been devastating. Although Michael Haslam has been convicted and has served a prison sentence, he has consistently denied any form of wrongdoing in relation to his patients. This denial applies not only to the cases where he has been convicted, but to all allegations made against him by any former patient referred to in this Report. We have no doubt that William Kerr likewise would deny all the allegations that have been made to the Inquiry. It is of course completely regrettable that the concerns and complaints, and these denials, were not examined fully and as contemporaneously as possible. It is regrettable from the perspective of the patients, the two consultants, and from the more general users of the local health service. However, that sense of regret did not dictate or influence the Inquiry. We must deal with the situation as we find it, not as we would wish it to be.

2   At the outset we posed these central questions:

- How could it be that the voices of the patients and former patients of William Kerr and Michael Haslam were not heard?

- Why were so many opportunities to respond and investigate missed?

- How could it happen that abuse of patients, evidenced by the convictions of William Kerr and Michael Haslam, went undetected for so long?

3   In order to attempt an explanation, this Inquiry has sought to examine the events that occurred in the hospitals, clinics and GP surgeries of North Yorkshire, primarily during the 1970s and 1980s.

4   The story that has emerged is not one of a deliberate conspiracy by healthcare professionals knowingly acting to conceal sexual misdemeanours (or worse) of two of their consultant colleagues. It is mainly but not entirely a story of committed and caring doctors, nurses, psychologists and others. But, for a complex of reasons that we attempt to unravel in our Report, no matter how committed and caring they may have been, many nevertheless ignored warning bells or dismissed rumours and some chose to remain silent when they should have been raising their voices.

5   It is also a story of management failure, failed communication, poor record keeping and a culture where the consultant was all-powerful.

6   While the majority stood back, there were, as in all such stories, some who stepped forward, and this account also seeks to examine why even those lone voices were not heard.

7   Above all this is an account of psychiatric patients, many in number, whose concerns and complaints fell on deaf ears. Added to that number were many more patients who, for a variety of understandable reasons, did not make any contemporaneous complaint, but who have found the strength and courage to come forward to the Inquiry. We know that there are others who have chosen to remain silent. As set out in the Report, there are many more alleged incidents identified by former patients than the five counts of sexual assault referred to above. Although, in accordance with our Terms of Reference, we record those concerns and complaints, whether or not raised at the time, we do not – nor could we – make any attempt to decide whether or not any concern or complaint is true or false. That is not our function.

8   Against this background of concerns and complaints that were dismissed at the time as incredible, ignored or simply not heard, we, as an Inquiry, have sought, at all times, to listen.

Nature and chronology of concerns and complaints raised concerning the practice and conduct of William Kerr and Michael Haslam

William Kerr

9   William Kerr started working as a locum Senior House Officer in psychiatry at Clifton Hospital in York in 1965; he was appointed as consultant in 1967, a post he held until his retirement in 1988.

10   During the course of the Inquiry we received evidence indicating that 38 former patients claimed they made disclosures to NHS staff of sexualised behaviour by William Kerr before his retirement. Not one of these led to any investigation of his practice.

11   The number of patients who have subsequently come forward alleging that they were subjected to some form of sexualised behaviour[1] by Kerr brings the total number of those who now make allegations against him to at least 67.

12   The first complaint against William Kerr in North Yorkshire was in his very first year in the post, 1965. This, as with so many subsequent cases, was a concern communicated by a patient to her GP. However, in a pattern that was to be repeated many times, no formal complaint was lodged by the patient with the hospital authorities or with William Kerr's employer, nor did any GP take the initiative to pursue the matter. The complaint progressed no further than forming part of the reserve of knowledge of one particular GP.

13   However, this was not the first time an allegation of sexual misconduct had been raised. William Kerr had left his previous post in Northern Ireland in 1964 after an internal disciplinary hearing concerning an allegation of inappropriate sexual conduct with a patient (the details of which remain unclear).

14   Concerns continued to be raised about William Kerr throughout his career. The accounts we heard from patients were strikingly similar. The allegations were of unscheduled domiciliary visits, or appointments being arranged for the end of clinics when there would be few nursing staff around. William Kerr would then

---

1 In this Report we have used the phrase "sexualised behaviour" to mean "acts, words and behaviour designed or intended to arouse or gratify sexual impulses and desires".

allegedly expose himself and "invite" patients to perform sexual acts (often of masturbation or oral sex) upon him, sometimes suggesting that this was part of their treatment. A number of patients also alleged that full sexual intercourse took place. A number of women described William Kerr's ability to make them comply with his wishes, leaving them confused and guilty about their own actions and afraid to complain in forthright terms.

15   In many cases the alleged recipients of these complaints, most typically GPs, but also community psychiatric nurses, hospital nurses and consultants, deny or have no recollection of any complaint. One of the major problems facing this Inquiry has been the passage of time since the events in question and the resultant fading memories. It has been difficult to conclude in each case, with any degree of certainty, whether a complaint was made – and if made, to whom, and in what precise terms. Were all these women mistaken when they told us that they raised concerns, that they made complaints? In our judgment the answer is clearly "No". We are satisfied that a significant number of concerns, whether or not raised as formal complaints, were voiced but not heard. Despite what appears to be a marked reluctance by recipients to make any contemporaneous note, even by some who acknowledge that they were very serious complaints of alleged wrongdoing, a few records have survived.

16   In the period prior to 1983, of the 30 concerns alleged to have been raised about William Kerr all but one fell on deaf ears.

17   The exception was the case of Patient A22[2]. In 1979 this patient complained to her GP, Dr Wade, about advances made by William Kerr, who allegedly propositioned her during a domiciliary visit. Dr Wade accepted Patient A22's concerns as being true, and linked the concerns with William Kerr's reputation of "potentially flirting with some [female] patients". It is one of the great ironies in this account that the consultant to whom Dr Wade chose to speak about his concerns regarding William Kerr was Michael Haslam. Perhaps unsurprisingly, given his attitude to sexual contact between patients and doctors, Michael Haslam did not take the matter any further or

2 From here onwards, we refer to the former patients of William Kerr and Michael Haslam specifically. To preserve confidentiality, as far as we can, and anonymity, we have adopted the practice of referring to them by a code. We did this both in correspondence with Inquiry participants and at the oral hearings. To increase confidentiality we have adopted different codes in our final Report.

raise it as an issue with the Regional Health Authority (William Kerr's employer).

18 In 1983 an account of an alleged sexual relationship between a psychiatric patient, Patient A17, and her treating consultant, William Kerr, was disclosed[3] to Deputy Sister Linda Bigwood – not by way of complaint, but as part of the patient's life story. Linda Bigwood, unlike so many of her colleagues, was not prepared to "turn a blind eye", and pursued her concerns about William Kerr's alleged sexual misconduct towards not only Patient A17 but a number of patients, with the hospital authorities, the District Health Authority and beyond that with the Regional Health Authority.

19 Despite letters and meetings setting out her concerns over a period of almost five years involving the most senior NHS managers, and despite the support of her union representatives, no investigation was ever made into William Kerr's practice and he retired in 1988 with a letter of thanks for his "valuable contribution" to the health service in the Yorkshire region. Linda Bigwood, in contrast – and as with many other so-called "whistle-blowers" – in personally raising the issue of how the complaints were handled, herself suffered professional detriment.

Michael Haslam

20 Michael Haslam took up his post as Consultant in Psychological Medicine at Clifton Hospital, York, and Harrogate District Hospital in 1970.

21 During the course of the Inquiry we received evidence indicating that at least eight patients had, during his time in York, raised concerns about his alleged sexual advances towards them. Many of the allegations involved offering friendship and social activities outside the clinical setting, leading later to the development of a personal, sexual, relationship.

22 The number of patients who have subsequently come forward alleging that they were sexually propositioned or assaulted by

3 We have also used the term "disclosure" to refer to information that passed between individuals. Some of those "disclosures" amounted to allegations against William Kerr and Michael Haslam. We make no comment on the veracity of those allegations but regard all such "disclosures" as information that should have been acted upon at the time.

Michael Haslam brings the total number of those who have now made allegations against him to at least 10.

23   The first complaint against Michael Haslam known to us occurred in 1974 when Patient B1 informed her GP, Dr Foggitt, that (allegedly) she had been having an affair with Michael Haslam. However, in a pattern that echoed the response to complaints regarding William Kerr, this was never pursued either by the patient herself or by Dr Foggitt as a formal complaint or as an issue that needed to be reported to health service management – even with the identity of the patient concealed.

24   While the number of patients who raised concerns about Michael Haslam was far smaller than in the case of William Kerr, concerns continued to be raised at intervals throughout his career, notably in 1976 (Patient B2), in 1981 (Patient AB) and in 1984 (Patient B3). It is to be noted that although the expressions of concern are very different from the allegations made in relation to William Kerr, they nonetheless share a striking similarity to each other.

25   Michael Haslam practised a range of treatments not widely known about or used within mental health settings. One such treatment was full-body massage (carried out without a chaperone). The Inquiry heard evidence on how on occasions this was carried out in isolated parts of the hospital or out of hours.

26   In three cases attempts were made to commence a formal complaint by means of letters (in the case of Patient B2, from solicitors) or a written statement. However, in none of the cases did matters progress to an investigation, no patient apparently being prepared to go through with a formal complaints procedure.

27   The stories of Michael Haslam and William Kerr, perhaps inevitably, overlap. Indeed, Linda Bigwood, whose efforts as a whistle-blower were concentrated on William Kerr, also brought concerns about Michael Haslam to the attention of management.

28   In 1987 Patient B5 complained to her GP of being propositioned by Michael Haslam. The GP concerned, Dr Moroney, raised the issue with the hospital management (Dr Kennedy). However, in a now familiar pattern, the disinclination of the patient to proceed with a

formal complaint marked the end of the matter and no investigation of Michael Haslam's practice was conducted.

29   It was not until the complaint by Patient B7 in 1988 of sexual assault that any real attempt was made to collate the previous allegations against Michael Haslam. Even at this stage, no investigation was launched and Michael Haslam was allowed, perhaps even encouraged, to retire from the NHS.

30   Unlike William Kerr, however, Michael Haslam's retirement from the NHS did not mark the end of his medical practice. He continued to work in the private sector and we are aware of at least one complaint that arose relating to the period when he was in private practice.

31   While Michael Haslam left the NHS under something of a cloud (though not according to Michael Haslam, and not known to many within the NHS), he was still subsequently appointed an honorary NHS consultant in 1989 in York. In addition, he was subsequently appointed as the non-clinical Medical Director in Durham. There was no investigation of his practice until the police investigation of William Kerr caused allegations about Michael Haslam to come into the open, prompting an internal NHS inquiry in 1997/98 (known as "the Manzoor Inquiry") and subsequently (following further allegations) a criminal trial. Michael Haslam finally retired from medical practice, and took voluntary erasure from the Medical Register, in 1999.

The procedures then in place for raising concerns about healthcare professionals

32   The systems (and procedures) within the NHS that enabled legitimate concerns and complaints to be raised were in fact part of the problem facing patients and staff from the 1960s through to the present day. The detail of the relevant systems and procedures and their operation is contained in Chapter 31 and Annex 5 of the Report. We describe the barriers that the organisation itself presented to complaints that were raised – see Section 5. We detail, at length, many of the individual specific complaints and how they were handled.

33   Very few patients wanted, or were robust enough, to make a formal complaint. Our clear impression is of a system that was difficult and obstructive. It was neither "user friendly" nor designed to ensure that patient safety was paramount. Those who came through it did so in spite of it, and were left damaged and disillusioned by it. Most never made it through the labyrinth of artificial barriers, unnecessary formalities and plain obstruction to any kind of resolution of issues. Patient complainants largely got nowhere; professional complainants often fared worse, attracting blame, criticism and a degree of professional ostracism that deterred others from following their lead.

34   Nowhere was the voice of the complainant listened to with enthusiasm or support. It is clear that procedures protected the status quo at the expense of much needed reform. It was a situation that changed all too slowly and, without doubt, resulted in damage and frustration for patients and their supporters alike.

Actions taken in response to concerns

35   The uncomfortable reality is that during the NHS employment of William Kerr and Michael Haslam:

- there was no detailed consideration/assessment of any complaint raised about their conduct and practice;

- any remedial action that might have been necessary was not taken, and;

- the consultants continued to practise without restraint, despite concerns having been reported.

The response of GPs

36   The response of GPs, who in many instances were the first and often only recipient of concerns expressed by patients of William Kerr and Michael Haslam, was varied.

37   Deputy Sister Linda Bigwood (one of the few key whistle-blowers in the William Kerr story) described a general concern among Harrogate GPs about William Kerr, such that some refused to refer female patients to him. Despite this, no attempt was made by NHS management at the time (whether at Regional or District level) to investigate whether or not the concerns were true. We are sure that William Kerr would have denied the allegations, but they were not

even put to him for his denial to be recorded. The failure by the local GPs to respond is a striking feature of the William Kerr story. In our Inquiry, some 20 years later, we found only one instance of a GP, Dr Wade, taking any active steps to pursue a complaint about William Kerr. This led Dr Wade, not unreasonably, to William Kerr's fellow consultant Michael Haslam, who did nothing to pursue Dr Wade's concerns. The complaint did not progress further.

38   The first complaint concerning Michael Haslam of which the Inquiry is aware was communicated to a GP, Dr Foggitt. In the same way as GPs had failed to forward their concerns about William Kerr to any higher authority, Dr Foggitt (although he took steps to refer his patient, Patient B1, to another consultant) did not seek to inform the authorities of Michael Haslam's alleged sexual relationship with Patient B1. Michael Haslam denies any wrongdoing in relation to Patient B1, but again the allegations we have heard were not put to any form of test, they were not the subject of any inquiry – they just became part of the unarticulated background to Michael Haslam's practice. On evidence received by the Inquiry, this 1974 allegation was the first; had it been investigated, admitted or found to be true, and suitable action taken, then patient safety might have been secured.

39   The later complaints against Michael Haslam, arising in 1987 and 1988, provoked a very different response from two GPs, Dr Moroney and Dr Moran. This is perhaps explicable by the gradual change of culture that had occurred by this stage. Both Dr Moroney (in relation to Patient B5's complaint) and Dr Moran (in relation to Patient B7's complaint) appear to have recognised both the severity of the allegation and the necessity of referring these matters on to the authorities (in the form of Dr Kennedy). Both were new GPs and, perhaps less restrained by the historical culture of a degree of tolerance towards sexualised behaviour by psychiatrists, were prepared to challenge the status quo.

40   In response to patient complaints and concerns, the first point we make is that many of those to whom they were made did not, or would not, hear them. GPs failed to pass on a complaint or concern. Material and relevant information was not properly received and actioned. Clear messages were ignored, hints were not taken up and silences were not explored.

41   As a culture we can characterise it as unhealthy. Professionals were reluctant to take action against consultants, through either a misguided sense of loyalty or fear of confrontation. Administrators felt powerless, and devised mechanisms to protect themselves, rather than the patients or those who raised concerns. Responsibility for action was fragmented and unclear; policy and protocols were confusing or were incorrectly implemented, if at all. As a consequence, responses at virtually all levels were inadequate and unconvincing. Some of this paucity of response was due to lack of ability or to lack of training; some of it arose through lack of clarity on how best to proceed. Sadly, some of the failure arose because it was easier, perhaps professionally safer, to do little or nothing at all.

42   As a consequence, patients were routinely disbelieved, were thought to have invented or exaggerated their concerns or complaints, and were treated neither fairly nor with the respect their situation required. Health professionals did not, in general, see their role as supporting patients in following through their concerns and complaints unless clear, unequivocal and incontrovertible evidence demanded it. In other words, if there was a possible "other side", or a mere denial by the consultant, the matter did not proceed. Even if there was any forward movement, procrastination and delay helped to diminish the impact of concerns and complaints – with damaging consequences. Nor, in general, did NHS staff initiate action in support of patient safety.

43   The result was that in both cases the consultants, despite considerable and widespread doubts as to the propriety of their behaviour, were able to retire, with some distinction, from the NHS. When it became apparent that all was not as it should be, the GMC was, it seems, unable to do more than grant them voluntary erasure from the Register and allow them to take an unscathed retirement. Indeed, retirement was seen as a solution by the authorities and as an end to a difficult and time-consuming problem. To the former patients it was seen as an escape, a trapdoor to freedom that they were loath to allow either doctor to use. It compounded the sense of injustice and grievance that many of them have told us they felt.

Contributing factors impeding appropriate investigation and action

44   In our view the root causes of this comprehensive failure to attend to patient concerns can be categorised under the following five headings.

Organisational

- Lack of rigour in recruitment and appointment practices
- Failure to examine/explore references
- Power and influence of defensive legal advice
- Poor and fragmented disciplinary procedures
- Lack of standard procedures and consistency for the writing and storage of records
- No formal process for supporting patients
- Several changes of NHS hospital and management structures
- Intermittent shortage of psychiatrists

Cultural

- Consultants had undue power and unclear accountability
- Prime loyalty to medical colleagues and a tolerance of sexualised behaviour
- Lack of knowledge (or acceptance of the knowledge) that doctors might abuse their patients
- No attempt to investigate/explore recurring rumours
- A predominantly male hierarchy of doctors and a predominantly female nursing cohort, which reinforced gender power relations
- Patient fears of retribution, punishment and/or withdrawal of treatment – or other adverse consequences

Structural

- Consensus management, which militated against leadership and pro-activity
- A separation of domains between general practice and hospitals, which made it difficult for GPs to identify how to raise concerns

- A management hierarchy for each function within the NHS, with no overview of the whole

- No requirement for continuous professional development learning or appraisal of senior doctors

Professional practice

- Absence of multi-disciplinary working

- Over-rigid interpretation, or even misinterpretation, of the legal position pertaining to the requirement for patient confidentiality – such that it overrode patient safety

- A belief that doctors could not harm patients – and a reluctance to discuss what was and was not acceptable behaviour

- Willingness to let doctors use therapies that were not understood by, or known to, colleagues and peers

- Lack of supervision/monitoring of domestic visits

- Lack of a structured and monitored appointments system

- Inadequate processes for GPs' sharing of information

- Different codes of practice for GPs and hospital doctors

- A willingness to resolve the issue of "problems with doctors" through retirement, promotion or a move to a different post

- Slowness and opacity of GMC processes

Individual failings

- Hospital doctors and GPs who did not act on concerns or complaints

- Nursing staff who failed to report concerns and ignored patient concerns

- NHS managers who neglected to take action, took a line of least resistance and failed to investigate expressed concerns

- Michael Haslam's failure to pass on concerns expressed by a GP

- A social worker, a counsellor and a psychologist, all of whom failed to report alleged disclosures by patients

- NHS managers who focused on the disciplinary issues raised by the actions of a whistle-blower, but failed to investigate to its conclusion the allegations and disclosures reported

45   So, we ask, how did this culture develop? To the rhetorical question "Do you think allegations of abuse by doctors should be ignored?" there is plainly only one answer, a resounding "No". Yet the culture did develop, or was allowed to develop, and that culture shaped the events upon which we have had to report. At times we felt that the structure of the NHS complaints system rendered the outcome of these events almost inevitable, if only because of the persisting requirement for a patient to be willing to make, and pursue, a formal complaint.

46   As stated, one recurring theme was the interpretation of the term "patient confidentiality" by those who were in a position to react positively to protect patients. All too often it was misunderstood, or used as an excuse to do nothing. We expand on the reasons for this in Chapter 28 of our Report

47   Our overall conclusion on this topic is that the way the NHS handled complaints in the 1970s and 1980s – perhaps even the 1990s – presented considerable barriers, so that all but the most determined and resolute were unable, or unwilling, to scale them.

What has changed?

48   We have detected a significant change – beginning in the 1990s and carrying through to the present day – in both attitudes and systems. The reasons for this change can be found in the pressure from public expectations, the impact of scandals (national and local), and the approach of new and different personnel to the needs of patients. Many professionals who gave evidence to the Inquiry describing their response to concerns and complaints in the 1970s and 1980s stated that they would act differently now. We think that this evidence reflects a broadly held view. Awareness at both a professional and a public level has heightened.

49   There is not only a willingness to change, but there are now in place systems throughout the NHS – some say too many systems – that treat the patient as consumer, entitled to be dissatisfied and to express dissatisfaction. During the time covered by this Inquiry such

systems, if they existed at all, were unclear or unworkable and were at best off-putting and fragmented. As a general statement, it is now true that professionals and patients know they can complain and receive some support, and they are not stigmatised for complaining. It is usual for their complaint to be treated with respect from the outset. In summary, we feel the climate is changing and improving, but patient safety demands that more still needs to be achieved.

50   Complaints systems are not the only way for the NHS to manage poor performance. Other governance systems have recently developed within the NHS, together with regulatory inspectoral bodies such as the Healthcare Commission. We are confident that scope for further improvement is to be found in this wider approach to improving standards, and protecting patient safety by identifying and addressing failings at an early stage, rather than allowing them to go unnoticed and/or unchecked for years, even decades.

51   Whistle-blowing policies for staff have existed since 1997. However, following high profile cases that identified failures to tackle issues highlighted by whistle-blowers (within and outside the NHS), there is greater confidence among some, but not yet all, staff in reporting their concerns.

52   Data from all these sources is now brought together for trend analysis and reported to Trust Boards through clinical governance arrangements. Risk management systems are regularly tested to meet standards by two external bodies – the risk pooling scheme (RPST) and the clinical negligence scheme (CNST).

53   Improved complaints systems, governance techniques, incident and "serious untoward incident" reporting systems all combine to produce this improved position. Serious work remains to be done in relation to ensuring that NHS staff are not only familiar with the systems and techniques but that they understand and appreciate why they are needed, and (most importantly) are prepared to learn and do learn from things that have gone wrong

The future

54   We are required by our Terms of Reference to make recommendations informed by our investigations as to improvements that should be made to the policies and procedures that are currently

in place within the health service, taking into account the changes in procedures since the events in question.

55   The situation is different from that which existed when William Kerr and Michael Haslam were working in the NHS. Further changes have of course occurred since they both retired. Today, mental healthcare is predominantly provided as a community based service within patients' homes and other non-hospital based settings such as resource centres.

56   We have considered the way forward against the following, we trust uncontentious, standard:

> Everyone has the right to be cared for and treated by medical professionals without fear of being subjected to sexual exploitation, sexual advances, and any form of sexualised behaviour.

57   In making our recommendations our guiding principles have been:

- a concern that the sexual abuse of vulnerable adult patients did not end with the retirement of William Kerr and Michael Haslam, and may be far more prevalent than hitherto realised or accepted;

- a recognition that the abuse of patients is, and should be treated as, very unusual, and that the vast majority of healthcare professionals (including consultant psychiatrists) are not and never have been guilty of any form of abuse;

- a recognition that allegations of sexual abuse, of whatever kind, are not all genuine;

- a recognition that allegations of sexual abuse are easy to make, and difficult to refute;

- an acceptance that doctors, and other healthcare workers, are entitled to expect protection from untrue allegations of sexual abuse;

- an acceptance that the complaints systems in place in North Yorkshire (and nationally) during the 1970s and 1980s have significantly changed over the years, and are still changing;

- a recognition that trust between patient and doctor is of central importance. Insofar as it has been damaged by the allegations made in recent years, including the allegations (whether true or not) listed in this Report, then every effort should be undertaken to restore that trust.

58   Although our recommendations are focused largely on psychiatrists, many will have a wider application to all mental healthcare professionals. We have been concerned to discover the lack of attention and resources given to the examination of the prevalence of sexualised behaviour (alleged or established). Such abusive behaviour is recorded neither consistently nor comprehensively. Given that it is the overwhelming view of the profession that an intimate relationship between doctor and patient is always harmful, this situation must be addressed immediately. The kind of behaviour that leads to what may become a charge of sexual assault needs to be detected at an early stage and action taken to prevent it developing into yet more serious and more harmful activity. To this end we feel that a code of ethics for all staff, most particularly in the context of our Inquiry for psychiatrists, detailing what is and is not acceptable, will be a valuable and useful tool for the profession and those monitoring it. We are sure that routinely offering trained chaperones to mental health patients whenever a doctor performs any kind of intimate personal examination is a move that will help address this issue.

59   There is an immediate need to address the issue of recording, storing and destroying records. Different standards apply across the NHS; this leads to confusion and inequity and provides a poor measure of monitoring and control.

60   We have briefly addressed in the Report the issue of discipline for doctors and the way it has recently changed. The new procedures will no doubt be controlled and monitored by the GMC. Given the new sense of transparency in its work, we anticipate that the GMC will report regularly and publicly on its assessment of the impact of the new regime on doctors – particularly in the area of patient abuse.

61   We have made a range of proposals relating to complaints – how they are made, received and processed, both by patients and by health professionals. This area must be addressed urgently if the necessary climate change for the improvement of patient care is to

be effected and maintained. Only when the content of complaints is generally regarded as providing a positive opportunity for improvement will that change be made. This means to us that health professionals acting as Linda Bigwood did should be regarded as people to be treated positively and given support. They are not threats to the NHS, but the essential catalysts that will bring about better patient care and better patient protection – goals to which everyone in the NHS today should aspire. We hope that, taken as a whole, our recommendations will promote and encourage this ongoing process of change.

Core concerns

62   We set out below a full list of the detailed recommendations arising from the evidence and submissions to the Inquiry.

63   The stories of William Kerr and Michael Haslam do not lead to simple answers. We also recognise and make no apology for the fact that the recommendations are wide ranging and, in some cases, represent only the first stage in initiating further discussion. We also recognise that this Inquiry takes its place as part of a wider picture and debate, informed in particular by the Ayling, Neale and Shipman Inquiries. However, we consider it fundamental to a Report of this nature and fundamental to our duty as a panel that the reader is left in no doubt as to what we determine are the key priorities. Impact can be lost in detail. We do not want to lose that impact. We set out below what we see as the "headline" concerns of this Report.

64   Prevention of patient abuse, our first headline, must be the short and long-term goal of all professionals and managers engaged in the care and treatment of the vulnerable – child, young person, or adult. This is and must be the basis of all other recommendations. However, without a clear understanding among those both working in and using mental health services, and a clear consensus as to where the boundaries actually lie between care and abuse, no sensible progress can be made. We have confined ourselves here to the consideration of mental healthcare professionals, though recognising the wider issue of sexualised behaviour or other boundary transgressions between health service users and healthcare professionals across other areas and disciplines.

Prevention of patient abuse

65 Managers, and mental health and social care professionals, must be left in no doubt that the breach of professional boundaries with regard to their patients (service users) is unacceptable, and must always be treated as harmful. Every effort must be made to prevent all patient abuse.

66 There are a number of ways of achieving this change of ethos. We here identify three:

- *Education:* of all staff at all levels on the identification and preservation of proper boundaries, and the harm caused by boundary transgressions, commencing at undergraduate level through all the relevant professions. The message must be reinforced in induction training, in continuous professional development and through employment contracts that detail specifically unacceptable behaviour. The message must be supported by clear and enforceable codes of conduct by NHS Trusts and by the regulatory bodies. There must be clear boundaries, clear sanctions, and no tolerance of the abuse of patients.

- *Promoting the obligation to speak out:* Patient safety requires a culture where speaking out (whether or not categorised as whistle-blowing) is welcomed, where minor transgressions can be addressed at early stages and (if possible) resolved. The NHS must fully support its staff, who in turn must be left in no doubt that the culture of turning a blind eye is unacceptable, and that to stay silent may be to perpetuate and thus participate in wrongdoing. There should be no career detriment for those who speak out to promote patient safety. To support these aims, a clearer knowledge of the requirements and limitations of confidentiality is essential, and must be achieved through continuing education.

- *Promoting knowledge and skills:* Managers must recognise their responsibility in minimising the risk of abuse, and maximising its detection. This responsibility is best fulfilled from a firm base of knowledge, including knowing what treatments and therapies are being used in their organisations, and by ensuring that there is in place adequate supervision of health and social care professionals. There should be systems in place to listen, hear and respond – not confined to formal concerns or complaints, but embracing consistent and specific but "soft" information. It is not just a case of waiting for abuse to be discovered, and then reacting. Proactivity is required if there is to be any real progress in this area. In order to build on the base of knowledge, and to create a culture in which both staff and patients feel able to speak and to listen, there must be, in addition to formal complaints and discipline structures, an informal channel of communication. It is only through knowledge of what is going on at ground level, together with the skill to monitor staff performance, that managers can truly play their role in ensuring that patient abuse is prevented.

67   Our second "headline" recognises the fact that unless patients are able to come forward to raise their initial concern or complaint, even the most sophisticated system or elaborate support network will lie redundant.

A clear point of contact

68   Patients should have a clear and well-publicised point of contact if they wish to raise a concern or make a complaint about a mental health or social care professional.

69   Where the matter goes from there, and how it is handled and by whom, will require a far more complex and wide-ranging review of the complaints system. However, without the first step nothing can be achieved.

70   We would like to see a situation where any member of the public, if asked what they would do with a serious concern about the abuse of a patient by a mental health or social care professional, would know how to access the first point of contact – as they would dial 999 in an emergency. Whether this should be a national or regional "patient-line" or a dedicated complaints manager in every NHS provider organisation is a matter for debate.

71   We also consider that a similar principle should inform the route for mental health and social care professionals wishing to raise concerns about a colleague or pass on patient concerns.

72   We do not specify whether there should be a single point of contact for *all* NHS complaints – whatever the subject matter; that is for

others to resolve. However, in the area of patient abuse we consider that a single gateway is achievable and helpful, enabling the patient or professional to take the essential first step in getting the concern about patient abuse documented for future reference.

73 But we emphasise that our view is not intended to recommend an exclusive gateway, merely one that is familiar and readily accessible. We do not wish to impede, *in any way*, the raising of concerns or complaints through other routes within, or from outside, the NHS.

74 Our final "headline" is related to the fact that the Kerr/Haslam Inquiry is unique among the various Inquiries we have cited – the others being Ayling, Neale and Shipman – which all looked at the raising of complaints and concerns. The unique feature is that in our Inquiry, all those patients who alleged abuse, were mental health patients. This raises the issue of not only whether the particular allegation of "sexual abuse" needs special handling (because of the sensitivity of the subject matter) but whether, as a matter of routine, such a potentially vulnerable class of individuals requires particular support, and the matters they raise specialised and skilled investigation.

An appropriate response

75 In all cases where a complaint is made or a concern raised by a mental health patient in relation to their alleged abuse by a mental health professional, appropriate support and assistance should be offered.

76 Such support and assistance will require, at least, access to a mental health support advocacy organisation, with the necessary aptitude and independence to advise on appropriate handling of the concern or complaint. The patients of William Kerr and Michael Haslam who raised initial contemporaneous complaints went on to withdraw them or, eventually, declined to pursue matters. Had someone been readily available to step in at the outset of their concern or complaint – "patient champions" as we describe them in the Report – to offer support and mentoring, refer them for appropriate assistance, and (where possible) ensure that any investigation/interview was appropriate to their vulnerabilities, this Inquiry might have been unnecessary.

77   But care and support is but one aspect of the appropriate response by a responsible health service. If concerns and complaints relating to allegations of abuse, raised by mental health patients, are to be investigated effectively, then it is imperative that those who are given the task of responding and initiating any investigation are themselves adequately trained, are equipped with the necessary skills to carry matters forward, and are of such seniority as to ensure that barriers and resistance are overcome. We cannot over-emphasise the need for raised awareness throughout the health service of the particular issues arising in the areas we have been considering. We believe there is a need for a change of culture surrounding psychiatric care, maintenance of patient dignity and personal boundaries, and an informed recognition of the potential for abuse at its highest, and misunderstanding and distress at its lowest: neither of which are conducive to delivering good patient care. Education and a nationally agreed set of guidelines and standards must start this necessary process of change.

Recommendations

78   Our recommendations are set out here without explanation, and without being put into context. The only reference is to the chapter in the Report where they appear. In the text of the Report we refer, where appropriate, to the conclusions that led to the recommendations from the evidence we received. We also reached conclusions from consideration of all the evidence; therefore some of the recommendations do not derive from a single evidential source.

We RECOMMEND that:

Chapter 6

One of the referees in any job application should be the consultant who conducts the applicant's appraisal, their Clinical Director, or their Medical Director.

Chapter 15

Procedures and policies should be put in place, within 12 months of the publication of this Report, to ensure that all NHS organisations are aware of the therapies being undertaken by all staff, particularly those where patients believe clinical

governance committees should be aware of them and making decisions about their use.

Within mental health services no member of the healthcare team should be permitted to use or pursue new or unorthodox treatments without discussion and approval by the team (such approval to be recorded in writing).

In relation to such identified "new or unorthodox treatments", patients should be given written explanations of the treatments, and why their use is appropriate.

The full range of physical, psychological and complementary therapies used by mental health professionals should be recorded and discussed through appraisal/job plans. Trusts should have a clear evidence base and protocols for guiding the use of these treatments.

The NHS should reconsider whether or not statutory regulation should be extended to cover hypnotherapy.

Chapter 17

When appointments to the NHS are considered, references should be obtained from the three most recent employers and those references should be properly checked.

Chapter 24

The Department of Health should develop and publish a specific policy, with practical guidance on implementation, to guide NHS managers in their handling of allegations or disclosure of sexualised behaviour. The policy should address the various issues and difficulties set out above and include examples of good practice, as well as the extended range of options for action that could be applied; where advice and assistance can readily be provided; guidance on record-making and keeping. The guidance should also include a range of preventative measures (for example, specific accessible information for patients on what they should and should not expect in consultations, and whom they can speak to for confidential advice and assistance).

In relation to disclosures of alleged abuse, voluntary advocacy and advice services (independent of the NHS) should be supported by central public funding to offer advice and assistance to patients and former patients (particularly those who are mentally unwell, or who are otherwise vulnerable).

All Trusts should develop, within their Code of Behaviour[4], guidance to reduce the likelihood of sexualised behaviour, and it should be incorporated into the contracts of employment of those staff, or contracts of engagement for all other persons providing mental health services within the NHS.

Chapter 27

Regarding mental health services, the NHS should review the cut-off period for registering a complaint, as well as the criteria for initiating an investigation of an old complaint and the procedures to be applied (see also Chapter 32 Recommendations).

Protocols should be established to ensure that psychiatric patients who raise concerns or complaints in relation to allegations of abuse are not treated in ways that are less favourable than the treatment advised for vulnerable or intimidated witnesses within the framework of *Achieving Best Evidence* (Action For Justice, 2002). Such psychiatric patients should be treated with care, consideration and integrity.

Because medical procedures that require benzodiazepines to be given intravenously (eg oral endoscopy and induction of anaesthesia) are potentially high risk in terms of false sexual fantasies and allegations, these should always be chaperoned (see Chapter 31, Chaperones).

Chapter 28

Trusts' confidentiality policies should include a section on disclosure within therapeutic interactions in psychiatric practice and should be supported by inter-agency information-sharing policies to be used in all cases of patient abuse.

---

4 See Creating a Patient-led NHS – March 2005.

Dedicated staff should be properly trained to carry out the investigations. This relates closely to the recommendations we make at the end of Chapter 33 regarding investigations generally.

The Secretary of State, within 12 months of the publication of this Report, should commission and publish guidance and issue advice and instruction (preferably in consultation with the professional regulatory bodies and healthcare colleges) as to the meaning and limitations of patient confidentiality in mental health settings. Such guidance should be kept under regular review.

Chapter 29

The NHS should convene an expert group to consider what boundaries need to be set between patients and mental health staff who have been in long-term therapeutic relationships, and how those boundaries are to be respected in terms of guidelines for the behaviour of health service professionals, and the provision of safeguards for patients.

Detailed, and readily accessible, guidance should be developed for medical professionals. The guidance should be framed in terms that address conduct which will not be tolerated and which is likely to lead to disciplinary action. Such guidance, if not provided at a professional regulatory level, should be supplemented by the NHS at an employment level.

Policies should be developed that enable health workers to feel able to disclose feelings of sexual attraction at the earliest stage possible without the automatic risk of disciplinary proceedings. Colleagues must also feel able to discuss openly and report concerns about the development of attraction/overly familiar relationships with patients. These policies should include all grade levels, including consultant.

The Secretary of State, within 12 months of the publication of this Report, should convene an expert group to develop guidance and best practice for the NHS on boundary setting, boundary transgression, sexualised behaviour, and all forms of abuse of patients, in the mental health services.[5]

5 This was also the view of the Ayling Inquiry – see paragraphs 2.30 and 2.31 of the Report.

The terms of reference of the expert group should not be restricted to sexualised behaviour between psychiatrists (or other mental healthcare professionals) and current patients, but should also address former patients.

Chapter 30

There should be detailed research carried out and published by the Department of Health to show the prevalence of sexual assaults, sexual contact, or other sexualised behaviour, between doctors and existing and/or former patients – particularly in the field of mental health.

The Department of Health should urgently investigate and report upon the need for a coordinated method of mandatory data collection and mandatory recording in relation to the area of abuse of patients by mental healthcare professionals.

Chapter 31

Mental health services should provide routine information to patients attending appointments on what to expect from a consultation with a mental health professional. This should apply to consultations in all settings, including home visits.

Where physical contact forms part of the consultation, or where there is a risk of loss of consciousness, there should be a national policy and implementation guidelines to safeguard patients and staff and support the maintenance of appropriate boundaries.

Chapter 32

The NHS should review current records management practice and ensure that a robust set of systems and practices are uniformly applied across the service.

Within 12 months of publication of this Report, the Department of Health should issue guidance as to how and where any disclosure or complaint of abuse by another healthcare professional made to a doctor or nurse should be recorded (if at all) in the patient's medical records and elsewhere.

A protocol should be produced and guidance issued within 12 months of the publication of this Report regarding the collection, collation and retention of data in relation to concerns and complaints covering sexualised conduct by mental health professionals – including, but not restricted to:

- the name of the mental health professional;

- the details of the concern or complaint;

- the date of the alleged sexualised behaviour;

- the date of the concern or complaint;

- if investigated, by whom and with what outcome;

- if not investigated, the reason.

Consideration should be given to the retention period of such data, stating our preference (subject to the advice of the Information Commissioner, and the terms of the Human Rights Act 1998) that such data be retained for the lifetime of the mental health professional. All NHS staff should be made aware regularly that this data is collected and retained.

The current regulations relating to complaints procedures should be amended to enable any person with a concern about the safety and effectiveness of the NHS to be allowed more readily to use the NHS complaints procedure. Further, the time limit applicable from the incidents complained of and the complaint being made should be relaxed.

The Department of Health should review the effectiveness of whistle-blowing policies and initiatives within NHS-funded organisations.

Chapter 33

As a matter of some urgency the NHS should clarify the context in which NHS staff have a positive obligation to inform NHS management of concerns in relation to the suspicion of the abuse of patients.

Policies and guidance should be drawn up to clarify the obligation to investigate (certainly in the case of suspicion of the abuse of possibly vulnerable patients) without the need for a complaint from, or one that identifies, a particular named patient.

Chapter 34

The NHS should, jointly with the appropriate National Standards bodies, produce a standardised complaints system to be implemented in all Trusts/organisations providing services to NHS patients.[6]

Themes and trends arising from the data of complaints, incidents, and patient and carer feedback should be analysed on a regular basis. This should form part of clinical governance and used to give early warning of emerging patterns of risk behaviour, in the interests of patient safety.

Information about the NHS complaints procedure and its relationship to other forms of regulation and clinical governance should be explained to all staff during their induction process and form a core part of continuing professional development programmes. This should include advice and training on how to deal with distressed and angry patients who want to make a complaint.

Frontline staff who receive complaints about issues that compromise patient safety – whether or not in the confines of a therapeutic disclosure – should be under an express obligation to report that matter to a complaints manager (in or beyond their own organisation), whether or not they work for the organisation named in the complaint.

Health and social care commissions should resource independent mental health advocacy as a priority.

---

6 This may be similar to the published guidance on consent.

Patient Advice and Liaison Services (PALS) and complaints staff should be actively linked into a clinical governance and information sharing network with regular access to data on performance issues drawn from such things as claims, patient satisfaction surveys, audit and peer review.

PALS and complaints staff should have direct access to a line manager at board level and to senior medical staff and they should be appointed at middle management level.

The roles of complaints officer and PALS officer should be distinct.

The Department of Health should introduce permanent arrangements for the provision of independent advice for mental health patients.

The Department of Health should be responsible for ensuring a standardised training programme for PALS and NHS complaints staff.

Those who are given the task of responding and initiating any investigation should themselves be adequately trained, equipped with the necessary skills to carry matters forward, and of such seniority as to ensure that barriers and resistance are overcome.

The revised regulations should require that all formal complaints should be directed to designated complaints managers in PCTs and NHS Trusts.

Formal complaints should be interpreted as any matter that the complainants would like to be treated as formal.

Current regulations should be amended to ensure that it is the duty of complaints officers to investigate complaints in a speedy, efficient *and effective* manner.

Current regulations should be amended to require complaints managers to consider the implications for clinical governance and patient safety of all complaints received. Where a clinical governance issue arises this should be reported to the relevant line manager and to the board.

Current regulations should be amended, and suitable guidance prepared, to allow and ensure that complaints managers consider the reference of any complaint received which, if true, would disclose the commission of a crime, to the local police force.

Current regulations should be amended to require complaints managers to take statements from all those staff involved in the investigation of the complaint.

Guidance issued under the regulations should clarify what constitutes a full and rigorous investigation, most notably that complaints officers be placed under a duty to raise additional issues for investigation.

All NHS staff should be placed under an obligation to cooperate with investigations carried out by complaints managers.

Where possible, the NHS should give clear advice and guidance on employment protocols following allegations of abuse.

Chief executives acting on the advice of their complaints managers should be given the authority to refer a complaint to the Healthcare Commission for further consideration.

Complainants should be allowed to pursue litigation at the same time as a complaint is being investigated.

The Department of Health should convene a working party to consider what information it is necessary to record about complaints in order for them to be of use in clinical governance, and the circumstances and form in which it is appropriate to record suspicions.

In line with the recommendations of the Shipman Inquiry, a centralised database capable of recording a range of information about the performance of individual doctors should be set up.

Chapter 35

Regulatory bodies (with responsibility for the regulation and discipline of psychiatrists and other mental healthcare professionals) and the Department of Health should be under a clear duty, in the public interest, to share information about disciplinary investigations or other related proceedings. This duty should extend to information known to the regulatory bodies and the Department of Health relating to disciplinary investigations and related proceedings, even if conducted outside the United Kingdom. Consideration should be given to the collection and retention of all information relevant to patient safety, including unsubstantiated complaints, unproven allegations and informal concerns.

The Department of Health should clearly state what information can be included in relation to electronic staff records relating to complaints, proven/unproven incidents, disciplinary investigations and findings. Such a record should be established in standard form and, once established, should move with the individual to reduce the risk of staff evading detection of past misdemeanours. The Department of Health should consider whether or not, and if so how and in what circumstances, any such information should be transferable between the NHS and the private sector.

The Department of Health in association with the National Institute for Mental Health in England (NIMHE) and the Royal College of Psychiatrists should publish guidance in relation to clinical supervision of consultant and career grade psychiatrists.

Any deviation from acceptable practice in mental health services should be identified by the relevant statutory regulatory body and, where appropriate, by Monitor, and a standard, fair and transparent set of rules governing conduct of all mental health NHS staff in all NHS bodies and Foundation Trusts be quickly established.

The Secretary of State should invite the Council for Healthcare Regulatory Excellence (CRHE) to consider (with a grant of additional powers if necessary), in relation to the regulation of healthcare professionals, the application of common standards, practices and procedures so that patient safety can more effectively be protected.

Chapter 36

Within 12 months of the publication of this Report the Department of Health should develop and publish national advice and guidance to Primary and Secondary Healthcare Trusts addressing the disclosure, by patients or other service users, of sexual, or other, abuse with particular emphasis on users of mental health services.

The GP curriculum should be reviewed to ensure that sufficient focus is given to the needs, treatment and care of patients experiencing mental health problems and illnesses and that all GPs should have some exposure to psychiatry.

Mental health issues should be part of the Nursing and Midwifery Council (NMC) Foundation Year 2.

Early consideration should be given to extending the remit of the National Clinical Assessment Service (NCAS) to cover other healthcare professionals, particularly those providing care and treatment in mental health services.

The NHS should review the curriculum content – at all education and training levels – to ensure that medical practitioners are able to undertake appropriate cross-sector working (including within NHS i.e. primary/secondary boundary) as part of their practice.

Those responsible for developing the curricula for education programmes of healthcare professionals should ensure that:

1) information about and discussion of the ethical responsibilities of healthcare professionals to bring poor performance to light is given due weight and

2) students are made aware of: forms of regulation and clinical governance operating in the NHS and the ethos which underpins them; the relationship between the different systems; and how they can be accessed.

Professional training includes: compulsory education and training on the maintenance of professional boundaries, awareness of boundary transgressions, sexualised behaviour as unethical conduct, response to expressions of concerns and complaints, complaints systems, what to do if a complaint is made but the person making the complaint declines to take an active part in a formal complaint, as well as the requirements of, and limitations on, patient confidentiality.

Duty of candour

The NHS should adopt and reinforce the recommendations in the Manzoor Report and in *Making Amends*, that there should be a duty of candour imposed on, and accepted by, NHS staff. This duty would mean that there is a responsibility to be proactively informative with patients and with their relatives and carers.

General

In relation to private inquiries for witnesses who make statements, and/or who give oral evidence, legal safeguards should be introduced to grant them immunity from action in relation to their evidence (whether fact or opinion), in the absence of malice.

If not already appointed, a multi-disciplinary committee should be established to collate, consider and report on the recommendations made in this Report, the Shipman Report, the Neale Report, the Ayling Report and the Peter Green Report, insofar as those Reports and the recommendations made in them relate to the common theme of handling concerns and complaints, and to patient protection.

All Strategic Health Authorities should set up a manned telephone helpline (perhaps called a "PatientLine"), where anonymised (or identified) concerns could be received and processed. Any information received through the helpline should be logged and received in confidence (unless there is express identification of the caller) and, if there is sufficient information disclosed, should be discussed with the relevant NHS Trust or PCT. Consideration should be given as to how this information could best be collated either regionally or nationally.

Information for patients

The Mental Health Trusts, together with the Primary Care Trusts, should draw up and distribute patient information leaflets, so that patients referred by their General Practitioners to the care of a consultant psychiatrist can better understand what to expect, and the circumstances – if any – in which the patient can expect to receive any physical examination or treatment from the psychiatrist. This leaflet information should include the following topics:

- when the patient can expect a physical examination by the psychiatrist;

- a description of boundaries, and what is and what is not acceptable behaviour by the psychiatrist;

- what the patient is likely to expect in the course of talking therapies (for example, questions and enquiries which some may consider too intrusive and intimate);

- what, if anything, is expected of the patient;

- the availability of trained chaperones and, if installed, the use of virtual chaperones;

- the contact details of the person to whom they may turn in confidence to discuss any issue that may give them concern before, during and after treatment.

Section One
The background

Chapter 1
Establishing the Inquiry

1.1 On 13 July 2001 the Secretary of State for Health announced the setting up of three separate, independent statutory Inquiries. None of these was to be held in public. The first of those Inquiries related to Clifford Ayling, a general practitioner and clinical assistant in obstetrics and gynaecology who worked in a number of hospitals in South East Kent; the second related to Richard Neale, a consultant obstetrician and gynaecologist who worked in a number of hospitals in North Yorkshire; and the third to William Kerr and Michael Haslam. We shall refer to the Inquiries jointly as 'the Three Inquiries', the name by which they have become known. The Three Inquiries had broadly similar Terms of Reference, which required in each case an investigation of how the NHS locally handled complaints about the performance and/or conduct of the doctors.

1.2 The Secretary of State's announcement indicated that, in relation to this Inquiry, the investigation would be chaired by Dame Fiona Caldicott, Principal of Somerville College, Oxford and a former President of the Royal College of Psychiatrists, its overall purpose being:

> "To assess the appropriateness and effectiveness of the procedures operated in the local health services (a) for enabling health service users to raise issues of legitimate concern relating to the conduct of health service employees; (b) for ensuring that such complaints are effectively considered, and (c) for ensuring that appropriate remedial action is taken in the particular case and generally."

1.3 The Inquiry was asked specifically:

- to document and establish the nature of and chronology of the concerns or complaints raised concerning the practice and conduct of William Kerr and Michael Haslam during their time as consultant psychiatrists in the North Yorkshire mental health services (and in William Kerr's case establishing where possible details from his past practice before this);

- to identify the procedures in place during the relevant period within the local health services to enable members of the public and other health service users to raise concerns or complaints concerning the actions and conduct of health service professionals in their professional capacity;

- to investigate the actions that were taken for the purpose of (a) considering the concerns and complaints which were raised; (b) providing remedial action in relation to them; and (c) ensuring that the opportunities for any similar future misconduct were removed;

- to investigate cultural or organisational factors within the local health services that impeded or prevented appropriate investigation and action;

- to assess and draw conclusions as to the effectiveness of the policies and procedures in place;

- to make recommendations informed by this case as to improvements which should be made to the policies, and procedures that are now in place within the health service (taking into account the changes in procedures since the events in question); and

- to provide a full report on these matters to the Secretary of State for Health for publication by him.

1.4 The Secretary of State's announcement made clear that it was not proposed to assess the culpability of William Kerr or Michael Haslam for each allegation that had been raised against the doctors. William Kerr's conduct had been tried before a jury in the Trial of the Facts at Leeds Crown Court the previous year. The police had investigated Michael Haslam and decided not to lay any charges against him, at the time that the Secretary of State announced the commencement of the Inquiry. (However, in June 2002 the police began a fresh investigation against Michael Haslam. He was subsequently charged and later tried in December 2003 at Leeds Crown Court.) The Secretary of State's announcement went on to say that the Inquiry would not be conducted through public hearings. The former patients of William Kerr and Michael Haslam were to be invited to provide evidence and submissions to the Inquiry Chairman. The Inquiry Chairman's findings were to be published in full by the Secretary of State.

1.5   Lawyers representing a number of former patients of William Kerr and Michael Haslam subsequently made representations to the Department of Health about the form the Inquiry should take. The Department took those representations seriously, and to ensure that all those involved had full confidence in the investigation it was agreed that certain changes would be made to the way in which the Inquiry would be conducted. In particular, those changes meant that there would be a modified form of private inquiry to allow interested parties or their representatives to attend the oral hearings and to establish a process whereby issues of concern could be raised with the Inquiry Chairman. Additionally, the Department agreed to appoint a QC or other demonstrably independent person to chair the Inquiry.

1.6   On 31 January 2002 the Secretary of State for Health announced that Nigel Pleming QC would chair this Inquiry. He also announced the appointment of two Panel members to support the Chairman. They were:

- Ros Alstead, Director Operations and Director of Nursing at the South Birmingham Mental Health Trust (now Director of Nursing at Birmingham and Solihull Mental Health Trust); and

- Ruth Lesirge, then Chief Executive of the Mental Health Foundation

1.7   The Inquiry Panel was to begin its work in the spring of 2002. Its Terms of Reference are set out at Appendix 5 of this Report.

1.8   In May 2002 the Chairman held separate meetings with the lawyers representing the former patients and the main NHS bodies in North Yorkshire who would be participating in the Inquiry. The purpose of both meetings was to give the Chairman an early opportunity to hear views about the expectations of those participants for the Inquiry and the work it was to perform.

1.9 Pauline Fox was appointed Secretary to the Three Inquiries and in October 2001 she established a secretariat to serve those Inquiries. She left the Three Inquiries in December 2002 to take up another appointment. Colin Phillips replaced her in March 2003. Kypros Menicou was appointed Assistant Secretary to the Inquiry. Dr Ruth Chadwick was appointed as Commissioning Manager (Experts) to the Three Inquiries. In the summer of 2002 Michael Fitzgerald was appointed Solicitor to the Three Inquiries; subsequently he was assisted by Duncan Henderson who was appointed Deputy Solicitor to the Three Inquiries. In the summer of 2002 Eleanor Grey was appointed to be Counsel to the Inquiry; she took maternity leave in the spring of 2004 and was replaced by Bruce Carr. In December 2003 Clare Brown was appointed Junior Counsel to the Inquiry. The role of the legal team was to assist the Panel in the investigation, advise on matters of law and evidence, and to present the evidence to the Inquiry at its hearings. A full list of those who worked on the Inquiry can be found at Appendix 2.

1.10 The Secretariat was initially located at The Sanctuary, Westminster, London SW1. In September 2002 the Secretariat moved to Hannibal House, a government building at Elephant & Castle, London SE1. The Secretariat was at all times housed in secure accommodation, which was kept entirely separate from other occupiers of the buildings.

Chapter 2
The conduct of the Inquiry

Form of Inquiry

2.1   The Secretary of State decided that the Inquiry should be conducted in private but subject to certain variations. This form of inquiry became known as a modified form of private inquiry. A further explanation of this form is contained at Appendix 4.

2.2   It was decided that the Inquiry would be divided into two parts. Part One would comprise the evidence-gathering process and would address paragraphs 1(a) to (c) of the Terms of Reference.

2.3   There is no statutory entitlement for any person to call witnesses, cross-examine or make submissions in an Inquiry of this sort. It was for the Chairman to decide what form the Inquiry should take and it was decided that the Inquiry would be inquisitorial, not adversarial, in nature.

2.4   Part Two would examine what appropriate recommendations could be made for the revision and improvement of the procedures operated in the local health services for the handling of complaints and concerns. Inevitably, that process lead to consideration of the wider, national picture in relation to some aspects of the Inquiry's work.

Delays to the Inquiry process

2.5   When this Inquiry was first announced by the Secretary of State in July 2001 it was against a background of some existing court and disciplinary proceedings as follows:

   i)   William Kerr's appeal to the Court of Appeal (Criminal Division) against his conviction in December 2000 following the Trial of the Facts in Leeds Crown Court before His Honour Judge Meyerson QC and a jury;

ii)   Civil claims brought by former patients of William Kerr and Michael Haslam against them and/or the North Yorkshire Regional Health Authority;

iii)   The General Medical Council's (GMC's) proceedings in relation to William Kerr consequent upon his application for voluntary erasure; and

iv)   Michael Haslam's civil proceedings for defamation against Times Newspapers Limited.

2.6   While it cannot be said that individually or collectively the above matters caused substantial delay to the Inquiry process, they were matters which the Inquiry had constantly to keep in mind. They did affect the timetable for the Inquiry and were considerations in the manner in which evidence had to be collected.

2.7   By contrast, delay (and in one case substantial delay) to the Inquiry process was caused by the following:

i)   The non-acceptance by the former patients of William Kerr of the private inquiry announced by the Secretary of State in July 2001;

ii)   The proceedings for Judicial Review commenced by the former patients of Clifford Ayling and Richard Neale (see below);

iii)   The criminal process concerning Michael Haslam; and

iv)   The Chairman's lack of compulsory powers before 2004.

2.8   In relation to ii), like the former patients of William Kerr, the former patients of Clifford Ayling and Richard Neale did not accept the initial decision of the Secretary of State to establish the three Inquiries as private Inquiries. However, unlike the former patients of William Kerr, the former patients of Ayling and Neale took proceedings against the Secretary of State for judicial review of his decision not to hold the Inquiries in public. Therefore, no real progress could be made with this Inquiry until the decision of the High Court was delivered on 15 March 2002.

2.9   That day Mr Justice Scott Baker (as he then was) decided that the decisions of the Secretary of State to set up each of the Inquiries were lawful and therefore both claims for judicial review failed. Accordingly, like the Ayling and Neale Inquiries, this Inquiry was to be held in private but would take account of the concessions made by the Secretary of State in September 2001. Namely, interested parties or their representatives would be allowed to attend all the Inquiry hearings and establish a process whereby issues of concern could be raised with the Inquiry Chairman.

2.10   In relation to iii), in June 2002 the Inquiry was informed that the police investigation into Michael Haslam was to be resumed. A preliminary hearing of the Inquiry was held in York on 3 and 4 September 2002 with a view to the rapid progress of the Inquiry. The following day the police announced that Michael Haslam was to be charged. The effect of that announcement, and the subsequent decision to charge Michael Haslam with criminal offences, delayed the Inquiry until January 2004.

Involvement of William Kerr and Michael Haslam

2.11   All contact with William Kerr by the Inquiry was through his medical defence organisation, the Medical Defence Union (MDU). In December 2002 the MDU told the Inquiry that it was of the view that, because of the focus of the Inquiry upon complaints handling, it was felt that the MDU on behalf of William Kerr need not contribute. In May 2003 the General Medical Council decided not to continue with its investigation of William Kerr; this followed the receipt of independent medical evidence it had commissioned. The Inquiry obtained a copy of the medical report commissioned by the GMC and considered it carefully. It became clear from that report that on grounds of ill health William Kerr was not fit to appear before the Inquiry to give evidence or answer written questions. It was concluded that, in view of the contents of the medical report, it would not be appropriate for the Inquiry to seek a contribution from William Kerr.

2.12   Michael Haslam had legal representation for the purposes of his dealings with the Inquiry. In the first instance this was through a firm of solicitors appointed by the MDU; latterly Michael Haslam's representation was by Philip Chapman of Mitchells, Solicitors, York. Michael Haslam provided witness statements to the Inquiry and gave oral evidence on 8 September 2004 when Mr Chapman, who had made opening oral submissions on Michael Haslam's behalf on 8 June 2004, represented him. Mr Chapman deemed it unnecessary to attend each day of the oral hearings, however he did appear before the Panel on occasions to raise procedural issues. Copies of the transcript of determinations of the Inquiry, affecting Michael Haslam's interests, were made available to Mr Chapman when he was unable to attend personally. Mr Chapman informed the Inquiry that Michael Haslam did not wish to attend each day of the hearings. The Inquiry would like to place it upon the record that facilities were arranged at the Hilton Hotel, York, to accommodate Michael Haslam in the daytime during the course of each day's hearings, to enable him to view the proceedings via a direct video camera link. Michael Haslam did not accept this offer and he was content only to attend to give his oral evidence to the Inquiry and for Mr Chapman to appear before the Panel as he deemed fit and to argue procedural matters. We place on record our thanks to the personnel at HMP Acklington and HMP Leeds who assisted us in making the necessary arrangements for Michael Haslam to give oral evidence.

2.13   Pursuant to the terms of paragraph 13 of our Procedures paper (set out at Appendix 6), allegations about Haslam's conduct, which had not been the subject of criminal or other investigations, were put to him through his solicitor. His responses to those allegations were then notified to the Inquiry by his solicitor in writing.

Scope of Terms of Reference

2.14   The Terms of Reference (TOR) invite the Inquiry to consider a number of issues relating to the NHS's handling of allegations relating to William Kerr and Michael Haslam. They cover what may be described as incidents, concerns and complaints. Not all incidents led to concerns, and not all concerns led to complaints. But where they did so, the TOR invite the Inquiry again to consider the handling of them by the relevant NHS personnel/authorities.

2.15   Michael Haslam's legal representative, Mr Chapman, argued that incidents or concerns that did not lead to contemporaneous complaints being made, lay outside the scope of our TOR. The Inquiry does not accept that proposition. The TOR clearly asks the Inquiry to look at any barriers that might have existed to prevent complaints being raised at the time of the events complained of. To accept Mr Chapman's view would be to remove completely the ability of the Inquiry to fulfil its TOR on those issues.

2.16   If the Inquiry could not take evidence about and examine incidents that did not lead to contemporaneous complaints, then it could not come to a view on what influences might or might not have prevented them from becoming complaints. For incidents that did not lead to contemporaneous complaints, the task was to examine the evidence presented regarding incidents that patients later decided were grounds for complaint.

2.17   Again the TOR refer to matters of "legitimate concern". The Inquiry therefore has to establish that the incidents were of some substance and, at a minimum, established in the minds of the witnesses a belief that they constituted grounds for complaint.

2.18   At this point it is important to record that the Inquiry had no remit, and did not seek to extend the remit, to establish the veracity of the incidents described by the witnesses. That was the task of the relevant NHS authorities where the complaint was, or could have been, made at the time. Or, if not for the NHS, for an appropriate investigating body such as the police or the GMC. The Inquiry had to examine what the NHS authorities themselves did to investigate the incidents to establish their veracity or, if they did not do so, why not.

2.19   Where the incidents or concerns did not lead to a contemporaneous complaint, the Inquiry was charged under its TOR with judging whether barriers existed to prevent the witness from taking their concerns forward and making a complaint. To do that, as outlined above, the Inquiry had to establish the broad nature of the incidents themselves and the concerns that the patients either did raise, or could have raised. Part of the Inquiry's task therefore was to assess from the evidence the incidents and concerns that never reached the level of a contemporaneous "complaint", why that was so, and whether negative factors came into play that acted against the interests of patients.

2.20   Where matters of legitimate concern were raised, the responses could range, and did range, from "it never happened" to "a criminal court was sure it did happen". Further, there could be a number of levels of response addressing the matters raised. For the record, unless by the nature of our examination of the issues and incidents the Inquiry necessarily have had to come to a conclusion on what happened, we make no comment on where in that range the concerns should be placed.

2.21 In this assessment of their role under the TOR, the conclusions the Inquiry Panel reached on this matter are as one with those reached by the Chairs of the Ayling and Neale Inquiries that, with the Kerr/Haslam Inquiry, form the Three Inquiries.

Part one: oral hearings

Venue

2.22 The hearings began on 8 June 2004 at The Hilton Hotel, York. As previously explained, the principal reason for the delay in the holding of the oral hearings was the requirement to allow the criminal process in relation to Michael Haslam to take its course following his arrest in September 2002 and the subsequent decision to charge him in December 2002. The conference suite which the Inquiry secured at The Hilton Hotel for the duration of the hearings provided a very serviceable hearing chamber. In the layout of the hearing room, and in the Inquiry's approach to the witnesses, every effort was made to make the hearings as informal as the circumstances permitted. The Inquiry was also able to utilise other accommodation at the hotel as offices for the secretariat and rooms for the use of the participants and their representatives.

Opening the Inquiry and hearing the evidence

2.23 Bruce Carr, Counsel to the Inquiry, made his opening statement on 8 June 2004. The statement identified the principal matters upon which, based on what was known at that time, the Inquiry would need to focus over the period of the hearings. Thereafter, other participants made opening statements. The first witness was called on 9 June 2004. In total 91 witnesses were called to give evidence over a total of 30 hearing days.

2.24 The written statements of a further 134 witnesses were put into evidence without the need for them to attend the Inquiry to give oral evidence.

2.25 The oral evidence was completed on 27 October 2004. A list of the witnesses who were called to give evidence and those whose statements were read into the evidence is set out at Appendix 9. The former patients who gave evidence are described collectively as "former patients", but not otherwise identified.

2.26 All oral evidence was simultaneously transcribed using a system called Livenote. This enabled the Inquiry Panel members and legal representatives to view and make notes on the transcript. The Inquiry is grateful for the work of the team from Smith Bernal – Helen Case, Pauline Phillips and Jacqueline Gleghorn – for their work in producing such a high quality daily transcript so quickly after the conclusion of the day's evidence.

2.27 Closing submissions from the participants were heard on 28 October 2004, following the earlier provision of written submissions.

2.28 Arrangements were made for representatives of the Leeds Mental Health Advocacy Group to be in attendance on each day of the oral hearings. Again the Inquiry is most grateful to them for agreeing to provide support for all those former patients attending the oral hearings.

Threat of proceedings by Michael Haslam

2.29 In a letter dated 5 June 2004, and received by the Inquiry on the day that it commenced its oral hearings in York, Michael Haslam referred to a comment about him which he had seen in a document supplied to him by the Inquiry for his consideration. He told the Inquiry that if the comment could not be substantiated then it was defamatory of him. He wrote: "I have already won a libel action against a colleague for similar unguarded remarks and am in no mood to stop now". The Chairman referred to this observation by Michael Haslam when making rulings on matters raised by his solicitor, Philip Chapman of Mitchells, Solicitors, York.

2.30 In his opening written and oral submissions to the Inquiry on behalf of Michael Haslam, Mr Chapman submitted that no evidence should be admitted about the incident which had led to a prosecution of his client on a charge of rape, and in respect of which Michael Haslam was convicted by the Crown Court in Leeds in December 2003. That conviction was set aside by the Court of Appeal (Criminal Division) in May 2004 as being unsafe. Mr Chapman submitted that the ventilation of evidence about the alleged incident, after the conviction had been set aside, would be likely seriously to prejudice the chance of a fair trial of Michael Haslam's action for libel against Times Newspapers Limited and also could amount to a further libel. He further submitted that a repetition of the allegations following the setting aside of the conviction would not be protected by any form of privilege in any subsequent defamation proceedings.

2.31 The combined effect of the observation made by Michael Haslam in his letter to the Inquiry of 5 June and the opening submissions made by his advocate in relation to the subject of defamation and the possibility of ensuing proceedings by Michael Haslam, caused considerable consternation amongst the former patients attending the oral hearings, some of whom were due to give evidence shortly thereafter. This was especially acute, of course, in the case of the former patients of Michael Haslam. The immediate impact was that one former patient felt quite unable to attend to give oral evidence. She subsequently withdrew her lengthy witness statement from the body of evidence gathered by the Inquiry and took no further part in the Inquiry process. This was a cause of considerable concern and regret to us.

2.32 Another former patient read a prepared statement in evidence. In it she referred to the threat of proceedings by Michael Haslam and her sense of "burning injustice" because she desperately wished to assist the Inquiry but, without a full indemnity from the Secretary of State in relation to any potential future defamation proceedings brought by Michael Haslam, she could not take the financial risk associated with giving evidence. She indicated that she would await developments before deciding whether she would give oral evidence to the Inquiry.

2.33 A further witness wrote to the Inquiry, after she had given oral evidence, to express continuing dissatisfaction. She did so on the basis that it was unsatisfactory for witnesses to any Inquiry such as this one to give evidence in the circumstances which existed at the time, namely with the threat of defamation proceedings hanging in the air.

2.34 The Chairman took the view that the letter from Michael Haslam, coupled with the written and oral submissions made by his advocate, could reasonably be interpreted as an attempt to intimidate witnesses to the Inquiry. As such he took a very serious view of this matter. Apart from the effect upon witnesses and their willingness to give evidence, it was a most unwelcome diversion from the essential task of hearing the oral evidence and complying with the Terms of Reference.

2.35 One of the immediate concerns for the Inquiry at this relatively early stage in the oral hearings was that written material had been supplied to Michael Haslam to enable him to assist the Inquiry in its work. As with all Inquiry material supplied to participants, it was supplied upon the terms of the standard Inquiry confidentiality undertaking, which Michael Haslam had signed, and which included the following clause:

> "I acknowledge that all material provided to me by the Secretariat to the William Kerr and Michael Haslam Inquiry is confidential and in consideration of the provision of that material to me I agree to take all necessary steps to preserve that confidentiality. I acknowledge that the material is provided to me solely for the purpose of assisting me in relation to my participation in the Inquiry and for no other purpose."

2.36 Of concern now was that Michael Haslam did not seem to appreciate that the undertaking prohibited him from using or considering any of the material so provided to him for any purpose other than assisting in his participation in the Inquiry or assisting the Inquiry in its deliberations and in the discharge of its duty. The Inquiry had the clear impression that Michael Haslam was receiving the information not solely for the purpose stated but potentially as a means of considering whether or not he should bring defamation proceedings against witnesses who were to come to the Inquiry to give evidence. The Chairman considered that to be a wholly unsatisfactory position so that, for several days, there was a considerable degree of uncertainty for potential witnesses, especially former patients of Michael Haslam, making it difficult for them to decide whether to tell the Inquiry fully of their experiences.

2.37 Mr Chapman, the advocate for Michael Haslam, addressed the Inquiry to the effect that witnesses who come to Inquiries such as this need have nothing to fear because if they tell the truth that will be a complete answer to defamation proceedings. But, as was made clear to Mr Chapman, that is of no assistance to patients who maintain that they are telling the truth but which is not accepted as such by Michael Haslam, with the consequence that there would be a continuing threat of proceedings.

2.38 In the difficult circumstances set out above, the Chairman decided he had to ask the Secretary of State for Health to consider as a matter of urgency the grant of an indemnity for the witnesses' costs of legal representation in defending any defamation action based on their evidence to our Inquiry. It was made clear that the indemnity would not extend to evidence that was malicious or deliberately untruthful. The Secretary of State treated the matter as one of considerable urgency and duly notified the Inquiry that such an indemnity was given. This had the effect of ensuring that, with the exception of the former patient referred to above, those former patients who had expressed doubt about giving evidence now felt able to do so. But another practical problem was rearranging the witness schedule so as to accommodate those witnesses who had previously stood down until the position was clarified.

2.39 The former patient referred to above, who elected not to give evidence and who withdrew from any involvement in the Inquiry, did so because she felt the indemnity given by the Secretary of State was not sufficient. Her point was that she did not wish to run the risk of being sued by Michael Haslam for defamation, with all the attendant anxieties associated with defending hotly contested litigation. What she required, in order to be in a position to give evidence, was immunity from the litigation itself, not simply the costs of it. Immunity from suit, as it is known, was not something that was open to the Secretary of State to grant to witnesses to the Inquiry. It is a subject that is addressed in the Inquiry's conclusions and recommendations.

Part two: seminars

2.40 The Inquiry held a series of seminars to explore further the themes and issues which the Inquiry Panel identified during the evidence-gathering process. They were designed to improve the Inquiry Panel's knowledge of current and prospective policy and practice, and to engage key agencies and others in dialogue to ensure that the Inquiry's recommendations are robust and consistent with best practice.

2.41 The seminars were held in two parts: local and national. The local seminars were held in the Hilton Hotel in York, on 1 and 2 December 2004. These seminars involved various medical and administrative staff from local NHS service providers, patient support groups, the General Medical Council, and other interested parties. The national seminars were held in the Church House Conference

Centre in Westminster, on 13 and 14 December 2004. These seminars included senior representatives of the NHS and other governing bodies, such as the GMC and the Royal College of Psychiatrists, along with organisations designed to support and promote patients' interests. A full list of attendees can be found at Appendix 11.

2.42 The local and national seminars explored identical themes: protecting patients; handling concerns and complaints by people with mental vulnerabilities; disclosure and the sharing of information; and complaints handling. The Inquiry Panel and attendees heard from an expert in the field of each of these identified themes by way of a 45-minute presentation. Participants were invited to comment on the presentation and were given the opportunity to take part in a stimulating and challenging discussion on the identified theme.

2.43 Throughout the seminars the Chatham House Rule applied, so as to promote open and honest discussion:

> *"When a meeting, or part thereof, is held under the Chatham House Rule, participants are free to use the information received, but neither the identity nor the affiliation of the speaker(s), nor that of any other participant, may be revealed."*

2.44 Before and after the series of seminars, participants provided the Inquiry with extensive written contributions. We are extremely grateful to each and every participant. The contributions made have provided invaluable assistance in undertaking our task.

Preliminary issues

Understanding and interpreting the past

2.45 We have sought to remain alert to the dangers of hindsight and retrospective vision. We also recognise that whilst we have sought to be as comprehensive in our Inquiry as possible, we have seen only a selection of what occurred. Events need to be viewed in their context and we have striven to maintain this sense of context, despite the distance from which we have inevitably had to examine the facts.

2.46 As the Bristol Inquiry commented: "We reconstruct the past from the building blocks left to us. But these can only ever give a partial picture." In particular we are conscious that at the time these events were happening, they were part of the blur of daily activity in the busy lives of healthcare professionals. Furthermore the events occurred at time of particular change within the Health Service.

2.47 Perhaps most significantly, given the advantage of extensive documentation and numerous witness statements, we have been able to construct a chronology of events that suggests a startlingly long list of complaints or concerns raised against both William Kerr and Michael Haslam. This creates a sense of progression and escalating concern, of which, if borne out, in most cases the individual GP or the hospital nurse would have been unaware. Criticism may still be made of those who failed to respond to an individual concern or complaint, but we have sought to remember that the picture they saw was a snapshot, not the detailed overview that we have now obtained of events.

The approach of this Inquiry

2.48 As an Inquiry we set out to conduct an investigation of how the NHS handled allegations into the conduct of William Kerr and Michael Haslam in a fair manner. We have sought also to contribute, to the best of our ability, to developing good and effective practice within the NHS today.

2.49 One of our aims at the outset, and something which was raised in the Preliminary Meeting in York on 6 February 2004, was to make it clear that there were certain parameters to the Inquiry. In particular, we have been at pains to emphasise (repeatedly) that it has not been our role to investigate whether or not the allegations of sexual assault and misconduct were true or whether the doctors acted unethically, or unlawfully. Those are matters for the criminal and civil courts and the GMC, not this Inquiry.

2.50 Another area that was of concern to a number of former patients related to entries in their medical records that they considered to be wrong or misleading. At one point in our investigation we had hoped to be able to address these concerns. However, whilst we have considered issues of record keeping and medical notes, in the end we had to conclude that it was not our role to make assessments on the truth and accuracy or otherwise of individuals' medical records, even were this possible so many years after the events.

2.51 Prior to the commencement of the oral hearings, we undertook a thorough examination of the considerable documentation available to us, in the material from the police, material from civil actions, GMC files, extensive documentation provided by the Trusts and of course numerous witness statements and exhibits from many of those concerned in the events in North Yorkshire. This paper exercise enabled us to produce a comprehensive summary of the facts, piecing together the various concerns and complaints that were raised and the response to these matters.

2.52 This summary then informed our choice of witnesses who would be called to give oral evidence, to clarify, expand or indeed contradict the story that had been told by the documents and written evidence alone.

2.53 We sought throughout the oral hearings to ensure that, as far as possible, the process of giving oral evidence was conducive to frank disclosure. However, we do not underestimate the ordeal that giving evidence under oath presented to both former patients and healthcare professionals.

2.54 Finally, prior to making this Report we have sought to test our conclusions and recommendations against those who, on a daily basis, are working or coming into contact with the mental health services provided by the NHS. Thus in the second stage of the Inquiry we have held both local (York based) and national seminars to which interested parties, including former patients and patient support groups, have been invited.

2.55 As already noted the overall purpose of our Inquiry has been to consider *local* health services, although our power to make recommendations is not so limited. We have inevitably therefore focused on practices and procedures in North Yorkshire, whilst considering the position in other NHS regions and nationally. However, and it is important to emphasise this at an early stage, it has not been possible or practicable to consider in detail present practice and procedures in more than a small handful of other regions. Even the London seminars could not provide the full national picture. We received information which clearly suggested to us that the overall position is mixed – some good, some not so good. Of particular concern is the fact that many of the areas of concern which were revealed in Part 1 – such as barriers to complaints, ineffectual and incomplete investigations – are still present today in many areas.

2.56 We acknowledge that there have been huge changes in the NHS since the 1970s and 1980s when most of the concerns and complaints were raised. We also acknowledge and accept that the position nationally, and in North Yorkshire particularly, has enormously improved. Focusing on North Yorkshire, we were informed that further work is already in train at local and national strategic level in respect of systems of clinical governance which – it is hoped and expected – should lead to patients' concerns and complaints being dealt with properly. At the conclusion of the Part 2 seminars we were provided with a short briefing paper provided by the local NHS authorities entitled: "What systems can be put in place to prevent a recurrence of similar events?" We found this paper to be helpful and encouraging. Coupled with more recent developments, anticipated changes and a favourable response to our recommendations, we are optimistic that, both locally and nationally, in future steps will be taken to ensure that patients who raise concerns and complaints will not be ignored.

Chapter 3
Introduction to concerns and complaints

The range of concerns and complaints

3.1   In this section of our Report we respond to that element of our Terms of Reference requiring us to document and establish the nature of concerns or complaints raised regarding the practice and conduct of William Kerr and Michael Haslam during their time as consultant psychiatrists in the North Yorkshire Mental Health Service.

3.2   We have interpreted our Terms of Reference to be restricted to concerns or complaints relating to alleged sexual misconduct by Michael Haslam or William Kerr. However, within that parameter we have sought to be inclusive, and have recorded in the chronology concerns and complaints that range from, at the one extreme, specific allegations of sexual intercourse to concerns about excessive questioning on sexual history. In most cases the evidence to the Inquiry (particularly from former patients of William Kerr) was that concerns, albeit expressed as relatively minor worries about questioning on sexual matters, were in fact tentative attempts to raise the issue of far more serious allegations of sexual assault.

3.3   We have also sought to be inclusive by asking witnesses about concerns regarding the practice of William Kerr and Michael Haslam that may, with the benefit of hindsight, have been warning bells. (For example, concerns regarding practices that would avail a consultant psychiatrist of a particular opportunity for abusing their position of trust). Thus we have listened to concerns about (in the case of William Kerr) unscheduled domiciliary visits and (in the case of Michael Haslam) unorthodox treatments and research projects. A common theme was the meeting of patients either in domestic or social settings or in deserted or remote parts of the hospital or clinic, often out-of-hours.

Defining a concern or complaint

3.4 Our Terms of Reference refer to concerns or complaints. This has enabled us to look beyond the rare instances of patients who raised what could truly be categorised as a complaint – that is, specific allegations of sexual advances being made by William Kerr or Michael Haslam, made in writing or raised orally with a healthcare professional or person in authority. Indeed, within this category of complaints, the sub category of what might be termed "formal complaints", where the patient had an expectation and desire that matters would be taken further (such as that initiated but not pursued by Patient B2), was even smaller.

3.5 Alongside complaints falls the more difficult issue of concerns. We interpreted concerns as including worries or anxieties about the two consultants, that were reasonably seen as falling short of complaints. We have interpreted concerns to include the rumours and gossip that circulated among certain health professionals, that "things were not right" with Michael Haslam's practice or that William Kerr was "a ladies' man". In addition, concerns were taken to encompass those situations where patients refused for reasons that were unexplained (at the time) to see either William Kerr or Michael Haslam or to have their relatives referred to these consultants.

3.6 There is of course no neat distinction between concerns and complaints and the two can to a large degree be used interchangeably. However the inclusion of both words in our Terms of Reference has caused us to look beyond what might be termed "a formal complaint" to the wider concerns regarding Michael Haslam and William Kerr.

3.7 We repeat here that we use the term "disclosure" to refer to information that passed between individuals. Some of those "disclosures" amounted to allegations against William Kerr and Michael Haslam. We make no comment on the veracity of those allegations but regard all such "disclosures" as information that should have been acted upon at the time.

3.8 Another difficulty we faced was that in some instances (most notably with Patient A17 who spoke to Linda Bigwood, a Deputy Sister at Clifton Hospital – see Chapter 8 for details), the disclosure of a sexual relationship with a consultant psychiatrist was not raised by a patient as either a concern or a complaint. Rather, a "disclosure" was made by a patient in the course of a therapeutic relationship about a past event that occurred. Nevertheless such a disclosure should, and did in the case of Patient A17 (and also Patient B3), cause the recipient healthcare professional to have serious concerns and pass the matter on as a formal complaint.

3.9 We do not accept the argument that where a patient raised the issue of having been involved in a sexual relationship with a consultant psychiatrist (particularly one still in practice), this should have been viewed as no more than a therapeutic disclosure. In such circumstances, once the disclosure was in the hands of a recipient healthcare professional, it should have become a concern that was raised by that individual with their superiors. We discuss this in greater detail in Section 5, "Barriers to making complaints".

Establishing whether a concern or complaint was in fact communicated

3.10 One particular difficulty faced by the Inquiry, exacerbated by the extensive passage of time, was the difficulty in establishing whether a concern or complaint was in fact communicated.

3.11 In a minority of cases there was written evidence such that it was possible to establish whether a complaint had indeed been made (for example in the case of Patient A17 or Patient B2). However, in the vast majority of cases (particularly in relation to former patients of William Kerr), there were apparently conflicting accounts between patients who claimed a clear recollection of telling a health professional (usually their GP) about their concerns regarding sexual advances by their consultant psychiatrist and the GP who had no recollection of any complaint.

3.12 In some cases a compromise situation was possible; the concern expressed may have been made in ambiguous terms and the GP may have failed to pick up on this worry. However, in other circumstances there has been no such compromise and in these cases we have had to make a judgement, doing the best we can after such a long period of time, to resolve whether or not any complaint was made. We regret that on occasions we have been unable to reach a conclusion – the evidence is simply incomplete, and straight conflicts of evidence cannot be resolved. After such a passage of time, an incomplete resolution is perhaps inevitable.

Assessing the response to concerns and complaints

3.13 We have sought in the Inquiry to assess the response to concerns and complaints in a number of ways.

3.14 In relation to concerns which arose at the level of rumour we have sought to consider the substance of these rumours and how widespread they were. We have gone on to examine rumour in a dedicated chapter, Chapter 33.

3.15 Regarding more specific concerns and complaints, particularly those that generated written statements or records, we have sought to go further and trace through the handling of the concern or complaint at all levels from hospital staff or GP surgeries up to the Regional Health Authority, who were the employers of the consultants. We have sought in the Report to set out both a factual chronology of how the concern or complaint was handled and also to consider and analyse the response, with a view to making recommendations that will produce real improvements.

Chapter 4
The Report in context

The vulnerability of psychiatric patients

4.1   It is to be borne in mind at all times when reading this Report that the Inquiry has focused on concerns and complaints made by, or made in relation to, women who were at the time psychiatric patients.

4.2   The vulnerability of these women manifests itself in many different ways. For example, as shown in some of the patient stories set out later in this Report, for many former patients there was great confusion and anxiety arising from the distorted relationship with a male consultant who is supposed to help, care for, and hopefully cure them, but at the same time (as alleged) subjecting them to various forms of sexual abuse. In the criminal trials of William Kerr and Michael Haslam much was made of the fact that former patients would return to the doctors *after* the occasions on which they allege the abuse took place. We of course do not know what effect this had on the juries in the criminal trial. We have no difficulty in understanding the principle involved in such situations – indeed, we would be surprised if, generally, psychiatric patients did not return, either believing the abuse was part of the treatment, or because they did not want to address the existence of the abuse, or because the doctor still remained the person who was there to make them better, or as part of the process of denial found in abusive situations. There would be patients for whom abusive sexualised behaviour was initially experienced as "flattering" – at least in the short term.

4.3   The vulnerability is also relevant to disclosure of abuse. We were struck by the approach of some doctors and other healthcare professionals, to disclosures of abuse by psychiatric patients. Some would reject, or at least considerably discount, the disclosures simply because the patient was mentally unwell – even where there was no evidence at all that the person was fantasising, or suffering from forms of mental disorder (such as psychosis) where lines between fact and fantasy may be distorted. Others, whether or not accepting the disclosure at face value, took the line of least resistance – treating the patient before them as not vulnerable, not in need of support and a caring, structured, environment. That line of least resistance involved saying to the patient – "if you have a complaint to make, make it to the proper authorities, to the police or to the GMC" – or to somebody other than to themselves. As one GP put it to us:

> *"I have no memory of any complaint to me of improper behaviour. If a patient had complained to me in terms as described, I would have said it was a serious matter and I would have advised the patient to go to the police."*

4.4 For the completely mentally well person, disclosure of sexualised behaviour by a consultant must be difficult and distressing enough – an additional traumatising experience, bringing with it feelings of guilt, lack of self-worth, embarrassment, humiliation and shame. In addition, there is the fear of consequences of "telling" – "Will I be believed?", "Will this go on my records?", "What will the GP think of me?", "What if I'm not believed – what then?", "Will I have to give evidence – in public?", "Will my family know about it?", "What will they think of me?", "What will happen to the consultant?", "What will happen to his family?" etc. For the vulnerable, psychiatric patient (who in addition may be on medication) that experience must be even more of an ordeal – those thoughts, those self-doubts compounded. To summon up the courage to say something about what had happened to her (or at least what she believed had happened to her) – not to a friend or family member which would be difficult enough, but to another, usually male, doctor – must (at least for some psychiatric patients) have been truly agonising. And, proceeding on the basis that the abuse did take place, this is without considering the additional impact of the extreme power imbalance between consultant psychiatrist and patient, a power imbalance which can carry with it the threat of withdrawal of needed treatment, or (at its extreme) the threat of loss of liberty – of Mental Health Act "sectioning".

4.5 There are, no doubt, still incidents of sexualised behaviour by treating medical professionals and there are, no doubt, still vulnerable psychiatric patients who are the victims of that behaviour.

In some ways they are more likely to be victims – more vulnerable, medicated, in need of care and affection, less likely to be believed.

4.6 Another important contextual point made to the Inquiry concerns the public perception of mental illness. The view of the general public of people with mental health difficulties was very negative throughout the 1960s–1990s. As one of the former patients put it, "we used to refer to it [Clifton Hospital] as the mad house". Many people working in mental health were dedicated to improving the lot of such patients and were caring and hard-working to that end. Others were less interested and were more dismissive of patients, particularly those who were more difficult. This could be said of any mental hospital at that time. The reality was that users of mental health services were seen as "mental patients", "awkward", "troublemakers" by some of those who were caring for them. It is against this background that the Panel learned from Professor Mortimer that, when she was a junior doctor, there would be a tendency not to believe something said by a patient on a mental health unit.

4.7 The culture today is different. The NHS today has well-established incident and serious untoward incident reporting systems. All staff need to be aware of them and know how to use them. Anonymous reporting is also encouraged.

4.8 Every NHS organisation has established whistle-blowing policies to enable staff to report concerns. The culture of the organisation or team is critical in encouraging the use of all of these policies without fear of incrimination.

The effect of the passage of time

4.9 At various places in this Report we refer to and comment upon the impact of the passage of time.

4.10 The requirements of the Inquiry's Terms of Reference have meant that we have had to consider events, meetings, conversations, which have covered a number of years.

4.11 In relation to William Kerr, the story goes back to 1964 when he was working in Northern Ireland – 40 years before our oral hearings in the summer of 2004. The first expression of concern, or any form of complaint, relating to William Kerr after he moved to North Yorkshire is alleged to have been in 1968 when Patient A4 complained that she had been attacked by William Kerr – the alleged assault was also in 1968. That is, 36 years before the oral hearings. The last recorded expression of concern to which a date can be attached, and when the complaint and incident are near contemporaneous, is by Patient A40 in 1988. This was in the year of William's Kerr's retirement from employment in the NHS – 16 years before the oral hearings.

4.12   In relation to Michael Haslam, the first recorded expression of concern, or complaint, was by Patient B1 around 1974, 30 years before the oral hearings. The last recorded expression of concern about Michael Haslam's practice as an NHS consultant, again when the concern/complaint and incident are near contemporaneous, was by Patient B7, in 1988 – shortly before Michael Haslam's retirement from NHS practice in early 1989. Again, 16 years before the oral hearings in 2004.

4.13   It is to be noted that there have been other fact-finding exercises in relation to these allegations. There have been two criminal trials – in relation to William Kerr in 2000, and in relation to Michael Haslam in 2003. In those trials the tasks of the juries were very different from those we have been tasked to undertake. In particular, the juries had to decide, to the criminal standard of proof, whether or not the alleged sexual assaults had taken place. As we will repeatedly make clear, this is not our role. William Kerr, through ill-health, was unable to give evidence in his own defence at his criminal trial. The 2000 Trial of the Facts for William Kerr involved allegations which covered the period 1968 to 1988. The 2003 trial of Michael Haslam covered the period 1981 to 1988.

4.14   We emphasise the Trial of the Facts (William Kerr), and the criminal trial (Michael Haslam), are very different procedures from this Inquiry. However, the trial judge's warning to the jury on the effect of delay is also relevant to our deliberations – particularly where we have had to decide whether or not there were disclosures by some of the former patients to their GPs, or others, and what was done (or not done) in response to disclosures, concerns or complaints. HHJ Myerson, in his Summing Up to the jury on 13 December 2000, asked them to consider whether they felt that delay was a reflection of the reliability of the complaints, or rather a result of the expressed views of many patients that they were not likely to be believed when William Kerr was a senior consultant with some standing in the community, and gave other valid reasons for not speaking out sooner.

4.15   Delay clearly had an effect on the ability of all witnesses to recall precise details of events many years previously. It emphasised too the importance of contemporaneous written records. The judge drew particular attention to whether there was particular disadvantage to William Kerr's case, especially given his inability because of his medical condition to recall events and advise those representing him. The judge further pointed out that mere delay in complaining when many former patients had explained why they had felt unable to act before was not of itself a ground for disbelieving their evidence.

4.16   In Michael Haslam's criminal trial, a warning to similar effect was given by Mr Justice Gray. He asked the jury to consider if the delay reflected adversely on the complainants, or otherwise raised questions about their credibility. Was there good reason offered for not coming forward earlier? He pointed out that all three complainants, in Michael Haslam's trial, said they had confided in a third party, but doubted whether they would be believed and did not feel strong enough to pursue their complaints formally.

4.17   All these issues had to be weighed carefully when considering the effect of time on the evidence which they, the jury, and we, the Inquiry, received.

4.18   Delay, the passage of time, is therefore very important, and we have constantly reminded ourselves of the need to exercise caution when considering what concerns and complaints were made, to whom and in what detail.

4.19   But the effect of delay is also important for another reason. The longer the gap between complaint and investigation, the more difficult that investigation becomes. It is perhaps significant that the only charge on which the jury were prepared to convict in the Trial of the Facts relating to William Kerr was on the evidence of Patient A40 – the most recent complainant, although even that was 12 years before the trial. The most striking example of "missed opportunity" examined by the Inquiry relates to Patient A36 and Linda Bigwood's complaint – addressed in detail in Chapter 8. If, in 1983/84, there had been full and detailed investigation within the NHS, we conclude that there would inevitably have been a wider investigation, perhaps including the police and the GMC. That investigation would in all probability have uncovered a series of concerns, and complaints, each adding support or credence to the other. We cannot but conclude that if there had been such a detailed investigation, prosecutions would have resulted and the guilt or innocence of both William Kerr and Michael Haslam determined by the mid to late 1980s.

4.20 The passage of time is also relevant to our consideration of the acts or omissions by the regulatory bodies. We recognise that an opinion expressed by us in 2005 on the merits or demerits of systems in place in the 1970s and 1980s is fraught with difficulties.

4.21 Finally, the question of delay has been raised as a reason for doubting the value of the Inquiry. It has been said that, so long after the events complained of and after all that has happened – not only to those involved with those events but also the massive changes in both the NHS and society generally – that an Inquiry such as ours was of little use and something of a waste of time and money.

4.22 We emphasise that this view has not been shared by others, particularly by the local NHS Trusts. In relation to those Trusts (and many other healthcare participants) we have no doubt as to the energy, effort and determination they have brought to address the problems highlighted by the events that led to this Inquiry, no matter how long ago.

Gaps in the story and the loss of documents

4.23 Our task of investigating whether concerns were expressed, or complaints made, at or near the time of the alleged incidents has not been made any easier by the absence of some contemporaneous records.

4.24 This lack of records has also had an impact on our Inquiry into the investigation of complaints which were made, and concerns which were expressed, in relation to both William Kerr and Michael Haslam.

4.25 Some documents were destroyed routinely, some unwisely, some as an inevitable consequence of NHS re-organisation: the net result to the Inquiry is one of loss. The Inquiry has, in many cases, only a partial account of a sequence of events, distorted by the accident of which documents remained, and who is alive and able to remember and comment. As Counsel speaking on behalf of the NHS Authorities invited us to, the Inquiry has had to *"exercise great caution before making findings of fact where documents are missing and memories are poor, particularly when a witness believes that records were made at the time."*

The nature of the allegations

4.26 In this Report we have spelt out in detail, on occasions in graphic detail, some of the alleged activities that were either the subject of criminal action against William Kerr and Michael Haslam, or formed the basis of concerns or complaints raised by patients. We are conscious that some of this makes uncomfortable reading, not least of all for the former patients. But we feel we owe it to them, who have made the difficult decision to speak out themselves, to show just what activities were alleged. When looking at the allegations in relation to William Kerr, this was not behaviour that could be described as light-hearted teasing or witty badinage; these would not be the actions of a playful "ladies' man"; if true, these would be degrading and oppressive physical assaults upon vulnerable and often distressed women by a man who is alleged to have exercised his power and control over patients in a way that would disgust and offend anyone who knew of them. With reference to the allegations relating to Michael Haslam, if true they would amount to behaviour that would at least be unethical and unacceptable and not at all the actions of a caring and supportive clinician.

4.27 In four instances a jury has accepted the allegations – and the verdicts speak for themselves. In cases where the jury has found William Kerr not guilty, or, in the case of Michael Haslam, the Court of Appeal (Criminal Division) has quashed the jury's verdict as being unsafe, the allegations themselves are briefly summarised to show what information may have been available at the time. More generally, and in relation to the allegations that have not been the subject of any court process, the detailed descriptions show the information that *may* have been discovered if the expression of concerns or the making of complaints had been the subject of swift and comprehensive investigation. The allegations made by the former patients could not be dismissed as being trivial or flippant. The allegations, whether expressed as concerns, complaints or just as "disclosures", raised issues of real concern. They demanded immediate attention, whether or not eventually proceeded with or dismissed. As explained later in this Report, some of the allegations called for wider investigation.

4.28 In the course of this Report we repeatedly emphasise that we are unable to reach conclusions on the truth or falsity of the disclosures – whether or not supported by statements to the Inquiry from the former patients. Michael Haslam disputes all allegations of sexual misconduct, or sexual relationships with his existing or former patients (save where expressly mentioned in the text of the Report). William Kerr, we must assume, also disputes all the allegations made in relation to him.

4.29 We also acknowledge, and here record, that allegations of sexual misconduct are often uncorroborated, and are difficult to disprove. We similarly acknowledge that allegations of sexual misconduct may be false – made maliciously, made to obtain financial gain, made innocently but based on a misinterpretation of events, made as a product of mental illness. We recognise that the debate continues in relation to "false memory", or "recovered memory". Indeed, there is a society in England (the *British False Memory Society*) dedicated to addressing this topic and "Serving People and Professionals in Contested Accusations of Abuse". However, we should also note that we are not here addressing any allegations of childhood abuse, and no former patient has suggested that her memory is "new".

4.30 We have received detailed letters, and expert reports, in support of Michael Haslam explaining why he was not guilty of the offences of which he has been convicted. We have read the documents, and we are grateful for them, but determination of the truth of the allegations is not a matter for us. We have also received letters of support from some of Michael Haslam's former patients.

The benefits and the limitations of a private inquiry

4.31 There are clear and obvious benefits from a private inquiry, where the material is particularly sensitive and there is a need to protect the identity of the former patients. We hope that the environment for the Inquiry's oral hearings, whilst not positively therapeutic, has been comfortable enough to enable *all* witnesses to give their evidence without being placed under too much stress.

4.32 However, there are some clear disadvantages when compared with a public inquiry. For example, the public does not have the opportunity to see the witnesses give their evidence, or to read the documents available to us. That disadvantage carries the additional chore for us, namely to sort and sift the evidence with additional care to ensure that the story is correctly told – knowing that there is no access to the supporting documentation, or to any transcript of the oral evidence.

4.33 There is an additional, perhaps less obvious, disadvantage. Although we have been assisted by extremely able and experienced experts, and we have been supplied with informed and very helpful submissions both in writing and at the four days of seminars, there has not been any ongoing public debate – no major media commentary, no (or very few) uninvited contributions (unlike, for example, the *Bristol Royal Infirmary* or *Harold Shipman* inquiries). The consequence is that this Report, even with clear recommendations, cannot be seen as the last word. Indeed, we would not want it to be. This is particularly the case in areas of the Report where we examine and express our views on complex issues such as boundary transgressions and sexual relations with former patients, and the regulation of medical professionals. In the Report, we refer to the way things are done in other parts of the world – for example in New Zealand and the United States. But what is considered to be the right approach there may be inappropriate for the UK. When it comes to some areas, such as those already mentioned, all we can do is recommend that there is an early and full investigation, with the government taking the lead.

Chapter 5
The factual background to the Inquiry

The organisation of the NHS in North Yorkshire
The North Yorkshire Mental Health Services

5.1   During the period from 1964 to the present, the North Yorkshire Mental Health Services, within which both William Kerr and Michael Haslam practised, underwent considerable organisational change. This organisational structure is set out briefly at the end of this section of the Report, together with a further chart detailing the identity, where known, of those holding certain posts of administrative responsibility.

5.2   In summary, the Leeds Regional Hospital Board (LRHB) was abolished in 1974 and replaced by the Yorkshire Regional Health Authority (YRHA). Below this, at area level, was the North Yorkshire Area Health Authority (NYAHA) and, parallel to this, the North Yorkshire Family Practitioner Committee (NYFPC). The NYAHA was further divided at district level, into the York Health District and the Harrogate Health District.

5.3   Up until the early 1990s, Mental Health Services for Harrogate were centred on Clifton Hospital, York. There was a small presence of mental health services elsewhere, including Scotton Banks Hospital at Knaresborough and outpatient clinics in Harrogate and Ripon.

5.4   In 1985 a transfer of services from York to Harrogate was agreed. This was finally achieved in 1992 when the Briary Wing at Harrogate District Hospital was opened and all Harrogate patients were being cared for in Harrogate.

5.5   In 1982 the North Yorkshire Area Health Authority was abolished and the York Health Authority and the Harrogate Health Authority were both created as District Health Authorities (DHAs).

5.6 In 1991/92 the NHS Trusts emerged, and in 1995 the Yorkshire Regional Health Authority was replaced by the NHS Executive Northern and Yorkshire Regional Office.

5.7 Consultant medical staff were employed under contracts initially with the Leeds Regional Hospital Board and then the Yorkshire Regional Health Authority until 1991. Thereafter, with the introduction of NHS Trusts, they were directly employed by the local Trusts that came into being, which in the case of York and Harrogate was in 1992.

5.8 From 1 April 2002, Mental Health Services were transferred from the York Health Services NHS Trust and Harrogate Healthcare NHS Trust to Selby and York Primary Care Trust and Craven, Harrogate and Rural District Primary Care Trust.

The North Yorkshire Hospitals and Clinics

5.9 The Hospitals within the York Health District and the Harrogate Health District with which Michael Haslam and William Kerr were principally involved were:

- Clifton Hospital, York
- Bootham Park Hospital, York
- Harrogate General Hospital, Harrogate
- Harrogate District Hospital, Harrogate
- York District Hospital, York
- Ripon Community Hospital, Ripon
- Scotton Banks Hospital, Knaresborough.

5.10 There were also community bases, such as Dragon Parade in Harrogate. In addition, there were private hospitals and clinics.

Clifton Hospital, York

5.11 Clifton Hospital opened in 1847 and closed in 1994. It has now been, for the most part, demolished. It was a psychiatric hospital. In the 1960s and 1970s, it contained some 700 or so inpatient beds (in the 1950s numbers reached over 1,000). It served not only York, but also Harrogate, Scarborough and a part of Northallerton.

5.12 Clifton Hospital was a training hospital for nurses, providing psychiatric nursing qualifications. It was also linked to the postgraduate and undergraduate schools of psychiatry at Leeds University, so that medical students and registrars would rotate through Clifton as part of their psychiatry training.

5.13 Clifton Hospital is described as having a lot of keys and locked doors, "like a prison", with the doctors/psychiatrists holding the master keys. William Kerr's office in Clifton Hospital was on the ground floor, to the right of the main entrance and with a bay window overlooking the main car park. The door was secured by a Gibbons deadlock and an individual Yale lock. William Kerr and his medical secretary (Kathleen Exton, formerly Spencer) held the keys to the office. His secretary said that he would lock his door during consultations to stop other patients wandering in.

5.14 Stuart Ingham was the District Administrator of York Health Authority from 1982 to 1985, after which he became District General Manager from 1985 to 1988. He then became the District General Manager for Leeds Western Health Authority and in 1991 was appointed Chief Executive of United Leeds Teaching Hospitals NHS Trust. Mr Ingham comments that when he was appointed in 1982, the psychiatric services at Clifton were "outmoded" and the facilities were in a poor state. The closure of Clifton Hospital in 1994 coincided with a general trend to close large mental health hospitals and a move to psychiatry being practised on a more localised basis. In 1992 multi-disciplinary community teams were introduced, including community psychiatric nurses (CPNs), clinical psychologists, psychiatrists, occupational therapists and social workers. In 1993 written care plans and key workers for patients (known as the Care Programme Approach) were introduced.

Ripon Community Hospital

5.15 Ripon Community Hospital (including an outpatient department) was a small community hospital in which medical cover was largely provided by local general practitioners. William Kerr held clinics at Ripon Community Hospital on Monday afternoons, between 2pm and 5pm. His consulting room was in a wooden building separate from the main hospital block; the two windows of the room were frosted glass and had black blinds.

Harrogate General Hospital and Harrogate District Hospital

5.16   Harrogate General Hospital was closed in 1999. William Kerr's clinics at Harrogate General Hospital were held in what was known as the antenatal clinic. This was a one-storey building situated towards the back of the hospital; the windows looked out on the walls of Nissen-type hut wards. The rooms were not locked and the windows had roller blinds. The clinics took place on Wednesday and Friday afternoons. In 1974, William Kerr transferred his patients to Harrogate District Hospital.

5.17   The first phase of the new Harrogate District Hospital opened in 1974. It was located about a quarter of a mile away from Harrogate General Hospital. William Kerr's clinic, held on Wednesday and Friday afternoons, was in the main outpatient department. There were no locks on the doors and the windows had blinds. Michael Haslam held clinics at Harrogate District Hospital on Tuesday and Thursday afternoons.

Scotton Banks Hospital, Knaresborough

5.18   Scotton Banks Hospital in Knaresborough was also part of the group of Harrogate Hospitals. The gynaecology ward was based at Scotton Banks until it was transferred to Harrogate General Hospital in 1988. Scotton Banks Hospital closed in 1990.

Duchy Nuffield Hospital, Harrogate

5.19   This was a private hospital where William Kerr saw his private patients during the years 1970 to 1975.

Bootham Park Hospital, York

5.20   Bootham Park, which opened in 1777, is a psychiatric hospital that shared a joint catchment area, primarily York, with Naburn Hospital from 1952. The superintendent until 1980 was Dr Arthur Bowen; he was the last superintendent. He was succeeded as a consultant psychiatrist by Dr Peter Kennedy. Bootham Park continues to be a psychiatric hospital with both inpatients and outpatients, and is adjacent to York District Hospital, now York Hospital.

Naburn Hospital, York

5.21 This was a psychiatric hospital, primarily serving York, that later operated in an integrated way with Bootham Park. This hospital closed in 1988.

Purey Cust Nuffield Hospital, York

5.22 Purey Cust was a general private hospital in York. It was closed when a new facility opened in 2004.

4 St Mary's, York

5.23 This was a private house in York located on a street opposite the main drive of Bootham Park Hospital. It was bought by a number of consultants and used as consulting rooms. The doctors who owned the premises also rented out the consulting rooms to other consultants, including Michael Haslam.

Whixley Hospital

5.24 Whixley Hospital, for people with learning difficulties, was originally part of the York health services but was transferred to the Harrogate health services in 1983; it closed in 1993. A letter from Browne Jacobson (solicitors for the Health Authority) dated 26 March 2004 informed the Inquiry that while neither William Kerr nor Michael Haslam had inpatient beds there, or held outpatient clinics on site, they would have attended Whixley when on call for emergencies, or if there were admissions.

The Psychosexual Disorder Clinic, York

5.25 This was a clinic that was set up in 1972 as an outpatient facility for people with marital and sexual problems. It was run by Michael Haslam and a psychologist, the late Dr Anne Pattie, and they were assisted by another psychologist, Charles Marsh. This clinic was initially based at Clifton Hospital, but later also at the newly opened York District Hospital in the Outpatient Department (on Friday afternoons). According to Michael Haslam the clinic was created as a result of research work by Masters and Johnson in the United States, and John and Judy Bancroft in the UK, into the psychology of sexual function. Clifton Hospital hosted the second international conference on psychosexual disorders in the UK in 1974. Patients attending this clinic would be seen without a chaperone unless there was an intimate examination.

Dragon Parade, Harrogate

5.26 13 Dragon Parade was a converted terraced house that was used by the Mental Health Team as a day centre for NHS patients. It was in use from the early 1960s. The house was privately owned and rented out to Social Services. There was one consulting room (with one curtained window) and a waiting room, both of which were on the first floor towards the back of the building.

5.27 The centre was initially staffed by William Kerr and Dr Munro, and later by Michael Haslam. Long-term rehabilitation and care was provided for some 20 patients with long-standing residual psychotic disabilities. An outpatient clinic was also held there. The centre organiser at 13 Dragon Parade was Harold Duncan Sykes. William Kerr used a room on the first floor at Dragon Parade on Wednesdays, from 2pm onwards, for some five or six years. This room was not used much except by consultants; normally it was used as an overflow room or a smokers' room. It was a carpeted room with a consultant's desk, a chair for patients and another desk in the corner. There were curtains in the room, which overlooked the rear yard of the premises. The main door to 13 Dragon Parade was locked with a latched Yale lock. William Kerr had his own key. The building was normally open Monday to Friday from 9am to 5pm, and no person had any reason or authority to enter the building outside these hours. On the doors to the consulting room there were old-type mortise locks on the door handles, but the keys were not readily available. Mr Sykes was unaware whether William Kerr had his own keys to the consulting room. On Wednesday afternoons there was no one to meet patients: they just let themselves in and went straight upstairs to the waiting room. There was no receptionist: patients had to find their own way to the clinic. At times, William Kerr would leave before the supervisor responsible for the building; at other times he would leave later.

5.28 At some point consultant psychiatrists, including William Kerr, stopped attending at 13 Dragon Parade.

NHS organisation structure – North Yorkshire

Year	Regional Level	Area Level	District Level	Local Level
1948 **(Consultant medical staff employed by RHB)**	Leeds Regional Hospital Board *LRHB*		York A Hospital Management Committee York B Hospital Management Committee Harrogate and Ripon Hospital Management Committee	Clifton Hospital, York Bootham Park Hospital, York Naburn Hospital, York Harrogate General Hospital Ripon Community Hospital Scotton Banks Hospital, Knaresborough Other community bases (eg Dragon Parade)
		North Yorkshire Executive Council *NYEC*		GPs Dentists Pharmacists Opticians
1974 **AHAs created** **(Consultant medical staff employed by RHA)** **ECs become FPCs**	Yorkshire Regional Health Authority *YRHA*	North Yorkshire Area Health Authority *NYAHA*	York Health District Harrogate Health District	Clifton Hospital, York *(MH services for Harrogate and York were centred on Clifton Hospital until Harrogate developed its own service in the period from 1985)* Bootham Park Hospital, York Naburn Hospital, York York District Hospital Harrogate General Hospital Harrogate District Hospital Ripon Community Hospital Other community bases (eg Dragon Parade)
		North Yorkshire Family Practitioner Committee *NYFPC*		GPs Dentists Pharmacists Opticians
1982 **AHAs abolished** **DHAs created**	Yorkshire Regional Health Authority *YRHA*		York Health Authority Harrogate Health Authority	Clifton Hospital, York Bootham Park Hospital, York York District Hospital Naburn Hospital, York – closed 1988 Harrogate General Hospital Harrogate District Hospital Ripon Community Hospital Other community bases (eg Dragon Parade)
		North Yorkshire Family Practitioner Committee *NYFPC*		GPs Dentists Pharmacists Opticians

Year	Regional Level	Area Level	District Level	Local Level		
1991/92 **NHS Trusts emerge** **FPCs become FHSAs** **(Consultant medical staff employed by NHS Trusts)**	Yorkshire Regional Health Authority *YRHA*	North Yorkshire Health Authority *NYHA*	York Health Services NHS Trust Harrogate Healthcare NHS Trust	Hospitals and community services Clifton Hospital, York – closed 1994 Harrogate continued to develop local mental health services		
		North Yorkshire Family Health Services Authority *NYFHSA*		GPs Dentists Pharmacists Opticians		
1996 **RHAs abolished** **HAs and FHSAs merged**	NHS Executive Northern and Yorkshire Regional Office *NYRO*	North Yorkshire Health Authority *NYHA*	York Health Services NHS Trust Harrogate Healthcare NHS Trust	Hospitals and community services		
				GPs Dentists Pharmacists Opticians		
2001 **PCTs emerge**	NHS Executive Northern and Yorkshire Regional Office *NYRO*	North Yorkshire Health Authority *NYHA*	York Health Services NHS Trust Harrogate Healthcare NHS Trust	Hospitals and community services		
			Selby and York Primary Care Trust *PCT*	GPs Dentists Pharmacists Opticians Community services	PCT in Selby and York but still HA elsewhere in county	
2002 **RO abolished** **Strategic Health Authorities established** **Mental Health Services transferred from York and Harrogate Healthcare Trusts to PCTs in York and Harrogate from April 2002**	Department of Health and Social Care North (abolished 2003)	North and East Yorkshire and Northern Lincolnshire Strategic Health Authority	York Health Services NHS Trust Harrogate Healthcare NHS Trust	Hospital services		
			Selby and York PCT Craven, Harrogate and Rural District PCT	GPs Dentists Pharmacists Opticians Community services Mental health services		

NHS personnel organisation structure – North Yorkshire

Year	Regional Level	Area Level	District Level	Local Level
1948 **(Consultant medical staff employed by RHB)**	Leeds Regional Hospital Board *LRHB* **Secretary to Board:** Mr W Bowring	North Yorkshire Executive Council *NYEC*	York A Hospital Management Committee	Clifton Hospital, York Bootham Park Hospital, York
			York B Hospital Management Committee	Naburn Hospital, York
				Harrogate General Hospital
			Harrogate and Ripon Hospital Management Committee	Ripon Community Hospital
			1948–1974	Scotton Banks Hospital Other community bases (eg Dragon Parade)
				In 1965 WK started as Locum Medical Officer at Clifton Hospital, York. Made full consultant in 1967.
				In 1969 WK appointed as Deputy Medical Superintendent at Clifton Hospital.
				In 1970 MH appointed as Consultant Psychiatrist at Clifton Hospital.
1974 **AHAs created** **(Consultant medical staff employed by RHA)** **ECs become FPCs**	Yorkshire Regional Health Authority *YRHA* **Regional Administrator:** Mr H Inman	North Yorkshire Area Health Authority *NYAHA* 1974–1982 **Area Administrator:** Mr W L Moore **Area Nursing Officer:** Miss E M Logan	York Health District Harrogate Health District 1974–1982 **District Administrator** in York: Mr A Holroyd (Mr Holroyd went on to become Regional Administrator)	Clifton Hospital, York Bootham Park Hospital, York
				Naburn Hospital, York
				York District Hospital Harrogate General Hospital
				Harrogate District Hospital
				Ripon Community Hospital Other community bases (eg Dragon Parade)
				In 1980 Dr P F Kennedy was appointed as Consultant Psychiatrist in York, based at Bootham Park Hospital.

Year	Regional Level	Area Level	District Level	Local Level
1982 **AHAs abolished** **DHAs created**	Yorkshire Regional Health Authority *YRHA* **Regional Administrators:** 1982 – Mr A Holroyd followed by: Mr K Punt Mr A Stokes Mr A Foster Mr K McLean **Regional Medical Officer:** Dr W Turner 1986 – Dr R Howard		York Health Authority **District Administrator:** 1982–1985 Mr S E Ingham **District General Manager:** 1985–1988 Mr S E Ingham 1988–1992 – Dr P F Kennedy **District Medical Officer:** 1982 – Dr A W McIntosh 1988 – Dr W Wintersgill 1989 – Dr J Beal 1990 – Dr M J M Carpenter, Director of Public Health **District Nursing Officer (Adviser):** 1982 – Mr J K Corbett 1985 – Mr K Darley, DNO (Adviser) 1986 – Miss A Whittington, DNO (Adviser) 1987 – Mr P Nicklin, Acting DNO (Adviser) 1989–1990 – Mr J W Gomersall, DNO (Adviser) **General Administrator:** 1983 onwards Mr G T Wood Harrogate Health Authority **District Administrator:** 1982–1985 Mr G E Saunders **District General Manager:** 1985–1992 Mr G E Saunders	Clifton Hospital, York Bootham Park Hospital, York Naburn Hospital – closed 1988 York District Hospital Harrogate General Hospital Harrogate District Hospital Ripon District Hospital Other community bases (eg Dragon Parade) York mental health services **Director of Nursing Services**, Mental Illness Unit, York: 1984 – Ray Wilk **Unit Administrator:** 1984 – Keith Parsons **Nursing Officer:** 1984 – Mrs A Tiplady

Year	Regional Level	Area Level	District Level	Local Level
1991/92 **NHS Trusts and HAs emerge** **FPCs become FHSAs** **(Consultant medical staff employed by NHS Trusts)**	Yorkshire Regional Health Authority *YRHA*	North Yorkshire Health Authority *NYHA* **Chief Executive:** 1992 – Mr R Brown 1994 – Mr B Fisher	York Health Services NHS Trust **Chief Executive:** 1992 to Sept 1999 – Dr P F Kennedy 2000 – Mr S Pleydell 2003 – Mr J Easton **Medical Consultant/Medical Director:** 1992 – Dr D J Wilkinson 1993 – Dr R L Marks 1999 – Dr M Porte **Director of Nursing:** 1992 – Miss H Coyne 1994 – Mrs P Hart 1998 – Mr M Proctor Harrogate Healthcare NHS Trust **Chief Executive:** 1992 – Mr G E Saunders 2001 – Mr M Scott	Hospitals and community services Clifton Hospital closed 1994. Harrogate continues to develop local mental health services.
1996 **RHAs abolished** **HAs and FHSAs merged**	NHS Executive Northern and Yorkshire Regional Office *NYRO* **Chief Executive:** Prof Liam Donaldson (also Regional Medical Officer) Acting for a short period: Mr D Flory 1998 – Mr P Garland	North Yorkshire Health Authority *NYHA*	York Health Services NHS Trust Harrogate Healthcare NHS Trust	Hospitals and community services GPs Dentists Pharmacists Opticians
2001 **PCTs emerge**	NHS Executive Northern and Yorkshire Regional Office *NYRO*	North Yorkshire Health Authority *NYHA*	York Health Services NHS Trust Harrogate Healthcare NHS Trust Selby and York Primary Care Trust *PCT*	Hospitals and community services GPs Dentists Pharmacists Opticians Community services } PCT in Selby and York but still HA elsewhere in county

Year	Regional Level	Area Level	District Level	Local Level
2002 **RO abolished** **Strategic Health Authorities established** **Mental Health Services transferred from York and Harrogate Healthcare Trusts to PCTs in York and Harrogate from 1 April 2002**	Department of Health and Social Care North (abolished 2003) **Chief Executive:** 2002–2003 Mr P Garland	North and East Yorkshire and Northern Lincolnshire Strategic Health Authority **Chief Executive:** 2002 Mr D Johnson	York Health Services NHS Trust Harrogate Healthcare NHS Trust	Hospital services
			Selby and York PCT **Chief Executive:** 2001–2004 – Dr S Ross 2004 – Mr J Clough **Director of Mental Health and Social Inclusion:** 2002 – Mr G Millard Craven Harrogate and Rural District PCT **Chief Executive:** 2002 – Ms P Jones **Director of Mental Health:** 2002 – Mr D Brown	GPs Dentists Pharmacists Opticians Community services Mental health services

Section Two
The William Kerr story

Chapter 6
William Kerr – the early years

Qualification

6.1   William Samuel Kerr was born on 8 October 1925 in India. He was educated in India, and after leaving school he served with the Army for approximately four years, including a year's active service in Burma. In 1947 he started studying medicine at Queen's University, Belfast. He graduated in June 1953.

Marriage

6.2   In 1953 William Kerr married Dr Beryl Bromham. She had also qualified as a doctor and, like William Kerr, worked at that time in Belfast City Hospital as a House Officer.

Northern Ireland

6.3   After a six-year period from 1955 to 1961 working in General Practice in Calcutta, India, William Kerr returned to Northern Ireland. On 11 September 1961, he commenced employment at Purdysburn Hospital, Belfast (now Knockbracken Healthcare Park) as a Senior House Officer on the Psychiatric Ward. Purdysburn was the main psychiatric teaching hospital in Northern Ireland, and worked closely with Queen's University. His wife, Dr Bromham, also took up psychiatry on the couple's return to Northern Ireland.

6.4   In September 1962, William Kerr was promoted at Purdysburn to be Registrar in Psychiatry, and in 1963 he obtained the Diploma in Psychological Medicine from the Royal College of Surgeons and Physicians, Dublin. In August 1964 he transferred to Holywell Hospital, Antrim, Northern Ireland as a Registrar.

Membership of the Royal College of Psychiatrists

6.5 William Kerr was elected a member of the Royal Medico-Psychological Association (the College's predecessor) on 3 July 1963 and subsequently became a foundation member of the Royal College of Psychiatrists on 1 June 1972 (he was never a Fellow). He resigned his college membership on 26 January 2001.

Complaint in Northern Ireland

6.6 In or about the latter part of 1964, William Kerr allegedly sexually assaulted a female patient of a GP, Dr Mathewson of Lisburn, Belfast. The assault was alleged to have occurred after Dr Mathewson referred the patient, who was suffering from anxiety and depression, for psychiatric treatment. An appointment was arranged for her with William Kerr at an outpatient clinic held at premises in the Lagan Valley Hospital, Lisburn, Belfast. The patient was in her late teens. It is alleged that William Kerr said he needed a longer consultation with her at the end of his clinic, and that this would take place in his car. Once in the car, he is reported to have told his patient that sexual intercourse would help her condition, and sexual intercourse is then alleged to have taken place.

Disciplinary proceedings

6.7 The patient took the matter to the local authorities after consultation with Dr Mathewson. Dr Mathewson gave evidence to a medical disciplinary committee in Belfast, a short time after the allegation came to light. Prior to this disciplinary hearing, Dr Mathewson described how William Kerr had approached him at home and asked him not to give evidence against him. Dr Mathewson refused to comply with William Kerr's wishes. According to Dr Mathewson's understanding, sometime after the medical disciplinary committee meeting, William Kerr was found guilty of professional misconduct and advised to leave Northern Ireland immediately, if he wanted to continue to practise medicine.

6.8 Dr Bromham's evidence to the Inquiry was that her husband informed her of the allegations. She also stated that she was aware her husband had, through family contacts, attempted to persuade Dr Mathewson to drop the complaint. This differed from Dr Mathewson's evidence that he had been approached both by William Kerr and friends of Dr Bromham. Dr Bromham denied making any attempt, either personally or through friends, to deter Dr Mathewson from pursuing the complaint.

6.9   Whilst Dr Bromham could not recall any formal disciplinary proceedings, she did recall a meeting with a Dr Robinson, shortly after the allegations had arisen, who suggested that William Kerr pursue his career in England.

6.10   Whilst we have had difficulties in obtaining accurate information relating to this early part of William Kerr's career, the Inquiry is satisfied that:

- whilst in Northern Ireland a complaint of serious sexual misconduct was raised against William Kerr;

- some form of disciplinary hearing was held, at which the patient's GP, Dr Mathewson, gave evidence;

- as a result of the disciplinary hearing, William Kerr was "advised" to leave Northern Ireland;

- Dr Bromham was aware of the fact of the complaint and the decision that William Kerr should leave Northern Ireland.

Appointment to North Yorkshire

6.11   On 7 December 1964, William Kerr made an application for the post of Registrar in Psychiatry at Leeds Regional Hospital Board (LRHB) (the predecessor of the Yorkshire Regional Health Authority), to be stationed at Clifton Hospital. The three referees named were all practitioners at the Purdysburn Hospital, which William Kerr had left in July 1964; none was provided from the hospital where he was then employed (Holywell Hospital, Antrim), and where he had been based when the complaint of sexual misconduct took place.

The interview process

6.12   On 17 December 1964, Dr Sippert, Assistant Senior Medical Officer, St James' Hospital and LRHB, interviewed William Kerr for the post at Clifton Hospital. There was no indication that references would be checked nor query made regarding William Kerr's most recent post at Holywell Hospital. It appears there was no knowledge by the interview panel in North Yorkshire of the circumstances in which William Kerr had left Northern Ireland.

6.13 On 1 January 1965, William Kerr was appointed as a Locum Senior House Medical Officer in Psychiatry at Clifton Hospital, York, apparently without any check of his references having occurred. The contract was to run for six months and then, subject to renewal, to be ongoing.

6.14 This is an appropriate point to note that, like William Kerr, Michael Haslam also failed to provide any references from his most recent previous post of consultant at Doncaster Royal Infirmary prior to obtaining employment at Clifton. The Inquiry does not suggest this is indicative of misconduct by Michael Haslam at Doncaster, but it does show a lack of any rigorous pursuing of references. Even more concerning was that in 1993, when Michael Haslam was appointed to the, albeit non-clinical, post of Medical Director of South West Durham Mental Health NHS Trust, references were not taken up.

6.15 We subscribe to the view that any gaps in an employment record should be carefully scrutinised; recent references should be required for all posts; and all references should be promptly and properly followed up, preferably by telephone but at least through correspondence.

We RECOMMEND that one of the referees in any job application should be the consultant who conducts the applicant's appraisal, their Clinical Director, or their Medical Director.

Career progression

6.16 William Kerr was appointed to the post of Consultant in February 1967, and was given the post of Deputy Medical Superintendent in 1969.

6.17 Six months after William Kerr's initial appointment in 1965, his wife, Dr Bromham, joined him from Northern Ireland. She became a registrar at Clifton Hospital and in 1973 she also, like her husband, became a consultant psychiatrist, both employed by the same regional health authority.

6.18 From 1979 to 1987 William Kerr was the Senior Consultant at Clifton Hospital (the title of Physician Superintendent having ceased with the retirement of Dr Quinn). William Kerr was succeeded by Michael Haslam, who held the post of Senior Consultant from 1987-1989.

Chapter 7
The expression of concerns and complaints by patients

Introduction

7.1   The Inquiry Terms of Reference instructed us:

> *"To document and establish the nature of and chronology of the concerns or complaints raised concerning the practice and conduct of William Kerr and Michael Haslam during their time as consultant psychiatrists in the North Yorkshire mental health services (and in William Kerr's case establishing where possible details from his past practice before this)".*

7.2   We have attempted to carry out that task by documenting all the concerns and complaints of which we are aware, whenever received and in whatever form, so long as they relate to the practice and conduct of the two psychiatrists when they were working as psychiatrists within the North Yorkshire mental health services, or, in relation to William Kerr, from his past practice in Northern Ireland. We have set them out chronologically, and the nature of the concerns and complaints should be clear.

7.3   We have interpreted the Terms of Reference so as only to include concerns and complaints relating to some aspect of alleged sexualised behaviour. The concerns and complaints have been gathered together from various sources. Some of the former patients provided the Inquiry with written statements, and some of these were invited to supplement those statements by giving oral evidence.

The rumours

7.4   In January 1965 William Kerr commenced his duties as a locum Senior House Medical Officer in Psychiatry, at Clifton Hospital in York. There is nothing to suggest that his new employer, the Leeds Regional Hospital Board (LRHB), had any knowledge of the complaint of a sexual assault of a female patient that had been made against him in 1964 or the resultant cloud under which he had left his previous post in Northern Ireland. However, within the first year in his new post, allegations of sexual misconduct were to arise (from Patient A1) and at or around this time it appears that rumours started to spread regarding William Kerr's "reputation".

7.5   The nature of the rumours was consistent, in that they all linked William Kerr with sexual advances towards women. However, within this broad category, the rumours ranged from gossip that he was "a ladies' man" and "a flirt", the implication being that this behaviour was confined to female members of staff, to more serious rumours of sexual advances towards female patients. Of the latter variety, one specific rumour, which was repeated to the Inquiry in a number of forms by various witnesses, was that William Kerr was known to have broken off a sexual relationship with a patient, who then became so distressed that she attempted suicide and, when admitted, recounted to Dr Bromham (the psychiatrist on call) the nature of her relationship with William Kerr (unaware, it is presumed, that Dr Bromham was the wife of William Kerr).

7.6   We were unable to link this story to any particular patient and did not investigate the truth of the rumour, although Dr Bromham denied any knowledge of such a situation. However, we were satisfied that from a relatively early stage in William Kerr's career in North Yorkshire there were rumours circulating about his inappropriate sexual advances towards patients and that these rumours, whilst not universally known amongst healthcare professionals, were widely spread, extending from GPs to hospital nurses.

7.7   Most witnesses who gave evidence to the Inquiry were questioned as to their awareness of rumours. It is plain that many people had heard a little. Some had heard a lot. However, the Health Authorities and NHS Trusts submit that most heard nothing. Due to the fact that evidence has been given, understandably, by those who had heard something, it is possible that a false impression has been given that most people had heard something. However an analysis, conducted by the representatives of the Health Authority, of all the statements submitted to the Inquiry (not merely those who gave oral evidence) suggests that the majority of healthcare professionals were not in fact aware of rumours.

7.8   Rumour is a dangerous thing. It can destroy people quite unnecessarily. Rumour and gossip is rife in hospitals and health authorities, as it is in many institutions. Decisions about events and reputations should not be made on the basis of rumour. The risk of rumour being malicious or unfounded is a strong reason not to act on the basis of gossip and it is difficult, except with hindsight, to criticise a failure to take action in response to rumour. To suggest that because someone is known as a "ladies' man" there should be a suspicion that he might be sexually assaulting people would be ill-advised. However, rumour has some value.

7.9   Much more useful is specific information, even if unsupported. For example "I have been told that X regularly takes his patients home in his car". Professor Sir Liam Donaldson characterised this as anecdotal rumour. It is not really rumour but second-hand information with detail. However characterised, it represents an important warning bell that should be heeded. For this reason, the rest of this chapter concentrates on those instances where patients made, or are alleged to have made, specific complaints about William Kerr, analysing the response of healthcare professionals who were the recipients of these complaints.

A summary of concerns and complaints raised by patients, 1965 to 1988

7.10   This summary sets out, in brief form, the concerns and complaints raised by patients throughout the career of William Kerr in North Yorkshire. It aims to give an overview of the number of concerns and complaints that were raised, yet largely ignored, throughout William Kerr's career in North Yorkshire.

7.11   However, this summary does not consider in any detail the uncertainty that is present in a number of cases, regarding whether the complaint was indeed raised as alleged. Nor does it seek to set out the explanations, where such exist, regarding the failure to progress or investigate complaints. This detail is an important aspect of the story and has instead been set out below.

7.12   During the period 1965 to 1988 the Inquiry is aware of at least 29 patients who alleged some form of complaint or concern concerning William Kerr's conduct. The majority of these patients expressed their concerns first, and usually solely, to their GP. A significant minority spoke to nursing staff about William Kerr's behaviour. Other recipients of isolated or small numbers of concerns were the hospital management, private therapists, the police and solicitors, with some patients raising their concerns with a number of different individuals.

1965

7.13   In 1965, William Kerr's first year in post in North Yorkshire, Patient A1 disclosed to a Harrogate GP, Dr Michael Moore, that William Kerr had made sexual suggestions to her. Dr Moore took advice from the Medical Defence Union and accordingly informed Patient A1 that she should report the matter herself. The complaint did not progress.

7.14   Also in the 1960s an unknown patient, Patient A2, is said (by a friend, Patient A22) to have informed Dr Rushton that William Kerr "tried it on" and "touched her bottom".

1968

7.15   Three years later a patient, Patient A3, whose identity we have also not been able to establish, alleged to Lynn Morgan (then Davey), a young nurse, that she had been raped by William Kerr. Miss Davey told no one.

7.16   In the same year Patient A4, a student nurse, disclosed to the Matron of Harrogate General Hospital that William Kerr, to whom she had been referred to seek approval for an abortion, had forced her to have oral sex. She was disbelieved and the complaint was not taken further.

1971

7.17   Just two years after Patient A4's complaint Patient A6, a student nurse, complained to the Matron of Harrogate General Hospital that William Kerr had persuaded her to have sexual intercourse with him as part of her "treatment". She was disbelieved and subsequently left her nursing course.

7.18   In the same year that Patient A6 complained, Patient A7 disclosed to Nurse Atkins (deceased) at Clifton Hospital that she had had sexual intercourse with William Kerr during a domiciliary visit. Patient A7 considered that Sister Atkins did not believe her. However it appears William Kerr learnt of the allegations and confronted Patient A7. The complaint was not progressed and no inquiry was made into William Kerr's practice.

1972

7.19 In 1972 a complaint against William Kerr reached the management, probably for the first time. Patient A8, a nurse and patient of William Kerr, wrote to the Leeds Regional Hospital Board accusing Kerr of making sexual advances towards her and sexually assaulting a fellow patient, Patient A5. This letter was one of a number written by Patient A8 complaining about a large number of issues. No substantive reply was received.

7.20 In the same year that Patient A8 was writing letters to the management, Patient A9 went to her GP to complain about William Kerr's behaviour. She had been referred to Kerr suffering from anxiety and depression. William Kerr allegedly asked her to wear a short dress for consultations and then exposed himself to her and asked her to place her hand on his genitals, claiming this was part of the treatment. According to Patient A9, her GP's response was that William Kerr was a senior figure, that it would be inappropriate to complain, and that in any event she would not be believed.

7.21 In the early 1970s, the precise date is unclear, Patient A10 allegedly received similar "treatment" from William Kerr. Patient A10 states that William Kerr would expose himself to her and invite her to touch his genitals. Like Patient A9, she also went to her GP, Dr Theo Crawfurd-Porter (deceased, and possibly the same GP that Patient A9 had seen). Dr Crawfurd-Porter allegedly responded "My God the fool", but appears to have taken no action to assist the patient in progressing a formal complaint.

7.22 Another patient who went to her GP in 1972 was Patient A11, then aged 21. She disclosed to her GP, Dr Phyllis Jones, that William Kerr had behaved inappropriately. Patient A11 described consultations where William Kerr would ask her to sit on his knee and kiss him to prove she had no problems relating to men.

1974

7.23 Patient A12 also claims she "tried to talk" to her GP, Dr Frank Young, in 1974, about sexual assaults by William Kerr which had allegedly occurred at Clifton Hospital in William Kerr's office, but received no encouragement. It is likely that any disclosure by Patient A12 to her GP was not made in explicit terms and Dr Young's evidence was that he had no recollection of a complaint.

1975

7.24 In 1975 Patient A13 complained to her GP, Dr George Crouch, about William Kerr. She alleged he made physical sexual advances to her during a domiciliary visit. No action was taken to further the complaint.

1976

7.25 The following year Patient A14 alleged to Sister Wearing at Clifton Hospital that she had been indecently assaulted by William Kerr. Patient A14 also believes she informed her GP, Dr Moss.

1978

7.26 Patient A15 made no explicit disclosure, but in 1978 she hinted to her GP, Dr Derek Jeary, at a concern about William Kerr. Her expressed concerns were confined to William Kerr's questioning on sexual matters, although her allegation to the Inquiry was that William Kerr sexually assaulted her, putting his finger in her vagina.

7.27 Patient A16 alleged that in 1972 William Kerr had inserted his finger into her vagina during an outpatient clinic, describing this as part of a "new treatment". She also alleged that William Kerr had sexual intercourse with her during a second appointment at the Dragon Parade Clinic. In 1978 when the issue arose of a referral of a family member to a psychiatrist, Patient A16 objected to the suggestion of William Kerr, and her recollection is she also specified to her GP the reason for her objection, namely that Kerr had made sexual advances towards her.

7.28 Also in 1978 Patient A17, an inpatient in Clifton Hospital, allegedly disclosed to Nurse Busby that she had been involved in a sexual relationship with William Kerr. Nurse Busby reportedly told Patient A17 to "keep quiet". This was the first disclosure by Patient A17, but she was subsequently to make allegations of a sexual relationship with William Kerr to both Sister Wearing and Deputy Sister Bigwood.

7.29 Patient A18 was a nursing sister who had worked at Harrogate. She was referred to William Kerr in 1978 for a psychiatric opinion prior to undergoing surgery. William Kerr attempted hypnosis of her during a domiciliary visit and she alleged that when she came round his hand was on her groin. Patient A18 went to her GP, Dr Day, and claims she requested that William Kerr was not to visit her at home, although it appears no express complaint of sexual assault was made.

7.30 Patient A19 was also a nurse working in Harrogate. She alleged that whilst she was an inpatient at Clifton hospital in 1978, William Kerr took her to his office and forced her to perform oral sex upon him. She complained, via her solicitor, to Clifton Hospital and was transferred away from William Kerr's care to that of Michael Haslam. However there is no record of any investigation of William Kerr, or any documentation recording the complaint. Patient A19's husband also informed Dr Theo Crawfurd-Porter of the allegation; Dr Crawfurd-Porter allegedly responded that Patient A19 was fantasising. Patient A19 subsequently informed a number of other healthcare professionals of William Kerr's alleged behaviour, including a disclosure to psychologist Marion Anderson in the 1980s, but never sought to pursue a formal complaint.

1979

7.31 The following year, in 1979, Patient A21 made similar allegations to those of Patient A19, namely that William Kerr attempted to force her to perform oral sex upon him. It is likely that Patient A21 made some attempt to inform her GP (probably Dr Michael Moore) about William Kerr, but failed to give any explicit account of his actions.

7.32 Another patient who informed her GP was Patient A20. She was referred to William Kerr in 1979, suffering from depression. She alleges that William Kerr "tried it on" with her, on one occasion undoing his trousers and exposing himself, on another suggesting during a domiciliary visit that they go upstairs. She rejected his advances and informed her GP, Dr Crawfurd-Porter who, she alleges, told her that he could not or would not do anything, as William Kerr was a friend of his.

7.33 In the same year, Patient A22 alleged to her GP, Dr Wade, that William Kerr made sexual propositions towards her. Patient A22 also informed the police, although she declined to make a formal statement for fear of becoming involved in court proceedings. Dr Wade reported Patient A22's concerns to a consultant colleague of William Kerr, Michael Haslam; however no action was taken to investigate William Kerr's practice. This particular complaint, representing the sole occasion when a GP took active steps to forward a complaint about William Kerr, is dealt with in greater detail in Chapter 22.

7.34 Patient A23 also complained to her GP, Dr Rosemary Livingstone, in 1979, claiming that William Kerr talked too much about sex. This did not raise alarm bells in Dr Livingstone's mind as she considered it to be a potentially legitimate part of taking a psychiatric history. Some time later, in 1983, Dr Angus Livingstone (husband of Dr Rosemary Livingstone) received a complaint from a patient, Patient A24, that William Kerr had made an unannounced visit to her home. Although no allegation was made of sexual assault by this patient, the fact of unannounced visits was a concern raised by a number of patients, a potential warning bell that went unheeded. Dr Angus Livingstone discussed his patient's concerns with colleagues, but neither he nor his wife took any action to forward any complaint about William Kerr.

7.35 Patient A25 does not allege any acts of sexual assault by William Kerr but did inform a doctor that she was unhappy that William Kerr only wanted to discuss her sex life. She also alleges William Kerr conducted an internal examination of her with no chaperone present. As a result of her concerns she ceased treatment by William Kerr.

7.36 Finally, in the same year as Patients A22 and A23 complained to their respective GPs, Patient A26 complained to hospital staff at Clifton. She complained to a nurse, Thomas English, about William Kerr visiting her at home and propositioning her. The complaint was passed on to the Nursing Sister, Pauline Brown, who informed William Kerr of the allegation. It appears that the complaint was dismissed as false without any investigation.

7.37 The timing of these complaints, all arising in 1979, emphasises the lack of coordination between concerns or complaints entering the system via different GP practices and those being raised within the hospital.

1981

7.38   In 1981 Patient A27 alleged to her private psychotherapist that some years previously (in about 1972) William Kerr had made sexual advances to her, rubbing his genital area against her face. It appears no action was taken in response to this disclosure. We refer in our conclusions on Michael Haslam leaving the NHS in Chapter 17 to the wider issues involved here.

7.39   A number of patients and healthcare professionals spoke of William Kerr's habit of making unannounced domiciliary visits to patients, and Patient A28 alleged that during domiciliary visits made at short notice William Kerr would touch her and masturbate himself. Patient A28's recollection was that in 1981 she informed her previous GP, Dr Visick, of this, although Dr Visick denied this and no action was taken to further the complaint.

1982

7.40   In 1982, seven years after receiving a complaint from Patient A13 about Kerr, Dr George Crouch was allegedly informed by Patient A29 that she refused to see William Kerr or his wife, Dr Bromham. She did not inform Dr Crouch of the reason for this refusal and was not questioned. Patient A29 alleged to the Inquiry that William Kerr had touched her breasts and pushed her hand against his crotch during an outpatient consultation.

7.41   In 1982 Patient A17, who had first mentioned her "relationship" with William Kerr to Nurse Busby in 1978, allegedly disclosed to Sister Wearing that she had been involved in a sexual relationship with William Kerr.

7.42   Also in 1982/83 Dr Rugg, a consultant psychiatrist in York, was informed by the probation officer that a patient, Patient A30, who allegedly found William Kerr too sexually suggestive, was being transferred to his care. We have not been able to identify this patient.

1983

7.43 The following year, in 1983, Patient A17 disclosed to Deputy Sister Bigwood at Clifton Hospital that she had been involved in a consensual relationship with William Kerr between 1973 and 1975. Deputy Sister Bigwood pursued this allegation with her superiors and this particular allegation is dealt with in detail in Chapter 8.

7.44 In the same year Patient A31 alleges she spoke to her GP, Dr Pamela Reed, accusing William Kerr of inappropriate behaviour at a domiciliary visit in 1981, when William Kerr allegedly forced her to hold his penis whilst he ejaculated. However, it seems unlikely that any concern she expressed to her GP took the form of a detailed complaint, and no action was taken.

7.45 Also in 1983 Patient A32 alleged to a nurse and to a personal friend of hers that she had been sexually assaulted by William Kerr during a domiciliary visit. Whilst the nurse offered to support her, Patient A32 declined to pursue a formal complaint and the nurse took no action to report the matter herself.

7.46 Finally in 1983, Patient A13, who had already complained to her GP, Dr Crouch, in 1975, repeated her allegations of sexual misconduct by William Kerr to a community worker, who in turn passed the information on to Deputy Sister Bigwood, who was already involved in pursuing the complaint raised by Patient A17.

1984

7.47 In or about 1984 Patient A36 alleged to a counsellor, Julie Levine, that she had been sexually abused by a consultant psychiatrist. This disclosure was not reported to the hospital authorities.

7.48 Also in 1984 Dr Rugg recalls seeing a patient, Patient A33 (whom it has not been possible to identify) on a private basis, who refused to see William Kerr due to the alleged inappropriate remarks he would make complimenting her dress and legs. Another patient (probably Patient A34) complained in about 1984 to a nurse, Peter Lister, about William Kerr visiting her at home and making sexual suggestions. The nurse thought at the time that these comments were part of the patient's delusional illness, although he believes he did discuss the disclosure with Dr Rugg.

7.49 Patient A35 states that, following an initial domiciliary visit in 1981, she would see William Kerr in his consulting rooms at Clifton. These consultations were, she alleges, dominated by questions about sex, and William Kerr attempted to kiss her and make sexual advances towards her. In 1984 Patient A35 says she disclosed this to a health visitor, Liz Edwards, and to her GP, Dr Witcher (who denies any disclosure).

1985

7.50 In 1985 Patient A37 alleged to her GP, Dr Nixon, that she had had sexual intercourse with her psychiatrist. Dr Nixon recorded this in her notes and advised her to report this to the authorities.

1986

7.51 The following year, 1986, Patient A37 (possibly in response to Dr Nixon's advice) telephoned George Wood at the Yorkshire Health Authority (YHA) to ask how to lodge a complaint against a psychiatrist at Clifton Hospital. She claimed she had had a sexual relationship with the consultant (whom she did not name). Despite the fact that during 1986 the hospital authorities should have been well aware of the similar allegations made by Deputy Sister Bigwood (to whom Patient A17 had made disclosures of a sexual relationship with Kerr), and the fact that it should have been a relatively simple matter to obtain Patient A37's medical notes to see whose care she had been under in order to question them, no further action was taken by the YHA. It appears that Patient A37 did not pursue the matter.

1987

7.52 In 1987, a year before William Kerr's retirement, Patient A38 alleged to a nurse, Colin Smith, that William Kerr had made inappropriate sexual advances to her. However she did not want to take matters further and the nurse did not report the complaint.

7.53 Finally in 1987 (as found by the Trial of the Facts in 2000), William Kerr sexually assaulted Patient A40. Although she informed her GP, Dr Bennett, in 1987 that things were "not going well" and she did not wish to see William Kerr again, she made no allegation of assault at that stage.

7.54 This summary of concerns and complaints gives, we hope, an overview of the number and type of complaints and concerns that were being raised about William Kerr. In the following section we consider these concerns and complaints, and the response to them in more detail.

The detail of the concerns and complaints, 1965 to 1988

Introduction

7.55 The nature of a private inquiry is such that the transcript of oral hearings is not publicly available. Accordingly, we have set out in this section, in some detail, the evidence of both patients and healthcare professionals who became recipients or alleged recipients of complaints.

7.56 In many cases there has been a discrepancy between the evidence of a patient with a firm recollection of making a complaint, and a healthcare professional, who denies being the recipient of such a disclosure.

7.57 We have sought to analyse in some detail the likelihood that a complaint was made; assess the content of the complaint; reconcile, where possible, conflicting accounts; and make findings on the evidence. Inevitably, this task has been materially hampered by the passage of time and fading memories, the early complaints dating back almost 40 years to the mid-1960s. For some patients we have very little detail, and in certain cases therefore we have not expanded upon what is set out in the preceding summary section. The table at the end of this chapter sets out a complete list of all those patients of whom the Inquiry is aware who alleged they complained about William Kerr. On occasion we have been unable to reach any conclusive view. For the ease of the reader we have highlighted those conclusions of a general nature which have a bearing on the story as a whole.

1965 – Patient A1

7.58 The first warning bell regarding the conduct of William Kerr sounded in a GP's surgery in Harrogate. A GP, Dr Michael Moore, was visited by one of his Harrogate patients, Patient A1, in 1965. She 'stormed' into his office protesting that William Kerr had made sexual suggestions to her. Dr Moore contacted the Medical Defence Union and said that he was advised firstly to tell Patient A1 to report the matter herself, and secondly not to do anything himself. Dr Moore duly advised Patient A1 to go to the police and, in accordance with the advice from the Medical Defence Union, took no further action himself. He heard nothing more regarding the allegations from Patient A1 and has no recollection of any other similar complaints concerning William Kerr, although, as set out below, it is possible that over 10 years later Patient A21 also voiced concerns to him about William Kerr.

7.59 It was not until the police investigation of William Kerr in 1998 that Dr Moore spoke to a police officer. He stated that he was not surprised that William Kerr was the subject of an investigation and described Patient A1's complaints. Patient A1 is now deceased and it has not been possible to discover whether she took Dr Moore's advice and contacted the police; certainly the Inquiry is aware of no investigation arising from her allegations.

7.60 In the six years following the complaint of Patient A1, from 1965 to 1971, four further complaints were to arise concerning William Kerr's behaviour towards patients.

1968 – Patient A3

7.61 In 1968 a young woman, Patient A3, a patient at Clifton Hospital, alleged to Lynn Morgan (then Davey), a young nurse, that she had been raped by William Kerr. Miss Davey told no one. She should have done. Her decision not to speak out was based entirely on her view that to take the matter further would bring nothing but trouble and further harm to the patient who was ill and in great distress. However, her decision not to speak out meant inevitably that there was no record of the allegation. Lynn Davey's reaction demonstrates the tension between the needs of the individual patient and the need to protect the wider patient population.

1968 – Patient A4

7.62 Two of the other four complainants between 1965 and 1971 were student nurses who had been referred to William Kerr as patients.

7.63 Patient A4 was a student nurse at Harrogate General Hospital. In 1968, aged 18, she discovered she was pregnant. She went to see the Home Sister, who provided pastoral care for the student nurses, who advised her to discuss the matter with her parents and the Matron. The Matron advised her she would need to see William Kerr in order to obtain approval for an abortion.[1]

7.64   Patient A4 visited William Kerr at his consulting rooms at Dragon Parade, Harrogate, on a Saturday afternoon. Her recollection is that she was the only person there, that he locked the front door behind her and took her to an upstairs room where he questioned her in detail on her past sexual experiences. Following this he attempted, unsuccessfully, to hypnotise her. He is said to have suggested she remove her clothes in order to assist her relaxation, a request that Patient A4 refused. She closed her eyes as she laid on a couch, and when she opened them, she alleges that William Kerr was completely naked and that he forced her to perform oral sex on him. Patient A4 ran out of the room in a panic and found herself trapped at the front door. Patient A4's account is that William Kerr came downstairs (now fully clothed) and when she threatened to report him, he replied in a calm manner that no one would believe her: "in the state you are in who would believe you? Would they believe you or me?"

7.65   Patient A4's evidence was in parts confused. It is unclear whether she told both the Home Sister and the Matron (both of whose names she was unable to recall), or just the Matron, about William Kerr's assault. It is also unclear precisely what details were conveyed regarding William Kerr's actions, although it appears she did not state explicitly that oral sex had taken place nor that William Kerr had been naked, rather she described William Kerr as having "touched" and "attacked" her. However, Patient A4 is clear and constant in her statements that she conveyed to the Matron that William Kerr had behaved inappropriately and that the Matron's response was that she was lying and would cause both herself and William Kerr a great deal of trouble by saying such things. Patient A4's recollection is that the Matron said that she was a: "nasty, dirty girl, who was ungrateful and upon whom a great deal of money had been spent in her training."

7.66   Patient A4's allegations formed one of the counts of Indecent Assault against William Kerr in the Trial of the Facts. The jury were unable to reach a verdict in respect of her allegations.

---

1 Nurses or student nurses requiring referral to a psychiatrist would, at that time, be referred to William Kerr.

1971 – Patient A6

7.67 Patient A6, like Patient A4, was a student nurse, aged 20, at Harrogate General Hospital. Her oral evidence to the Inquiry was that she was referred to William Kerr suffering from depression and homesickness and that he visited her at her student accommodation on two occasions. On both occasions he allegedly informed her that part of her treatment involved having sexual intercourse with him. Patient A6 states that sexual intercourse took place on each of his two visits. Following the second visit by William Kerr, Patient A6 went to the Home Sister, Sister Thornton, and also to the Matron, Ms Farnsworth, to complain about William Kerr's behaviour. Patient A6 was disbelieved, and considers that it was as a result of complaining that she was asked to leave her nursing course, being told that she "did not fit in". Patient A6 was subsequently referred for inpatient psychiatric treatment at Bradford.

7.68 Patient A6's evidence as to the exact sequence of events was imprecise which, given the passage of time, is perhaps unsurprising. However, her medical notes confirm that on 15 September 1971 she saw her GP requesting to see a psychiatrist, complaining of being tense and anxious and having been ill for three years.

7.69 Patient A6's medical notes also reveal that she had health problems prior to her referral to William Kerr and that doubts had previously been expressed about her reliability and ability to complete her training. It is also apparent that in September 1971 she took at least two overdoses, which were attributed to a break-up with a boyfriend. Subsequent entries in her medical notes suggest that it was as a result of the overdoses that she was seen by William Kerr and advised to give up nursing (having already been off work at this stage for six weeks). Accordingly, Patient A6's belief that she was dismissed from the nursing course solely due to her complaint about William Kerr's behaviour seems unfounded. Whether it played a part in her dismissal from the nursing course remains uncertain.

7.70   The story of Patient A6 demonstrates the difficulty facing staff when informed of an apparent account of sexual abuse by a respected consultant, by a patient who may be perceived as or was indeed having fantasies. However had the history of past allegations against William Kerr been known, or if already known, heeded, Patient A6's account may have been given more serious consideration.

7.71   The stories of Patient A4 and Patient A6 are striking in their similarity. They occurred within three years of each other and it is highly likely that Matron Farnsworth was a recipient of both Patient A4 and Patient A6's complaint. In both cases there appears to have been no investigation as to the substance of their complaints, despite the fact that, according to Patient A6, William Kerr was already known by senior nursing staff to have a reputation as "a ladies' man".

7.72   Even by the early 1970s, a pattern had begun to emerge:

- The complaining patients were automatically disbelieved.

- No action was taken.

- No attempt was made to "join up" the accounts of different patients telling similar stories, and opportunities to carry out investigations were missed.

7.73   Elements of this pattern are repeated throughout the following narrative. Concerns and complaints were repeatedly raised and repeatedly dismissed without any investigation.

1971 – Patient A7

7.74   In the same year that Patient A6 was complaining about William Kerr's behaviour to senior nursing staff at Harrogate General Hospital, at Clifton Hospital, York, Patient A7 was raising concerns with a senior nurse.

7.75   This demonstrates the potential problem where different geographical sites may contribute to a lack of co-ordination regarding the recording and "joining-up" of complaints.

7.76 In about 1968, Patient A7 was referred to William Kerr by her GP, Dr Albert Day, following a suicide attempt. She first saw William Kerr at Harrogate Hospital. She was also treated as an inpatient at Clifton Hospital and subsequently at Dragon Parade, Harrogate, where William Kerr would question Patient A7 on her sex life. Patient A7 alleges that William Kerr then visited her at home unannounced whilst her husband was at work. He proposed sexual intercourse, to which she agreed. Sexual intercourse is said to have taken place on three separate visits, probably during the period 1968 to 1970. Patient A7 recalls William Kerr being insistent that she should tell no one.

7.77 Following a further suicide attempt in 1971, Patient A7 was re-admitted to Clifton Hospital. She says that whilst an inpatient she informed Sister Atkins of the sexual relationship with William Kerr. Patient A7's recollection is that Sister Atkins did not believe her, however it would appear Sister Atkins did inform someone of the disclosure, as Patient A7 recalls William Kerr: "accusing me of telling Sister Atkins about the affair," and asking, "Who else have you told?"

7.78 Sister Atkins is deceased and the Inquiry therefore has limited knowledge about the alleged disclosure by Patient A7.

1972 – Patient A8

7.79 Patient A8 had been a theatre sister employed at Harrogate General Hospital. In 1969 she began to encounter difficulties at work, as a result of which the Matron, Ms Farnsworth, arranged through her GP, Dr Fountain, for Patient A8 to be referred for a psychiatric consultation with William Kerr. In 1970, Patient A8 was dismissed from her employment on grounds of psychiatric illness. Patient A8 herself disputes that she had any psychiatric problem and a long-running dispute commenced regarding her pension rights and retirement on grounds of ill health.

7.80 At the end of one of the last sessions between Patient A8 and William Kerr (probably late 1969), Patient A8 alleges that William Kerr put his arm around her shoulder and asked her if she wanted to stay. In oral evidence to the Inquiry Patient A8 accepted that her complaint, in summary, was that William Kerr had been "flaunting himself, giving her the come-on", and inviting her into a "sexual liaison".

7.81   Patient A8 wrote a large number of letters, over the next (at least) 18 years to a number of people in positions of authority, complaining principally about her pension. However some of her letters also made reference to the conduct of William Kerr.

7.82   In a letter dated 20 March 1972 to the Secretary of the Leeds Regional Hospital Board, Harrogate, Patient A8 included the following passage:

> *"As I was leaving the clinic, I turned at the door to ask Dr Kerr something, and he put his arm around me, and asked me (very softly) if I wanted to stay! I would not dream of making a fuss about a man putting his arm around me, but I hardly need point out that I could hardly be staying for anything but a "session" with Dr Kerr.*

> *"Much later, he was visiting a friend, Patient A5 in her home, whilst her husband was away in the Lake District. Patient A5 never wished to see a psychiatrist. She also had Dr Kerr "inflicted" upon her. According to Patient A5, she was sexually assaulted by Dr Kerr. At first I did not believe her, but later she told me that Dr Crawfurd-Porter had spent Sunday afternoon (his off-duty) trying to brain-wash her. Apparently he kept repeating "it did not happen, did it?" over and over again. Dr Crawfurd-Porter did the same thing to me on 15 January 1970. He called at my house and tried to urge me to accept the pension. In front of my mother, he kept repeating "you are not well enough to work, are you?" Later Patient A5 told me that Dr Kerr had said that he had only tried it on to see if she missed sex! ... He [Dr Kerr] used words that she did not understand. Apparently obscenities. Later, Dr Kerr apologised to both Patient A5 and her husband. Patient A5's husband apparently reported him to his senior at Clifton."*

7.83   The letter also stated:

> *"I also met the Health Visitor at Killinghall. She said 'My God, he [Dr Kerr] has done "something terrible" to a friend of mine.' I did not ask what."*

7.84   There is no record of any response to this letter. It is to be noted that Patient A8's description of her own experience was moderately stated. It is not obvious to us why her expression of concerns and complaints was not investigated.

7.85 The reference to William Kerr's conduct towards the friend of the health visitor at Killinghall was repeated in a letter from Patient A8 to the Officer of the Health Service Commissioner on 6 October 1973, a letter in which Patient A8 also noted:

> *"I have also heard other complaints about Dr Kerr and think it is time that Dr Kerr's activities were looked into."*

7.86 It appears there was a response to this letter on 2 November 1973, but that the suggestion to look into William Kerr's activities was ignored.

7.87 On 10 November 1973, Patient A8 wrote again, this time directly to Sir Allan Marre, the then Health Service Commissioner, and repeated the allegation that Patient A5 had been sexually assaulted by William Kerr. The response to this letter, dated 20 November 1973, was that the matters complained of fell outside the Health Service Commissioner's jurisdiction and that Patient A8 might instead wish to approach the Department of Health and Social Security. Following this response, Patient A8's mother wrote to the Health Service Commissioner in a letter dated 30 November 1973:

> *"I have just recently been in touch with the Chairman of the Leeds Regional Hospital Board and he informs me he is aware of the complaints my daughter has made to you regarding Dr Kerr and other medical personnel at Harrogate General Hospital. Would you kindly inform me of the results of the enquiries you have made of the hospital authorities."*

7.88 There is no evidence that any enquiries were made.

7.89 The response of the authorities to Patient A8's letters was described by counsel for the former patients as an "abject failure to pick up and investigate what were clear and unambiguous complaints about Kerr's behaviour". That there was a failure to investigate is without doubt. We are satisfied that Patient A8's account of her own experience with William Kerr has been reasonably constant over the years – whether true or not. However the clarity of the complaints against William Kerr's behaviour contained within the letters is more apparent with hindsight. The letters from Patient A8 contain a number of complaints extending over a number of pages against a variety of healthcare professionals, one of whom was William Kerr. Further, the letters arose in the context of a clearly aggrieved former member of staff who had been dismissed on grounds of psychiatric ill health. We conclude that to say the letters made "clear and unambiguous complaints" is to overstate the case. In fact their clarity was obscured by the profusion of other complaints and issues raised in Patient A8's letters.

7.90   Nevertheless, we accept that complaints were made, and that they extended beyond Patient A8's own experience and covered another former patient, and named a GP (Dr Theo Crawfurd-Porter) who could have provided further information.

7.91   Had there been a proper system of record-keeping, such that the complaints against William Kerr by Patient A8 (and in relation to Patient A5) could have been related to the previous allegations, the letters would have been less readily dismissed, as they were, as the ramblings of a disaffected public servant who had reluctantly taken retirement on grounds of ill health.

7.92   In 1973 Patient A8 requested that William Kerr's activities be "looked into". If there had been a more sympathetic and informed response, then it might not have been necessary for there to have been a delay of another 24 years before it came about. We have little doubt that this attitude was an example of how the culture at the time operated against the best interests of the patients.

7.93   We must conclude, therefore, that this was another opportunity missed.

1972 – Patients A9 and A10

7.94   Whilst Patient A8 was pursuing her grievances through the Hospital Authorities and Health Service Commissioner, complaints about William Kerr were also, we were told, being communicated to GPs.

7.95   Patient A9 was referred to William Kerr in 1972 by her GP, suffering from anxiety and depression due to marital problems. Initially Patient A9 and her husband were both referred to William Kerr. However, according to Patient A9, William Kerr then suggested he see her alone at her home and specified that she should wear "a short dress and not any form of trousers or jeans".

7.96   Patient A9 describes William Kerr exposing himself and asking her to place her hand on his genitals, alleging this was part of the treatment. Patient A9 describes William Kerr then concentrating on intimate sexual matters in their discussions. After a number of "treatments", Patient A9 says she went back to her GP to complain about William Kerr's behaviour. The response of the GP, she said, was to "shrug off the complaint", saying that William Kerr was a senior figure within the local National Health Service, that "it would be inappropriate to make any formal complaint" and that she would not be believed. Further, it was said by the GP that William Kerr's statements could all have been part of the treatment. Patient A9's evidence was that the GP she complained to was either Dr John Givans or Dr George Crouch, although both of these doctors denied being the recipient of such a disclosure or of responding as Patient A9 alleged.

7.97 Patient A9's account bears a striking similarity to that of Patient A10. Patient A10 was referred to William Kerr in the early 1970s by Dr Theo Crawfurd-Porter, a doctor in the same surgery as Dr Givans and Dr Crouch. Patient A9 describes William Kerr sitting behind a large desk and inviting her to sit at the side of the desk. She alleges that William Kerr then exposed himself to her with the words: "What about some of this, this is what you need", inviting her to touch his genitals, which she refused. William Kerr thereafter discussed sexual matters, rather than focusing upon Patient A10's problems. Patient A10 informed Dr Crawfurd-Porter that she would not go back to William Kerr. Indeed according to Patient A8 (to whom Patient A10 recounted her story in 1982), Patient A10 told Dr Crawfurd-Porter of William Kerr's behaviour, to which his response was: "My God, the fool".

7.98 A number of other patients had allegedly received similarly dismissive responses from Dr Crawfurd-Porter to their concerns about William Kerr. Dr Crawfurd-Porter allegedly tried to persuade Patient A5 that the sexual assault she complained of had not happened. In relation to Patient A19's complaints about William Kerr (regarding being forced to perform sex), Dr Crawfurd-Porter allegedly made obscene jokes and informed Patient A19's husband that his wife was fantasising.

7.99 We conclude that it is likely that Patient A9 did make a complaint to her GP. However, on the evidence, we are unable to conclude who that GP was. Patient A9 refers to Drs Crouch and Givans. We consider that her description describes the likely response of Dr Crawfurd-Porter, the then senior partner.

7.100 What is clear is that, if there was any form of complaint to the GP, it was not taken further – and indeed there was active discouragement.

1972 – Patient A11

7.101 In 1972, Patient A11 was referred to William Kerr for treatment by her GP, Dr Phyllis Jones, following an overdose. During the consultations, which took place at the Duchy Nuffield Hospital, Harrogate, Patient A11 alleges that William Kerr suggested to her that she had difficulty relating to men and that she should prove that she had no problem by sitting on his knee and kissing him. We here include Patient A11's written description of events:

> "He asked me to go round the desk to where he was. I didn't want to go any further. He went on to say how I didn't want to get close to men and I could prove I did if I went round to him and sat on his knee. He took hold of my hand when I walked round to his chair and I stood near him. He said something like 'There you are, that's progress', basically encouraging me to go further. I wanted to prove that there wasn't a problem in that area. I felt uncomfortable, shaky and became tearful. He was very clever by making me approach him, resulting in me moving to him rather than him moving towards me. He wanted me to go further by sitting on his knee, put my arm around him and kiss him. I became a bit frightened because I didn't feel in control of the situation, he was meant to make things better and seemed to be making them worse."

7.102 At that time, Patient A11 was 21 years old – William Kerr was in his mid 40s.

7.103 Patient A11 was not happy with the "treatment" and asked a friend to accompany her on future sessions, at which William Kerr behaved appropriately.

7.104 Patient A11 returned to her GP, Dr Phyllis Jones, at Leeds Road Surgery, Harrogate and explained what had happened in her consultations with William Kerr, asking whether there had been other complaints. Patient A11 says of Dr Jones:

> "I think she believed me but I got the impression that she believed if a complaint went further Dr Kerr would probably be believed rather than me."

7.105 Dr Jones, in her police statement dated 1997, stated she recalled discussing with Dr Foggitt, a fellow partner, the fact that patients had made allegations that William Kerr was over-familiar or over-friendly. In particular she was able to recall three patients making allegations directly to her. She describes her response to these patients:

> *"as they did not wish to take the matter any further, I would not have made any notes about the allegations."*

7.106 In her oral evidence to the Inquiry, Dr Jones claimed she could no longer recall the number of complaints which she had told the police about in 1997, neither could she recall a partners' meeting where serious concerns about William Kerr had been voiced. Her memory was apparently confined to Patient A11's complaint, which she said amounted to William Kerr being "slightly suggestive", although she accepted that this was sufficient to make her more "cautious" about referring female patients to William Kerr.

7.107 Given the content of Dr Jones' police statement in 1997, combined with the evidence of Dr Scatchard and Dr Foggitt, both of whom had some recollection of a partners' meeting – where it seems likely there was discussion of a patient complaining about William Kerr exposing himself – the Panel finds that Dr Jones, with her fellow partners (including Dr Foggitt and Dr Scatchard) were collectively aware of a number of allegations concerning William Kerr's conduct towards female patients. Despite the knowledge that concerns had been raised by more than one patient, as a surgery and as individuals they failed to take any steps to report these concerns to the hospital authorities or the Regional Health Authority which employed William Kerr.

7.108 Thus it would appear that by the mid-1970s there was concern in at least two surgeries in Harrogate, Dr Moss and Partners at King's Road (which included Dr Crawfurd-Porter, Dr Crouch and Dr Givans) and Dr Chave Cox and Partners at Leeds Road (which included Dr Jones, Dr Foggitt and Dr Scatchard), that William Kerr was in some way "suspect" in relation to his conduct towards female patients. It is unclear whether the concerns had been communicated to all partners within those surgeries, although without doubt such concerns should have been shared.

7.109 It is not surprising that for many patients the most accessible means of expressing a concern or complaint was to speak to their GP. However in the case of the majority of patients, and certainly in the case of Patient A11, the concerns fell on stony ground and were disregarded. Moreover, it is likely that this process of disclosure and rejection added yet further distress.

1974 – Patient A12

7.110 Patient A12 was referred to William Kerr's outpatient clinic at Harrogate General Hospital on 30 November 1973 by her GP, Dr Frank Young of Beech House Surgery, Knaresborough. She was in turn referred on from the outpatient clinic to Clifton Hospital, where she was treated as an inpatient. Patient A12 alleges that in December 1973 at Clifton Hospital she was indecently assaulted by William Kerr during a consultation in his office, a pattern that was repeated a number of times during her stay. Patient A12 describes the first incident as follows:

> "The first time I saw Dr Kerr in his office was on 2 December 1973. He tried to discuss my sex life in detail, and refused to listen to my complaints about the things that were bothering me. I cried with frustration and put my head in my hands but at this point he pushed my head into his crotch, and simulated oral sex. He continued to talk only of sexual matters."

7.111 Patient A12 said she was noticeably reluctant to go and see William Kerr in his office, but none of the nurses ever questioned the reason for this reluctance.

7.112 Following discharge from Clifton Hospital, Patient A12 continued to see William Kerr as an outpatient at Dragon Parade, allegedly under duress from her husband. During one of these consultations William Kerr is said to have masturbated whilst standing behind her chair.

7.113 Patient A12 alleged at the Trial of the Facts that she tried to talk to her GP, Dr Young, who seemed not to want to know. Dr Young had no recollection of any complaint about William Kerr from Patient A12. It seems likely that Patient A12 in fact made no complaint in express terms, hence Dr Young's lack of recollection. Indeed Patient A12's statement to the Inquiry says she made no contemporaneous disclosure to any healthcare professional, repeating remarks in a statement made for civil proceedings where she stated that she felt unable to confide in her GP.

7.114 Patient A12 did disclose to her parish priest a number of years later (in about 1976) what she alleged had occurred, and the priest confirmed during the police investigation a "vague" recollection of a disclosure concerning sexual misbehaviour by William Kerr.

7.115 The other health professional apart from Dr Young to whom Patient A12 disclosed was a clinical psychologist, Marion Anderson, although this disclosure did not take place until 1991.

7.116 In the Trial of the Facts, the jury concluded that William Kerr was not guilty of the facts alleged by Patient A12.

7.117 This is the first of the former patients referred to in this Report where, at the Trial of the Facts, there was a "not guilty" verdict. Of course, the basis for that verdict remains unclear. There could be no guilty verdict unless the jury were sure (to the criminal standard of proof) that William Kerr had done the acts alleged against him, and that those acts amounted to the criminal offence of sexual assault (or, in some cases, rape). The jury, therefore, may have disbelieved Patient A12, or concluded that she was consenting to William Kerr's advances.

7.118 Any attempt by us to investigate the reason for the jury's verdict would be speculative in the extreme, and wrong. We do, however, note that the Trial of the Facts was in 2000 – many, sometimes tens, of years after the events in question. Notwithstanding submissions to the contrary made by counsel for the health authorities, we are satisfied that if investigations had been carried out in the 1970s or 1980s, charges may then have been laid against William Kerr. We cannot, of course, predict the outcome of a trial at that time, when (we assume) William Kerr would have been well enough to take an active part. What we can say is that, whatever the verdict(s), a trial then would have been fairer to all involved – to William Kerr and to the former patients.

7.119 After giving evidence in relation to Patient A12, Marion Anderson also described to us an incident which gave some indication of the overbearing position and status of William Kerr, and casts light on the then prevailing culture. The incident, William Kerr's behaviour, and Marion Anderson's over-tolerant reaction at the time, is disturbing.

7.120 The incident related to an unnamed and unidentified patient who had been referred from William Kerr to Marion Anderson. The patient was believed to be suffering from psychosexual fantasies. The patient arrived at the hospital as an outpatient, when in front of Marion Anderson and outside his office, William Kerr asked the patient if "beards turned her on". She did not respond. William Kerr, according to Marion Anderson's account, then went up to the patient and rubbed his beard all over her face. Her description of the incident concluded as follows:

> "Dr Kerr then looked at me almost as if to ask what I was going to do about it."

7.121 Marion Anderson told us that she "did not feel the incident was very serious". Her response led to the following exchange with Counsel to the Inquiry:

Q. The incident being that he asks the patient if beards turned her on, and then goes up to the patient and rubs his beard in her face. You described that as "slightly inappropriate behaviour". Is that as far as you regarded it? It was just something a little bit odd, a little bit out of the ordinary, slightly inappropriate? From a non-medical perspective, it looks like a piece of fairly extraordinary behaviour.

A. It is very difficult at this stage to put the same judgment on it as I did at the time. I know that I was concerned, but the patient was a bit surprised, but was not concerned.

Q. It is an extraordinary piece of behaviour: somebody who is in the position of a psychiatrist who is dealing with psychosexual problems of a female patient goes up to her and rubs his beard in her face. That is bizarre beyond belief, is it not? Or maybe you did not see it that way, maybe you saw it as part of the rough and tumble of being a psychiatrist?

A. This is what I was trying to explain to you earlier: you are in an environment, you are in a setting where, because of what is going on all around you all day, it is difficult to see things in the perspective that you would see them.

Q. Do I take it from that that looking at it now and, as it were, re-rationalising what you think of it, you have probably a slightly different view of the appropriateness or otherwise of that behaviour than you did when it occurred?

A. Yes. But a lot of things have changed.

7.122 This incident was picked up in questions from the Chairman:

> Q. *When you described the incident when Dr Kerr rubbed his beard over the patient's face, and you were trying to tell us that it is difficult to understand that without being there at the time. Looking at it now, I think we are all agreed that that was a very unusual, perhaps even very inappropriate, behaviour. What it also conveys, or may convey, is domination of a patient; domination to such an extent that a man could rub his beard over her face and she would not complain. You did complain to him, as I read your statement, and the response was, "What has it got to do with you? Who do you think you are?"*
>
> A. *"Who do you think you are?" That was the attitude I was up against at that time with the psychiatrists.*
>
> Q. *There you had one or two men who were in control, and control was very important; is that right so far?*
>
> A. *Yes. There was a third, junior psychiatrist, who we have mentioned, Dr Rugg, but he came along later, and he was a different school.*

7.123 We accept the accuracy of the description of the "beard rubbing" incident. When looked at in its proper context, it shows an institution out of control, where values are inverted, where seriously inappropriate behaviour is accepted, where control and domination is tolerated.

7.124 Add to the description of the incident Marion Anderson's evidence that in the 1960s to the 1980s patients who had mental disorders (of whatever nature) were *routinely* disbelieved as fantasisers, where psychiatrists could blame it all on problems of "transference", and there is in place a culture and environment where abuse can flourish, and where a failure to respond to concerns and complaints becomes the norm.

1975 – Patient A13

7.125 In October 1975 Patient A13 (then 23 years old) was re-referred to William Kerr, having been treated in Clifton Hospital earlier in the year. William Kerr made a domiciliary visit and it is alleged that during this visit he attempted to persuade her to go upstairs to the bedroom, away from her children. When she refused, he allegedly touched her breast and tried to force her legs open with his knees. She resisted his embrace and ordered him to leave the house, despite his protests that he was only seeking to comfort her and that she was imagining things due to her distraught state. The following is taken from Patient A13's police statement made in 1997 (she gave oral evidence to the same effect in William Kerr's Trial of the Facts in 2000):

> "I remember Dr Kerr visited me in the morning at home and the children were around. I answered the front door and let him in. I was crying as I opened the door and obviously distraught. Dr Kerr immediately placed both his arms around me, in what I at first thought was a comforting gesture. I didn't reject the embrace at first because I was so distressed that I needed the comfort and support. I remember welcoming the power and strength from the embrace.
>
> I recall that the children were demanding my attention and screaming, I was also still crying. I therefore suggested that we went through to the front room, where the children were. He still kept his arms around me, and he said that we needed to be alone to talk and suggested that we went upstairs to our bedroom. I remember saying 'no' because we couldn't leave the children in the front room alone. He again tried to encourage me to leave the children and to go upstairs so that we could talk.
>
> I realised that something was not right at this stage, and inwardly I felt uneasy and the alarm bells started to ring. Something was not right. I had also become aware of Dr Kerr's knees trying to force their way between my legs. I tried to pull away from Kerr, but I was unable to, he was still holding me very tightly. I remember becoming more fearful. He told me that I needed to be comforted. I again told him that we were not going upstairs, and I could still feel that his knees were pushing between my legs even more forcefully.

I was then aware of his hand cupping my breast. This happened very quickly. I know that both our bodies were very close at this time. I definitely knew that his hand was cupped around my breast. As I have said, the alarm bells inside me were ringing very loud. I then wriggled to get away from Dr Kerr and pushed him away. I also brought my knee up, and kicked him in the groin area. I was very angry at this time, and I shouted at him to get out of my house, and not to come back."

7.126 We have set out Patient A13's evidence in some detail as the prelude to what followed. Patient A13's evidence to the Inquiry was that, having considered the matter for a couple of hours, she went to her GP's surgery and complained directly to Dr Crouch. She was clear that she conveyed to Dr Crouch the sexual nature of the assault on her. She states that she told Dr Crouch that she:

"hoped he was going to document it in my notes and that if he did not believe me, then whenever the next lady came through his surgery door, whether it be next week, next year or in 10 years' time he would believe them."

7.127 Patient A13 stated that Dr Crouch's response was dismissive and that he did not believe her, suggesting to her that as she was on medication she might have imagined things. In his evidence to the Inquiry Dr Crouch denied that Patient A13, or indeed any patient, had complained to him about William Kerr's behaviour.

7.128 In about 1977 Patient A13 states she approached Dr Crouch for a further psychiatric referral and on this occasion was referred to Dr Bromham. According to Patient A13, at the time of this referral, she told Dr Crouch that she refused to see William Kerr and repeated her account of William's Kerr's alleged assault on her five years previously. Patient A13 was unaware that Dr Bromham was William Kerr's wife and at the consultation with Dr Bromham, Patient A13 informed her of William Kerr's alleged assault. Dr Bromham allegedly listened to the allegations against William Kerr, appearing to accept Patient A13's account, but offered no assistance in terms of progressing a complaint. Dr Bromham in her evidence to the Inquiry had no recollection of Patient A13, although she accepted it was possible that Patient A13 could have made an allegation against her husband which she dismissed as a fabrication.

7.129 Patient A13's account highlights the difficulties surrounding the issue of believing patients. She herself recognised the difficulty and states that at the time of the alleged assaults she felt:

> "*who is going to believe me, a young lady who is on a long list of medication who has just come out of a psychiatric hospital or a doctor of his high standing at the time.*"

7.130 The difficulty faced by a GP when confronted with an allegation of sexual misconduct made by a patient with mental health problems is also illustrated by Patient A13's evidence. She acknowledged that her behaviour was "not normal", and while criticism can be levelled at a GP for failing to believe her, Patient A13 accepted that even her own husband did not believe her account of abuse by William Kerr.

7.131 However, perhaps the principal significance of Patient A13's account is the extent to which it represents an opportunity missed.

7.132 In about 1983, Patient A13 was introduced, through a mutual friend who was a community worker, to a nurse, Deputy Sister Linda Bigwood, who was pursuing a complaint against William Kerr concerning his alleged sexual impropriety towards female patients. Patient A13 agreed that she would be happy to assist Linda Bigwood and produce a statement. Linda Bigwood recorded her contact with Patient A13 (albeit not mentioning her name) in a typed note dated 20 August 1983:

> "*Indirectly, I have heard that it is well known in Harrogate that Dr Kerr abuses his trust in young female patients. Without any prompting, a social worker from Harrogate told me that a friend of hers, while she was living in Harrogate, had gone to Dr Kerr with a problem, and had been immediately propositioned by him, and that she had been very upset by it and refused to see him again.*"

7.133 In March 1985 Linda Bigwood repeated this account in a further typed document (which, like her earlier account, was sent to the York Health Authority). This account in particular makes it clear that the patient she is speaking of must be Patient A13:

> *"Coincidentally, I was informed by a Community Worker from Harrogate that a friend of hers had been sexually propositioned by Dr Kerr during a domiciliary visit to her home when she was suffering from depression. She would be prepared to put this in writing."*

7.134 However, as we set out in some detail in the next Chapter, Linda Bigwood's repeated calls for the York Health Authority to investigate William Kerr's practice were not heeded and no one sought from Linda Bigwood names of witnesses (such as Patient A13) who might have been prepared to make a complaint, had they been approached.

7.135 Had the York Health Authority sought to follow up Linda Bigwood's well-documented concerns about William Kerr, it seems highly likely that enquiries would have led them to Patient A13 (a witness seemingly prepared to make a written statement). This in turn would have led them to Dr Crouch's surgery, which was likely to have uncovered yet further complaints. In particular, Patient A5, Patient A9, Patient A10, Patients A19 and A29 all allegedly made complaints or raised concerns about referral to William Kerr to one or other of the doctors at Dr Crouch's surgery (Dr Moss & Partners).

7.136 In the Trial of the Facts Patient A13's allegations formed one of the counts of indecent assault. The jury was not able to reach a verdict in respect of Patient A13's allegations.

7.137 In analysing what complaint, if any, was made by Patient A13, the Inquiry was faced with a direct conflict of evidence between Patient A13 and Dr Crouch as to what was said some 27 years ago. Dr Crouch was firm in his written and oral evidence to the Inquiry that he had not received any complaint from Patient A13 at all. For example, in his written evidence he said this:

"I can say categorically that at no time did Patient A13 ever complain to me about Dr Kerr's behaviour towards her. Her description of arriving at my surgery and demanding to see me immediately would not fit with how our surgeries were organised. Had any patient reported the type of episode which Patient A13 is suggesting she reported to me, I would have recorded this in her notes and then discussed what had been disclosed with my partners. I had been a principal in General Practice for approximately 18 months at that time and would have felt duty bound to consult with my partners with regard to such a serious allegation."

7.138 This statement is perhaps a little stronger than the statement made to the police in 1997 when Dr Crouch said this:

"From the time that I joined Dr Moss and Partners as a partner, in August 1973, I have referred many patients to Dr Kerr until his retirement in the mid-1980s. I can recall no patient making any complaint to me about any impropriety by Dr Kerr."

7.139 Dr Crouch's oral evidence to the Inquiry re-emphasised the point:

"I was a young doctor then and not long in the practice [he had joined the practice two years earlier in 1973]. I had never come across a patient being sexually assaulted by a doctor before. It would be so far out of my knowledge that I would have noted it and I would have made enquiries of my partners as to what I should do about it. I would not, in any circumstances, have ignored it."

7.140 The documentary evidence adds further confusion, recording that Patient A13 saw William Kerr in January 1976, several months after the alleged assault (although Patient A13 denies she saw William Kerr after the alleged assault). Further, the alleged 1977 referral of Patient A13 to Dr Bromham appears to have in fact been made by Dr Givans, not by Dr Crouch as Patient A13 alleges.

7.141 Nevertheless, there are a number of factors that have led us to conclude that, on the balance of probabilities, Patient A13 did, as she alleges, complain to her GP – probably to Dr Crouch – in 1975 regarding William Kerr's conduct. First, Patient A13 has a specific recollection of going to the surgery with her two children in the pushchair in the rain and demanding that the receptionist let her see the doctor at once without an appointment. This not only has the ring of truth to it, but is consistent with her anger described above. Second, and more significantly, at the time of the alleged abuse Patient A13 told her friend what had occurred. Her friend gave a statement to the police in 1997 confirming that, shortly after the alleged assault, Patient A13 had described to her how she had gone to Dr Crouch to complain. Third, Patient A13's husband also gave a statement to the police in 1997 to the effect that Patient A13 had been assaulted by William Kerr, and had been to see Dr Crouch. Both the friend and Patient A13's husband gave oral evidence in the Trial of the Facts. Fourth, whilst there is doubt as to whether Patient A13 repeated the complaint to Dr Crouch in 1977, as the referral letter to Dr Bromham seems to come from Dr Givans, it is significant to note that rather than being referred back to her previous treating consultant (William Kerr) a change was made and she was referred to a female psychiatrist. Whilst this could perhaps be attributed to chance, it certainly fits with Patient A13's account that she was only prepared to see a female psychiatrist and informed her GP of this fact. We attribute some significance to the exclamation mark at the end of the following extract from the letter by Dr Bromham to Dr Givans in relation to Patient A13:

> "Thank you for referring this patient with the information that she had seen Bill [a reference to William Kerr] and had in-patient treatment with electroplexy in 1975 for menopausal depression; the situation throughout her marriage had not been very satisfactory and she now felt she again required psychiatric help, but had suggested that a female psychiatrist might be more appropriate!"

7.142 Returning to Dr Crouch, Patient A13's evidence is that he did not believe her allegations against William Kerr. Significantly, Patient A13 accepts that even her own husband did not believe her, as her behaviour at the time was, in her own words, "not normal", Assuming Dr Crouch considered that Patient A13's concerns could be attributed to her mental state and/or medication and thus made no note of the matter in the GP notes, we consider it is entirely possible that almost 30 years and no doubt thousands of patient consultations later, he might (as he claims) have no recollection of Patient A13's report of William Kerr's conduct. We make it clear that we are not concluding that Dr Crouch has deliberately sought to mislead the Inquiry.

7.143 However, there are a number of factors that lead us to conclude that Dr Crouch must have been aware in the 1970s and 1980s of at least some concerns regarding William Kerr's behaviour towards female patients. The senior partner, Dr Moss, admitted to the Inquiry that he considered William Kerr to be suspect. According to Dr Moss, Dr Crawfurd-Porter (another partner) had mentioned on two occasions William Kerr's "unorthodox" practices and another (unidentified) partner had been present at this disclosure. In such circumstances, where at least three partners seem to have been aware of rumours, the Inquiry considers it likely that all the partners would have discussed the matter, even if informally, and have been aware of some level of concern. The Inquiry has also taken into account the fact that a further patient, Patient A29, similarly claims that she saw Dr Crouch following alleged abuse by William Kerr.

1976 – Patient A14

7.144 Patient A14 was referred to William Kerr by her GP, Dr Moss, in 1972, suffering from post-natal depression and agoraphobia. During domiciliary visits Patient A14 alleges William Kerr touched her breasts and spoke about sexual matters. In or about 1976, following a deterioration of her psychiatric condition, Patient A14 was admitted to Clifton Hospital for treatment as an inpatient. During consultations Patient A14 alleges that William Kerr would ask her to touch his genitals and discuss sexual matters. Patient A14 believed she informed Sister Wearing about William Kerr's behaviour and also spoke to Dr Moss, whom she felt did not believe her. Sister Wearing had no recollection of Patient A14 or any such disclosure; likewise Dr Moss had no recollection of a complaint from Patient A14, although he did consider William Kerr's conduct to be "suspect", based on remarks made by one of his partners, Dr Crawfurd-Porter.

1978 – Patient A15

> **7.145** The account of Patient A13 set out above demonstrates the difficulty surrounding the issue of "believing patients", even in the context of what appears to have been an explicit complaint about a consultant's behaviour. Patient A15's account demonstrates how these problems are magnified when the patient feels unable to complain, in clear terms, of sexual impropriety (perhaps due to fear of being disbelieved, fear of adverse consequences, and misplaced guilt or embarrassment) and simply "hints" to a GP at a problem, a hint which may easily, and in some cases understandably, be overlooked.

7.146 Patient A15 had considerable contact with the psychiatric services since about 1971. In 1977 she was admitted to Bootham Park Hospital, York by her GP, Dr Jeary. In relation to her admission to Bootham Park, Dr Jeary noted that Patient A15 was unhappy that few tests had been done, that she had been upset by questions relating to sexual matters and had been assaulted by another patient. In September 1977 Dr Jeary, in light of Patient A15's concerns about her treatment at Bootham Park, referred her to William Kerr (who had not been involved in her treatment at Bootham Park), noting in the referral letter that:

> *"Patient A15 has been upset by some of the questioning she received at Bootham Park."*

7.147 Patient A15 was first seen by William Kerr's Senior Health Officer, Dr Tom Donaldson, on 13 October 1977. He conducted a full review and once again recorded Patient A15's complaint about her treatment at Bootham Park, noting that she:

> *"expressed several doubts about the validity of the questions asked at Bootham as they referred mainly to sexual problems."*

7.148 Patient A15 was probably first seen by William Kerr in late October 1977, when she alleges that he subjected her to detailed and intrusive questioning about her sex life, asked her to lie on a couch and remove her top layer of clothing and her bra. He then "examined me with a light feathery touch, over both my breasts and my front, feeling around and inside the top of my knicker elastic tights". She then returned to her chair, where she alleges William Kerr forcibly restrained her whilst he assaulted her by stroking her clitoris and vagina, and putting his finger in her vagina. He then allegedly barred her exit from the room as he groped her from behind.

7.149 On her second and subsequent visits (in total approximately six), Patient A15 says she sat further away from William Kerr and kept her legs crossed. Her account is that when she acted in this way:

> *"he [William Kerr] did not pursue it and returned to his seat."*

7.150 It would appear that Patient A15's last session with William Kerr was in February 1978, as William Kerr wrote a discharge letter to Dr Jeary on 22 February 1978. Patient A15 subsequently spoke to Dr Jeary but mentioned only that she had been concerned about William Kerr's line of questioning to which he replied:

> *"he is entitled to ask those questions."*

7.151 In his evidence, Dr Jeary accepted that he recalled Patient A15 complaining about sexual questioning, but considered that this would have formed a normal part of psychiatric history-taking. He added that in retrospect he accepted that he:

> *"did not do her justice, that I should perhaps have given more importance to what she was saying and I did not deliver the goods on that."*

7.152 Dr Jeary also accepted in oral evidence that he had previously been made aware of a patient who had complained to Dr Keyworth (a GP in the same surgery) about William Kerr, although his evidence was that at the time of Patient A15's concerns about sexual questioning he did not put the two together.

7.153 Patient A15, like Patient A13, had real concerns that her account would not be believed and that she would be thought of as "loopy". In her oral evidence to the Inquiry she added that she was concerned about not being believed, and further:

> *"I could not open up to the GP. I was frightened that, had it got referred back to him [William Kerr], he would then have me admitted into York and I would be under his control. He frightened me."*

7.154 Later, in 1981, Patient A15's husband required referral to a psychiatrist. Patient A15 informed the referring GP (Dr Dixon) that her husband would not see "the psychiatrist at Ripon [William Kerr]". Accordingly, Patient A15's husband was referred to Dr Bromham. Allegedly, at Dr Bromham's clinic, Dr Bromham herself raised the issue of an onward referral to William Kerr, to which Patient A13 says she responded:

> *"No way is my husband going to see him. I wouldn't even take my cats to see him."*

7.155 Dr Bromham had no recollection of Patient A15 or of any such remark being made to her.

1978 – Patient A16

7.156 Dr Jeary was allegedly the recipient of a further complaint by a patient, Patient A16, also in 1978. Patient A16 was referred to William Kerr in about 1972 by her GP, Dr Heatley. Her first appointment with William Kerr took place at the Harrogate General Hospital and on this occasion he allegedly sat opposite her at close quarters. He allegedly told her to open her legs and then he inserted his finger into her vagina, breaking through her tights. This first assault was interrupted by a porter knocking on the door. William Kerr is said to have explained his actions as "a new treatment" brought back from a recent trip to America. The second appointment took place in what Patient A16 describes as: "a small house opposite the Dragon Parade clinic". Patient A16 comments that the clinic seemed deserted (just as it had to Patient A4 when she visited Dragon Parade seeking approval for an abortion) and that she had sexual intercourse with William Kerr on the floor. The third appointment took place at the Duchy Nuffield Hospital and Patient A16 states that William Kerr collected her from her home before driving her there. Once at the hospital, he allegedly undressed and asked her to perform oral sex upon him, which she refused. He then asked her to lie down on the couch and, she thinks, masturbated behind her. Patient A16 had become increasingly uneasy about this "new treatment", until on this third occasion she formed the opinion he was behaving improperly and she attended no more appointments.

7.157 It was not until 1978 that Patient A16 alleges she spoke to Dr Jeary, prompted by Dr Jeary's suggestion that he refer one of her family members to William Kerr. She states that she disclosed to Dr Jeary that William Kerr had made sexual advances to her. According to Patient A16, Dr Jeary's response was: "Oh, some of these people are very strange".

7.158 The following extracts from Patient A16's evidence are particularly relevant:

> *Q. I appreciate you cannot remember the exact words, but it is quite important to the Inquiry to know whether what you did specifically say to Dr Jeary was "sexual advances" or whether you just said, "I did not like him".*
>
> *A. It was "sexual advances". I was trying to put it in a polite way. I did not want to talk about the detail. I thought he would get the message enough from that term.*
>
> *Q. You are completely clear in your mind, are you, that you at least conveyed to Dr Jeary that it was sexual impropriety by William Kerr?*
>
> *A. Absolutely.*
>
> *Q. What did you feel about Dr Jeary's reaction to that? Did you feel that it surprised him or that he was aware of it already?*
>
> *A. I was aware of no silence whatsoever. He just said, "Oh, some of these people are rather strange". I was shocked.*
>
> *Q. You are clear there he was talking about William Kerr as being rather strange?*
>
> *A. I assumed he was talking about psychiatrists in general.*
>
> *Q. What were you intending by that? Clearly, you were intending for [the member of your family] not to be referred, but were you in some ways making a formal complaint, thinking, "If I tell Dr Jeary, he is obviously still around, this will stop him"?*
>
> *A. I thought it was an opportunity to tell him. I had thought I should tell someone for a long time and put it off, and I thought this is the ideal time to say something.*

Q. In your mind, what did you think Dr Jeary would do about it?

A. I thought he would tell me either to report it, or that he would report it, not just a rebuff answer like that, offhand.

Q. When he did not say to you, "Would you like to report it?", did you think about doing anything more? Did you think, "Maybe now I should write a letter"?

A. No. I thought if he is not going to do anything, how can I do anything? He was the one person I expected would have taken the matter up.

7.159 Dr Jeary disputed Patient A16's account. He stated:

"I am quite definite that if she had mentioned the words 'sexual advances', it would have pressed alarm bells in my mind and I would have acted completely differently. ... I would have asked her to make a full statement in writing, and I would have discussed it with all my partners. I may well have discussed it with the representative of the Medical Protection Society. I may have discussed it with the LMC – I am not sure if I would have done in this situation."

7.160 In the case of Patient A16 we have been faced with a straight conflict of evidence of whether or not a disclosure of sexual misbehaviour was made. Unlike other such clashes, there are here no reference points, no other witnesses whose statements may assist us in reaching a reliable conclusion. We see no reason to doubt that Patient A16 made some complaint to Dr Jeary or expressed some concern about the treatment she had received at the hands of William Kerr, so that her relative would not be put at risk. However, it may be that, as with other witnesses to the Inquiry, she did not use the words "sexual advances", or similar clear statements of sexual impropriety. But that does not mean that Dr Jeary should not have inquired further. Indeed, quite the contrary. Dr Jeary told the Inquiry: "It was not uncommon for people to say, 'I do not want this consultant', for various reasons". But this was an unusual situation. Dr Jeary is not disputing that Patient A16 informed him that she did not want her relative to see William Kerr, he merely disputes the claimed reason. But that leaves no reason being given, which would have been very odd.

7.161 We conclude that, even in the 1970s, it would not have been unreasonable to have expected a GP such as Dr Jeary to have made some attempt to discover the reason why a female patient would feel so strongly about her recent experience with a male psychiatrist that she either refused to attend any more appointments herself, or objected to a relative's referral to the same consultant.

1978 – Patient A17

7.162 Patient A17, whilst an inpatient at Clifton Hospital, allegedly made a disclosure to Nurse Busby in 1978 about the fact she had been involved in a sexual relationship with William Kerr. Nurse Busby is said to have told Patient A17 to "keep quiet". Patient A17 subsequently told Sister Wearing (in 1982) and Deputy Sister Bigwood (in 1983) of her sexual relationship with William Kerr. The case of Patient A17 is considered in greater detail in Chapter 8.

1978 – Patient A18

7.163 Patient A18 was a nursing sister, who had worked at Harrogate. She was referred to William Kerr in 1978 by a surgeon, Mr Hannah. She had endured pain following a fall and surgery in 1972. The symptoms of pain from which she suffered were thought to be psychosomatic and Mr Hannah wished to have a psychiatric opinion before considering amputation of an apparently viable limb and foot.

7.164 Patient A18 saw William Kerr on a number of occasions, one of which was a home visit when she was at her parents' home on 23 February 1978. On that occasion, as William Kerr accepts in his letter to Dr Roger Calvert (Patient A18's GP), he attempted hypnosis. Patient A18 states that, when she opened her eyes after the hypnosis, William Kerr's hand was on her groin.

7.165 William Kerr's letter to Dr Calvert of 2 March 1978 is interesting, not just because it confirms that he used hypnosis, but also due to the comment: "I hope to call in and see her later this week", which is suggestive of the unplanned domiciliary visits of which a number of patients spoke. The letter also mentioned that Patient A18 would need a number of further hypnosis sessions, "in her own home".

7.166 Patient A18's recollection was that a week later she attended her GP's surgery and saw Dr Albert Day. The GP notes confirm that on 11 March 1978 (just over two weeks after William Kerr's visit) Patient A18 saw Dr Day and the entry reads:

> *"Says she's at the end of tether. Really no evidence of pressure. Wants to go into Clifton. Told her to contact Dr Kerr's secretary."*

7.167 Patient A18's account of this visit is that she told Dr Day she did not want to see William Kerr at her own home. However, before she could provide further details as to her reasons, Dr Day allegedly "exploded", saying:

> *"Why do women patients always complain about psychiatrists?"*

7.168 Dr Day denied that he would have responded in this way, and stated further that had Patient A18 made a complaint about William Kerr's sexual impropriety (which Patient A18 says she did not do due to Dr Day's reaction) he would have recorded it and advised the patient to go to the police.

7.169 The medical notes reveal that whilst Patient A18 did see William Kerr again in 1978 and subsequently in 1980 and 1982 she was, as at 28 May 1978 (three months after the alleged assault), attending his clinic "reluctantly". Patient A18 does not allege any further impropriety by William Kerr and accepts that he assisted her in obtaining a recommendation for a move to a council flat with better access.

7.170 In the William Kerr Trial of the Facts, Patient A18's allegation formed one of the counts of indecent assault. The jury reached a verdict that William Kerr was not guilty of the facts alleged.

7.171 We have had to consider the recollections of Patient A18 and Dr Day, and whose recollection we prefer. For the patient, this was an important event – a "significant event", to adopt a familiar term. For Dr Day, she was one of very many patients, who was (on any view) expressing a degree of disquiet. Dr Day's reasoning was a combination of the following – "I have no memory of this"; "If it had happened I would have put the complaint in the notes"; "It is not in the notes, therefore it didn't happen"; and, finally, in relation to the alleged remark: "This is not something I would say, or did say". Dr Day's reliance on his notes has to be treated with some caution.

Patient A18 saw him during a consultation that was not, according to Dr Day, time-limited. The consultation could, therefore, have lasted for somewhere between 10 and 30 minutes. Assuming, favourably to Dr Day, that the duration was only 10 minutes, it is to be noted that the entire note of that meeting – including the advice given – is 24 words long, taking about 10 seconds to read or write. There is a clear danger for a witness who places such strong reliance on incomplete contemporaneous notes as evidence of the complete interview.

7.172 Fortunately, however, we find that the apparent conflict between Patient A18's evidence and that of Dr Day is, to a large extent, reconcilable. Patient A18 accepts she did not go on to complain about William Kerr in express terms, which would account for Dr Day's lack of recall of any such complaint. However, Dr Day recorded in the notes Patient A18's distress and her desire to go into Clifton (which probably reflects Patient A18's request that there be no more home visits). The fact that the home visits for hypnosis planned by William Kerr in his letter of 2 March 1978 never took place suggests that (as noted) Patient A18 may have contacted William Kerr's secretary to change arrangements.

7.173 Counsel for Patient A18 has advanced detailed arguments as to why we should prefer his client's recollection. However, we do not find it necessary to resolve the conflict over whether Dr Day in fact uttered the words "women patients always complain about [their] psychiatrists". It is not an issue that needs to be resolved by the Inquiry. We note and record that Dr Day was clear in his evidence that the remarks, which he denies saying, are factually incorrect.

1978 – Patient A19

7.174 Patient A19 was a nurse working at Harrogate Hospital when she came into contact with William Kerr. On 18 June 1978 she attempted suicide by taking antidepressants and her GP, Dr Theo Crawfurd-Porter, referred her to William Kerr. William Kerr visited her at home and then arranged for her to be admitted to Clifton Hospital, where she stayed for approximately a month. During that time she alleges she saw William Kerr alone between three and four times (there is evidence in the medical notes to show that this is likely to be correct). On the first occasion she was escorted to his room. He was alone and locked the door after her arrival. He then allegedly informed her that he had fallen for her and knew that she had feelings for him also. She also recalls him telling her that they would have an affair (and that he had a caravan and she would want for nothing). Finally, he stressed that she must tell no one else or he would lose his job.

7.175 According to Patient A19, on the second visit to see William Kerr in a remote room in the hospital, he was seated behind his desk but was naked below the waist. He allegedly tried to make her perform oral sex on him. It is not clear whether on that first alleged occasion he succeeded, but Patient A19 states that on three occasions oral sex took place.

7.176 During her admission Patient A19 was approached by a nurse who asked if everything was all right, but she felt unable to disclose to him. However she did mention the alleged assault to a friend during a home visit. This friend in turn informed Patient A19's husband who attended a solicitor, Mr Reah. Mr Reah telephoned Harrogate District Hospital and recounted the alleged assault to a man identified only as "Bill". It hasn't been possible to establish who that was. The response of "Bill" was apparently to ask whether it was William Kerr or Michael Haslam that was being complained about. There are no records of this phone call and the Inquiry has had to rely on the evidence of Patient A19, Patient A19's friend and Patient A19's husband. It is documented that following a complaint, Patient A19 was changed from being under William Kerr's care to Michael Haslam – the records also note that Patient A19 was unhappy about this change. There is therefore clear contemporaneous support for the existence of a complaint about William Kerr's conduct – but the records do not reveal the nature of the complaint. Further, the hospital records do not reveal the level of investigation (if any) – with the following being the only entry referring to the complaint being put to William Kerr:

> "*Saw Dr Kerr yesterday – denies knowledge of what complaint is about*".

7.177 Patient A19's husband (accompanied by his wife's friend) also attended the GP, Dr Crawfurd-Porter, who said that Patient A19 was fantasising about William Kerr, but added that he would speak to William Kerr that evening as the two families were meeting for dinner. The friend's evidence to the Inquiry was as follows:

*"Following the appointment with [the solicitor], I went to see
[Patient A19's] GP, Dr Crawfurd-Porter, about Dr Kerr. Dr
Crawfurd-Porter did not seem to take our complaint seriously
and he just laughed it off and said 'I'll have a word with him'."*

7.178 It seems likely that Dr Crawfurd-Porter did indeed pass on the
complaint to William Kerr (directly or indirectly) who went on to
confront Patient A19 over the allegation.

7.179 Patient A19 states that, having made a complaint, she was subject to
threats. She states that she was confronted by Sister Pauline Brown
who accused her of "making trouble" for William Kerr. This was
denied by Pauline Brown, who says she did not start as Sister on the
ward until September 1978 after Sister Atkins' retirement. Further,
William Kerr himself allegedly confronted Patient A19 with the
words:

*"What are you bloody trying to do to me, you are going to
reduce me to a bloody dustbin man."*

7.180 After her discharge, Patient A19 describes visiting Dr Crawfurd-Porter.
His alleged comment to her was vulgar and uncaring in the extreme:

*"Oh, (Patient A19) you don't want a big ginger penis shoved at
you, do you?"*

7.181 The apparent lack of concern for Patient A19 has echoes of the
response Dr Crawfurd-Porter allegedly made to Patient A10 in 1969
or 1970. When Patient A10 disclosed an alleged assault by Kerr he is
said to have responded: "My god, the fool", showing apparently no
concern for Patient A10's feelings.

7.182 As Dr Crawfurd-Porter is deceased, we obviously could not get his
version of events. However, we are satisfied that Dr Crawfurd-Porter
was well aware of William Kerr's activities even before Patient A19's
allegations arose, having allegedly received specific disclosures from
Patient A5, Patient A10 and possibly Patient A9. We consider it likely
that Dr Crawfurd-Porter's reaction and comments were as described
to the Inquiry by Patient A19.

7.183 Partly in consequence of Dr Crawfurd-Porter's reaction and partly
due to a dispute concerning an incident when Dr Crawfurd-Porter
allegedly refused to come out to see Patient A19, Patient A19

changed GPs and moved to Dr Albert Day (in partnership with Dr Roger Calvert) at Park Parade Surgery, Harrogate. Patient A19 has no recollection of discussing her complaint against William Kerr with Dr Day and his evidence was that he did not become aware of the allegation made by Patient A19 (he also denied knowledge of any complaint by Patient A18). This is despite the fact that a letter from Michael Haslam to Dr Day dated 17 April 1980 opens with the words:

> "This lady initially under Dr Kerr's care in 1978 came under myself following a disagreement with my colleague."

7.184 According to Dr Day, he never enquired either of Patient A19 or Michael Haslam as to what this disagreement might have been.

7.185 A number of years later in 1984, Patient A19 spoke to a Community Psychiatric Nurse, Stephen Cook, stating that she had had a sexual relationship with William Kerr. She also told him that she had made a complaint. His impression was that the complaint had been managed, albeit not to her satisfaction, at a high level and he considered that in those circumstances there was little he could do. His evidence was that he passed on the account to his line manager, Mr Thomas Welsh, who made a "mental note" of the incident. This contradicts Mr Welsh's statement stating he had no recollection of any staff or patient complaining to him about William Kerr. In the light of Mr Cook's subsequent evidence that Patient A19 was insistent she did not want to make a complaint, we cannot be satisfied that Mr Cook did pass on the matter to his line manager, Mr Welsh. Alternatively, if we are mistaken and the complaint was passed on by Mr Cook, we conclude that he conveyed the information in such an informal manner that its significance was not appreciated. Mr Cook explained his failure to act, despite believing that Patient A19 had been subject to a serious assault by William Kerr (who to his knowledge was still practising), in the following terms:

> "I clarified with Patient A19 whether she wanted to make another complaint. But she was clear that she did not. I got the impression that, had I taken it further myself, she would not have co-operated with that. She wanted to draw a line under it and sort of move on."

7.186 In response to a question as to his concern about the potential threat of William Kerr to other patients, Mr Cook was frank:

> *"I am not sure how much I did consider it really. I mean, it certainly was partly because Patient A19 did not want me to move it forward. But also the allegation had been made many years before, and my recollection was that it had been investigated. I am not really sure what could have been done."*

7.187 There were two other healthcare professionals to whom Patient A19 complained, both of whom cited as their reason for not pursuing the allegations against William Kerr the reluctance of Patient A19 to do so. The first, Marion Anderson, a clinical psychologist, acknowledged she had received the disclosure in the early 1980s whilst Patient A19 was working as a nursing colleague. Patient A19 spoke of William Kerr's alleged sexual misconduct but said she did not want the matter to be taken any further.

7.188 Marion Anderson's evidence is important insofar as it casts some light on how she considers she should have responded to a disclosure of sexual misconduct, drawing a distinction (reflected elsewhere in the evidence) between disclosure of conduct which could be described as criminal, and conduct which could not. When it did not amount to criminal conduct, she thought it could only be taken forward with the consent of the patient. According to Marion Anderson, "inappropriate" behaviour that fell short of a criminal assault could not be examined further – because of patient confidentiality – unless the patient agreed.

7.189 The second healthcare professional to whom Patient A19 allegedly complained was Dr Derek Pheby, then a locum Accident and Emergency doctor, who gave evidence to the Inquiry that Patient A19 had, as a nursing colleague, disclosed to him that she had been subject to a serious sexual assault by William Kerr. Dr Pheby considered that, given Patient A19's reluctance to pursue the matter, there was little he could do. Patient A19 herself has no recollection of her disclosure to Dr Pheby, and indeed it would appear that Dr Pheby's employment at Clifton Hospital predated Patient A19's admission, casting doubt on the reliability of Dr Pheby's recollection.

7.190 The case of Patient A19 is particularly informative. It highlights the failing of the system at every level over a period of time, because at the outset it appears serious attempts were made to pursue a complaint to the hospital authorities via a solicitor. The effect of this process, apart from a change of consultant for Patient A19's care, was not to launch any form of inquiry into William Kerr's behaviour, but, if anything, to make life more difficult for Patient A19. If the hospital authorities route was unresponsive, the GP route was just as unsuccessful. A complaint to the GP, Dr Crawfurd-Porter, by Patient A19's husband and also her friend, which should have produced some serious response, was met with the comment "I'll have a word with him" – as if the complaint was of the most flippant kind, hardly worth even that effort. Patient A19's own disclosure to her GP, Dr Crawfurd-Porter, was met with disbelief and a crude and dismissive comment. Given these responses, it is not surprising that, whilst Patient A19 did speak to others (to Stephen Cook, to Marion Anderson and possibly to Dr Pheby), in all her subsequent disclosures she stressed the fact that she did not want to pursue matters. Further, in the criminal investigation in 1997/98 when Patient A19 was asked to make a written statement, she declined.

7.191 In summary, Patient A19's complaint in 1978 – we believe clearly made at the time by her and on her behalf by others – was an opportunity missed. Not only was there a total failure to take her complaints seriously – and they were extremely serious complaints – but also (so far as we can discover) no investigation was carried out and no record at all was made at any time. Any attempt made by her to complain, certainly in the late 1970s, was met with obstruction and inaction, almost with derision. If there had been at least some contemporaneous record made, some attempt to take the matter seriously, then even if a full investigation was not possible at that time (because Patient A19 had been so discouraged from progressing her complaint), there would have been an obvious reason for taking Patient A17's remarks far more seriously when her disclosure was made in 1983.

7.192 What is also to be noted is that Patient A19's complaint was dismissed, without any investigation, even though she was supported by her husband, her friend, and her solicitor. Many of the former patients did not have that network of support. In the climate and culture that prevailed in the NHS in the late 1970s and early 1980s in North Yorkshire and is evidenced by the treatment of Patient A19's complaint, there was little prospect of any of their concerns and complaints receiving serious attention.

1979 – Patient A21

7.193 Shortly after Patient A19 had complained about William Kerr, another patient, Patient A21, was also allegedly reporting similar matters to her GP. Patient A21's account is notably similar to that of Patient A19. She was admitted to Clifton Hospital as an inpatient following an emergency referral by a GP on 12 October 1978 for alcohol-related problems. She remained as an inpatient until 24 November 1978 and was subsequently treated by William Kerr at Harrogate District Hospital until approximately March 1979. According to Patient A21, William Kerr told her that all her problems were due to "sexual hang-ups". Whilst she was being treated at Harrogate, William Kerr allegedly exposed himself to her and attempted to force her to perform oral sex on him. Her description of that event, taken from her 1997 police statement is as follows:

> "*I was sent through for a consultation with Doctor Kerr, I recall going into his office, where initially he said 'All your problems are due to sexual hang-ups' and that 'I will be able to help you'. The next thing I remember is Doctor Kerr standing up and unzipping his trousers, and pulling out his penis. I saw immediately that his penis was erect and he appeared to be offering it to me …*"

7.194 Patient A21's evidence is that the alleged sexual behaviour ended there, without any further assault, and was not repeated.

7.195 Patient A21's evidence to the Inquiry was that she spoke to another patient at Clifton Hospital who had experienced a similar incident with William Kerr.

7.196 Patient A21 alleges that she subsequently reported "the incident" to her GP, but without giving the details set out above. She stated that the GP seemed to know it was William Kerr she was talking about. Patient A21's GP at the time was Dr Michael Moore. Allegedly, the GP said that another person had complained about William Kerr and that if Patient A21 wanted to take it any further she would have to be prepared to go to court, something Patient A21 felt unable to do.

7.197 As already noted, Dr Michael Moore had received a previous complaint, from Patient A1, over 10 years earlier in 1965 and the advice he had given on that occasion was that Patient A1 should go to the police. However, Dr Moore (whilst accepting he had been the recipient of Patient A1's complaint) denied that Patient A21 had ever complained to him. Patient A21 does not specifically name Dr Moore as the GP to whom she disclosed there had been an "incident". In the early 1980s, Patient A21 told her daughter of William Kerr's alleged sexual abuse, and that she had discussed the issue with her then GP, Dr Thornton. Dr Thornton has no recollection of such a discussion.

7.198 Against that factual background, we are unable to conclude with any degree of certainty that any detailed disclosure was made by Patient A21 to either Dr Moore (in 1979) or to Dr Thornton (in the early 1980s). However, we have no reason to disbelieve Patient A21's evidence that she did make some limited attempt to inform her GP (probably Dr Michael Moore) of her concerns in relation to William Kerr. This conclusion is supported by the similarity of the account of both Patient A1 and Patient A21 regarding the response from their GP.

1979 – Patient A22

7.199 The account of Patient A22 is of particular significance in the documentation of complaints raised against William Kerr, for it is the first known account of a GP referring a patient's complaint "up the line". The GP in question, Dr Wade of Eastgate Surgery, Knaresborough, referred Patient A22's complaint against William Kerr to a fellow Consultant Psychiatrist, Michael Haslam. Perhaps unsurprisingly in the light of what is now known of Michael Haslam's own conduct (in respect of which he was convicted), the complaint progressed no further.

7.200 Patient A22 had first seen William Kerr in 1974 without incident, but was re-referred in 1979 by her GP, Dr Barry Wade. She described having a very good relationship with Dr Wade and in light of what was to unfold subsequently it is interesting that Patient A22's evidence was that he had been "reluctant" to refer her. As Patient A22 preferred not to visit a psychiatric unit, the visits took place at her home. During the first visit nothing untoward occurred although William Kerr did allegedly inquire about her sex life. In March 1979 at a domiciliary visit, William Kerr is alleged to have groped Patient A22's breast and thigh, tried to kiss her on the lips and said words to the effect of:

"the thought of going to bed with you is delightful."

7.201 That brief description of the alleged sexual assault has been repeated by Patient A22 over the years, and so far as we can discover – from written statements, and from the transcript of the criminal trial – has not changed at all.

7.202 Patient A22 requested that William Kerr leave, which he did. He telephoned the next day and tried to arrange another meeting but she refused.

7.203 On 28 March 1979, Patient A22 attended Dr Wade's practice. The purpose of that visit was two-fold; first, to explain why she no longer wished to see William Kerr and, second, to alert Dr Wade to the perceived danger of referring other women to him. Her evidence to the Inquiry was that she informed Dr Wade that William Kerr had tried to get her into bed with him. According to Patient A22, Dr Wade's response was:

"Oh no, it has happened before. Of all the people I did not think it was going to happen to you."

7.204 Dr Wade allegedly went on to say he would make a note in her records that she did not wish to see William Kerr. Patient A22 objected to this, as she was concerned William Kerr might manage to obtain sight of her records and use them against her. Patient A22's fear was: "He [William Kerr] might say 'this woman is unstable and she is making it up'".

7.205 Despite not wishing to make a formal complaint in her own name, Patient A22 informed the Inquiry that her expectation (having made her concerns known) was that Dr Wade would be able to take some action to protect other patients:

> *"If you told a member of the [medical] profession, you would expect them to know the ropes, what to do to protect other people."*

7.206 In Dr Wade's evidence to the Inquiry he made it clear that by 1979 he and those in his practice in Knaresborough (Drs Rushton, Bennie, Wade, Iddon and Plowman) were already aware of William Kerr's reputation for flirting with female patients.

7.207 This accords with Patient A22's evidence that, subsequent to her own alleged assault, she learnt that a friend of hers, Patient A2, had allegedly been the victim of similar treatment by William Kerr in the 1960s and had reported the incident to Dr Rushton, the senior partner in Dr Wade's surgery. Dr Rushton had allegedly responded that women tended to imagine such things when they were in a distraught state.

7.208 Dr Wade did go on to describe Patient A22's complaint in anonymised form with practitioners in the Harrogate area at meetings and was clear that the information would have been disseminated.

7.209 Patient A22 also reported the incident with William Kerr to the police, again with the intention of making sure that if any other women complained they would take them seriously. She was not prepared to give a statement herself, believing that if she did so she would be obliged to attend and give evidence in court.

7.210 The police then contacted Dr Wade and whilst they did not disclose the name of the patient, due to the co-incidence of timing he formed the clear impression the police complainant was Patient A22.

7.211 Dr Wade, after being visited by the police, went to see Michael Haslam personally on 3 April 1979 at Harrogate District Hospital to discuss the complaint against William Kerr. It seems that this visit must have been discussed with his fellow GP partners – certainly Dr Plowman was aware of the meeting. The meeting, according to Dr

Wade, was in order to "put a marker down". Michael Haslam's response to the complaint was said to be non-committal and Dr Wade neither asked for, nor received, any follow-up.

7.212 Michael Haslam's written evidence to the Inquiry on his reaction to the complaint from Dr Wade was as follows:

> "I am not personally aware of ANY complaint against Dr Kerr in the years I worked with him, save for one woman who was referred to me by her GP having previously been under Dr Kerr, for some amorous episode to which she had presumably objected. The patient did not wish to discuss it with me. I do not know what, if anything, the GP did about it. Frankly, if every psychiatric patient who has a go; makes a pass or takes umbrage at something, were to lead to a formal complaint, one might as well close down."

And

> "I do not recall any detail of the interview with Dr Wade. I doubt he would have gone into any detail without the patient's consent to do so, which would have been recorded in his notes."

7.213 Michael Haslam gave oral evidence to the Inquiry, insisting that he did not receive any complaint, as such, from Dr Wade, but merely an invitation to take on a new patient. Although he acknowledged that he was also given information concerning an alleged sexual assault by William Kerr, he did not regard it as his role to deal with, as Dr Wade and the police had the information too.

7.214 Dr Wade and his partners, in spite of the concerns they had about William Kerr, continued to refer female patients to him. They seem to have taken the view, and Dr Wade gave evidence to that effect, that on balance, having a consultation with William Kerr despite its attendant risk of his 'flirtatious' behaviour was in some circumstances better than no consultation at all.

7.215 Dr Wade was asked questions about the issue of continuing referrals, given his concerns about William Kerr. We have concluded that Dr Wade was not the only GP in Harrogate or York who was faced with this dilemma.

Q. You would have done so [made a referral] in the knowledge of his reputation as being somebody who might try it on with a female patient?

A. Yes. What I had to do was to weigh up the option of the benefit that the patient would obtain by the consultation with him as opposed to not having a consultation, or some considerable delay and therefore exposing the patient to potential risk.

Q. It sounds almost like a risk analysis, weighing up the risk of being subject to flirtatious behaviour, on the one hand, against the speed of treatment on the other?

A. It was indeed, yes.

Q. It is a slightly dangerous situation to send a patient into, is it not –

A. I am fully aware of that.

Q. – if you had decided that the urgency required them to be sent into what one might have thought was a bit of a lion's den?

A. Yes, indeed, it was the real horns of a dilemma.

Q. You remained on the horns of that dilemma for a number of years, by the sound of it?

A. Yes, indeed.

Q. As far as you are aware, that was equally the case with others in your practice?

A. There must have been, yes.

Q. And others who practised at the health centre coming from other surgeries?

A. And other Harrogate surgeries and Knaresborough surgeries, yes.

7.216 Although there is cause for concern in relation to Dr Wade's failure to act to protect other female patients by continuing to refer them to William Kerr, he does deserve some credit for taking action when aware of Patient A22's experience – whether or not stirred by police involvement. He was not to know that Michael Haslam would be incapable of, or unwilling to, take the matter further. It was a reasonable assumption that passing the matter on to a colleague – particularly a colleague as senior as Michael Haslam – would result in something being done.

7.217 Patient A22 was later admitted to Harrogate District Hospital on 4 June 1980. She was asked by the SHO (who has not given evidence to the Inquiry) whether she wished to see a psychiatrist. She refused, with words to the effect:

"No, because Kerr can't keep his hands off female patients"

7.218 Again, there seems to be a failure to pick up on this comment or make any enquiries as to whether there was any substance to it.

7.219 Many years later, in 1995, Patient A22 raised the issue of William Kerr's behaviour with Dr Iddon, stating that William Kerr had assaulted her. Dr Iddon was already aware of Patient A50 (see below) who had also made allegations against William Kerr. By this time, William Kerr had retired and thus (assuming Dr Iddon knew William Kerr was no longer seeing patients) there was no longer the imperative of patient protection to motivate forwarding the complaint. However, it has not been possible to determine whether the fact of William Kerr's retirement influenced Dr Iddon's response, as he had no recollection of Patient A22 ever complaining to him about William Kerr. Whether or not Dr Iddon was informed, it is clear that issues of counselling and support for Patient A22 in addition to the possibility of criminal responsibility of William Kerr remained unaddressed.

7.220 Finally, in 1996, Patient A22 disclosed to a clinical psychologist, Christine Williams, about William Kerr's behaviour. Although this was a disclosure in a therapeutic context, and came eight years after William Kerr's retirement from the NHS, it is still notable that no steps were taken to forward the complaint.

7.221 In the William Kerr Trial of the Facts, Patient A22's allegations form one of the counts of indecent assault. The jury was not able to reach a verdict in respect of Patient A22's allegation.

7.222 Patient A22 was a prolific and plausible discloser. Her GP, who knew her well, accepted her account. However, despite disclosing both to her GP and the police, contemporaneous to the incident, no action was taken to address the potential danger posed by William Kerr to other patients. Patient A22's voice, perhaps more articulate than some, was not heard.

1979 – Patient A23

7.223 Dr Wade was not the only GP receiving complaints about William Kerr in 1979. Patient A23 was referred to William Kerr by her GP, Dr Rosemary Livingstone. Patient A23 alleges that William Kerr insisted on talking about sex at the sessions, suggesting she find herself a lover as her husband was not adequate. Whilst Patient A23 did not consider William Kerr was helping her, she continued to see him until he asked her what she would do if he was sitting before her naked. This prompted Patient A23 to speak to Dr Livingstone about William Kerr's behaviour. She formed the impression her GP did not believe her. The GP notes for 6 December 1979 record that Patient A23 had a "fraught time" with a psychiatrist (William Kerr).

7.224 When the issue of a referral to a psychiatrist was raised again in 1984, Patient A23 refused to see William Kerr and, on being asked the reason, informed Dr Livingstone that William Kerr talked too much about sex. Dr Livingstone referred Patient A23 instead to Consultant Psychiatrist Dr Rugg, mentioning Patient A23's problem with the previous psychiatrist in the letter (dislike of being asked sexual questions).

7.225 When asked why the complaint about talking too much about sex had not raised alarm bells, Dr Livingstone stated that: "talking to a patient about sex in psychiatry is part of the psychiatric history. Clearly it would be highly inappropriate in a cardiologist". This emphasises the particular difficulty in the field of psychiatry where sexual matters may potentially be of relevance, providing practitioners with a legitimate "opening", enabling them to move a consultation towards a situation of sexual abuse.

7.226 Of some relevance here is that Dr Rosemary Livingstone was in partnership with her husband, Dr Angus Livingstone. In 1983 he was to receive a complaint from a patient, A24, who said that shortly after being seen in the afternoon clinic at Ripon by William Kerr, he made an unannounced visit to her home. Dr Angus Livingstone agreed with the patient that this was inappropriate behaviour and sought to encourage her to complain. However the patient refused, and apparently took the matter lightly. Dr Angus Livingstone also recalls in the period prior to 1982 two or three female patients complaining to him about William Kerr's line of questioning on sexual matters. Dr Angus Livingstone discussed this with his wife and with Dr Grey, a GP from a neighbouring practice who had previously worked with William Kerr. Dr Grey said he was not aware of any concerns about William Kerr and neither Dr Rosemary Livingstone nor Dr Angus Livingstone forwarded their concerns about William Kerr.

1979 – Patient A26

7.227 In the same year as Patient A22 and Patient A23's complaints to their respective GPs, another patient, Patient A26, was raising concerns about William Kerr with the staff of Clifton Hospital. The timing of these incidents emphasises the lack of coordination between complaints entering the system via the GP route and those being raised within the hospital.

7.228 Patient A26 complained to a psychiatric nurse working on Nidderdale ward at Clifton Hospital, Thomas English, in about March/April 1979. Patient A26 said that she did not want to be discharged and to have William Kerr make a home visit, as on the last occasion he had propositioned her. Mr English was sufficiently concerned to call his superior, Sister Pauline Brown, at her home to discuss the issue. According to Mr English, Sister Brown called him back some minutes later, allegedly having raised the matter directly with William Kerr and told Mr English that the accusation was malicious.

7.229 In her evidence to the Inquiry Sister Brown had no recollection of this incident, although she stated that, had she received such a complaint, she would have gone first to the Nursing Officer and then discussed the matter with William Kerr. Of itself, this revealed a failure to appreciate the vulnerable position in which this could leave the patient, and the potential risk that William Kerr, having been "alerted" to the complaint at the earliest stage, could use his influence to quash it. Pauline Brown also said she was unaware of William Kerr's practice of making unscheduled visits to patients at their own homes, a lack of awareness that Mr English dismissed as "inconceivable". Linda Bigwood in her written complaint in 1983 referred to an incident where Pauline Brown had been informed of an allegation by Patient A17 of a sexual relationship with William Kerr. It appears that the only action taken in relation to that disclosure was to alert William Kerr that the allegation had been made. Let us state here for the record and in some mitigation, the actions of Pauline Brown have to be seen in the context of the culture of the time where it was not uncommon for staff to fail to take complaints from psychiatric patients seriously.

7.230 We prefer Mr English's recollection. His evidence was modest, restrained, and compelling. It follows that Pauline Brown's recollection is mistaken. It is probably that Mr English did raise Patient A26's concerns with her, and when raised, her only response was to alert William Kerr that the allegation had been made.

7.231 Mr English's evidence goes to the heart of the problem, describing a culture prevalent at the time, where patient safety was *not* of central importance. Patient A26 was a patient who was expressing a concern and specifically saying that William Kerr had propositioned her during a domiciliary visit, and she was fearful he would do this again. She was soon to be discharged from hospital. Her concerns were simply fobbed off – Mr English spoke to Pauline Brown, Pauline Brown spoke to William Kerr (who denied any wrongdoing). End of concern.

7.232 The timing of Patient A26's complaint is striking. It was at almost the same time as Patient A22's complaint to her GP, Dr Wade. The descriptions are also remarkably similar. Two complaints in the same year, against the same consultant psychiatrist, alleging the same sexualised behaviour. But no connections were made, and no action was taken.

1981 – Patient A27

7.233 Patient A27, who did not give oral evidence to the Inquiry, is an example of a patient who took a number of years to feel able to come forward with her complaint. However, as with so many others, when she did so, no action was taken.

7.234 Patient A27 had been referred to William Kerr in 1972 by her GP, Dr Pamela Heatley (later Reed), of East Parade Surgery, Harrogate, suffering from postnatal depression. Patient A27 alleges that William Kerr indecently assaulted her on a domiciliary visit. As with other former patients, the account of her allegation is brief and has been constant over the years. This is taken from her 1997 police statement:

> *"I can remember very little about the session but I clearly remember Dr Kerr asking me to put [my 9 month-old baby] on the floor. This was at the beginning of the session. I said 'No'. He then repeated it again. I again said 'No'. Straight away I felt scared, frightened, wondered what he was going to do to me, wondering why he needed [the baby] on the floor.*

> *"I was wondering what was the point in this. I felt so frightened that I felt safer with holding [the baby] on my knee, he was like a shield to me, I refused to put him on the floor. Dr Kerr then stood up, walked towards me and [the baby], as he was immediately on my left side, he lifted the bottom right hand side of his jacket and slightly lent his genital area toward my cheek and rested it there for a very short time as I told him 'You can pack that in'. 'If there is anything you want to know about my sex life you just have to ask'."*

7.235 Patient A27 was subsequently admitted to and discharged from Clifton Hospital. She thereafter sought treatment from her GP, rather than seeking specialist assistance.

1981 – Patient A28

7.236 Patient A28 was referred to William Kerr on 24 March 1981 by her GP, Dr Whitcher. She says she saw William Kerr twice at Clifton Hospital and that thereafter, for an eight-month period, he made irregular domiciliary visits which do not appear to be recorded in her medical notes. According to Patient A28, the visits were not planned and William Kerr would telephone shortly before arriving. She alleged that during the sessions he would touch her and masturbate himself – a description of sexual misconduct very similar to that given by others. Her account, taken from her police statement, is as follows:

"All these home visits lasted for about eight months and they were all very similar. I was on my own in the house, Dr Kerr and I would sit in the lounge. He would sit on the settee, I would sit on a chair. He asked if I was wearing stockings. He invited me to go and sit next to him or stand up near him, which I did. He would put his hands up my skirt and touch my legs above my stocking tops and suspenders, and at the same time his trousers were undone and he masturbated himself. On most occasions he became very flushed. On occasions he put my hand on his erect penis and with his hand on top of mine he would masturbate. I pulled my hand away and kept telling him I didn't want to do it, he carried on masturbating and ejaculated in his handkerchief. He then went upstairs to the bathroom, came downstairs all dressed up and proper again in an official capacity, said 'thank you very much', picked up his briefcase and went."

7.237   She felt she could not tell her GP, Dr Whitcher, but alleges that she did disclose to her former GP, Dr Visick. Dr Visick allegedly responded that he could not take it further unless she made a statement. He also asked her if she was prepared to stand up in court and speak about it. Dr Visick's evidence to the police was that he had no recollection of any allegation.

7.238   In the Trial of the Facts, the jury could not reach a verdict regarding Patient A28's allegations.

7.239   Dr Visick's evidence to the Inquiry went further than his evidence to the police (a statement that was read out at the criminal trial). To the Inquiry he said this:

"Although I have no independent recollection of [Patient A28] returning to see me after she had left the practice, I would accept that she may well have done so. However, I have had the opportunity to consider her Section 9 witness statement dated 4th August 1998, together with a transcript of her evidence at Court. I can say categorically that if [Patient A28] did attend to see me she did not relate these various matters to me as she has alleged in her statement and evidence at all. I have no doubt that, had she done so, I would be able to recall the information and the circumstances surrounding her disclosure of it to me. Had anyone related such information to me at any stage I would have been appalled."

7.240 There is an oddity here. There is little doubt that Patient A28 made disclosure to her friend in about 1986, many years after the alleged abuse, but also many years before the media references to William Kerr. And if Patient A28's disclosure was a fabrication, she would surely have said she made it to her then GP, Dr Whitcher, rather than to Dr Visick?

7.241 However, in the light of Dr Visick's firm denial, we are unable to conclude that Patient A28 gave to her GP sufficient information upon which he could have been expected to take any action. We do not consider that this fact is likely to affect our overall conclusions on missed opportunities in the late 1970s and early 1980s.

1982 – Patient A29

7.242 Patient A29 was referred to William Kerr by her GP, Dr Crouch, in 1981 (then in her late 20s), and saw him at an outpatient clinic at Harrogate Hospital on two or three occasions in late 1981 and early 1982. During the final consultation she alleges he indecently assaulted her, asking her to lie on a couch then touching her breasts and pushing her hand against his crotch. Patient A29 informed Dr Crouch that she did not want to see either William Kerr or his wife, Dr Bromham, (whom Dr Crouch had mentioned as an alternative). Patient A29 told the Inquiry that she considered Dr Crouch to be a very good doctor. Whilst Patient A29 accepts that she did not tell Dr Crouch the reason for her refusal to see William Kerr or Dr Bromham and does not consider that Dr Crouch had any concerns about William Kerr, she states that Dr Crouch asked no more searching questions to understand the reasons behind her decision, and she was "surprised he did not ask me why I wanted to change psychiatrists at the time". Dr Crouch took Patient A29's request not to be referred to either William Kerr or Dr Bromham sufficiently seriously to refer her outside the region to a Leeds psychiatrist. At the very least, the Inquiry concludes that in relation to Patient A29, (even if he was not aware of, or had even forgotten, Patient A13's complaint) Dr Crouch should have been alerted to a potential problem with William Kerr and should have sought to elicit the reason for Patient A29's refusal to see either him or his wife. We do not accept Dr Crouch's oral evidence that he had no concerns at all about William Kerr during his time in practice in North Yorkshire (although we note that Dr Givans similarly denied any knowledge of the "unorthodox" behaviour of William Kerr which Dr Crawfurd-Porter had mentioned to Dr Moss).

7.243 Further we conclude that Dr Crouch, along with his fellow partners, were aware of concerns about William Kerr which they neither sought to report nor investigate.

1982 – Patient A17

7.244 Patient A17, an inpatient at Clifton Hospital, disclosed to Sister Barbara Wearing in 1982 that she had had a sexual relationship with William Kerr. It is recorded (by Linda Bigwood) that Sister Wearing took no action in relation to this disclosure. In her oral evidence to the Inquiry, Sister Wearing had no recollection of Patient A17 making such a disclosure.

1983 – Patient A17

7.245 A year later, in 1983, Patient A17 repeated the disclosure in the previous paragraph and informed Deputy Sister Bigwood that she had been involved in a consensual sexual relationship with William Kerr while she was his patient between 1973 and 1975.

7.246 We deal fully with the details of the disclosure of Patient A17 to Linda Bigwood in Chapter 8.

1983 – Patient A31

7.247 In 1981, Patient A31 was referred to William Kerr by her GP, Dr Pamela Reed (née Heatley). William Kerr – then a stranger to Patient A31 – made a domiciliary visit. At the end of the visit, Patient A31 alleges, William Kerr used the bathroom, called her in and forced her to hold his penis whilst he urinated and eventually ejaculated. He told her not to tell Dr Reed about the visit. Approximately six months later Patient A31 bumped into William Kerr in the course of her work at Harrogate District Hospital, where he allegedly reminded her not to tell anyone of the visit. About two years after the incident, in about 1983, Patient A31 says she informed Dr Reed as to what had occurred at the domiciliary visit. Dr Reed allegedly asked Patient A31 if she wanted to report it. Patient A31 declined as she "could not see the point", and felt she would not be believed. Dr Reed told the Inquiry that she had no recollection of this disclosure, indeed had no recollection of even referring Patient A31 to William Kerr. She stated it was not until after Kerr's retirement that she heard rumours that he was: "fond of the ladies". She recalled hearing a nurse, Sister Watson, speaking about such matters to a patient in about 1990, but could recall no more details.

7.248　This is, again, an example of the former patient saying that she disclosed to her GP, and the GP either denying the disclosure or (here) having no recollection of the disclosure. At the criminal trial of William Kerr, this absence of supporting evidence from the GPs was used by the defence team to undermine the prosecution evidence. In his summing-up to the jury, the trial judge (HHJ Myerson QC) said this:

> "It was at this point Mr Smith [counsel for the Defence] drew your attention to what has become obvious as this case has gone on, that many of the doctors to whom it is said complaints were made at this point in time have no recollection of those complaints being made.

> "There are two opposing views, members of the jury, urged upon you. The Defence say that when such complaints are made of this nature, it is unbelievable, if they were made, that a doctor, even at this length of time, would not remember something of what, after all, his patient was saying – even more strongly, Mr Smith suggested, in the case of Dr Visick, to whom of course a special visit had been made. The Prosecution, on the other hand, say these were busy general practitioners, who must have seen umpteen patients every day of the week, who are now being asked to refer back many, many years to what has been said to them, and which they have, for one reason or another, chosen not to record at the time in the notes of the patient, and therefore it is not at all peculiar that they do not now have any recollection. Well, members of the jury, those are the rival contentions, so to speak, which you have to consider, and I can do no more really, I am afraid, than outline them to you."

7.249 We can see the force of those comments, and the competing arguments. However, we have had the opportunity – not available to the criminal trial jury – of considering not only a mass of written and oral evidence (expert and lay) which the jury did not see, but also hearing far more about the culture within the GP community at the time. We are not surprised at all to hear that some GPs have little recollection of probably hesitant and incomplete disclosures made to them by distressed patients, in the course of busy surgeries. That absence of recollection does not mean, always, that the disclosure was not made. We are inclined to the general view that the former patients are more likely to be correct in their recollection of disclosures. We are also not impressed, one way or the other, by the absence of any note of the disclosure in the medical records. It is to be remembered that even Dr Wade, who did, on his own evidence, receive a disclosure from Patient A22, only recorded on her medical notes the four words "rational and still coping".

7.250 On balance, we conclude that Patient A31 did make some form of disclosure to her GP, probably not detailed, and probably some time after the incident.

7.251 Proceeding on the assumption that some form of complaint was made to the GP in about 1983/84, this is a further example of a doctor either failing to take forward an expression of concern or a complaint, on grounds of lack of patient's consent. Or, and perhaps more appropriately, it provides an example of a failure to listen and at least make some record, somewhere, so that if and when there was an investigation – as for example in 1983/84 following the Linda Bigwood allegations – then there would be some material from which a wider and more accurate picture could be drawn. Then, when former patients were perhaps more willing and able to give formal statements, at least the treating GPs would have had some record of their first disclosure.

1983 – Patient A32

7.252 Patient A32 was a former patient who alleged that William Kerr, during the course of a hypnosis session at her home in approximately 1983, indecently exposed himself and sexually assaulted her. Shortly following the incident Patient A32 informed a nurse, Sarah Cotterill. The nurse alleges she tried to encourage Patient A32 to report the matter, but without success. The nurse took no steps to raise the matter herself with anyone in authority despite the fact William Kerr was still practising.

7.253 Sarah Cotterill was one of the very few health professionals who refused to give evidence to the Inquiry. She wrote to us in August 2004 to confirm she would not attend to give evidence, despite several requests from the Chairman to do so. This was unfortunate, and meant that we were unable to explore with her the response to Patient A32's disclosure and the reasons for her action.

7.254 Patient A32 also alleges she informed her GP, Dr Plowman, that William Kerr had not behaved properly; however, Dr Plowman has no recollection of any such disclosure. It is difficult for us to resolve this conflict of recollection. It is clear that Patient A32 did make contemporaneous, or near-contemporaneous, disclosures to a nurse and to at least three friends. She gives a detailed description of Dr Plowman's casual reaction to the disclosure. On the other hand, we were impressed by Dr Plowman's evidence and feel that, in the light of her experience within the partnership (see below), she had good reason to remember, and act on, any disclosure if it had been made. She said this:

> "I know that she did not tell me about something improper happening. I would have remembered, I know I would. I knew her very well. She was a near neighbour; she was the mother of one of my son's friends. I knew her well. If she had told me, I would have remembered, and I do not remember her telling me."

7.255 On balance, we prefer Dr Plowman's recollection of what Patient A32 disclosed to her.

7.256 In the William Kerr Trial of the Facts, Patient A32's allegations formed a count of indecent assault. The jury decided that William Kerr was not guilty of this charge.

7.257 Before leaving Patient A32 and Dr Plowman, we draw attention to how Dr Plowman, as one of Dr Wade's partners, responded to his disclosure that there had been a complaint from Patient A22 of sexual assault by William Kerr. Dr Plowman acknowledged that she felt female patients were at risk and did not refer them to William Kerr. Neither within the practice nor the wider GP community did they pass on sufficient information by way of warning to other doctors.

7.258 Although she learnt, informally, that some other doctors were adopting similar changes in practice, the result was very much "hit-or-miss", and although there seemed to her to be a "general awareness" of a cloud over William Kerr's behaviour, some doctors continued to refer female patients to him.

7.259 From Dr Plowman's evidence, it is clear that there was some firm support for the comment in Linda Bigwood's written complaint in 1983 that Harrogate GPs were not referring female patients to William Kerr.

7.260 We suggest Dr Plowman's evidence is typical of the response of GPs to disclosure in the late 1970s and early 1980s. Her evidence is an important general indicator of the failure by local GPs to respond in any meaningful and structural way to the information they were receiving. Their apparent inaction was a product of lack of training, and the cultural and professional impediments discussed later in the Report.

1984 – Patient A36

7.261 Another former patient, Patient A36, claims that in about 1984 she informed Marion Anderson, a consultant clinical psychologist from whom she was receiving counselling, about sexual misconduct that had occurred approximately five years earlier. William Kerr had allegedly exposed himself to Patient A36 during a consultation. On subsequent occasions it is alleged that he asked Patient A36 to masturbate him or engage in mutual masturbation and on one occasion sexual intercourse is said to have taken place. Patient A36 also alleged that William Kerr had made an unannounced visit to her in the evening, although nothing untoward occurred on this occasion as her partner had been present. Patient A36's evidence was that Mrs

Anderson believed her and had responded that she was aware of Kerr's actions. Patient A36 described feeling "stonewalled" by Marion Anderson's response.

> "I was just shocked by the way she said, 'I know'. And it just seemed that was it … I had been cut off, I had been stonewalled."

7.262 However, we have concluded that we cannot be satisfied that Patient A36 did disclose to Marion Anderson, rather than to a counsellor/therapist, Julie Levine. Extracts from the oral evidence to the Inquiry illustrate the conflict on this point. In her police statement and a further statement in 2001, Patient A36 was unsure whether she had spoken to Marion Anderson or Julie Levine about William Kerr's behaviour. It was only in her evidence to the Inquiry that Patient A36 was sure she had informed Marion Anderson.

7.263 In contrast, Marion Anderson was clear in her evidence that no disclosure was made to her by Patient A36.

7.264 In the light of the apparent conflict between Patient A36's earlier statements, and her later statement to the Inquiry (although it is of course possible that there has been an improvement in her recollection), it is also possible that the original uncertainty reflects the correct position. Insofar as further confirmation is needed, we note that Julie Levine does recall that she was the recipient of a disclosure from Patient A36 that she had been the victim of sexual abuse by a consultant psychiatrist. (Julie Levine was unable to recall whether the accused psychiatrist was William Kerr or Michael Haslam. She also treated the disclosure as confidential and did not consider Patient A36 was making a formal complaint. Accordingly, after discussion with her supervisor, she took no action to pursue the matter).

7.265 In those circumstances, we are not satisfied that Marion Anderson was the recipient of a disclosure from Patient A36.

1985/86 – Patient A37

7.266 In 1985 Patient A37 alleged to her GP, Dr Nixon, that William Kerr had sexually assaulted her during a consultation at Clifton Hospital and that sexual intercourse had taken place. Dr Nixon recorded the allegation in her GP notes dated 30 July 1985:

> *"Claims to have had sex with her psychiatrist and that money has been claimed by him unethically."*

7.267 Dr Nixon's evidence was that he had advised Patient A37 that these were serious matters and if they were true she ought to report them to the appropriate authorities, namely the police or the GMC. Patient A37's response to this advice (according to Dr Nixon) was:

> *"What good will that do? All you doctors stick together."*

7.268 Patient A37's evidence at the Trial of the Facts (she did not give oral evidence at the Inquiry) was that she had not been given such advice by Dr Nixon.

7.269 Dr Nixon was questioned when he gave oral evidence to the Inquiry as to whether he accepted Patient A37's allegations. He said that he had "no reason to believe or disbelieve her". This is consistent with his actions at the time. Having noted the allegations in Patient A37's medical notes, Dr Nixon went on to raise the matter with his fellow partners. Dr Nixon did not immediately dismiss the account as a fabrication. It is worth setting out in some detail Dr Nixon's oral evidence, as it shows the lack of clarity amongst the GP community and the confused position they had reached. The exchange with Counsel to the Inquiry went as follows:

> *Q. Did you not feel that you had a responsibility to ensure that you did something to try to see that this was investigated because of, for one matter, the risk to other patients potentially, if he carried on practising?*
>
> *A. I think it was very difficult to – where would one take it? I do not think the GMC in 1985 would have taken a report from the practice or from me without having some form of affidavit or sworn oath from the patient, to take things further. Likewise, I do not think the police would pursue an investigation if I went and told them what would be, I suppose, I do not know, hearsay evidence.*

Q. That is dealing with the police and the GMC. Did you consider going to William Kerr's employers? Did you consider going to the hospital and, through that route, alert someone at the hospital to what you had heard?

A. That was not an option that I thought of, no.

7.270 The following is in response to questions from the Chairman.

Q. Your evidence is that after the disclosure, your view is that she [Patient A37] may have been telling the truth?

A. Yes.

Q. The allegations she made, whether they be of rape or of oral sex, were of the most serious kind?

A. Right.

Q. You continued – that is you and your practice – continued to refer patients to William Kerr, even though the allegations may have been true and they were of the most serious kind? Is that accurate?

A. That is true.

Q. When it came to doing anything about what you had been told, you spoke to your partners, and that would be Drs Hazell, Green and Osmond. And that is all. You did not do anything else; is that right? You thought about things that you could do or could not do, but you did not do anything else?

A. That is right.

7.271 In summary, Dr Nixon (and his partners) did not know what to do with the information they had received, and effectively did nothing. Whether some action would have made any difference in relation to this former patient remains unclear, but it is another example of an opportunity missed to pass on information to hospital, or health authority management, which may (or, we suspect, may not) have been joined up with other information – such as that received from Linda Bigwood – so that alarm bells started sounding, and a full investigation was carried out.

7.272 Patient A37 repeated her allegations against William Kerr to a number of other healthcare professionals, including to another GP, Dr Osmond, who was in the same practice as Dr Nixon. It seems likely that Dr Osmond was first made aware of the allegations by Patient A37 when Dr Nixon discussed the matter with his partners in 1985. Patient A37 subsequently made a specific allegation of rape to Dr Osmond. It is unclear when this was, although it was not until approximately 1993 that Dr Osmond informed Dr Givans (Secretary of the North Yorkshire Local Medical Committee) of Patient A37's allegations; this did not lead to any action being taken. Dr Givans accepted that he had been told of the allegation by Dr Osmond and had responded that he was aware of other allegations. However Dr Givans felt that, having received the information second- or third-hand it was not for him (Dr Givans) to take the matter forward. Dr Givans' recollection was that he did advise Dr Osmond to speak to the Medical Defence Union about the matter.

7.273 Patient A37 also made allegations to Dr Larkin, a consultant cardiologist, that she had "had to pay that man [William Kerr] for sex".

7.274 Dr Larkin accepts that he did not question Patient A37 further as he did not believe her. He said his reasons for his lack of belief were the mental state of Patient A37, the "inconceivable" notion that a consultant would do such a thing, and the "ludicrous" idea that Patient A37 would pay William Kerr for sex.

7.275 Although Dr Larkin was no doubt doing his professional, medical, best for a difficult and demanding patient, his evidence does have some disturbing features.

7.276 First, his approach to such a disclosure (even if received now) seemed to be that he would filter out most disclosures and not contact the GMC if 1) he disbelieved the patient, and 2) the patient did not want him to take it further.

7.277 Second, his explanation in relation to Patient A37's disclosure is less than satisfactory. He dismissed the disclosure as ludicrous, in part because of his perception of Patient A37's mental state. But, as a caring physician, he referred her to Dr Vivian Deacon (a psychiatrist) and received back information which took away a main plank of his reason for dismissing the disclosure. That left him with two reasons for not doing anything: firstly, consultants do not do things like this, and secondly, the demand for money. We would not have seen either of these points as significant. However, we do accept that at the end of the day, Dr Larkin had to make a judgement. On balance, his decision was perhaps understandable, but unwise in terms of patient safety.

7.278　Perhaps most significantly, it appears that Patient A37 did take some preliminary steps towards making a complaint to hospital managers. On 4 August 1986 she telephoned George Wood, District Planning Manager for the York Health Authority, to ask how to lodge a complaint against an unnamed psychiatrist at Clifton Hospital. She gave her name and address during the course of the conversation and indicated that the complaint concerned the fact that she had had a full sexual relationship with the doctor and had been asked for considerable sums of money. Mr Wood advised Patient A37 that she could set out her complaint in writing, or that arrangements could be made for her to see senior members of staff. She indicated that she would probably prefer the latter and was told to ask for Mr Ingham, District Administrator of the York Health Authority, when she called back. There is no record to suggest that Patient A37 ever did call back. It would have been prudent for Mr Wood to have followed this up with her at the time, at least by getting a contact telephone number for Patient A37 to enable him to do so.

7.279　On 6 August 1986, Mr Wood wrote an internal memo to Mr Ingham, outlining the conversation that had taken place[2]. Mr Ingham, by this date, was well aware of other allegations against both William Kerr and Michael Haslam, which had been brought to his attention by Linda Bigwood. When questioned as to his response to this memo, which recorded a serious allegation of sexual misconduct by a consultant psychiatrist (unnamed), he had little recollection save that an unsuccessful attempt had been made to trace Patient A37's medical notes, and that a decision was made not to contact Patient A37 herself to follow up the complaint.

2 Mr Wood advised that Mr Wilk, Director of Nursing, and Dr Kennedy were also made aware of the complaint. Mr Wilk's recollection was that he had been in the room when Mr Wood received the phone call from Patient A37 and the matter had been discussed. It was Mr Wilk's expectation that there was to be a further investigation into this, although he was not involved in handling the complaint in any way. Dr Kennedy accepted from the documents that he had discussed the matter with Mr Wood, but had no independent recollection of the incident.

7.280 In the William Kerr Trial of the Facts in 2000, Patient A37's allegations formed counts of indecent assault and rape. The jury was unable to reach a verdict in respect of Patient A37's allegation of indecent assault and reached a verdict that William Kerr was not guilty of the rape allegation.

1987 – Patient A38

7.281 In 1987, a year after Patient A37's complaint to Mr Wood, another former patient, Patient A38, alleged to a nurse, Colin Smith, that William Kerr had made inappropriate sexual advances to her on a domiciliary visit, but that she did not want to take the matter further.

7.282 Colin Smith's evidence to the Inquiry displays the dilemma facing a healthcare professional when made the recipient of a disclosure by a patient who insisted that the matter remain confidential and not be taken further. He was specifically asked about the issue of balancing the interests of the individual patient, who did not want to pursue a formal complaint and whom he felt would not cope well with the process of a complaints procedure, and the protection of the wider patient population from a potentially abusive doctor.

> *"That was the dilemma that I faced at the time, and it was whether Patient A38 was expendable in the interests of the greater good. Patient A38, I think, was courageous in pointing out that her trust in a male clinician had been betrayed, and I could not let that happen again."*

7.283 Mr Smith reached this conclusion against the background of what was perceived as the failure, in the course of the Patient A17/Linda Bigwood disclosures, to carry out any meaningful investigation, and where Patient A17's confidentiality was not protected but her disclosure was immediately revealed to William Kerr.

> *Q. Thinking back on it now, does it concern you that you did not take a step, because other patients were then put in a position of actual or potential risk with William Kerr?*

> *A. Yes. I feel very sad that we did not have systems around that could protect other patients at that time. Very troubled.*

7.284 We note that although Mr Smith was very dissatisfied with the systems and culture which prevailed in York and Harrogate in the mid-1980s, he had no such reservations in relation to the present system.

1980s – Patient A39

7.285 It has not been possible either to date the alleged disclosure made by Patient A39 regarding William Kerr or to conclude with any certainty that there was any disclosure at all. Patient A39, who suffered from schizophrenia, was first referred to William Kerr in 1967. It is alleged that between approximately 1981 and his retirement, William Kerr would make unannounced domiciliary visits (approximately every eight weeks) where he would expose himself and indecently touch Patient A39. Patient A39 accepts that she "had a crush" on William Kerr and did not try to complain or prevent these visits.

7.286 In 1991 a Community Psychiatric Nurse (CPN), Nicholas Owens, became Patient A39's keyworker. In his statement to the Inquiry, Mr Owens said that he had been informed by another CPN that she had disclosed to Ken Randall (a CPN and previous keyworker) that William Kerr had behaved inappropriately towards her. However, Ken Randall denied being the recipient of any such disclosure and it was not possible to clarify this discrepancy. At the suggestion of Dr Marilyn Loizou, a consultant psychiatrist, Patient A39 gave a statement to the police in 1997. She does not refer to any disclosure to Ken Randall or any other healthcare professional in this statement.

1987 – Patient A40

7.287 In 1987, Patient A40 was referred by her GP, Dr Christopher Bennett, to William Kerr. She saw William Kerr on a monthly basis until the summer of 1988. William Kerr sexually assaulted Patient A40. Patient A40 described what has now become a familiar story. After consultations with William Kerr which were without incident, his questioning began to be dominated by reference to sex. She described him on one occasion sexually assaulting her by putting his fingers into her vagina and on another occasion forcing her to hold his penis and pushing her head down towards his penis, again during the consultation. On one occasion he also telephoned her, asking her to meet him at Ripon racecourse – she declined. At the final consultation, Patient A40 was conscious of William Kerr locking the door and making advances to her. She unlocked the door and left and did not return to see William Kerr after this incident. Patient A40 wrote to William Kerr saying the sessions were not helping her and she wanted to end them, although the letter made no reference to the sexual assaults. She also saw her GP, Dr Bennett, on 14 July 1988 and informed him she would not be seeing William Kerr again. There is some dispute about exactly what was said at this consultation, but it seems clear that Patient A40 at least expressed some disquiet about William Kerr's behaviour. Dr Bennett's recollection is that Patient A40 informed him that William Kerr had "invited her out in a non-professional sense". Dr Bennett's evidence was that he sought to explore matters further, but that Patient A40 gave few details and denied that there had been any sexual advances. Patient A40's medical records for July 1988 have this entry:

> *"Psychiatric disillusionment!!!"*

7.288 Clearly there was some discussion, although probably limited. We do not find that Dr Bennett had sufficient information to put him on notice, in 1987 or 1988, that William Kerr had sexually assaulted Patient A40.

7.289 Patient A40 had already told her brother of the sexual assault by William Kerr.

7.290 In the 2000 Trial of the Facts, Patient A40's allegation of indecent assault was found proved to the criminal standard.

7.291 We note here that the allegation made by Patient A40 was the only one accepted by the jury to a criminal standard of proof in the 2000 Trial of the Facts. Two points are significant:

7.292 First, this assault was the most recent – having taken place in 1987 or 1988. It may be that the jury were more comfortable with a recent allegation (although 12 years old by the time of the trial), rather than allegations which extended back into the late 1960s and early 1970s. This provides some support for our general concern that by taking the opportunities that were missed in those earlier years the allegations about William Kerr could have been brought to the attention of the police far earlier than 1997.

7.293 Second, proceeding on the basis that William Kerr did sexually assault his Patient A40 in the course of consultation, there is real concern that the failures to act, the failures to investigate years earlier (for example in response to Linda Bigwood's written complaint in late 1983), allowed William Kerr to continue practising in the belief that he was effectively immune from discovery and apprehension.

Uncertain disclosures

7.294 In some cases it has been difficult to trace the healthcare professionals to whom disclosures are said to have been made. In other cases it has been difficult to establish whether in fact a disclosure was made. In yet others it is clear that a patient's recollection of a disclosure is erroneous, an example being one patient, A41, who recalls a disclosure to her GP, Dr Keenleside, at a date when Dr Keenleside was still a medical student. That is not to say there was no abuse or no disclosure to a GP. We make no finding on that, but clearly recollection of events has been confused. Some healthcare professionals were faced with a problem when they were the recipients of ambiguous comments from patients. One CPN describes a patient, Patient A43, who had paranoid schizophrenia, informing her that William Kerr had treated her in a "very special way" and taken her out. Despite the CPN attempting to explore the matter further, Patient A43 would not elaborate and the CPN, in consultation with colleagues, felt that more evidence would be needed to proceed further. We recognise that there were sometimes difficulties in this area. We address elsewhere in this Report the issues of general believability and communication of complaints by psychiatric patients.

Confrontation with William Kerr

7.295 In only one case that came to the attention of the Inquiry did an alleged victim confront William Kerr about his behaviour. Perhaps significantly, Patient A42 was not a psychiatric patient but was the mother of a patient of William Kerr. Her contact with William Kerr arose in the context of discussing her child's treatment. Patient A42 alleged that on two occasions William Kerr visited her at her home address and raped her and that on other occasions at a clinic he exposed himself to her and touched her indecently. Some years after the incidents, Patient A42 was at Harrogate District Hospital due to an unrelated physical injury and she recounts that she forced her way into William Kerr's clinic and confronted him about his behaviour and then left. It would appear there were no witnesses to this confrontation and no formal action against William Kerr arose as a result.

Disclosures after William Kerr's retirement

7.296 In some instances disclosures, although made prior to the police investigation (and not prompted by that investigation), were not communicated until after William Kerr had retired. The dilemma facing healthcare professionals who were the recipients of such complaints, from patients who insisted that "no one be told", was less stark. Assuming they were confident that William Kerr was not practising in any capacity (NHS or private), then maintaining a patient's desire for confidentiality did not put any other patients at risk of potential harm from the activities of William Kerr. Nevertheless, the failure to pass on these complaints was not without consequences – most significantly, it was instrumental in the delay between the reported events and the Trial of the Facts involving William Kerr that ultimately took place.

7.297 One of the consultants, Dr Loizou, who was the recipient of a number of allegations following William Kerr's retirement, explained her actions and failure to pursue any of the complaints in the following terms:

> "All of the complaints I received about Dr Kerr were after his retirement when he was no longer working in the NHS. In all cases I confirmed to the women who made the disclosures that I would provide them with support should they wish to come forward. If I had thought Dr Kerr was still in a position to abuse women I would have tried to persuade the patients in question to let me disclose the details or the fact of the assaults on their behalf. If I had felt that Dr Kerr was a danger to others I would have breached patient confidentiality in order to make the police and managers aware of the information I was receiving. By the time of the Police Investigation in 1997, it was clear that a number of women had come forward and that those women making disclosures to me after that date would simply be adding to the body of evidence rather than bringing something new. If they felt unable to come forward, I had to respect their wishes."

Patient A44

7.298 Patient A44 was one of the patients whose disclosure about alleged sexual misconduct by William Kerr, said to have occurred fortnightly in the period from 1985 to 1988, was not made until after he had retired. She acknowledged the power William Kerr had over her and the inability she felt to complain whilst she was still his patient.[3] She described what he allegedly made her do (perform oral sex upon him) as "shameful" yet acknowledged that she still felt reliant upon him. In moving evidence to the Inquiry she told us that "he would not speak to me before he had done it", and said this:

> Q. *Can you remember talking to anyone about it?*
>
> A. *When it was going on?*
>
> Q. *Before he retired.*
>
> A. *I do not think I mentioned it to anybody, no.*
>
> Q. *Why did you think that was? Did you not feel you should tell someone and then it would stop and you could maybe see another psychiatrist?*
>
> A. *It was disgusting. But he still used to have about 12 minutes to listen to me. And I thought, well, he used to say that his willie really loved me and I thought I was the only one, and he liked me so much because I was innocent.*

7.299 It was not until 1992/93, following a breakdown, that Patient A44 made a disclosure of alleged sexual abuse. She informed a nurse and also Dr Vivien Deacon, a consultant psychiatrist, who in turn informed Dr Ryan (Patient A44's treating consultant psychiatrist). Dr Deacon's view was that it was a matter for Dr Ryan. Dr Ryan's response was:

> *"Despite several enquiries by me, the patient declined to speak to me about Dr Kerr. I was aware that she was speaking to a staff nurse on the unit and a community psychiatric nurse about this and therefore determined that, as her needs in this respect were being met elsewhere, I would leave the matter there."*

---

3 She describes the sexual abuse as occurring on every appointment, for approximately 2½ years, continuing right up until his retirement.

7.300 Sometime after William Kerr's retirement in 1988 Patient A44 also informed her GP, Dr Graham Foggitt, who believed that he discussed the matter with his partners (Dr Clement Chave-Cox, Dr Michael Scatchard and Dr Phyllis Jones). Finally in 1996, Patient A44 alleged to Dr Rugg's registrar that her previous psychiatrist had made her perform oral sex on him during her outpatient appointments. The Registrar, on reading Patient A44's notes, established that the accused psychiatrist was William Kerr and wrote, referring to the allegations, to Patient A44's then GP (Dr Peter Banks), her CPN and her consultant, Dr Ryan. The Registrar's view was that, as Patient A44 did not want to take the matter further and as William Kerr had retired, his action need not extend beyond notifying her GP, consultant and CPN of the allegations.

Patient A45

7.301 Another patient who did not make any disclosure until after William Kerr's retirement was Patient A45. She alleges that in about 1982 she began a sexual relationship with William Kerr who had been treating her with relaxation classes in relation to her anxiety problems. Sexual intercourse allegedly would take place either in consulting rooms in Clifton Hospital or in her flat in York. Patient A45 states that William Kerr told her that if she said anything to anyone she would be in as much trouble as him. This frightened Patient A45 who felt she would not be believed. The relationship is said to have lasted until 1985, when Patient A45 broke it off, having by then met her future husband.

7.302 It was not until she started seeing a psychologist, Elaine Middleton, in about 1991 that Patient A45 disclosed the nature of her relationship with William Kerr. Ms Middleton's evidence was that she informed Patient A45 that she had "every right to take it forward" as a complaint. However, Patient A45 was concerned that her husband would find out about the matter and declined to pursue the complaint.

Patient A39

7.303 Patient A39 was referred to William Kerr in 1967 and saw him at infrequent intervals thereafter, both as an inpatient and an outpatient. She alleges that from 1981, during domiciliary visits, William Kerr would touch her inappropriately, pushing up her skirt, although matters never proceeded to sexual intercourse. There is some confusion regarding any disclosure, but it appears she may have informed a CPN, Ken Randall, of William Kerr's behaviour, probably after William Kerr's retirement. (Mr Randall denies ever receiving such information.)

Patient A46

7.304   It was not until 1992 that Patient A46 alleged to a CPN, Peter Kidd, that 10 years previously she had been visited by William Kerr in her flat and that they had had sexual intercourse. In his police statement, Peter Kidd states that Patient A46 was adamant that he should tell no one else, and he respected her wishes. Patient A46 repeated her allegations to a psychiatric nurse, Jane Lucas, in 1995. Again, she was insistent the matter be taken no further, although she did agree to Ms Lucas informing her consultant, Dr Loizou, of the matter. Patient A46 was not prepared to take the matter forward and despite Dr Loizou being informed, no further action was taken.

Patient A47

7.305   Patient A47 was referred by her CPN, Sarah Harris, to a consultant psychiatrist in 1995. This prompted a conversation in which Patient A47 stated that she had, in the past, seen William Kerr and that he had made suggestions of a sexual nature to her. In her police witness statement, Sarah Harris noted: "[Patient A47] told me that she did not want to share this information with anyone else and I respected that".

Patient A48

7.306   Patient A48 alleges that from 1981, when she was treated as an outpatient by William Kerr (usually in his Friday afternoon clinic), she was subject to inappropriate questioning on her sex life and William Kerr would masturbate in front of her. On one occasion (probably 1988) during a "relaxation session", she alleges she opened her eyes to see William Kerr semi-naked and that he then raped her. Patient A48 alleges that William Kerr telephoned her after this incident to try to arrange a meeting, but she declined. According to Patient A48, she informed a CPN, Peter Kidd, of William Kerr's "wandering hands" in 1995, although Peter Kidd himself makes no reference to this in his police statement.

Patient A12

7.307 Sometime in 1991, according to her witness statement given to the police, Patient A12 stated that she had made a disclosure to Marion Anderson, a clinical psychologist, alleging that William Kerr had sexually assaulted her. Marion Anderson stated that she does not recall any such allegation being put to her by Patient A12, but stated that Patient A12's account was in keeping with some second- or third-hand accounts that she had received about William Kerr.

Patient A49

7.308 On 3 December 1971, Dr Pamela Reed (née Heatley) referred Patient A49 to William Kerr. On 10 December 1971, Patient A49 went to William Kerr's consulting rooms at Harrogate General Hospital. Patient A49 alleged that William Kerr discussed sexual matters with her and masturbated whilst she was present. The second consultation was held at Dragon Parade, Harrogate, on 29 December 1971, and she alleged that William Kerr sexually assaulted her on that occasion, insisting on sexual intercourse before granting a termination. Patient A49 believed that she had to do what William Kerr told her to do because she wanted an abortion and William Kerr was the person with the "power" to refer her for it.

7.309 In 1972, William Kerr again gave his opinion in respect of a termination of a pregnancy. On this occasion, according to Patient A49's evidence in civil proceedings, she spoke to William Kerr only on the telephone and was not abused. It appears that this contact with William Kerr was initiated by her, rather than her GP.

7.310 Patient A49 did not report the alleged abuse to any authorities until 1997 when she spoke to a social worker, Ann Clark, who was treating her for depression. Shortly after this disclosure, the police and media became involved in the allegations against William Kerr, and Ms Clark encouraged Patient A49 to speak to the police.

7.311 In the William Kerr Trial of the Facts, Patient A49's allegations formed a count of rape. The jury could not reach a verdict in respect of Patient A49's allegations.

7.312 Patient A49 provided a written statement to the Inquiry, attaching her civil statement, which stated that her reason for not complaining was that she thought the details were too awful to talk about and did not think that she would be believed.

Patient A50

7.313 Whilst the failure to alert the authorities remained an almost uniform response of GPs, it is not correct to say that all GPs refused to acknowledge the complaints that were raised.

7.314 Patient A50 was referred to William Kerr by her GP, following concerns being raised by counsellors at the college where she was studying. The appointments took place at Harrogate District Hospital and continued between 1983 and 1986. Patient A50 alleged that William Kerr would instruct her to perform oral sex upon him, stating that this was part of her treatment. This "treatment" continued until Patient A50 informed her fiancé of what was going on and he said she should cease to attend the appointments. There was, according to Patient A50, one subsequent contact with William Kerr when he made a domiciliary visit in January 1988, following Patient A50's depression after an ectopic pregnancy. According to Patient A50, William Kerr raped her on this occasion.

7.315 Patient A50 did not make any complaint at the time, alleging that William Kerr had made her promise she would not tell anyone what had happened and she felt bound by that promise.

7.316 However, in approximately 1989, Patient A50 informed Dr Loizou that she believed her problems were a direct result of her "experiences" with William Kerr. Dr Loizou, having previously (in late 1988/89) received an allegation from Patient A17 who claimed a consensual sexual relationship with William Kerr, assumed that Patient A50's references to "experiences" related to sexual misconduct on the part of William Kerr. Dr Loizou's evidence to the Inquiry was as follows:

"Patient A50 and I discussed what options were open to her. This included the possibility of her coming forward and making a complaint about Dr Kerr. However, Patient A50 was clear that she did not want her husband to know what had been going on. My concern was to look after Patient A50's well-being. Dr Kerr was no longer a danger to her and Patient A50 was unwilling to give any detail of the 'experiences' that she had raised with me. I decided to try to get Patient A50 to come to see me at my clinic to discuss this matter further. However, Patient A50 did not attend and therefore the matter was not followed up.

"Following my initial consultation with Patient A50, and before it became clear she would not be attending any further appointments, I raised with colleagues the possibility that a complaint about Dr Kerr may be forthcoming. This was done on an informal basis with Dr Anthony Rugg and Dr Vivien Deacon. When I raised the possibility of a complaint, my colleagues said 'he is known for it'. There was no elaboration on this statement and I am unable to recall who said it. My sense was that the comment was due to Dr Kerr's reputation as a ladies' man and not to any knowledge of untoward behaviour. Relationships with patients were then and are now not acceptable."

7.317 From May 1987, Patient A50's GP was Dr Iddon, a GP in the same practice as Dr Wade. He gave evidence that he had no suspicions regarding William Kerr prior to Patient A50's disclosure which, if correct, shows a concerning lack of communication between partners. Dr Iddon was unable to date Patient A50's disclosure, save that correspondence suggests he was aware of the allegations by at least December 1991. He accepted that he discussed the allegations with Patient A50 over a long period of time on a great many occasions, although there is a concerning lack of any notes recording the "counselling" sessions. It would appear that his failure to forward the allegations of Patient A50 was partly due to her reluctance to initiate proceedings at that stage and also because he knew William Kerr had retired. However, in his evidence to the Inquiry, he accepted that he should have contacted the GMC and that he should if necessary have overridden patient confidentiality to contact the authorities. The following exchange with Counsel to the Inquiry adequately illustrates his evidence on this topic:

Q. The second point is the question of your understanding of the duties to report actions and to take action in relation to concerns about other medical practitioners. That is really directed towards the point we addressed earlier on, about you not taking any action when the disclosure was first made. Is there anything you want to add in relation to that point?

A. In hindsight, it would have been the appropriate thing to do, whether or not the particular person had wished me to do it or not. I had not taken on board really the fact that William Kerr was licensed by the GMC as opposed to his – sorry, what I was trying to say is that my assumption, and it was wrong, was that in 1988 when he retired from NHS practice, that that was an end of his patient involvement. I had not realised that there was a potential for him to continue in practice and seeing patients.

Q. With regard to notifying the police that what he had done was a criminal offence, is there any comment you would like to make about that?

A. I think, from what I have learnt through this process, clearly I should have overridden this particular patient's reluctance and picked the phone up. I would certainly do it now.

7.318 Some years later (in 1994) Patient A50 also informed her Community Psychiatric Nurse, Carmel Duff, of William Kerr's alleged sexual abuse. She also subsequently informed a further CPN and a student nurse (in order to explain her fear of being left alone with a doctor). In addition, she spoke to a number of non-medical people, including to two journalists.

7.319 Finally, in 1997, she went to the police.

7.320 Due to Patient A50's disclosure to the police, an investigation was started that was to lead to extensive investigations, the contacting of many of William Kerr's former patients, and ultimately his trial and conviction of indecent assault.

7.321 In the William Kerr Trial of the Facts, Patient A50's allegations formed counts of indecent assault and rape. The jury could not reach a verdict in respect of these allegations.

Other non-complainants

7.322 Once the police investigation began and letters were sent out to former patients of William Kerr, a large number of women came forward who had previously made no disclosure to any healthcare professional. The accounts of those 21 patients who came forward for the first time, in response to the police investigation, are summarised in Chapter 10.

Conclusion

7.323 In the preceding paragraphs, we have identified 59 former patients of William Kerr who allege they were the victims of sexual assault, or inappropriate sexual behaviour. In the period between 1965 and 1983 we are satisfied that at least 30 concerns or complaints, ranging from unhappiness at questioning on sexual matters or an unexplained refusal to see William Kerr, to explicit disclosures of sexual assault, were raised with at least 11 different GPs. Only one of these GPs took any action to forward the complaint and he, Dr Wade, having referred the complaint to a consultant colleague of William Kerr, Michael Haslam, took no further action.

7.324 Prior to 1983, we are satisfied that complaints were also raised with no less than 11 hospital staff, as well as the Secretary of the Leeds Regional Hospital Board and Sir Allan Marre, the then Health Service Commissioner. None of these complaints led to any investigation into William Kerr's practice. Indeed, one of the few complaints that was referred "up the line" to the Sister in Charge, was subsequently referred by the Sister to William Kerr himself, and then, unsurprisingly, instantly dismissed as "malicious".

7.325 It was not until 1983 that a complaint fell into the hands of a nurse, Deputy Sister Linda Bigwood, who was not prepared to let the matter drop. However, despite Deputy Sister Bigwood's persistence, it was not until 1997, almost 10 years after William Kerr's retirement and over 30 years after the first concern was raised in North Yorkshire, that any serious investigation was undertaken into his practice. This was an investigation by the police that was to lead to him being found guilty of sexual assault and being placed on the Sexual Offenders Register.

7.326 What is immediately striking about the list of names and dates is the regularity of the expressions of concerns and complaints – particularly during the 1970s. Although the Inquiry is not concerned to investigate the truth of the allegations, it is also striking that a number of women, apparently completely unconnected with each other, made similar allegations of sexual assaults by the same psychiatrist. We of course have the benefit of seeing a sequence of alleged incidents, and seeing some accounts not available to the jury. Also, we have had the advantage over all the GPs and other healthcare professionals identified in the previous paragraphs. What, to them, may have been a single complaint, or an isolated incident, can now be seen in its chronological place, as part of an emerging pattern of alleged abusive behaviour. The similarities we have identified may not have been sufficient to satisfy a criminal trial jury of William Kerr's guilt in relation to all the charges made against him, but they may well, and certainly should have, led an investigating team – at local or national level – to conclude that there was here a pattern of alleged abusive behaviour which merited very close analysis, and (if possible) the careful collection of written statements from all concerned.

Summary of concerns and complaints raised by patients, 1965 to 1988, at a glance

Date of disclosure	Patient	Alleged recipient
1965	A1	GP – Dr Michael Moore
1965	A2	GP – Dr Rushton
1968	A3	Nurse – Lynn Davey
1968	A4	Nurse – Matron of Harrogate General Hospital
1969/1970	A5	GP – Dr Theo Crawfurd-Porter
1971	A6	Nurse – Matron Farnsworth (Harrogate General Hospital) Nurse – Sister Thornton
1971	A7	Nurse – Sister Ann Atkins
1972	A8	Management – Letter to Leeds Regional Hospital Board
1972	A9	GP – Unknown
?1972	A10	GP – Dr Theo Crawfurd-Porter
1972	A11	GP – Dr Phyllis Jones
1974	A12	GP – Dr Frank Young
1975	A13	GP – Dr George Crouch
1976	A14	Nurse – Sister Barbara Wearing GP – Dr Moss
1978	A15	GP – Dr Derek Jeary
1978	A16	GP – Dr Derek Jeary
1978	A17	Nurse – Nurse Busby

Date of disclosure	Patient	Alleged recipient
1978	A18	GP – Dr Albert Day
1978	A19	Solicitor GP – Dr Theo Crawfurd-Porter (Subsequently to Psychologist – Marion Anderson)
1979	A21	GP – Unknown
1979	A20	GP – Dr Theo Crawfurd Porter
1979	A22	GP – Dr Wade Police
1979	A23	GP – Dr Rosemary Livingstone
1979	A24	GP – Dr Angus Livingstone
1979	A25	Doctor – Unknown
1979	A26	Nurse – Thomas English
1981	A27	Private Psychotherapist – Kath Horton
1981	A28	GP – Dr Visick
1982	A29	GP – Dr George Crouch
1982	A17	Nurse – Sister Wearing
1982/83	A30	Consultant – Dr Rugg
1983	A17	Nurse – Deputy Sister Linda Bigwood
1983	A31	GP – Dr Pamela Reed
1983	A32	Nurse – Sister Cotterill GP – Dr Margaret Plowman
1983	A13	Community Worker
1984	A36	Counsellor – Julie Levine
1984	A33	Consultant – Dr Rugg
1984	A34	Nurse – Peter Lister
1984	A35	GP – Dr Whitcher Health Visitor – Ms Liz Edwards (untraced)
1985	A37	GP – Dr Nixon
1986	A37	Consultant – Dr H Larkin Management – George Wood, District Planning Manager, Yorkshire Health Authority
1987	A38	Nurse – Colin Smith
1987	A40	GP – Dr Bennett

Chapter 8
The Bigwood concern – a written allegation of serial sexual misconduct

Introduction

8.1   In the summer of 1983, a patient (Patient A17) made a detailed disclosure to Deputy Sister Linda Bigwood at Clifton Hospital. She alleged that for a number of years (between approximately 1973 and 1975) she had been having a consensual sexual relationship with her treating psychiatrist, William Kerr.

8.2   It should be noted and recorded at the outset that, as with other allegations of sexual misbehaviour made against William Kerr (or Michael Haslam), we have not attempted to determine whether or not Patient A17's story was true or false. Indeed, Linda Bigwood herself did not decide whether the disclosure was true or false, merely noting what she had been told, and not dismissing the account as untrue.

8.3   Patient A17's disclosure was subsequently withdrawn (more than once) and the factual picture is further clouded by the fact that we have not heard from Patient A17 (who has not taken any part in the Inquiry), nor, of course, from William Kerr. In those circumstances, even if it was proper for us (and in accordance with our Terms of Reference) to investigate the truth of the disclosure, it would have been impossible to do so with any degree of certainty.

8.4   The reason Patient A17's story has been given such prominence in this Inquiry is not due to the content of the allegations she made (and later retracted) of sexual misconduct by William Kerr. Her story of alleged abuse by William Kerr is not substantially different from the accounts given by a large number of other patients. However, largely thanks to Linda Bigwood's detailed and near-contemporaneous notes, the Patient A17 story offers a unique insight into how the hospital authorities and the district and regional health authorities responded, when faced with allegations in writing about the sexual misconduct of one of their consultant psychiatrists.

8.5 The immediate response to Patient A17's disclosure set the tone and standard for what followed. Instead of a considered investigation, centred on support for Patient A17 and considerations of patient safety, Patient A17 was 'thrown into the lion's den' when, following her disclosure to Linda Bigwood, a one-to-one interview with William Kerr was arranged. After that interview she wrote: "I wish to retract any allegations I made against William Kerr." Whether that retraction was made of her own free will or under duress is one of many unanswered questions. Suffice it to say that the retraction should have been treated with considerable scepticism, coming as it did after a psychiatric patient had expressed fear of reprisal and had then been subjected to a one-to-one interview with the person about whom she was complaining. Witnesses to the Inquiry have largely accepted that the meeting between Patient A17 and William Kerr should not have taken place.

8.6 Had Patient A17's allegations been confined to her alleged affair with William Kerr, the story may have ended there. She had, after all, retracted her account of the affair, albeit in questionable circumstances. However, what Patient A17 told Linda Bigwood went far beyond her own case. Patient A17 told Linda Bigwood that William Kerr had had sexual relationships with a number of other female patients. According to Patient A17, William Kerr's alleged sexual misconduct was known to his wife (who, significantly, was also a psychiatrist working in the same region) and was so well known in Harrogate that some of the Harrogate GPs would not refer young women to him.

8.7 Linda Bigwood was not a person to let matters rest, and in August/September 1983 she compiled a detailed document, both in relation to Patient A17's disclosure of an affair and the wider allegations of serial sexual misconduct by William Kerr.

8.8 By the end of 1983, Linda Bigwood's complaint had gone from the local level at Clifton Hospital, to the district and up to the regional level. However, no investigation of William Kerr was ever launched and he continued practising until his retirement in 1988, when he was thanked for his "valuable contribution" to the Yorkshire Region.

8.9 What is revealed by the Patient A17 story is a disturbing picture of inaction, or part action, amounting in the end to a total failure by hospital staff and administrators to investigate the allegations against William Kerr (despite Linda Bigwood's dogged pursuit of the issue). Our task is to set out part of the overall story in some detail, draw some conclusions, and make any necessary recommendations that may assist in ensuring that this sorry episode is not repeated. From any point of view, Patient A17 was a vulnerable person suffering at the time from mental disorder – she deserved better treatment. As is now recognised by the health authorities in written submissions to the Inquiry, Linda Bigwood was "courageous, persistent and determined in her fight to have a proper investigation into Patient A17's allegations to her". Linda Bigwood deserved a better hearing.

8.10 The Patient A17 story also provides an object lesson in failing to offer support and understanding, not only for the person making the disclosure (whether or not a complaint is made) but also the staff member in the difficult position of responding to the disclosure.

The Bigwood story in detail

June and July 1983

8.11 Patient A17 had been a regular patient at Clifton Hospital over a number of years. The relevant admissions were in June and July 1983.

8.12 During that admission, in June 1983, Dr Ann Mortimer (then William Kerr's Senior House Officer, and now Professor Mortimer), asked Linda Bigwood (then working on Ash Tree House Ward) if she would see Patient A17 on a regular basis for counselling. Patient A17 was then on Langdale Ward; however, Linda Bigwood had previously nursed and counselled Patient A17 when she had been an inpatient on Ash Tree House Ward, Clifton, in October 1982, and had established a good rapport. The counselling sessions were to take place once a week.

8.13 At the second counselling session, Patient A17 spoke to Linda Bigwood about a sexual relationship she claimed to have had with William Kerr. According to Patient A17, the relationship lasted from approximately 1973 to 1975. William Kerr would allegedly book her in for the last appointment of the day at his outpatient clinic at Dragon Parade, when the building would be empty, leaving them free to engage in a physical relationship without fear of interruption. In addition to their encounters at Dragon Parade, Patient A17 described William Kerr visiting her flat and taking her out in his car. It appears that the end of the alleged sexual relationship coincided with a time when William Kerr started to see his outpatients at Harrogate Hospital rather than at Dragon Parade.

8.14   The date of the disclosure is not absolutely clear, and nothing appears in the contemporaneous medical or nursing records. As far as we can ascertain, it was 23 or 30 June 1983.

8.15   Patient A17's "fraught divulgence" to Linda Bigwood was made in the context of therapeutic counselling. Patient A17 felt that, as a result of the past relationship, William Kerr "wanted her out of the way" and that this was detrimental to the care she was receiving. Patient A17 said she was afraid of making any formal complaint, for fear of reprisals from William Kerr or from other staff who might want to protect his position.

8.16   Patient A17 asked that her disclosure be treated as strictly confidential. In the first instance Linda Bigwood agreed to this; however, as she states: "When I thought about it afterwards I decided it was something I could not keep in confidence according to my own conscience."

8.17   Accordingly, shortly after Patient A17's disclosure, Linda Bigwood went to her Nursing Officer, John Monk-Steel, and told him exactly what she had been told by Patient A17. Linda Bigwood emphasised that she was unaware whether the allegation was true or false, but that at the very least it was a matter of concern that Patient A17 remained under the care of William Kerr. Linda Bigwood returned to see Patient A17 and informed her that she had felt obliged to pass the allegation on to John Monk-Steel.

8.18   John Monk-Steel's initial response was: "Let's get the bastard". John Monk-Steel had come into conflict with William Kerr in the past over the issue of multidisciplinary working, to which Kerr was opposed, and due to what John Monk-Steel perceived as William Kerr's attitude that he was "actually in charge of the hospital".

8.19   John Monk-Steel went to see his immediate superior, Senior Nursing Officer Anne Tiplady. She decided that John Monk-Steel should speak to Patient A17 himself. She also informed the Sector Administrator, Keith Parsons, of her actions.

8.20 Dr Ann Mortimer was informed of Patient A17's allegation. According to Linda Bigwood's August/September document, Dr Mortimer was informed on Anne Tiplady's instructions. However, Dr Mortimer's oral evidence to the Inquiry was that Linda Bigwood had informed her of the allegation and that she had subsequently heard the disclosure directly from Patient A17:

> *"I remember Patient A17 disclosing that she and Dr Kerr had been engaged in a sexual relationship for years, and she was very blasé really about it, in a way that I found was really quite shocking, because I knew that consultants were not supposed to be having sexual relations with patients."*

8.21 William Kerr was also informed of Patient A17's allegation, although there is some confusion over who first informed him. It seems most likely that it was Dr Mortimer. Her evidence was as follows:

> *"My recollection is that I did telephone Dr Kerr and I said, 'Patient A17 has made certain allegations, Dr Kerr.' He said, 'Oh God, not that again, that is all old hat, she has been saying these things for years', which was in a sense even more shocking to me, that he had apparently been aware of Patient A17's allegations on previous occasions, yet he was still the consultant."*

8.22 This is supported by Linda Bigwood's contemporaneous record of events:

> *"I said [...] 'Has he [Kerr] been told officially?' And Monk-Steel replied: Dr Mortimer told Dr Kerr on the telephone, and his reply was 'Oh God, that's all old hat'."*

8.23 Dr Mortimer went on to recount that, having spoken to William Kerr on the telephone, she saw him in his office and volunteered to make arrangements for Patient A17 to be transferred to a colleague. William Kerr allegedly refused to countenance such action.

8.24 Dr Mortimer accepted that she was not certain whether Patient A17 was telling the truth; indeed, on the whole she stated that she did not believe what Patient A17 said was true. However, she felt that it was important that William Kerr knew what had been said "so that he would then have the opportunity to defend himself or take whatever actions he felt were necessary".

8.25 It seems that John Monk-Steel (presumably after Dr Mortimer had spoken to William Kerr) also discussed the allegations with William Kerr, apparently at Anne Tiplady's instigation. This discussion seemed to be no more conclusive than the discussion between Dr Mortimer and William Kerr. John Monk-Steel described the conversation in the following terms:

> "We engaged in dialogue about the allegations and what they might mean. I do not remember what he [Kerr] said, but I do remember that I was in there for [half an hour] discussing this...

> "My view of the substance of the allegations remained unchanged because he had not really told me anything."

8.26 John Monk-Steel, as agreed with Anne Tiplady, also saw Patient A17. At this meeting Patient A17 retracted her allegation against William Kerr, a retraction that John Monk-Steel found unconvincing, due in part to her body language (poor eye contact and restlessness in her chair when discussing the issue).

8.27 There is an unresolved dispute as to who instigated the one-to-one meeting between William Kerr and Patient A17, which took place in early July 1983. Both John Monk-Steel and Anne Tiplady deny organising it. Indeed, Anne Tiplady's oral evidence was that she would have viewed such a meeting as entirely inappropriate and considered it as tantamount to "putting the ferret in with the rabbit".

8.28 Dr Mortimer was unable in oral evidence to recall the detail of how this meeting was arranged. Linda Bigwood's August/September document suggests that the meeting was arranged by Dr Mortimer at the instigation of Anne Tiplady. The other near contemporaneous document (Mr Wilk's report dated February 1984 – see below) states that the meeting between William Kerr and Patient A17 was arranged by Dr Mortimer, although there is no record of whether this was at anyone's instigation. It is certainly possible that William Kerr himself decided to see Patient A17 alone. As Dr Mortimer accepted in her evidence, "I could not prevent the consultant from seeing Patient A17." Nor, one assumes, could the nursing staff, who had no authority over William Kerr.

8.29 Leaving aside the issue of who arranged the meeting between William Kerr and Patient A17, which we find unnecessary to resolve, it is clear that there was such a one-to-one meeting, and it is likely that Dr Mortimer, John Monk-Steel and Anne Tiplady all had some role in organising this meeting or knowledge that such a meeting was to take place.

8.30 It is also clear that Patient A17 retracted her allegation both orally (to John Monk-Steel) and subsequently in writing. Whether the first oral retraction to John Monk-Steel took place prior to Patient A17 having seen William Kerr is again unclear. The 1983/84 documents cloud rather than clarify this issue. The investigation by Mr Wilk, carried out in late 1983/early 1984 is somewhat contradictory. The report implies that John Monk-Steel saw Patient A17 prior to the one-to-one meeting with William Kerr. However, the report also records John Monk-Steel's evidence as being that Patient A17 changed her story and withdrew her statement after a private interview with William Kerr.

8.31 While these discrepancies are noted for completeness, we find that, given the passage of time, such inconsistencies are inevitable. To our mind, the important facts are the following, all of which have been established to our satisfaction:

- Patient A17 made a detailed disclosure of a long-term consensual sexual relationship with her consultant, William Kerr.

- Despite Patient A17's desire that this matter be kept confidential, the nurse to whom the disclosure had been made, Linda Bigwood, felt duty-bound to report the matter.

- The disclosure was reported by Linda Bigwood in the first instance to Nursing Officer John Monk-Steel. He in turn consulted with his senior Nursing Officer, Anne Tiplady, who in turn informed the Sector Administrator, Keith Parsons.

- John Monk-Steel, Anne Tiplady and Keith Parsons, having been informed of the disclosure, took a number of steps, the order of which is unclear:

  - Patient A17 was informed by Linda Bigwood that she had felt bound to pass on the disclosure.

  - Dr Mortimer was informed of the disclosure.

  - William Kerr was informed of the allegation made by Patient A17 (probably by Dr Mortimer).

  - John Monk-Steel saw Patient A17 to discuss the matter. Patient A17 orally retracted her allegation against William Kerr.

  - William Kerr saw Patient A17 in a one-to-one meeting, very probably on Monday 4 July 1983 (there is an entry in Patient A17's nursing notes for that date, which reads "Went to see William Kerr in his office this morning").

Patient A17's written retractions

8.32 Following these events (post-dating the one-to-one meeting with William Kerr), Patient A17 made the first of two written retractions. In a handwritten note, that was signed and dated as 18 July 1983 (the day she was again seen by William Kerr, and the day before she was discharged from Clifton) she stated: "I wish to retract any allegations I made against Dr Kerr."

8.33 The relevant part of Patient A17's nursing notes for that day read as follows:

> *"Saw Dr Kerr this morning. For discharge tomorrow. Looks miserable. Found lying on her bed at 9pm – tearful and disturbed. Said she was unable to tell me the 'position' she was now in, but felt terrible."*

8.34 The written retraction on 18 July 1983, had it not been for the persistence of Linda Bigwood, would no doubt have marked the end of the matter.

8.35 Three principal factors appear to have played a part in fuelling Linda Bigwood's sense of grievance in the early stages of the handling of the disclosure, which in turn appear to have contributed to her taking the matter further. Firstly, it appears she was not given any adequate feedback on how Patient A17's disclosure was being handled. She was not called upon to give any written statement or take part in, or contribute to, any investigation. She was not even able to speak to Anne Tiplady for a number of weeks (partly due to holiday arrangements) and, even when a meeting was arranged, Linda Bigwood claims that Anne Tiplady refused to discuss the handling of the disclosure by Patient A17, save to state that the matter had gone to the Sector Administrator and nothing more could be done. Although Anne Tiplady in her oral evidence did not agree with this characterisation of her actions, she accepted that she may have said "I cannot discuss this now." Secondly, shortly after she had passed on Patient A17's disclosure to John Monk-Steel, Linda Bigwood was informed she was to be moved from Ash Tree House Ward, an acute admissions ward, to Rosedale Ward, a geriatric ward. Linda Bigwood viewed this move as a demotion and felt she was being punished for raising Patient A17's disclosure. Finally, she felt strongly that it was improper that William Kerr should have been permitted to have a one-to-one meeting with Patient A17 following

Patient A17's disclosure and attributed Patient A17's retraction to pressure being placed on her by William Kerr. Her grievance on this point was aggravated by the fact that, prior to the one-to-one meeting, she had expressly informed John Monk-Steel of her concerns about such a meeting – concerns that were ignored.

8.36 Linda Bigwood was not alone in her unease at the one-to-one meeting between William Kerr and Patient A17, or in her belief that this meeting had played a significant role in Patient A17's retraction. Dr Mortimer, in her evidence to the Inquiry, said she believed that, if William Kerr had not had the meeting with Patient A17, the retraction would not have occurred when it did.

8.37 When the complaint subsequently reached district level and legal advice was sought, the possibility that Patient A17's retraction had been obtained under duress was explicitly recognised, so much so that a decision was made to re-interview Patient A17 (see below).

8.38 Whether Linda Bigwood's other principal concern, namely that she was being "punished" for reporting Patient A17's disclosure by being moved to a different ward, was well-founded is difficult to establish. Anne Tiplady's evidence was that Linda Bigwood's move was due to a breakdown in the working relationship between her and other staff on Ash Tree House Ward, in particular with Charge Nurse Alan Greenfield. Linda Bigwood's contemporaneous documents substantiate the fact that there was a breakdown in working relationships. She states that she had lost faith in both Alan Greenfield (who she describes in her written complaint as "totally pseudy, bullshit remarks all the time") and John Monk-Steel. In such circumstances it is difficult to see how she could have remained as an effective part of the Ash Tree House Ward team (assuming Alan Greenfield was to continue on that ward). However, given the coincidence of the timing, it seems likely that, by reporting Patient A17's disclosure and forcefully expressing her concern at the way subsequent "investigations" were handled, matters were brought to a head and her "whistle-blowing behaviour" played at least some part in her transfer to a different ward.

8.39 By late July 1983, Patient A17's disclosure had been made and withdrawn. On 25 July 1983, as Senior House Officer to William Kerr, Dr Mortimer wrote to Patient A17's GP (Dr Smith) saying:

"Deputy Sister Lynn Bigwood was asked to renew counselling sessions with Patient A17, and kindly consented, but it was felt that Patient A17 manipulated this one-to-one situation, and there was no apparent improvement."

Records

8.40 There have been suggestions from some witnesses that some records were made of Patient A17's disclosure and the immediate handling of it, for example by Anne Tiplady in "diary notes which she placed on the Senior Nursing Officer Complaints File". That file has not survived. We have examined Patient A17's hospital records for the period, and there is nothing there to show the existence of any disclosure, or any reference to any form of investigation. Of even greater significance, there is nothing in the Wilk Report made in February 1984 (see below) to suggest that there were any official contemporaneous records – indeed, one of Mr Wilk's findings was that Anne Tiplady "failed to keep any record of this incident or the investigation". Our conclusion is that Anne Tiplady's recollection is probably mistaken, and there was no record made at the time, at all, by anybody. There was no record of the disclosure, no record of action taken (if any) and no record of William Kerr's response. This conclusion also applies to John Monk-Steel, who told us that he made, and kept, notes of his discussion with Patient A17 and of his lengthy (30-minute) meeting with William Kerr. It is said that these notes "have not survived". Our conclusion is that it is more likely that they were never made. We cannot accept that, if they had been made at all, the notes would not have surfaced and been referred to in the Wilk Report.

8.41 Dr Mortimer, then a very junior doctor, had also heard from Patient A17 that she had had a longstanding sexual relationship with William Kerr. Dr Mortimer also made no note of that disclosure. Her reasons, openly stated to the Inquiry, go some way to explaining the prevalent culture of the time, and the likely reasons for the absence of any records by others. In her evidence, she explained that the prevailing culture at the time required loyalty to a fellow doctor, coupled with the knowledge that a junior doctor relied on the references from their consultants to progress in the profession.

8.42 It is for readers of this Report, with knowledge of current practices and attitudes, to decide for themselves whether a junior doctor today would in all cases act differently from Dr Mortimer in 1983.

Linda Bigwood's written complaint

8.43 On 18 August 1983, Linda Bigwood, concerned at both the way in which Patient A17's disclosure had been handled and her own treatment in being transferred to work on a geriatric ward (which she perceived as an unfavourable career move), made a tape recording of her version of events. This was subsequently transcribed, with added notes made on 20 August 1983 and 1 September 1983, into a 13-page, closely-typed document. The document was entitled

> *A complaint against the Nursing Management of Clifton Hospital, York concerning:*
>
> *a. The abuse of a patient's trust and possibly person;*
>
> *b. The abuse of a member of staff making known to management that patient's allegations.*

8.44 The document ("the written complaint") set out the detail of Patient A17's allegation and the manner in which John Monk-Steel and Anne Tiplady had dealt with the matter.

8.45 The written complaint also set out other significant information, which can broadly be divided into three categories:

- allegations by Patient A17 suggesting William Kerr's abuse was not confined to her but was both widespread and widely known;

- the names of other healthcare professionals who had been recipients of consistent allegations made by Patient A17 over a significant period about a sexual relationship with William Kerr; and

- details of other evidence and sources (beyond Patient A17) that suggested William Kerr was serially sexually abusing patients.

8.46 The allegations by Patient A17, suggesting she was not an isolated case and that concerns about William Kerr's actions were widespread, were as follows:

- Other patients had been subject to abuse by William Kerr.

- Allegations of William Kerr's abuse of female patients were well known to GPs in Harrogate, such that some would no longer refer young female patients to him.

- Allegations of William Kerr's abuse of patients were known to the Samaritans.

- Dr Bromham was aware of her husband's abuse of female patients and on one occasion had "hushed up" a situation where she had treated a female patient who had attempted suicide following a sexual encounter with William Kerr.

8.47   The details of the other staff members who had allegedly been party to consistent disclosures from Patient A17 about a sexual relationship with William Kerr were set out by Linda Bigwood in the written complaint as follows:

- In 1978, Patient A17 allegedly told Nursing Officer Jillian Busby. Jillian Busby allegedly told Patient A17 to keep quiet about it.

- At an unknown date, prior to June 1983, Patient A17 had allegedly informed an unnamed member of staff about her sexual contact with William Kerr. This in turn had been passed on to Sister Pauline Brown. Patient A17 was then seen by William Kerr on a one-to-one basis and was forced to retract her allegation.

- In 1982, Patient A17 allegedly told Sister Barbara Wearing, who had been sympathetic. Linda Bigwood herself spoke to Sister Wearing about this. Sister Wearing is said to have accepted that she had received an allegation and had believed Patient A17, but felt there was nothing she could do about it, as she could not prove anything. Furthermore, Sister Wearing allegedly informed Linda Bigwood that she had come across similar complaints from many female patients over the years and she was prepared to put in writing what she had been told by Patient A17.

- At about the same time as her disclosure to Linda Bigwood, Patient A17 also allegedly informed her GP, Dr Margaret Smith, about her sexual relationship with William Kerr. The GP's response was said to have been that she should write a story to a woman's magazine about it.

8.48   Finally, the written complaint compiled by Linda Bigwood contained a number of other details and sources (beyond Patient A17) leading to suspicions that William Kerr was a serial sexual abuser. These details were as follows:

- A second patient (not Patient A17) had, in about August 1983, informed Linda Bigwood that she had in the past consoled a fellow patient who claimed to have been "dragged into a linen cupboard by Dr Kerr".

- A third patient had complained to Linda Bigwood in about August 1983 that William Kerr had flirted with her during a domiciliary visit.

- Dr Mortimer had informed Linda Bigwood that she had been warned when she started to work for William Kerr to "watch out for him" because he was a womaniser, although she (Dr Mortimer) had "never had any trouble with him".

- A social worker had informed Linda Bigwood that a friend of hers had been propositioned by William Kerr (a reference to Patient A13).

- Meg Jones, the Senior Social Worker at Clifton, informed Linda Bigwood that she and her colleagues had heard rumours about William Kerr. Linda Bigwood also documented that Meg Jones had reported Michael Haslam to the Sector Administrator some years earlier over a similar incident of improper sexual contact with a patient (a reference to Patient AB).

8.49　The written complaint transformed what had started as a specific disclosure by one patient to a nurse in a therapeutic context into a detailed complaint of the most wide-ranging and serious nature. It suggested that other staff had been the recipients of disclosures by Patient A17 about a sexual relationship with William Kerr, but had taken no action. Of even more concern, it suggested that William Kerr was serially sexually abusing his patients, that knowledge of this was widespread, and that there were a number of potential witnesses who would be able to confirm this account. It also, almost by way of a footnote, raised the possibility that William Kerr's fellow consultant psychiatrist, Michael Haslam, should be investigated in respect of Patient AB's allegations against him of similar behaviour.

Circulation of the written complaint

8.50　The written complaint was circulated by Linda Bigwood to her union, the Confederation of Health Service Employees (COHSE) (who in turn forwarded the document to John Corbett, the District Nursing Officer), Dr Mortimer, the Head of the Social Work Department (Meg Jones) and Sister Wearing.

8.51 The allegations against William Kerr, and the involvement of Linda Bigwood, were also communicated to a fellow consultant psychiatrist of William Kerr, Dr Rugg, who sat on the Hospital Management Committee. At the time of the circulation of the written complaint, Dr Mortimer (under the rotation scheme) had moved from being SHO to William Kerr to work for Dr Rugg, and it was she who informed him of these matters. Dr Rugg, in his evidence to the Inquiry, had no recollection of the written complaint, but recalled Dr Mortimer speaking to him both about the fact that she had been warned when she arrived to watch out because of William Kerr's reputation with women (the implication being his reputation with female staff) and about Patient A17's disclosure. Dr Rugg accepted that, having been informed of these matters, he spoke first to Linda Bigwood and then to William Kerr. Dr Rugg recognised that it appeared Linda Bigwood was being sidelined and demoted, due to her "whistle-blowing" behaviour. However, he denied that his contact with Linda Bigwood was in any way intended as a threat to her. His evidence was as follows:

> *"I spoke to her [Linda Bigwood] with the intention of trying to say, look, what you are doing at the moment is actually making you the complaint, and it may be you that will suffer...*

> *"I was going to her with the intention, and I do not think this came across, of suggesting that if she had a complaint against a doctor and had some evidence for it and if the people that she had taken it to were not doing anything about it – or it appeared to her they were not doing anything about it – perhaps she should consider taking it somewhere else. I remember suggesting possibly the GMC, not actually knowing how you do that...*

> *"I may have said, and probably did say, 'look, if you carry on with the present course that you are on at the moment, Dr Kerr is still going to be sat there doing his job in six months' time, the same way he is doing it now, you run the risk of getting the sack,' or something like that. I certainly did not threaten her with it."*

8.52 For the record, we conclude that Dr Rugg was not intending to threaten Linda Bigwood – it may well be that his words and actions were motivated by concern for her. However, Linda Bigwood reasonably interpreted Dr Rugg's words as warning her that she was in danger of losing her job if she took the matter any further. Dr Rugg's words undoubtedly confirmed to Linda Bigwood her belief that the move to a geriatric ward was related to her having complained.

8.53 Dr Rugg spoke to William Kerr, who he described as being "rattled" by the allegation, threatening to resign if an investigation were launched. However, despite what was at best an ambiguous response by William Kerr, certainly short of any convincing explanation or denial, Dr Rugg took no action to pursue either William Kerr's alleged behaviour or the apparent treatment of Linda Bigwood, despite being a member of the Hospital Management Committee.

The initial response to Linda Bigwood's written complaint

8.54 The story of what happened to Linda Bigwood's written complaint is one that spans almost five years. The story itself is a salutary one of management failures at every level. It is a story that ended in 1988 with the words:

> *"With regard to Dr Kerr, as he will be leaving the employment of this authority in six months [due to retirement], there is little effective action the RHA [Regional Health Authority] could take against him, even if we subsequently felt it was justified."*

8.55 However, it would be incorrect to characterise what occurred following submission of the written complaint as total inactivity. Indeed, four apparently positive actions were taken at the outset:

- Steps were taken to meet with Linda Bigwood.

- Patient A17 was visited.

- The matter was referred to the Regional Health Authority.

- An investigation was instigated, carried out by Mr Wilk, Director of Nursing Services (Mental Illness).

Meeting with Linda Bigwood

8.56 The District Nursing Officer, Mr John Corbett (now deceased), had been one of the recipients of the written complaint, sent to him under cover of a letter dated 26 October 1983 from Mr Kineavy of COHSE, acting on behalf of Linda Bigwood.

8.57 Mr Corbett responded to COHSE the following day to inform them that "an enquiry will take place, the exact nature of which is not yet decided... [I] will make every endeavour to ensure a rapid resolvement of the stated grievances."

8.58 From the outset, it appears, perhaps due to COHSE's involvement, that the focus was on "the grievances of Linda Bigwood" and there was a failure to focus on the patient safety issues raised by the extremely serious allegations against William Kerr. Of particular significance is that no attempt was made to analyse the written complaint and set out the number of allegations against William Kerr and the potential sources of information and lines of inquiry. In other words, there was no investigation: in concentrating on the messenger, the substance of the message was both lost and ignored.

8.59 Soon after receiving the written complaint, Mr Corbett discussed the matter with Mr Ingham, the District Administrator (and later District General Manager). Mr Ingham's oral evidence to the Inquiry was that, because Linda Bigwood's written complaint was not an easy document to get into (he described it as long and wandering) and because the covering letter from COHSE referred to a grievance, he believed that:

> "Mr Corbett saw it as primarily, until he met Sister Bigwood, a complaint about the way Sister Bigwood had been treated, rather than primarily a complaint about the way a patient had been abused."

8.60 Mr Corbett invited Linda Bigwood to attend an interview, accompanied by Mr Kineavy. The expressed purpose of the meeting, according to Mr Corbett, was to "establish, as clearly as possible, the facts arising from [Linda Bigwood's] complaints, in order that I may process these further". The meeting was originally set for Monday 7 November 1983; however, this was inconvenient for Linda Bigwood, and the meeting was therefore rescheduled for 21 November 1983.

8.61 Linda Bigwood described how a written retraction by Patient A17 was "waved under [her] nose" at this meeting.

8.62 As set out above, on 18 July 1983 Patient A17 had written a short note: "I wish to retract any allegations I made against Dr Kerr." There had been a suspicion that this written retraction had been instigated by William Kerr in the one-to-one meeting he had had with Patient A17 on 4 July 1983. However, the written retraction presented to Linda Bigwood at the meeting on 21 November 1983 was a far more comprehensive retraction, reading as follows:

> *3.11.83*
>
> *Dear Sir,*
>
> *I am writing to you concerning a disturbing matter which arose during the time I spent recently in Clifton Hospital.*
>
> *Whilst talking to one of the nurses I made allegations against Dr Kerr which were unfair and were interpreted by the nurse to be of a sexual nature.*
>
> *I would like to assure you that there was in fact no sex involved and whatever I said was done so out of bitterness at the time on my part which I regret completely.*
>
> *I just wish the matter to be forgotten and to treat Dr Kerr with the respect he has always commanded.*
>
> *Yours faithfully*
>
> *[Patient A17]*

8.63 Despite being addressed as "Dear Sir", the letter had in fact been addressed and sent to Anne Tiplady.

8.64 Linda Bigwood was immediately suspicious that this letter had not been freely sent by Patient A17, and arrived just before the time when the issue of an inquiry was being considered. It was possible that someone had applied pressure to her to write such a letter. The obvious suspect was William Kerr.

8.65 In fact, correspondence reveals that in November 1983 Dr Wintersgill, Specialist in Community Medicine of the District Health Authority, and Mr Price, consultant surgeon and member of the District

Management Team (DMT), met William Kerr at Clifton Hospital to inform him of what was going on.

8.66 According to Mr Ingham's oral evidence to the Inquiry, Dr Wintersgill was highly thought of and was a senior member of the District Health Authority team. He was perceived to be someone suitable to deal with such a matter in Dr McIntosh's (the District Medical Officer (DMO)) absence on holiday and then due to sickness. However, Dr Wintersgill was not a member of the DMT, and it seems likely that this was the reason the decision was taken that he should be accompanied by a member of the DMT, Mr Price. The decision to send two people may also have been a reflection of the fact that, according to Dr Wintersgill, "Consultants were seen by the DMT as not untouchable exactly, but very difficult to get to, assuming there was any reason to do this."

8.67 It appears from the correspondence that, at this meeting, the second (3 November 1983) letter of retraction from Patient A17 had not been received, suggesting this meeting must have taken place during the first few days of November 1983 (before the letter of 3 November 1983 was received). Dr Wintersgill's evidence to the Inquiry was that the meeting with William Kerr took place on 3 November 1983, the letter of retraction being written on the same day and posted on the next day. The timing strongly suggests to us (as it did to Anne Tiplady) that the letter of retraction was written at the instruction of William Kerr (or of his unidentified "supporters"). This point is perhaps an indicator of a wider malaise: the investigation in relation to the disclosure was so superficial, so "shallow" (to use Mr Wilk's word in the February 1984 Report), that in truth it was no investigation at all. The coincidence of the letter of retraction being written very shortly after William Kerr had been alerted to the ongoing inquiries about him is striking. Indeed, Linda Bigwood felt so concerned that someone had put pressure on Patient A17 to obtain the retraction that she drove straight from the meeting (held at Bootham Park) to Clifton Hospital, where she first attempted to see William Kerr, and after failing to obtain any response from knocking on his door, went straight to Anne Tiplady's office where she accused Mrs Tiplady of participating in a "cover-up".

The referral to the Regional Health Authority

8.68 Despite the production of the written retraction from Patient A17 at the meeting on 21 November 1983, Linda Bigwood's complaint was not entirely dismissed, and neither were her concerns that the retraction had been obtained under duress. A decision was taken at the meeting that Mr Corbett would refer the matter to "the Authority" (presumably the Regional Health Authority) and recommend "an enquiry to be carried out by an unbiased committee".

8.69 Mr Ingham explained that, despite the fact that his role as District Administrator included controlling the secretarial aspect of dealing with formal complaints, he had little involvement at this stage because:

> *"it was not regarded as a complaint in that sense. It came in as a grievance. And in that grievance was seen the possibility of major disciplinary action or investigation, potentially disciplinary action against a consultant. So I do not think the people who were ever involved, or indeed I, ever regarded it as a complaint in that sense."*

8.70 The referral up to Region was, according to both Dr Wintersgill and Dr Turner, the normal procedure. Complaints against doctors would go first to the DMO (Dr McIntosh) or, in the present case, Dr Wintersgill, who effectively stood in as a deputy on this issue. The DMO would then refer the matter on to the Regional Health Authority where it would become the responsibility of the Regional Medical Officer (RMO).

8.71 It seems likely that it was Dr Wintersgill who took the step of communicating the complaint by Linda Bigwood to Dr Turner, the RMO, on 29 November 1983. While Dr Wintersgill's evidence was that he first heard of the matter from Hugh Chapman (the Regional Legal Adviser), this does not fit easily with the fact that he had already, in early November, been involved in seeing William Kerr on behalf of the DMT.

8.72 Dr Turner responded to Dr Wintersgill on 1 December 1983 in the following terms:

"My involvement as RMO concerns the serious allegations made by the patient against the consultant, Dr Kerr, which, if substantiated, would lead to consideration either by GMC or through other disciplinary procedures. The letter from [Patient A17] dated 3 November 1983 indicates that there is no matter of complaint.

"Unless this position alters either through any investigation of the nursing elements of the complaint or, alternatively, by further approach to [Patient A17], then there would seem no action that I should take and I am grateful for your information."

8.73 Dr Turner's evidence was that he was never shown the written complaint of Linda Bigwood and thus was never made aware of the more wide-ranging allegations of sexual abuse by William Kerr of a number of patients. His evidence to the Inquiry was that he, as RMO, would have been responsible for matters of serious misconduct by a consultant, such as sexual relationships with patients, and that he would have instigated an investigation and taken steps to alert the GMC:

"Any person in my position seeing a document of this kind [Linda Bigwood's written complaint], the alarm bells would have been ringing like Westminster Abbey."

8.74 A criticism of Dr Turner made by Mr Ingham was that he:

"rapidly absented himself from the scene and said 'Complaint withdrawn, nothing to do with me, over to you'."

8.75 It appears that the Regional Legal Adviser, Hugh Chapman, also became involved and is recorded as giving the following advice:

• There should be an inquiry into the complaint by Linda Bigwood against nurse management at Clifton Hospital.

• There should be an interview with Patient A17 to assess the possibility that her retraction had been made under duress.

8.76 It was Mr Ingham's view that Mr Chapman effectively started to direct affairs on behalf of the Region. However, Mr Chapman's evidence to the Inquiry was that he too was not aware of the detailed content of

Linda Bigwood's written complaint because, if he had been made aware of it, he would have advised the immediate involvement of the police. We will return to Mr Chapman's involvement later in this section of the Report.

8.77   In accordance with Mr Chapman's advice, steps were taken to arrange for Patient A17 to be interviewed – but by this time it was almost six months after the initial disclosure. Speed was clearly not of the essence. A letter was sent to Patient A17 on 5 January 1984 enquiring whether she would be prepared to meet Dr Wintersgill and a psychiatric nurse, Miss Armitage. This letter was copied to Patient A17's GP, Dr Smith, on the basis that Patient A17 might wish to discuss the matter with her GP, who, according to the letter, had been forewarned that an approach was to be made to Patient A17.

8.78   This letter strongly suggests that Dr Smith (contrary to her oral evidence to the Inquiry) was fully aware of the disclosures made by Patient A17 about William Kerr and the concern surrounding the possibility of duress being applied to her in order to secure a retraction. Although Dr Smith denied any recollection of the letter, an inspection of Patient A17's GP notes revealed that it had been received by Dr Smith's surgery.

Patient A17 meets Dr Wintersgill and Miss Armitage

8.79   Patient A17 agreed to see Dr Wintersgill and Miss Armitage, and the meeting took place at her home on 12 January 1984. A report was made of the meeting. This recorded that Patient A17 repeated that her allegations against William Kerr were untrue and that they had been made out of bitterness. She explained that this bitterness was due in part to the role he had played in advising her to have a termination of pregnancy some years previously, and partly as she feared he would not accede to her request to stay longer in hospital. She also stated that she had made similar allegations about William Kerr on previous occasions, all of which were untrue. Her explanation for sending a second written retraction, dated 3 November 1983, was that she had received a postcard from Linda Bigwood indicating that further action was being taken and she (Patient A17) wished to stop this going ahead. Apparently no request was made to see the postcard, and, almost unbelievably, Linda Bigwood was not even asked to confirm that a postcard had been sent.

8.80 The assessment made by Dr Wintersgill and Miss Armitage in their report dated 15 February 1984 was as follows:

> "Patient A17 was apparently honest and frank throughout the interview and showed a very clear and firm understanding of her mental state at the time she had made her allegations. We recognise the limitations of an interview between doctor/nurse and a patient in such circumstances since it might present a clinical rather than a non-clinical atmosphere with the influence this could have in reaching conclusions. Patient A17, however, gave no indication at any time that her retraction of the allegations had been inappropriate or that the retraction had been made under duress. Accordingly, we must accept what she says.
>
> "In our view it must be questioned whether the decision to ask Dr Mortimer to arrange a private interview between Patient A17 and Dr Kerr was wise, given that the allegations made had not at that stage been considered fully. There must also be some doubt about the interview having taken place in private. These, however, are separate points."

8.81 This interview marked the end of any further consideration of Patient A17's allegation, although, according to Mr Ingham, there remained at least for himself "a sort of uneasy feeling". Patient A17 had retracted her statement and had stood by that retraction, leaving the authorities with little option but to accept her stance. What is less understandable is the fact that, given the unease that continued to surround Patient A17's retraction, no attempt was made to investigate the written complaint by Linda Bigwood that William Kerr was serially abusing other patients.

8.82 Mr Ingham described the pursuit of the complaint of sexual misconduct by William Kerr in the following terms:

> "In terms of the substantial allegation of sexual abuse, it was taken further in the sense that Dr Wintersgill and Ms Armitage saw the patient, who withdrew the allegation, and, not only that, gave a credible explanation for her behaviour. All roads in the complaint, I think here and in Sister Bigwood's original document, led to the patient, with the possible exception of the Meg Jones comment."

8.83   On this, Mr Ingham was, of course, mistaken – there were a number of allegations against William Kerr that stood independent of Patient A17. His description continued:

> *"Once the patient had withdrawn, credibly, I presume that Mr Chapman in discussion with Dr Wintersgill – but I would guess the predominant figure would be Mr Chapman – took the view that no further avenues could or should be taken."*

The Wilk Inquiry

8.84   In accordance with Mr Chapman's legal advice, in addition to interviewing Patient A17 there was an inquiry into the complaint by Linda Bigwood against nursing management. This inquiry led to a report entitled *Report of a Nursing Management Enquiry into a Written Complaint Submitted by Deputy Sister Bigwood.*

8.85   At the request of John Corbett, the inquiry was chaired by Mr Ray Wilk, the Director of Nursing Services (Mental Illness). Accompanied by Mr C Flanagan, Authority Nurse, Mr Wilk conducted a number of staff interviews.

8.86   The Wilk Inquiry considered the attitude of nursing staff to psychiatric patients and the system for handling complaints. However, without any explanation, it entirely excluded from its remit the most concerning aspect of Linda Bigwood's complaint, namely that a consultant psychiatrist was allegedly sexually abusing his female patients and that knowledge of these allegations was widespread among other healthcare professionals, including GPs. It also excluded from its remit any consideration of the one-to-one interview of Patient A17 by William Kerr, although Mr Wilk (when giving evidence to the Inquiry) was at a loss to explain why this matter was excluded.

8.87   In his evidence to the Inquiry, Mr Wilk was clear that his remit was limited to investigating the way nursing management had handled the complaint (relating to Patient A17) that Linda Bigwood had raised. He was clear that his remit excluded any consideration of the substance of Patient A17's allegation (whether she had in fact been having a sexual relationship with William Kerr); neither would it appear that he ever considered it his role to investigate the allegations that William Kerr was having sexual relationships with other patients (although he must have been aware of the allegations, having been given a copy of Linda Bigwood's written complaint).

8.88 Mr Wilk was completely at a loss to explain to us why, given that his task was to investigate the way the complaint was handled, he did not examine why and how William Kerr came to have a one-to-one meeting with Patient A17 as soon as he learnt of her allegations.

8.89 He acknowledged in his evidence that his jurisdiction reached beyond simply nursing staff and extended, for example, to Mr Parsons as an administrator and Dr Mortimer as a member of the doctors' team. He was unable to explain to us, therefore, why William Kerr was excluded from his investigations.

8.90 All staff interviewed by Mr Wilk were given the opportunity to be accompanied by a representative of their trade union or professional organisation. The report that Mr Wilk subsequently produced consisted of brief summaries of these interviews, followed by a number of findings of fact and seven conclusions.

8.91 Mr Wilk interviewed the following members of staff:

- John Monk-Steel, Nursing Officer;

- Jill Busby, Nursing Officer (nights);

- Pauline Brown, Ward Sister;

- Barbara Wearing, Sister (nights);

- Keith Parsons, Unit Administrator;

- Dr Ann Mortimer, Senior House Officer;

- Alan Greenfield, Charge Nurse, Ash Tree House Ward;

- Anne Tiplady, Senior Nursing Officer; and

- Linda Bigwood, Deputy Sister.

8.92 Mr Wilk found the following facts:

1. Mr Monk-Steel was asked to carry out the initial investigation into a potentially very serious complaint. He did not have the necessary training/experience and skill to undertake this task.

2. The patient, Patient A17, was not "protected" when subjected to a "private interview" with William Kerr, after he became aware of her complaint.

3. Although Miss Bigwood expressed dissatisfaction with the way in which the complaint was being handled, no positive steps were taken to remedy this matter.

4. The subject matter of Mr Monk-Steel's appraisal/counselling was not recognised.

5. Mr Monk-Steel was not involved in either the decision to allocate Miss Bigwood to Ash Tree House Ward or the decision to transfer her to Rosedale Ward at Clifton Hospital.

6. There was a generally "dismissive attitude" displayed in response to the complaint. Because Patient A17 was a psychiatric patient, she was not taken seriously.

7. Mrs Busby did not consider it necessary to pursue comments made by Patient A17 over several years.

8. There was a totally dismissive attitude on the part of Sister Brown. She was unable to "respect" the view that a psychiatric patient could relate a story that had to be taken seriously.

9. Sister Wearing did not reach a conclusion on whether the facts as given by Patient A17 were true or false.

10. Sister Wearing failed to share Patient A17's disclosure about a sexual relationship with William Kerr with another senior member of the nursing staff.

11. The discussion on this complaint between senior officers was so informal that no positive action was taken or suggested by the Unit Administrator (Mr Keith Parsons).

12. The Unit Administrator did not follow up or get involved in a serious complaint regarding a consultant psychiatrist at Clifton Hospital.

13. Dr Mortimer, in retrospect, felt that she had not satisfied herself fully on the level of skills Miss Bigwood had in counselling.

14. There was real evidence of a breakdown in relationships between Mr Greenfield and Miss Bigwood.

15. Both Mr Greenfield and Miss Bigwood made no "real effort" to resolve their different points of view.

16. The Unit Nursing Officer failed to address himself to the inter-personal relationship problems on Ash Tree House Ward, which were inevitably having an effect on its functioning.

17. The Unit Nursing Officer failed to carry out any system of staff appraisal that actively involved staff, and, therefore, staff were not informed of their strengths/weaknesses.

18. There was ineffective monitoring of the developments of nursing staff roles.

19. Mrs Tiplady asked an inexperienced nursing officer to investigate "a complaint" that was potentially very serious.

20. Mrs Tiplady failed to discuss in detail this very serious matter with another senior officer.

21. Mrs Tiplady failed to keep any record of this incident or of the investigation.

22. There was a dismissive attitude towards a psychiatric patient with a "track record" and therefore the allegation was not fully investigated.

23. The patient was subjected to an interview alone with William Kerr.

24. Mrs Tiplady, as the Senior Nursing Officer and the officer accountable for the outcome of the investigative interviews, did not complete the process by discussing the outcome with Miss Bigwood.

25. Counselling, as an extension of the role of the nurse, was not properly monitored by the Unit Nursing Officer.

26. Nursing staff on Ash Tree House Ward were not adequately prepared for their counselling role.

27. The timing, reasons and decision taken to transfer Miss Bigwood to Rosedale Ward were unplanned.

28. The motives for the selection of Miss Bigwood [for transfer to Rosedale Ward] were unclear.

29. There were apparent inconsistencies in the handling of the report [by Linda Bigwood of Patient A17's disclosure].

30. The "report" became a "complaint" because Miss Bigwood felt that Mrs Tiplady and Mr Monk-Steel were mishandling the information.

31. The "normal" procedure of requesting a written statement on a serious complaint was not followed.

32. There were serious staff relationship problems on Ash Tree House Ward.

33. There was a serious breakdown in communication/relationships between Miss Bigwood and nursing management.

8.93 The seven conclusions of Mr Wilk in his report dated 15 February 1984, were as follows:

1. There was a serious problem in the attitudes of the staff dealing with a complaint from a psychiatric patient.

2. The shallowness of the investigation resulted in the dismissal of the complaint.

3. It would not be untoward to question the motives of staff and the investigative model they adopted as this led to the impression that there was a "closing of ranks" and consequently a cover-up.

4. A lack of understanding of the monitoring role of the Senior/Unit Nursing Officer contributed to the lack of resolution in the staff relationship problems on Ash Tree House Ward.

5. The absence of a staff appraisals system for staff on the Acute Unit contributed to staff continuing to work in roles they did not clearly understand and for which they did not receive critical comments.

6. Senior nursing management did not properly discharge their responsibilities in connection with the handling of a serious complaint.

7. Senior nursing management was unable to offer an acceptable account of the reasoning used in the deployment of staff.

8.94 The first three conclusions are particularly damning and should have produced some substantial response at a higher, regional, level. The conclusion, in summary, was that the attitude and motives of the staff were subject to serious question and concern – there had been a shallow investigation and at least the impression of a cover-up.

Where did patient safety fit into the "investigative model"? It seems to have been a low priority, if even considered at all.

Investigations not pursued

8.95 There were three strands arising from the Patient A17/Linda Bigwood story:

1. the disclosure by Patient A17 of her own alleged sexual relationship with William Kerr;

2. the reaction by the health authorities (at hospital, district and regional levels) to that specific disclosure, and to Linda Bigwood as the messenger; and

3. the wider allegations of sexual abuse by William Kerr (and also by Michael Haslam) set out in Linda Bigwood's detailed complaint.

8.96 Strand 1 effectively ended in early 1984 with the visit to Patient A17 by Dr Wintersgill and Miss Armitage – confirmed in the letter to William Kerr dated 11 April 1984.

8.97 Strand 2 effectively ended with the Wilk Report in February 1984, and the letter to Linda Bigwood from Mr Ingham dated 29 July 1985 stating that "it is possible for a consultant to decide to see a patient alone, even when a complaint of this nature has been made".

8.98 Strand 3 was to all intents and purposes ignored or disregarded by the recipients of the Linda Bigwood written complaint, or the wider allegations were simply not communicated to people who needed to know – such as Graham Saunders, and (possibly) Hugh Chapman. But even if Hugh Chapman had seen the wider allegations (and we suspect that he did), his likely response would have been as set out in his oral evidence:

A. If I concentrated on the third strand, as you put it, the allegations were very vague, and I think I would have looked at the matter from a practical point of view of the necessity in disciplinary proceedings of consultants of getting absolutely firm evidence; the difficulty of persuading patients who might have been abused to come forward with statements; if they came forward with statements, the difficulty of persuading them to give oral evidence in proceedings; the cost of the exercise, the waste of management time and money, and the certain resolute defence of the practitioner by either the British Medical Association or one of the defence organisations. Those are practical considerations, and those would have put out of my mind the suggestion we follow up the third strand complaints.

Q. In effect, you are saying that those various practical considerations, all of which militate against taking further the points raised by Linda Bigwood, would have been the features that would have caused you to say we are not going to take this any further?

A. It was not for me to say we are not taking it any further.

Q. Or for you to advise?

A. I would have advised the District Management Team that on balance, in terms of cost effectiveness, it was not a route to go down.

Q. Because it was going to be very difficult, very expensive, very strongly resisted by Kerr?

A. And very time-consuming.

Q. And that would have been your advice, would it, even if the likes of Mr Corbett, Dr Wintersgill and Mr Ingham had said to you, look, we think there is a cloud over this doctor, we are worried that he might in fact be abusing patients? Those features that you identified as militating against an investigation would have done so even if they had said to you things of the sort I have just put to you?

A. I do not think I ever learned of the views of Mr Corbett. Stuart Ingham in his evidence, I think, speaks of some feeling of unease. If I had been aware of Mr Corbett's objection and Stuart Ingham's unease – and I do not think I was – I do not think my advice to the DMT would have been different.

Q. You do not think it would have been?

A. I do not think it would have been different.

Q. Even if they had said to you we are uncomfortable, we think he might be up to something, you still would have said there is nothing we can do?

A. Yes.

Q. Sorry, that there is nothing that should be done by way of further investigation?

A. Yes.

8.99 An analysis of the steps that were taken in response to the written complaint reveals in stark form the matters that were not investigated. We have attempted to reconstruct, insofar as this is possible after such an interval, what might have been revealed had an attempt been made to investigate the wider allegations made by Linda Bigwood, namely that Patient A17 was not an isolated case and that William Kerr was serially sexually abusing his patients, and that rumours as to his behaviour were widespread.

8.100 As set out above, the written complaint made it clear that Patient A17 had complained to at least four other healthcare professionals. However, it appears that even those who were questioned by Mr Wilk were not pressed as to their information concerning William Kerr's practices.

Jill Busby (Nursing Officer)

8.101 According to Linda Bigwood, Patient A17 had informed Jill Busby about her alleged sexual relationship with William Kerr in 1978. The Wilk Report concluded that Patient A17 had indeed made comments regarding William Kerr "over several years", but that Mrs Busby, who was found to have a dismissive attitude towards psychiatric patients, had not pursued these comments. Mrs Busby informed Mr Wilk that she "had heard other comments regarding Dr Kerr" but that "she did not wish to quote them".

8.102 There is no indication that she was pressed on this matter and/or informed of any obligation to give details as to any behaviour that may have had implications for patient safety.

8.103 Had she been pressed, Mrs Busby may have been able to offer more information regarding allegations of sexual misconduct by William Kerr.

Sister Pauline Brown

8.104 According to the written complaint, at an unknown date, prior to June 1983, Patient A17 had informed an unnamed member of staff about her alleged sexual contact with William Kerr. This had, in turn, been passed on to Sister Pauline Brown. However, Patient A17 was then seen by William Kerr on a one-to-one basis and retracted her allegation.

8.105 Mr Wilk did question Pauline Brown as to whether Patient A17 had ever made any complaint to her regarding a sexual relationship with William Kerr. Sister Brown denied this, adding that she would not have believed it in any event as she considered Patient A17 to be a troublemaker. There is no evidence that Sister Brown was questioned on the specific issue of whether an allegation by Patient A17 concerning William Kerr had been passed to her by another member of staff, or whether she had been involved in a situation where Patient A17 had retracted an allegation following a one-to-one meeting with William Kerr.

8.106 We heard evidence from Pauline Brown, who, consistent with her evidence to Mr Wilk, denied any knowledge of any complaints by patients of sexual misconduct by William Kerr. We were thus faced with two broadly contemporaneous accounts, one that Pauline Brown had been the recipient of a complaint by Patient A17 (forwarded to her by another nurse, according to Patient A17's account as recorded in Linda Bigwood's written complaint) and one (Pauline Brown's own evidence to Mr Wilk) that she was aware of no such complaint.

8.107 For reasons we set out below, we prefer the account set out in Linda Bigwood's written complaint, namely that Pauline Brown had been the recipient of complaints about William Kerr. In Chapter 7 we have referred to the Patient A26 story. That story is here repeated. Thomas English was a nurse who worked at Clifton Hospital. In his evidence to the Inquiry, he referred to a specific incident in approximately March 1979 when he had received an expression of concern from a patient (whose identity he could not recall) who did not want William Kerr to visit her at home, as she alleged he had previously attended her home unannounced and she had felt sexually intimidated. In summary, the patient (who was then an inpatient) stated that William Kerr had sexually propositioned her in her own home, and she was fearful that, following her discharge, he would do it again.

8.108 Thomas English reported this matter to Pauline Brown, who responded by informing William Kerr of the allegation. Thomas English was subsequently taken by Pauline Brown to William Kerr's office and questioned about the matter. William Kerr convinced Mr English that the complaint was malicious and the matter was taken no further. While this account does not fit entirely with Linda Bigwood's written record and possibly relates to a different patient, it does convince us that Pauline Brown was aware of allegations by at least one patient regarding William Kerr's behaviour towards female patients. It is also significant that, in her oral evidence to the Inquiry, Pauline Brown, while she could recollect no instance of receiving a complaint from a patient about William Kerr's sexual advances, did accept that had she done so she would have acted broadly in the way alleged by Mr English, namely by referring the complaint to William Kerr himself. This adds credence to Mr English's recollection of events.

8.109 Mr English's evidence has further consequences. As we have noted elsewhere, the concerns of the patient he referred to were simply fobbed off. He spoke to Sister Brown, she spoke to William Kerr, William Kerr denied any wrongdoing – end of inquiry and end of complaint. We do not know what happened to Patient A26 – she is not known to the Inquiry and we have only her first name. The effect of Mr English's evidence is that the concerns of the patient were entirely discounted (even suppressed) by the joint effort of William Kerr and Sister Brown. At almost exactly the same time, in the spring of 1979, Patient A22 was making a very similar complaint to her GP, Dr Wade, and to the police of a domiciliary visit by William Kerr and of a sexual proposition. That complaint was taken by the GP to Michael Haslam on 3 April 1979, when, so we conclude, the complaint came to a dead end. There is now evidence not only of a cultural problem at Clifton Hospital (and in the wider local NHS) that allowed concerns and complaints not to be investigated, but, arguably, of something close to conspiracy to suppress expressions of concern, disclosures of sexual misconduct and tolerance of sexualised behaviour towards patients.

8.110 Had disclosures of sexual misconduct by William Kerr been more actively pursued, the account of the patient who had voiced concern to Mr English may have come to light.

Sister Barbara Wearing

8.111 According to Linda Bigwood's written complaint, in 1982 Patient A17 told Sister Barbara Wearing about her alleged sexual involvement with William Kerr. Sister Wearing's response was said to have been sympathetic.

8.112 Sister Wearing was asked about this matter by Mr Wilk and she stated that she recalled a conversation with Patient A17, "part of which related to a sexual relationship the patient had with Dr Kerr whilst attending the outpatient department in Harrogate". Sister Wearing said she reached no conclusion on whether the facts were true or false (although she noted that Patient A17 was coherent and lucid at the time of the disclosure). She accepted that she did not report the matter to any other staff.

8.113 Linda Bigwood's written complaint recorded her own interview with Sister Wearing who, on that occasion, apparently accepted that she had received an allegation and had believed Patient A17, but felt there was nothing she could do about it, as she could not prove anything. Further, Sister Wearing informed Linda Bigwood that she had come across similar complaints from many female patients over the years and she was prepared to put in writing what she had been told by Patient A17. None of these matters, all of which were noted in the written complaint, were put to Sister Wearing by Mr Wilk.

8.114 Had Sister Wearing been questioned specifically on the similar complaints she had heard from other patients, she may have referred, among others, to the case of Patient A14.

8.115 Patient A14 was seen by William Kerr on a domiciliary visit in 1972. She alleges that on that occasion she was indecently assaulted. Patient A14 claims that she informed a nurse, "Rachel", the following day, who is said to have responded that "everyone knew what Bill Kerr was like". At subsequent domiciliary visits, William Kerr allegedly insisted on discussing her sex life, not the specific problem that she suffered from (agoraphobia). Patient A14 was admitted to Clifton Hospital under the care of William Kerr in February 1976 and alleges that it was on this occasion she alleged to Sister Wearing that she had been indecently assaulted.

8.116 We have had the advantage of considering a whole range of allegations against William Kerr, and thereby seeing for ourselves links and connections, similarities of description, etc. We accept that the decision makers in 1983 and 1984 did not have this information. However, at least part of the explanation for their lack of knowledge is because of the poor quality of the investigation. Opportunities to gather information were missed. For example, had Sister Wearing been asked by Mr Wilk (or by some other investigator) to put in writing the other disclosures she had received (as she was apparently prepared to do) a number of other victims may have been revealed. The difficulty of carrying out any useful investigation in 2004, so long after the event, was particularly apparent in the case of Sister Wearing, whose oral evidence was that she had no recollection of any patient ever complaining to her about sexual advances by a consultant. We accept that memories may have faded after such a period of time, and thus do not conclude that Sister Wearing was obstructing the Inquiry. However, insofar as there was a discrepancy between her recollection as at 2004 and the contemporaneous documentary evidence, which suggested that she was in fact the recipient of a number of complaints about William Kerr's sexual misconduct but failed to take any action, we prefer the contemporaneous evidence.

8.117 A further line of inquiry that could have been followed but was not, despite Sister Wearing's evidence, was an investigation into the running of the Dragon Parade clinic, which was the stated location of many of the alleged incidents of abuse by William Kerr, some of which are said to have occurred out of hours – often on a Friday afternoon/evening.

Dr Margaret Smith

8.118 According to Linda Bigwood's written complaint, Patient A17 had informed her GP about her alleged sexual relationship with William Kerr. The GP had allegedly responded that she should write a story for a woman's magazine about it. Patient A17's GP was Dr Margaret Smith and it is assumed that this is the GP who is referred to in the written complaint, although she is not specifically named. Dr Smith was not questioned by Mr Wilk, or by anybody else, about this allegation. Dr Smith's evidence to the Inquiry was confused. Her first written statement said this:

> "Patient A17 consulted me at my surgery in November 1983 and January 1984, and told me of a long-term sexual relationship between herself and William Kerr. She did not wish to make any complaint but rather seemed concerned that it had ended."

8.119 That account is entirely consistent with Linda Bigwood's recollection of the terms of the disclosure made to her in June 1983, and also fits comfortably in time terms with the letter written by Dr Wintersgill.

8.120 Dr Smith changed her evidence from that initial acceptance that in 1983/84 Patient A17 had disclosed to her a sexual relationship with William Kerr to a position where she denied any knowledge of the allegations against William Kerr until a time shortly prior to his retirement in 1988. In summary, she gives the following reasons for fixing on that date rather than the earlier date:

- The disclosure was made around the time of William Kerr's retirement, which we know to be in September 1988.

- At the time of the disclosure, Patient A17 was living opposite Harrogate District Hospital.

- By that time, Patient A17 was seeing a female consultant psychiatrist, Dr Marilyn Loizou.

- There had been a recent admission to Clifton Hospital, which was from 28 December 1988 to 9 January 1989.

8.121 Notwithstanding those reasons, and Dr Smith's insistence, the Inquiry is entirely satisfied that the *original* disclosure was sometime in 1983, and that Dr Smith was aware of Patient A17's disclosures about a sexual relationship with William Kerr in 1983 (if not earlier) but failed to take any action. Dr Smith may have been re-informed in 1988, at about the time of William Kerr's retirement – this would be consistent with Patient A17's disclosure to Dr Loizou (and to Vicky Sparks). It is important to note that Dr Loizou's recollection – clear after all the passing years – is that shortly after William Kerr's retirement, Patient A17 disclosed to her a sexual relationship with him.

8.122 Dr Loizou said this:

> *"Shortly after my arrival in late 1988 or early 1989, I saw as an outpatient Patient A17. Sometime after I began seeing Patient A17, Vicky Sparks, Unit General Manager of Harrogate District Hospital, informed me that Patient A17 had made a complaint against Dr Kerr. During subsequent consultations with Patient A17, it became clear to me that she was extremely cross that Dr Kerr, who had treated her previously, had left and had not contacted her since his retirement. Patient A17 disclosed to me that she and Dr Kerr had had a consensual, sexual relationship. I was very shocked by this."*

8.123 Patient A17 also made a late disclosure of her alleged affair with William Kerr to Marion Anderson, a clinical psychologist, as well as to Dr Loizou. Marion Anderson's response when questioned as to why, unlike Linda Bigwood, she did not pursue the matter with the authorities, was that Patient A17 had spoken to her "in confidence".

8.124 Dr Smith's accepted confusion as to dates may well have extended to the details of Patient A17's disclosure. She saw Patient A17 many times over the years – there are, for example, 15 entries in the surgery notes for 1983, and 19 entries for 1988. It is very likely that, in the course of those consultations, Patient A17 told her story more than once. Indeed, it would be surprising if she had not told her story more than once. Patient A17 trusted her GP, and the GP was clearly sympathetic and caring, accepting that Patient A17 was telling her the truth.

8.125 Again, had Dr Smith been interviewed at the time, she may have been prepared and able to voice concerns about William Kerr from her standpoint as a GP, in relation not only to Patient A17 but possibly also to other patients.

The Harrogate GPs

8.126 One of the potentially most alarming aspects of Linda Bigwood's written complaint was the suggestion that rumours of William Kerr's alleged abuse of female patients were well known to GPs in Harrogate, to the extent that some would no longer refer young female patients to him. Not only was the allegation alarming, we now know that it was consistent with, at least, the evidence of Dr Wade and the evidence of Dr Plowman, Dr Wade's junior partner in the Knaresborough practice (adjacent to Harrogate). Dr Plowman's evidence to the Inquiry made it clear that the refusal to refer young female patients to William Kerr was widespread.

8.127 Any investigation in the early to mid-1980s involving the Harrogate GPs would also have resulted in contact with Dr Givans, who was in practice in Harrogate and in Knaresborough. At the relevant time, Dr Givans was, and indeed still is, an active member and officer of the Local Medical Committee, being Medical Secretary from 1984. The investigation, if it had taken place, may have (and we emphasise "may have") received a different picture from Dr Givans. His evidence was that, until the 1990s, he was not aware of any allegations.

8.128 No attempt was made to contact the Harrogate Health Authority to investigate whether there was the reported concern among GPs or, if such concern existed, the reasons and the evidential support (if any) for these concerns. This was a serious allegation, and it could have been investigated – with little inconvenience, and probably at little cost. The investigation may have ended with Dr Givans, or it may have resulted in contact with Dr Wade and Dr Plowman (and others). If Dr Wade had been contacted, he would have mentioned the complaint in 1979, and the referral of that complaint to Michael Haslam. Michael Haslam's apparent failure to do anything in relation to that complaint would then have been revealed. Pieces would have fallen into place, alarm bells should have been sounded. But, as nothing whatsoever was done, it is only possible to speculate as to the outcome.

8.129 Graham Saunders, the District Administrator of Harrogate Health Authority from 1982 to 1985, informed the Inquiry that Linda Bigwood's complaint was never forwarded to him, nor was he ever made aware of any concerns about William Kerr. While Mr Ingham's evidence was that he had discussed the issue with Graham Saunders (the pair met frequently on a social basis), he accepted that the mention would not have extended to a detailed account of the fact that GPs in Harrogate were said to have concerns. Mr Ingham viewed this sort of communication between districts as falling to Dr Wintersgill, or those at Region, to instigate.

8.130 Graham Saunders' evidence was that, had he been informed that there was a concern that Harrogate GPs were not referring patients to William Kerr due to worries about his sexual conduct, his response would have been as follows:

> "I would have wanted to talk to Stuart Ingham about the arrangements that they had put in place within York to investigate this complaint which had come to them, and how they were seeking to follow up this alleged statement about the behaviour of GPs in Harrogate in relation to referrals, and offer either to support their investigation in terms of the behaviour of the Harrogate GPs or to offer to work with them, or take over that element of the investigations."

8.131 Had that investigation of Harrogate GPs taken place, it is likely that at least some of the GPs who had been recipients of complaints, some of whom had changed their referral practice in response (notably Dr Wade), would have, when approached directly, been able and prepared to provide details that would have provided grounds for, at the very least, a proper and thorough investigation of William Kerr's practice.

Dr Bromham

8.132 According to Linda Bigwood's written complaint, Dr Bromham was aware of complaints about her husband, William Kerr, regarding sexual advances made to patients. Indeed, she was said to have treated a patient who had attempted suicide following a sexual relationship with William Kerr. In her oral evidence to the Inquiry, Dr Bromham denied any contemporary knowledge of allegations surrounding her husband and sexual contact with female patients and also said that she had been entirely unaware of the complaint pursued by Linda Bigwood implicating her husband.

8.133 We find it surprising that Dr Bromham was not aware of allegations and rumours concerning her husband. Indeed, Dr Rugg, a fellow consultant psychiatrist, told the Inquiry that he found it difficult to believe that at the time when the Linda Bigwood complaint was being pursued in 1983/84 Dr Bromham could have been entirely unaware of the issue. In addition to the general talk in the hospital, a number of patients (notably Patient A13 and Patient A15) also allege that they had specifically told Dr Bromham about concerns they had regarding William Kerr.

8.134 Certainly, had Dr Bromham been asked about whether she had any awareness of any such allegations against William Kerr during his career, she would, in order to have answered truthfully, have had to have disclosed the circumstances leading to William Kerr leaving Northern Ireland.

8.135 However, it is unnecessary for us to explore Dr Bromham's state of knowledge any further. Whether or not she was aware of the concerns and complaints, it is clear that she was not interviewed in 1983/84 nor at any time before her husband's retirement in September 1988.

Other consultants

8.136 While not specifically referred to in Linda Bigwood's written complaint as a source of potential information, an obvious route for anyone investigating the allegations would have been to speak to consultant colleagues of William Kerr. In addition to Dr Bromham, the others approached could have included Dr Rugg and Michael Haslam.

8.137 Dr Rugg had a number of concerns about William Kerr, ranging from general gossip concerning wandering hands (towards female members of staff), to two specific cases where patients were referred to him, having expressed disquiet at alleged sexual overtones during William Kerr's consultations. He was clear in his oral evidence that, while he accepted that he had not initiated any investigation into

William Kerr's practice, had he been approached for his views he would have passed on his concerns.

> **8.138** Had Michael Haslam been asked whether he was aware of any concerns being expressed about William Kerr, in order to answer truthfully, he would have had to reveal the conversation he had had with Dr Wade in 1979, that a patient had made an allegation of sexual assault against William Kerr.

Linda Bigwood

8.139 In her written complaint, Linda Bigwood refers to two other patients, one of whom had been informed by a fellow patient of an alleged sexual assault by William Kerr in a linen cupboard and another who complained that William Kerr flirted with her during a domiciliary visit. Mr Wilk did not question her about either of these accounts.

> **8.140** We have not been able to establish who these patients were, given the passage of time. However, had there been a contemporaneous investigation, there is the possibility that this may have produced a statement by a patient or patients prepared to make complaints against William Kerr.

Dr Mortimer

8.141 Dr Mortimer was questioned by Mr Wilk, but this questioning did not extend to her alleged remark to Linda Bigwood that she had been warned that William Kerr was a womaniser. Such questioning would have alerted an investigator to the significant amount of rumour that we heard about concerning William Kerr's reputation as a "ladies' man" and a "flirt". At this point, we refer back to the evidence of Mr Monk-Steel, who told us – based on a lengthy career in mental health nursing – that William Kerr and Michael Haslam "were the only two consultants of whom I have heard any vague rumours in relation to their sexual impropriety whilst working in the psychiatric service".

Social worker

8.142 One of the very specific references in the written complaint is to the "friend of a social worker" who claimed to have been propositioned by William Kerr. Had Linda Bigwood been pressed for the name of this social worker, it would have led to Patient A13. Significantly, Patient A13's evidence to the Inquiry was that, had she been approached in the mid-1980s, she would have been prepared to pursue a complaint against William Kerr.

Meg Jones

8.143 At the very end of the written complaint, Linda Bigwood refers to Meg Jones, the Senior Social Worker at Clifton Hospital. According to Linda Bigwood, Meg Jones and her colleagues "had all heard similar things in the past about him". Had Meg Jones been approached, then it is likely (based on her evidence to our Inquiry) that she would not have supported Linda Bigwood's account. She told us:

> "Linda Bigwood was reporting facts of which I knew nothing. Neither I nor my colleagues had ever had a complaint against Dr Kerr and I would have known because my job by this time was supervision of my social workers. I saw them every week; we discussed their cases. Anything like this would have come up in our supervision sessions, and we had a very close relationship anyway in our department, and I was angry that she used a casual remark of mine to include me without permission in her report. She seemed to me to be throwing accusations around in an irresponsible way and I did not want to be identified with it."

8.144 However, there may have been more fertile ground in relation to that part of Linda Bigwood's written complaint which refers to Meg Jones having received a similar (i.e. concerning sexual misconduct) complaint about Michael Haslam. Had she been questioned about this it would have been revealed that this complaint, concerning Patient AB, had been referred to Mr Holroyd in 1981 but that no action had been taken, and it is possible that at this stage a link would then have been made between the previous complaint by Patient B2, leading to an investigation of Michael Haslam.

Events after the Wilk Report

8.145 Following completion of the Wilk Report, and having interviewed Patient A17 regarding her retraction, an attempt was made to close down the issues in Linda Bigwood's written complaint. On 5 April 1984, a letter was sent to Mr Kineavy of COHSE from Mr Corbett (the initial written complaint having been forwarded by Mr Kineavy to Mr Corbett in late October 1983). This letter stated as follows:

Complaint by Deputy Sister Bigwood

Further to the above complaint, all investigations have now been carried out and the decisions reached are as follows:

In the light of the fact that the patient who made the original complaint to Deputy Sister Bigwood subsequently withdrew this complaint, stating that there was no truth in her accusation, we are left with little alternative but to ignore the original complaint laid.

With regard to the handling of the complaint by nurse managers at Clifton Hospital, the senior nurse managers in this district were dissatisfied with the handling of such a complaint, and they have counselled those senior managers in consequence of their failures in this direction so that, in future, complaints raised by staff are dealt with in the prescribed manner in all units in this district.

8.146 Anne Tiplady's personnel file records that she was counselled regarding the management of the complaint when it was initially raised, and advised that poor judgement had been exercised in allowing an inexperienced nursing manager (John Monk-Steel) to carry out interviews in a potentially serious situation.

8.147 A few days later, on 11 April 1984, a letter was sent from Dr Wintersgill to William Kerr (Dr McIntosh, Mr Ingham and Mr Corbett being copied in to the letter). This stated:

Dear Dr Kerr,

You are aware that investigations have been taking place into allegations by Deputy Sister Bigwood that a complaint she had made on a patient's behalf was mishandled. The patient had claimed that there had been an improper relationship between you and herself so Mr Price and I met you at Clifton Hospital in November to acquaint you with what was happening.

I am now writing to let you know that the statement made by the patient was withdrawn by letter and subsequently at interview when she said that there was no truth in any allegations that she had made. The original complaint has therefore been ignored.

Enquiries showed, however, that the nurse managers at Clifton Hospital had not used appropriate procedures for dealing with complaints and have been counselled about their failures and advised to use prescribed methods in future.

I am sorry that the investigations have taken so long and for any anxieties that this unfortunate occurrence may have caused.

8.148 Therefore, in summary, the only response to the Wilk Report appears to be that "nurse managers… have been counselled about their failures" (this is a reference to Anne Tiplady and John Monk-Steel) and that William Kerr received an apology for any anxiety he had been caused.

8.149 So far as we have been able to discover, there was no management response to the conclusions that there had been a shallow investigation, the appearance of a cover-up, the automatic disbelief in psychiatric patients, and the arranging of a one-to-one meeting between Patient A17 and William Kerr. We were not offered any explanation for that lack of response. There is also a concern here that nurses were being asked to undertake an investigation into issues that were not, primarily, their responsibility. They were then blamed when the investigation proved flawed.

Linda Bigwood continues to pursue her complaint in 1984

8.150 Linda Bigwood was not content with the handling of her written complaint. Indeed, only 10 days after the letter of 5 April 1984, in which Mr Corbett had sought to conclude the matter, stating that investigations (the Wilk Inquiry) had been carried out, Linda Bigwood was writing to Jim Docherty, Branch Secretary of COHSE, reporting allegations that Michael Haslam was having an affair with a patient and that this had been reported to Nurse Alan Greenfield (although Linda Bigwood was not aware of the details, this was in fact a reference to Patient B3) and voicing her disquiet that William Kerr had been told that the matters she had raised (concerning his alleged sexual misconduct) would not be taken any further.

8.151 Linda Bigwood's concern at the handling of her written complaint was formally communicated to Mr Corbett, by means of a letter dated 20 July 1984 from Mr Robinson, the Regional Officer of COHSE. This letter requested a meeting with Mr Corbett to discuss the original complaint. No response was received and Mr Robinson therefore chased Mr Corbett for a reply on 15 August 1984.

8.152 According to Linda Bigwood, there was a meeting between Mr Robinson and Mr Corbett to discuss her dissatisfaction at the handling of the complaint. At this meeting, Linda Bigwood alleges that Mr Corbett informed Mr Robinson that "Kerr intended to 'crucify' me, that he would sue me" – if true, intimidation in the extreme.

8.153 In March 1985, Linda Bigwood compiled a further summary of events, stating that in her view the Wilk Inquiry had been "bogus" and that the matters she complained of remained "unresolved".

8.154 This summary set out Linda Bigwood's version of events, month by month, between June 1983 and October 1984. It also set out the following "notes", which make it clear that the allegations being made went far beyond the case of Patient A17, and indeed beyond William Kerr, to include allegations against Michael Haslam.

NOTES

1. *During the course of events outlined in the previous pages, three senior members of staff made it known to me that they had each received reports of a similar nature concerning the sexual abuse of psychiatric patients by Dr Kerr and also Dr Haslam, also a consultant at Clifton Hospital.*

   Sister Wearing – stated that many patients had, over the years, informed her of sexual abuse by Dr Kerr, including the patient concerned in my case. She had never acted upon these allegations, although she believed them to be true, as she had had no evidence.

   Staff Nurse Gallagher – stated that a patient had informed her of sexual abuse by Dr Kerr and that this patient had transferred to Dr Rugg because of this. Staff Nurse Gallagher would be prepared to put this in writing.

Meg Jones, Head of Social Work – stated that she had received many reports over the years from both patients and colleagues concerning sexual abuse by both Dr Kerr and Dr Haslam. She had at one time reported an allegation concerning Dr Haslam to the Administrator and also persuaded the patient [Patient AB] to go to a solicitor, which the patient duly did. Nothing came of the case as, Meg Jones believes, the solicitor in cahoots with Dr Haslam 'watered down the case' until it was meaningless. Meg Jones was angry with me for mentioning this in my original report and asked me to withdraw it from the report, which I refused to do.

2. *Coincidentally I was informed by a community worker from Harrogate that a friend of hers [Patient A13] had been sexually propositioned by Dr Kerr during a domiciliary visit to her home when she was suffering from depression. She may be prepared to put this in writing.*

3. *I was also informed by the patient [Patient A17] in my report that Dr Kerr's behaviour is well known to GPs in Harrogate to the extent that some will not send young women to him, to the Samaritans in Harrogate, to other patients and to his wife, Dr Bromham, also a consultant at Clifton Hospital, who had admitted a young girl who had taken an overdose following her relationship with Dr Kerr.*

4. *Following the original allegations made to me by the patient [Patient A17] in my report, I was informed by another patient that she had once had to comfort a young girl in Harrogate District Hospital who had been dragged into the linen cupboard by Dr Kerr. This information was relayed to me during the course of a casual discussion between myself and three other patients. The other two each alluded to knowledge of similar events which I did not pursue.*

8.155 On 10 June 1985, a meeting was called by COHSE, which was concerned about the response that had been given to Linda Bigwood's written complaint. The meeting was attended by Linda Bigwood, Mr C Brace (Branch Chairman of COHSE), Mr Whyte (Branch Secretary of COHSE), Mr Wilk (Director of Nursing Services) and Mr Ingham (District General Manager). It appears that the summary and accompanying notes (set out above) were handed over by Linda Bigwood at this meeting.

8.156 Mr Ingham's note of the meeting records that Linda Bigwood stated at this meeting that she wanted the following:

- to establish further information on the handling of the complaint against nurse managers (she had never been shown a copy of the Wilk Report);

- to ensure that there had been no detrimental effect on herself in raising the complaint;

- to establish what prompted the patient (Patient A17) to write a letter withdrawing her complaint against William Kerr;

- to ascertain whether William Kerr had been reported to the BMA and, if not, why not; and

- to know whether William Kerr had been disciplined in any other way for seeing the patient (Patient A17) on her own after she had raised the complaint.

8.157 Mr Ingham agreed at the meeting to write a further letter to Linda Bigwood, amplifying the letter sent by Mr Corbett on 5 April 1984, and that this letter would:

- give a more detailed reply regarding the investigation/counselling of the nurse managers;

- see if it were possible to do anything further about the investigation into William Kerr's conduct; and

- state that it was accepted that Sister Bigwood had made the original complaint in good faith and that her career prospects would not be prejudiced by having brought this complaint.

8.158 This last point was in respect of a specific grievance Linda Bigwood had about an unfavourable remark in her personnel file (made by John Monk-Steel) that she considered had been made in response to her making a complaint. She wished the remark to be erased from her file.

8.159 Mr Ingham sent a memo to Dr Wintersgill attaching a note of his meeting with Linda Bigwood. Mr Ingham asked Dr Wintersgill to "consider what further action we can take in this matter and what more we might say to Sister Bigwood about the investigations into Dr Kerr's behaviour. It seems to me that we need to make the Regional Medical Officer aware of this latest approach."

8.160 In drafting the letter to Linda Bigwood that had been promised at the meeting on 10 June 1985, Mr Ingham sought and received input from Mr Wilk and Dr Wintersgill.

8.161 Dr Wintersgill's input was to agree with the letter in essence but to suggest an addition of what was in effect a "gentle" criticism, stating that "not all consultant psychiatrists might have thought it wise to see a patient alone".

8.162 Mr Ingham also sent a copy of the draft letter to William Kerr for his comments prior to it being sent out. Unsurprisingly, William Kerr objected to the additional words suggested by Dr Wintersgill and these were duly deleted from the final draft.

8.163 Dr Wintersgill sent a memorandum to Mr Ingham, setting out William Kerr's amendment and commenting:

> *"As anticipated, he [William Kerr] was disturbed to learn that the matter had been raised again, and talking about what action he might take. He eventually accepted that his approach at present, should be limited to sending a copy of whatever letter is sent to Miss Bigwood to his Medical Defence Organisation for information. There is no doubt, however, that he will be asking his Defence organisation to pursue the matter aggressively if the subject is re-opened."*

8.164 In spite of the tenor of that letter, Mr Ingham denied suggestions that fear of the reaction of William Kerr in any way acted as an inhibitor to any investigation.

8.165 The final draft of the letter was sent from Mr Ingham to Linda Bigwood on 29 July 1985 and purported to address the concerns raised at the 10 June 1985 meeting. The letter read as follows:

> *Dear Miss Bigwood,*
>
> *Further to our discussion on the 10th June, I have made further enquiries into the handling of your complaint and I am writing to give you further information.*

On receipt of your complaint, the District Nursing Officer, Mr Corbett, instructed Mr Wilk, the Director of Nursing Services, to carry out a thorough investigation into the complaint as it affected nurse management and to report back to him on his findings.

Mr Wilk interviewed a number of nursing, medical and administrative staff and, in the course of the enquiry, established that the complaint could have been handled in a much more positive manner by nurse managers. He found that previous investigations were far too shallow and would not have established the validity of such a complaint. At the conclusion of the enquiry, Mr Wilk reported his findings to the District Nursing Officer and, subsequently, appropriate disciplinary action was taken against the nurse managers involved.

You asked particularly to know whether any action had been taken against Dr Kerr in the light of his decision to see the patient alone, following your complaint. This issue was considered at the time of the original complaint and I have also recently confirmed with another Senior Psychiatrist, whose judgement I trust, that the relationship between a Consultant Psychiatrist and a patient is such that it is possible for a Consultant to decide to see a patient alone, even when a complaint of this nature has been made. Thus, whilst a member of staff of another discipline, who interviews a patient alone in such circumstances, would lay themselves open to criticism, the same cannot be said about Consultant Psychiatrists. The relationship between a Consultant Psychiatrist and a patient is different, in kind, to the relationship between any other member of staff and a patient. Because of this, it is within the bounds of reasonableness for a Consultant Psychiatrist to see the patient alone, as Dr Kerr did.

You also asked what prompted the patient to write a letter withdrawing her complaint against Dr Kerr. It is difficult to be absolutely certain about this, but the patient herself stated that she wrote the letter as a result of receiving a postcard from yourself (I believe you were on holiday abroad at the time). The contents of that postcard made it clear to the patient the seriousness with which her complaint was being taken and she said that, as a result, she realised the consequences of her false allegation and decided to withdraw it. This withdrawal was confirmed by the patient, directly, to two independent senior members of staff of the Authority who had been asked to investigate the areas of your complaint other than those directly the concern of Mr Wilk.

Finally, can I confirm that I accept, absolutely, that you made and have pursued your complaint in good faith and that your career prospects within the York Health Authority will not be prejudiced by your actions.

8.166 Of particular significance in this letter is the reference to a "Senior Consultant" who is described as confirming that "the relationship between a Consultant Psychiatrist and a patient is such that it is possible for a Consultant to decide to see a patient alone, even when a complaint of this nature has been made".

8.167 Mr Ingham's evidence was that this description followed advice he had sought from Dr Peter Kennedy at the Region, on how best to deal with the issue of William Kerr, although he acknowledged that they had discussed it "almost, if you like, as though it was a theoretical question".

8.168 Dr Kennedy's evidence on this described the conversation as more "hypothetical". While he thought there might be an urgent situation where a consultant's intervention alone could be appropriate, he thought it more sensible to have somebody else there.

8.169 Dr Kennedy's recollection that the issue of seeing a patient alone was not raised is supported to some extent by Mr Ingham being unable to be sure whether the use of the word "alone" came from Dr Kennedy.

8.170 The letter from Mr Ingham to Linda Bigwood (set out above), rather than settling the matter, inflamed the situation yet further.

8.171 Mr Whyte responded to Mr Ingham by a letter dated 14 October 1985. The letter made a number of points. It requested a fuller report of Mr Wilk's investigation. It also set out that COHSE would be taking the matter of William Kerr seeing Patient A17 alone to the Region, and possibly to the BMA. The letter refutes the suggestion that Patient A17's written retraction of 3 November 1983 was motivated by a postcard from Linda Bigwood, and finally the letter addresses the issue of the allegedly "defamatory" entry on Linda Bigwood's personnel file.

8.172 Mr Ingham's response to this letter, dated 24 October 1985, did not answer the points raised; rather, he sought to separate out what were issues that COHSE wished to raise, and what matters related to either the complaint by Linda Bigwood about the care of a patient or issues of her career prospects being prejudiced.

8.173 The matter was then left in abeyance until September 1987. Tony Brownbridge (COHSE) resurrected the issues and wrote to the Regional General Manager, Mr Stokes, with copies to the Regional Chairman and the RMO (Professor Haward). This letter in essence repeated the matters raised in Mr Whyte's letter of 14 October 1985 that had not been addressed by Mr Ingham in his response of 24 October 1985. However, significantly, the letter from Mr Brownbridge enclosed a letter from Linda Bigwood, which set out as follows:

> *Dear Sir,*
>
> *During the course of events surrounding the complaint outlined in the enclosed report, certain information was volunteered to me concerning allegations of sexual misconduct by Dr Kerr and, in one case, by Dr Haslam (also a Consultant Psychiatrist at Clifton Hospital). I have brought these matters to the attention of various managerial staff in previous statements and reports but, for the sake of clarity, I outline them below.*

1. *I was informed by Mrs Jones, then Head of Social Work at Clifton Hospital, that both herself and her colleagues had received allegations by patients of sexual misconduct on the part of both Dr Kerr and Dr Haslam over a period of many years. She believed them to be true but had taken no action due to lack of evidence. She had once assisted a patient in pursuing a case against Dr Haslam through a solicitor but the patient had been finally persuaded by the solicitor to drop the case.*

2. *A Nursing Sister stated that many patients had, over the years, informed her of sexual misconduct by Dr Kerr, including the patient in the current case. She had not acted upon these allegations, although she believed them to be true, due to lack of evidence.*

3. *A Staff Nurse stated that a patient had informed her that she had been transferred from Dr Kerr to Dr Rugg because of sexual misconduct on the part of Dr Kerr.*

4. *I was informed by a former Community Worker in Harrogate that a friend of hers had been sexually propositioned by Dr Kerr during a domiciliary visit he made to her home when she was suffering from depression.*

5. *The patient in the current complaint alleged that Dr Kerr's behaviour is well known to GPs in Harrogate to the extent that some will not send young female patients to him; to the Samaritans in Harrogate; to other patients; and to Dr Kerr's wife, Dr Bromham, also a Consultant Psychiatrist at Clifton Hospital, who, the patient alleged, had admitted a young girl to hospital after she had taken an overdose following a sexual relationship with Dr Kerr.*

6. *Another patient at Clifton Hospital alleged that she had once had to comfort a young female patient at Harrogate District Hospital who had been 'dragged into the linen cupboard by Dr Kerr'. This allegation was made to me during the course of a casual discussion between myself and three other female patients on the Admission Ward. The other two patients each alluded to knowledge of similar events but I did not pursue this information.*

8.174 This letter again repeated in clear terms that the allegations about sexual misconduct by William Kerr were not related to only one patient; that knowledge of this sexual misconduct was known to a number of staff, and to Dr Bromham and was well known to GPs in Harrogate; and, further, that a patient had been transferred to Dr Rugg from William Kerr due to allegations of sexual misconduct. The letter also mentioned the Patient AB complaint of sexual misconduct against Michael Haslam in which Meg Jones, Head of Social Work at Clifton Hospital, had been involved.

8.175 The letter from COHSE, containing Linda Bigwood's letter, provoked a response from the Regional Health Authority, albeit not a particularly prompt one.

8.176 It seems that Dr Green was given charge of the matter at the Regional Health Authority. Dr Green was employed by the Yorkshire Regional Health Authority between 1987 and 1995 in a role that included specific responsibility for dealing with "problem doctors". Dr Green, having acknowledged that allegations against William Kerr and Michael Haslam had been made, wrote to Mr Ingham (District General Manager) on 25 November 1987, stating:

> *"I know you are well aware of these allegations and I would be grateful for your advice as to how the RHA should now respond to them."*

Advice is again sought from the Regional Legal Adviser

8.177 On 3 December 1987, advice was again sought from Mr Chapman, the Regional Legal Adviser, this time by Dr Green.

8.178 A number of issues are clear from the memo from Dr Green to Mr Chapman:

- The RMO (Professor Haward) was aware of the allegations against William Kerr and Michael Haslam relating to sexual misconduct.

- There was the mistaken view that Linda Bigwood's naming of Meg Jones as a recipient of allegations of sexual misconduct by William Kerr and Michael Haslam was a new piece of information (in fact Linda Bigwood included this information in her first written complaint in September 1983).

- The allegations refer to incidents that occurred some years ago.

- Mr Ingham, the District General Manager, recognised that the allegations were potentially criminal matters and queried whether the police should become involved (Mr Ingham was unable to give any explanation to us of why the thought of contacting the police or the recognition of the potentially criminal nature of the alleged acts of the two named consultants were not considered before when Linda Bigwood made the same allegations at the outset, over four years earlier).

- William Kerr and his wife Dr Bromham had written to resign from their posts from autumn 1988.

8.179 Dr Green poses two questions to Mr Chapman: firstly, should the allegations be investigated; and secondly, should the police be involved.

8.180 In a letter of 8 December 1987 to Dr Green, Mr Ingham appears at pains to draw a distinction between Linda Bigwood's allegations in her letter of 22 September 1987 and the previous allegations she had made. In fact, a cursory overview of the documents reveals the matters of which Linda Bigwood was complaining in 1987 – in essence alleged serial sexual abuse by William Kerr of his female patients and the raising (to a lesser extent) of concerns about Michael Haslam's alleged sexual conduct towards patients – were expressed in her first written complaint in 1983. Nothing had changed over the four-year period.

8.181 On 15 December 1987, Dr Green responded to Mr Ingham enclosing the advice he had received from Mr Chapman. The advice of Mr Chapman was as follows:

> *"There are so many separate allegations of improper conduct, and so many potential sources of information which might be identifiable if proper enquiries were made, that I feel bound to advise that the police should be informed of the contents of her letter of 22 September 1987, at least so far as Dr K is concerned.*

> *"If only one patient made, and later retracted, allegations against Dr H, I question whether his name needs to be brought to the attention of the police.[1]*

> *"If the police decline to take action or, having carried out an investigation, consider that a prosecution would not be justified, we shall need to think again about Dr K's position."*

8.182 Mr Chapman was questioned in his oral evidence to us as to why the advice he gave on this occasion, namely that there were a large number of potential sources of information and that the police should be informed, had not been given when he was first involved in the issue back in 1983. His response to this was that it was possible he had never seen the 1983 written complaint by Linda Bigwood, and as such would have been unaware that the allegations extended beyond the case of Patient A17. We would be very surprised if Mr Chapman had not received the written complaint in 1983 when acting as legal adviser to the District and/or to the Regional Health Authority. It would have been extraordinary (although not impossible) if he were not shown the written complaint, but was still asked to offer legal advice on the conduct of any investigation. However, that said, having seen and heard from relevant witnesses, such an elementary absence of communication – although extraordinary – was not impossible.

8.183 It is curious that, despite having specifically referred to the decision to await Mr Chapman's advice, Mr Ingham in fact chose to telephone the police on 15 December, prior to receiving a copy of Mr Chapman's advice. His file note, dated 21 December 1987, records as follows:

---

1 This advice fails to recognise that other patients may have made allegations – or that those allegations were known to the police. It is also regrettable that, had proper investigations been made and files kept, it would have been appreciated that there was not just one patient making allegations against Michael Haslam.

"I telephoned the local police and spoke to Sergeant Ellerker before I read John Green's letter of the 15th December and, as a result, didn't send the police a copy of Mrs Bigwood's letter but did discuss its contents and the background of the case with Sergeant Ellerker, who was clearly of the view that unless we could obtain more specific complaints from Mrs Bigwood, certainly in terms of the complainants and preferably in terms of the patients concerned, then the police wouldn't feel that this was a case worth investigating by them. I informed Dr Green of this and he undertook to take further advice from Mr Chapman before we consider what steps to take next."

8.184 It was put to Mr Ingham in his oral evidence to the Inquiry that he deliberately failed to send Linda Bigwood's letter to the police as he feared being criticised for failing to have brought the matter to their attention in 1983 or 1985. Clearly, if the police declined to investigate in 1987, he could not be criticised for failing to act earlier. Support for such criticism also potentially comes from the fact that, in the summary of events he subsequently prepared to send to the Regional Health Authority, it appears he omitted to enclose Linda Bigwood's original 1983 written complaint, which would have shown that the complaints against William Kerr that were independent of Patient A17 had been raised at this stage, not (as he suggested in his conversation with Dr Green on 3 December 1987) only in 1987.

8.185 Mr Ingham refuted such allegations and emphasised that he had been the only person to approach the police. He was, however, unable to offer any explanation as to why the invitation of Sergeant Ellerker to obtain more specific details of complaints and patients involved was not taken up.

8.186 We found Mr Ingham to be an unconvincing witness. We have concluded that he was dismissive of Linda Bigwood's written complaint – far too quickly, and merely on the basis of the withdrawal of the specific Patient A17 complaint, in unsatisfactory circumstances. He was keen to place responsibility on others, particularly Dr Turner and Mr Chapman. Further, our conclusion is that William Kerr (in 1985) was being exonerated on a false basis – it was not the professional view that it was reasonable for William Kerr to see Patient A17 alone. That view is not supported by the contemporaneous note of the conversation with Dr Peter Kennedy, and was not supported by Dr Kennedy when he gave oral evidence. Mr Ingram's actions in 1987 were too little, too late – there was no significant new evidence in 1987. By that time, there had been years of inaction, and no doubt evidence trails would have gone cold. Patient safety should have been at the forefront of their minds but was not, and (in case the allegations were true) patients were entitled to better protection. It is to be remembered that the sexual assault on Patient A40, of which William Kerr was found "guilty" on a Trial of the Facts, took place in 1987.

8.187 We do not conclude that Mr Ingham deliberately obstructed the involvement of the police. However, we do consider that he is to be criticised for failing to pursue even the most preliminary of investigations with Linda Bigwood, with regard to the details and sources of the allegations independent of Patient A17.

8.188 Mr Ingham wrote to Dr Green repeating the content of his memo and this was passed on by Dr Green to Mr Chapman, with the request that Mr Chapman give his views on Mr Ingham's suggestion that Linda Bigwood be seen again by someone from outside the York District Health Authority.

8.189 This request for advice from Mr Chapman went unanswered for a number of months. It was not until 2 March 1988 that Mr Chapman responded. While recognising the possibility of wasting time pursuing possibly groundless allegations, Mr Chapman's advice (which was sent to Dr Green and copied to Professor Haward, the RMO) is clear that:

- The allegations of misconduct against William Kerr are extremely serious.

- The Regional Health Authority has an obligation to investigate.

- Sister Bigwood should be seen possibly by a male/female medico-legal team.

- Sister Bigwood should be told in advance that she would need to provide names and dates so that steps could be taken to contact the individuals concerned.

8.190 Dr Green, having received this advice, wrote to Mr Ingham requesting a summary of the earlier investigation regarding William Kerr. Mr Ingham responded as asked with a summary sent on 26 April 1988. Significantly, while a number of enclosures were sent with the summary (such as the Wilk Report), no copy of Linda Bigwood's original written complaint of 1983 was sent. As set out above, this would, of course, have revealed that the allegations made in her most recent letter of September 1987 were no more than repetitions of matters set out in that document, circulated over four years previously.

8.191 On 3 March 1988, Dr Green wrote a letter to Mr Brownbridge of COHSE. The letter states as follows:

> *"I am replying to your letter to the Regional General Manager of 17 September. I apologise for the delay in responding but you will appreciate that the issues you raised are complex.*
>
> *With regard to the allegations of sexual misconduct made against Dr Kerr, these have been carefully considered by officers of this Authority. These allegations are taken seriously, but in considering what action should follow, those concerned with the investigation have had to recognise the lack of corroborating evidence, which Sister Bigwood acknowledges. I do not propose to add further to these comments on this aspect of your letter and I am sure you will appreciate the propriety of this.*
>
> *With regard to the other issues you raise, I must first respectfully reject the role you appear to be claiming with respect to the way in which a health authority deals with its patients, except insofar as such policies affect your members. The question of the circumstances under which a Consultant interviews a patient is a matter for Health Service Management together with the patient and those who may properly be representing the patient..."*

8.192 The letter makes no reference to any future investigation or to Mr Chapman's suggestion that Linda Bigwood be seen by a medico-legal team and advised of the need to provide names and dates. However, Dr Green's evidence was that the prospect of further investigation into Linda Bigwood's allegation of sexual abuse by William Kerr was still live at that stage; he was simply seeking to close down the issue of the one-to-one meeting by William Kerr that was being pursued by COHSE.

The end of the Patient A17 story

8.193 The story of Patient A17 ends (in terms of evidence to the Inquiry) with the following memo from Dr Green to Mr Chapman. Even at this stage it appears that Linda Bigwood's original 1983 written complaint had not reached the Regional Health Authority.

> *From: Dr Green*
>
> *To: Mr R H D Chapman*
>
> *Date: 27.4.88*
>
> *DR KERR*
>
> *Following your memo of 2 March, we agreed to ask the York District for an account of their investigation of an allegation against Dr Kerr before deciding how to deal with the later statement from Sister Bigwood.*
>
> *Stuart Ingham has responded and I attach a copy of his letter and the papers that accompany it.*
>
> *The Wilk's investigation is primarily concerned with the earlier mishandling of Miss Bigwood's report of the allegation against Dr Kerr. In the process of considering this secondary issue, senior officers and the Chairman of the DHA became aware of the allegation against Dr Kerr and the basis for it; they clearly felt that that allegation could not be substantiated. It appears to have been at this time, when Miss Bigwood felt her report was not being taken seriously, that others reported other allegations to her. She states that these were reported to Management, but, with the possible exception of para 5 of the summary of events, the papers from York do not appear to refer to other allegations.*

I would be grateful for any further comments you would care to make and whether you still feel Miss Bigwood should be seen. I have the impression that Miss Bigwood was primarily concerned to justify her own actions and ensure her career did not suffer; I hope we have satisfied her and her union on this latter point.

With regard to Dr Kerr, as he will be leaving the employment of this Authority in six months, there is little effective action the RHA could take against him, even if we subsequently felt it was justified. You will gather that I have little enthusiasm in the circumstances for pursuing issues that are now so dated.

8.194   The change of attitude in this memo, from the earlier references to contacting the police and setting up a male/female medico-legal team to question Linda Bigwood on the allegations (beyond the case of Patient A17), is stark. Dr Green was questioned on this and responded as follows:

Q. ...you end the memo by saying: "You will gather that I have little enthusiasm in the circumstances [that is pending William Kerr's retirement] for pursuing issues that are now so dated." This seems to be a dramatic change from the "let's pursue it, go to the police, medico-legal team." We are now, "Let's kick it into touch because he is about to retire."

A. I think I was very frustrated at this time. We had been six months looking at this issue, and at least two people had delayed responding to my inquiries, one was Hugh Chapman and the other was Stuart Ingham, and each had taken a couple of months to reply to my memos. So here I am now, within four months of seeing Dr Kerr leave us, we have on the face of it some vague allegations, they are, by all accounts, very dated allegations, I do not see how we can conclude anything within the four months that were left to us – summer months at that.

8.195   There is no response to this memo, and Mr Chapman was unable to assist the Inquiry as to whether there was any further discussion of this issue. He said:

"I have no recollection of writing to Dr Green, I might have spoken to him on the telephone but I have no reliable recollection."

8.196   At this point the documents cease and it appears that the issue died away with William Kerr's retirement.

8.197 Although, even following William Kerr's retirement, a number of patients continued to raise concerns and make disclosures to healthcare professionals as to alleged incidents of sexual assault, it was not until Patient A50 went to the police in 1997 that the issue of conducting an investigation into William Kerr's practice was to be raised again.

8.198 In marked contrast to the lack of enthusiasm expressed by Dr Green in 1988 to investigating 'dated' issues concerning William Kerr, in 1997 the health authorities cooperated with the police in undertaking an extensive review of medical records and contacting large numbers of William Kerr's former patients, including the setting up of helplines, in order to assist with the investigation.

8.199 In the next chapter, we look at the wider response to the Patient A17 story.

Conclusions

8.200 We have set out our factual conclusions in this chapter as the Patient A17 story has unfolded.

8.201 It is unnecessary to set out more generalised conclusions. The story speaks for itself. There was here a failure to respond and investigate at all levels. Individual tasks may have been discharged adequately at some stages of the story. But, overall, there was a failure of leadership. Patient A17's story, and Linda Bigwood's dogged pursuit, extended over several years. We were unable to identify any sense of urgency, any overriding consideration of patient safety.

8.202 With our advantage of hindsight, the Patient A17 saga looks like a half-hearted attempt to go through the motions of responding to an irritant – Linda Bigwood.

8.203 The response by the NHS management at the time (reflected to a more limited extent in evidence and submissions to our Inquiry) was that there was no complaint to which they could respond. As Patient A17 had withdrawn her disclosure and was herself making no complaint – formal or otherwise – the attitude was that there was nothing that could be done. Therefore, so the argument goes, there can be no basis for criticism.

8.204 We reject this approach. It is, of course, correct that Patient A17's disclosure was withdrawn – but the circumstances of the withdrawals were troublesome and cast doubt on their genuineness. Our concern, and we conclude that this was a concern that should have been shared by NHS management at the time, is that the Linda Bigwood written statement coupled with William Kerr's one-to-one meeting with Patient A17 had enough content and leads that it deserved investigation. Such an investigation did not require a formal complaint from a willing patient.

8.205 For the reasons set out in the body of this chapter, this was an opportunity missed, and missed by a considerable margin.

8.206 We pick up these points in the next chapter.

Chapter 9
The response to complaints/concerns about William Kerr

Introduction

9.1   While the complaints and concerns regarding William Kerr extend far beyond the Patient A17 story, we have set out that story in some considerable detail, as it provides such a well-documented example of the opportunities raised and missed. We can understand how the initial Patient A17 disclosure, when withdrawn, was not pursued. However, it is far more difficult to understand the overall reaction to Linda Bigwood's detailed written complaint, containing as it did allegations that William Kerr was serially sexually abusing patients.

The response to the Linda Bigwood complaint

9.2   What we read and heard in relation to the response to Linda Bigwood's written complaint caused us to conclude that there was poor reaction and positive inaction. We do not find that there was a deliberate cover-up or suppression of Linda Bigwood's written complaint, but such a perception is not unreasonable. What seems to have happened is that those who could and, we find, should have carried out investigations did not do so for a variety of reasons – reasons that probably did not stand alone, but flowed together. These include:

- an over-respectful attitude towards, possibly even fear of, confronting a senior and powerful consultant such as William Kerr;

- coupled to the first point, a failure to ensure that Region were involved early, and at all stages, to ensure that the consultant's employers were engaged;

- strict adherence to processes that were not designed to address the kind of complaints raised by Linda Bigwood;

- lamentable lack of communication and leadership at regional and district levels – there was nobody in control, or prepared to take control, so that an investigation could be carried out;

- inadequate training of administrators (at district and regional levels) in relation to the initiation and conduct of investigations – particularly concerning consultants;

- concentration on looking after the interests of other members of the health profession, rather than focusing on the risk to patient safety;

- coupled to the previous point, exaggerated loyalty by doctors to their (particularly senior) colleagues at the expense of patient safety;

- a tendency to disbelieve the patients, simply because they were suffering from mental illness or had mental health problems;

- a concentration on the messenger (Linda Bigwood), rather than attempting to understand and respond to the message;

- a failure to set in place a simple, straightforward and consistent process by which concerns and complaints were documented;

- alternatively, a deliberate failure to make contemporaneous written records so that there would, literally, be no record of the disclosure.

9.3   Overall, the impression we are left with is of something akin to maladministration, almost an institutional moral failing or a widespread failure of the system. We are unable to ascribe responsibility to individuals, because we accept that poor communication may have led to the position that individuals who could have, and should have, made a difference were not involved at the appropriate time.

9.4   The following represents a reasonable first response to Linda Bigwood's written complaint:

> *"There are so many separate allegations of improper conduct, and so many potential sources of information which might be identifiable, if proper inquiries were made, that I feel bound to advise that the police should be informed ..."*

9.5   That is the kind of response we would expect from NHS management interested in patient safety and anxious to ensure that a proper investigation was carried out. Regrettably, that extract comes from an internal memo from Mr Hugh Chapman (the Regional and District Legal Adviser) to Dr Green (Specialist in Community Medicine at the Yorkshire Regional Health Authority), dated 11 December 1987, four years after Linda Bigwood's written complaint. We have received no adequate explanation, indeed no explanation at all, as to why that obvious response was not made in 1983. Even in 1983 there was no reason why it should not have been recognised, and accepted, that an allegation of sexual misconduct against a consultant was clearly a matter for Region, and possibly for the police.

9.6   It was not suggested to us that some form of wider investigation was impossible, or inappropriate – indeed, several witnesses expressed regret that such an investigation had not been carried out. There is, therefore, no general disagreement with the evidence to the Inquiry from Sir Liam Donaldson and Dr Patricia Cresswell as to the benefit of such investigations. It should not be necessary for those who initiate, or who conduct, such investigations to require a formal complaint, or to see a disciplinary outcome as the reason for inquiring. Such an approach is to prejudge the results of the investigation, and to confuse discovery of the facts with a response to them. It may also have the wholly undesirable effect of paralysing action. For example, as in GMC disciplinary proceedings the case must (still) be proved to a criminal standard, and until very recently the case for dismissal of a consultant for professional misconduct had to be proved to a criminal standard, administrators may decline to authorise investigation unless there is a near certainty that such clear and compelling evidence is forthcoming. We strongly favour patient safety as the touchstone for investigations. We agree with what Sir Liam Donaldson said in a 1994 *British Medical Journal* article:

"It is far too simplistic to imply, as some have done, that misconduct or incompetence should be tested by using the formal procedures and if not found to be present, then no problem exists. I fully accept that concerns have been expressed by some members of the profession ... that doctors should have the right to be 'tried' under existing procedures (ideally in public), and to deny them this, whether by prolonged suspension or other means, could be unjust and amount to victimisation. This position fails to acknowledge that existing procedures which could result in a doctor's dismissal are, however, a deterrent to action by employing authorities, potential witnesses, and others. Intolerable situations are thus allowed to prevail rather than being dealt with..."

9.7 In his oral evidence to the Inquiry, Sir Liam said the following in response to a question asking what practical steps could be taken to reassure a patient wishing to complain, but concerned about public knowledge of both her involvement with the psychiatric services and her allegation of sexual abuse. We agree with his response, and see no reason why some similar steps were not taken in 1983:

A. ... I think there are two broad approaches that you can use, and the two come together. One is to identify somebody trusted, a clinical psychologist or somebody who is possibly from a neighbouring service that would give particular explicit reassurances to the patient that they were going to treat anything they said in complete confidence, they would not divulge it unless they wanted them to. So you build a system of support around the patient. The other option is to say these allegations are so serious, they are allegations of what seems tantamount to rape, to forming inappropriate relationships with patients, possibly to using drugs and things of this sort to sedate them while assaults were being made, this is big league stuff and it needs either the police to be informed or it needs an investigation of the service, not just of the individual doctor. I think those are the two routes to go down, but basically to try to get a clearer picture, so that at the end of getting a clearer picture you can decide which of the formal mechanisms could be put into play.

Q. *That is a process that you could envisage happening in the 1980s without there being any structural or professional inhibitions which might prevent such an exercise being carried out?*

A. *The short answer to that is yes. In a way, I do not see – maybe this is a non-legal mind at work, and I think some of the processes put in place by the health service, including myself, have not always been legally that sound, but in a genuine attempt to try to tackle a problem, I would not have thought it at that point out of the question to establish a wide ranging investigation or inquiry, perhaps using experts from outside, without having open sworn testimony of patients, but simply to have a recording of concerns in confidence.*

And

Q. *The question again: is there any reason that at any level an investigation could be undertaken, district, regional or whatever, has there ever been an obstacle to investigation?*

A. *No, none whatsoever, unless you receive some legal advice that – there may be some thought needs to be given to how the procedure was designed for taking it further, but with that qualification, there would be no impediment whatsoever. Indeed, from a purely – I would not tend to look at the world like this, but from a purely self-interested point of view, any chief executive receiving a dossier is – and not doing anything with it, is potentially sitting on a time bomb that is going to explode at some point in the future, from a self-interest point of view, let alone from a service of interest.*

Q. *Let me take it a step further. I am trying to remove all my training as a lawyer and trying to get away from the slightly confrontational process that you appear to have been the victim of at some time, which is bringing somebody to give evidence and grill them. There are many ways of investigating and one is not to bring people to you but to go to them to investigate in a caring, helpful, compassionate way, but gather information. So there are no constraints as far as you can recall as to how an investigation is carried out?*

A. *Absolutely none whatsoever, no.*

9.8 At this point it might be relevant to state that we welcome the new procedures outlined in *Maintaining High Professional Standards in the Modern NHS*. We discuss this further in Chapters 30 and 32 of our Report.

9.9 We have already mentioned in the previous chapter the failure to conduct a wider inquiry into William Kerr's practice following the serious allegations made by Linda Bigwood. However, even in relation to Patient A17, more could easily have been done, and in our judgment should have been done. The picture may have been very different, and the outcome different, if the following had occurred – all simple steps and using systems in place at the time, and some common sense, and patient sensitivity.

9.10 We start from the factual position that Patient A17 had made her disclosure of the longstanding (but by then long ended) alleged sexual relationship with William Kerr to Dr Mortimer, to Linda Bigwood, and also to her GP, Dr Smith (we do not here include disclosure to other nurses, or to Marion Anderson).

9.11 The disclosure to Dr Mortimer seems likely to have pre-dated the disclosure to Linda Bigwood; if that is right, Dr Mortimer ought to have made a note of the disclosure and revealed it to a senior colleague – not to, or at least not just to, William Kerr.

9.12 Linda Bigwood received Patient A17's disclosure and then went to speak to Mr Monk-Steel. He, or Mrs Tiplady, should immediately have instructed Linda Bigwood to make a detailed written report, signed and dated, before any other step was taken.

9.13 Mrs Tiplady should then have spoken to her line manager, Mr Corbett – who was responsible for managing complaints – and Linda Bigwood should then have been instructed to keep talking to Patient A17, picking up and developing any missing detail of the story – in other words, facilitating the disclosure and caring for the welfare of the patient. During this process, Linda Bigwood (or some other person with whom Patient A17 had a good rapport) should have informed Patient A17 that the disclosure was important, that doctors should not, and must not, have sexual relationships with their patients, and that Linda Bigwood would have to share the information with relevant others at the hospital.

9.14 It was also the role of medical managers who managed complaints to take the matter to the senior manager of health services and invite him, on advice, to consider the exclusion of William Kerr from clinical work while enquiries were made.

9.15 During the disclosure, every effort should have been made to reassure Patient A17, to explain that her disclosure was being treated as nothing more than that – a disclosure that may or may not be acted on. It was not being treated as a complaint, because it was not a complaint.

9.16 In addition, every effort should have been made to ensure that William Kerr did not see Patient A17 alone, and that if he saw her at all (with, for example, Dr Mortimer or Senior Nursing Officer Tiplady present), the topic of the disclosure was not to be raised. This means:

a. William Kerr should have been told of the existence of the disclosure at an early stage. This should have been done at a formal meeting, a note taken of the meeting, with a copy of the note given to William Kerr.

b. At, or before, that meeting William Kerr should have been advised not to see Patient A17 alone. This would suggest that someone from Region should have been at the meeting. It is accepted that such advice was not enforceable, but at least it could have been given, William Kerr's reaction could have been noted, and if he then did see Patient A17 alone, some disciplinary step may have been available to Region.

c. Following such a disclosure, irrespective of its truth and as much for the protection of the consultant as the patient, Patient A17's care should have been transferred to another consultant.

9.17 If the Patient A17 disclosure continued, then Linda Bigwood (or perhaps some other person, possibly Dr Mortimer) might have suggested taking a statement from Patient A17 – to be signed, witnessed, and dated. In addition, statements should have been taken from Linda Bigwood and any other recipients of Patient A17's disclosure. These documents should then have formed the basis of a preliminary report to Region.

9.18 If, on the other hand, Patient A17 refused to speak, refused to make a statement, or withdrew the disclosure, then it is probably correct that no further attempts should be made to press Patient A17. At least there would be a contemporaneous record – from Linda Bigwood and from Dr Mortimer – of the disclosure in case Patient A17 changed her mind, and wanted to resurrect the disclosure, or if another disclosure or complaint was made. Even in this situation it would perhaps have been advisable for a report to have been submitted to Region, noting the initial disclosure but noting that it had subsequently been withdrawn.

9.19 What should not have happened, and what we conclude did happen, is that Mr Monk-Steel (or someone in a similar position) was sent to see William Kerr on his own, and Mr Monk-Steel then spoke to Patient A17 on his own. William Kerr said it was all "old hat", and Patient A17 withdrew the disclosure – a completely unsatisfactory situation.

9.20 Perhaps the most fundamental practical and early error in relation to Patient A17's story (rather than the wider concerns referred to in Linda Bigwood's written complaint) was to allow there to be a one-to-one interview between William Kerr and Patient A17. This error probably emanated in part from the fact that there was no-one handling the complaint who had authority over William Kerr to prevent such a meeting. The magnitude of this error is even more apparent when seen in the context of Patient A17 as a vulnerable psychiatric patient receiving inpatient care, who had expressed herself to be fearful of reprisals. In contrast, William Kerr was a powerful consultant, described by various witnesses as "a bully", "autocratic" and "overbearing".

9.21 This error went on to haunt those handling the complaint, which Linda Bigwood refused to drop. Linda Bigwood had from the outset opposed the one-to-one meeting, to no avail. The suspicion that Patient A17's complaint was withdrawn under duress following a one-to-one meeting with William Kerr was not hers alone, and was expressly recognised once the complaint reached district level, and legal advice was sought.

9.22 Despite this contemporaneous recognition of the risk of duress, and the unanimous evidence to the Inquiry that such a one-to-one meeting would not be appropriate following the making of a serious allegation (for the protection of both the patient and doctor), in July 1985 Linda Bigwood was sent a letter that stated:

> *"You asked particularly to know whether any action had been taken against Dr Kerr in the light of his decision to see the patient alone, following your complaint. This issue was considered at the time of the original complaint and I have also recently confirmed with another Senior Psychiatrist, whose judgement I trust, that the relationship between a Consultant Psychiatrist and a patient is such that* it is possible for a Consultant to decide to see a patient alone, even when a complaint of this nature has been made.*" (emphasis added)*

9.23 We do not accept that proposition. In fact, as explained elsewhere in our Report, the statement itself is suspect and arises from, at least, a misunderstanding of the information upon which it was based.

9.24 In our list of concerns set out above we have identified absence of communication as a key failing.

Dr Turner

9.25 Dr Turner was Regional Medical Officer (RMO) for the Yorkshire Regional Health Authority between 1976 and 1986. As RMO he was responsible for, and dealt with, complaints against consultants.

9.26 Dr Turner's evidence to the Inquiry was that he was unaware of Linda Bigwood's written complaint. When shown the document by the Inquiry, his evidence was that he would have expected not only to have had it referred to him, but also to have undertaken, or at least to have taken responsibility for, an investigation into the allegations himself.

9.27 Mr Ingram in his evidence said that "Dr Turner absented himself from the scene". In the light of the evidence from Dr Turner as to what he would have done, this becomes a very serious allegation. We found Mr Ingram to be a very defensive witness, keen to put responsibility on others. We concluded that he was dismissive of Linda Bigwood's complaint – far too quickly, and merely on the basis of the somewhat dubious withdrawal by Patient A17 of her complaint. We conclude that Mr Ingram's criticism of Dr Turner is misplaced. However, we are strongly critical of the system – the organisation – then in place that would not and, we conclude, did not enable the Linda Bigwood written complaint to be brought to the immediate attention of the then RMO. We are appalled that Dr Turner was not kept fully informed of Linda Bigwood's written allegations.

The Patient A17/Linda Bigwood story – an end piece

9.28 The inadequate response to the disclosures made by Patient A17, and the complaints made by Linda Bigwood, cast a long shadow. It seems to have been known – admittedly not by all, but by a number within Clifton Hospital – that allegations had been made that fitted in with the more general rumours and gossip circulating in relation to William Kerr. But when the complaint was raised and Linda Bigwood was prepared to take it further, Patient A17 withdrew her allegation, and Linda Bigwood was moved from the ward (and eventually removed), and William Kerr continued in practice. The effect on the morale of the nursing staff who knew of the Patient A17 allegations must have been bad.

9.29 A direct consequence of this mishandling was that when, in 1987, another patient (Patient A38) raised her (similar) concern with her Community Psychiatric Nurse (CPN), Mr Smith, in relation to the alleged sexual assault by William Kerr – when discussing trust when in contact with men – Mr Smith felt that he could do nothing. He felt he could not even speak to his immediate line manager, for fear of causing harm to Patient A38 and destroying whatever trust she may have had in male professionals. Mr Smith's written and oral evidence to the Inquiry is important and eloquent. In his written statement referring to his time at Bootham and Naburn hospitals he said this:

> *"Nursing staff simply did not raise issues about practice in York. If you attempted to raise issues, it was not looked upon favourably by your colleagues. The advice given to staff was to report anything untoward up through line management. However, it seemed that if you reported anything up the line you were quickly moved on to a different position.*
>
> *"There was a culture amongst staff that you did not complain about colleagues. Anyone who had attempted to make a complaint would have felt very vulnerable. There was very much a culture of 'I dare you to make a complaint'.*

"As far as patients making complaints went there was very much a culture that patients should not be believed because they were psychiatric patients and may be lying. If patients had brought a complaint, they would have undoubtedly felt that it was their word against the psychiatrist's and they were unlikely to be believed."

9.30   From his oral evidence, we emphasise the following:

Q. ... You go on then to talk about the culture that patients should not be believed because they were psychiatric patients and may be lying. Again, this is a theme that the Panel have been exploring, so we would be interested to have your views on why you felt it was that there was this culture, which, again, is a fairly strong term, of disbelieving psychiatric patients. Where did that come from, this understanding?

A. Where did it come from? It felt to me as if it was a culture that had always been there, way before my time. I do not know how to answer that any better really. It was a very uncomfortable culture ...

And

Q. In your statement, what you are there describing is a culture which was not patient-based, insofar as we are dealing with complaints and concerns, but an organisation that was geared more to the protection of the medical professional, particularly the doctors. Would that be a fair summary?

A. Yes, broader than that. I think it just felt very much of an institution where everybody wanted to maintain the status quo, yes.

Q. Don't rock the boat, don't bang on the doors?

A. That is what it felt like from where I was.

Q. You said this: "There was very much a culture of 'I dare you to make a complaint'."

A. That is a personal interpretation.

9.31   We share that view of both the culture and organisational structures in place at the time.

9.32 One final point. We have in this, and the preceding chapter, concentrated almost exclusively on William Kerr. It is to be borne in mind – as developed later in the Report – that the Patient A17 story flows into concerns and complaints about Michael Haslam. In paragraph 9.28 above we have observed that the effect on the morale of the nursing staff who knew of the Patient A17 story (and the outcome for Linda Bigwood) must have been devastating. It must not be forgotten that it is also likely to have had an adverse effect on those who had to respond to near-contemporaneous concerns and complaints into the practice of Michael Haslam.

Chapter 10
Patients who made no contemporaneous complaint

Introduction

10.1 During the course of the Inquiry we have become aware, either through written statements, reports of third parties or oral evidence from the women involved, of over twenty further former patients who made no contemporaneous complaint about William Kerr. Some of these women came forward in response to the police investigation and others have come forward for the first time to the Inquiry.

10.2 Their allegations range from inappropriate sexual suggestions including obscene telephone calls, to full sexual intercourse, sometimes presented as "part of the treatment" and in other cases as the physical aspect of an "affair" in which William Kerr made unfulfilled promises of marriage.

10.3 Accounts of abuse also included William Kerr allegedly exposing himself, forcing women to masturbate him or perform oral sex. There were also complaints of unnecessary internal examinations and incidents where he allegedly groped women's breasts or kissed them.

10.4 Each allegation was shocking due to the alleged behaviour itself (if true) and, in most cases, the extreme vulnerability of the victims. The patients' feelings of abuse of trust has in many cases had devastating effects on the women concerned.

10.5 Our focus in hearing the allegations of those who had not made a complaint in the many years before, was in order to try to obtain a better understanding of why they had not made any contemporaneous complaint.

10.6 All those who gave oral evidence, and indeed those who submitted written statements, were asked to express why they had felt unable to raise a complaint at the time.

10.7 The responses were varied. A recurring theme was one of embarrassment and of feeling ashamed. As one woman described: "I was just so embarrassed, I could not have told anyone." This feeling was exacerbated by the particularly vulnerable position of many of the women. In some cases they felt there was no one to turn to; ironically some perceived the very psychiatrist who was the alleged abuser as their only source of help. In other cases women feared the consequences if their families or partners were to learn of the alleged abuse, blaming themselves as being in some way responsible for William Kerr's behaviour.

10.8 There was an almost universal lack of knowledge among the former patients as to how one would lodge a complaint, or what this would involve – a lack of knowledge that is readily understandable when it is appreciated that even the health professionals themselves, including GPs, had only the sketchiest of understanding as to how to progress a complaint.

10.9 In some cases women wanted to bury the issue, not to "create another set of problems" by complaining. Indeed one woman explained that her fear of these matters being investigated, even by the Inquiry team, had led to her initially being hostile to the Inquiry and seeking for it to be stopped.

10.10 Other women had very specific fears that were said to have been played upon by William Kerr. One woman alleges William Kerr threatened her that if she told anybody (about the alleged sexual assault) "I would never see my children again". Others spoke of the fear of being "sectioned" and forcibly detained, and in at least one case a woman feared that the abortion she sought would not be approved unless she acceded to William Kerr's alleged demands for sexual intercourse.

10.11 The allegations and concerns not raised at the time have been carried silently by the patients of William Kerr (and Michael Haslam). We do not seek to judge the veracity of the allegations but recognise the distress that these patients – and maybe others who have not come forward – have experienced in carrying their allegations in silence. We cover this in more detail in Section Five of our report entitled "Barriers to Making Complaints". They have made clear to us in their evidence the extent to which they feel this has blighted their lives.

10.12 We have not set out the accounts of each of these patients in detail as our focus is not on the allegations made against William Kerr and the truth or otherwise of these matters. However their participation in the Inquiry has been essential in enabling us to understand the barriers to complaints and to making recommendations that we hope will break down some of these problems. We discuss this further in Chapter 36.

The patients who did not complain at the time

Patient A51

10.13 On 22 September 1969, Patient A51 was referred by a GP in Harrogate to a psychiatrist. It appears from the records that the first psychiatrist seen by Patient A51 was Dr Bromham. However after one consultation she was referred to William Kerr at his Dragon Parade clinic. The notes show outpatient appointments at Dragon Parade on dates between September 1969 and October 1970.

10.14 The appointments were allegedly arranged for late afternoon or early evening when William Kerr and Patient A51 were the only people in the building. Patient A51 alleged that on each occasion William Kerr had sexual intercourse with her and told her that it was part of her treatment.

10.15 Patient A51, who gave evidence to the Inquiry, did not complain about William Kerr's conduct to anyone since she believed that William Kerr was treating her and that he was the only one who could help her. She also said that she was too ashamed to mention it. It was not until the press releases in 1997 that Patient A51 disclosed the alleged assaults.

10.16 In the William Kerr trial of the facts, Patient A51's allegations formed a count of rape. The jury found William Kerr not guilty in respect of Patient A51's allegations.

Patient A52

10.17 Patient A52 was referred to William Kerr in 1969 at Ripon Hospital. She saw him at various locations, including Ripon Hospital, Clifton Hospital and Harrogate General Hospital. However, the majority of the consultations took place at Dragon Parade. At a consultation at Dragon Parade, having discussed sex, William Kerr allegedly exposed himself to Patient A52 and requested that she expose herself to him, which she agreed to. William Kerr is said to have presented this as part of her treatment. Patient A52 alleged that sexual intercourse then took place, after which William Kerr went to the lavatory and asked Patient A52 to watch him masturbate. William Kerr is said to have impressed upon Patient A52 that she should tell no one about what had happened. Patient A52 also recalled treatment by William Kerr that allegedly involved her lying on a bed with a face mask on, and being very distressed and screaming when she came round.

10.18   The sexual activities are alleged to have continued (at Dragon Parade) for a period of 18 months. On one occasion Patient A52 described meeting William Kerr in Ripon Market Square, and said that he suggested they go to her parents' home; she refused. Patient A52's treatment by William Kerr ceased in 1970/71 although she alleged that he visited her bedsit on one final occasion but she refused to let him in, as she had an ex-boyfriend with her at the time.

10.19   When the court case and Inquiry were announced, Patient A52 wrote letters to try and halt the procedure and also started to correspond with William Kerr and his wife offering support. She later came to view William Kerr's alleged acts as abusive.

10.20   Patient A52 gave evidence to the Inquiry and stated that her reason for not complaining about William Kerr's conduct was that she felt that she was a willing participant and therefore had nothing to complain about.

Patient A53

10.21   Patient A53 refused to make a formal statement to police, as her husband was unaware of a "relationship" with William Kerr. She was referred to William Kerr by her GP, Dr Parks. Her first appointment with William Kerr was 18 March 1969. Thereafter he allegedly suggested she accompany him in his car as he was busy and they could talk there. Patient A53 alleged that William Kerr telephoned her at home, asking her what underwear she had on, and that in May/June 1969 he drove with her in his car to some secluded woods and they had sexual intercourse. Patient A53 stated that she continued to see William Kerr on a regular basis over the next couple of years (having sexual intercourse on most occasions they met).

10.22 When Patient A53 moved away she still continued to see William Kerr in Ripon and Harrogate and alleged that the sexual relationship continued. She stated that he assured her he loved her and would leave his wife and marry her in 10 to 15 years. In about 1976, Patient A53 decided William Kerr was not fulfilling his promise to marry her and was just using her. She considered Kerr had abused his position of trust and taken advantage of her when he knew she was going through a rocky period in her marriage. She had disclosed the nature of her relationship to friends but was not prepared to name them to the police.

Patient AB

10.23 On 22 June 1972, Patient AB, a nurse, took an overdose and was referred to William Kerr at his Dragon Parade clinic, Harrogate. At that time she had previously heard "rumours" about William Kerr's alleged sexual impropriety.

10.24 Patient AB alleged that on the first occasion that she visited William Kerr, he placed his hand on her groin saying "you are very tense aren't you." He allegedly went on to suggest she go to London and have sex with hundreds of men. After discussing the consultation with her husband, Patient AB returned for a second consultation and took her young daughter with her. Patient AB alleged that William Kerr was "disgruntled because the child was there" and that, although he did not touch her inappropriately during that consultation, he stared at her breasts, telling her she was a "big girl".

10.25 Patient AB, who gave oral evidence to the Inquiry, did not return to see William Kerr and did not tell her GP, as she did not want to be labelled a "trouble-maker". The post that she held as nurse in the local area meant that she was reserved in telling the authorities.

10.26 Not until about 1997 did Patient AB speak to a key worker at a therapy session, although this was not pursued. In or about 1999, she disclosed the allegations to a doctor, Dr Adam, in group therapy. Patient AB said that seeing news articles prompted this disclosure. It was at this stage that Patient AB decided to take the matter further and reported her allegations to the Community Health Council, Harrogate and gave a statement to the police and the GMC.

10.27   Patient AB's allegations did not form a count in the William Kerr trial of the facts. However she was also a former patient of Michael Haslam and her allegations did form two counts (both of indecent assault) in the criminal trial of Michael Haslam. The jury found Michael Haslam guilty of both counts of indecent assault of Patient AB.

10.28   So far as we are aware, Patient AB is the only patient who alleges to have been a victim of sexual abuse by both William Kerr and Michael Haslam.

Patient A54

10.29   In September 1972, Patient A54 was referred to William Kerr by a gynaecologist, Ms Hutcheon, regarding a pregnancy. William Kerr visited Patient A54 at her home on 22 September 1972 and stated that he needed to perform an internal examination. Patient A54 agreed to this, and it took place in her bedroom.

10.30   William Kerr subsequently indicated by letter dated 25 September 1972 that he had "examined the patient myself" and that he felt "She was quite depressed and in need of psychiatric assistance. The marriage is a difficult one, she herself says that she has to accept all the responsibilities for running the home and there are emotional difficulties with her husband." The pregnancy was not terminated.

10.31   Patient A54 subsequently attended William Kerr's rooms at the Harrogate General Hospital for further treatment as an outpatient. The Harrogate General Hospital medical records showed appointments during October and November 1972 and January 1973.

10.32   On these occasions William Kerr allegedly talked mainly about sex and on one particular occasion exposed his penis to her. After this, Patient A54 did not return to see William Kerr for treatment.

10.33   It was not until Patient A54 read the newspaper reports outlining the investigation in 1997 that she came forward to speak of her alleged abuse. In a statement to the police, her GP, Dr Thornton, confirmed that there was no mention of any complaint in her medical records, and she had never made any to him.

10.34 Patient A54's eldest son stated in his police witness statement that in approximately 1992/3 his mother told him that the psychiatrist who had visited her had made her strip off and had conducted an internal examination. Her son had a vague recollection of a man visiting his mother when he was eleven years old, but was unable to say if he was a psychiatrist.

10.35 In the William Kerr Trial of the Facts, Patient A54's allegations formed two counts of indecent assault. The jury could not reach a verdict about Patient A54's allegations.

Patient A55

10.36 Patient A55 was referred to William Kerr, by her then GP Dr Hugh Jackson Houston (a partner of Dr McCluskey and Dr Cornford) of Grey Street, Harrogate. She attended one appointment with William Kerr at Harrogate District Hospital in 1977. During the 30-minute appointment he allegedly made sexual innuendos and Patient A55 formed the impression he was not listening to her but was "getting a kick out of talking dirty to me". She did not report the matter (although she told her husband) as she felt that she would not be believed and felt she had enough problems in her life without adding further stress.

Patient A56

10.37 On 16 March 1978, Patient A56 was referred by a GP to William Kerr. William Kerr saw her on 21 March 1978 at her home.

10.38 On 10 April 1978, Patient A56 saw one of William Kerr's Registrars, as an outpatient at the Ripon clinic. On 8 May 1978 she saw William Kerr at the Ripon clinic. Her appointment was the last of the day, about 3.30pm. Patient A56 alleged that William Kerr indecently assaulted her by exposing his erect penis to her and asking her, "what would you like to do?". William Kerr allegedly threatened her with detention in hospital if she did not do what he told her to. He said that he would call the nurses, say that she had made advances at him, and have her sectioned. Patient A56 was then instructed by William Kerr to perform oral sex on him.

10.39 Subsequently, William Kerr allegedly arranged to meet Patient A56 on Harrogate Road. Patient A56 alleged that William Kerr instructed her to get into his car and then drove down the road for a short distance. After stopping, he instructed her to masturbate him.

10.40 Patient A56 did not see William Kerr after that event, although she said that he telephoned her on a couple of occasions trying to get her to agree to a meeting. However, the medical records show two subsequent visits from Patient A56 to the Ripon outpatients' clinic on 5 June and 26 June 1978. She denied that the records were correct or that these visits had taken place.

10.41 At the end of 1996, Patient A56 told her daughter that a psychiatrist had exposed himself to her, later stating that in fact it was more serious than that but her husband did not know and it was "too embarrassing" to repeat.

10.42 Patient A56, who gave oral evidence to the Inquiry, did not tell anyone in authority of the above events, due to the fact that she thought "no-one would believe me". On hearing about the police investigation in 1997, she disclosed to her GP, Dr Morag Shelagh McDowell of North Street Surgery, North Street, that she had oral sex with William Kerr.

10.43 In the William Kerr Trial of the Facts, Patient A56's allegations formed a count of indecent assault. The jury could not reach a verdict in respect of Patient A56's allegations.

Patient A57

10.44 Patient A57 was referred to William Kerr by her GP, Dr Moss, in 1978 suffering from depression. William Kerr asked her questions about her sex life and she questioned the relevance of this. She did not return for a further consultation.

Patient A58

10.45 Patient A58 was treated by her GP, Dr Moss, with medication and she was then referred to a psychiatrist in Leeds in March 1969. After a period of approximately three weeks as an inpatient at Leeds General Infirmary, Patient A58 was discharged.

10.46 Some time passed until, in November 1976, Dr Moss referred her to Dr Bromham. Dr Bromham admitted her into Clifton Hospital. After her discharge, Patient A58 saw Dr Bromham as an outpatient at Harrogate General Hospital.

10.47 After a lengthy period of treatment by Dr Bromham, Patient A58 was referred to William Kerr in around February 1979. She was given a choice of two doctors, William Kerr and Michael Haslam, and chose William Kerr, who she knew was Dr Bromham's husband. The first consultation occurred at her home on 16 February 1979, with her husband present. Thereafter, she saw William Kerr at the outpatients' clinic at Harrogate Hospital. She continued to see William Kerr as a regular outpatient at the Hospital until discharged on 26 June 1988, when he retired. At one time, she was briefly admitted to Clifton Hospital from 25 October to 12 November 1982. William Kerr, in a letter of 27 October 1982, said he had admitted her following a domiciliary visit where she was "very tearful and distressed". He adds "she has been abusing drugs for a long time now, and indeed getting prescriptions both from the surgery and me."

10.48 Patient A58 alleged that subsequent to the first few consultations in which no inappropriate activity occurred, William Kerr indecently assaulted her during the consultations. This alleged abuse continued up until William Kerr retired in 1988.

10.49 Patient A58, who provided a written statement to the Inquiry, said that she allowed the alleged abuse to continue because she felt that otherwise she would not get the help and medication that she thought she needed. She also felt that if she spoke to anyone she would not be believed, as she was suffering from a mental illness. She did not consider the possibility of asking to be referred to another psychiatrist.

10.50 In June 1997, Patient A58 received the letter from Harrogate Healthcare in respect of William Kerr. As a result of this and a television programme relating to the allegations against William Kerr, she decided to come forward and telephoned the Healthcare Hotline.

10.51 Her allegations against William Kerr formed a count of indecent assault in the Trial of the Facts. The jury was not able to reach a verdict in respect of Patient A58's allegations.

Patient A59

10.52   Patient A59 was referred to William Kerr by her GP in the late 1970s/early 1980s. Her first contact with William Kerr was on a domiciliary visit and thereafter follow-up was arranged at Ripon Hospital Outpatients. Patient A59 recalls William Kerr asking questions about her sex life, which she felt were inappropriate. She attended outpatient appointments on a monthly basis and on the sixth or seventh visit, William Kerr allegedly took hold of her hand and asked her how she would feel if he put his arms around her and gave her a kiss. Patient A59 was embarrassed, rejected his suggestions of a kiss and made an excuse to leave the consultation and did not make any further appointments.

Patient A60

10.53   Patient A60 was referred to William Kerr in November 1979 by her GP, Dr Sheila Young. William Kerr made an initial domiciliary visit. Shortly after this visit, Patient A60 attended Harrogate District Hospital for a follow-up appointment. On this occasion, William Kerr allegedly greeted Patient A60 with a hug, which she took at the time as a "fatherly" gesture. She continued to have appointments initially on a weekly basis, reducing then to fortnightly. At one of these appointments, William Kerr put his arms around Patient A60 to hug her and in doing so allegedly groped her breast. At a subsequent appointment William Kerr tried to persuade her to lie on the examination couch, behind a screen; she refused and comments that William Kerr then behaved coldly towards her. She also alleged that on several occasions, William Kerr invited her to go with him to his caravan, which she believed was located in the Lake District or the Yorkshire Dales. Patient A60 refused these invitations.

10.54   Patient Patient A60 commented that having rejected his "advances", William Kerr stopped making approaches to her. She continued to see William Kerr for a two-year period, although she remained uneasy in his presence.

Patient A61

10.55   On 26 March 1980, Patient A61 was voluntarily admitted to Clifton Hospital under the care of William Kerr. She was discharged on 1 April 1980.

10.56 On 24 May 1980, William Kerr prepared a psychiatric report of Patient A61, having examined her on 13 May 1980 at Clifton Hospital for that purpose. On 1 July 1980 her GP, Dr Walter, referred her to William Kerr's outpatient practice in Ripon District Hospital. At the Trial of the Facts, Patient A61 stated that this was at the suggestion of her solicitors.

10.57 On 21 July 1980, Patient A61 says she was urged by William Kerr to talk about her sex life and he allegedly asked if he could take her out for dinner and visit her at home. She declined.

10.58 On 28 July 1980, Patient A61 attended a further consultation with William Kerr at Ripon. It is alleged that William Kerr indecently assaulted her on this occasion. It is said he locked the door and began to kiss her. She alleged that William Kerr threatened her with the loss of custody of her children if she did not obey his requests.

10.59 On 18 August 1980, Patient A61 attended the Ripon clinic to consult William Kerr. She alleged that on this occasion, William Kerr indecently assaulted her again. She described the door being locked and William Kerr threatening her with loss of her children if she did not co-operate. He allegedly kissed her and rubbed himself against her leg until he ejaculated.

10.60 Patient A61, who gave oral evidence to the Inquiry, said that she reported the alleged sexual assaults by William Kerr to her solicitor, Mr Martin Clarke of Hudson, Hart and Borrows, who was annoyed and said that he would have William Kerr "struck off". However, when Mr Clarke was asked to give evidence in the criminal proceedings against William Kerr, he was unable to recall any allegations being made. Patient A61 made complaints to family and friends but did not feel able to make a formal complaint due to her mental state.

10.61 A friend of Patient A61, in her police witness statement, said that Patient A61 went into Clifton Hospital in about 1980. When she came out she told the friend that William Kerr had cuddled her and groped her breasts, saying that if she didn't meet him then he would have her children taken away. The friend says she did not know what to do and told Patient A61 to pull herself together as she was now out of hospital. The friend heard about the investigation into a Clifton

Hospital Psychiatrist on the News in July 1997 and phoned Patient A61 to tell her.

10.62   In the William Kerr Trial of the Facts, Patient A61's allegations formed a count of indecent assault. The jury found William Kerr not guilty in respect of Patient A61's allegations.

Patient A62

10.63   Patient A62 was referred to William Kerr by her GP, Dr Moss. William Kerr visited her at her home on 4 February 1981 and asked her intimate questions about her sex life. He allegedly asked her to sit on the floor in front of him and he massaged her neck and fondled her breasts. She asked him to leave and told her mother and husband about the incident but they did not believe her.

10.64   Patient A62 provided a written statement to the Inquiry and explained that her husband had told her that if she reported the incident she may be "locked up". She made no formal complaint, and commented that she was unaware how one would make a complaint against a consultant.

Patient A63

10.65   In March 1977, Patient A63 was admitted to Clifton Hospital, under the care of William Kerr. On 18 July 1977 she was admitted to Clifton Hospital again. On 4 August 1977, she was discharged from Clifton Hospital and attended the outpatients clinic on a regular basis thereafter.

10.66   In November 1980, Patient A63 returned to the outpatients' department for treatment by William Kerr after an assault by her then boyfriend. On 3 August 1981, she was again admitted to Clifton Hospital.

10.67   On 12 October 1981, Patient A63 had a domiciliary visit by William Kerr. She was surprised to see him, as she was not expecting a visit. Patient A63 alleged that William Kerr indecently assaulted her during the visit, fondling her breasts and putting his hand between her legs. Subsequent to the domiciliary visit, she made her own way to Clifton Hospital for treatment. She did not report the allegations to anyone as she thought that she would not be believed.

Patient A64

10.68 Patient A64 was referred to William Kerr by her GP, Dr Roz Marshall, for a domiciliary visit, on 27 January 1986. She subsequently saw William Kerr approximately once a fortnight, at one of the Harrogate Hospitals (unsure which) for a period up to 8 August 1988. William Kerr would allegedly ask inappropriate questions about Patient A64's sex life and on the occasion of her last visit, she states that he grabbed her as she was leaving, putting his arms around her and trying to kiss her and fondle her breasts. According to Patient A64, she pulled away, started shouting and rushed out of the room. She collected her children who were waiting in the canteen for her and left the hospital crying. She informed her husband of what had happened and states he telephoned William Kerr, telling him not to touch his wife again. William Kerr is said to have informed Patient A64's husband that he was being friendly and just giving her a hug.

10.69 The ex-husband of Patient A64 confirmed in his police statement that he had telephoned William Kerr as stated by his ex-wife and that William Kerr had said the hug was just a friendly gesture.

10.70 Patient A64 never made any allegations against William Kerr to her GP.

Patient A65

10.71 Patient A65 was admitted to Harrogate General Hospital and diagnosed by William Kerr as suffering from depression.

10.72 After a few months, Patient A65 became very tearful and her GP, Dr Foggitt, arranged for William Kerr to visit her at home. She subsequently visited him about six times at Harrogate District Hospital on Friday afternoons. During the consultations, William Kerr allegedly asked about her sex life and relationships and on one occasion asked if she wanted to go up to his caravan at Pateley Bridge. She dismissed his comments.

10.73 On one occasion, William Kerr arrived unannounced at Patient A65's house and said he was considering forming a support group for Clifton Hospital. Patient A65 agreed to help. A support group was indeed formed, helping provide transport for relatives to patients, fund raising etc.

10.74 Patient A65 then allegedly started to receive telephone calls at home from William Kerr. She claimed these were calls with sexual connotations, telling her he was masturbating and mentioning he would like to go to bed with her.

10.75 On one further occasion, Patient A65 states that William Kerr arrived at her house unannounced. He apparently smelt of alcohol. She let him in, however when he allegedly grabbed hold of her by the waist she resisted and threw him out of the house.

Patient A66

10.76 Patient A66 was referred to William Kerr by her GP, Dr Brown, 20 November 1973. After she had finished her initial treatment with William Kerr, she had cause to call out a psychiatrist to attend to her mother at home. William Kerr attended and having seen her mother he then asked Patient A66 to go into the dining room with him where he would complete the paperwork. Patient A66 mentioned that she had a stomach ache and claims that William Kerr then placed his hand on her breast, asking if the pain was there. He then allegedly proceeded to move his hand down to her groin area. Patient A66 immediately moved away and told him to stop. Patient A66 informed her husband what had happened but they decided to take no further action.

10.77 In his police statement, Patient A66's husband confirmed his wife's account.

10.78 Patient A66 stated that she recalled that a friend of hers during the 1970s had referred to William Kerr as a womaniser when his name was mentioned. Patient A66 assumed something of a sexual nature had also happened to her friend, but she did not pursue the subject.

10.79 Patient A66 contacted the police, having received a letter from Harrogate Healthcare in 1997.

Patient A67

10.80 Patient A67's husband recalled his wife coming back from an appointment with William Kerr and saying she did not want to visit again. Some time later, he recalls his wife telling him that William Kerr exposed himself to her. She also expressed her dissatisfaction with William Kerr's behaviour to a friend (Patient A39).

10.81 Patient A67, who gave oral evidence to the Inquiry, said she felt a stigma attached to psychiatric patients, referring to the fact that in her childhood, Clifton Hospital had been referred to as the "mad house". She described how she felt William Kerr to be "in control" and "blamed herself" when he made advances. Patient A67 also described how her fear of being "locked up" in Clifton meant she felt unable to complain at the time.

Patient A68

10.82 Patient A68 was referred to William Kerr by her GP, Dr Nixon. She alleges that William Kerr forced her to perform oral sex. She also makes other, somewhat confused, allegations of sexual assault.

Patient A69

10.83 Patient A69 was referred to William Kerr by her GP, Dr Houston, of Alexander Road, Harrogate. William Kerr made a home visit and Patient A69 said he smelt of whisky. He admitted Patient A69 to Clifton Hospital. She was unhappy with the treatment and, with the help of a friend, discharged herself. She continued to be treated by Dr Houston who felt she needed to see a psychiatrist and she therefore attended William Kerr as an outpatient on three occasions at Harrogate District Hospital. Her medical notes contain domiciliary and outpatient visits. On each occasion, Patient A69 recalls William Kerr making sexual innuendos to the point where, on the last occasion, she walked out of the consultation.

10.84 At some point, Patient A69 also saw Dr Bromham and mentioned that she did not like William Kerr and did not want to see him, although she did not specify the reason (and was unaware that Dr Bromham was married to William Kerr).

10.85 A number of other patients have subsequently raised issues and allegations. We have not sought, except where the allegation was markedly different in character from the others, to pursue each of them in turn. Suffice to say, there remain other unresolved matters that patients have disclosed.

Chapter 11
The retirement of William Kerr and voluntary erasure

William Kerr's retirement

11.1 On 9 September 1987, William Kerr wrote to the Secretary of the Yorkshire Regional Health Authority (YRHA) to give notice of his intention to retire from the YRHA with effect from 10 September 1988 (12 months hence). He also wrote on behalf of his wife, Dr Beryl Bromham, who intended to retire with effect from 7 September 1988. According to his police statement, William Kerr had made a decision a considerable time earlier to retire on the day of his wife's 60th birthday.

11.2 On 22 September 1987, Dr Green wrote to William Kerr to acknowledge receipt of William Kerr's letter dated 9 September 1987 and also to make note of Dr Green's gratitude for the "valuable contribution" both William Kerr and Dr Bromham had made to the Yorkshire Region. This was just six days before Linda Bigwood sent notice of the complaint relating to William Kerr and Clifton Hospital to the Chairman of the YRHA.

11.3 On 10 September 1988 William Kerr retired from his employment with the NHS at the age of 63 years.

William Kerr's ill health

11.4 The Inquiry was provided with approximately 18 medical reports relating to the physical and mental health of William Kerr. The reports spanned the period from December 1998 until April 2000. The legal representatives in relation to the criminal investigations and the Trial of the Facts commissioned these various reports. On 4 February 2003 Professor Dora Kohen, Consultant Psychiatrist from the Lancashire Postgraduate School of Medicine, saw William Kerr at the request of the GMC. The GMC wished to ascertain William Kerr's fitness to plead or give evidence to the Professional Conduct

Committee (PCC). The GMC did not request a report from a general surgeon to inquire into Kerr's state of physical health.

11.5 Professor Kohen's opinion was that William Kerr was not fit to plead, provide instructions to his legal counsel or give evidence. Professor Kohen stated that:

> *"His [Kerr's] memory problems, his limited attention and poor concentration would make it impossible for him to scrutinise any written information, to retain any form of verbal information or to give any evidence to the court. I do not believe that he may appreciate the effect of any evidence [advice?] from his legal team. I do not believe that he can give instructions to his legal team. I do not believe that he is able to [give] evidence."*

11.6 Professor Kohen thought that William Kerr's prognosis was poor. Professor Kohen believed that there had been deterioration in William Kerr's condition since the last assessment in 1999. On the basis of the opinion of Professor Kohen the GMC decided to accept William Kerr's application for voluntary erasure and to thereby discontinue the disciplinary proceedings, which had been referred to the PCC.

Voluntary erasure

11.7 In June 1997 the GMC received a complaint about William Kerr from Patient A22. The GMC, having established that William Kerr was subject to criminal investigation, contacted the police in August 1997 and asked to be kept informed of developments.

11.8 By April 2001 the GMC had received complaints about William Kerr from a further eight former patients.

11.9 In April 2001, following his conviction for indecent assault, William Kerr applied for voluntary erasure. The GMC responded by suspending his registration pending full investigation of the case.

11.10 William Kerr's application for voluntary erasure referred to his ill health and the GMC appointed its own specialist to prepare an up-to-date medical report, which was obtained in February 2003. In evidence before the Inquiry, a number of former patients disclosed their opposition to William Kerr being granted voluntary erasure by the GMC.

11.11 To investigate and advise generally on the actions of the GMC is not within the Terms of Reference of this Inquiry. Under our Terms of Reference, we cannot make recommendations to the Secretary of State for Health about non-NHS bodies, although we can examine the interaction between those bodies. However, the limitations on our jurisdiction do not prevent us from recording evidence received by the Inquiry and, where appropriate, expressing our concerns.

11.12 On the issue of William Kerr's voluntary erasure from the Register, we here record one former patient's letter to the GMC:

> "... to escape suspension from the Register by possible voluntary erasure by Dr Kerr, the Committee should consider the message it is giving to current and potential abusing doctors."

11.13 The Inquiry is charged with looking at the situation today to ensure that as far as possible similar situations will not occur. The effect on the actions of practising NHS doctors of any decision of the GMC in relation to William Kerr therefore falls within our Terms of Reference, as would similar action regarding Michael Haslam. We deal with the general issue of voluntary erasure later, but here seek to address the specific points raised by the former patients in relation to William Kerr.

11.14 Patient A22 was not alone in expressing her disquiet. Another said to the GMC:

> "If the GMC accepts an application for Doctor William Kerr's voluntary erasure it would appear to me that they would be permitting him to influence them in their decision making, by allowing him to resign keeping his dignity and respect. This would be an inappropriate outcome when he took away by his actions, from his patients, their dignity and respect."

11.15 And another said:

> " [William Kerr] has been placed on the sex offenders register and should therefore have to face the consequences of his gross misconduct. He himself should be held accountable for his actions and face up to his disciplinary body in person. He has abused a position of trust as he himself knows and should be struck off, perhaps then he may show an atom of remorse."

11.16 In May 2003 the GMC concluded that, taking into account the medical evidence, William Kerr's application for voluntary erasure should be granted.

11.17 In response to that decision, one former patient wrote in anger to the GMC, saying:

> *"This decision, although not unexpected, has caused great disappointment and despair amongst those ladies who suffered at his hands during his years of practice as a Psychiatrist.*

> *"It is our hope that the loophole which allowed this man to remain on the Register in spite of having been found to have committed a sexual act on a patient and then later apply to remove his name voluntarily, thereby preventing the GMC from taking action against him, be looked at and closed."*

11.18 The Inquiry understands and appreciates the frustration and anger that the former patients must have felt, and communicated to the Inquiry in their evidence, at the application for voluntary erasure.

11.19 However, it is clear from the independent medical evidence on William Kerr's mental and physical condition which led to the Trial of the Facts – evidence accepted by the Court – that he was in no position either to defend himself or to advise others on his defence. The GMC commissioned a further independent psychiatric report, which reached a similar conclusion: that William Kerr had a long list of physical and neurological conditions, including dementia, depression and memory loss, and was therefore unfit to plead or attend a hearing due to his ill health. William Kerr has rights to a fair trial, and to a fair hearing before the GMC's disciplinary committees – under common law and under Article 6 of the European Convention on Human Rights (ECHR), as was made clear to the GMC by its solicitors and a separate advice from Queen's Counsel. For the GMC to have done other than acknowledge and accept William Kerr's deteriorating condition would have produced an injustice. This would clearly have been unacceptable. Galling though it clearly is, even now, to some of the former patients, fairness and natural justice left the GMC with no option other than to accept the application for voluntary erasure, thereby ensuring patient safety. Indeed, given that the PPC hearing may have been halted due to William Kerr's ill health, the end result could have been that William Kerr would have remained on the register, because once the PCC hearing was under way, voluntary erasure could not be granted. Furthermore, there was no apparent mechanism to bring William Kerr's application for voluntary erasure back before the PPC, unless he resubmitted his application. We do not believe that the actions of the GMC, when looked at in their entirety, could reasonably be interpreted as any indication to the medical profession that voluntary erasure should be taken as an easy way to avoid being called to account by the relevant professional body.

11.20   As noted in paragraphs 4 to 6 above, we also took steps open to us to ensure that the conclusions made by others in relation to William Kerr's current state of health were correct. Accordingly, we asked for and received copies of medical and psychiatric reports that showed, clearly and to our satisfaction, that he was unable to take any meaningful part in our Inquiry. This conclusion is entirely consistent with the decisions of the Crown Court and the GMC's disciplinary and health committees.

11.21   In summary on this issue, we sympathise with the former patients but conclude that the GMC was not in a position to call William Kerr to account due to his proven medical condition and agree with its decision – the only one open to it to ensure patient safety for the future – to grant William Kerr voluntary erasure.

Chapter 12
The trial of William Kerr

1997 police investigation

12.1   On 25 February 1997, Patient A50 spoke to Detective Constable Moore at Harrogate and complained that William Kerr had sexually assaulted her during the period from 1982 to 1986. Her allegations included one of rape, which allegedly took place in her home in 1986.

12.2   Patient A50 informed the police that she had informed a CPN, Carmel Duff, about the assaults and that she had, in fact, first contacted the police in 1995 and spoken to a Detective Constable Porter (a female officer) when she confirmed indecent assaults had taken place, but had decided not to pursue the matter at that time.

12.3   On 17 March 1997, Detective Constable Moore contacted Carmel Duff who confirmed the information provided by Patient A50. In addition, she stated that "dozens" of females in the Harrogate area had disclosed to CPNs that they were victims of sexual assaults by William Kerr.

12.4   On 18 March 1997, Assistant Detective Superintendent Bye and Detective Constable Moore had a preliminary meeting with executives from Harrogate Healthcare Trust to discuss these allegations. Mr Graham Saunders, the Chief Executive, wrote on 19 March 1997 informing Professor Liam Donaldson, the then Regional Director of NHS Executive, Northern and Yorkshire, that there had been a report of indecent assault made to the police and that the Trust had set up a strategy group.

12.5   The strategy group consisted of Mrs J M Holbrey, Director of Corporate Development and Nursing, Harrogate Healthcare, Dr Rugg, Director of Mental Health Services and Consultant Psychiatrist, Harrogate Healthcare, Mrs P Jones, Assistant Director, Joint Planning,

North Yorkshire Health Authority and Mr J Lovell of Hempsons Solicitors (acting on behalf of Harrogate Healthcare and North Yorkshire Health Authority). Also part of the group were Detective Inspector Ali, Superintendent Bye and Detective Constable Moore.

12.6 Having consulted with the Trust, a decision was made by the police to investigate the matter further. On 19 March 1997, DI Ali was appointed as Senior Investigating Officer.

12.7 On 21 May 1997, Dr Kennedy sent to Mr Graham Saunders, "the entire file on investigations carried out in the 1980s into allegations against Dr W S Kerr by the then District Administrator, Stuart Ingham" (the Bigwood/Patient A17 file).

12.8 On 16 June 1997, the Health Authority sent out a standard letter to female former patients of William Kerr between 1975 and 1985 (this was about 1,200 women) as well as to various interested parties.

> *The Harrogate Healthcare NHS Trust has been asked to cooperate with a North Yorkshire Police investigation regarding alleged incidents of misconduct concerning Dr William Samuel Kerr, a former National Health Service employee.*
>
> *As a result of these allegations being made, a decision by the North Yorkshire Police in consultation with ourselves, has been made to contact former patients of Dr Kerr in order that anyone who has information to offer may be given every opportunity to do so and to speak with the Police. To protect your confidentiality, I have agreed to send you this letter. The Police have not been given any details about you.*
>
> *If, having read this letter, you have any relevant information which you wish to draw to the attention of the Police, you may wish to contact the Investigating Officer on telephone number xxx. This telephone number will operate until 11 July 1997, between the hours 12.00 noon and 3.00pm, Monday to Friday. Outside these hours, an answer machine will take messages. Alternatively, you can complete the enclosed proforma and return it to the Police in the enclosed stamped, addressed envelope.*

I recognise that receiving this letter may cause understandable stress and concern. If you would find it helpful to have a discussion with a healthcare professional, there is a helpline operating on xxx. The line will be manned daily, 7 days a week, between 1.00pm and 9.00pm.

Please accept my apologies for troubling you, but I am sure you will appreciate these alleged incidents need to be fully investigated.

Yours sincerely

G E SAUNDERS

Chief Executive

12.9 In addition, press releases were made appealing for information. The Director of Corporate Development and Nursing also wrote to all Consultant Psychiatrists, Community Psychiatric Nurses and Psychologists informing them of the police investigation. All GPs in the Harrogate district were also written to by Graham Saunders in June 1997, informing them of the fact that former patients of William Kerr had been contacted by letter (as set out above).

12.10 In addition, a Helpline was set up for former patients. Forty-five patients phoned to make direct allegations against William Kerr, whereas forty-two called to say either they had no complaint and/or had positive experiences with William Kerr.

12.11 There were also various articles in the press about the investigation. In the early stages, William Kerr was not mentioned by name.

12.12 In April 1997, the Harrogate Healthcare Trust established the Serious Incident Strategy Group (SISG) in relation to the allegations against William Kerr. At the same time, the police commenced interviews of the Harrogate Healthcare Trust staff.

12.13 Following the extensive investigations, William Kerr was arrested on suspicion of the rape of Patient A49; indecent assault on Patient A56; indecent assault on Patient A18; and rape and indecent assault on Patient A50. He was formally charged with 15 counts of serious sexual assault (including rape) on 15 July 1998 and bailed to appear before Harrogate Magistrates on 18 August 1998.

12.14 William Kerr appeared on 18 August 1998 and the case was adjourned to 10 December 1998.

12.15 William Kerr was later charged on 20 November 1998 with a further four offences arising from four people who had come forward since the original charges. He was bailed in line with the other offences until 10 December 1998.

12.16 On 10 December 1998, 7 January 1999 and 11 February 1999 the case was adjourned and the issue of William Kerr's fitness to plead was raised.

12.17 The next appearance of William Kerr in court was on 1 July 1999. The case was referred to a Stipendiary Magistrate for a hearing of four days commencing on 14 September 1999.

12.18 The Stipendiary Magistrate committed William Kerr to the Crown Court on 25 October 1999. It was anticipated there would be a pre-trial review when William Kerr would be expected to plead, and the issue of his fitness to stand would be raised again. A pre-trial hearing was set for the week commencing 14 April 2000, when the Trial Judge was to determine the fitness of William Kerr to stand trial or to plead.

12.19 William Kerr appealed to the Attorney General that he was not fit to stand trial. This was not accepted. However, on 17 April 2000, at a hearing before Hooper J in Leeds Crown Court, the jury found William Kerr not fit to plead.

The Trial of the Facts

12.20 A trial date was set for the week commencing 27 November 2000. His Honour Judge Meyerson QC conducted the proceedings in Leeds Crown Court pursuant to Section 4A of the Criminal Procedure (Insanity) Act 1964, otherwise referred to as a Trial of the Facts.

12.21 Due to the fact that he was "not fit to plead", William Kerr was not able to be tried by a jury in respect of the charges laid before the court and either acquitted or convicted of the allegations. However, the prosecution was permitted to place before the jury the evidence it would have presented in a normal trial and ask the jury to decide whether the alleged "facts" had been proved, beyond reasonable doubt, by the evidence. Kerr's defence team was permitted to test the evidence or present his own case, just as he would have been able to do in a normal trial.

12.22 The allegations in the indictment consisted of fifteen counts of indecent assault and four counts of rape. All the counts related to the period between January 1968 and September 1988 and concerned 16 complainants who had all been patients of William Kerr. William Kerr did not give evidence and no evidence was called on his behalf.

Outcome of the trial

12.23 The hearing concluded on Monday 18 December 2000. The jury found proof beyond reasonable doubt that William Kerr had committed one of the acts forming the basis of the charges against him, namely that of indecent assault of Patient A40. The jury found that two counts of rape and four counts of indecent assault had not been proved by the prosecution. The jury could not reach a decision on the remaining 12 charges, consisting of 10 counts of indecent assault and two counts of rape.

12.24 A decision was made by the Crown Prosecution Service on 19 December 2000 that there would be no rehearing of the matters on which the jury could not reach a decision.

12.25 William Kerr was granted an absolute discharge and his name was placed upon the Sex Offenders Register for five years.

Chapter 13
Overview and timeline

Overview

13.1 In the preceding chapters we have set out, briefly, the disclosures made by William Kerr's former patients. Later in the Report, we turn to consider gossip and rumour, and the investigation that could have taken place at various times but did not.

13.2 The concerns and complaints cover the whole period of William Kerr's employment as a consultant psychiatrist in North Yorkshire – from his first arrival from Northern Ireland to his retirement in 1988. In the preceding chapter, we have attempted to pin down the disclosures to a particular year, or years, when it is said that the sexualised behaviour occurred – whatever the detail of the allegation. However, some of the disclosures refer to sexual relationships taking place over a number of years. Similar information was revealed in relation to Michael Haslam – although the number of patients is greatly reduced.

13.3 We have inevitably received far more information than considered by the judge and jury in William Kerr's criminal trial, and more information than was considered by the GMC.

13.4 To illustrate the pattern of alleged behaviour, we set out below, using single years only, where the various stories fit on a timeline of William Kerr's employment in North Yorkshire. The timeline only shows the year in which the disclosures were made; it does not attempt to show how long or how often they were made. Nor does it attempt to identify the years when the alleged sexualised behaviour is said to have taken place. Often, but not always, the year of the disclosure and the year of the alleged sexualised behaviour are the same. To complete the picture, it is the very last entry – Patient A40 – which forms the subject matter of the only finding of guilt.

13.5 An investigation in the 1980s (as early as late 1983, early 1984, after Linda Bigwood's dossier) might have uncovered the same kind of information disclosed to us; it might not. It is likely, in our opinion, that a detailed investigation – carried out with an open mind – would at least have revealed some of this information.

Timeline

William Kerr timeline – dates of concerns and complaints raised with NHS staff

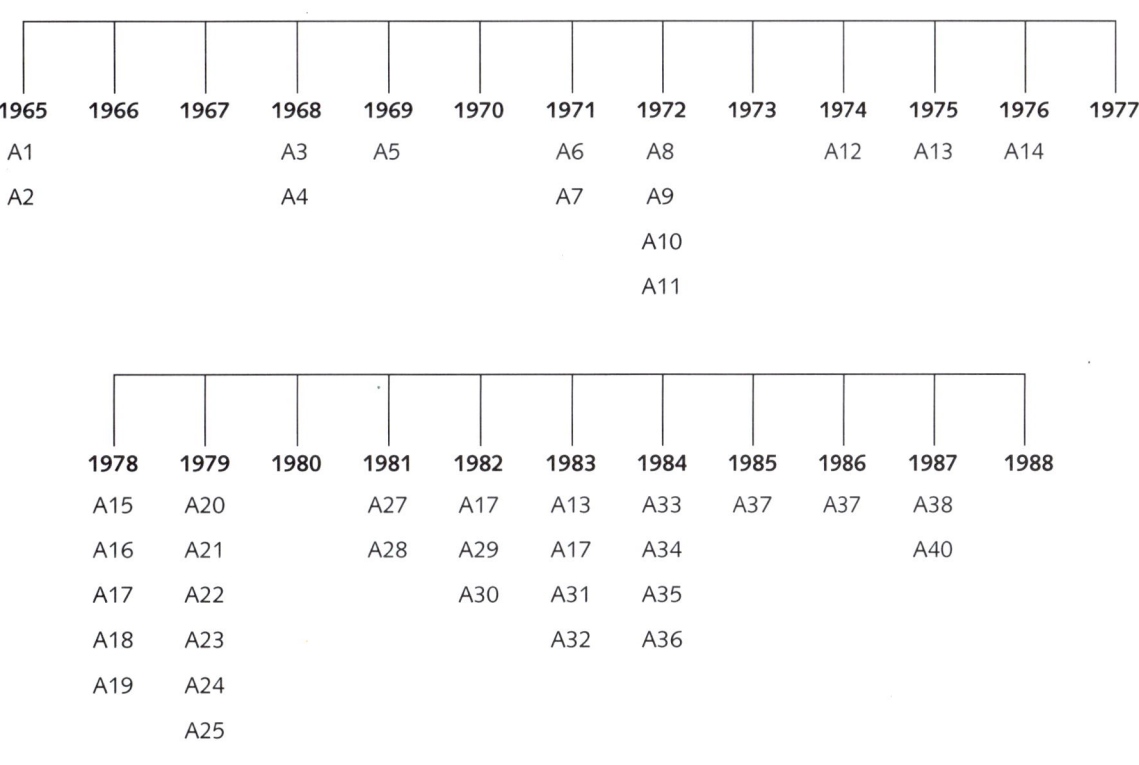

1965	1966	1967	1968	1969	1970	1971	1972	1973	1974	1975	1976	1977
A1			A3	A5		A6	A8		A12	A13	A14	
A2			A4			A7	A9					
							A10					
							A11					

1978	1979	1980	1981	1982	1983	1984	1985	1986	1987	1988
A15	A20		A27	A17	A13	A33	A37	A37	A38	
A16	A21		A28	A29	A17	A34			A40	
A17	A22			A30	A31	A35				
A18	A23				A32	A36				
A19	A24									
	A25									
	A26									

Section Three
The Michael Haslam story

Chapter 20: The trial of Michael Haslam and libel proceedings

Introduction and early police investigations

Second police investigation and trial

Appeal

Libel proceedings

Chapter 14
Michael Haslam – the early years

Qualification and early career

14.1 Michael Haslam was born on 7 February 1934. He studied at Cambridge University and then at St Bartholomew's Hospital, London, qualifying as a doctor in 1959.

14.2 On 1 January 1963, he was elected a member of the Royal Medico Psychological Association (the predecessor organisation to the Royal College of Psychiatrists). In 1967 he was appointed as MRCP Glasgow and was elected as FRCP Glasgow in 1979. In 1972 he became a Foundation Member of the Royal College of Psychiatrists. He was registered as a Fellow of the College in 1980.

14.3 Between 1959 and 1960 he spent a year as a House Officer in general medicine, surgery, gynaecology and paediatrics at Harrogate General Hospital. He also undertook some obstetrics at the Rotunda Hospital in Dublin. Between 1960 and 1962 he undertook his National Service, during which time he began to specialise in psychiatry. During part of that time, he worked as a junior psychiatrist at the Royal Victoria Hospital, Netley.

14.4 On completion of his National Service, he worked from 1962 to 1964 as a Registrar in Psychiatry at Bootham Park and Naburn Hospitals, York. In May 1964 he became a Senior Registrar in Psychiatry at the Psychiatric Unit, Newcastle General Hospital. In May 1965 he was appointed a Senior Registrar in Psychiatry at St Nicholas Hospital, Gosforth, where he remained until September 1967.

Doncaster Royal Infirmary

14.5 Michael Haslam was appointed Consultant in Psychological Medicine at the Doncaster Royal Infirmary in 1967, and remained there until 1970.

Arrival in North Yorkshire

14.6   In 1969 Michael Haslam was appointed to the post of Consultant in Psychological Medicine at Clifton Hospital, York, and Harrogate District Hospital. He took up his post in 1970.

Career in North Yorkshire

14.7   While he was based at Clifton Hospital in York, Michael Haslam also ran clinics at Bootham Park Hospital, York, and he also worked in Harrogate.

14.8   In 1972 Michael Haslam and Anne Pattie, the Senior Clinical Psychologist, set up an outpatient facility for marital and sexual problems known as the PSD (Psycho-Sexual Disorder) Clinic, based initially at Clifton Hospital but later also at York District Hospital Outpatients when this hospital was opened. In 1974 Clifton Hospital hosted the Second International Conference on Psycho-Sexual Disorders.

14.9   Following Dr Quinn's retirement in 1979, Michael Haslam left the Harrogate catchment area to cover the North Sector of York, including the Thirsk outpatient clinic. Later, the Thirsk outpatient clinic was taken over by another doctor, and Michael Haslam took over two sessions at the Neuro Psychiatric Unit at Bootham Park.

14.10   From 1980 Michael Haslam was appointed as a Consultant in Psychological Medicine at Bootham Park Hospital, York. It was in the 1980s that Michael Haslam began to undertake private work, with consulting rooms in Harrogate and York. At various times he worked from premises at The Retreat (a private psychiatric hospital), 4 St Mary's, York (a private house used as consulting rooms by a number of doctors) and the Purey Cust (a private general hospital in York).

14.11   Michael Haslam left his NHS Consultant post in 1989. He went on to practise in the private sector. The circumstances of his resignation from his NHS post and his subsequent private practice are set out in later chapters.

Chapter 15
Treatments and procedures carried out by Michael Haslam

Introduction

15.1   In the following sections of this chapter of the Report, we will briefly describe the treatments and the research project – paying particular attention to massage. We do not seek to express any views on the efficacy of any of the treatments – although they all appear to be "fringe" treatments, unheard of by many psychiatrists and psychosexual therapists practising at the time. We are also very keen to emphasise that we do not seek to discourage innovative treatment practices in psychiatry – where there is an evidence-based approach and cycles of audit and monitoring. Our concern is that the treatments were being used by Michael Haslam without monitoring, without any form of chaperoning, in quiet parts of the hospital, in one-to-one sessions, without any effective controls in place. The treatments formed the background to the three criminal sexual assaults of which he was convicted.

15.2   Witnesses to the Inquiry have expressed concerns in relation to three treatments carried out by Michael Haslam, and the conduct of one research project. What the treatments and project have in common is that they illustrate the considerable degree of consultant freedom and lack of monitoring of anyone overseeing Michael Haslam's practice at the time. This was in keeping with the psychiatric practice of consultants at the time. However, the impact of this was that it allowed Michael Haslam to have close, unchaperoned, contact with his younger female patients – this particularly applies to carbon dioxide inhalation therapy, massage and Kirlian photography. The other treatment, Somlec (or electro-sleep) therapy, seems to have been administered by nursing staff – although the picture is not wholly clear.

15.3   In the course of the Inquiry we asked Michael Haslam for his views on the awareness by hospital authorities of his use of massage, carbon dioxide therapy, etc. He responded as follows:

> *"It would not be a matter for managerial knowledge since (with respect) clinical treatments are not matters one would expect lay management to have any knowledge or judgement about. If one means the clinical tutor or the chairman of the medical advisory committee, then I held both of those posts at various times."*

15.4   It goes further. It was not just management who were in the dark. The evidence and advice we have received during the course of the Inquiry has led us to conclude that the treatments described in this chapter and being used by Michael Haslam were not only unknown to management and to many colleagues, but were unheard of at the time by many practising psychiatrists, and by practising psychosexual therapists.

15.5   This comes through in the evidence from GPs who did not know (or did not explain to their patients) what treatment they should expect from the psychiatrist. Several GPs and a number of the NHS managers who gave evidence did not understand the treatments that Michael Haslam was using, even when they (the managers) were involved in approving the purchase of specialist equipment. As one witness made clear, it was a small price to pay for having a consultant on the patch, and the treatment seemed to be in the vanguard of modern practice. The evidence to the Inquiry suggests that the belief that the treatments were "in the vanguard" was mistaken.

15.6   There appears to have been a general failure to enquire as to the treatments that Michael Haslam was undertaking (e.g. carbon dioxide treatment, Somlec, Kirlian photography – and hypnosis as practised by William Kerr). What follows are examples of the evidence we received – taken from three separate, but representative, witnesses.

> *Q. Do you recall any discussions with Dr Haslam about the sort of treatments that he was using and the developments that he was trying to make in psychiatric treatment?*
>
> *A. Not at all.*

Q. Would Michael Haslam discuss these sort of treatments with you, if you were not fully familiar with them?

A. He would have explained, I think, what they were.

Q. Just a few others. Carbon dioxide treatment?

A. No.

Q. Kirlian photography, have you heard of that?

A. No.

Q. Using massage on his patients, were you aware that Michael Haslam was doing that?

A. No.

Q. The Panel have also heard evidence concerning Michael Haslam taking patients out for social occasions, according to Michael Haslam as part of their treatment. Is that something that you were aware was going on?

A. No.

Q. Because the picture that seems to be being painted at present is that Michael Haslam's treatments, that included Somlec, carbon dioxide and the use of Kirlian photography as a diagnostic tool, were something that it appears very few of the witnesses we have heard from had any understanding of.

A. I think that is right.

Q. Is it fair to say that even the Medical Ethics Committee, and even you as the chairman of that, also had very little understanding of what Michael Haslam was doing with his practice?

A. I think that is probably right.

15.7 This all led to a system that was not open to challenge and where professionals were working in isolation rather than in multidisciplinary teams, thus giving rise to circumstances where this behaviour could go relatively undetected.

15.8 We would be extremely concerned if consultants, and other medical professionals, were still permitted the degree of autonomy and lack of accountability enjoyed by Michael Haslam (and William Kerr) in NHS employment during the mid to late 1980s.

Somlec

15.9 This treatment involved the use of a low voltage current intended to develop within the central nervous system the same rhythm of pulse as found in a normal sleep EEG.[1] It was intended to create a sense of relaxation in patients with anxiety states, or who were trying to end dependency on alcohol or other drugs. Treatment with Somlec or standard electroplexy took place in the Electroplexy Unit near the Villa Ward at Clifton Hospital.

15.10 In his evidence to the Inquiry, Michael Haslam described the treatment as follows:

> *"The technique of using subliminal electrical stimulation of the forebrain to induce relaxation was widely used and researched in Europe and in the USA 25 to 30 years ago. International symposia were held on the subject. We have very many papers and references. I have a paper published with my assistant Dr S while I was working in York. As regards the hospital authorities, they knew the treatment was used for some years at Clifton Hospital. It was administered by the nursing staff as a tension relief treatment, after lunch on the Villa Ward. Hundreds of patients, I guess, had it, so many of the nursing staff would have been aware of it. The hospital purchased the machine, so the hospital secretary and stores manager would also know about it. I lectured on the uses of Somlec at the Post-Graduate Centre."*

15.11 According to the evidence of Sister Anne Tiplady at Michael Haslam's criminal trial, the Somlec treatment was administered by nursing staff.

---

1 Electroencephalogram (EEG) is a method of recording electrical impulses/activity coming from the brain. The pattern of "brainwaves" may enable a diagnosis of certain conditions, such as epilepsy or states of consciousness, to be identified.

15.12 Mrs Veronica Mackley (née Ward), Staff Nurse on Villa Ward at Clifton Hospital at the relevant time, described to the Inquiry how the Somlec treatment was administered by the nursing staff. She said that it was normal for a nurse to administer the treatment – doctors were not present. A small portable machine was used and attached to the patient via electrodes. She thought that, during her training, probably only Michael Haslam had taught the technique.

15.13 Dr Adrian Skinner, Consultant Psychologist, who was employed by the Harrogate Health Authority as Principal Psychologist from 1985, described his impression of Somlec, in his evidence to the Inquiry, as follows:

> *"I guess I thought of the Somlec and the carbon dioxide treatment as kind of extended relaxation therapy."*

15.14 Mr Stephen Brooks, Community Psychiatric Nurse (at the relevant time), who treated Patient B7, gave the following evidence in relation to Somlec:

> *Q. ... Somlec was something about which you heard beneficial feedback from the patient?*
>
> *A. Yes.*

15.15 However, some at Clifton Hospital who were working directly with consultants had little or no idea about the treatment or its function. Dr Rowena Yates, Clinical Assistant in the Department of Psychiatry at Clifton between 1979 and 1990 and who worked in the Psycho-Sexual Disorder Clinic run by Michael Haslam and Dr Ann Pattie, gave the following evidence:

> *A. Yes, I knew he was using a treatment called Somlec, but I did not know what it was. I assumed it was, as I say, a biofeedback, but I do not know, and still do not know what it is.*

15.16 There was a general lack of curiosity to find out. In the modern day we hope consultants and other senior doctors would be curious about the efficacy of treatments being offered to patients by their colleagues. It is the responsibility of the clinical director to know what range of treatments is being offered by medical colleagues.

Carbon dioxide inhalation therapy

15.17 The aim of carbon dioxide therapy was to reduce anxiety and panic states (a sophisticated form of breathing into a paper bag to control a panic attack). The claimed advantages of carbon dioxide therapy were that it was non-addictive and could be given during a short session (20 minutes) at an outpatient appointment. Different versions of carbon dioxide therapy were developed between the 1930s and the 1980s. There were different theories as to the appropriate mix of carbon dioxide to oxygen, with some techniques aiming at inducing unconsciousness for short periods. It was stated at the criminal trial that Michael Haslam followed the "Wolpe" technique[2]. The carbon dioxide/oxygen mix in this technique was given in a mix of 50% carbon dioxide to 50% oxygen through a mask and the patient would take up to eight inhalations in a session of 20 minutes while reclined (fully clothed) on a couch. A course of 12 sessions over a period of one month (two or three sessions a week) would be usual.

15.18 Michael Haslam started using carbon dioxide therapy when he was in Doncaster in 1967, and continued at Clifton Hospital. He lectured about its use – in York and at the World Psychiatric Association Conference (in 1971). It is obvious that the hospital administration was well aware of its use (or should have been) – equipment (oxygen and CO_2 cylinders and apparatus) had to be ordered, maintained and stored. However, Dr Peter Kennedy, Consultant Psychiatrist and, from 1986, Unit General Manager in Mental Health, gave evidence that contrary to that assumption, the clinical administrators did not actually know of its practice.

2 A reference to Joseph Wolpe MD, who wrote extensively on the topic from the 1950s to the 1980s. The Inquiry has been supplied by Michael Haslam with a 1986 paper from Dr Wolpe, "Anxiolysis by Single Inhalations of Carbon Dioxide", which does not advocate loss of consciousness. The paper includes the following description of the administration of CO_2/oxygen mix:

"First, the patient is shown how to empty his lungs, and then to fill them to capacity through an anaesthetic mask that he applies to his face. The standard mixture nowadays consists of 50 per cent each of carbon dioxide and oxygen. When his lungs are full, he removes the mask from his face. Hyperventilation reaches a peak in a few seconds and substantially ends within 15 seconds. The patient is left to relax undisturbed for half a minute or more. During the hyperventilation he will have felt other sensations, such as flushing of his face and neck, tingling in his extremities and genital organs, visual phenomena such as flashes, coloured lights and blackness, and sometimes momentary dimming of consciousness, all of which quickly subside."

Q. ... When you had your concerns about Michael Haslam, which were pretty concrete by 1984, he was not only treating patients as a general psychiatrist, he was operating the sexual therapy clinic as well?

A. Yes.

Q. Was that an area of particular additional concern?

A. I thought that all his work – I understood at that time that all his work in psychosexual problems was done in partnership with a female therapist.

Q. That means you did not know about the massage, CO₂, et cetera?

A. Not at all. Dr Pattie was a pretty straight lady who would not have countenanced anything like that, so I guess my concerns were not so alerted in that particular area.

15.19 Further, those who were working with Michael Haslam had little or no knowledge of the administration of CO_2 treatment, despite its obvious equipment needs. For example, Dr Rowena Yates (mentioned above) stated:

Q. You were asked about treatments. This is part of why you did not know, why other colleagues did not know. I only want to look at two of them, and that is the carbon dioxide therapy and massage. First of all, the CO₂ therapy, you told us that was something which was in the past, in the days of coma treatment?

A. Yes.

Q. When you heard about it at the trial, in the newspapers, the words you used were that you were "shocked" that it was going on. But how could it go on without your knowledge? I find that curious.

A. Well, I cannot understand that myself.

Q. It would involve a tank of gas, it would involve an opportunity to use the ECT suite or some other room. Is there any way that you can explain?

A. Well, Clifton Hospital is a big place, and I was both at Clifton and the District.

Q. Are you surprised that it was not discussed with you?

A. I am, yes.

Q. So surprised that you are horrified that your senior consultant was using a treatment which presumably he believed in, unless it was for exploitative purposes, he would want you to know about it, would he not?

A. I know it sounds strange, but I did not know really.

15.20 The evidence to the Inquiry indicates that Michael Haslam was administering CO_2 inhalation therapy to patients generally, and not only to patients attending the psychosexual clinic.

15.21 In his criminal trial, Michael Haslam accepted that he gave the CO_2 treatment to female patients without any nursing attendance and without any chaperone present. It is clear from the evidence we have heard that Michael Haslam used the carbon dioxide therapy technique alone, at the end of the day, and with vulnerable female patients. There is no suggestion that the treatment was administered in secret – indeed, Michael Haslam wrote to GPs to explain that the treatment was being used. However, it is also clear that the use of carbon dioxide therapy could potentially be abused by a psychiatrist – by changing the mix of gases to cause loss of consciousness, to exploit the one-to-one meetings, and to exploit the known side-effects referred to above in the footnote (although probably not known to the patient).

Kirlian photography

15.22 Kirlian photography is the production of an image of the electromagnetic field around living tissue. The theory is that the type of pattern produced in the electromagnetic field varies and that this may be used as a diagnostic tool.

15.23 Michael Haslam's research project (funded by the York Health Authority Research Committee) consisted of building up a library of pictures to determine whether there were consistent patterns that were diagnostic of mood, etc. Michael Haslam used a large camera called a K829, which consisted of a portable trolley with a white box on top of it and a black box beneath that. The patient would place their hand on the photographic paper and images were produced which needed to be developed in darkroom conditions (Michael Haslam would develop and "fix" the photographs in the Kirlian room).

15.24 In his evidence on this subject, Michael Haslam said: "The technique is used and known world wide, and much research is available and published."

15.25 The Inquiry has been provided with documents used by the defence at Michael Haslam's criminal trial. They show that Kirlian photography was the subject of a six-day conference in London in 1990: the Second International Conference for Medical and Applied Bioelectrography. Michael Haslam was a speaker at that conference.

15.26 Expert evidence was presented by the defence at the criminal trial in 2003. Mrs Rosemary Steele, Vice-President of the International Union for Medical and Applied Bioelectrography, gave evidence to confirm that the technique was widely used in acupuncture. She said: "There are probably in the region of 2,000 practitioners in Europe and all over the world … who use the fingertips and toetips for the acupuncture balances."

15.27 The issue, therefore, does not appear to be in relation to research into the efficacy of Kirlian photography, but rather that Michael Haslam's use of the Kirlian photographic process, including the locked and darkened room, led to some women patients raising concerns or complaints about alleged sexual impropriety. And this was in relation to a psychiatrist who was the subject of expressions of concerns and complaints, regarding alleged sexual relationships with some of his female patients.

15.28 The use of Kirlian photography formed the background to the complaint of rape by Patient B7 (eventually dismissed by the Court of Appeal, Criminal Division), and to the concerns expressed by Patient B12.

Massage

15.29 This topic deserves more detailed attention. Again, we emphasise that there is no intention to criticise massage, or even assess its use, for bona fide purposes by bona fide practitioners. It is generally likely to be relaxing, and may have many other benefits. However, its use by Michael Haslam, a male consultant psychiatrist, in the one-to-one, private "treatment" of his female patients and in the context of a psychiatric therapeutic consultation, should have been known to hospital staff and administrators and should have been the subject of careful monitoring and close scrutiny.

15.30 At his criminal trial, Michael Haslam called Dr Michael Crowe, an eminent psychiatrist who specialised in psychosexual treatments. He has also provided assistance to the Inquiry as an independent expert witness. At the criminal trial, in relation to the use of massage, Dr Crowe was of the opinion that it was both unwise and capable of misinterpretation for a consultant to ask a patient to remove all her clothing in preparation for a massage. Indeed, the Inquiry recognised that it was not a usual component of psychiatric practice.

15.31 The Inquiry proceeds on the admitted basis that Michael Haslam was carrying out massage on patients during the relevant period. The Inquiry is aware that his use of massage was limited but, where it occurred, it clearly gave rise in some instances to concerns. He states that he had completed a course on massage therapy, and had a certificate of competence. We do not consider this to be relevant to whether or not Michael Haslam should have used massage on his patients, and whether or not its use should have been monitored.

15.32 In his statement to the Inquiry dated 17 March 2004, Michael Haslam says this in relation to massage:

"I have accepted in court that my introduction of massage therapy for the relief of tension, with outpatients, and sometimes without a chaperone (for practical reasons, not sinister reasons) was unwise ... Any outpatient who accepted the treatment did so in a purely voluntary way and could have discontinued the treatment at any [time?]. I feel that I should point out that I only used this treatment for a couple of years because of its impracticality and some ethical concerns ... Twenty years on, massage treatment is now widely used. A lot of treatments first introduced by doctors are subsequently taken up and handed over to other professionals. Most of the public are aware of its value."

15.33   Whether Michael Haslam used massage for "a couple of years" or longer, it is unlikely that such massages were a rare event, and most likely that the massages were carried out flesh-to-flesh (Michael Haslam admits the use of baby oil and/or talcum powder) and without any other person present. The patients were naked (or semi-naked), covered (if at all) by a towel or blanket. How the towel/blanket was manoeuvred (or not) with such treatments could readily be misinterpreted (or correctly interpreted) by the patient. At best, as described during an exchange at Michael Haslam's trial, it was probably always something of a "rigmarole" and a potential source of discomfort to both doctor and patient.

15.34   Even without the experiments with Kirlian photography, and the use of carbon dioxide therapy, the massaging of patients by a treating consultant psychiatrist seems to us to be a recipe for disaster, creating a clear opportunity for sexual contact or, at least, sexual grooming. What is the female patient to think, given that it is likely to be a patient who is mentally unwell, also likely to be on medication, suffering from some degree of distress, and possibly unhappy at home or in her personal relationships? This kind of massaging of such patients by a person in a relationship of such power imbalance was bound to encourage confused thoughts of affection/domination, and lead to some degree of sexual arousal.

15.35   Based on the conviction of Michael Haslam for the offence of sexual assault in relation to a patient, the Inquiry considers it safe to proceed on the basis that sexual arousal or sexual grooming was Michael Haslam's intention, at least in relation to that patient. But even if it was not, the massage procedure was inherently dangerous and should not have happened, nor should it have been allowed to happen.

15.36 Michael Haslam was asked, at the oral hearings, to comment on the topic of massaging his patients. He had already accepted, in the criminal trial and in written statements to the Inquiry, that the massaging was "unwise". He further accepted that with physical contact it created a real risk of boundaries being blurred and eventually crossed if the physical contact became extensive.

15.37 We have formed the clear view that Michael Haslam's use of massage was not only "unwise", but was part of his attempt to seduce or sexually groom female patients, as evidenced by the conviction for a sexual assault that occurred during one of the massage sessions. The massage by a consultant psychiatrist of women patients with baby oil and talcum powder, when they were naked (or semi-naked) and unchaperoned, was simply wrong and would have been seen as wrong by fellow consultants and by the doctors and administrators at the hospital where it was carried out – if known to them.

15.38 The massaging of a naked (or semi-naked) female psychiatric patient by a male psychiatrist (particularly unchaperoned) is a clear and obvious crossing of the boundaries that should exist between psychiatrist and patient. That kind of physical touch could potentially arouse complicated feelings in the patient, feelings that might be likely to be sexualised by her even if the practitioner had no intention to sexualise the contact. It would very rarely, if ever, be appropriate or wise for a psychiatrist to provide massage to a patient for therapeutic purposes.

15.39 Michael Haslam's wife, in her correspondence with the Inquiry, said: "The much maligned massage technique is now used for stress problems in health clinics without chaperones." But this comment, and comments to similar effect by Michael Haslam (and those who have contacted the Inquiry on his behalf), are missing the point of concern. The technique of massage is not being "maligned" at all. It is of course accepted that massage may be very relaxing, and may well reduce stress. It may also be the case that male to female massage can be carried out, and is carried out "in health clinics without chaperones", although we have sought no evidence on that issue. What causes us concern, and seems also to have caused concern for professional witnesses to the Inquiry, is that Michael

Haslam, as a consultant psychiatrist with responsibility for the care and well-being of vulnerable and unwell women, chose to offer them one-on-one massage as a "special" service. We have not seen any evidence in this Inquiry, or in the GMC investigation, or in the criminal trial of Michael Haslam, to suggest that the additional massage service was offered by Michael Haslam to, or delivered by Michael Haslam to, male patients. We would be extremely surprised if such a service, by a person in such a position of power and responsibility, was offered to such patients within the current mental health services of the NHS. If, as may be suggested by Mrs Haslam, it is currently happening in the NHS, then we strongly advise that the practice should be reviewed and very closely monitored. Similarly, if, as suggested by Michael Haslam, "massage treatment is now widely used" by psychiatrists, again there should be an early review of that practice.

15.40 What is also a cause for concern is that doctors, nurses and other staff working at Clifton and Bootham Park Hospitals at the relevant time did not appear to be aware that Michael Haslam was massaging his female patients. Witness after witness was asked about this topic. The response was consistent – they knew nothing of the practice, and if they had known they would have been concerned.

15.41 Michael Haslam's use of massage on hospital premises should have been known about, and should have been monitored – and, we believe, immediately stopped.

Hypnotism

15.42 The evidence before the Inquiry shows that both William Kerr and Michael Haslam used hypnotism, or hypnotherapy, as part of their treatment of, or dealings with, their patients. There is clear evidence to show that William Kerr used hypnotism in the course of domiciliary visits – when he was alone in a house with a female patient. We do not here seek to question the therapeutic value of hypnotism – we are prepared to proceed on the basis that there is a sound evidence base for the use of hypnotherapy in the control of pain and, for example, in the cessation of addictions such as smoking.

15.43 The value of hypnotism is not our concern. Our concern is that the use of hypnotism within the NHS is not regulated and, so far as we are aware, there is no guidance from bodies such as the GMC, the BMA or the Royal College of Psychiatrists (RCP) on when, in what circumstances, or in relation to what (if any) mental disorders, it can properly and reasonably be used. It is for the National Institute of Clinical Excellence (NICE) and the RCP together, not the Inquiry Panel, to decide the efficacy of such treatments in psychiatric practice.

15.44 It also seems to us that it is a therapy that is unlikely to be appropriate for use in the course of a home visit, or in any situation where there is no chaperone present.

15.45 The response from the Department of Health when contacted about regulation of hypnotherapy was as follows:

- At present, there is no regulatory framework governing the practice of hypnotherapy in the UK. The Department encourages all complementary therapists, including hypnotherapists, to register with a reputable voluntary regulatory body. This body should have transparent, effective and rigorous codes of conduct and ethics.

- The Department of Health is aware of a number of voluntary regulatory bodies with regard to the practice of hypnotherapy. However, the Department does not endorse any of these bodies.

- The Government has no current plans to extend statutory regulation to other complementary and alternative medicine (CAM) therapies. It expects unregulated CAM therapies, including hypnotherapy, to develop their own unified systems of voluntary regulation. In order to achieve this, individual therapies must come together under a single regulatory body.

- The Government's first priority is to put in place statutory regulation for herbal medicine and acupuncture. It agreed with the House of Lords Select Committee on Science and Technology that these two therapies were at a stage where it would be of benefit to them and the patients to work towards statutory regulation.

Recommendations

We RECOMMEND that procedures and policies should be put in place, within 12 months of the publication of this Report, to ensure that all NHS organisations are aware of the therapies being undertaken by all staff, particularly those where patients believe clinical governance committees should be aware of them and making decisions about their use.

We RECOMMEND that within mental health services no member of the healthcare team should be permitted to use or pursue new or unorthodox treatments without discussion and approval by the team (such approval to be recorded in writing).

We RECOMMEND that in relation to such identified "new or unorthodox treatments", patients should be given written explanations of the treatments, and why their use is appropriate.

We RECOMMEND that the full range of physical, psychological and complementary therapies used by mental health professionals should be recorded and discussed through appraisal/job plans. Trusts should have a clear evidence base and protocols for guiding the use of these treatments.

We RECOMMEND that the NHS should reconsider whether or not statutory regulation should be extended to cover hypnotherapy.

Chapter 16
The expressions of concerns and complaints by patients

The detail of the patient concerns and complaints

Introduction

16.1 As with William Kerr, here we set out in some detail the concerns and complaints known to the Inquiry regarding Michael Haslam, without attempting to reach any conclusion as to the veracity of the accounts. We are well aware that this necessary restriction of the scope of our Inquiry has caused some distress and anxiety for former patients who wanted not only their voices to be heard, but also their stories to be believed.

16.2 This approach does not apply to the allegations against Michael Haslam, which form the subject matter of the three convictions for sexual assault upheld by the Court of Appeal.

16.3 Unlike the position with William Kerr, the Inquiry has received some response from Michael Haslam in relation to the factual allegations. We have identified in the text of the report his denials of any wrongdoing or inappropriate behaviour.

16.4 Michael Haslam took up the post of Consultant in Psychological Medicine at Clifton Hospital, York, and Harrogate District Hospital in 1970. A few years later, in 1974, the first complaint (of which the Inquiry is aware) concerning Michael Haslam was brought to the attention of a local GP. It is clear from the lack of surprise, which was the reaction of at least one consultant to whom the disclosure was made, that predating 1974 there were already rumours, at least in the consultant community, that: "Michael Haslam's behaviour with patients was less than appropriate."

Patient B1

16.5 Patient B1 first saw Michael Haslam in January 1973 at Harrogate General Hospital following a referral from her GP, Dr Ann Jones. She had been diagnosed as suffering from depression. Patient B1 was a university-educated, married woman in her early 30s with two children. She was treated by Michael Haslam with prescribed medicine and advised to attend his psychotherapy clinic at the Royal Bath Hospital.

16.6 Patient B1's written statement to the Inquiry explained:

> *"He [Haslam] became more and more familiar with me. I do know that I have a very hazy recollection of a lot of the consultations because I was taking so many drugs at the time, I was not really with it. He used to make me feel special, he would be flattering. I was in a very low ebb at that time and the fact that somebody was complimenting my appearance, how I looked and started to make suggestions about having a relationship, I suppose was quite flattering at the time.*

> *"I would say that we had sexual intercourse on about four or five occasions. I remember that we went to a place close to York racecourse but I cannot tell you where it is. I remember we used to go to the sauna together."*

16.7 Medical records confirm that Patient B1's last appointment with Michael Haslam was on 14 March 1974. Patient B1 described coming out of a consultation with Michael Haslam on this occasion and seeing a blonde-haired woman waiting for the next appointment. According to Patient B1, Michael Haslam made a reference to "one blonde in, one brunette out", which caused Patient B1 to speculate that Michael Haslam was having an affair with this woman as well. Patient B1's evidence was as follows:

> *"I realised that it was not just me that he was having a relationship with. It made me realise actually that this had not been a special relationship, he was just using me as one of his patients."*

16.8 Indeed Patient B1 subsequently made contact with the "blonde woman" who confirmed that Haslam was "propositioning her", flattering her and suggesting they have an affair, although Patient B1 was unclear as to whether matters ever progressed to a sexual relationship.

16.9 Patient B1, having concluded that she was not the only patient whom Michael Haslam had been propositioning, ceased appointments and told her husband of her sexual relationship with Michael Haslam. Patient B1 and her husband decided that all appointments with Michael Haslam should cease immediately and that Patient B1 should instead seek help, in the first instance from her GP, Dr Foggitt.

16.10 Accordingly on 18 March 1974, four days after her final appointment with Michael Haslam, Patient B1 went to see Dr Foggitt. Patient B1's recollection is that she informed Dr Foggitt that she had been having an affair with Michael Haslam. The following is an extract from her oral evidence to the Inquiry:

> *Q. What were you wanting Dr Foggitt to do? What was your expectation?*
>
> *A. I think I probably wanted help. This had happened and he had started this relationship with me, then he had sort of rejected me, like everybody else had. I thought, in my mind at the time, and probably I was going to him to get help.*
>
> *Q. Help from a different medical practitioner?*
>
> *A. Yes.*
>
> *Q. Rather than looking to Dr Foggitt to make some sort of formal complaint about Michael Haslam's behaviour?*
>
> *A. I think probably I thought that he would have made a complaint. What I remember telling him about what had happened, he did not say anything. I remember trying to tell him about what had been going on – I cannot remember how many months it was – and trying to tell him, and he just did not answer me, he just sort of sat there. And I remember thinking, "Oh well, they are all closing ranks, he will not do anything against Dr Haslam, because they are all doctors together."*

Q. Beyond a silence, what was it that gave you that impression that there was going to be a closing of ranks? Is there anything in particular you can remember?

A. I think I remember asking him whether he should be reported, Dr Haslam. I think he probably said, "Well, it is very difficult to prove." I do not think he believed me. I think he probably thought I was a neurotic woman, which I was, and I was making this whole thing up.

Q. In terms of what you wanted, what would have been the reaction, if you could have chosen the reaction from your GP, what would you have been looking for?

A. I think the GP should have reported Dr Haslam and there should have been an investigation, he should have been struck off for what he had done.

16.11   Due to problems with recall caused by a medical condition, Dr Foggitt was not required by the Inquiry to give oral evidence. However, he was able to provide the Inquiry with a written statement setting out his recollection of Patient B1's disclosure of a relationship with Michael Haslam. Some of his evidence was inconsistent with that of Patient B1 and her husband. In particular, we prefer the evidence of Patient B1 and her husband, that Patient B1 herself informed him of the alleged affair, which is contrary to Dr Foggitt's memory that Patient B1's husband was the informant. However, the Panel were assisted by Dr Foggitt's evidence regarding his response to Patient B1's disclosure. This evidence chimes with the accounts we have received from other GPs describing the attitude and culture of the time.

"It seemed to me that Haslam had been very foolish. It was human weakness, quite possibly professional misconduct, but not a crime. I was probably not in favour of reporting the matter to the authorities because I probably did have concerns about Patient B1 and her husband going public on the matter, especially with Patient B1 being vulnerable. I would have been concerned that further stress might wreck their marriage. Reporting the matter to the authorities was likely to do more harm than good as far as Patient B1 was concerned and that was what troubled me most. In order to understand my thinking at the time, it must also be remembered that as far as I was concerned this was a one-off. There was nothing to alert me to a bigger problem. I did not know Haslam to be other than a good psychiatrist.

"I do not believe that I discussed Patient B1's affair with Dr Haslam with my partners. I think I kept it to myself. As to why I did not report what I had learnt to the authorities, I have a feeling that it was probably not part of the culture at the time to report another doctor to the GMC and, if Patient B1 was not in a position to pursue the matter any further, she and her husband had no wish to do so, it would have been virtually impossible to proceed."

16.12 Following his wife's appointment with Dr Foggitt, Patient B1's husband telephoned Michael Haslam. He threatened Haslam that any further contact with his wife would lead to him being reported to the regulatory authorities.

16.13 The evidence of the husband of Patient B1 was that following this telephone call he received a letter from Michael Haslam, suggesting that it would do irreparable damage to Patient B1 to take action against him, due to her current illness, and appealing to Patient B1's husband not to take action, due to the effect such action would have on Haslam's own wife and children. Unfortunately this letter is no longer in existence.

16.14 Patient B1's husband expressed regret to the Inquiry that he had not come forward at the time to make a complaint, but explained that he felt his wife was too ill to be put through any form of local or national inquiry and that foremost in his mind was the welfare of his wife and their children.

"I had a wish to take it further, because I felt that this unprofessional conduct was quite unforgivable and was a danger to other patients, having seen the disturbance to my wife. But, as I have said in my statement, it was absolutely of paramount importance to me to make sure that I did not upset her again."

16.15 In April 1974, Michael Haslam wrote to Dr Foggitt with a summary of Patient B1's treatment. This letter describes Patient B1's problems, suggesting an extramarital affair, without making any allusion to the identity of her lover. It explains Patient B1's alleged relationship with Michael Haslam in terms of "transference" and "counter transference" and even acknowledges "a chance conversation" with an outpatient leading to Patient B1's feelings of "rejection" and of her husband's decision that treatment by Haslam should cease. The letter ends with a suggestion that, "supportive psychotherapy perhaps with a female psychotherapist would be helpful".

16.16 As set out at the beginning of this section, and has been constantly emphasised in this Report, we do not seek to make findings of fact as to whether alleged sexual misconduct took place. However, this letter demonstrates the difficulty encountered where a complaint is not immediately acted upon and the patient and notes removed to a new consultant (for the protection of both patient and doctor).

16.17 We find as a fact that a disclosure of a sexual relationship had been made by Patient B1 to Dr Foggitt – indeed that much is common ground between Patient B1 and Dr Foggitt. We also find that Patient B1's husband telephoned Michael Haslam, alerting him to the fact that Patient B1 had made a disclosure of a relationship. This left a situation where Michael Haslam, despite being aware of the disclosure, was still in a position to contribute to Patient B1's medical notes and to her medical history, in this case by writing a letter to her GP to summarise her condition. We find that the April 1974 letter was written some time after the disclosure by Patient B1 to Dr Foggitt, and some time after the conversation between Michael Haslam and Patient B1's husband. Whether or not the April letter was deliberately drafted to be self-serving remains unclear. However, its terms produce strong feelings of unease. The letter does, however, reveal a further potential detriment to any patient, where there is an unresolved allegation of an intimate or sexual relationship with a treating consultant psychiatrist – particularly where that patient is vulnerable. The consultant has an opportunity to contribute to the patient's medical history – by notes or letters – in a way which may not tell the whole story, or the true story, and which may be intended to serve the interests of the clinician rather than the interests of the patient. And, of course, the vulnerable patient is unlikely to be aware of the contents of the notes or letter.

16.18   Whilst Dr Foggitt did not pursue the complaint against Michael Haslam through any formal channels, he did take the step of referring Patient B1 to an "out of region" psychiatrist, Dr Clarkson at Scalebor Park, and informed Dr Clarkson of the reason for the change of consultant.

16.19   Dr Foggitt had no specific recollection of the referral, but accepted in his written statement:

> *"I am sure that I would have told Dr Clarkson about the matter and the family's wish not to take the matter further; after all he would want some explanation as to why Patient B1 was changing consultants and being referred out of the area."*

16.20   This is consistent with the tone of a letter sent by Dr Clarkson to Dr Foggitt on 20 March 1974, which makes an oblique reference to the alleged affair with Michael Haslam, in his diagnosis of Patient B1:

> *"Mild reactive depression to a situation with which you are familiar."*

16.21   Patient B1 herself had a recollection of discussing her alleged "affair" with Haslam with Dr Clarkson during her brief admission to Scalebor Park:

> *Q. ... So you went in on the 20th and came out on the 21st, having had a brief discussion with Dr Clarkson?*
>
> *A. An unsatisfactory discussion.*
>
> *Q. Why was it unsatisfactory?*
>
> *A. Because I do think he did not believe me. He gave me no comfort. I was looking for some support and comfort from doctors, which I did not get.*

Q. When you say he did not believe you, that was about the relationship between yourself and Michael Haslam?

A. Yes, he was trying to cover it up, and, again, no comment.

16.22 Dr Clarkson was also able to recollect the circumstances of the referral of Patient B1 from Dr Foggitt:

A. My recollection, such as it is, is that he [Dr Foggitt] called me on the telephone and explained that he had a patient that he would like me to see, who had been seeing Dr Haslam and did not wish to see him again, and there was a rather indirect allusion to the reasons for that.

Q. Whilst it was indirect, it was an allusion that you readily understood as being an allegation of sexual misconduct of some sort?

A. Yes.

Q. That allegation of sexual misconduct, did you form the view that it was likely to be of the same character that you understood to have been the subject of rumours relating to Michael Haslam: namely, that this was inappropriate touching?

A. That is what I assume, yes.

Q. Can I press you a little bit more on what your understanding was of inappropriate touching and what you thought might have been going on with this particular psychiatrist?

A. Yes, I suppose touching would have been of a sexual nature, either on the breasts or other parts of the body that one would not normally do.

Q. This would, in your mind, presumably, have amounted to a form of sexual assault?

A. I would say so, yes.

Q. Therefore, a criminal activity rather than just, as it were, simple misconduct?

A. Again I find that somewhat difficult to answer, because I do think customs and attitudes were different in those days. Whether it would have been seen as criminal or just stupid, I am not sure.

16.23 Dr Clarkson's recollection of his discussion with Patient B1 was that she admitted that there had been inappropriate contact by Michael Haslam, but that she did not discuss it in detail and did not wish him (Dr Clarkson) to do anything about it. His evidence was that he remained unclear as to the nature of any relationship or inappropriate contact.

16.24 Dr Clarkson was questioned by Counsel to the Inquiry as to why he had taken no action in response to learning that Michael Haslam had allegedly been behaving inappropriately towards one of his female patients, consistent with the rumours he had previously been aware of:

Q. But there must have been in your mind some appreciation that the reactive depression that she was suffering from may be a reactive depression that other patients might suffer in future if they were referred to this same doctor who exhibited this same behaviour who had been the subject of rumours?

A. Certainly, yes.

Q. Did that not override any obligation you felt with regard to this patient, because there must have been other patients who were at risk?

A. I am sure it was something that occurred to me. But I think that – I can only assume my clinical judgment was that she – that I had to respect her wishes [that the matter be taken no further].

Q. Beyond her immediate clinical position there is a wider concern, is there not? Is there not a wider duty to other patients who might be exposed to the same risk that she had been exposed to when referred to Michael Haslam?

A. Yes.

Q. Could not that have been addressed by, for example, going to Region and saying, "I cannot tell you the name of this individual patient, but I think it is right that you be aware that a consultant operating in North Yorkshire is a cause of concern to me, having seen a particular patient"?

A. Yes, that is possible. I do not know. I suspect if I had gone to the Region with that, they would have told me to produce evidence.

Q. I am just trying to explore the reasons why you might not have done that. That is one possible reason, that you felt you might be sent away and told to get evidence. Is there any other reason you can think of that might have deterred you from taking it further.

A. I think that was the attitude of Region in those days to that sort of complaint, it was seen as having no substance.

Q. One other possibility – and I do not want to be unfair to you in putting this to you, but I think it is right that I do put it to you – that has been suggested by other witnesses to the Inquiry is that the culture was: doctors do not snitch on other doctors. Was there any extent of that which may have impacted on your thinking? You may not use a word such as "snitch", but you used the word "loyalty" yourself. Was there an element of loyalty that might have precluded you from taking a concern to region?

A. I think that there is some degree of that, there must be, yes.

16.25 Dr Clarkson did not take any steps to report his concerns about Michael Haslam to any of the authorities. However, it is clear that the case of Patient B1 remained firmly in his mind. Six years later, in 1980, when Dr Kennedy commenced at York, Dr Clarkson informed him that he had once taken over a patient of Michael Haslam's due to "some kind of sexual allegation". The patient to whom he was referring was Patient B1.

16.26 When questioned about why he had not made any report of the matter earlier than 1980, Dr Clarkson's explanation was that at the time of the disclosure he had respected Patient B1's wish not to pursue the matter, but that when Dr Kennedy arrived in York, a person he knew and trusted, he felt it proper to pass the matter on, in the expectation that it would assist Dr Kennedy in the enquiries he was making. It is clear to us that Dr Clarkson felt that he should have done *something*. It was not only the knowledge of the alleged sexual relationship that was gnawing away – it was the concern that there may be other patients, other vulnerable patients, who may have been taken advantage of by Michael Haslam, if the original allegation was true.

16.27   We consider it regrettable that both Dr Foggitt and Dr Clarkson, well aware of the allegation that Michael Haslam had behaved in a sexually inappropriate way towards Patient B1 (a current, and vulnerable, patient), did nothing to alert the responsible authorities to the potential risk of danger to other patients. Dr Foggitt's evidence-free conclusion (in 1974) that this was a "one-off", and that Michael Haslam had merely been "foolish", echoes down the years. Had Dr Foggitt made some kind of report and had Dr Clarkson made some kind of report, then subsequent expressions of concern may have been taken more seriously. We do not find that there was a deliberate cover-up between Dr Foggitt and Dr Clarkson. However, their individual and combined inaction does give the unfortunate impression of doctors sticking together – or as Patient B1 put it "doctors closing ranks".

16.28   Michael Haslam's response to the allegations of Patient B1 (whose name he was shown), put to him in the context of this Inquiry, was as follows:

> *"I have not the slightest idea who [Patient B1] is – 32 years ago? Heaven help us! I must have seen thousands of people since then."*

16.29   Michael Haslam had no recollection of receiving any telephone call from Patient B1's husband, and his response to Dr Clarkson's suggestion that there were rumours in the consultant community concerning his practice was that the various senior appointments and posts he held during his career contradicted this.

Patient B2

16.30   Two years after Patient B1's disclosure of her alleged sexual relationship with Michael Haslam, another allegation came to the fore.

16.31 Whereas Patient B1's disclosure had remained within the team of those treating her, namely Dr Foggitt and Dr Clarkson, Patient B2's disclosure in 1976 was of a far more formal nature. She instructed solicitors to act on her behalf and an official letter of complaint was sent to York Health District.

16.32 Solicitors instructed on behalf of Patient B2 wrote to Mr Holroyd, District Administrator to the York Health District (1974–1982), on 4 June 1976, stating that Patient B2 had been referred to Michael Haslam by Dr Warren in February 1974. The letter alleged that whilst Patient B2 was under the care of Michael Haslam, he had instigated a sexual relationship that lasted from July/August 1974 until May 1976. It was said that sexual intercourse took place at hospital premises, particularly at the end of the Friday clinic, and also at other locations. Patient B2 was said to have been on strong anti-depressants and tranquillisers during this sexual relationship.

16.33 Patient B2 did not come forward to the Inquiry, and we have not received any written or oral evidence from her. Our knowledge of Patient B2's complaint is confined to 1976 and 1977 letters and memos, and the evidence of Mr Holroyd, the District Administrator at York.

16.34 Mr Holroyd's oral evidence to the Inquiry was that he, "could not have been more surprised" by the letter concerning Patient B2 and that he recognised it as being "the most serious possible sort of issue, if established". Prior to receipt of this letter, Mr Holroyd had believed that Michael Haslam's Psychosexual Clinic was the "jewel in the crown" at Clifton Hospital and he had heard of no negative rumours. Mr Holroyd's recollection was that immediately having received the solicitor's letter he, in all likelihood, discussed the matter with Dr McIntosh, the District Medical Officer, before speaking to Michael Haslam.

16.35 We pause here to note the similarities between Patient B1 and Patient B2. Both women were well educated and/or held positions of professional responsibility. In both cases they were referred to Michael Haslam suffering from depression and some sexual problems. Patient B1 was said to have suffered, according to his patient notes, in Michael Haslam's words, "loss of libido" and Patient B2 was specifically referred due to psychosexual problems. Finally both women make particular comment that their treatment included strong medication affecting their behaviour (Patient B1 describes being unable to look after children, and Patient B2 was unable to continue in her work due to the effects of the drugs). Patient B2 makes the specific allegation that the drugs she was prescribed were intended to "facilitate intercourse". It is also of note that in terms of chronology, the alleged relationships appear to be closely consecutive. Patient B1's alleged affair with Michael Haslam is said to have ended in March 1974, and the relationship with Patient B2 allegedly commenced in July/August 1974.

16.36 The Inquiry commissioned an independent audit of William Kerr and Michael Haslam's prescribing practices. The pharmacist, who had experience of working during the relevant period through to the present day, found prescribing as recorded on prescription charts to be within the normal limits for the period.

16.37 Evidence from expert witnesses also concludes that although prescribed oral medication may have had an impact on concentration and recall, it would not have affected the reliability of former patients' accounts.

16.38 In the letter from Patient B2's solicitors to Mr Holroyd, reference is made to one particular incident on 5 May 1976, when it is claimed Michael Haslam visited Patient B2 at home and sexual intercourse took place. Patient B2 was said to have been left in a suicidal state. Patient B2 allegedly informed Michael Haslam that she was suicidal and did subsequently take an overdose, being admitted to Pontefract General Hospital. The solicitors' letter stated that Michael Haslam himself, and Dr Warren, were both aware of the possibility of Patient B2 making a complaint, and expressed concern that she had received anonymous phone calls threatening her with trouble if she took any action regarding her complaint (the clear implication being that Michael Haslam had made or instigated these threats).

16.39 Dr McIntosh, whilst acknowledging that the documents revealed his involvement, had no independent recollection of the complaint by Patient B2:

Q. Do you recall that in the mid 1970s there was some sort of complaint against Michael Haslam or do you have absolutely no recollection at all?

A. I have a complete blank in my mind about that. It is clear that there were two meetings and I was present at both of them, so I have to accept that I was there. But I do not remember the complaint or any detail about it.

16.40 Mr Holroyd's rationale for immediately telephoning Michael Haslam on receipt of the solicitors' letter was in order to give him the "right to reply". Mr Holroyd's evidence was as follows:

"It was not my role to investigate. I was clear as soon as I read that letter that it would go to the Regional Health Authority (RHA) in one way or another. It was not for me to investigate. But I was giving him the right to reply and I was wanting to ensure that I knew his reply in order to pass that on to Region."

16.41 Handwritten notes made by Mr Holroyd record the conversation with Michael Haslam on 7 June 1976. It appears that Michael Haslam accepted that he had made a home visit on 5 May 1976 at Patient B2's request and that on this occasion she mentioned suicide, although he considered there was no serious intent to carry out such action. Michael Haslam denied that sexual intercourse had taken place. The telephone note does record Michael Haslam describing his "working relationship" with Patient B2 (who, it is said, was assisting him in producing a book on his psychosexual work) and also his "social relationship" with Patient B2 and her husband. The note also records that Patient B2's GP, Dr Dobey, was aware of her intention of complaining.

16.42 Also on 7 June 1976, Patient B2's solicitors telephoned Mr Holroyd to inform him that there was some "supporting evidence", including photographs, and that the purpose of their client's complaint was to halt Michael Haslam's activities for the benefit of others. Mr Holroyd's recollection was that Michael Haslam accepted he had been involved in transvestite activities when the issue of photographs was raised, and accordingly Mr Holroyd inferred this was the subject matter of the photographs referred to. It seems that Mr Holroyd accepted, without question, Michael Haslam's explanation that the photographic evidence related to "an entirely social cross-dressing event attended by him at a club", an event that was "outside work and had no connection with patients". How the photographic evidence got into the possession of a patient, Patient B2, who was complaining of sexual impropriety, does not appear to have troubled Mr Holroyd at all.

16.43   Michael Haslam was formally notified of the complaint by Mr Holroyd in a letter dated 9 June 1976. Mr Holroyd informed Michael Haslam that he had shown Patient B2's letter of complaint to Dr McIntosh, Dr Bertie Moore (the Area Medical Officer) and Mr Bill Moore (the Area Administrator) and that it had been decided that no action would be taken until Michael Haslam had had a chance to contact the Medical Defence Union. Michael Haslam responded, through his then solicitors, by letters of 1 and 13 July 1976, denying any sexual relationship with Patient B2 and then expanding upon this denial:

> "Dr Haslam unequivocally denies that he instigated a sexual relationship with Patient B2 and that at any time that sexual intercourse between them took place."

16.44   Michael Haslam's response to the allegations of Patient B2 were again put to him in the context of this Inquiry and his comments in his written statement were as follows:

> "Indeed I remember [Patient B2]. She worked for the Health Authority. She is the woman I referred to in one of my witness statements as having made a complaint in the 1970s but chose to withdraw it. You gave some details and papers sent to me at the beginning of the Inquiry. Of course I saw her. She worked for the Health Authority. Mr Holroyd also referred to it in a letter to me with regard to the court case at which he gave evidence in November 2003. However, I have to say that Patient B2 is lying when she says that there was any sexual contact on the occasion that I called to give her a prescription. I remember the occasion well, but without her written permission, I would not deem it proper to comment further and indeed shall not. She withdrew her complaint for reasons best known to herself. Mr Holroyd can hardly press her complaint as it ceased to be one and which would be against the wishes of the ex-complainant. I know nothing of any telephone calls. They certainly would not be from me if they existed. It is not my style. I did not see her professionally after the date she refers to."

16.45 On 19 July 1976, six weeks after first receiving the solicitors' letter, and having by this time also discussed the matter with the Chairman of the Area Health Authority, Mr Hazell, Mr Holroyd referred Patient B2's complaint to Mr Inman, the Regional Administrator of the Yorkshire Regional Health Authority.

16.46 Mr Holroyd explained that his decision to wait for Michael Haslam's response before referring the matter to Region, was approved by Mr Hazell. Their view was that, to have any real prospect of engaging Region, they would need to send a "considered reply". Anything less would have been returned to them for further investigation.

16.47 On 12 April 1977, 10 months after the initial letter of complaint from Patient B2's solicitors, Mr Inman responded to Mr Holroyd, stating that he had been informed by the patient's solicitors that she had decided not to press her complaints against Michael Haslam, although she was not prepared to sign any formal withdrawal of complaint, rather wishing to let matters simply rest.

16.48 We have been unable to discover what, if any, investigation or action took place in the period from July 1976 to April 1977, whilst the Regional Health Authority were in possession of the complaint against Michael Haslam. This lack of information or any documentary record strongly suggests that in fact there was no investigation of Michael Haslam's practice. Indeed Michael Haslam told us in his oral evidence that he had no recollection of even being interviewed by the Regional Health Authority.

16.49 Mr Holroyd's response when asked about the delay was that although it was possible contact was made with Michael Haslam without his involvement, that was unlikely and nothing was in fact done.

16.50 When questioned about unease at the existence of an unresolved complaint against Michael Haslam, Mr Holroyd's response, perhaps naturally, was to place responsibility with Region, who he correctly recognised as Michael Haslam's employer:

> "So we had the message from the most senior person possible [Mr Inman] that the matter had come to an end and no caution, warning or whatever guidance, had been given to us either formally, as part of the letter, or informally."

16.51 Significantly Dr Turner, who took over as Regional Medical Officer in 1976, had no knowledge of the complaint. This would suggest that not only did the Regional Health Authority fail to launch any investigation into the complaint (whilst still live) or into Michael Haslam's practice, they also failed to keep any file of past complaints. This is of particular concern as Dr Turner, who as Regional Medical Officer was charged with responsibility of handling serious complaints of professional misconduct against consultants, subsequently came to deal with the complaint by Patient B3 against Michael Haslam in 1984. As Dr Turner accepted in his oral evidence, had he known of the Patient B2 complaint, his handling of the Patient B3 complaint would have been different.

16.52 We accept that Mr Holroyd is not to be criticised for the failings at Regional level. He performed his (limited) role by passing on the complaint (with Michael Haslam's response) to Region.

16.53 Counsel for the Health Authorities accepted in her closing submissions to the Inquiry that "it did not appear that any investigation was carried out by Region". We agree. Our conclusion, therefore, in relation to the investigation of Patient B2's complaint made in 1976, was that there was no investigation worthy of the name – at District or Regional level. Serious allegations were made, Michael Haslam denied them, and that appears to have been the end of it. There is nothing to suggest that Patient B2 was interviewed – with or without her solicitor. There is nothing to suggest that the corroborating evidence (such as photographs) was sought and examined. There is nothing to suggest that there was even any attempt to seek any expansion of the allegations set out briefly in the June 1976 letter.

16.54 It is highly regrettable that the Region file has been lost, or has been destroyed – if there was any such file. However, we expect that, if there was a file, it contained little else other than correspondence and memos.

16.55 Against a background of unexplained inactivity, it is hardly surprising that Patient B2 discontinued her formalised complaint. Of course, that left Region in difficulties – without a complainant, how could they process the complaint? Based on what we have read and heard in relation to Region's handling of this complaint, and subsequent disclosures, we conclude that it was Region's own lack of investigative zeal which caused or contributed to the withdrawal.

16.56 In written and oral submissions, Counsel for the Health Authorities drew our attention to the fact that Patient B2 is an example "of a complaint coming to a halt because the complainant is not prepared to participate in the process". We are not convinced that this was the reason – or at least the sole reason. There is no evidence to suggest that the patient was offered any support, any counselling, any proactive response by the National Health Service at any level, anything at all. Pointing to the withdrawal of the complaint, we conclude, is an over-simplification of the position. However, we do accept that the systems (if there were systems) in place were heavily dependent on there being a willing complainant. We will turn later in the Report to consideration of this problem, and whether there are any recommendations we can make to facilitate investigation, when there is no such willing and able complainant.

16.57 It may be that Patient B1's complaint alone (in 1974), or that of Patient B2 alone (in 1976), would not have led to any action against Michael Haslam. But, as all the relevant witnesses to the Inquiry accepted, an accumulation of concerns and complaints changes the situation. That would, of course, particularly be the case here where there was an existing background of rumour and gossip in relation to the practice of Michael Haslam. Both Patient B1 and Patient B2 were opportunities missed, opportunities which may well have led to a more robust managerial response, to the Patient AB story in 1981, to the Patient A17 story in 1983 (which raised allegations against both Kerr and Haslam), or to later, more specific, allegations of sexual misconduct levelled against Michael Haslam. If the Patient B1 and Patient B2 stories had been put together then, by the time of the Patient AB disclosure in 1981, Mr Holroyd or Region would have been dealing with three complaints, all of a similar nature, made about the same consultant in less than 10 years. And all this in a climate in which (as almost every witness who has given evidence on the point has emphasised) complaints of sexual misconduct, in particular concerning consultants, were a rare event.

Patient AB

16.58 Patient AB is the only patient, of whom we are aware, who has made allegations against both William Kerr and Michael Haslam (see Chapter

10). She was treated by William Kerr in the early 1970s, following an overdose, and alleges he placed his hand on her groin, stared at her breasts, and suggested that she go to London to have sex with hundreds of men.

16.59   Some years later, in November 1979, Patient AB was admitted as an emergency to "the Retreat", a private psychiatric hospital in York. Due to concerns about funding, she was transferred to the care of Michael Haslam at Clifton Hospital, where she completed a course of ECT and was discharged on 3 January 1980. She was followed up by Michael Haslam at the Thirsk outpatient clinic. Patient AB was again admitted to Clifton Hospital on 16 March 1980 and remained an inpatient until 23 April 1980. Thereafter, Michael Haslam continued to treat Patient AB in 1980 and 1981, as an NHS patient.

16.60   It is alleged that Michael Haslam informed Patient AB at some point that he was writing a book on sexual dysfunction and discussed issues of that nature with her. He also asked her whether she would consider massage as a mechanism to reduce her anxiety. She recounts that Michael Haslam arranged to see her on a Saturday afternoon in January or February 1981 at an outbuilding at Clifton Hospital, believed by her to be the day-patient building. She states that he unlocked the building, no one else being present, and proceeded to undress her (pulling her dress over her head). He is then alleged to have massaged her all over using baby oil, caressing her genitals and, as she got down from the couch, kissed her on the mouth. Similar inappropriate touching was said to have occurred approximately two weeks later, in about February 1981. Again the appointment was on a Saturday afternoon at Clifton Hospital in the day-patient outbuilding. On this occasion, Patient AB claims she undressed herself, and that Michael Haslam massaged her, placing his finger in her vagina. She says he also took her hand to touch his genitals and kissed her.

16.61   These allegations of sexual assault formed two counts in Michael Haslam's trial in December 2003. He was convicted and sentenced to 18 months' imprisonment. The convictions, and the sentence, were upheld by the Court of Appeal (Criminal Division).

16.62   Following the second alleged "massage treatment", Patient AB confided in a friend who was a psychiatric nurse, Lynne Davy. Lynne Davy told Patient AB that what was going on was wrong and offered to attend the next appointment, which had also been scheduled for a Saturday afternoon. On this occasion, the third Saturday appointment, Patient AB, accompanied by Lynne Davy, entered Michael Haslam's room and said that she was not coming back to see him as what was going on was wrong. Patient AB recalls that Michael Haslam made no response to this statement, and that she and Lynne Davy therefore left.

16.63 Between 24 April 1981 and 18 May 1981, Patient AB was an inpatient in Clifton Hospital and she received Somlec therapy. Patient AB described this treatment as a group of people in a room being plugged into a machine in order to help them relax.

16.64 Patient AB says that when she was re-admitted to Clifton Hospital during this period, Michael Haslam put his arms around her and said "welcome back to the fold", although nothing was said by either her or Michael Haslam during this period about the massage.

16.65 After she was admitted to Clifton Hospital, Patient AB decided to make a complaint about the "massage treatment" she had received. As she was unsure how to make a complaint, she decided to ring the social worker at Clifton Hospital, Margaret Jones, with whom she had had considerable contact, for advice.

16.66 According to Patient AB, Margaret Jones advised her that because of her vulnerability and fragility, she might not be strong enough to be involved in any court case. She did advise her to go to see a firm of solicitors and get them to draft a letter, which she could then take or send to Mr Holroyd.

16.67 Patient AB's understanding was that solicitors would assist her in drafting a letter, "so that it did not get into the realms of legal proceedings".

16.68 The area social services officer, Margaret Jones (based at Clifton Hospital from 1975 onwards), recalled the interview with Patient AB, although there was some discrepancy as to the details of what was said, and what advice was given.

16.69 Margaret Jones did recall being shocked and upset by what she was told. Her evidence was that the complaint was such that it was the only occasion in the 12 years she was at Clifton Hospital that she actually took a case to her line manager.

16.70　Margaret Jones' recollection of the content of the complaint (according to her police statement) was that Patient AB was alleging "clitoral stimulation against her will" during the course of "relaxation treatment".

16.71　Margaret Jones duly went to see her line manager, Mr Jim Maguire, the divisional officer based at Northallerton, to seek advice. He advised that the correct route was to report the matter to Mr Holroyd, who, as the District Administrator, was perceived as the most senior person at Clifton Hospital.

16.72　Margaret Jones had a clear recollection of her subsequent interview with Mr Holroyd which took place at Bootham Park, where he was based. She recalls clearly giving him details of the complaint.

16.73　Margaret Jones denied that she ever suggested to Patient AB that she seek the advice of solicitors, and said she was "amazed" to learn she had allegedly done so.

16.74　When questioned by Counsel to the Inquiry as to why, having learnt that the complaint had "fizzled out", she did not take any action, due to the potential risk to other patients, Margaret Jones said that going to Mr Holroyd with the complaint meant it was being dealt with.

16.75　Patient AB states that having seen Margaret Jones, she contacted solicitors in York who drafted a letter for her which was sent to Mr Holroyd.

16.76　We do not find it necessary to resolve the dispute as to whether or not it was Margaret Jones who recommended the involvement of solicitors, suffice it to say that we are satisfied that the letter, set out in full below, was drafted with the assistance of legal advice. The letter, although not dated, was apparently written on 1 March 1981.

Dear Sir,

Regretfully I feel that I must bring to your notice the conduct of Dr Haslam of Clifton Hospital, York who has, in my consideration, acted in an extremely unprofessional manner and in breach of the privilege of Doctor/Patient relationship, which existed between us.

I was referred to Dr Haslam in December 1979 whilst suffering from reactive depression. I remained in his care as an outpatient until February 1981. From the Autumn of 1980, the appointments with Dr Haslam began to take on what I considered to be sexual overtones. I was not at any time suffering from any condition which required such treatment and I have subsequently been informed that if such kind of treatment is given, a third party should be present. At no time was such a third party present in my treatment sessions.

I was at first confused by this treatment, being in a position of trust in regard to my psychiatrist, but after a particular attendance in February 1981, I was upset and disturbed by the said treatment I was receiving and I discussed the matter with a third party and later with my Social Worker. On their advice, I have not returned to the said Doctor for treatment and I now make this formal complaint of unprofessional conduct against him.

I will be happy to assist you further in this matter at the above address.

Yours faithfully,

[Patient AB]

16.77 That seems to us to be clear enough – and anyone reading the letter must surely have regarded its content as both important and disturbing.

16.78 Mr Holroyd had no recollection of receiving this letter, although he accepted that it was possible he did receive such a letter. He notes in his police statement that had such a letter been received, it would have been replied to, although no reply has in fact been discovered.

16.79 Mr Holroyd's evidence was that he had no recollection of either the meeting with Margaret Jones or with Patient AB, although he did not dispute that these meetings may have occurred. He did have a recollection of a patient coming to him to complain about a psychiatrist, although his memory was that this patient was accompanied by a supporter, and he was unable to confirm whether the patient was Patient AB. Whilst there is a discrepancy as to the number of people present at the meeting, it seems likely that Mr Holroyd's recollection of a meeting with two women (a patient and a supporter) in fact relates to his meeting with Patient AB.

16.80   For the avoidance of doubt, we find that Mr Holroyd did have meetings both with Margaret Jones and subsequently with Patient AB. We find it unnecessary to resolve the disputed fact of whether Patient AB was accompanied by a friend.

16.81   Patient AB's recollection of the meeting with Mr Holroyd is that she specifically told him about the "massage treatment", not in graphic detail but "enough for concern, enough for him to look into it, I would have thought".

16.82   Patient AB's impression from her meeting with Mr Holroyd was that, although she was wary of taking matters further, something would be done regarding Michael Haslam's practice. Mr Holroyd's recollection differed, his view being that he had made it clear to the patient that further particulars would be necessary before the matter could be taken forward. In other words, Mr Holroyd's recollection is that when he left the meeting, the initiative as to whether to proceed was left with Patient AB. In summary, as submitted on behalf of the patients, although he had before him a credible and very serious complaint against a senior consultant who was treating many vulnerable female patients, he effectively ceded responsibility for the safety of all those patients to Patient AB.

16.83   Insofar as Mr Holroyd's lack of response can be attributed to a misunderstanding, then it is an almost inevitable consequence when there is no clearly laid out process of complaint, clear to both patients and healthcare professionals. When challenged by Counsel to the Inquiry regarding his lack of action following Patient AB's complaint, Mr Holroyd accepted that: "on the balance of probability, I did not take any initiative after this letter and after a meeting". His view remains that the letter did not provide a specific basis for investigation. We cannot agree; it clearly gives real cause for concern.

16.84 Mr Holroyd also made the comparison with the Patient B2 complaint. He said:

> *"I reached the view that [in relation to the Patient AB complaint] that I had not got enough on which to initiate an investigation as we had initiated in 1976 [regarding Patient B2]."*

16.85 It appears, consistent with Mr Holroyd's recollection, that there was no investigation, and that Michael Haslam was never shown or informed about such a letter or informed of any complaint made by Patient AB in 1981.

16.86 It is difficult to see any justification for Mr Holroyd's inaction, or his conclusion that there was not even enough to "initiate an investigation". He had a formal complaint of professional misconduct, a direct reference to sexual overtones, and (through Meg Jones) more detailed disclosure.

16.87 True it was that Patient AB was reluctant to make a statement, reluctant to develop her complaint, but the mere existence of such a serious complaint – particularly against the background of the 1976 complaint – should have prompted some more positive action from Mr Holroyd. It should not have been allowed to die, completely uninvestigated, on his desk.

16.88 There is no suggestion that he had forgotten Patient B2's allegations between 1977 and 1981 – his oral evidence was that it was likely that he remembered the earlier incident. Looking back at that disclosure, Mr Holroyd's evidence was that any sexual involvement between a patient and a psychiatrist was very serious. Patient AB's evidence was clear in that the issue of sexual impropriety was discussed. In any event, it is there for all to see in the letter. In his oral evidence to the Inquiry, Mr Holroyd sought to explain his inaction by reference to the difficulty in managing consultants on a District level because they were employed by Region, and that a reference to Region, unless it was supported by a complaint in clearest, fully documented, terms, was a waste of time. There may be a degree of truth in both of these observations, but they come nowhere near to a justification for no action.

16.89 Patient AB told us that she left the meeting with Mr Holroyd believing that there would be an investigation into Michael Haslam, but that she "simply did not have the emotional strength to take matters any further".

16.90 In his written evidence to the Inquiry, Mr Holroyd said this:

> "I cannot believe that I would have walked away from a graphic complaint such as the one which is now made by Patient AB."

16.91 Putting it shortly, we conclude that Mr Holroyd did have a sufficiently graphic complaint, and he did "walk away". Why that happened we cannot be sure – disappointment at the response by Region in 1977? Perhaps. Not wishing to make waves? Perhaps not satisfied that the allegation was "serious enough" to pass on to Region? Perhaps. More likely, a combination of the three, together with the hope that if he did nothing, it would go away.

16.92 Counsel for the Health Authorities submitted that Mr Holroyd should not be criticised for his apparent inaction, saying this:

> "The question was asked, why was the letter not sent direct to Region? Surely it is obvious that that letter would have received no attention. If, contrary to all expectation based on previous experience, it had received attention, the request would have come back – get a complaint."

16.93 Although that may well paint an accurate, and entirely depressing, picture of the inadequacies within Region, it provides no excuse for Mr Holroyd's failure to pass on the letter – supported (at the very least) by a report of his conversations with Patient B2 and Meg Jones.

16.94 We conclude that Patient AB was poorly dealt with, and badly let down.

16.95 Patient AB was subsequently seen by Dr Kennedy on two occasions in 1982 and there is a reference in her GP notes to a letter from Dr Kennedy about her having "transference problems with a previous psychiatrist who treated her and she ended up worse". Patient AB's impression was that Dr Kennedy was unsympathetic to her problems and she interpreted this as him considering her as a "troublemaker" due to her earlier complaint against Michael Haslam. In fact

Dr Kennedy's evidence was that he had no knowledge of her earlier complaint, and whilst he accepted that he may have considered that Patient AB could be more properly treated outside the psychiatric service, this was in no way due to a lack of sympathy. According to Dr Kennedy, despite the reference to transference problems with her previous psychiatrist (Michael Haslam), he had no concerns at that stage that there had been any impropriety by Michael Haslam towards Patient AB and no such issues were raised by Patient AB.

16.96 We do not see any basis here for any criticism of Dr Kennedy. However, it is to be noted that Patient AB's contact with Dr Kennedy reveals a fear (reflected in evidence from several former patients) that they are stigmatised as troublemakers if they complain, and that this will affect their future treatment.

16.97 Patient AB was seen again by Michael Haslam on 5 June 1984 and 3 July 1984 but failed to attend a further appointment in August 1984. She then referred herself to Michael Haslam privately in May 1987 and saw him at St. Mary's consulting rooms on 5 May 1987 for regular appointments (approximately once a month) up to June 1988. In her evidence at the criminal trial, Patient AB said she did not pay the usual amount for these visits but a reduced sum of about £5. She states that no further untoward incidents occurred and that a nurse was present throughout each of her sessions with Michael Haslam.

16.98 As noted at the outset of this section, in the Michael Haslam criminal trial, Patient AB's allegations formed two counts of indecent assault, both said to have occurred in 1981 in the course of "massage treatment". The jury found Michael Haslam guilty of both counts. In the light of those convictions, we do not here set out Michael Haslam's detailed response to Patient AB's complaint, save to record his continuing denial of any impropriety and this extract from the written statement to the Inquiry:

"...In the case of Patient AB, she claims I had been over-familiar on an occasion in 1981 during treatment. Fine. So she returns two weeks' later and has the identical treatment, quite voluntarily, and then says a quarter of a century later that that too was an assault. Yet in the following five years until 1987 she continued to attend me – quite voluntarily – and indeed for some nine months as a (paying) private patient – if that isn't consent implied then I am a Dutchman. So she comes forward in 1999 after she fails in an attempt to get compensation out of Dr Kerr, and has been interviewed by The Sunday Times *against whom we have a libel action, and suddenly comes up with this story. Are we that naïve? Evidently the jury were."*

Patient B3

16.99   In the criminal trial of Michael Haslam, Patient B3's allegations formed one count of indecent assault, said to have occurred in 1981, during an inappropriate internal examination. The jury found Michael Haslam guilty of this count.

16.100   In 1976, Patient B3 and her then husband were referred to Michael Haslam in connection with sexual problems in their marriage. The first appointment was at York District Hospital. After two or three sessions with her husband, Patient B3 continued to see Michael Haslam for individual appointments. She attended regular appointments from 1976 to early 1977. She then ceased appointments, but commenced treatment with Michael Haslam again in 1981 at the District Hospital in York. On recommencing treatment, Patient B3 states that Michael Haslam conducted an inappropriate internal examination in the course of investigating whether she suffered from the condition of vaginismus (no chaperone was present). When Patient B3 confronted Michael Haslam about this examination at her next appointment, two weeks later, she alleges that he said: "You knew exactly what was going to happen when you got onto that couch", and then added that if she informed anyone she would not be believed or it would be thought she had led him on and that such a complaint would ruin her reputation. Michael Haslam stated at the criminal trial that he recalled Patient B3 complaining about his familiar manner, but went on to say he informed Patient B3 of his usual practice at such examinations (trying to put the patient at ease) and that as far as he was concerned, it was a misunderstanding and that was the end of the matter.

16.101 In her statement to the police, Patient B3 described Michael Haslam as making an uninvited approach to her in early 1982, putting his arms around her when they were alone in his office at York District Hospital. In the summer of 1982, Michael Haslam, again, according to Patient B3, put his arms around her whilst they were alone in his office at Clifton Hospital. On this occasion, Patient B3 responded and this marked the beginning of a physical relationship.

16.102 Patient B3 continued to see Michael Haslam in his rooms at Clifton Hospital. She states:

> *"I continued to see Michael Haslam for my regular appointments until February 1983. We often went to another room within Clifton Hospital which was more private. My appointments continued on the whole to take place in the evening after work."*

16.103 In the criminal trial, Patient B3 stated the appointments were generally the last appointment on a Friday. In addition, they would meet in a social context, playing squash together.

16.104 In a letter of 4 October 1982, Michael Haslam informed Patient B3's GP, Dr Scott, that he had agreed to give Patient B3 some relaxation sessions, which would be conducted at "The Retreat", where he carried out his private practice, because it was "not practical to do this at the District". Such a letter ought, with hindsight, to have rung alarm bells. In fact, Patient B3's evidence was that she had already informed her GP of her relationship with Haslam but that Dr Scott had not reacted. Dr Scott denied having ever received such a disclosure. Patient B3's evidence at the criminal trial was that Michael Haslam suggested she attend The Retreat, in order that he could hypnotise her, suggesting that this might help to relax her. Patient B3 recalls that: "Michael Haslam had a private room where we would not be disturbed, for example by nurses." Patient B3 says she was hypnotised on two occasions but that she did not pay for these sessions as a private patient. She states: "Although I was still talking about my problems with Michael Haslam, he was no longer really treating me as a psychiatric patient." Patient B3 accepted that: "it was more like friends than a doctor/patient relationship," and that she had become "infatuated" with Haslam. At these sessions Patient B3 states that a physical relationship (stopping short of sexual intercourse – but on one occasion involving both being completely naked and engaging in "heavy petting") developed between her and

Michael Haslam. Following this physical intimacy, Michael Haslam allegedly commented:

"This isn't ethically right but you'll never say anything will you?"

16.105 Michael Haslam accepted at the criminal trial that he had kissed and cuddled Patient B3 at the last occasion he saw her at The Retreat, but denied a relationship of the extent described by Patient B3.

16.106 Throughout 1983, Patient B3 continued to see Michael Haslam as an outpatient and also spent at least three periods as an inpatient in Clifton Hospital. Patient B3 was again admitted to Clifton Hospital in March 1984, following an overdose.

16.107 On 14 March 1984, whilst Patient B3 was an inpatient, Nurse Alan Greenfield was interviewed by Mr Terry Beverton, Assistant Director of Nursing Services "in connection with his inappropriate use of counselling techniques on his ward and in particular his counselling of Patient B3". It appears there were concerns regarding Mr Greenfield's lack of note taking, a lack of a care plan and fears that issues of transference were not being correctly handled (indeed Patient B3 later accepted that she became over-fond of Nurse Greenfield). During the course of the interview, Alan Greenfield informed Mr Beverton that the previous year, on 11 March 1983, he had been told by Patient B3 that Michael Haslam had "kissed and fondled her body". Alan Greenfield said he had raised the matter inferentially with Michael Haslam and received a "somewhat blasé" response. He explained that he had not taken the matter further, in part because he did not wish to damage his relationship with Michael Haslam and in part because having discussed the matter with fellow nurse, John Monk Steel, he had decided that the allegation was "fantasy".

16.108 Following the meeting on 15 March 1984, Mr Beverton compiled a report, noting the disclosure of an inappropriate relationship between Patient B3 and Michael Haslam and setting out Mr Greenfield's counselling inadequacies. This report made a recommendation that Alan Greenfield be removed "immediately" from Ash Tree House Ward. It was also suggested that the matter be discussed with Michael Haslam at a forthcoming multi-disciplinary team meeting (although it seems this never occurred).

16.109 What is striking to us is that the focus seemed to remain upon Nurse Greenfield's counselling skills, and there was a failure to respond to the underlying allegation concerning Haslam's behaviour towards Patient B3.

16.110 Mr Beverton was questioned about this at some length during the oral hearings. His explanation was that his remit had been to investigate the counselling carried out by Mr Greenfield and that insofar as there was a disclosure about Michael Haslam, he had noted this fully and passed that note on to his superior, Mr Wilk.

16.111 The similarity with the Patient A17 and Deputy Sister Bigwood story, addressed earlier in the Report, is disturbing. At about the same time in 1983/1984, Patient A17 and Linda Bigwood had also raised serious questions in relation to allegations of sexual misconduct (by William Kerr and, later, by Michael Haslam), but the focus was on Linda Bigwood's performance, and on nursing matters more generally. Again, the underlying message was either deliberately ignored, or filed under "too difficult" and not investigated. To see this happen in two cases, so close together, strongly suggests an institutional failing.

16.112 A few days later on 19 March 1984, whilst she was on Ash Tree House Ward (an acute psychiatric ward situated in a Victorian house forming part of Clifton Hospital), Patient B3 spoke to Acting Sister Catherine Little about her relationship with Michael Haslam. Sister Little, presumably appreciating the gravity of what was being said, compiled a statement, which was signed by Patient B3 and witnessed by Student Nurse Andy Cattell and Nursing Officer Brian Cottingham. The statement set out as follows:

Date: 19/3/84

Time: 6.40pm.

2/3 years ago I suffered from vaginismus. Dr Haslam, whilst examining me started to fondle me. I was so shocked, I did nothing then. The next time I saw him, I told him what a fool he'd been and that he must never do it again. Relations with my husband had got very bad and Dr Haslam started showing me more emotion and kindness. We always got on extremely well and he started coaching me at squash. One day he kissed me and I didn't push him away. At every available opportunity, he would go further until we used to meet privately at The Retreat, (where he holds his private clinic) and it went as far as it could sexually, apart from full sexual intercourse. He would never go as far as that, and I wouldn't. I thought I loved him, but he always made it plain he would never leave his wife.

It's been hell seeing him all this time. But I don't love him any more. I told my GP and [my husband] knows, (Alan [Greenfield] made me tell [my husband]) and one or two close girlfriends know. Meeting him (and any contact) stopped when I came to Ashtree House. He probably treated me worse because he was putting up a front. I thought our relationship would still continue and things would be great when I was admitted.

Signed:..........................[Patient B3] ....

Witnesses: *Catherine A Little...*
                     Brian Cottingham...
                     Andy Cattell...

THIS STATEMENT WAS DICTATED BY [Patient B3] IN THE PRESENCE OF THE ABOVE SIGNATORIES AND WRITTEN BY DEP SISTER C. LITTLE

16.113 Having signed a written statement, Patient B3 was then interviewed by Ray Wilk and Terry Beverton. She describes this as an aggressive interview, with Mr Wilk suggesting she had led Michael Haslam on. Mr Beverton's evidence was that the rationale for this interview was to see if Patient B3's account was going to "stand up" in order to be confident that the complaint would "get somewhere", and in order that Mr Beverton and Mr Wilk's credibility in pursuing the matter was not destroyed. Mr Beverton himself did not take notes of the interview and was unable to recall whether Mr Wilk took notes, although he assumed so. In fact no notes have been found and it seems likely none were made. Contrary to Patient B3's evidence, Mr Wilk's oral evidence was that Sister Little would have been present at the meeting. He denied that he used aggressive questioning, stating that he had come into the hospital whilst off duty in order to protect Patient B3, which he had tried to do by ensuring a statement had been properly recorded and that she was transferred away from Haslam to a different consultant. Mr Wilk's evidence was that he was unaware at the time of the disclosure previously made by Patient B3 to Mr Greenfield. This may be explained if Mr Beverton's report on

Mr Greenfield was sent, not to Mr Wilk, but to Mr Corbett (which is supported to some extent by subsequent correspondence). However, it would seem likely that Mr Beverton, when asked to attend an interview of Patient B3, would inevitably have discussed her earlier disclosure to Nurse Greenfield.

16.114 Accordingly we find that Mr Wilk would have, at the time, been aware of the earlier disclosure by Patient B3 to Nurse Greenfield. We do not find that Mr Wilk intentionally sought to interview Patient B3 in an aggressive manner in order to dissuade her from complaining about Michael Haslam. However, we do conclude that the interview of Patient B3 was unfortunately handled. Patient B3 had already had a traumatic day that had involved giving a written statement about the most intimate matters. It is likely that the meeting with Mr Wilk took place late in the evening, the statement having been timed to begin at 6.30pm. The interview was in a formal setting, and we find that Cath Little was not present. Patient B3 had made a detailed, and written, disclosure of sexual misconduct. Instead of being supported, and cared for, she was instead subjected to an interview with two men and we find that there was an element of "testing" her account to see if it "stood up", which may well have appeared to Patient B3 as aggressive. Whilst we accept that a gentle probing of an account, to see if it appeared to be at least superficially credible, may be legitimate, prior to taking steps such as changing a patient's consultant, the timing and manner of such an interview needs to be handled with far more care and sensitivity than was the case with Patient B3. Patient B3 must have been greatly disturbed by the experience.

16.115 The following day, on 20 March 1984, Patient B3 was moved to Bootham Park Hospital under the care of Dr Kennedy, who had taken over her care at the request of Dr Wilson McIntosh, the District Medical Officer. It would appear that having moved to Bootham Park on 20 March 1984, Patient B3 was then discharged to home on the same day. Patient B3's admission sheet for Bootham Park records the comment "Fear – proceedings re Michael Haslam getting public".

16.116 Mr Wilk had informed Dr McIntosh by telephone of Patient B3's complaints on the evening of 19 March 1984. It was Dr McIntosh who gave instructions that she be immediately removed from Michael Haslam's care.

16.117 Dr McIntosh's evidence was that, despite there being no mention in any of the correspondence concerning Patient B3 of any previous complaints about Michael Haslam (by Patient B2 or Patient AB), he was confident he did make the link between Patient B3's complaint and Patient B2's complaint, in which he had been involved eight years earlier.

16.118 Dr McIntosh saw Michael Haslam on 20 March 1984 and gave him a copy of Patient B3's signed statement. He informed Haslam that he was reporting the matter to the Regional Medical Officer, Dr Turner. This Dr McIntosh duly did, writing Dr Turner a detailed letter setting out the Patient B3 complaint.

16.119 Also on 20 March 1984, Mr Beverton learned that Michael Haslam had apparently been in contact with Patient B3's husband. According to a telephone call made by Mr Beverton, Michael Haslam was "trying to put the pressure on". Mr Beverton's oral evidence was that his understanding was that Michael Haslam knew Patient B3's husband socially and had been trying to use that relationship to suppress whatever had happened. There was also a suggestion that Michael Haslam was using his Senior House Officer to try to obtain information about the complaint from the nursing staff. Mr Beverton passed on this information to Mr Corbett, although it is unclear whether the information was then relayed to Dr Turner; there is no documentary record to suggest it was. Mr Beverton's involvement in the complaint effectively ended following the interview of Patient B3 conducted with Mr Wilk. He left his post two years later in 1986, by which stage no action had been taken against Michael Haslam. His oral evidence was that, whilst he had no evidence to prove it, he remained suspicious that the medical powers had suppressed the complaint.

16.120 The reference to Michael Haslam "trying to put pressure on" Patient B3's husband is important for another reason. Dr McIntosh told us that if he had seen the document (which he says he did not see) on which this information was recorded it would have made a significant difference to his response to, and dealing with, Patient B3's disclosure. He said:

> "No, I think we would have been duty-bound to pursue it further. This was – if this is correct, it was an instance of the witness being pressurised."

16.121 Having examined with care the relevant correspondence, we find that Dr McIntosh (and Dr Turner) did receive the report saying that Michael Haslam had being putting pressure on Patient B3's husband. But, notwithstanding that information, nothing was done to protect Patient B3, or to tackle Michael Haslam's alleged conduct, conduct which so closely echoed the alleged behaviour of William Kerr in relation to the disclosure by Patient A17. We are also satisfied that Dr McIntosh and Dr Turner were aware that the pressure from Michael Haslam preceded the decision by Patient B3 not to pursue her allegation.

16.122 The final letter from Michael Haslam to GP, Dr Scott, concerning Patient B3 is dated 23 March 1984 and follows her period as an inpatient at Clifton Hospital, and her written disclosure. In the light of the recent history, it is a surprising letter, beginning:

> *"This lady has been giving us further problems while as an inpatient on this last occasion."*

16.123 In this letter, Michael Haslam refers to Patient B3 as having "relationship problems [with her husband] and with various therapists with whom she develops rapid transference involvement". The letter also refers to "some crisis recently between herself and the nurse therapist" and speaks about her "manipulative behaviour". As set out above, following the making of the written statement, Patient B3's care was transferred to Dr Kennedy at the request of Dr Wilson McIntosh. Dr Kennedy stated that he was aware the complaint had gone to the Regional Health Authority.

16.124 Dr Turner wrote to Patient B3 on 23 March 1984 stating that he had received from the District Medical Officer of the York Health Authority a copy of her statement and that he would be studying the documents before recommending any course of action. Dr Turner's evidence (in contrast to that of Dr McIntosh) was that he was unaware of the previous complaints against Michael Haslam (Patient B2 and Patient AB). In the light of what we have read and heard about communication and record-keeping, Dr Turner's recollection is likely to be correct. It appears to us that only those who were personally involved kept information – and that information was probably not recorded in any formal sense. However, what is abundantly clear to us is that Dr Turner ought to have known of the previous complaints, and ought to have known of the very recent allegations made in the written statement of Linda Bigwood. On 25 March 1984, Patient B3 and her husband wrote to Mr Wilk stating that the circumstances in which she had made written statements were "disturbingly unusual" and that permission for her written statement to be used was not given until there was some clarification of the purpose for which such statement would be used. The letter also stated that any further interviews "may have to be conducted in the presence of our solicitor".

16.125 On 26 March 1984, Patient B3 and her husband duly contacted a solicitor in York. The solicitor says in his police statement that he regarded the matter as serious and spoke by telephone to Dr Mackie and Dr Turner.

16.126 Dr Turner wrote to the solicitor on 6 April 1984, stating that the matters raised in Patient B3's statement of 19 March 1984 raised the possibility of referral to the General Medical Council. Dr Turner suggested arranging an appointment with Patient B3 and her husband to discuss matters. On 11 April 1984, the solicitor replied to Dr Turner, stating that Patient B3 did not want to take the matter further and that the statement she had signed was not prepared by way of complaint but as a part of the treatment she was undergoing. Mr Turner replied to the solicitor acknowledging his letter of 11 April 1984 and stating that in the light of its contents, no further approach would be made to Patient B3, nor any formal action undertaken. The letter also stated that this position would be communicated to Michael Haslam.

16.127 On 13 April 1984, Dr Turner wrote to Dr McIntosh to inform him of the contents of a letter he proposed to send to Michael Haslam, which stated that Patient B3 did not wish to take the matter further and that no action was therefore proposed.

16.128 On 19 April 1984, Dr McIntosh wrote to Dr Turner in reply to the letter of 13 April 1984, stating that there appeared to be little alternative to the line that was being taken and suggesting that Dr Kennedy was:

> *"very concerned that further involvement by [Patient B3] in this affair would seriously damage her mental health".*

16.129 Dr Turner did, however, have a meeting with Michael Haslam. He said that he wanted to confront Michael Haslam and to tell him "not to open himself to things of this kind". But he also told us that he acknowledged he had missed an opportunity to open up the issues of Michael Haslam's wider practice.

16.130 We agree, and find that there clearly was an opportunity missed, but it is more worrying than that. It seems to be accepted, at least by Dr Turner, that there was a significant failure of communication between District and Region – either a deliberate failure, or sloppiness to a surprising degree. What is particularly disturbing to us is that Region failed to act on the combined effect of information which was either received, or should have been received, and retained in relation to Patient B3, Patient B2 and Patient AB (and also from Linda Bigwood). Even taking Patient B3 alone, there is real concern that her disclosure was not followed up. She did not withdraw the disclosure, did not say it was untrue, or fantasy – merely said that she did not consent to the information being used. But, at that time, Patient B3 was unwell and distressed and allegedly her husband was under pressure from Michael Haslam. Nobody seems to have considered a wider investigation, or at least offered support and comfort to Patient B3, so that she could be encouraged to pursue her disclosure when she felt better able to cope with whatever pressure she was under. Again, nothing was done – exposing a culture where psychiatric patents were disbelieved simply because they were mentally unwell, and where doctors were protected.

16.131 Patient B3 did subsequently write to Mr Wilk, largely it seems due to a concern that Alan Greenfield, to whom she had formed a strong attachment, had been wrongly "punished" for his role in counselling her. Mr Wilk, on 15 May 1984, wrote to Patient B3 stating that the reason for the transfer of Alan Greenfield was "as a result of my own appraisal of him and his current level of functioning". He also stated:

> *"Your placement on Ward Ash Tree House at Clifton Hospital was a medical decision arrived at to meet your particular clinical needs. Alan Greenfield's movement from Ash Tree House was a quite different professional matter."*

16.132 There were a number of other people who were also party to Patient B3's allegations of sexual misconduct by Michael Haslam. One of these was a Senior Administrator at Clifton Hospital who was also a former school friend of Patient B3. She recalled the incident when Patient B3 came into her office at Clifton Hospital in a distressed state and spoke about incidents with Michael Haslam. She formed the view that these were of a sexual nature and that Michael Haslam was abusing his position of trust, but that Patient B3 was consenting to the "relationship". She advised Patient B3 that she could make a complaint and also had the right to change consultant; she also told her that there was gossip in the hospital about Michael Haslam's behaviour in relation to other patients. She pointed out to Patient B3 that Michael Haslam would have the defence available to him that her allegation was a consequence of her psychiatric problem and that she should be prepared for this if she was going to complain.

16.133 In addition, Linda Bigwood also became aware of the complaint made by Patient B3 and she refers to this complaint (although not to Patient B3 by name) in her letter of 15 April 1984 to Jim Docherty, the Branch Secretary of the Confederation of Health Service Employees (COHSE). She makes reference to a patient (presumably Patient B3) who had confided in Alan Greenfield that she was having an affair with Michael Haslam and was subsequently moved to Bootham Park. Linda Bigwood also notes that Sister Little was horrified by the events concerning Michael Haslam.

16.134 Finally, Patient B3 also confided in James Maxwell, the nurse to whom she was referred by Dr Kennedy. James Maxwell made detailed notes of his counselling sessions with Patient B3 which included details of her relationship with Michael Haslam. Whilst James Maxwell was aware that Patient B3 had decided not to pursue the complaint, he did not raise the matter of Michael Haslam continuing to practise, as:

> *"I presumed that he [Kennedy] knew, the senior nurse managers knew and folk at a higher level in the authority knew what was happening, that they knew what they were doing with it."*

16.135 In resisting criticism, the health authorities and witnesses relied on the strictures placed on investigating consultants by the terms of DH Circular (61)112. However, it is clear to us that the mere withdrawal of consent to rely on a disclosure was no justification for the absence of any action or any investigation. The attitude of Region (and possibly District) seems to be that they could not investigate unless they had clear, unequivocal, written statements from the patient, and some supporting evidence. But that cannot be a correct approach. As Dr Turner eventually recognised, cause for concern should have lead to some form of investigation – even at a low level. This was particularly the case where there was more than one disclosure. In his oral evidence to us, Dr Turner agreed that, even if the requirements of Circular (61)112 meant a formal inquiry was difficult, the evidence was already such that some kind of further – and detailed – investigation was essential.

16.136 But as with William Kerr, there was no investigation, no further action – nothing at all was done.

Patient B5

16.137 In 1987, Patient B5 went to her GP, Dr John Moroney of Monkgate surgery, to complain about Michael Haslam's alleged sexual suggestions – inviting her to go away with him for the weekend – and his alleged escalating use of physical contact, in particular putting an arm around her shoulders, kissing her and inviting her to touch his chest after he had unbuttoned his shirt.

The detail of Patient B5's evidence is important because it alleges conduct (whether true or not) which falls into the category of "grooming", and could have illustrated the subtle potential process of crossing patient/clinician boundaries.

16.138 In her written evidence to the Inquiry, Patient B5 said this:

> *"I developed a close relationship with my psychiatrist, Dr Haslam. He treated me as if I was special and made it very clear that he thought I was an attractive woman. He would make comments that I was attractive and about how I looked. One example of my being special was that he gave me a book about psychiatry which he inscribed, 'To [Christian name] from Michael in hope!'*

"I used to see him at Clifton Hospital. Sometimes he would see me in his main office but at other times he would take me to other rooms away from the main part of the hospital. On one occasion, he took me to a photocopying room where he photocopied my hand and told me it was to do with a hand aura. He made it plain that this was not part of my treatment but rather that I was specially privileged that he would do this for me...

"On one occasion, I think it was around April 1987, he took me to a small sparsely-furnished room and asked me to sit on a chair whilst he sat on the floor. He then persuaded me to sit close by him on the floor. He unbuttoned his shirt and asked me to touch his chest.

"On the last visit to see him in June 1987, he asked me to go away with him for a weekend on his boat. He asked me to have an affair with him. He said we could go swimming from the boat."

16.139 Patient B5's account, set out above, has been rejected by Michael Haslam in his submissions to the Inquiry. As with other disclosures by other former patients, we do not here make any finding as to whether or not the allegations are correct.

16.140 When Patient B5 made her disclosure to Dr Moroney, she felt he believed her. However, whilst he explained to her the complaints procedure, she was influenced by his view that it would be hard to prove her case and it might be to her detriment to go through the complaints procedure.

16.141 Dr Moroney recorded in Patient B5's GP notes on 18 June 1987:

"? change psychiatrist. Pt. Feels threatening physical relationship is developing between Michael Haslam and herself. Dr Kennedy phoned."

16.142 Dr Moroney phoned Dr Kennedy twice (on the advice of a fellow doctor, Dr Jackson) and was advised that the patient would need to be prepared to address a disciplinary hearing. Dr Moroney accepted in his evidence that his knowledge of the complaints system was poor:

"I had had very little to do with complaints procedures, and I certainly had not dealt with them on the training scheme, apart from complaints against GPs personally, and it was a long-winded system. But I had no idea how to cross the boundary and go into the hospital."

16.143 Dr Moroney told Dr Kennedy that although the patient did not want to make a formal complaint, she wanted the matter noted on the record, should there be another incident. In keeping with this wish, Dr Kennedy made a typed note, dated 26 June 1987, recording Dr Moroney's telephone call. However, Dr Moroney felt that his action in passing the complaint on was not welcomed. In his oral evidence he described this unease:

"It was the fact that I felt I had got very important information which needed to go back into the system to get an appropriate response, and I was made to feel I was acting beyond my status and my information was not welcomed. It certainly was not acknowledged on a professional level as appropriate. It felt like I was struggling to be heard. I accept that is not necessarily the same as the patient's difficulty in being heard, but I did find the whole process very difficult."

16.144 Dr Kennedy advised Dr Moroney to see Patient B5 again and explain the complaints procedure, reassuring her that enquiries would be made by a professional and would be tactful, but could result in a disciplinary hearing, at which her evidence would be crucial. Dr Kennedy further advised that if Patient B5 was still emphatic that she would not repeat her allegations or make a complaint, then Dr Moroney should discuss with her whether to cease her outpatient appointments with Michael Haslam, and whether Dr Kennedy had permission to let Michael Haslam know that serious questions had been raised about his professional conduct by a named patient and named GP.

16.145 Dr Moroney spoke to Dr Kennedy again and confirmed that Patient B5 would not proceed with a complaint but would stop attending Michael Haslam's clinic. Dr Moroney was to refer her to another clinician. It was recorded that Patient B5 had agreed that Dr Kennedy could speak to Michael Haslam on her behalf and this course of action was agreed with Dr Wintersgill (District Medical Adviser).

16.146 Dr Moroney, however, continued to consider not only that his complaint had not been welcomed, but that there was a culture that such matters should not be raised.

> *"I still do not feel that I was treated with respect, let alone the patient's allegations treated with proper respect. But that is how I feel. I do not have objective evidence on that.*

> *"But it was not just that. It was other meetings where I raised the issue of Haslam, always preserving confidentiality, but asking if other people had picked up any whispers or ideas. It just felt like there was a brick wall.*

> *"The overwhelming feeling was that really: was this valid? Was it worth addressing? Was it a bit of a storm in a teacup? I did get the feeling of who was I, as this new general practitioner, to be raising such issues about well-established members of the medical community.*

> *"It is always very difficult interpreting this, because I have no idea of a lot of the actual words that were used and I have no idea what the intent was and I have no idea, as I have already said, whether Peter Kennedy was representing a bankrupt system or whether the words truly were from his own heart.*

> *"But there was no little talk, you know, 'Hello, how are you?' whatever, 'How are you doing?'. There was no, 'Thank you for calling,' there was no, 'Yes, I acknowledge this.'. It was very much silence from the other end of the phone when I was trying to go through what I felt I must act on. That was both from the DMSC officer and Peter Kennedy."*

16.147 Following the complaints made by Patient B5 via her GP, Dr Moroney, Dr Kennedy held an interview with Michael Haslam on 24 June 1987. He described the allegations to Michael Haslam and explained that Patient B5 would not be keeping her next appointment, but would not pursue her complaint. Dr Kennedy's note records that Michael Haslam's response was that he was amazed. Michael Haslam said he had seen Patient B5 about six times and that all he had done was to put a consoling arm around her when she needed comfort on her third visit, when she was very upset. Dr Kennedy notes that he discussed the matter with Michael Haslam *"in relation to previous allegations"* and Michael Haslam's response was: *"perhaps I do sail close to the wind, only to give* *comfort – will have to think about that and stop any possible gesture that could be misunderstood."* Dr Kennedy notes that he concluded the meeting with Michael Haslam, saying he would simply have to record these events. Dr Kennedy states he then informed Dr Moroney of what had been done, although Dr Moroney had no recollection of this.

16.148 Patient B5 was subsequently treated by Dr Reilly, a consultant psychiatrist, although she states that the reason for the change of consultant was never openly discussed. Dr Moroney did speak to Dr Reilly about Patient B5's reasons for transferring consultants although he accepted that in his referral letter he was oblique because: *"I was made to feel very much that passing serious allegations on was not acceptable unless there was incontrovertible evidence."*

16.149 Michael Haslam's response to the complaints by Patient B5 was to dismiss it as "absurd", and "she had deemed my conversation flirtatious", and "I apologised [to Patient B5] if there was any misunderstanding about my having removed my jacket and tie. The truth is that before doing so, I had asked for and obtained her permission."

16.150 The Patient B5 disclosure did not go beyond District level. If it had been forwarded to Region, perhaps some connection may have been made with previous incidents. Dr Kennedy recognised the significance of this failing, accepting that a consequence was that if it had not been for Patient B7 (see below), Michael Haslam would have continued to practise until normal retirement age. In response to questions, he said: "It's appalling, isn't it." Dr Kennedy should have passed on his concerns to Region.

16.151 Dr Moroney, following this incident, did not refer any more patients to Michael Haslam, and neither did his GP colleagues. He described making discreet enquiries of colleagues as to Haslam's reputation and was "delighted" when he heard he had retired and then "utterly horrified" when he "popped up again at the Harrogate Clinic".

16.152 At about the same time as Dr Kennedy was dealing with the complaint from Patient B5, Linda Bigwood was continuing to raise concerns about Michael Haslam. In her letter of 22 September 1987 to the Chairman of the Yorkshire Regional Health Authority (YRHA), Linda Bigwood states that she was:

" ...informed by Mrs Jones, then Head of Social Work at Clifton House, that both herself and her colleagues had received allegations by patients of sexual misconduct on the part of both Dr Kerr and Dr Haslam over a period of many years. She believed them to be true but had taken no action due to lack of evidence. She had once assisted a patient in pursuing a case against Michael Haslam through a solicitor but the patient had been finally persuaded by the solicitor to drop the case."
(A reference to Patient AB.)

16.153 Issues about Michael Haslam were also being raised by fellow doctors. Dr Christopher Simpson, a consultant who took over psychiatric responsibilities in Northallerton previously covered by Michael Haslam, stated that within a month of taking up the post of Consultant Psychiatrist at the Friarage Hospital in Northallerton in October 1987, he met a group of local GPs. They told him that they welcomed his arrival as they "could now start referring young female patients back to psychiatry" which they had not done previously, as Michael Haslam had invited patients to hotels and had sex with them. Dr Simpson was sufficiently concerned by this that he "informed senior doctors in the York Health Authority".

16.154 In addition, Dr Wintersgill recalls interviewing Michael Haslam at Clifton Hospital (in the period 1987 to 1989) about an allegation of sexual interference with a female patient. He believes the interview was at the instigation of Chris Reid, the Unit Administrator. Unusually, it was an oral request. He says that he would have made a written report. In the course of the interview, Michael Haslam stated that he would have discussed matters of a sexual nature with the patient concerned but that no inappropriate physical contact took place.

16.155 It has not been possible to trace who the patient was; however, it confirms the building picture that many in senior positions were well aware of the unease at Michael Haslam's practice by 1987, and in some cases significantly earlier.

16.156 In addition to describing her own circumstances – and the impact on her self-esteem of the treatment she alleges she received from Michael Haslam – Patient B5 provided the Inquiry with interesting and helpful evidence on the professional cold-shouldering she experienced. As she says, whether or not the disclosure she made was accepted as true or untrue, it was an important part of her, it was part of her "truth". Her complaint is that when she made her disclosure to her GP, and (quite correctly) she was referred on to a different consultant, neither her GP nor her consultant were prepared to talk to her about the disclosure and the impact the disclosure may have had on her. We set out her evidence in some detail, as we believe it is relevant today. She said this to the Inquiry:

> "There was one thing that definitely did not happen with me and which I think should happen in a subsequent situation like this, is that when the patient is referred to another consultant or on to another health professional, then the disclosure that they have made should become part of the overall treatment plan with the patient. What I mean by that is it should not be excluded from the picture as if it has never happened, because it has happened and, whatever the truth of it, it is true for the patient. Therefore, it needs to be considered as part of the ongoing therapeutic plan and treatment."

And

> "I am saying that in order for somebody, particularly somebody who is vulnerable, in the mental health services, in order for them to make a disclosure about abuse, whether that is actually subsequently founded or not, it is part of that person's experience, otherwise they would not be making that disclosure. So therefore, even if they are transferred to a different consultant, the fact that they have made that disclosure needs to be investigated from a therapeutic point of view, as well as from a professional point of view. In the process of exploring it from the therapeutic point of view, more issues may come to light that inform any subsequent professional decisions. That is very different from – I am going to use the word – pretending that it almost does not exist and is separate from the person and their needs."

And

> "Because, of course, I came to therapy initially because I had difficulties. That is why I was referred to Dr Haslam. When I left Dr Haslam's care I had additional difficulties, which were actually caused by the relationship I had had with Dr Haslam. Those difficulties were then not addressed. It was as if they had not happened, when I went into my next period of therapy."

16.157 Patient B5's evidence was to the effect that the impact of the alleged abuse could have been lessened by more care and understanding in relation to that disclosure. Whatever the intention, the impact of this failure to address the allegations of abuse was that Patient B5 believed she had been marginalised, and made to feel guilty, because she had dared to disclose.

Patient B6

16.158 Patient B6's identity is not known to us and neither have we been able to conclusively fit the limited facts known about her circumstances to any of the patients who are known to us. We include her story, sparse as the details are, to illustrate how warning bells rung by her fell upon deaf ears.

16.159 Patient B6 complained to Michael Haslam's Senior House Officer (SHO), Dr Hanslip, in about July 1987 that Michael Haslam had propositioned her when he met her in York, suggesting they book an hotel for the night. The patient declined but was upset and did not want to see Michael Haslam again. She saw Dr Hanslip in a distraught state. Dr Hanslip advised her to make a formal complaint and to ask to be seen by the SHO in future instead of Michael Haslam. However, it would appear no formal complaint was ever made and Dr Hanslip did not herself pursue the matter. Dr Hanslip produced a written statement to the Inquiry addressing this topic. She said this:

> "I recall advising the patient she should write to the hospital management and, as she was reluctant to do so, that she should talk to her GP. I gained the impression that the patient would not proceed with a formal complaint. I did not myself at the time feel in a position to report the complaint as the details were not substantial and would involve a breach of patient confidentiality. At a later date, I did report what the patient had told me to Dr Reilly."

16.160 The reporting to Dr Reilly on that "later date" must have been some time after the event, possibly the next year or later. By that time, in 1988/1989, other events had led to Michael Haslam's departure from NHS practice.

16.161 At the time of the disclosure to her, Dr Hanslip was a very junior doctor, and clearly unsure of her role and her function, in relation to the information she had received. In the light of the prevailing culture at the time, perhaps her inaction is excusable. Her reaction was not dissimilar to that of Dr Mortimer – see the Patient A17 story in relation to William Kerr. We do not consider it necessary to criticise her in this Report. However, her reasons for not passing on the information are interesting and, we believe, may still prevail today notwithstanding advice and instruction from the GMC – particularly for a doctor in such a junior position. She gives two reasons:

a. The details of the disclosure "were not substantial"; and

b. Reporting the complaint "would involve a breach of patient confidentiality".

16.162 The details may not have been "substantial" to Dr Hanslip, but they were real and substantial to the patient, and (when joined with other information) may well have been substantial for hospital administrators. As for "patient confidentiality", we address this reason elsewhere in the Report. In our opinion, it provides no good reason now, and provided no good reason in 1987. Indeed, although Dr Hanslip says it was an impediment at the time, we note that it did not prevent her later disclosure to Dr Reilly.

16.163 This short story also demonstrates, yet again, the need for clear guidelines, for clear and continuing education of medical professionals, so that even new SHOs are well aware that any complaint of sexual misconduct has to be reported – in the same way as any allegation of child abuse would always be reported. The fact that this was only a complaint of a proposition does not dilute that obligation. If made, such a proposition (consistent with other allegations by other former patients – see Patient B5, for example) would clearly be unprofessional, and may be symptomatic of a willingness by the consultant to breach doctor/patient boundaries.

Patient B7

16.164 Patient B7's allegations formed the subject matter of two criminal charges against Michael Haslam – one of sexual assault, and one of rape. In December 2003, at Leeds Crown Court, Michael Haslam was convicted of both offences. He appealed to the Court of Appeal (Criminal Division), and in May 2004, the conviction for rape was set aside as being unsafe. The conviction for sexual assault was not set aside.

16.165 We mention this at the outset because it is relevant to Patient B7's involvement with the Inquiry and how we summarise her story. Patient B7 provided a lengthy and detailed written statement to the Inquiry and was scheduled to give oral evidence. However, Patient B7 became extremely concerned that Michael Haslam would take civil proceedings for libel against her if her allegations of rape were repeated to the Inquiry. At that time, Michael Haslam's libel proceedings against *The Sunday Times* had not been withdrawn. We accept that there was some basis for Patient B7's concerns – indeed they were fuelled by comments made by Michael Haslam, and by his legal representative. Against that background, Patient B7 withdrew her written statement and declined the invitation to give oral evidence.

16.166 We were then, and are now, placed in a difficult position in relation to Patient B7's account. Our obligation, in accordance with our Terms of Reference, is "to document and establish the nature of, and chronology of, the concerns or complaints" raised in relation to Michael Haslam. There is no doubt that Patient B7 has raised concerns and complaints – not confined to the allegation of sexual assault on which Michael Haslam remains convicted. In the circumstances, we have concluded that it would be appropriate to take the summary of Patient B7's factual allegations from the decision of the Court of Appeal which is in the public domain. We can then set out, in greater detail, how those concerns and complaints were responded to.

> *"1. The third complainant [Patient B7], had suffered a number of sexual assaults in her adolescence. She had also experienced emotional difficulties after the birth of twins in 1984. In 1987 she began to harm herself and was referred to a psychiatrist [outside Yorkshire] where she then lived. She was admitted to hospital and had ECT treatment. She subsequently moved to Yorkshire and was referred to the appellant [Michael Haslam] after her condition deteriorated. On 31 December 1987 she was admitted to hospital as an inpatient and started an ECT course. Her condition improved and she returned home. On one occasion when she was with the appellant he told her he would aid her with her sex problems and showed her a number of vibrators and other sex aids, at which point she left. She was concerned about the appellant's interest in her sexual problems, as she did not believe she had any.*

"2. Her condition again deteriorated in May 1988. In July 1988 she commenced carbon dioxide treatment during which she was to undress, put on a gown and lie on a couch. The appellant would hold her hand and cover her nose and mouth with a mask. She would lose consciousness and wake up with a headache and feeling 'woozy'. During the final treatment of that kind she awoke to find the appellant spread-eagled on top of her. That was the evidence on count 4, the indecent assault.

"3. At the appellant's request she agreed to take part in a research project which he was conducting into something known as Kirlian photography. In September 1998 she attended Clifton Hospital and accompanied the appellant to a small room. After photographing her hand, the appellant forced her to the floor and raped her. During the attack the appellant's hairpiece had come loose. That was the evidence on count 5. She said that she returned home and later the same day cut her wrist. The following day she told her community psychiatric nurse that the appellant had frightened her, behaved unprofessionally and had lain across her. The nurse persuaded her to see her GP. She told him that she never wanted to see the appellant again. The general practitioner asked if the appellant had behaved unprofessionally and she said: 'That must be the understatement of the century', adding, 'It was physical on his part, I just lay there and froze.' She did not make a complaint to the police.

"4. She did complain to her then husband and he interpreted her complaint as being akin to rape, although she had not used that word. In cross-examination he was to accept that she had once made a false allegation of assault against him.

"5. It was suggested to [Patient B7] in cross-examination that she was making false allegations because she blamed the medical profession generally and the appellant in particular for her troubles. Much of that cross-examination was conducted on the basis of entries in her medical records.

"6. The case for the appellant was that he had not behaved improperly towards [Patient B7]. He had administered carbon dioxide but the complainant had never become unconscious. He accepted that he had taken a Kirlian photograph of her hand for use in research and produced a paper which he had subsequently presented at a conference on that subject in the 1990s."

16.167 We turn now to put that summary in the context of Patient B7's treatment. Patient B7 had first been referred to Michael Haslam in October 1987 by her GP, Dr Moran. Michael Haslam diagnosed her as having psychosexual problems and saw her on a number of occasions before admitting her to Bootham Park for ECT treatment on 31 December 1987. The allegations of abuse relate to periods when Patient B7 was an outpatient during 1988.

16.168 In March 1988, Patient B7 was referred to a Community Psychiatric Nurse, Stephen Brooks, whom she saw very frequently, one to three times a week. She was also reviewed by a female psychiatrist, Dr Yates, on 12 April 1988 at Michael Haslam's outpatient clinic and was subsequently referred by Haslam to Dr Reilly, a consultant psychiatrist, for assessment for a course of supportive psychotherapy in May 1988. Dr Reilly saw her on a number of occasions in July and August 1988, diagnosing her as suffering from borderline personality disorder.

16.169 The sexual assault and allegation of rape, summarised above, are said to have occurred in the late summer and autumn of 1988, after Michael Haslam's return from a trip to the United States.

16.170 Patient B7 states that she complained to both the Community Psychiatric Nurse, Stephen Brooks, and her GP, Dr Moran, about the carbon dioxide treatment and about Michael Haslam becoming increasingly physical in these sessions, although neither Stephen Brooks nor Dr Moran had any recollection of such complaints. Stephen Brooks, did, however, recall that Patient B7 had mentioned to him that Haslam had discussed her sex life and sexual aids with her and also said she received a postcard from Michael Haslam. On 26 September 1988, Patient B7 informed Stephen Brooks that she had had problems with Michael Haslam and was frightened to see him. This is recorded in Stephen Brooks' therapist notes.

16.171 Stephen Brooks was clear in his evidence that he had a duty to take this matter further and that he explained this duty to Patient B7. This is in marked contrast to the evidence of some other witnesses, who told us that they felt so constrained by patient confidentiality that they could not pass on the concerns. The clarity of Stephen Brooks' evidence as to his duty to inform where there is potential risk to patients, serves to highlight the confusion which then (and probably now) exists as to what should be done in such circumstances.

Stephen Brooks spoke to his Senior Nursing Officer who advised that Patient B7 should, if possible, be admitted and that once in this secure environment, she could be encouraged to give a statement. Patient B7 said that she was content to be admitted to Bootham Park Hospital, but wished to go to Ward 1 under Dr Reilly, not Ward 2 (Michael Haslam's ward).

16.172 Patient B7 visited Dr Moran on 27 September 1988 to have her self-inflicted wounds dressed. She informed him that there had been improper behaviour by Michael Haslam: "It was physical on his part, I just lay there and froze." She also, a few days later, informed her then husband that Michael Haslam had taken her to a small room, had lifted her skirt, and had "messed about" with her.

16.173 On 28 September 1988, Patient B7 told Stephen Brooks that she had told her GP, Dr Moran, that Michael Haslam had been unprofessional and that she "just froze". However, she did not at this stage refer to rape, nor according to Stephen Brooks, did she give any details of the assault which she subsequently alleged occurred during the course of the Kirlian photography session.

16.174 Also on 28 September 1988, Patient B7 was admitted to Bootham Park. According to Dr Reilly, this was by pre-arrangement with himself. Patient B7 informed Dr Reilly about what had happened to her during carbon dioxide therapy, with Michael Haslam putting his arms around her and on one occasion pulling her to the floor.

16.175 At the end of September 1988, Patient B7's GP, Dr Moran, spoke to his GP partners and contacted Stephen Brooks. Dr Moran and Stephen Brooks met on 29 September 1988 to discuss the matter and took the decision to inform Dr Kennedy. Stephen Brooks' recollection was that, on this occasion, they discussed the fact that there had been at least one other complaint or concern raised about Michael Haslam. This seems likely as Dr Moran was aware of Patient B5's complaint, because she had recently joined his practice and informed him of her complaint about Michael Haslam's alleged inappropriate sexual advances. Dr Moran had believed that Patient B5's complaint had already been investigated and thought the problem was one of a specific relationship. It was not until he heard Patient B7 that he suspected this could be a potentially wider problem and risk to patients. Stephen Brooks also had some, albeit very limited, knowledge of prior question marks over Haslam's behaviour. He was able to recall an incident a number of years earlier when, at a union meeting, there had been a reference to Haslam's "mistress" being admitted for psychiatric treatment. This seems likely to have been a reference to Patient B3.

16.176 Although his recollection is that he spoke first to Dr Kennedy, it seems that Dr Moran's first step was probably to contact the "Three Wise Men" – appointed by a special professional panel that health authorities set up to ensure "prevention of harm to patients resulting from physical or mental disability of hospital or community medical or dental staff". Raymond Lawrence Marks, an anaesthetist, a member and subsequently chairman of the "Three Wise Men" committee, recalls being contacted by Dr Moran about a patient (who was not named) who had made allegations of sexual misconduct by Michael Haslam. Dr Marks decided this was not a matter for his committee and referred the matter to Dr Kennedy. This corresponds with Dr Kennedy's evidence that once alerted to the complaint, he was clear it was a matter that fell within his remit, as opposed to that of the "Three Wise Men". In any event, Dr Moran did contact Dr Kennedy who advised him to hand-write everything that had been said and personally deliver the letter. This Dr Moran did. Dr Kennedy made a detailed note of his phone call with Dr Moran.

16.177 Dr Kennedy later returned Dr Moran's telephone call and Dr Moran formed the impression that a decision had been taken that Michael Haslam would be asked to resign.

16.178 Stephen Brooks, accompanied by Dr Reilly, saw Patient B7 on the ward on 29 September 1988. Dr Reilly informed Patient B7 that Dr Kennedy was aware of her complaint. He explained to her the procedure for making a complaint, following which she indicated that she did not wish to take the matter further. Dr Reilly stated at the criminal trial that he considered Patient B7 was too emotionally unstable to cope with any formal interviews with the police or even hospital managers. Stephen Brooks subsequently saw Patient B7 on her own; on this occasion she told him that Michael Haslam had been lying across her and kissing her face during a 6.00pm appointment at Clifton Hospital. Stephen Brooks took a signed statement on this occasion although this has subsequently gone missing. Stephen Brooks' recollection was that the statement was largely a repetition of matters he noted in his records.

16.179 At the criminal trial, when asked why she made no formal complaint "to the police or someone like that", Patient B7 replied:

> *"Once Stephen Brooks, Dr Moran and Dr Reilly knew, they reassured me that they would – well, they didn't reassure me they actually asked my permission to take the nature of my complaint to the authorities at Bootham Park, and I always assumed, as did my husband, at that point that the police would naturally be involved as part of that enquiry anyway."*

16.180 Following his role in taking a statement, Stephen Brooks' involvement in Patient B7's complaint ceased. His evidence was that he was told that he would have a continuing supportive role for Patient B7, but that he should not discuss the allegations with her as these were to be dealt with by Dr Reilly, who would be taking the matter further.

16.181 Stephen Brooks was left with a deep feeling of frustration. Having forwarded the complaint and played such a significant role in the handling of an extremely difficult issue, he was never informed of the outcome. In his oral evidence he said this:

> *"What concerned me was, and still does to this day, that there did not seem to be a clear and transparent process; that my client Patient B7 had not heard what had happened; members of staff involved had not heard what had happened. So whether Dr Haslam was exonerated, whether the complaint had been taken further, nobody knew."*

16.182 We understand that sense of frustration, and here record that Stephen Brooks, unlike some of his colleagues, recognised a clear obligation to report the concerns set out in the disclosure he had heard.

16.183 Dr Kennedy, having been informed of the complaint on 29 September 1988, immediately wrote to Dr W J Green, Specialist in Community Medicine of YRHA in a letter dated 30 September 1988 concerning the allegations against Michael Haslam. Dr Green had specific responsibility for medical staff including consultants, with a particular remit to consider "problem doctors". Dr Green had previously been alerted to complaints against Michael Haslam in about October 1987, by Linda Bigwood, on which occasion no action had been taken.

16.184 Dr Green responded to Dr Kennedy by letter on 4 October 1988 requesting statements from Dr Moran and Stephen Brooks as well as Patient B7's medical records. Later on that afternoon, Dr Kennedy spoke to Dr Reilly who informed him that the patient was "quite upset but did not wish to make a formal complaint as yet!". Dr Kennedy also spoke to the Regional Medical Officer, Dr (later Professor) Haward, about the procedure that should be followed.

16.185 Dr Kennedy also communicated the fact of the complaint to Michael Haslam, himself. Michael Haslam responded by letter on 2 October 1988, stating that he had contacted the Medical Defence Union and "strongly denied any impropriety" in the treatment of Patient B7. He went on to say that he was rather unclear as to just what Patient B7 was saying and added, "would it not be simplest to have an adult discussion with Patient B7 yourself and myself and ask her what she is dissatisfied about?".

16.186 On 12 October 1988, Dr Kennedy wrote again to Dr Green in reply to the latter's letter of 4 October 1988, enclosing the statements of Dr Moran and Stephen Brooks. The letter stated that Patient B7 no longer wished to pursue her complaint against Michael Haslam. Also enclosed with the letter were Patient B7's medical notes concerning the treatment she received from Michael Haslam and a memorandum made by Dr Kennedy of previous concerns raised about Michael Haslam dating back to 1980. This included the concerns raised by Patient B3 and Patient B5, noting also that in early October 1988, he had been approached by a consultant anaesthetist in York who stated that a patient of his was thinking of making a complaint about Michael Haslam. Dr Kennedy also noted that he had also heard (via Dr Wintersgill) of concerns that had been expressed about Haslam to Dr Simpson. In the course of one of his introductory meetings with a GP's surgery in Thirsk (Dr Harrison, Dr Donald and Dr Thiede), Dr Simpson had been informed of Haslam's reputation for sleeping with his female patients (although no names were quoted, the Thirsk GP's knowledge probably stems from the case of Patient B4 (a patient of Dr Donald – Marion Anderson, a psychologist, had previously raised concerns with Dr Donald about Patient B4's relationship with Michael Haslam). Dr Simpson was shocked by the Thirsk GPs' response which appeared to him to amount to "it's not illegal" and that consequently nothing could be done. Dr Simpson was clear in his mind that the alleged behaviour of Haslam was unacceptable (irrespective of legality) and having first discussed the matter with fellow consultant psychiatrist Dr Richardson, referred the matter on to Dr Wintersgill.

16.187 The view expressed by Dr Kennedy was that Michael Haslam should be "counselled to consider retirement fairly soon, or restriction of his practice which could be discreetly monitored by someone else". He acknowledged that this solution was crudely tactical and "a far from satisfactory conclusion". He might have added still that it left patients at risk.

Patient B4

16.188 In the early/mid 1980s, Michael Haslam commenced treating Patient B4. He referred her to Marion Anderson, a psychologist who was working at the outpatient clinic in Thirsk. During the course of her therapy with Marion Anderson, Patient B4 announced that she was pregnant and did not know whether the father was her fiancé, her next-door neighbour, or Michael Haslam. Marion Anderson comments as follows regarding this disclosure:

> "I discussed the situation with her and told her I was very concerned. She said that she was enjoying all three relationships and seemed to me, almost proud of her relationship with Dr Haslam. She stated categorically that she did not want me to break her confidence and pass the information on to anybody else. Accordingly I did not.

> "About this same time, or possibly just before, I was told by a nurse at the Thirsk clinic about another patient whose name I do not think I ever knew. The nurse told me that she had been told by the patient that Dr Haslam had made a pass at her and had taken her out a couple of times, but had then suddenly dropped her. The thing that was upsetting the patient was not that she had been out with Dr Haslam a couple of times, but that she had been suddenly dropped. The nurse told me that apparently when the patient was seeing Dr Haslam, she had told her and one of the other nurses, about Dr Haslam and Dr Haslam had found out that the patient was talking about the relationship. For this reason he had ended the relationship with her. When the nurse spoke to me about it, she claimed that the patient's complaint was not that Dr Haslam had taken advantage of her, rather that he had ended the affair as soon as she had told somebody else about it. I was again told this information in confidence and

did not pass it on. However, this information made [Patient B4's] claims about Dr Haslam the more believable.

"[Patient B4] started to say that she was concerned about what she would do about the baby's father. At this point [Patient B4] was becoming more and more disturbed and I had evidence that she was also talking to other people about what she claimed was going on. At this point I took the decision to discuss the matter with [Patient B4's] GP, who I think was a Dr Donald. He was a Thirsk GP and worked in a nearby medical practice, though not the one at the Lambert Hospital where I saw my outpatients. Dr Donald told me that [Patient B4] had also talked to him about her affair with Dr Haslam. He said that he was appalled by the situation but also said that [Patient B4] had said that she did not want to do anything about it. He said that due to the need for patient confidentiality, and the fact that the only information he or I had was hearsay, he felt that he could not do anything about [Patient B4's] allegations. He also told me that he was of the view that at that time [Patient B4] was sufficiently precariously balanced that she should not be forced into making statements that she did not want to make. He also said that he did not think that she would repeat her story if confronted by any authority. I must say I agreed with him in all the points that he made."

16.189 Dr Donald's evidence confirmed that Patient B4 had told him she was having sexual intercourse with Michael Haslam. He discussed that matter with his senior partner who was of the opinion that Patient B4 was making the story up. Whilst Dr Donald did not share this view, Patient B4 was insistent that no action be taken, and he accordingly did not take the matter any further.

16.190 Marion Anderson remained concerned about the alleged relationship between Patient B4 and Michael Haslam and decided to confront him. Her recollection of this confrontation was that Haslam denied having a sexual relationship with Patient B4 and also claimed that she was no longer officially his patient, "he was just keeping an eye on her".

16.191 Patient B4 continued to confide in Marion Anderson, informing her of weekends away in London with Michael Haslam, and a holiday in Scotland, that she claimed he had suggested as a "last fling" before she got married. During this holiday in Scotland (Autumn 1985), Patient B4 phoned Marion Anderson in a distressed state saying she and Michael Haslam had been involved in a car crash but that he had not let her go to hospital for fear of a scandal. Patient B4 was concerned that her unborn baby may have been injured.

16.192 Marion Anderson also treated another woman with marriage difficulties (Patient B8) who decided to see Michael Haslam privately. Marion Anderson warned Patient B8 of the rumours surrounding Haslam, but later learned from the woman's husband that an affair had nevertheless commenced with Haslam and that accordingly the husband was seeking a divorce. Ten years later, Patient B8 sought further assistance from Marion Anderson, due to depression caused by being dropped by Michael Haslam very suddenly. She claimed she understood that he had been involved with other women (mentioning Patient B4 by name) but that they had had a "wonderful 10 years" and she did not want any action taken against Michael Haslam. When Marion Anderson questioned Patient B8 as to whether she had been Michael Haslam's patient during the relationship, her response was that it was difficult to say, because whilst he told her she was not his patient, he continued to prescribe for her if she had any problems.

16.193 Patient B4 went on to make subsequent disclosures about Michael Haslam. She also informed a GP, Dr Martyn Harrison (at the same practice as Dr Donald), of their sexual relationship, who in turn spoke to his senior partner Dr Thiede and another GP, Dr McClellan, although despite this, no action was taken.

16.194 Much later in 1993, Patient B4 disclosed to a consultant clinical psychologist, Mark McFeteridge in Scarborough, that she had had sexual intercourse with her former psychiatrist, Michael Haslam, as, she believed, part of her therapy. Mr McFeteridge informed Patient B4 that sexual intercourse could never be part of the therapy provided by a psychiatrist to a patient. He also reported Patient B4's disclosure to his line manager, Janet Martin, who herself had been the previous recipient of a disclosure from Patient B9 who claimed to be in a consensual relationship with Michael Haslam. Janet Martin was, however, unable to recall the identity of Patient B9. It is possible that Patient B9 and Patient B8 are the same person.

16.195 Ms Martin advised Mr McFeteridge to contact the trust legal department, the British Psychological Society and Dr Timperley, Consultant Psychiatrist, in order to establish what should be done following receipt of such an allegation. In fact Patient B4 did not return to Mr McFeteridge for any treatment and the matter went "cold". In February/March 1996, Patient B4 was seen by Dr Timperley. She told him that she had been seen by Michael Haslam as a patient and that they had engaged in consensual sexual intercourse which she believed was part of the therapy. According to Patient B4, the relationship had ended in 1994.

16.196 Dr Timperley discussed the incident on an anonymous basis with colleagues and was surprised that repeatedly colleagues rightly assumed his concerns were about Michael Haslam. On 11 March 1996, Dr Timperley wrote to the GMC.

16.197 Michael Haslam responded to the Inquiry protesting that "any personal relationship he had with [Patient B4] was not during the time that he had a professional relationship with her". He objected to the Patient B4 disclosure being included in the Report on that basis – "that she was not a patient of [his] at the time in question".

Other patients

16.198 In addition to those patients mentioned above, various other information came to the attention of the Inquiry concerning Michael Haslam's treatment of female patients. Some of this information came to the Inquiry indirectly, not from the patients themselves, other concerns related to private patients of Michael Haslam. The Inquiry is grateful for all the assistance it has received, enabling it to build up a comprehensive picture. However, as has been repeatedly stressed, it is not the function of this Inquiry to look into the truth or otherwise of allegations against Michael Haslam, and thus we do not find it necessary to document these in detail save to acknowledge there were some other issues raised and not properly investigated.

Chapter 17
Michael Haslam leaves the NHS

Circumstances of his retirement

Introduction

17.1 By October 1988, it would appear that Michael Haslam had secured the post of Medical Director at the Harrogate Clinic. On 24 September 1988, John Hughes of Gateway Residential Services plc had written to Michael Haslam enclosing a draft contract for the post of Medical Director at Harrogate Clinic. A letter was sent to Dr Kennedy on 12 October 1988 advertising the forthcoming opening of the Harrogate Clinic. Dr Kennedy copied the letter to Dr Haward on 3 November 1988, with a suggestion that whilst it appeared that Michael Haslam was to retire from the health service, it might be that the NHS still had some responsibilities in respect of his work in the private sector.

17.2 A meeting was held on 3 November between Dr Green, Hugh Chapman (legal adviser), Dr Haward and Carole Teitjen (Director of Personnel) to discuss the need to take urgent action. Dr Green's recollection of this meeting was as follows:

> "I am sure we decided at that point that Dr Haslam should be seen, and I believe at that meeting we decided that the best outcome would be to get him to resign. Bear in mind that at that stage we had no complainant who was prepared to persist with an allegation.

> "I think we all felt that we were in a very weak position in taking forward disciplinary action, but equally convinced that we had to bring Michael Haslam's career in the NHS to an end."

17.3 As an important aside here, Dr Green adds that he made a handwritten record of the meeting but that it was destroyed when he retired in 1995. Neither has the Inquiry seen any record of the "council of war meeting" as Dr Green described it, which took place on 3 November between Dr Green, Dr Haward, Carole Teitjen and Hugh Chapman. Again we stress the importance of making, maintaining and being able to review contemporaneous records of what, even without the benefit of hindsight, must have been transparently important decision making meetings.

17.4 On 11 November 1988, Dr Green wrote to the Medical Defence Union (MDU), Manchester, and confirmed an earlier telephone call agreeing to meet informally to discuss, *"our disquiet about Michael Haslam's behaviour prior to formally seeing him with his representatives with regard to these further allegations."* This meeting was to take place at 9.00am in the office of the District Medical Officer in the Leeds Eastern Health Authority Headquarters on 24 November 1988.

17.5 On 24 November 1988, presumably as a result of that meeting, Dr Green wrote to Michael Haslam to inform him that *"serious allegations have been reported to this authority of your impropriety in relation to female patients under your care".* Dr Green invited Michael Haslam to attend a meeting with the Regional Medical Officer on Monday 5 December 1988 and he was invited to bring a representative of his medical defence organisation with him. This letter from Dr Green was blind copied to Dr Haward, Mr Chapman, Miss Tietjen and Dr P J Hoyte at the MDU.

17.6 On 8 December 1988, following the meeting with Dr Green and Dr Haward on 5 December 1988 concerning the complaints against him, Michael Haslam wrote, on 8 December 1988, to resign from the Health Service with effect from 1 April 1989. Dr Green, in his police statement, recalls that Michael Haslam denied all allegations of inappropriate behaviour and that he was offered the opportunity to resign, or to face an investigation where many of the people he worked with would be spoken to as well as the patients. In his oral evidence Dr Green speculated (although he had no clear recollection) that there may have been a "deal" whereby the resignation was in return for a dropping of the investigation. This, however, was denied by Michael Haslam, who said that he was presented with no ultimatum of "resign or face investigation" – on the contrary, he said he informed the meeting that he would be resigning in any event to take up a post at the Harrogate Clinic.

17.7 For Professor Haward the essential problem was that there was no formal evidence which could form the basis for an inquiry at regional level, or disciplinary proceedings under HM 61/112. Therefore, in terms of patient protection (by this, Professor Haward must be referring to NHS patients – see below) "it was concluded that the best solution would be to try and secure Dr Haslam's resignation". He continued:

> "The strategy we were pursuing acknowledged the serious nature of the allegations and the fact that the complainants were not prepared to pursue their allegations further. Our assessment was that it was more likely than not that there was some truth in the allegations. We were aware that he was coming up to retirement and we considered that the best available option open to us at the time was to try and secure his retirement."

17.8 Referring to the meeting with Michael Haslam, he said:

> "We challenged him to resign and that if we did not receive his resignation within a week then he would face a further investigation."

17.9 In Professor Haward's words, Michael Haslam preferred to resign rather than see "these difficult and problematic complaints pursued further." There is near-contemporaneous and other pre-Inquiry support for this account. In his reference letter to Dr Saunders dated 21 March 1989, Professor Haward said this:

> "In discussion with Dr Haslam he felt he would prefer to resign his NHS appointment, having reached the age of 55 with mental health status, rather than see these difficult and problematic complaints pursued further."

17.10 In his oral evidence to the Inquiry, Professor Haward emphasised that he, and others, were keen to ensure that Michael Haslam no longer practised in the NHS, and they were effectively prevented from achieving this by any form of direct action. He said:

> "... we had no complaints which, if you like, one had any firm evidence of the sort one could put before an HM(61)112 tribunal or action of that sort. We simply did not have the ammunition. We had the taint, if you like, we had the sense that there was something going on here that was a bad story, but we did not have the evidence and, therefore, to go down the formal route would have been unlikely to succeed. Now, whether or not, if we looked at it, looked at some of those old complaints afresh, we might have got anywhere, I cannot comment. I think we concluded that the complainants had not been willing to go forward, that was their decision as complainants.
>
> "It was not that we were hostile to going down that route or looking for an easy life. We actually reached a considered judgment on the difficult question when we were unhappy about the situation we were in."

17.11 He added:

> "I think we formed the view, rightly or wrongly, that because the allegation was not backed up, as the individual was not prepared to take their complaint forward, we therefore were in a position – it was not a position we wanted to be in, but we were in a position where allegations had been made, withdrawn, things had been inconclusive, but cumulatively, you got the feeling that this was not a good story. Our challenge, if you like, was to draw it to a conclusion some way, and that was what we did."

17.12 Dr Green's explanation of the course of action taken was similar:

> "I think what carried weight with us was that, at that present time, we had no complainant prepared to go forward. If we had gone down the road of investigating, we might well possibly have found patients willing to stick by a complaint. We would have had to explain to them that, whether it was through the disciplinary procedure of HM(61)112 or the GMC, they would have to give evidence that would be tested in the legal fashion. Now, going down that road, would we at that time have found anybody willing to stick by an allegation? At a disciplinary meeting or at the GMC, would that allegation have stood? If it did not, might we still be stuck with Dr Haslam as an employee, now almost immune from further action, and some of his patients stigmatised as false accusers or fantasists?

"I think those sort of thoughts would have gone through our mind. The option of a quick resignation from Dr Haslam seemed to us the best option at the time. And when it was achieved, I think all of us felt it was a good day's work."

17.13 Clearly Dr Green was concerned about the allegations/complaints as described to him. In his oral evidence to the Inquiry Dr Green said:

> *A. Can I say that I was very concerned when I got this initial correspondence from Dr Kennedy. He speaks of the sort of pattern of complaints that you mentioned earlier, going back a number of years. He mentions the regional inquiry. And I am conscious, and I am sure Dr Haward and others were conscious, that this was a very serious issue that we had to address. Although at that time there was no firm evidence, I think I believed at that time that we had a bad doctor on our hands and that patients were at risk.*
>
> *Q. Just stopping you there, that was your belief there, and you have put it very graphically, you believed you had a bad doctor on your books and something needed to be done?*
>
> *A. Yes.*

17.14 This evidence has caused us some concern. If Michael Haslam was believed to be a "bad doctor" within the NHS, why was the decision made merely to obtain his resignation or retirement, rather than ensure that there was at least some form of investigation, and some reference to the GMC, or contact with the police? Even if the Inquiry accepts that there was some degree of focus on patient safety, there is at least a reasonable suspicion that the main concern was to get Michael Haslam off Dr Green's "patch".

17.15 The consequence of all this dithering was of course, that not only was Michael Haslam allowed to retire, without facing any investigation, he was also allowed to work out his notice, as opposed to being suspended pending resignation. We come back to that consequence later.

17.16 Even without looking at the evidence from Michael Haslam, there is material to suggest that a deal was done with Michael Haslam whereby, in exchange for the tendered resignation (after he had indicated that he was going to retire in any event and go to the

Harrogate Clinic) any possible investigation would be brought to an end, and not pursued.

17.17 The supporting evidence comes first from the contemporaneous correspondence. On 5 January 1989, Dr Green wrote the following letter to Dr Kennedy:

> *"In consideration of Dr Haslam's resignation, the RHA will not be pursuing the allegations made against him by [Patient B7] and I return her medical notes."*

17.18 The following is a further extract from Dr Green's oral evidence to the Inquiry:

> *Q. Why was there no investigation?*
>
> *A. I have asked myself whether that was part of the deal.*
>
> *Q. Just expand on that – part of the deal between who and who?*
>
> *A. That if he resigned we would not pursue any further inquiries. I do not know whether that was the case.*
>
> *Q. Was that maybe something that you were saying to the MDU, that is the sort of thing that could be informal discussions, keep it informal but –*
>
> *A. It could have been, yes. Please do not misunderstand me, I am not saying that that deal, if I can call it that, happened. Looking back, I wonder if it was part of the agreement with Dr Haslam that if he gave us his notice we would not pursue the issue. Certainly we did say to him, and I am sure I said to Dr Hoyte, "We are minded to pursue this very vigorously. It is going to be very unpleasant. All your colleagues" – I am sure we said, "You will be suspended, all your colleagues will be aware of what is going on, your medical colleagues, your nursing colleagues; many of your patients will be approached, and in general it will be a tough time for you." That was certainly the pressure that was put on him. Whether there was also a carrot, I cannot remember.*

17.19 Having considered all the evidence (including the evidence from Dr Kennedy – see below), we conclude it is likely that there was an offer – at the very least an implied offer – made to Michael Haslam along the lines of, "You are intending to retire to take up the appointment at the Harrogate Clinic; if we have early confirmation in writing that you are in fact going to retire, then we will not take any further action in relation to the complaints made."

17.20 If the general question is asked at this point "Why did Region not carry out an investigation into the practice of Michael Haslam – even at this stage?", the likely answer is that there was no appetite for such an investigation within the District and within the Region. This may have been driven by pessimistic internal legal advice, but we do not think that was the only reason. The decision not to investigate in 1988, even with some new managers in place, fits comfortably with the decision not to investigate at any time in the past – in relation to Michael Haslam's practice, or in relation to William Kerr's practice. We do not accept the suggestion for the absence of an investigation put forward to the Inquiry on behalf of the NHS – "Why did Region not investigate even at that stage? Because Haslam was quick-witted, as ever. He announced his retirement before they had got round to considering his position. All subsequent consideration was done against the background of his impending departure." The last sentence is undoubtedly correct, but it was not a quick-witted Michael Haslam who avoided the investigation, it was the NHS itself, even in 1988/89, at both District and Regional level, wanting an easy and quiet life.

The evidence of Dr Kennedy

17.21 Dr Kennedy had no direct involvement in the meetings to discuss Michael Haslam's possible retirement or resignation. In his written statement to the Inquiry he said:

> *"My recollection as to what happened next is a little hazy, but I believe that I was telephoned by Dr Haward to say that he had seen Dr Haslam and had confronted him. He told him that if he received his resignation within a week, he would not pursue matters, if not, he would make life difficult for him. He told me that this threat was a bluff on his part because he had no firm evidence with which to proceed with a formal disciplinary investigation. He did say, however, that we shall see what will happen."*

17.22 However, it could be said that it was Dr Kennedy who initiated the retirement route. In his important letter dated 12 October 1988, after referring to the five or six complaints received over the previous years, he said this:

> "Whether, or not, in the legal sense there is, or will ever be, a case to answer of professional misconduct, one has to conclude that Dr Haslam has problems with young and middle-aged female patients, who he sees for more than one or two outpatient sessions on his own. The kindest interpretation is that he doesn't know how to handle the kind of erotic transferences that every psychiatrist in training is helped to recognise and avoid. If so, it is my considered opinion that training will not change things now. The repetitiveness of these allegations makes it clear that his behaviour is not influenced by fear of exposure. Indeed, the problem appears to be getting more frequent.

> "I just wonder whether for the sake of patients, and to avoid his career ending in a public scandal, Dr Haslam might be counselled to consider retirement fairly soon, or restriction of his practice, which could be discreetly monitored by someone else. He has intimated that he might retire at 55 and if there is only a year or two to go, with his agreement, it might be practically possible for his practice to be arranged such that certain patients requiring certain kinds of treatment are dealt with by another consultant. These, of course, are just very preliminary thoughts on this very difficult matter and I shall be happy to discuss them further if you wish."

17.23 In his oral evidence to the Inquiry, Dr Kennedy expressed considerable disquiet about the circumstances of the resignation, in particular the fact that Michael Haslam gave notice in early December 1988, but was able to work out his period of notice. He said that the decision to allow Michael Haslam to retire, and then continue practising, but outside the local NHS, was "a crudely tactical decision, but a far from satisfactory conclusion".

17.24 The following exchanges between Counsel to the Inquiry and Dr Kennedy reflect his evidence:

Q. From 8 December 1988 to 1 April 1989 is a period just short of four months. Are you aware of any restrictions or restraints put on Michael Haslam's practice in the period from 8 December 1988 to the date of his resignation in April 1989?

A. No.

Q. Would it be fair to say that there were further opportunities for the abuse of patients which might have presented themselves in that four-month period or three-and-a-half-month period?

A. One can only say yes.

Q. Do you have any concerns about that situation having arisen and did you have any concerns at the time that there was an even greater risk to patient safety?

A. I mean, for two and a half years I had had concerns, they had not changed. I had put the ball in the court of his employer, and the issue was, "Give me your resignation quickly," which he did, but not, "and leave forthwith." He was allowed to serve his notice.

Q. And allowed to work unrestricted. That does not really answer my question. You have told us – and I am not making any comment about the appropriateness of this – that the Region as the employers, it is much for them to handle. I just want to know what your view was.

A. I do not think it was right.

Q. Did you say to Professor Haward, "This man could be seeing other women and there could be further opportunity for abuse"?

A. I think the fairest answer – let me think about it. By that stage, I was so pessimistic that the Health Service would ever get its act together and do anything about this, that the fact that his resignation had been brought about and he was off soon seemed better than expected. But as we have said before, it was unsatisfactory that he was going to get away without his reputation being affected, he was allowed to practise for another three months. We still had problems about stopping him practising outside the health service.

Q. Would you agree with me that, even in terms of confrontation, it would not have been a huge confrontation to say to Michael Haslam, not even that "We are suspending you until your resignation," just that, "You can have pay in lieu of notice, you are not required to fulfil your duties"?

A. Yes.

Q. That would have at least sent a bit more of a message to anybody familiar with the circumstances of his resignation that his behaviour was in no way being condoned or accepted?

A. Yes.

Q. There is no technical reason why that could not have been done, that you are aware of?

A. I do not think so.

17.25 This evidence does not address the issue – why no investigation, even at that stage, referred to above? However, Dr Kennedy's position was reasonably clear. As recently appointed acting District General Manager, he had made his contribution by bringing material together, and passing the burden over to Michael Haslam's employers. It was for Region, and its advisers, to decide what to do with that information. We will address the question of references later in this section. However, before we leave the evidence of Dr Kennedy, we wish to record that he readily accepted to the Inquiry that there were things he did that he regrets, and actions he regrets not taking. But it is to be noted that it was Dr Kennedy who collated information and provided the material which could have lead to some form of investigation if Michael Haslam had not decided to take early retirement. In her closing submissions on behalf of Dr Kennedy, counsel for the NHS bodies said this:

"Dr Kennedy is an impressive man and was, it is submitted, an impressive witness. His contribution to the improvements in services to mental health service users in the last 25 years is enormous. That contribution continues. He took on the role of a manager in the late 1980s so that he could bring about change. He succeeded. He does not suggest that everything he did was right. He was finding his way in a difficult area. Nonetheless it is submitted that here was a man who made a real difference.

"The panel is invited to reread his statements and his oral evidence, together with the papers he provided. His description of conditions in York is powerful and convincing. His reservations about Haslam's practice, and his frustration at his and the system's inability to do something about it in the early 1980s is palpable. His determination to root out bad practice and stand up to consultants required courage and determination, both of which he displayed in large measure throughout his time as a manager.

"It was Kennedy who collated complaints. It was he who provided them to Region. It was he who provided the memory. His contribution to getting rid of Haslam should be acknowledged."

17.26 We agree with much of what is said there. In relation to Michael Haslam's parting from the NHS, to use a neutral word, we here readily acknowledge it was Dr Kennedy who collated the complaints against Michael Haslam, who provided them to Region, and who provided the memory to expand the story in the October 1988 letter. Without that letter, there may have been no confrontation with Michael Haslam, and he may not have resigned. Where there have been failings, such as allowing Michael Haslam to take early retirement without any suspension, Dr Kennedy readily accepted responsibility. That cannot be said of all the witnesses to the Inquiry.

The evidence of Michael Haslam

17.27 We turn now to look at Michael Haslam's version of the enforced resignation/retirement issue.

17.28 In relation to the meeting of 5 December 1988, Michael Haslam said this to the Inquiry:

"This meeting was, as I understand it, an informal Hearing and it did not go on to the Hearing of a formal complaint, nor did I receive a formal warning, nor was I suspended. Indeed I was granted an honorary consultantship in York when I retired a few months later."

17.29 In his witness statement in his libel proceedings against Times Newspapers Limited (now discontinued) he said:

> "Dr Moran reported the [Patient B7] matter to Dr Peter Kennedy who was then District Manager of the York NHS Trust, who in turn referred it to the Regional Health Authority who investigated the complaint and interviewed me but found no reason to process the matter further. This episode was understandably an embarrassment to me as I was about to take up the job of Medical Director in Harrogate… However, I was able to obtain appropriate references from my employers and take up my new appointment. Furthermore, in August 1989 the Health Authority wrote to me appointing me as Honorary Consultant in the area of the York NHS Trust."

17.30 In his statement to the Inquiry on 17 March 2004, Michael Haslam said this:

> "Finally I am asked to comment on the circumstances surrounding my retirement in 1989. This is perfectly straightforward and simple enough, but has been the subject of some adverse comments from certain colleagues, who should know better than to make public statements in ignorance of the facts, and this includes a certain MP.

> "1. Doctors in the Mental Section of the Health Service were able to take retirement with full pension rights at the age of 55 years if they had worked for sufficient years. I had, and I was 55 years old on 7 February 1989.

> "2. I was headhunted by a private healthcare company (Cygnet Health Care, managing director John Hughes) in early 1988 and was offered the post of Medical Director of the hospital which was to be opened in 1989 in Harrogate, for private psychiatric care. My wife and I considered this matter and met with the company on two or three occasions in July and again in September 1988. It would be a considerable increase in my salary (in addition to my NHS superannuation). We decided to accept the offer.

> "I signed a two year contract with them to start in February 1989, but to do some work for them in the three months leading up to that date, in order to set up the unit; interview staff etc.

"I informed Peter Kennedy verbally and I wrote to Chris Reid, who was at that time Administrator, in early September 1988. I started two sessions a week for Cygnet Health Care from September 1988. I handed in my formal notice to the health authority three months before the start of my new contract, ie November 1988. My solicitors have pay chits and all the relevant letters confirming those dates. The episode of [Patient B7's] allegation, processed in October 1988 was an embarrassment, but of no relevance to the new post to which I was already committed. References had already been obtained for this new post, naturally."

17.31 Michael Haslam gave oral evidence to the Inquiry on this topic, particularly in relation to the 5 December 1988 meeting,

A. Professor Haward discussed with me the allegations that had been made and asked for my views, and I gave my opinions as to what had or had not happened. I think the gist of it was that they were aware that I was – that I had been offered the post of medical director of a private clinic and was therefore resigning from the Health Service. Now, I cannot say to what extent that did or did not influence their subsequent actions, but I think they were aware of that at the time and they were aware of the complaint that Patient B7 had made and they were aware of my comments in reply. That was the last I personally heard of it.

Q. Can you help me with this: you have not told us very much about what the tone of the meeting was, but I want to put to you what we understand from Professor Haward's perspective to have been the tone of the meeting. The tone of the meeting was: if you do not go, you will face the mother of all inquiries or investigations. Was it your feeling that great pressure was being put on you to force you out?

A. There was no need for pressure because I had already resigned.

Q. Was the tone of the meeting amicable or one where they were reasonably hostile?

A. Professor Haward was amicable. Dr Green, whatever his name is, was brusque. Dr Green, or anyway the medical representative there.

Q. Did you understand yourself, as it were, to be striking a bargain with them, that if you handed in your resignation they would back off from any inquiry?

A. No. I do not think that was the case. I mean, that may have been in their mind, for all I know, but that is not what was put to me, because I had already pointed out that I was engaged to be medical director of the Harrogate Clinic, starting – in fact I think the contract started 31 March 1989. And since I continued in the post without being suspended from the date of this meeting which was, did you say, December 1988?

Q. 5 December.

A. Yes, from 5 December 1988 until 31 March 1989, I was still in the employment of York Regional Health Authority and that was two months.

Q. No restriction placed on your practice at all during that time?

A. No.

Q. No suggestion that you should go on what we call gardening leave and that you would not be asked to attend?

A. No, there were not.

Q. It was not, as it were, put to you as an ultimatum that you must resign or be investigated?

A. No.

Q. Did you make it clear in that meeting that you were leaving in any event?

A. Yes.

Some conclusions

17.32 From that statement by Michael Haslam, there are some differences in the accounts that are readily resolvable. First, Michael Haslam did *not* hand in his formal notice in November 1988. It was not until after the key meeting on 8 December that he did so. All he had put in writing until then was in a letter dated 31 October 1988 addressed to the Unit General Manager of Bootham Park Hospital, a statement that he would be "putting in his resignation and retiring early from the NHS as of 1 April 1989".

17.33 Second, the question of references had *not* been resolved before the meeting in December 1988. However, what is reasonably clear is that the Harrogate Clinic position was discussed and taken up before the complaint by Patient B7 was drawn to the attention of Michael Haslam in October 1988, and before the reaction to that complaint was made by the District and Region between October and December 1988. It is likely that a Letter of Agreement between Michael Haslam and Cygnet Healthcare (the owners of the Harrogate Clinic) was signed on 23 September 1988, with the appointment taking effect on 1 March 1989. The appointment was as Medical Director, a part-time engagement – "the time commitment overlapping to a considerable extent with your attendance to inpatients and outpatients at the clinic".

17.34 Once again our conclusions, this time concerning the 5 December meeting, are not assisted by the absence of a contemporaneous – or indeed any – written record of it.

17.35 However, it seems to us that Michael Haslam's account appears broadly correct, but we conclude that it was in all probability made clear to him that if there was no written resignation/retirement within a few days, some (unspecified) further action would be taken.

17.36 What is abundantly and manifestly clear, is that there was no investigation, and Michael Haslam was allowed to leave the NHS in 1989 without any written record of disquiet about his practice in respect of women patients, and with every indication to the outside world that he was leaving without any criticism from District or Region, and with the apparent good wishes of all concerned.

17.37 Michael Haslam had continued to see NHS patients (including female patients) until his retirement, there was no supervision of his practice, there was no requirement that he should only see women patients if there was a chaperone present, he was not suspended at all, and, on receipt of his letter of resignation, he was not invited or instructed not to work out his notice (put on gardening leave). He was instead offered an honorary consultancy. References were also provided.

The honorary consultancy and the provision of references

17.38 The position reached immediately after the retirement/resignation letter of 8 December 1988 may be summarised as follows:

- There had been no meaningful investigation by District or Region in relation to any complaint or concern in relation to the practice of Michael Haslam.

- Michael Haslam had not been suspended from practising.

- Even although Michael Haslam had given his notice, he was not invited to leave immediately without working out that notice – in other words, take "gardening leave".

- No restrictions were placed on his practice for the remaining three and a half months of his NHS practice.

- Michael Haslam's use of CO_2 therapy, massage, Somlec etc was not questioned, nor was his investigation of the value of Kirlian photography – even though CO_2 therapy and Kirlian photography featured strongly in the complaint by Patient B7.

- There was no suggestion that Michael Haslam should not see women patients without at least offering them a chaperone. In summary, Michael Haslam's practice continued as if nothing had happened to call his conduct into question.

- Michael Haslam asked for, and was granted, an honorary consultancy.

- The owners of the Harrogate Clinic requested and were given a written reference to the effect that Michael Haslam was a fit and proper person.

17.39 We now will deal with the last two issues in greater detail.

Issue one: the honorary consultancy in psychiatry

17.40 We know that Michael Haslam used this appointment as an indicator that the NHS had no complaint about his performance, and were prepared to hold him out, effectively, as a former consultant who was worthy of "honour", of this honorary title. As already noted, the title was even used in the libel proceedings to demonstrate that, so far as his employers were concerned, there was nothing in the complaint by Patient B7.

17.41 The question of becoming an honorary consultant following his retirement was raised by Michael Haslam in his letter to the Unit General Manager of Bootham Park Hospital dated 31 October 1988.

17.42 How that appointment eventually came to be made is perhaps best covered in the evidence of Dr Kennedy. In his written evidence to the Inquiry he said:

> *"The awarding of honorary consultancy was standard practice. I discussed this with the Health Authority. We decided that if we vetoed it, this would have stirred up the consultant body. Tactically, therefore, we decided there was no need to fight a battle that did not need to be fought. The consultants were awarded honorary consultants contracts and shortly afterwards we abolished the honorary consultants contracts system and put an end to all honorary contracts."*

17.43 The letter setting out the District's position on Michael Haslam's application for an "honorary contract" was written by Dr Kennedy to Mr Harris at YRHA on 19 June 1989 (worryingly, just a few weeks after he had expressed serious doubts as to his suitability to be a "fit person" to treat patients). The letter reads:

> *"This request has now been supported by the medical Executive Committee, the District Medical Committee and by the Authority; I should therefore be pleased if you would issue Dr Haslam with an honorary contract."*

17.44 In his oral evidence, Dr Kennedy said this:

> *Q. In relation to the question of the role of honorary consultant, you give this answer: that it was not worth the effort really not to give him honorary consultancy because that had been given to lots of people over the years, and then you abolished honorary consultancy. Surely you realised that the message that was being given out by honorary consultancy, by the very body that is expressing serious doubts about his suitability, is completely the wrong message?*
>
> *A. Yes. I remember taking this to my health authority – what would it be, 16 people appointed by the Secretary of State from the general public, from professions, from local business, and discussing it with them, and the upshot of that discussion was, "It is just not worth the – tactically it is not worth the hassle of*

having the consultant body rise up in objection to picking off one or two of their number, so why do we not just let it go through and then abolish the whole lot?"

Q. Is it your evidence that the decision of the establishment was to give him this honorary consultancy because it just was not worth the effort with other consultants to deny it to him?

A. That was the corporate decision of my governing bodies, yes.

17.45 In the scheme of things, this is probably a small point, but whether taken alone, or taken with the other matters listed above, this seems to be a classic case of the NHS giving out mixed messages. It is to be borne in mind that at the time Michael Haslam was being granted an honorary consultancy, Dr Kennedy was firm in his view that Michael Haslam was "an abuser of patients".

Issue two: the references and the Harrogate Clinic

17.46 In her written submissions to the Inquiry, counsel for the health authorities said this:

"There is no doubt that by the time Drs Kerr and Haslam left the health service alarm bells were ringing in every direction from hospital to Region."

17.47 This view was shared by a number of witnesses, including Drs Donald, Turner and McIntosh, who said this to the Inquiry:

Q. From what you said earlier, would it be fair to conclude that, as far as the individual patient was concerned, there was a limited extent to which alarm bells were ringing in your mind, given that it was consensual and outside the clinical environment?

A. Oh, alarm bells were ringing yes; I was concerned about it.

Q. Were those alarm bells ringing in respect of the individual patient?

A. Yes, at the time I focused on the individual patient, I am afraid I did not look any further than the individual patient.

Q. If someone had said to you, we have a document – they might have said, a rambling, difficult to read document that seems to make – they may have put it in pejorative terms – makes wild allegations – you would have nevertheless said, I must see that document?

A. Not only that, but any person in my position seeing a document of this kind, the alarm bells would have been ringing like Westminster Abbey, *they really would.*

Q. The problem seems to be – we will come to this later when we deal with Patient B3 – when that complaint was raised, it seems to have been treated as a first complaint, and there seems to have been – between hospital level, district level and regional level – a lack of any one person who is coordinating matters of concern to raise, so when one might get a third or fourth complaint, there is a record of that. Is that something you can help with or express a view on?

A. I would have thought at regional level, if a series of complaints were coming in about one consultant, then the alarm bells would start to ring *and they would pay much more attention to it.*

17.48 Although the remit of this Inquiry is essentially focused on what happened in the NHS organisations, we still need to examine the evidence dealing with Michael Haslam's activities in the private sector and to see how NHS employees – healthcare administrators and doctors – handled his transition from NHS to private practice. If the view of Dr Kennedy and others in 1988/89 was to the effect that Michael Haslam could be seen as a possible danger to women – whether NHS or private patients – we do not believe that the NHS should simply have washed their hands, and said nothing or done nothing. This is obvious for several reasons:

- A consultant psychiatrist such as Michael Haslam (then only 55) could return to NHS work either locally or elsewhere.

- Existing NHS patients could be referred to Michael Haslam privately. Whatever the legal position, the NHS clearly owed a moral duty to ensure that such patients were not exposed to a possible risk of harm that the NHS managers had already foreseen. It would be disgraceful if the NHS was merely allowed to wash its hands of a suspect doctor, without at least taking some steps to protect existing and future patients.

- It was expressly contemplated by Michael Haslam and the Harrogate Clinic that the clinic may take "patients for care from the NHS on some contract basis".

- For the protection of vulnerable women generally.

17.49   Before we consider the appropriateness of the NHS references in detail, we make these preparatory remarks. It is to be borne in mind that in 1988/89, although there were concerns in relation to Michael Haslam's practice, and his safety with women patients, the evidence was considered to be weak. The view taken was that the women patients were not prepared to pursue the concerns and complaints. Also, and this was clearly a very important factor, legal advice from Region and District was a heavily moderating influence. It is very difficult to be critical of Dr Kennedy, when he was being advised by the Region's solicitor to tone down any adverse comments in relation to Michael Haslam – advice given presumably on the basis that comments made without clear supporting evidence could lead to litigation.

17.50   Mr George Wood (Deputy Chief Executive) summarised the position as follows in his 1999 letter to Michael Haslam's solicitor:

> "Whilst certain complaints were made by patients regarding Dr Haslam in the 1980s, the patients concerned decided that they did not wish to pursue, and indeed did not pursue, those complaints. If any such complaints had been pursued (and I repeat they were not) then that would have been a matter for the former Yorkshire Regional Health Authority. The complaint would not have been the subject of local investigation and decision."

17.51   Similarly, we believe that it was pessimistic and defensive legal advice which drove, or at least heavily influenced, the decision by Harrogate Health Authority not to object to, or reject, the application for the registration of the Harrogate Clinic with Michael Haslam as their medical director.

17.52   We know that Professor Haward's evidence to the Inquiry was that Michael Haslam should be taken out of "clinical circulation if we could manage it": "We wished to make it clear to Harrogate Health Authority that there was a problem with this consultant. We did not think he should be in charge of Harrogate Clinic, treating patients." We know that Dr Kennedy's evidence was that he did not believe in 1988/89 that Michael Haslam was a fit person to treat patients, and was prepared to express "serious doubts". So that may be taken as our starting point from December 1988. How those views came about we now outline.

17.53 From the evidence received by the Inquiry, the detailed chronology in relation to the provisions of references is as follows:

17.54 On 8 March 1989, shortly before Michael Haslam left the NHS, Graham Saunders wrote to Dr Kennedy informing him that Michael Haslam had been appointed "Medical Director and Person in Charge" of the Harrogate Clinic, and asking for his views as to Haslam's suitability as a "fit person" to fill those roles. At that time, Mr Saunders was aware of rumours in relation to alleged sexual misconduct with patients

> *"So I would have been aware that there were complaints of this nature which [Dr Kennedy] had found difficult to investigate because the complainants were not in all cases prepared to allow them to be fully investigated, and I was aware, because of what [Dr Kennedy] told me, that discussions were taking place with the RMO, the regional medical officer, about how this could be handled, and I was aware that Dr Haslam had retired."*

17.55 Following that initial request for information, Dr Kennedy wrote a short reference, in which he mentioned the "series of complaints about unprofessional behaviour by Dr Haslam towards female patients", and concluding with the sentence:

> *"Dr Haslam is an extremely well-qualified and experienced consultant psychiatrist, who is competent to manage a clinical facility, but I have no alternative but to raise serious doubts about his suitability as a 'fit person' to treat patients."*

17.56 This sentence is consistent with the telephone conversation between Dr Kennedy and Mr Saunders, from which Mr Saunders understood that Michael Haslam could carry out management responsibilities but should not be allowed to treat patients:

> *"I accept the comments in the sections in Dr Kennedy's statement that Dr Kennedy's approach to me in that conversation is 'I do not think this particular person should be treating patients'."*

17.57 That expression of "serious doubts" by Dr Kennedy never saw the light of day. The withdrawal of the public expression of those doubts probably arose from advice given in late March 1989 by John Lovel, the Regional Health Authority's solicitor, to Dr Haward and to Dr Kennedy, in the light of concerns relating to defamation. The draft letter was amended to read as follows (now dated 30 March 1989):

> *"Since I came to York eight and a half years ago, I have been made aware indirectly as a fellow consultant psychiatrist and later, directly as a manager of the service, of a series of complaints about unprofessional behaviour by Dr Haslam towards female patients. In no case was the complaint confirmed on further investigation. However, within a confidential reference of the kind you require, I feel I have to bring this to your attention because the number of unsubstantiated complaints of this kind is unusual. I have records of six such incidents spread over the years, three of which were in the last two years in the run-up to Dr Haslam's retirement, which he decided to take at the age of 55, after a discussion with the Regional Medical Officer.*

> *"Dr Haslam is an extremely well-qualified and experienced consultant psychiatrist. I hope you will understand the considerable difficulty in composing a reference which is both fair to Dr Haslam and an honest response to your request for confidential information, relevant to your task of deciding the suitability of an application for charge of a nursing home and having personal care of patients."*

17.58 Although this letter does give some more detail of the numbers of complaints, there is no reference to any detail, and no longer any mention at all of "suitability as a 'fit person' to treat patients". The letter reflects "option 2" of the advice given by John Lovel, to which Dr Haward refers in his letter to Dr Kennedy dated 24 March 1989 as "an option which recognises the facts of our involvement with the complaints. It doesn't pursue their content". The letter continues:

> *"If you wish to say anything about the content, then I suggest you have a quiet word with John Lovel as to how far you may go".*

17.59 It is likely that Dr Kennedy did speak directly to John Lovel, and his letter was rewritten in light of that conversation.

17.60 At about this time, the formal letter from the Region (Dr Haward) was being written to the Harrogate District Health Authority (Mr Saunders), which had the task of deciding on registration. The Inquiry has seen the draft of that letter dated 20 March 1989, approved by John Lovel, although "he would have done so had there been more explicit reference to the unsubstantiated allegations that have been made".

17.61 We have no reason to doubt that this was the letter as sent.

17.62 Dr Haward also referred to the complaints and to the fact that they remained "unsubstantiated". However, there is no reference to the detail of the complaints, no reference even to the fact that they were of sexual misconduct, not even to the fact that the patients were women. The letter contains these passages:

> "It is in the nature of psychiatry that clinicians can be vulnerable to certain sorts of complaints by patients, and although these have been investigated within York, patients were neither willing to see the complaints go forward to an arena in which they could be properly tested nor prepared to withdraw them... The complaints, spread over years, were not regarded by us in any sense at all as constituting proof or as providing a basis for evidence which we could have used through any of the normal procedures open to a consultant's employer."

17.63 Perhaps there was some clue for Harrogate to latch onto in the following passage:

> "In discussion with Dr Haslam, he felt he would prefer to resign his NHS appointments having reached the age of 55 with mental health status, rather than see these difficult and problematic complaints pursued further."

17.64 This was an indication as to the real reason for Michael Haslam's retirement, but no more than an indication, and Dr Haward refused to give a character reference himself, suggesting instead to Dr Kennedy that:

> "You would be advised to approach colleagues within the district in which he worked for this greater level of detail."

17.65 That route, if taken up, would no doubt have lead to the revised, John Lovel approved, letter from Dr Kennedy set out earlier.

17.66 What was Mr Saunders to make of this information? His understanding of the authority's role in the approval process is important. He emphasised to the Inquiry that the authority was not seeking to employ Michael Haslam, rather it was being asked to approve the registration of the Harrogate Clinic with Michael Haslam as the medical director.

17.67 In relation to that approval role, in Mr Saunders' oral evidence, he said this:

> Q. He said there were six complaints, of which there are records, which you never sought to pursue?
>
> A. Which are unsubstantiated. I do not think it is the responsibility of the health authority, in its registering of nursing homes, to seek to investigate complaints in another area. We need to take account of the fact, in determining whether or not we think this person is a fit person, about whether there have been complaints, whether they were substantiated or unsubstantiated, how they were pursued. I do not think now, and I did not think then, that it would be the registering authority's responsibility to investigate complaints in another organisation.
>
> Q. However, serious allegations that came to you in a reference, incredibly serious allegations made about someone, you would never think, "This means I have to take more steps to investigate," or to say, "I simply cannot recommend him as a fit person." That is the logical –
>
> A. I reflected on what would be issues which would actually allow the health authority to defensively say: this is not a fit person. If they were not appropriately professionally qualified, if they were not on the register, they would not be a fit person. If there was evidence of a relevant criminal conviction, in other words, something which has been tested out through a court of law and is a relevant criminal conviction; if the individual had been dismissed for a relevant reason and had not appealed, and therefore it was accepted that the reasons for dismissal were correct; if there had been a complaint that had been investigated and was reported to us as a serious complaint which was

investigated and had been found to be proven, that would give you evidence to say that was not a fit person; if there was a complaint which had not been investigated and had not been substantiated and which was denied by the person, I think it is very difficult to say that is evidence the health authority can rely upon, in terms of deciding to register or not register mental health nursing homes on the basis that person is not a fit person.

And later:

"The criteria which the health authority had to use in deciding, not whether to employ Dr Haslam – in determining whether or not it registered the Harrogate Clinic as a registered mental health home, were a whole series of criteria, including the fitness of Dr Haslam as the person in charge. That was just one of a whole series of numbers of criteria that had to be met. If the health authority determined not to register, then the next route would be an appeal to a nursing homes tribunal, that worked on the basis of evidence. The judgment, rightly or wrongly, that I made was that, when I reviewed the references, as part of the procedure where other people had seen them, so it was not just me."

Q. The other people who had seen them would be who?

A. The other people would be the nursing inspectors and the members of the Panel. If you put together these three references which talked about unsubstantiated allegations, there was not enough in there to actually say: "we should decline to register".

17.68 The references before Mr Saunders were as follows:

a. from Dr Hayward – who, in terms of any detail, merely referred the reader to District and Dr Kennedy;

b. from Dr Kennedy expressing concern, and providing some details;

c. from Sir Martin Roth.

17.69 We have mentioned, in some detail, the first two references. The third reference, from Sir Martin Roth, read as follows:

"This letter has in fact to be dictated while I am being driven to the airport and I regret not being able to sign it.

"I thought I would send a brief reply to make it known that I have a high opinion of Dr Haslam's professional skill as a psychiatrist, his administrative ability and his personal qualities. He is a man of high intelligence and unquestionable integrity.

"I am not able to complete the form you have sent until after my return from Portugal."

17.70 So far as can be discovered, the "form" was never completed. Had it been completed it would have revealed that, from the limited information available to the Inquiry, that in answer to the question "Please state how long you have known the applicant and in what capacity", Sir Martin worked closely with Michael Haslam in 1969 – some 20 years earlier, and does not appear, from the evidence we have, to have done so since then. There was no more detailed reference, nor any follow-up. The Inquiry has seen no information available to the decision makers at the time which showed any more recent knowledge.

17.71 Therefore, the comment by Sir Martin that Michael Haslam was a man "of unquestionable integrity", should have been considered in the light of the fact that the reference was based on close knowledge some 20 years earlier and gave no information as to when there was more recent knowledge, or even contact.

17.72 It was put to Mr Saunders that, faced with the three references, and the oral expression of concern from Dr Kennedy, there should have been a refusal to register. The exchange with the Inquiry Chairman was as follows:

Q. I think you have now agreed with me that what you had is one irrelevant reference, because of these three words, one bad reference that would be so bad that you would not employ the man, and another one which says, "There are question marks, check those with York." What I wanted to take you to is really this question: if Professor Kennedy had said, "We suspect, although we cannot prove it, that Dr Haslam has sexual relations with his patients," so making it less ambiguous, if he had said that, and the other two references said exactly the same, or the other two references only dealt with his intelligence and his ability as a general psychiatrist, would you have said that this man was a fit person, moving on to make your registration decision?

A. I think if it was as explicit as that and it was actually written down in the way in which you have described it, then what I would be looking to do is to say, "If we decide not to register the clinic on the basis that this person is not a fit person, have we got enough evidence if we get to a nursing home tribunal so that a reasonable court would actually say that is a reasonable decision?". I think if it is as explicit as the way you have said it and it was written down, and Peter Kennedy was prepared to stand by that and be called as a witness, then the answer to that is probably yes.

17.73 When correctly analysed, the effect of the three references seems to us to have been as summarised in the question from the Chairman.

17.74 Counsel for the health authorities submitted to the Inquiry:

"So far as Mr Saunders was concerned, therefore he had a doctor whose name was on the register and against whom no disciplinary action had been taken. Note the support for his stance from Mark Baker [District General Manager of Bradford Health Authority at the relevant time, now Professor Mark Baker, Medical Director of West Yorkshire Strategic Health Authority]. He would have made the same decision. He said in a written statement to the Inquiry – "In the absence of proven misdemeanour, he did not feel able to act on the advice received." As a former Registering Officer myself, I believe he was correct in that a subsequent Tribunal would not have backed his refusal to register.

"It is easy in 2005 to criticise Mr Saunders. It is easy to suggest that, given what he knew of Haslam, he should have taken the decision anyway and lived with the consequences. It was his honest judgment that he could not justify refusal. The panel's judgment may have been different, even in 1988, but that does not mean that Mr Saunders should be castigated. Before making decisions adverse to Mr Saunders, the Inquiry is asked to consider the whole of his evidence, and in particular the very significant work he did to improve procedures in Harrogate. He is not a man to take patient safety lightly.

"As to the desirability of engaging Michael Haslam, the clinic knew what his reputation was. They asked him about it and he no doubt reassured them. There is no doubt that by the time Drs Kerr and Haslam left the health service, alarm bells were ringing in every direction from hospital to Region. Yet even then, disciplinary action was not possible, in the absence of complainants."

17.75 The final decision was made by resolution of the Harrogate Health Authority on 12 April 1989:

"That on the recommendation of the Nursing Homes Inspectors and the Authority's Nursing Home Member Panel, approval be given to the registration of the Harrogate Clinic in the name of Cygnet Health Care PLC for the care of 34 inpatients and five day patients with the category mentally ill. The registration would include patients sectioned under the Mental Health Act 1983."

17.76 There seems here to be a combination of factors, all of which allowed Mr Saunders to make a decision (or more correctly allowed the health authority to make a decision) – to approve the registration of the Harrogate Clinic, with Michael Haslam as a "fit person" to be Medical Director – which, in our opinion, was wrong. A decision that the Harrogate Clinic would be suitable for registration, even with Michael Haslam in a position where, despite the widespread concerns, he could treat vulnerable female patients. The factors are as follows:

- a pessimistic and defensive view of the legal difficulties;

- a failure by Dr Kennedy, no doubt in the light of legal advice, to express more clearly his own view as to the suitability of Michael Haslam to be accepted as a "fit person";

- a failure by Mr Saunders to follow up the short reference from Sir Martin Roth, which sat so uncomfortably with the other, more recent, references;

- an incorrect weighing up of the references (and Dr Kennedy's oral remarks) by Mr Saunders.

17.77 We have here again referred to the three references before Mr Saunders. In the light of Mr Saunders' oral evidence, the evidence of Mr Baker, and the submissions made on Mr Saunders' behalf (summarised above), we doubt whether the references really did have much practical effect on the decision. Even if all three references had said "we have doubts about this man's professional integrity", or "we do not consider he is suitable", or similar, Mr Saunders and the Harrogate Health Authority would, in our view, still have accepted the registration of the clinic, with Michael Haslam as Medical Director. They would have done so because, as we know, they thought as there were no women patients who were then prepared to make formal complaints, or give evidence against Michael Haslam and, in any event, as Mr Saunders told us, Michael Haslam was "a doctor whose name was on the register and against whom no disciplinary action had been taken".

17.78 The outcome was, to put it at its best, unfortunate, and accepted as such by witnesses to the Inquiry. When Dr Peter Kennedy was asked his views upon hearing of the appointment, he said merely that he was "disappointed". In the light of his firmly held view that Michael Haslam was an abuser of patients; that he believed he had communicated that view to Graham Saunders, but nevertheless Michael Haslam was free to treat patients in the considerably less regulated atmosphere of private practice, this expression of disappointment is perhaps not surprising, if a little understated.

17.79 When Dr Green was asked about his view of Michael Haslam's freedom to continue in practice, the exchange with Counsel to the Inquiry was as follows:

> Q: Once Michael Haslam had left the NHS and was then working in a private clinic, during that period he was seeing private patients, had anybody asked you, you would have had misgivings about the fact that he was seeing patients to the extent that, had someone asked you to recommend a consultant psychiatrist, he would probably have been last on your list?

> A: He would not have been on the list at all, I am sorry.

The Inquiry's conclusions on the retirement of Michael Haslam

17.80 Michael Haslam's appointment to the role of Medical Director at the Harrogate Clinic may have been inevitable under the registration procedures then (and now) in place. We also recognise and accept, that it is a strong step to take for a former employer (here the NHS) to interfere in a person's right to take up employment. Whether or not Michael Haslam continued to practice as a consultant psychiatrist was a matter for the GMC, not for the North Yorkshire NHS. That said, we take the view that women patients in the Harrogate area (actual or potential), would have had cause for real concern if they had known that the newly-appointed Medical Director of the Harrogate Clinic was considered, by at least some of his former colleagues in the NHS, to be a real danger to women. The North Yorkshire NHS not only failed to take any steps to prevent Michael Haslam taking up that appointment, but it went further, and allowed Michael Haslam to leave the NHS not under a cloud, but with all the indicators of a perfectly normal departure – no gardening leave, no suspension, no control of his practice during the notice period, being allowed to remain on ethics committees, remaining as one of the "Three Wise Men", and finally, being granted an honorary consultancy.

17.81 To that we add one more feature. The effective decision maker on the approval of the registration of the Harrogate Clinic, with Michael Haslam as a Medical Director was Mr Saunders. He was the man who, in 1984, had not been told of the Linda Bigwood dossier which referred to Michael Haslam and Harrogate patients.

17.82 What is striking is that even in 1988, when senior NHS managers had very real concerns about Michael Haslam, not one of them considered it appropriate to mention their concerns to the GMC.

Recommendations

We RECOMMEND that when appointments to the NHS are considered, references should be obtained from the three most recent employers and those references should be properly checked.

Chapter 18
Michael Haslam in private practice (the Harrogate Clinic)

The Harrogate Clinic and the South Durham NHS Trust

18.1 As set out above, Michael Haslam left the NHS in 1989 in somewhat strange circumstances, and with mixed messages to the outside world. It was believed, at least by some at District and Region in North Yorkshire, that he had retired rather than face an investigation into allegations of sexual misbehaviour with patients. But, insofar as it was within the power of the NHS to do so, his appointment as Medical Director to the Harrogate Clinic had not been blocked. Further, he had been awarded an honorary consultancy. Insofar as attempts were made to control his otherwise unlimited access to private patients, it was merely "through informal networks", at a local level – for example, by Dr Kennedy to The Retreat and the Purey Cust in York. There was no disciplinary process, no complaint to the GMC, and no police investigation. Further, Michael Haslam continued to see patients privately, in Harrogate, and in York, writing as follows to Dr Kemp in August 1989:

> "Incidentally, I have not retired, but simply moved into full-time private practice and am still available for consultation at the Purey Crust and shortly at 4 St Mary's in York, and also, of course, at the Harrogate Clinic, the brochure of which I enclose for your interest."

18.2 He continued his writing, and was the Honorary Secretary and later Chairman of the Society of Clinical Psychiatrists. He was on the Journal Committee of the Royal College of Psychiatrists. There was more. Michael Haslam continued to practice in two publicly-funded areas – as a Second Opinion Appointed Doctor under part IV of the Mental Health Act 1983, a role which he described as follows:

"I am on the Mental Health Act Commission, giving second opinions to consultants in the Region on section cases, and this takes me, approximately once a fortnight, to a wide variety of hospitals within the Region."

18.3   Michael Haslam also continued to be a medical assessor to the Disabled Living Allowance Board.

18.4   Michael Haslam resigned from the post of Medical Director at the Harrogate Clinic from mid-1990, but continued to see private patients there on a full-time basis until late 1992, when he moved from resident to visiting consultant. He continued to have outpatient clinics and admission rights until they were suspended in October 1996, following allegations by Patient B11, a private patient at the Harrogate Clinic, that she had had a sexual relationship with Michael Haslam.

18.5   Against that background it is perhaps not surprising that Michael Haslam was able to return to the NHS, in December 1993, when appointed as Medical Director of the South Durham NHS Trust – although this was a non-clinical position. The appointment process was somewhat unorthodox – for example, there was no interview, and no references were taken up. It seems to be the position that Michael Haslam simply met some members of the management team and was appointed.

Suspension, termination, and Employment Tribunal

18.6   Michael Haslam was suspended on 7 October 1997 when his name arose in the course of police investigations into allegations relating to William Kerr.

18.7   An alert letter (HSG(97)36) was issued on 21 October 1997 by Professor Donaldson as Regional Director of Public Health.

18.8   Michael Haslam was dismissed from his post at South West Durham Mental Health NHS Trust in July 1998 following the production of the Manzoor report. He then brought proceedings in the Employment Tribunal claiming that he had been both wrongfully and unfairly dismissed. His wrongful dismissal claim succeeded (such that he was able to claim six months payment in lieu of notice) but the Tribunal found that he had not been unfairly dismissed. The essence of the

Tribunal's decision on wrongful dismissal is contained in paragraphs 14 and 15:

> "As to the sanction of dismissal, it is not of course for us to seek to substitute our view for that of an employer in any given case, but rather to ask ourselves whether the decision to dismiss falls within that band of reasonable responses of a reasonable employer acting reasonably. Faced with the findings of the independent review panel and the failure on the part of the applicant to further explain the matter, we are satisfied that the employer in this case had little option but to dismiss, bearing in mind the serious nature of the allegations and the responsibility for patient care. Certainly, we have no hesitation in saying that the dismissal falls within the band of reasonable responses.

> "However, this does not end the matter, because the applicant has also brought a claim of wrongful dismissal. The decision to dismiss was based upon an alleged breach of contract, which we find was not a breach, because the conduct complained of pre-dated the term of the contract. For this reason and this reason only, we find that despite the fact that we have come to the conclusion that the dismissal was not unfair, it was nevertheless wrongful and contrary to the applicant's employment terms because the conduct could not for those reasons, be gross misconduct under those terms and therefore could not justify summary dismissal. Under the terms of the applicant's employment he was entitled to six months' notice of termination. This was not provided."

18.9 Despite his dismissal from his post in July 1988, following the Manzoor report, Michael Haslam remained on the GMC Register and thus, in theory, able to continue practice (although as will be recalled, an alert letter had been issued back in October 1997). It was not until April 1999 that Michael Haslam's name was removed from the Register, in the circumstances set out in the following chapter.

Chapter 19
Michael Haslam investigated

The Manzoor Inquiry

The reasons for the investigation

19.1 At the end of 1997, in view of the seriousness of the allegations, Professor Sir Liam Donaldson, who was then Regional Director NHS Executive Northern and Yorkshire, determined that the Regional Office should convene an independent review of the circumstances surrounding the allegations of sexual misconduct against Michael Haslam between 1984 and 1988, and the response of healthcare professionals and NHS organisations to those allegations. An Inquiry was duly set up, chaired by Mrs Zahida Manzoor, Regional Chair, NHS Executive Northern and Yorkshire. The panel included, as a clinical assessor, a consultant psychiatrist from another Region, with expertise in psychosexual counselling.

19.2 The Inquiry's terms of reference were as follows:

(i) to investigate the complaint made to the York Health Services NHS Trust and three complaints made via the North Yorkshire Police relating to the allegations of sexual misconduct/assault between 1984 and 1988 and to make appropriate responses to the complainants;

(ii) to investigate the responses of individual healthcare professionals and managers to any allegation made known to them at that time (1984–88) and to determine whether such responses were appropriate;

(iii) to investigate the cultural and organisational factors within local health services at the time (1984–88) which may have prevented proper investigation and action;

(iv) to make recommendations about any necessary changes in current practice; and

(v) to make a confidential report to the Regional Director of the NHS Executive who will make public the findings and recommendations of the panel, whilst ensuring that full patient confidentiality is maintained.

The handling of the investigation

19.3 It is important to note at the outset that the Manzoor Inquiry was not hindered by the decision of the local police not to prosecute Michael Haslam. This is a recognition, which we endorse, of the fact that a decision by the police not to prosecute does not necessarily preclude an internal NHS inquiry, or disciplinary proceedings, or even GMC proceedings.

19.4 The Manzoor panel expressly stated that they would be mindful of the (then) current guidance on the handling of complaints set out in *Complaints, Listening, Acting, Improving – Guidance on Implementation of the NHS Complaints Procedure*. It was also decided that the Manzoor panel, in order to encourage openness, would not seek to allocate blame to named individuals. Patients and individual complainants would be kept anonymous.

19.5 The Manzoor panel met for two days on 15 and 16 January 1998 at a non-NHS venue near York. They interviewed four complainants, Patient B7, Patient B3, Patient B5 and Patient B12, and four key NHS staff from the period in question – Dr Kennedy, Dr Haward, Andy Cattell and Stephen Brooks.

19.6 Michael Haslam, although invited to participate, did not do so (refusing, on the advice of his solicitor, to answer questions at the hearing on 15/16 January 1998), save to provide the original file and notes of Patient B3 and to appear before the Manzoor panel on 20 March 1998, accompanied by a solicitor, to read a prepared statement. In his written statement to the Manzoor panel, Michael Haslam stated that the complaints of Patient B3, Patient B5 and Patient B7 had already been investigated and matters not pursued. With regard to Patient B12, he did not deny a sexual liaison but said there was no doctor/patient relationship at the time. More generally, Michael Haslam complained that the procedures of the Manzoor Inquiry were fundamentally flawed and unfair to him.

19.7   The Manzoor panel had available to them contemporaneous material relating to the four complaints, including relevant medical records and management records. These records, plus copies of witness statements and other material provided by the North Yorkshire Police were circulated in confidence to the Manzoor panel members. The NHS staff called to give evidence were given copies of contemporaneous records or statements made by themselves. It was noted by the Manzoor panel that important records of the handling of the complaints against Michael Haslam by the then Yorkshire Regional Health Authority had been destroyed in 1995.

19.8   In addition, Patient B12 provided to the Manzoor panel copies of letters written to her by Michael Haslam.

The Manzoor Report

19.9   An interim report was sent to Professor Donaldson on 2 March 1998. He sent the interim report (minus a confidential section) to the GMC on 4 March 1998. Patient B3 and Patient B12 gave consent for their confidential statements to be forwarded to the GMC; Patient B12 also agreed to the letters from Michael Haslam to herself being sent.

19.10   The Manzoor panel stated that they were struck by considerable similarities between the four complainants. Each complainant described herself as depressed and vulnerable and there were consistent themes of low self-esteem and relationship difficulties, with sexual relationship difficulties as a secondary issue in two cases. All of the complainants stated that they felt "labelled" or "stigmatised" by their mental illness at the time and all described worsening feelings of confusion, guilt, loss of self-esteem and distress which they felt were caused by Michael Haslam's alleged behaviour.

19.11   From evidence to our Inquiry, we have learned that the members of the Manzoor panel saw Michael Haslam as using "grooming techniques" in his alleged seduction or attempted seduction of his patients – in the same way that paedophiles groom young children. It was noted that all the witnesses talked about being sat on the floor, Michael Haslam putting his arm around them and gradually building up to something more serious.

19.12 It was noted by the Manzoor panel that there were contemporaneous statements in the management records. In the case of Patient B3, she herself had made a statement, in addition to there being a statement by a member of NHS staff. In the case of Patient B7 and Patient B5, there were contemporaneous statements by NHS Staff. Patient B12 was noted to have made no contemporaneous complaint.

19.13 It was noted from the management records that in relation to all three patients who made contemporaneous complaints (Patient B3, Patient B5 and Patient B7) Michael Haslam was made aware at the time of the complaint. However, in all three cases the complaints were not pursued by the complainants.

19.14 The Manzoor panel, having been impressed by the consistency of the accounts and the pattern of events described, concluded that Michael Haslam had taken advantage of his position as a doctor to sexually exploit the complainants who were vulnerable patients.

19.15 In relation to the issue of the response of healthcare professionals and managers to allegations made to them, the Manzoor panel reached the following conclusions:

- Although there was clear acknowledgement that, at the time they made their original complaints, the Manzoor panel concluded that the three complainants were vulnerable and distressed, they were not offered any form of support at the time of making their complaint nor in pursuing their complaint at some later date. There seemed to be little understanding of how difficult it would be for the complainant to make a complaint about staff upon whom, at that time, because of their emotional state (or psychological difficulties) they were very dependent. Individual staff including two GPs, a community psychiatric nurse, two consultant psychiatrists and a nursing manager could be said to be at fault. However, the fact that such a wide range of clinical and managerial staff failed to act supportively suggests that at the time, there was no clear understanding as to how such allegations or complaints made by patients should be properly dealt with. It was confirmed to the Manzoor panel that at the time there was no explicit policy in the unit.

- The second criticism which the Manzoor panel made related to the lack of information given to the women following their allegations/complaints. They were not informed of any action taken, other than the fact that their care was transferred to a different psychiatrist. The women were then left with the perception that their complaints had not been taken seriously and that there had been no adequate investigation. This was despite the fact that, although formal investigations had not been carried out, there had been some action taken.

- According to the Manzoor panel, comments made by others were too readily accepted by senior management as a reason not to investigate allegations. Although the women may have been perceived by their doctors as not being robust enough to withstand an adversarial investigation, this should not have prevented formally recorded interviews with Michael Haslam and other staff.

- The Manzoor panel felt that senior staff who dealt with Michael Haslam's retirement should have informed the GMC, in view of the level of concern expressed in the correspondence between senior professionals and managers at the time.

19.16 With regard to their investigation of the cultural and organisational factors within local health services during the period (1984–88) which may have prevented proper investigation and action, the Manzoor panel concluded as follows:

- Although at the time of the complaints there had not been full development of multidisciplinary teams, the panel would stress the importance of proper multidisciplinary working, both to safeguard patients' welfare and also to protect staff.

- On the basis of the information available to it, the Manzoor panel did not consider that the local health services, at the time, behaved differently from the way in which the health service in general would have behaved in responding to such unusual and serious allegations and complaints.

- However, the Manzoor panel felt that there are many areas where practice fell short of what would now be considered good practice, for example: failure to support complainants and in particular to inform them of the external support available (for example through the Community Health Council or Mental Health Advocacy or the Mental Health Act Commission); failure to respond to the complainants; failure to support junior staff to whom disclosure had been made.

- The Manzoor panel also felt that issues had arisen in terms of organisational response to complaints made by vulnerable individuals, which point to areas where good practice needs to be developed.

19.17 The final report was dated 19 May 1998 and the Manzoor panel suggested that it be made available (with the section detailing specific evidence of named complainants and staff removed) to:

- the GMC;

- the complainants;

- NHS Staff interviewed by the panel;

- Michael Haslam;

- the Chief Executive of Durham County Priority Services NHS Trust;

- the Chief Executives of York Health Authority, York NHS Trust, Harrogate Healthcare NHS Trust;

- the North Yorkshire Police;

- the Chief Officer of the York Community Health Council;

- the Secretary of State for Health; and

- the President of the Royal College of Psychiatrists.

19.18   The relevant Manzoor panel recommendations were:

- that when serious allegations are made about clinical staff, clinical records should be immediately secured and copied by the Medical/Nurse Director. This recommendation arose out of the fact that it came to light in the review that Michael Haslam had in his personal possession the original hospital notes of one of the complainants (Patient B3) (including notes for a period when the patient was under a different consultant) which included a description of the contemporaneous complaint;

- that systems should be put in place in Medical Records Departments to ensure that records cannot be removed by staff who are not at that time responsible for the patient, unless some proper reason is given. Robust tracing systems should be implemented so that the whereabouts of medical records is known and recorded;

- that patients, particularly those with complex needs, have an appropriate multidisciplinary assessment and are given a care plan which clearly delineates the roles of those involved in their care. Proper implementation of the Care Programme Approach will assist in this;

- that NHS organisations should develop clear and explicit policies to ensure:

  - that patients have access to information about their treatment, what they should expect from staff and how to raise any concerns they may have;

  - that support by a non-involved, appropriately trained staff member is offered to patients who allege sexual misconduct/abuse/assault;

  - that written information is available to patients not only about the NHS complaints procedure but also about support available from external organisations e.g. Mental Health Advocacy, the Community Health Council, the Mental Health Act Commission;

  - that all staff are aware of a named senior member of staff to whom they may speak in confidence about any concerns they may have about the personal or professional conduct of colleagues;

– that staff are aware of the duty to report an allegation or complaint of sexual misconduct/abuse/assault, even if the patient is unwilling or unable to pursue the complaint, and that any such allegation should be brought to the immediate attention of the Chief Executive or a nominated deputy;

– that when such allegations or complaints are brought to the attention of senior management, proper formal and fully documented investigation is undertaken, leading when appropriate to disciplinary investigation, including referral to professional bodies; and

– that proper feedback is given to patients alleging sexual misconduct/abuse/assault as to the progress of investigations and this is done sensitively;

- that NHS organisations should establish systems, in particular through training and regular supervision, to ensure that staff are clearly aware of boundaries within the therapeutic relationship. Staff experiencing difficulties with boundaries should be encouraged to come forward and seek assistance, which should be given sensitively; and

- the Health Authorities should ensure that advice is available to GPs on the handling of serious allegations made by patients against healthcare professionals.

19.19 These are the formal conclusions and recommendations of the Manzoor Report. We asked Dr Patricia Cresswell for her personal response to what she had read and heard in the course of that Inquiry:

"There are two things I took away very strongly, both personally and professionally. One was the NHS' duty, and I do mean duty, to ensure that people who have had an adverse experience as extreme as this one or even at lower levels of severity, that people can be heard in a non-adversarial situation. I do know that evidence has to be tested later if there is going to be disciplinary or criminal issues. But the NHS has to be very sure that its processes do support vulnerable patients and clients to come forward. The other thing, which very much links in, is the importance to NHS staff of that process as well. We felt very strongly that two of the staff who came forward had suffered a great deal from them not being able to feel that they had taken the issue forward properly because the situation did not allow them to."

19.20 We received in evidence a detailed letter from the Chief Medical Officer that explained the way in which the recommendations of the Manzoor Inquiry had been addressed. From that reply, we have been assured that the policies and practices needed to deal with the above recommendations have been implemented and that implementation by a number of bodies and organisations has been monitored by the Department of Health.

Our conclusions on the Manzoor Report

19.21 The first point to be made in respect of the report is to use it as an illustration of the need to set up some sort of sound investigation quickly. It shows that a report covering the essential issues is of much more practical use if done speedily.

19.22 Having said that, it was clear to us that setting up an Inquiry contemporaneously required determination, leadership and a degree of managerial, and individual, commitment. Those characteristics seem to have been missing in a number of those responsible in the local NHS for most of the period covered by our report.

19.23 The Chief Medical Officer, in his evidence to us, confirmed that there was no bar to an investigation then, referring to the 1980s, provided the will to establish one existed. We saw little evidence that such will did exist. We were also impressed by the evidence of Dr Patricia Cresswell, a member of the Manzoor Inquiry panel, when she said:

> "I refuse to believe that there was not the capacity to look at general clinical performance of what is a high risk area in 1988. There seems to have been no divorcing of the individual complaint [which may not have been taken forward] from the professional performance issues thrown up by them."

19.24 We are in little doubt that if an investigation along the lines of, or with similar Terms of Reference to, the later Manzoor Inquiry had been set up in the 1980s, outcomes could have been very different. Not only would the evidence have been contemporaneous and memories clearer, but any follow-up action would have exposed problems at a much earlier stage. At the very least, the mere existence of an investigation would have made it clear to all those connected with it that their actions were being monitored and scrutinised.

After the Manzoor Report

19.25 Michael Haslam was dismissed from his post at South West Durham Mental Health NHS Trust in September 1998 following the production of the Manzoor Report.

19.26 He brought proceedings in the Employment Tribunal claiming that he had been both wrongfully and unfairly dismissed. His wrongful dismissal claim succeeded (such that he was able to claim six months payment in lieu of notice) but the Tribunal found that he had not been unfairly dismissed. It is clearly a matter of concern that Michael Haslam was able to return to employment within the NHS despite the concerns surrounding his departure in 1988. We comment on this elsewhere, in Chapter 17 of our report.

GMC proceedings

19.27 We first set out the story in some detail, but without reference to the oral evidence, and without comment from us.

Complaints by fellow consultants

19.28 On 11 March 1996, Dr Timperley wrote to the GMC advising them of an allegation he had received from a current patient of his, Patient B10. The patient described to Dr Timperley a sexual relationship with Michael Haslam continuing up until 1994, following the patient having been referred to Michael Haslam for treatment. The GMC instructed its solicitors to interview Dr Timperley to obtain a statement. A meeting was convened between Dr Timperley and a representative of Field Fisher Waterhouse (FFW) solicitors on 2 October 1996.

19.29 On 23 September 1996, Patient B11 wrote to the GMC to complain about the treatment she had received from Michael Haslam whilst a patient of his from 1990 to 1996. Patient B11 alleged that a physical relationship commenced in 1992.

19.30 In late January 1997, after receiving a letter from the GMC advising her that their solicitors would be in touch with her to obtain a statement, Patient B11 decided to withdraw her complaint stating that any publicity of her allegations would have disastrous repercussions upon her current family life.

19.31 However, after some further discussions with a representative from FFW, Patient B11 changed her mind and, in March 1997, decided to pursue the complaint against Michael Haslam. Unfortunately, in May 1997 the pressure became too great, and her concerns relating to the possible damage any inquiry into her complaint may have upon her family life, caused Patient B11 to withdraw her complaint for the final time and it was never recommenced.

19.32 On 24 June 1997, the GMC wrote to Mr Saunders, Chief Executive of the Harrogate NHS Trust, to enquire whether the recent newspaper articles describing police investigations into a local consultant psychiatrist were related to Michael Haslam.

19.33 On 9 July 1997, Dr Peter Kennedy, Chief Executive of the York NHS Health Trust, wrote to the GMC enclosing a note of an allegation against Michael Haslam. This note documented that earlier that month (July 1997), Patient B12 had requested an appointment with Dr Kennedy in order to make a complaint about Michael Haslam. The patient alleged to Dr Kennedy that the relationship she had with Michael Haslam was a sexual one and had commenced after she was referred to Michael Haslam for treatment. The patient described the relationship as having taken place during a period between 1987 and 1990.

19.34 On 12 August 1997, Dr Patricia Cresswell, Consultant in Public Health from the NHS Executive of Northern and Yorkshire, wrote to the GMC to advise it that the police had concluded their investigations in relation to Michael Haslam and had decided not to proceed with laying charges against him, based upon the evidence to hand. Dr Cresswell advised that the NHS had decided to undertake its own investigations into the circumstances surrounding the allegations against Michael Haslam (this became the Manzoor Inquiry).

19.35 However, on 1 September 1997, the police reopened their investigations in relation to Michael Haslam, upon receipt of further evidence from Patient B7. Due to Patient B7's reluctance to proceed to give evidence in court, the police were forced to discontinue their investigations in November 1997, without laying charges.

19.36 Accordingly, the NHS inquiry was put at the top of the agenda and any investigation by the GMC was put on hold, to be periodically reviewed until the completion of the NHS investigations.

19.37 However the GMC's solicitors continued to investigate the allegations, which it was aware of. Specifically, the GMC instructed its solicitors on 8 December 1997 to interview Patient B3, with respect to her allegations against Michael Haslam relating to an alleged relationship between 1981 and 1983.

19.38 On 10 December 1997, Dr Richardson wrote to the GMC to outline rumours amongst his colleagues, which he was aware of, in relation to Michael Haslam. In response to receiving a copy of the letter, Michael Haslam refuted the allegations as being untrue and claimed that they were politically motivated, in light of his campaign for the presidency of the York Medical Society.

19.39 On or about 19 January 1998, Dr Cresswell spoke with the GMC to advise them of the heightened concerns the health authority had in respect of Michael Haslam following the deliberations of the Manzoor panel.

19.40 On 12 February 1998, the GMC wrote to Dr Richardson to request that he obtain further details from his colleagues in relation to the allegations that they had received from Michael Haslam's former patients.

19.41 On 16 February 1998, Dr Richardson wrote to Dr Kennedy to advise him of his dealings with the GMC and Michael Haslam and to invite any comments he may have.

19.42 In support of Dr Richardson's actions, Dr Adams, Consultant Psychiatrist at York NHS Trust, wrote to the GMC on 23 February 1998 detailing the allegations which had been raised with him by Patient B12. Dr Simpson, Consultant Psychiatrist at Northallerton Health Services NHS Trust, wrote to the GMC on 23 February 1998 to advise it that whilst he had not received any complaint from a patient who was prepared to give evidence against Michael Haslam, he had heard from a number of local doctors (GPs) that they had patients who had allegedly been sexually involved with Michael Haslam. On 2 April 1998, Dr Donald, General Practitioner at Lambert Medical Centre, Thirsk, wrote to the GMC noting that a patient of his (confirmed in oral evidence as Patient B4) had told him of a sexual relationship she had with Michael Haslam. That relationship probably continued from about 1985 to about 1994.

19.43 On 4 March 1998, the health authority wrote to the GMC providing it with the interim report of the Manzoor Inquiry. Attached to the report were the synopses of the evidence of Patient B3 and Patient B12, together with the photocopies of the various letters that had passed between Michael Haslam and Patient B12.

19.44 In late April 1998, Dr Timperley wrote to the GMC to follow-up whether there had been any progress on the initial complaint lodged by him in March 1996. He was concerned that whilst Michael Haslam was no longer practicing in the NHS, he still had private patients and the GMC were not taking into consideration their interests that were outside the scope of the Manzoor Inquiry. In its reply dated 17 June 1998, the GMC stated that it would await the result of the NHS inquiry, which would test the relevant evidence, before conducting its own investigation.

19.45 On 22 June 1998, Professor Sir Liam Donaldson, by now Chief Medical Officer (CMO), sent a copy of the final Manzoor Report to the GMC. The report had not been published by the CMO and was provided on a confidential basis. The GMC's solicitors advised that due to a number of omissions of relevant evidence in the report, it could not, of itself, form the basis of evidence to be tendered to the Preliminary Proceedings Committee (PPC) for disciplinary proceedings under the GMC's rules. Then and now, proceedings before the GMC's disciplinary committees require proof to a criminal standard. Accordingly, the GMC instructed its solicitors to recommence their investigations relating to the allegations against Michael Haslam.

19.46 On 10 August 1998, Michael Haslam instructed his solicitors to write to the GMC to ask whether it would accept his voluntary erasure (VE) from the GMC Register.

19.47 On 13 August 1998, the GMC wrote to Mrs Manzoor to state that the report she had produced to the CMO was not 'prima facie evidence' to justify referral to the PPC. The GMC required an unedited version of the report in order to proceed further.

Complaints by former patients

19.48 During the intervening period the GMC's solicitors interviewed Patient B3 and Patient B12. They had made contact with and arranged to interview Mr James Maxwell, nursing staff, Mr Andrew Cattell, nursing staff, and Patient B7.

19.49 On 11 November 1998, the health authority sent the GMC various documents and material relating to the Manzoor Report that had not been disclosed in June 1998.

19.50 On 18 January 1999, Michael Haslam instructed his solicitors to make an application for VE of his name from the GMC Register.

19.51 On 25 February 1999, FFW advised the GMC that they had completed their investigations in respect of the allegations made by Patient B12 against Michael Haslam. FFW opined that the evidence was sufficient to warrant referral of the Patient B12 complaint to the PPC for consideration. Having recently received Michael Haslam's application for VE, the GMC, through its medical screener, Dr Robin Steel, decided that it would be inappropriate to grant Michael Haslam's VE in light of the advice from FFW in relation to the Patient B12 complaint. In accordance with the advice from FFW, Dr Steel referred the complaint to the PPC. Dr Steel thought it would be proper for the GMC to obtain Patient B12's opinion on Michael Haslam's application for VE. However, the GMC did not seek the opinion of the other complainants.

19.52 On 1 March 1999, the GMC wrote to Michael Haslam to formally place him on notice of the referral of the complaint by Patient B12 to the PPC and to advise him of the date of the PPC hearing, 1 April 1999.

19.53 On 5 March 1999, Patient B12, unsurprisingly, instructed her solicitors to advise FFW that she strongly objected to Michael Haslam's application for VE. FFW relayed Patient B12's opinion to the GMC.

19.54 On 18 March 1999, Michael Haslam's solicitors furnished to the GMC his submissions in reply to the allegations made by Patient B12 in her complaint, the subject of the referral to the PPC. In those submissions, Michael Haslam admitted he had treated Patient B12 as a patient in York from 28 November 1986 until 4 February 1987.

During this period, Patient B12 had alleged that Michael Haslam had inappropriately "cuddled and kissed" her whilst taking photographs of her hands with a Kirlian photography machine at Clifton Hospital on 13 January 1987. Michael Haslam denied this allegation. Michael Haslam stated that from 4 February 1987 he considered that the "professional relationship" had ceased and shortly thereafter a sexual relationship had commenced. Notwithstanding this assertion, Michael Haslam acknowledged that he had sent prescriptions for medication to Patient B12, in accordance with her requests, on 18 February 1987, 23 May 1987 and 2 January 1988. On each of these occasions, Michael Haslam declared that he had prescribed the medication in his position as Patient B12's "friend", not her doctor.

19.55 In those submissions Michael Haslam was saying the professional relationship had ended on 4 February 1987, and that Patient B12 had then written to him. The submission continues:

> "Dr Haslam wrote a response dated 18 February 1987. He accepts that this is flirtatious in its tone but it was a response to the letter written by Patient B12…"

19.56 The GMC by then had a copy of that letter – written, even on Michael Haslam's account, within a few days of seeing Patient B12 as a patient. The letter was clearly flirtatious in tone, and in content – for example, with an "I'm jealous" reference to Patient B12's boyfriend. The beginning and ending of the letter are as follows:

> Dear [Patient B12' first name]
>
> Thanks for your nice letter. I enclose a prescription […]. Are you on one or two a day? Anyway I've written it for two and if not it will last longer!
>
> …I'm glad to hear things are ticking over and hope your mood is lifting with my wonderful medication. How is your concentration?!!
>
> I look forward to hearing from you again soon. Be good (not too much?).
>
> Love
>
> Michael

19.57 Michael Haslam confirmed in his solicitor's submissions that he had a sexual relationship with Patient B12, which is said to have commenced in May 1987 after he had arranged to meet her in London for dinner. The relationship, according to Michael Haslam, continued until the middle of 1988.

19.58 Michael Haslam alleged that in August 1989 he was asked by Patient B12's mother to see her for treatment. Michael Haslam states that he "somewhat reluctantly agreed" and did so under correspondence with Patient B12's GP at the time, Dr Kemp. Michael Haslam saw Patient B12 on nine occasions until 3 January 1991 and alleged that he did not see her again, in any capacity, after that date. This treatment it would seem was conducted at the same time as Patient B12 was under the care of another NHS consultant.

19.59 The submissions to the GMC by Haslam's solicitors concluded by requesting that the PPC grant the application for VE made by Michael Haslam – "in view of his age and the fact that his NHS employment has been terminated".

Voluntary erasure

19.60 On 1 April 1999, the PPC considered the complaint against Michael Haslam and decided that charges should be formulated and referred to the Professional Conduct Committee (PCC) for hearing "with offer of Voluntary Erasure". In a letter dated 6 April 1999, Dr Richard Clifford, Assistant Registrar of the GMC, wrote to Michael Haslam to advise him of the PPC's decision and to invite him to lodge an application for VE, saying:

> "...[if] you do not wish to undergo a public hearing, they [the PPC] would instead accept an application from you to remove your name from the Register. The voluntary removal of a doctor's name carries no stigma and some doctors, particularly those who have permanently retired or are about to retire permanently from medical practice, decide to apply for this."

19.61 Mr Finlay Scott (Chief Executive of the GMC) was asked about this letter:

> *Q. Would you agree with me that the signal that letter sends to the doctor is: you should not worry about the consequences of voluntary erasure because it does not mean there is any stain on your character?*
>
> *A. That is correct. I think this is an unfortunate form of words.*

19.62 On 14 April 1999, Michael Haslam wrote to the GMC and forwarded his formal application for VE.

19.63 On 15 April 1999, the GMC wrote to Michael Haslam to advise him that it had granted his application and removed his name from the Register on 14 April 1999, stating:

> *"As matters stand, the inquiry by the Professional Conduct Committee into a charge against you will not take place."*

After the voluntary erasure, including oral evidence and panel comment

19.64 On 28 May 1999, Dr Kennedy wrote to the GMC to ask it to explain why Michael Haslam was granted a VE, despite what Dr Kennedy believed was the policy of the GMC not to allow such applications to doctors who were subject to disciplinary proceedings. Dr Kennedy said:

> *"There was some perturbation in York when we heard the news that Dr Haslam would not have to answer the serious complaints against him, simply because he had sought and had been granted removal from the register."*

19.65 A letter to similar effect was sent by Dr R E Kendell, the then President of the Royal College of Psychiatrists. He said:

> *"I am concerned about the GMC's handling of this doctor... Subsequently Dr Haslam was allowed to remove his name from the Register, thus conveniently putting himself beyond the reach of the Conduct Committee".*

19.66 The GMC responded to Dr Kennedy by letter dated 4 June 1999. Dr Nisbet, Director of Fitness to Practice, stated that it was the policy of the GMC not to offer VE before a doctor's case was referred to the PPC. Accordingly, the GMC did not break with any policy in offering the VE to Michael Haslam when it did.

19.67 Dr Nisbet went on to say that in relation to the various reasons why the GMC will offer a VE to a doctor:

> *"The main one is that it is a speedy way to make sure that doctors do not practice. It has also proved useful in the cases of doctors whose performance has declined towards retirement, who are the subject of multiple complaints about inadequate treatments and who have themselves said that they do not want to practice again. In other cases where there is a risk that a case against a doctor might not be found proven, Voluntary Erasure can be a safer way to protect to public."*

19.68 We observe that, in relation to Michael Haslam at least, this was an interesting explanation. Whilst Dr Nisbet did not suggest that it was an exhaustive list of reasons, those that are proffered can easily be refuted in the case of Michael Haslam. Dr Nisbet stated earlier in her letter that the GMC's investigations had produced a "well-documented allegation of a sexual relationship with a patient conducted over several years". Accordingly, it could not be suggested by the GMC that they had reservations about the potential success of their case against Michael Haslam.

19.69 In his application for VE, Michael Haslam stated that he was making the application due to "retirement". Therefore, the GMC did not have to grant VE to "make sure that (Michael Haslam) did not practice"; he was intending to do that himself, albeit with his hand forced by the referral to the PPC.

19.70 Further, the allegations make no suggestion that Michael Haslam's performance was in decline or that he had provided inadequate treatments. The simple fact of the allegation was that he had been involved in a sexual relationship with a patient, which was contrary to the conduct rules.

19.71 The decision to invite Michael Haslam to apply for VE, and the subsequent granting of VE, produced further letters of protest from former patients, and from a local MP. The following extract from a letter from Patient B12, the patient who would have been the subject of the charge against Michael Haslam, is instructive:

> "Whilst I appreciate that he is no longer able to practice, he is still carrying out the posturing role of pillar of the community, social secretary of one of the University colleges and actively involved in the Schizophrenia Association. It would appear that the matter has been conveniently swept under the carpet and a man who used his position to systematically abuse vulnerable patients has once again got away scot-free and failed to have been called to public account. Even if this is not the case, I feel personally cheated of any justice and feel that once again there has been a cynical disregard for the suffering of the patient".

19.72 The correspondence rumbled on until at least the end of 2000. One former patient [Patient B3] was particularly troubled that her complaint had not been processed at all by the GMC. The letter from the GMC dated 21 December 2000 set the record straight:

> "It is, as I now see, absolutely untrue to suggest that not all of those making allegations against Mr Haslam were prepared to make written statements. It is very clear that yourself and Patient B3 were both extremely helpful and cooperative to our solicitors in preparing the information in the required form.

> "As I now understand the position, in February 1999, David Worrall was in the process of taking witness statements from a number of individuals. These were in different stages of preparation towards the end of February, when a decision was made by a medical member of Council that, given the seriousness and age of the allegations, we should take as much of the case as possible forward to the Preliminary Proceedings Committee (PPC) as soon as possible. At that stage, only one of the statements (that of another of your clients) was in a form which was ready to proceed to the PPC. As with many other cases, we therefore took this part of the case forward, with a view to joining it up with the other elements of the case, including [Patient B3]'s, at a later stage. It should be said that it was not envisaged at this point that the PPC would grant voluntary erasure in this case, hence David Worrall's work at around this time with a number of former patients including [Patient B3].

"Once Mr Haslam was erased, in the manner with which you will now be familiar, he ceased to become a registered medical practitioner, and therefore no longer fell under statutory powers. In short, we no longer had any power to take any action against Mr Haslam once he was erased, notwithstanding the seriousness of the allegations against him, raised by, for example, [Patient B3]."

19.73 Concerns about the GMC's handling of the allegations against Michael Haslam, and his VE, were raised by several witnesses to the Inquiry in their oral evidence. We will here only refer to one, Dr Timperley, referred to above. At the end of his oral evidence, Dr Timperley's overall concerns were clearly and forcefully expressed in the following passage:

"I have given a great deal of thought to this. Most of my involvement in trying to make things happen has related to my dealings with the GMC. I have found the GMC to be opaque and uninterested. I think it is worth stating that, apart from one rather anodyne press release, I have seen nothing in which anyone has actually said the word sorry for this. It is also worth stating that if Haslam had not sued The Sunday Times, he would have got away with it. None of these procedures actually did anything to stop what happened. There is a lot of talk about – you can read Donaldson's statement about the Manzoor Report's findings raising the fear of Haslam suing the NHS and of Haslam having his human rights breached. Nobody says anything about the human rights of patients. They really do not seem to be considered in this at all. I find it very difficult to be objective about it, in that I have had an awful lot of time and effort put into achieving precisely nothing. On a personal level – and this is not a digression – the Inquiry needs to know that I come from Hyde and six people in my parents' street were murdered by Shipman, of which three I knew personally. So I am very well aware of the total failure to deal with medically qualified sociopaths, and I use those words specifically. At no point does it seem that Haslam was actually confronted. That is the point... I would like to believe that in the future the GMC will take complaints seriously, as I do not believe they did so here."

19.74 In the light of the evidence we received expressing such concern in relation to the VE of Michael Haslam, we sought details of the decision of the PCC taken on 1 April 1999 so that we could try to understand their reasoning – or at least the material being considered by the Committee.

19.75 We were surprised to discover the following:

a. None of the members of the PCC sitting on that day has any recollection of the reasons for the decision – or indeed any recollection of the discussion at all (the Chairman of the Committee, who may have had some recollection, is now retired and unwell).

b. No reasons were given for the decision – this was, apparently, normal practice at the time.

c. Although the Committee meeting was attended by a panel of between five and seven members, a legal assessor, a solicitor from Field Fisher and Martineau, and a GMC secretary, there are no notes, no record of the discussion at the Committee meeting, indeed nothing to explain why the invitation to Michael Haslam to apply for VE had been made;

d. Therefore, it is unclear whether the PPC (before inviting VE) were informed that there were other complaints "in the pipeline", or informed that the patients who had expressed concerns were opposed to VE.

19.76 It was readily accepted by the GMC that the situation was "clearly unsatisfactory". The extent of the problem is illustrated by the following exchanges between Counsel to the Inquiry and Mr Finlay Scott, addressing the information which could lead to a referral to the PPC, and the interest of the former patients in knowing about the offer of VE:

Q. [There was] a sufficient case for Patient B12 to be referred [to the PPC]?

A. Yes.

Q. The very strong foundations of a sufficient case in relation to Patient B7 and Patient B3?

A. Yes.

Q. The GMC had the complaints of Patient B11 and Patient B4 which, although withdrawn, given the history in relation to the other three complaints that were live, must still have remained a matter of concern. You could not just say: well, they have withdrawn, therefore there is nothing to worry about?

A. Yes.

Q. You had the concerns raised by Dr Richardson and his reference to six psychiatrists and one clinical psychologist?

A. Yes.

Q. And, therefore, those original components that we identified as in place when the very first complaint came in from Dr Timperley were there writ large: serious misconduct, multiple misconduct, and possibly ongoing misconduct.

A. Yes.

Q. The next feature we had was that prior to a decision to offer Michael Haslam voluntary erasure, the views of Patient B12 were taken?

A. That is correct.

Q. And the view of Patient B12 was, no, she did not want him to be offered voluntary erasure?

A. That is correct.

Q. The views of Patient B3 and Patient B7 were not expressly taken in order to establish whether they had a view on voluntary erasure?

A. That is correct.

Q. Even though, would you accept, that they would have an interest in that decision, given the fact that their complaints would effectively come to an end the moment voluntary erasure was granted?

A. It is undeniable that they had an interest.

19.77 It was also wholly unsatisfactory, and accepted as such by the GMC, that complaints first raised in 1996 took three years to investigate, and in the meantime, Michael Haslam continued to practice without restriction.

19.78 We are told that the position in relation to records of Committee meetings is now vastly improved. We know that extensive reasons were given in relation to the VE of William Kerr.

19.79 We are greatly indebted to the GMC for their detailed responses in answer to our many requests for information and documentation. The Inquiry has received considerable assistance by the provision of two detailed written statements, by letters, by the helpful oral evidence of Mr Finlay Scott, and many files of documents. In the course of providing that assistance, the GMC has readily accepted that as Mr Finlay Scott said in his evidence to the Inquiry:

> "We could have been more effective in our handling of the various complaints and potential complaints against Dr Haslam."

19.80 There are clearly lessons to be learned by the GMC from the Michael Haslam case. One particular concern is whether or not there is any justification, in the interest of the public and of patients, for the retention of the *criminal* standard of proof at GMC disciplinary proceedings, and generally treating those proceedings as if the GMC was engaged in some form of pseudo-criminal process. Of course, where the allegations are particularly serious – amounting, if the subject of police investigation, to a serious crime – it is less likely that the doctor will have acted as alleged. But that difficulty can be addressed without the need to adopt any recourse to criminal standards of proof, or the trappings of a criminal trial. Where the allegations would also amount to serious criminal wrongdoing, probability is, rightly, not easily established.

19.81 As there have been detailed recommendations in relation to the GMC in the *Fifth Report of the Shipman Inquiry*[1], and the government is now engaged (at the time of writing this Report) in an extensive investigation into the role and workings of the GMC, it is unnecessary for us to add yet further recommendations. In the course

---

1 CM 6394-1, presented to Parliament in December 2004.

of that investigation, no doubt the working party will have regard to the accounts given by patients and their relatives in the various Inquiries, public and private, that have taken place over the last few years. In our Inquiry, the former patients made their disappointment over the conduct of the GMC very clear. The working party should at least be aware of their view expressed to us so forcefully:

> "Having regard to all that had gone before, the GMC's conduct was little short of incredible. A show of support for patients which amounted to nothing less than a concerted and determined decision not to investigate what were by then universally well known accounts of Haslam's abuse; a steadfast refusal to respond to those who had made complaints in the past; complete disregard for the safety of the patients. Those patients who thought that doctors would stick together and cover for one another could scarcely have guessed that if and when a doctor did take the complaint forward, then it would be treated in such an off-hand manner by the very authority charged with regulation of the medical profession."

19.82 There were similar views expressed to us by the representatives of the NHS – although more briefly:

> "It is extraordinary that even with the information from Manzoor the GMC did nothing. With all the informal procedures in the world, if Haslam was not struck off he was free to practise in the private sector or abroad. The risk to patients could only be stopped if his registration were taken away... Patient safety could only be guaranteed by the GMC."

19.83 When patients and the NHS are speaking with the same voice, it is to be hoped and expected that the GMC will heed the criticisms and put their house in order. If not, their house must be put in order for them.

19.84 We end this section of the Report with a sentence from the oral evidence of Dr Timperley, referred to above. Whilst we, of course, accept that no system can produce a guaranteed totally risk-free environment for patients in the care of psychiatrists, experience over recent years ought to have taught invaluable lessons in the area of boundary transgression and sexualised behaviour. This may not be the case. The words of Dr Timperley sound a clear warning against which any reform of the regulation of the medical profession must be judged:

> *"I am still quite convinced that a highly intelligent and manipulative abuser would be able to get away with it again."*

19.85 We address the problem raised by this particularly damaging comment later in our Report, when we look ourselves at the situation today, and the role of the GMC in the regulation of doctors.

Chapter 20
The trial of Michael Haslam and libel proceedings

Introduction and early police investigations

20.1   In total (including Patient B12) four women contacted the police helpline, set up in relation to the investigation against Kerr, to complain about Michael Haslam. The other three women were Patient B7, Patient B3 and Patient B5.

20.2   The Harrogate Healthcare minutes of a meeting on 29 April 1997 (held to discuss the case of Kerr) show that there was, certainly at this stage, an awareness of allegations against Michael Haslam and of the fact that he now worked in private practice.

20.3   A review of the management files in 1997 revealed four allegations against Michael Haslam. The first complaint in the files was the 1976 complaint made by solicitors acting for Patient B12. This complaint (as set out above) was noted in the files as being withdrawn and the files contained no further information relating to her case. The other three allegations on the files were those of Patient B7, Patient B3 and Patient B5.

20.4   A meeting was held between Barrie Fisher (Chief Executive, North Yorkshire Health Authority) and George Wood (Deputy Chief Executive, York Health Services NHS Trust) on 20 June 1997 where it was suggested that York NHS Trust set up its own serious incident committee to consider the issues relating to Michael Haslam and to liaise with the police.

20.5 On 13 August 1997 the Police formally stated that they had completed their inquiries into allegations against Michael Haslam. Detective Chief Inspector Hunt wrote to Mr Wood stating:

> "I refer to our meeting of this date concerning the allegations received. I can now confirm that having caused inquiries to be made by my Officers since the reports received there appears to be no evidence of a criminal nature sufficient to support a prosecution through the criminal courts."

20.6 Enclosed with the letter were copies of pro formas, notes and statements by the women who had contacted the police.

20.7 At the end of August 1997, Patient B7 contacted the police and this led to them reopening an investigation of Michael Haslam in response to her allegation of rape. However, on 5 September 1997, Patient B7 declined to make a statement or give evidence.

20.8 On 3 November 1997, the North Yorkshire Police informed George Wood that they had ceased their inquiries and that, with the consent of the women involved, they were passing the information in relation to the complaints against Michael Haslam to the NHS for further investigation. George Wood wrote to Patient B12 on 10 November 1997 to inform her that the way was now clear for the NHS review to start in relation to Michael Haslam.

Second police investigation and trial

20.9 Following the commencement of the libel proceedings by Michael Haslam, Patient B7 agreed to make a statement to the police containing her allegations of rape (she had declined to make a formal police statement in the earlier 1997 investigation). This led to a reopening of the police investigations.

20.10 Michael Haslam was charged with four counts of indecent assault and a fifth count of rape. The first two counts related to two indecent assaults against Patient AB in 1981. He was found guilty on both counts and sentenced to 18 months' imprisonment on each. The third count related to an indecent assault against Patient B3, again in 1981. He was found guilty and sentenced to 18 months. The fourth count related to an indecent assault against Patient B7 in 1988. He was found guilty and given a sentence of three years. The fifth count related to the rape of Patient B7 again in 1988. He was found guilty and sentenced to seven years' imprisonment. The judge directed that the first four sentences should run concurrently with each other and that all four should run concurrently with the rape conviction. The total sentence was therefore seven years. The judge also directed that Michael Haslam should serve at least half of that sentence before he could be considered for parole.

Appeal

20.11 Michael Haslam appealed against all convictions. On 20 May 2004 the Court of Appeal upheld the convictions on the four counts of indecent assault, referring to them as "safe verdicts of guilty". The appeal against the fifth count of rape was allowed, the Court finding it "unsafe" and quashing the conviction and sentence. The Court of Appeal also declined to order a retrial of count five on the grounds that there were safe verdicts on counts one to four and, taking into account the age of Michael Haslam, it was not considered that the public interest required a retrial on the count of rape. Accordingly, the overall result of the appeal was that the conviction was quashed, the seven-year sentence was set aside, but the convictions for sexual assault and the total sentence of three years' imprisonment remained.

20.12 He was released from prison on parole under licence in June 2005.

Libel proceedings

20.13 On 24 January 1999, the *Sunday Times* published an article headed "Psychiatrists accused of serial rapes", which commenced as follows:

> *"Two senior psychiatrists are being investigated on suspicion of raping or sexually assaulting dozens of female patients. Up to 30 women are alleged to have been attacked by Michael Haslam ..."*

20.14 The article also stated that Michael Haslam was being investigated by the GMC. It quoted one complainant as "having complained repeatedly to hospital authorities without success. She was given the impression that doctors believed her and that, although she was considered too vulnerable to talk to police herself, an investigation would take place." It quotes the victim as saying "I was told I was one in a long line of victims but nothing whatsoever happened. I just trusted them to follow the correct procedure."

20.15 On 20 January 2000, Michael Haslam issued libel proceedings against Times Newspapers Ltd. The Particulars of Claim were amended in July 2001 to include a reference to a second article published by the *Sunday Times* and headed "Doctor too ill to face trial".

20.16 In its defence to the libel proceedings, Times Newspapers Ltd said that the article it had printed was true. It is unnecessary here to set out the detail of those proceedings.

20.17 The claim was listed for a 10-day trial, due to commence on 14 May 2001 but vacated on Michael Haslam's application on 11 April 2001.

20.18 In October 2004, after the decision of the Court of Appeal (Crime Division), the *Sunday Times* and Michael Haslam agreed to resolve the libel court case without proceeding to trial. The terms of the settlement were that Michael Haslam would not prosecute any further or outstanding claims against the *Sunday Times* and would make a substantial contribution towards payment of the legal costs incurred by the *Sunday Times* in defending the actions brought by Michael Haslam. The agreement stipulated that if either party, or their respective legal representatives, were asked to provide a statement, then such statement would be that which was agreed between the parties. The Inquiry asked the *Sunday Times* for a statement regarding the resolution of the libel proceedings. The statement issued was:

> "*Michael Haslam has discontinued his libel action in relation to an article published in the* Sunday Times *in January 1999. Dr Haslam has agreed to make a substantial contribution to the newspaper's legal costs.*"

Section Four
The response of the GPs

Introduction

21.1 In previous chapters we have set out, in some detail, the concerns and complaints raised by William Kerr's and Michael Haslam's former patients over a number of years. The usual, but not the only, recipient of those concerns and complaints was the patient's GP. The responses by the GPs were, to put it kindly, mixed. In this chapter we look more specifically at the role of the GPs, and try to discover reasons for that mixed response.

21.2 In the course of the Inquiry, we received written responses from 35 GPs, 23 of whom were invited to give oral evidence. With very few exceptions we were impressed by the cooperation we received, and the way in which GPs gave their evidence to us and responded to what must have been searching and difficult questions. We are acutely conscious that the GP witnesses (indeed many of the witnesses) were being asked to recall events and conversations that occurred up to 30 years ago – often without patient notes to refresh their memories. Furthermore, the GPs who received concerns and complaints (or who are said to have received them) did not have the benefit of hindsight – they could not know that William Kerr and Michael Haslam would be subject to criminal investigation and prosecution, and generally did not know that there were many similar (indeed, strikingly similar) concerns and complaints being raised by different patients with other doctors, nurses, social workers, etc. We bear these factors very much in mind when considering the actions and reactions of the local GP community.

21.3 Our starting point is that all the GPs were competent, caring professionals. Indeed, many former patients have expressed admiration and gratitude. We also accept that the reason some GPs did nothing is that they knew nothing – some patients who remember making complaints may not have done so as clearly or as expressly as they now recall. Further, some patients who wanted to express concerns, or make complaints, were unable to do so. However, this cannot be a complete answer. While there were clear instances of GPs taking action to pursue concerns, notably Dr Wade, Dr Moran and Dr Moroney, this represented the minority. The more characteristic picture was of GPs who were well aware of patient concerns about the practices of William Kerr and/or Michael Haslam, and who did nothing or very little.

21.4 There are, of course, a number of possible situations that could have resulted in a GP failing to act:

- No complaint had been made, thus the GP was unaware of the problem.

- The GP heard only hearsay or rumours, and deemed it inappropriate to act on such information.

- The patient informed the GP of a complaint, but insisted that no action be taken.

- The patient wanted action taken and informed the GP, who decided to take no action.

- The patient informed the GP, who discussed it with partners or colleagues, but no action was taken.

- The patient informed the GP, who excused or rationalised the behaviour of the psychiatrist.

21.5 All the GPs who gave evidence to the Inquiry accepted that their duty to their patients centred on safety. Dr Givans, the current (at the time of oral hearings in 2004) Secretary of the North Yorkshire Local Medical Committee, speaking on behalf of many of the local doctors, said this in his written evidence:

"Doctors have always had a professional responsibility to take appropriate action if they had reasonable certainty that a colleague was acting unethically, but until recently doctors were given stern warnings about making accusations about colleagues. Unless they were in possession of strong evidence to support those accusations, they were advised that hearsay was not acceptable."

21.6 Some of the GPs in their oral evidence went further, accepting that if they had evidence of sexual assaults, or sexually inappropriate and unethical behaviour, which *may have been* true (i.e. was not obviously absurd or incredible), they should have done something with that information to protect that patient, and to protect existing and future patients who were being treated by, or could in the future be treated by, that "suspect" doctor.

21.7 GPs did not know enough about psychiatric practice in order to ask patients more about the detail and sort of questions William Kerr in particular was asking his patients. Had they done so, concerns might have surfaced sooner.

21.8 Despite the concerns of many GPs about disclosures made by patients, the evidence given to the Inquiry indicated:

a. a general failure to take personal responsibility for pursuing the disclosure;

b. a lack of clarity about whether it was their duty to do so or merely to hear the disclosure and "do what the patient wanted" – including making no report of alleged sexual misconduct – if that was what the patient wished;

c. confusion or lack of knowledge about what the range of options were for taking action.

Dr Simpson

21.9 From the previous chapters we conclude that GPs were aware of concerns in relation to allegations of sexual misconduct in relation to Michael Haslam by 1974 (the undisputed disclosure by Patient B1 to Dr Foggitt), and regarding William Kerr by at least 1979 (the undisputed disclosure by Patient A22 to Dr Wade). However, we were struck by the following more recent account which, at least in our view, illustrated the paralysis that had taken hold of some members of the local GP community when it came to complaints of sexual misbehaviour.

21.10 Dr Simpson began work as a Consultant Psychiatrist at Northallerton NHS Trust in October 1987. By this time William Kerr had indicated that he would retire the following year, and at about this time Michael Haslam was considering his retirement from the NHS, and moving to the Harrogate Clinic.

21.11 The following is taken from Dr Simpson's written evidence to the Inquiry:

> "When I became Consultant Psychiatrist in October 1987 I made a point of going out and introducing myself to all of the GPs within my area. The GPs would be the individuals responsible for referring patients and I wanted to get to know them. Within a few weeks of taking up the post, some time in October 1987, I went to the Picks Lane Practice (now Lambert Medical Centre) in Thirsk to meet with GPs. Most, if not all, of the GP partners were present at the meeting. Of those partners only two are still alive. One, Dr Donald, still works at the Lambert Medical Centre. The other, Dr Harrison, is retired.

> "During the course of the meeting with the GP partners one of them, I cannot recall which, told me they were pleased that I had been appointed as they could now refer young women to a psychiatrist. Dr Haslam, they informed me, had sex with female patients.

> "I was very shocked by this revelation and asked them why they had not done anything about it. The GPs informed me that Dr Haslam's approach was to suggest to the young women he was treating that they have a night away with him. It seemed this was suggested to them as part of their treatment. On these nights away, Dr Haslam would have sex with these women. The GPs' view was that this was not illegal and there was therefore nothing they could do about this. The GP partners did not give me the names of any of the patients Dr Haslam had gone away with.

> "I was clear that something had to be done about this and, even though I was a young, new arrival I was prepared to be the one to bring this to the attention of the appropriate people."

21.12 In his oral evidence, Dr Simpson developed that written evidence, describing his meeting with the local GPs in some detail. Again, we are not (nor was Dr Simpson) setting out this information to demonstrate, or even suggest, that the information was true. Instead, it shows what information was available at the time: information that should have been subject to contemporaneous examination, investigation and scrutiny. What the account shows is that, at least from Dr Simpson's perspective, some GPs were aware of concerns (true or not), and either did not know what to do or, knowing what to do, did nothing.

21.13 What Dr Simpson did, and when, is discussed elsewhere in this Report (see Chapter 23, paragraphs 57 and 58). Dr Simpson, as he explained to the Inquiry, was shocked by what he heard, and rightly so. His evidence is even more important in that he describes the Thirsk GP practice as *not* atypical, although more communicative than others. He received the clear impression in 1987 that GP practices (or even the local GP community) were well aware of allegations that Michael Haslam had sex with his patients. The response "it is not illegal, we cannot do anything" has been confirmed to the Inquiry by Dr Harrison (of the Picks Lane Practice). We also know from the evidence of Dr Harrison that this response was not confined to one surgery, for when he sought advice from a GP in a neighbouring practice the same response was given. The opinion of Dr Givans was that the attitude "it's not illegal, we can do nothing" would have been the view of the majority of GPs at that time.

Contributing factors

21.14 We conclude that there were a variety of contributing factors, ranging from inertia and failure to believe patients to unwavering faith in consultants, all combining to produce the situation where the rights and interests of patients were downgraded, and their expressions of concern and complaint went unheeded. We discuss these further below under the heading: "Key factors explaining GPs' responses".

21.15 What is striking is that the GP community seems to have failed to grasp at least three fundamentals:

- These female patients were vulnerable – having been referred to William Kerr and/or Michael Haslam by their GPs, because the GPs believed they were suffering from some form of mental disorder.

- Consultant psychiatrists were capable, even in the 1970s and 1980s, of conduct that was not in the best interests of their patients – which was professionally and morally wrong, even if not a criminal assault.

- In order to protect their patients fully they needed to take concerns about sexual misconduct of consultants seriously and ensure they were passed on, in some form, in order to prompt an investigation.

Key factors explaining GPs' responses

The old-boy network

21.16 Professional loyalty was an influential factor. Known colloquially as the old-boy network, doctors were not keen to say or do something that might damage the reputation of another doctor for fear of:

- getting it wrong, particularly where they may have felt there was a lack of "hard evidence";

- having to endure the possibility of protracted disciplinary measures;

- the threat of an action for defamation from the doctor;

- the threat of damaging their own career, being perceived as disloyal or a troublemaker.

21.17 Patient B1, who spoke to her GP, Dr Foggitt, about an alleged sexual relationship with Michael Haslam, described the old-boy network in the following terms:

> *"I remember thinking [after making her disclosure about Haslam to Dr Foggitt] – oh well, they are all closing ranks, he [Dr Foggitt] will not do anything against Dr Haslam, because they are all doctors together."*

21.18 Another particularly striking example of the "old-boy network" is to be found in the response a GP allegedly gave to Patient A9. Following Patient A9's complaint of sexual abuse by William Kerr, the GP (whose identity has not been established) allegedly shrugged off the complaint, with the remark that William Kerr was a senior figure and that it would be inappropriate to make a formal complaint. The GP allegedly added that, in any case, the patient would not be believed.

21.19 The role of the senior partner was potentially significant in perpetuating the old-boy network. A senior partner would be older and experienced in general practice. Significantly, he (and they were predominantly male during the period in question) would often be the first port of call for a more junior GP faced with an allegation from a patient about a fellow healthcare professional. Evidence presented to the Inquiry suggested that senior partners strongly influenced culture and working practices within the practice. A negative response by the senior partner generally ensured that the complaint was not taken any further.

21.20 Two factors that, in our view, resulted in the particular strength and influence of the old-boy network in North Yorkshire at the period in question were the low turnover of GPs, and the overlap between professional and social roles.

21.21 The doctor population was described as being very stable, leading in some cases to two generations of GPs in one family, and husband and wife teams of GPs. It was also predominantly male, particularly at the senior partner level. We also heard evidence of overlapping histories between consultants and GPs; where they had trained together or worked together as house officers in the same hospitals.

21.22 While we do not in any way suggest collusion, and while this pattern of relationships between doctors was not uncommon throughout the NHS, the culture of familiarity between health professionals fuelled those who sought to uphold the old-boy network. We recognise again that this is a common feature of many professions. However, we consider that it is one of the factors that may have acted as a disincentive to disclosure and full investigation. While it made for a very cohesive community, the evidence suggests that it also resulted in an unspoken social pressure not to "rock the boat" and an expectation that people would fit in.

21.23 All these factors, these subtle influences to the general advice to GPs at the time and reluctance to act, may be more readily understood if not condoned. Dr Moroney said this in his evidence:

> " ... as a new recruit to general practice, my voice was less important than that of more established colleagues."

21.24 Many local GPs shared his view and considered themselves bound by it. When this instruction is added not only to the factors already mentioned but to a tolerance, by some local GPs, of consensual sexual relations between doctors and patients, the moral confusion revealed by the evidence of Dr Simpson, it becomes reasonably clear why the activities alleged against William Kerr and Michael Haslam could go unquestioned and unchallenged.

21.25 The Inquiry also heard evidence from GPs and other health professionals about the interrelationship of professional and social life in the York/Harrogate and surrounding areas – for example, the annual summer event held at the Kerrs' home to which many local doctors were invited.

21.26 In addition, we heard from a number of GPs of meetings and seminars held by the York and Harrogate medical societies, where they met their local consultants. There was also one patient who described a GP as having shared interests – such as golf and shooting – and participating in them with William Kerr. While in itself that may not be remarkable, and indeed in a local community they are all normal and positive things, it nevertheless presents a potential barrier to action regarding complaints or concerns by a GP when the relationship with the person concerned is itself a friendly and social one.

21.27 In this regard it is also noteworthy that the evidence given by the women GPs indicated quite strongly that they were not part of the social network that included William Kerr and Michael Haslam, although there was no indication that there was any conscious act to exclude them.

21.28 There was little to suggest that GPs and consultants, in their social encounters, exchanged information about patients or discussed individual cases. We accept that in a small and relatively stable community there will inevitably be some movement between professional and social contacts. The issue of concern here is to what extent this may have created a) a disincentive to believe patients when they raised concerns – about William Kerr in particular, and b) a reluctance to pursue concerns and complaints that were expressed.

Isolation of GPs

21.29 A second factor is what we describe as the isolation of GPs. We include here both the absence of any coordinated process for exchange of information between partners of a single practice, and more widely between different practices working in the same region.

21.30 During the entire period covered by this Inquiry, GPs were independent contractors providing general medical services in accordance with a standard national contract.

21.31 Family Practitioner Committees (FPCs), which came into being in the 1970s, had very little control over GPs. Until 1980 FPCs had no management role or any responsibility for professional competence or quality of care by GPs. Although their role was more active in the 1980s, their control over GPs remained limited throughout the relevant period.

21.32 Without any unifying structure, a complaint that crossed sectors was difficult to navigate and individual GPs, from their isolated position, had to have specific time and motivation to handle such matters. Some GPs had limited knowledge of how the complaints system within a hospital operated or to whom complaints should be forwarded. Further, large hospitals, such as Clifton, were seen as fairly closed systems – this acted as an additional inhibiting factor.

21.33 It appears from the evidence given by the GPs that the prime focus of internal information-sharing within a GP practice in the 1970s and 1980s was the morning coffee break, lunch or end of the day chat. These informal gatherings were commonly used to exchange information about patients and other matters of concern to partners in the practice. This was described to us as being an informal practice and not a meeting; there was no agenda and no notes were taken.

21.34 However, this system of informal exchanges was liable to break down in the case of large practices, where all partners could not meet together. Where GPs ran satellite surgeries in different towns and villages away from the main practice, communication was further hampered.

21.35 Significantly, there does not seem to have been any structure, informal or otherwise, to extend communication outside the individual surgery to neighbouring practices.

21.36 One specific means of communication between GPs within the same practice, at least in relation to the frequent situation where one patient would be seen by a number of different members of the practice, is that of patient notes. However, there was evidence that when serious disclosures were made, GPs were in a dilemma as to whether they should record the concerns in the patient's record. Practices and views on what was the appropriate thing to do varied widely. In some cases no notes were made on the record, or only coded references such as "psychiatric disillusionment" (Patient A40), which, while clear to the author, may have been obscure to a doctor taking over the care of that patient.

21.37   There was little or no systematic recording of complaints in an incident log held at practice level. There was no readily accessible record of complaints that could have been drawn together to form a wider picture of concern. The knowledge of such concerns resided within individuals rather than on any system. This knowledge was lost when individual GPs retired or patients moved practices. At best, knowledge of complaints was communicated within a single practice, but we found no evidence of any surgery actively seeking to systematically inform other practices.

21.38   The Inquiry's view is that the absence of a coordinated or written process for the collation and exchange of information between GPs, both within practices and between practices, lack of knowledge of hospital complaints systems, and unsatisfactory note keeping, contributed to the failure to recognise the incremental nature of the allegations about William Kerr and Michael Haslam. Had records been kept, it might have enabled GPs to approach William Kerr's or Michael Haslam's employers with enough evidence to trigger a proper investigation of the allegations.

21.39   The lack of a coordinated system of record keeping was not the preserve of GPs. Throughout the mental health service during this period there appears to have been a failure to collate information and see trends. One of the striking factors, particularly in the case of William Kerr, was the number of domiciliary visits he carried out. Visits were sanctioned, sometimes retrospectively, by GPs (thus securing the consultant an entitlement to an additional home visit fee). Had there been a central system of recording the total number of domiciliary visits by all practitioners, any marked increase by a particular consultant would have been noted and should have been the subject of some investigation. As we know, that never occurred in the case of William Kerr. We do not suggest that domiciliary visits should be curtailed; clearly they provide an invaluable service. However, any doctor who is making excessive visits (when compared to contemporaries) should be required to provide an explanation.

21.40 Instead of a coordinated approach, the response of many GPs to complaints concerning consultants who were working within hospital settings (and conducting domiciliary visits) was that this represented "someone else's problem". There were other mental health professionals and managers working in much closer proximity with the consultants than GPs, and they assumed that if there was a more serious problem with the behaviour of either doctor, it would be tackled from within the mental health system. This is an understandable response. However, as we know from the situation with William Kerr and Michael Haslam, they were overly optimistic in their assumption – appropriate investigations were not carried out.

21.41 The presence of large psychiatric hospitals seen as "closed communities", together with the stereotypical image of psychiatrists in the 1970s as being eccentric or wacky, were both factors cited by GPs in their evidence. What arose within the North Yorkshire GP community in particular was a tolerance of sexualised behaviour by the two psychiatrists being passed off as "the norm".

21.42 Other GPs in evidence gave a clear view that they thought a consensual relationship between a doctor and a patient was acceptable. Dr Simpson, a new consultant psychiatrist, immediately recognised that professional boundaries had been violated.

Lack of external support

21.43 A third key factor in explaining the response of GPs is, we believe, to be found in the lack of external support, both at local level from the Local Medical Committee (LMC) and at national level from the GMC.

The Local Medical Committee

21.44 The Inquiry explored the role of the LMC in relation to GPs. In his expert evidence to us, Dr Michael Jeffries described the role and responsibilities of the LMC:

"For many GPs faced with the problem of how to best deal with a patient complaint concerning sexual assault by a consultant, the obvious source of help would be the LMC secretary or chairman, both of whom are GPs. LMCs are the bodies set up to represent the interests of GPs within an area and do not represent hospital or public health doctors of any grade. Although they have statutory right to exist, they have no statutory obligation to process complaints against doctors. An LMC secretary would, even in 1970, be expected to offer advice and support to a GP concerned about the unethical behaviour of a consultant but there would have been, and still is, no statutory obligation on an LMC secretary or member to further or facilitate a complaint."

21.45 We are aware of two instances where GPs sought advice from an LMC representative regarding complaints about William Kerr or Michael Haslam. Dr Harrison sought advice from Dr McClellan concerning Michael Haslam and allegedly received the response that as the alleged acts (consensual sexual relationships) were not illegal, nothing could be done. Much later, after William Kerr's retirement, Dr Osmond went to Dr Givans and reported Patient A37's allegation of rape by William Kerr. Dr Givans was aware of other similar concerns by this time and his recollection is that he told Dr Osmond to seek advice from his medical defence organisation.

21.46 However, for the most part, it seems that during the period when GPs were faced with concerns about William Kerr and Michael Haslam, the LMC was not where they turned. We do not know how the LMC might have responded had they been faced with a group of GPs who had recorded and collated their concerns about William Kerr and/or Michael Haslam, because this never happened.

21.47 It is difficult to say whether the LMC failed in its role, as we have not been able to establish with any certainty what its state of knowledge was regarding the complaints against William Kerr and Michael Haslam. However, we would find it surprising in the extreme if it was completely unaware of the concerns that were found to be relatively widespread among GPs. Certainly the LMC took no proactive steps to act as a unifying voice for GPs in relation to their concerns or to further test the veracity of the information it was hearing.

The General Medical Council

21.48 Another aspect of the lack of external support was a common consensus among the GPs that reporting their concerns to the GMC was unlikely to be productive. There were repeated references in the evidence of doctors regarding their relationship with the GMC. The most consistent message we received was that doctors (and some patients too) were aware of the role of the GMC in regulating the profession, but were unaware of the practical implications of that role. There was a lack of clarity among GPs as to what the procedures were for reporting concerns and complaints. What was surprising in their evidence was the predominant sense of resignation about the length of time it would take to get a response from the GMC and the degree of detailed or hard evidence that would be required to trigger any action by the GMC.

21.49 The Inquiry heard from Mr Finlay Scott, the current Chief Executive of the GMC. He confirmed the need for a patient who was prepared to "stand behind the complaint" before the GMC was able to act. He asserted: "We did not see ourselves, at that point in our history, as investigating concerns. We saw ourselves as reacting to complaints. In the absence of a complaint, because there was no complainant, there was no basis for taking something forward."

Tolerance of sexualised behaviour

21.50 Dr Simpson's evidence demonstrates the importance of a new person coming into a relatively stable workforce and challenging what had become the status quo, expressed as "the way we do things around here!" The GP community, rather than challenge unacceptable behaviour, simply turned a blind eye to practices they had some concerns about.

21.51 Dr Simpson was quite clear that what the GPs were reporting was totally unacceptable practice for a consultant psychiatrist. For unclear reasons the GP community at large had come to accept (condone) this behaviour. A variety of reasons for this were heard by the Inquiry. Psychiatry was not widely understood and some psychiatrists were known to be eccentric.

21.52 Consensual relationships between doctors and patients are not illegal. Psychiatrists were like gold dust and very difficult to recruit. There were fears that there might not be any psychiatrists to replace William Kerr or Michael Haslam.

Insufficient expertise in psychiatry

21.53 From the evidence we have received, there was a clear lack of focus on mental health issues in GP training and insufficient knowledge of psychiatric consultations. (Indeed, until 1979 GP training was not mandatory for a qualified doctor moving into that field.) This, in our view, was a fourth factor in explaining the response of GPs. Put simply, GPs did not always have the background of knowledge to form the necessary treatment plans that would best suit some of their patients with mental health difficulties. They needed the help and expertise of those better qualified in that field. While there is no criticism of referral to specialists, when those specialists were the consultants about whom the concerns and complaints were being raised, the conflicts and difficulties were obvious.

21.54 Further, GPs' limited knowledge of mental health issues in some cases led them to believe that patients complaining about their psychiatrists was a feature of their illness. This is demonstrated by the alleged response of one GP to a patient who complained about William Kerr's alleged sexual advances. Faced with a distressed female patient who made an allegation of a sexual assault, the GP allegedly responded: "Why do women always complain about their psychiatrists?" Patients were too readily believed to be fabricating or embellishing stories about their psychiatrists when in fact they could just as easily have been telling the truth. Allegations were all too easily rationalised, rather than being explored in an inquisitive way to establish the validity of what was being said.

21.55 The failure to believe patients or, in some cases, to interpret or question the concerns expressed by patients was sometimes compounded by the GP's poor understanding of what could reasonably be expected of a psychiatric consultation undertaken by a consultant psychiatrist. Had this been better understood, some of the accounts given by the women at the time might have been put into context and some of their tentative expressions of concerns might have been more readily identified as being indicative of serious problems.

21.56 Women were outlining to their GPs that both William Kerr and Michael Haslam were asking them to talk in detail about their sex lives. This was taken at face value, rationalised as psychiatrists understandably asking questions about libido as this was relevant in an assessment of mood. The GPs in question rarely probed in depth the nature of the questions being asked relative to the woman's presenting problem and did not ask for details of what happened in the consultation. This led to complaints being shut down at a very early stage and women feeling disbelieved.

21.57 It was evident that what was being reported to these GPs was outside all of their known experiences; it was not a foreseen risk that consultant psychiatrists could be doing something that was harmful to their patients. There was no general perception of offences by consultants, or indeed any doctors in this area, rates of offending were not known, and there was limited professional guidance forthcoming from the GMC.

Confidentiality

21.58 Another explanation, and a fifth factor explaining the reluctance of GPs to go to the GMC or, indeed, any other authority to pursue a complaint, was a genuine concern regarding patient confidentiality.

21.59 Of the GPs who gave evidence, some clearly emphasised their duty to the individual patients who were in a fragile state of mind, and who wished to preserve confidentiality. Other patients were perceived by doctors to be not in a strong enough state of mind to progress their concerns through the complaints system at the time (something that patients themselves acknowledged). Some GPs felt their responsibilities to the individual patient, and confidentiality, took precedence over wider safety considerations towards other patients and the potential continued risk of not following up a complaint. In some cases this dilemma was clearly expressed by GPs; in others, GPs indicated that they did not even consider any possible wider safety concerns about allowing William Kerr or Michael Haslam to continue to practise. The issue of patient confidentiality is a particularly complex one and for that reason we deal with it at greater length in Chapter 28 of this Report.

Power of consultants

21.60 A sixth influence was undoubtedly the perceived power of consultants, although this seemed to us to have a larger influence within the non-GP fraternity, mainly because of the ability of consultants to make career-changing decisions affecting their juniors. However, there was evidence among the GP community that this was a factor in some decision making.

21.61 The GPs who gave evidence to us were divided in their views as to whether there was a power differential between hospital consultants and general practice that made complaints harder to raise. This notion was strongly denied by some GPs, who felt there might have been an inequity in resources rather than in the power dynamic. However, both operated in separate domains, with patients being the common factor passing from one to the other.

21.62 We were left with a general impression that consultants, in the perception of many GPs, occupied a higher, more privileged position in the hierarchy of the medical profession. Any approach that questioned their behaviour – perhaps even beyond the field of clinical judgement to include personal activities – was difficult and problematical. It was never to be undertaken lightly and only to be contemplated in extreme circumstances where proof of inappropriate behaviour could be backed up by detailed and usually written corroboration.

Ambivalent attitude to relationships between doctor and patient

21.63 A seventh and final factor, one that we found disturbing and closely linked to tolerance of sexualised behaviour, was the ambivalent attitude to doctors forming relationships with patients and ex-patients. The Inquiry heard doctors offer a variety of views with regard to this issue. At one end of the spectrum was the view that any personal engagement with a patient or ex-patient by a doctor was completely unprofessional and detrimental to the long-term well-being of the patient. Other GPs were not clear in their own minds, so sought advice from their senior partners. At the opposite end of the spectrum was the view attributed to the GPs of the Picks Lane Practice at Thirsk that consensual sexual relationships between doctors and patients "were not illegal" and nothing could be done.

21.64 Michael Haslam gave evidence to us that in his view friendship between a patient and psychotherapist could be very supportive and rewarding. The acceptable level of "friendship" was not explained.

21.65 A good example of the serious lack of clarity that existed among some doctors about what could be considered "unethical behaviour" in the field of personal relationships between doctor and patient appears in the evidence given to the Inquiry by Dr Foggitt, who, in 1974, was the recipient of a disclosure by Patient B1 of an alleged sexual relationship with Michael Haslam. Dr Foggitt said:

> "It seemed to me that Haslam had been very foolish. It was human weakness, quite possibly professional misconduct, but not a crime. I was probably not in favour of reporting the matter to the authorities because I probably did have concerns about Patient B1 and her husband going public on the matter, especially with Patient B1 being vulnerable. I would have been concerned that further stress might wreck their marriage. Reporting the matter to the authorities was likely to do more harm than good as far as Patient B1 was concerned and that was what troubled me most. In order to understand my thinking at the time, it must also be remembered that as far as I was concerned this was a one-off. There was nothing to alert me to a bigger problem. I did not know Haslam to be other than a good psychiatrist.

> "I do not believe that I discussed Patient B1's affair with Dr Haslam with my partners. I think I kept it to myself. As to why I did not report what I had learnt to the authorities, I have a feeling that it was probably not part of the culture at the time to report another doctor to the GMC and, if Patient B1 was not in a position to pursue the matter any further, or she and her husband had no wish to do so, it would have been virtually impossible to proceed."

21.66 As with the issue of confidentiality, the Inquiry considered the issue of sexualised behaviour, and in particular the nature of the relationship between the psychiatrist and the patient, to be a complex area that warranted further consideration. Accordingly, this is dealt with more fully in Chapter 29 of this Report.

Chapter 22
GPs who passed on the complaints

Introduction

22.1 In an earlier chapter we considered the response of the GP community at large and explored some of the factors that explained their failure to examine properly the concerns about William Kerr and Michael Haslam that were then in general circulation.

22.2 However, it would be misleading to suggest that there were no GPs who sought to report matters and to bring their concerns, or the concerns of their patients, regarding William Kerr or Michael Haslam to the attention of the authorities.

22.3 We set out here the stories of three of the doctors, each of whom to a greater or lesser extent sought to pass on their concern and, in modern terminology, "blow the whistle". Their stories are extracted from the evidence summarised in earlier chapters.

Dr Wade

22.4 A significant number of GPs received concerns or complaints about William Kerr's behaviour directly from patients. The concerns or complaints ranged from worries about inappropriate questioning on sexual matters to explicit allegations of sexual abuse.

22.5 It is a disturbing fact that only one GP, Dr Wade, took any steps to forward the complaint he received about William Kerr. Even then the steps he took were limited and, as it turned out, completely ineffectual.

22.6 Dr Wade's evidence to the Inquiry was that by 1979 he was already aware of Kerr's reputation for flirting with patients. We should state here that we believe the use of the term "flirting" tends to underplay the seriousness of the reputation. William Kerr was a consultant psychiatrist and the patients with whom he was allegedly overstepping the boundaries and "flirting" would, in many cases, have been vulnerable and fragile women. On any view, they had all been passed into his care because the referring GP was of the opinion that they were so unwell that they needed the specialist attention of a consultant psychiatrist. Many of the patients were suffering from some form of mild to severe mental illness and were taking prescribed medication to alleviate their symptoms.

22.7 The rumours were of sufficient concern to Dr Wade to cause him to carry out a risk analysis before sending patients to William Kerr. His evidence was startling in its candour. He was specifically aware of the potential danger to female patients, so that when he referred them to William Kerr, he described it as putting him "on the horns of a dilemma". He told the Inquiry:

"I tried to be selective in the type of patient I referred.

"What I had to do was to weigh up the option of the benefit the patient would obtain by the consultation with him [William Kerr] as opposed to not having a consultation, or some considerable delay and therefore exposing the patient to potential risk."

22.8 Dr Wade made it clear that he was not isolated in his concerns. His fellow partners "must have been aware" of the rumours regarding William Kerr. Likewise, other GPs in Knaresborough and Harrogate practices would have known of the concerns surrounding William Kerr's behaviour towards patients. Indeed, he went as far as to say that he was sure that on dozens, if not hundreds, of occasions, fellow GPs wrestled with the same dilemma he faced.

22.9 While there must have been an understanding among the GP community of the power imbalance between psychiatrist and patient, and the potential for harm if the rumours about William Kerr had substance, no action was taken either by individual GPs, by GP practices or by the Local Medical Committee to examine the rumours with any degree of diligence. Dr Wade's assumptions about the knowledge of fellow GPs were shown, during the course of the Inquiry, to be accurate.

22.10 Despite Dr Wade's concerns about William Kerr – concerns that were sufficiently serious to make him reluctant to refer patients – and his belief that there was unease among substantial numbers of GPs, he felt unable to report the situation to the health authorities at District or Region. He explained why in the following terms:

> "It was just incomprehensible that someone could behave in this way and one would never have imagined that this behaviour would have been from a professional colleague, particularly a consultant professional colleague."

22.11   The GP community, Dr Wade among them, failed to contact the hospital authorities to notify them of the dilemma they were in and the unease they felt at referring patients to William Kerr. When asked whether he considered contacting the hospital, Dr Wade responded as follows:

> "I considered that. But I felt that really it would not get me anywhere … so far as I was aware there was no definite form of making a complaint in that way. The consultant staff in the hospitals were completely separate and had their own system of dealing with complaints, as opposed to general practitioners."

22.12   Dr Wade went on to explain his lack of action as follows:

> "The evidence that I had prior to referring Patient A22 was based on rumour, and I do not think tittle-tattle is too strong a word to put upon it, in other words, very superficial rumour. There was certainly nothing substantive that I felt I, as a medical practitioner, could have taken action upon in order to take it further against a colleague, another medical practitioner, in the climate of that time, 1979."

22.13   Dr Wade's view was that the Local Medical Committee would have similarly felt unable to go to the District on behalf of GPs:

> "I think that in the period that we are talking about the attitude would have been that, unless they had names, dates and this sort of thing, they [the LMC] would not have gone further, because they would have been, I presume, ridiculed for not presenting evidence in a factual manner."

22.14 This reluctance to complain was explained in part, said Dr Wade, by the stern warnings received when he was training to become a doctor that:

> *"You would never criticise a colleague, whether they be a GP or a consultant."*

22.15 He also acknowledged that the reluctance to complain about a consultant was exacerbated by the power imbalance between GPs and consultants, an attitude towards consultants fostered and encouraged in his student days.

22.16 Although Dr Wade's candour can be praised and he should be credited with being the only GP who sought to forward a complaint about William Kerr, Counsel for the former patients submitted that there were "grotesquely illogical" processes at work in Dr Wade's mind.

22.17 Despite his awareness of the potential danger in referring patients to Kerr, Dr Wade continued to refer them. His belief that they would disclose to him how Kerr behaved (and we received evidence from many witnesses who said they felt unable to make any disclosure to their GP) could only apply to those patients who had allegedly suffered at William Kerr's hands. He did little to prevent a potential danger he had already foreseen for those who had not already accused William Kerr of abuse.

22.18 Before 1979, Dr Wade was in a similar position to many local GPs. He was aware of rumours surrounding William Kerr's conduct with female patients and he had serious concerns about these rumours – so much so that he altered his referral system – but he had no specific complaint or details to rely upon. He is no more or less to blame than a large number of his colleagues who were similarly inactive in raising any concerns about William Kerr. That inactivity changed when he received a visit from Patient A22.

22.19 Patient A22 disclosed to Dr Wade that William Kerr had visited her in her own home, that he had groped her, tried to kiss her and propositioned her with the words: "the thought of going to bed with you would be delightful". Her story is set out in greater detail in Chapter 7.

22.20 Dr Wade's first response was that he would discuss the matter with William Kerr. This was a course that Patient A22 objected to. Further, Patient A22 told Dr Wade quite clearly that she did not want him to take the matter any further. Despite this, Dr Wade was sufficiently concerned to consult his senior partner, Dr Rushton. Dr Wade's evidence was that Dr Rushton was shocked. This conflicts to some extent with Patient A22's evidence that a friend of hers, who had seen William Kerr for treatment for postnatal depression in the 1960s, had complained to Dr Rushton about William Kerr's alleged sexual misconduct, to which Dr Rushton had responded that women tended to imagine things when they were in a distraught state.

22.21 Dr Rushton is deceased and so we were unable to reach any firm conclusion on his state of knowledge of complaints against William Kerr prior to Dr Wade discussing the case of Patient A22. However, it was Dr Wade's evidence that, prior to the Patient A22 disclosure, he felt his fellow partners "must have been aware". Even if Dr Rushton had not been party to prior concerns about William Kerr, which we find unlikely given his role as senior partner, he should have responded with positive advice when Dr Wade raised the case of Patient A22 with him. In fact it appears that Dr Rushton neither gave any positive advice nor took any action regarding the allegation of sexual assault. Here is an apparent example of a senior partner who should have been supporting and encouraging his more junior colleague (Dr Wade), but who seems rather to have been taking the side of the consultant, a fact possibly explained by a personal friendship between the two men, about which Patient A22 gave evidence.

22.22 Following her disclosure to Dr Wade, Patient A22 went to Knaresborough Police Station and explained to a female police officer what had happened. However, she declined to make a statement for fear that she would then be obliged to attend court to give evidence. The police in turn contacted Dr Wade and informed him that a complaint had been made (anonymously) against William Kerr. Dr Wade assumed, it appears correctly, that the police complainant was Patient A22.

22.23 Dr Wade, having received no guidance from Dr Rushton, yet having had the severity of the matter impressed upon him by receiving a visit from the police, was faced with a dilemma. Patient A22 had clearly expressed her view that she did not want the matter taken further. Dr Wade felt that "foolish action" on his part could have exacerbated her anxiety and depressive state. Nevertheless, he felt he had to notify someone in authority. He decided to take the matter to a senior consultant colleague of William Kerr, Michael Haslam. Dr Wade's evidence was that this action was his attempt at "putting a marker down". He said he reported the matter to Michael Haslam "similar to a forces situation where you report to your immediate superior officer … in the hope that he would know how to proceed on the hospital protocol of dealing with the situation, which I did not."

22.24 Dr Wade made an appointment to meet Michael Haslam alone during his outpatient clinic at Harrogate District Hospital. He told us he did not mention Patient A22 by name when he spoke to Michael Haslam, merely stating that a patient of his had made a serious complaint about William Kerr, and that there had also been a complaint to the police, although matters had not progressed.

22.25 Dr Wade described Michael Haslam's reaction at their meeting as being "non-committal". He said that Michael Haslam thanked him for the information and the meeting ended. Dr Wade neither requested nor received any follow-up.

22.26 In his evidence to the Inquiry, Michael Haslam said he recollected being visited by Dr Wade. However, his recollection was that Dr Wade simply asked him to take over the consultant care of Patient A22 and explained the circumstances surrounding her refusal to continue to see William Kerr, which included a reference to an alleged sexual assault, although details were not given. Michael Haslam denied that he was ever charged with the task of forwarding the complaint and stated that he did not see it as a colleague's role to make judgements about another.

22.27 The medical records show that Patient A22 was not referred to Michael Haslam until two years later, in June 1981, apparently by Dr Rushton. Accordingly we do not accept Michael Haslam's evidence that the principal purpose of Dr Wade's meeting with him was to ask him to take over Patient A22's care. When Patient A22 was seen by Michael Haslam in 1981 she recalls him referring to "my esteemed colleague" William Kerr. From this Patient A22 inferred that Haslam was aware of the fact she had complained about William Kerr. Assuming that Patient A22 is right in her recollection and inference, it would seem that either Dr Wade is mistaken and he had informed Michael Haslam of the identity of Patient A22 back in 1979 and this had been recalled by Haslam, or that Dr Rushton, when referring Patient A22 to Michael Haslam, had informed him of the background of a complaint by Patient A22 against William Kerr. Alternatively, of course, Michael Haslam could have spoken to William Kerr and obtained the identity of Patient A22 from him.

22.28 Following Patient A22's disclosure, Dr Wade continued to refer patients to William Kerr, but would do so only when there was an urgent need for a domiciliary visit if William Kerr was on duty, or where there was no other psychiatrist available (the alternatives being Michael Haslam and Dr Bromham).

Conclusions

22.29 We accept that Dr Wade was well intentioned in reporting the complaint to Michael Haslam, and was not merely aiming to warn William Kerr to "watch out" in the future. However, and perhaps understandably in light of Patient A22's desire that the complaint should not be progressed, we consider that Dr Wade did not present the complaint with any force and failed to convey to Michael Haslam in clear terms that he was making a formal complaint that he expected to be raised with the hospital, district or regional authorities. Nevertheless, we do not consider that this exonerates Michael Haslam from severe criticism for failing to take any steps to forward the serious concerns, and clear potential issues of patient safety, that had been raised with him concerning William Kerr.

22.30 We find that Michael Haslam must have been aware that Dr Wade was informing him of the concern about William Kerr with the intention that "something be done" – there is no other sensible interpretation. He failed to forward that concern to the hospital authorities, or to Region (as William Kerr's employers), with the result that nothing was done. The complaint raised by Dr Wade ought to have led to inquiries being made in 1979 into William Kerr's practice.

22.31 We have set out all this in some detail because it illustrates many of the factors discussed in the last chapter. Dr Wade's account is that of a GP who was, on his own admission, unfamiliar with the hospital complaints system. He had concerns (prior to Patient A22's complaint) about making any report based on hearsay and rumour, and refers indirectly to the old-boy network, saying: "You would never criticise a colleague, whether they be a GP or a consultant." Dr Wade also acknowledged the power imbalance between GPs and consultants. Like many of his colleagues, his first port of call when faced with a specific complaint from a patient about the alleged sexual misconduct of a consultant was his senior partner, although this did not prove to be a source of any positive advice. Finally, Dr Wade also had to grapple with the problem of patient confidentiality.

22.32 We recognise that Dr Wade was unique among his fellow GPs in believing that he had to take, and in taking, some positive action to forward the complaint. This is all the more striking given that he faced the same obstacles as his fellow GPs of the old-boy network, lack of knowledge of the complaints system and problems of confidentiality.

22.33 Insofar as it is possible to speculate on why Dr Wade acted differently from his contemporaries, the answer perhaps lies in the fact that he had a particularly good relationship with the patient who complained and was thus convinced of the truth of her account. Further, he had received a visit from the police and this could have left him in no doubt of the potential seriousness of the allegations. His failure to act might have been exposed if there was any police investigation and prosecution.

22.34 Having acknowledged that Dr Wade did act differently from his contemporaries, we must also consider whether the action he took was adequate in all the circumstances. Even when we consider that he was proactive to some extent when others were not, which we applaud, we are driven to the conclusion that the action he did take was incomplete. This may seem to some to be a harsh conclusion, but we have considered what he did know very carefully.

22.35 In spite of a serious complaint of sexual misconduct, which he believed to be true and suspected was not an isolated incident, Dr Wade continued to refer female patients to William Kerr, accepting "inevitably" the risks that he placed them under. Further, having raised concerns with Michael Haslam about William Kerr's practice, he took no steps to satisfy himself that an investigation had taken place, despite knowing that William Kerr was continuing to practise without restriction.

22.36 We reach this conclusion even in light of the expert advice we have received that in the absence of a formal complaint by Patient A22 and her formal consent to disclose her complaint, Dr Wade may have believed "in the face of available information from the GMC and the BMA ... he was making unfounded criticism of a colleague that could result in him being criticised or even disciplined".

22.37 Dr Wade's evidence also goes to the heart of the problematic issue of rumours. At what point should concerns be raised with authorities? Doctors should not be faced with unsubstantiated or malicious rumours that can blight their career, yet to refuse to listen to rumour may be to ignore important warning signs. We discuss this issue in more detail later in our Report.

Dr Moroney

22.38 Dr Moroney was one of the GPs who forwarded his concerns about Michael Haslam to the hospital authorities. Significantly, in the view of the Inquiry, the complaint he received occurred in 1987, towards the end of Michael Haslam's career as an NHS consultant. Both his and Dr Moran's responses to a complaint about Michael Haslam in 1988 (see below) show a markedly different approach from that of many of the GPs who were the recipients of concerns a decade or more earlier. The most obvious comparator is with the actions of Dr Foggitt, who, when faced with a complaint from Patient (B1) in 1974 about her alleged sexual relationship with Michael Haslam, took no steps to inform the authorities.

22.39 Both Dr Moroney and Dr Moran were aware of the existence of a complaints system. While they may not have been familiar with the detail (indeed Dr Moroney accepts he was not), they recognised the importance of forwarding the concern and were able to establish (in

Dr Moroney's case after consulting a colleague) to whom they should address the complaints. In both cases this was Dr Kennedy, the Unit General Manager of Mental Health for York Health Authority, and subsequently District General Manager. Likewise, both were aware of the need to make a clear written note of the complaint.

22.40 When Patient B5 made her disclosure to Dr Moroney, she felt he believed her. However, while he explained the complaints procedure to her, she was influenced by his view that it would be hard for her to prove the case and that it might be to her detriment to have to go through the complaints procedure.

22.41 Dr Moroney recorded in Patient B5's GP notes on 18 June 1987:

> *"?change psychiatrist. Pt. feels threatening physical relationship is developing between Michael Haslam and herself. Dr Kennedy phoned."*

22.42 Dr Moroney phoned Dr Kennedy twice (on the advice of a fellow doctor, Dr Jackson), and was advised that the patient would need to be prepared to address a disciplinary hearing. Dr Moroney accepted in his evidence that his knowledge of the complaints system was poor:

> *"I had had very little to do with complaints procedures, and I certainly had not dealt with them on the training scheme, apart from complaints against GPs personally, and it was a long-winded system. But I had no idea how to cross the boundary and go into the hospital."*

22.43 Dr Moroney told Dr Kennedy that although the patient did not want to make a formal complaint, she wanted the matter noted on the record, should there be another alleged incident. In keeping with this wish, Dr Kennedy made a typed note dated 26 June 1987 recording Dr Moroney's telephone call. However, Dr Moroney felt that his action in passing the complaint on was not welcomed. In his oral evidence he described this unease:

"It was the fact that I felt I had got very important information which needed to go back into the system to get an appropriate response, and I was made to feel I was acting beyond my status and my information was not welcomed. It certainly was not acknowledged on a professional level as appropriate. It felt like I was struggling to be heard. I accept that is not necessarily the same as the patient's difficulty in being heard, but I did find the whole process very difficult."

22.44 Dr Kennedy advised Dr Moroney to see Patient B5 again and explain the complaints procedure, reassuring her that enquiries would be made by a professional and would be tactful, but could result in a disciplinary hearing at which her evidence would be crucial. Dr Kennedy further advised that if Patient B5 was still emphatic that she would not repeat her allegations or make a complaint, then Dr Moroney should discuss with her whether to cease her outpatient appointments with Michael Haslam and whether Dr Kennedy had permission to let Michael Haslam know that serious questions had been raised about his professional conduct by a named patient and a named GP.

22.45 On 18 June 1987 Dr Moroney spoke to Dr Kennedy again and confirmed that Patient B5 would not proceed with a complaint but would stop attending Michael Haslam's clinic. Dr Moroney was to refer her to another clinician. It was recorded that Patient B5 had agreed that Dr Kennedy could speak to Michael Haslam on her behalf and this course of action was agreed with Dr Wintersgill (District Medical Adviser).

22.46 Dr Moroney, however, continued to consider not only that his complaint had not been welcomed, but that there was a culture that such matters should not be raised.

"I still do not feel that I was treated with respect, let alone the patient's allegations treated with proper respect. But that is how I feel. I do not have objective evidence on that.

"But it was not just that. It was other meetings where I raised the issue of Haslam, always preserving confidentiality, but asking if other people had picked up any whispers or ideas. It just felt like there was a brick wall.

"The overwhelming feeling was that really: was this valid? Was it worth addressing? Was it a bit of a storm in a teacup? I did get the feeling of who was I, as this new general practitioner, to be raising such issues about well-established members of the medical community.

"It is always very difficult interpreting this, because I have no idea of a lot of the actual words that were used and I have no idea what the intent was and I have no idea, as I have already said, whether Peter Kennedy was representing a bankrupt system or whether the words truly were from his own heart.

"But there was no little talk, you know, 'Hello, how are you?' whatever, 'How are you doing?' There was no, 'Thank you for calling,' there was no, 'Yes, I acknowledge this.' It was very much silence from the other end of the phone when I was trying to go through what I felt I must act on. That was both from the DMSC officer and Peter Kennedy."

Conclusions

22.47 It is perhaps simplistic to attribute the different reaction of Dr Moroney, compared with that of Dr Foggitt 13 years earlier, purely to the passage of time, although many GPs did speak of how their approach had changed over the years due to a growing awareness both of the prevalence of abuse (particularly in the context of child abuse) and the duty to speak out. However, we do find that the passage of time was a factor that goes some way to explaining the reactions of Dr Moran and Dr Moroney when compared to their predecessors.

22.48 Dr Moroney was perhaps ahead of his time, but we conclude that he is representative of the more proactive stance towards forwarding complaints that is now present among healthcare professionals. However, as his story demonstrates, all was not well even by 1987. Dr Moroney himself was not satisfied with the response he received. Ultimately there was no investigation of Michael Haslam that was prompted either by the concerns he had forwarded (relating to Patient B5) or by the concerns raised by Dr Moran, that were to arise in 1988 (although this complaint did lead to Michael Haslam's retirement from his NHS consultant post).

Dr Moran

22.49 Patient B7 complained in September 1988 both to her community psychiatric nurse (CPN), Stephen Brooks, and her GP, Dr Moran, about sexual misconduct by Michael Haslam. Dr Moran immediately spoke to his GP partners and contacted Stephen Brooks. Dr Moran and Stephen Brooks met on 29 September 1988 to discuss the matter and took the decision to inform Dr Kennedy. Stephen Brooks' recollection was that on this occasion they discussed the fact that there had been at least one other complaint or concern raised about Michael Haslam. This seems likely as Dr Moran was aware of Patient B5's complaint because the patient had recently joined his practice and informed him of her complaint about Michael Haslam's alleged inappropriate sexual advances. Dr Moran had believed that Patient B5's complaint had already been investigated and thought the problem was one of a specific relationship. It was not until he heard Patient B7's complaint that he appreciated the potential of a wider problem and risk to patients. Stephen Brooks also had some, albeit very limited, knowledge of prior question marks over Haslam's behaviour. He was able to recall an incident a number of years earlier when, at a union meeting, there had been a reference to Haslam's mistress being admitted for psychiatric treatment. This seems likely to have been a reference to Patient B3.

22.50 Although his recollection is that he spoke first to Dr Kennedy, it seems that Dr Moran's first step was probably to contact the "Three Wise Men" – appointed by a Special Professional Panel that health authorities set up to ensure "prevention of harm to patients resulting from physical or mental disability of hospital or community medical or dental staff". Dr Raymond Lawrence Marks, an anaesthetist, a member and subsequently chairman of the "Three Wise Men" committee, recalls being contacted by Dr Moran about a patient (who was not named) who had made allegations of sexual misconduct by Michael Haslam. Dr Marks decided this was not a matter for his committee and referred the matter to Dr Kennedy. This corresponds with Dr Kennedy's evidence that, once alerted to the complaint, he was clear it was a matter that fell within his remit, as opposed to that of the "Three Wise Men". In any event Dr Moran did contact Dr Kennedy, who advised him to handwrite everything that had been said and personally deliver the letter. This Dr Moran did. Dr Kennedy made a detailed note of his phone call with Dr Moran.

22.51 Dr Kennedy later returned Dr Moran's telephone call and Dr Moran formed the impression that a decision had been taken that Michael Haslam would be asked to resign.

22.52 Stephen Brooks, accompanied by Dr Reilly, saw Patient B7 on the ward on 29 September 1988. Dr Reilly informed Patient B7 that Dr Kennedy was aware of her complaint. He explained to her the procedure for making a complaint, following which she indicated that she did not wish to take the matter further. Dr Reilly stated at the criminal trial that he considered Patient B7 too emotionally unstable to cope with any formal interviews with the police or even hospital managers. Stephen Brooks subsequently saw Patient B7 on her own; on this occasion she told him that Michael Haslam had been lying across her and kissing her face during a 6pm appointment at Clifton Hospital. Stephen Brooks took a signed statement on this occasion, although this has subsequently gone missing. Stephen Brooks' recollection was that the statement was largely a repetition of matters he noted in his records.

22.53 At the criminal trial, when asked why she had made no formal complaint "to the police or someone like that", Patient B7 replied:

> *"Once Stephen Brooks, Dr Moran and Dr Reilly knew, they reassured me that they would – well, they didn't reassure me they actually asked my permission to take the nature of my complaint to the authorities at Bootham Park, and I always assumed, as did my husband, at that point that the police would naturally be involved as part of that inquiry anyway."*

Conclusions

22.54 The fact that, although Michael Haslam did retire, no investigation was conducted into his practice, and he then went on to work in the private sector, demonstrates that even by 1988 the system of dealing with serious concerns about consultant conduct was far from satisfactory.

22.55 However, in relation to the response of GPs, Dr Moran's story paints a more positive picture than that of GP responses in the 1970s and early 1980s. Dr Moran appears to have readily recognised the need to forward the complaint and produced a detailed written statement at Dr Kennedy's request. Further, there appears to have been communication and co-operation between the GP (Dr Moran), nursing staff (CPN Stephen Brooks) and management (Dr Kennedy) in order to document and progress the complaint, although there is no indication that Dr Moran (or Stephen Brooks) were kept "in the loop" and informed of developments.

Summary

22.56 In this chapter we have set out the stories of three GPs who did take positive steps to report complaints made to them by patients about the alleged sexual misconduct of consultants.

22.57 It is true that Dr Moran and Dr Moroney were practising in the late 1980s, to some extent a different climate from the 1970s when some of the other complaints by patients appear to have fallen on deaf ears.

22.58 However, the so-called "change in culture" should be used neither to discredit their stance nor to excuse their predecessors who failed to report and pursue serious concerns and complaints about both William Kerr and Michael Haslam.

22.59 It is perhaps appropriate to end this chapter with a reference back to the GP who, as far as the Inquiry can establish, was in fact the first "whistleblower". In 1964 Dr Mathewson, a GP practising in Northern Ireland, ignored express pressure that he should not give evidence against a colleague, and pursued a complaint by a young female patient (who alleged that sexual intercourse had taken place in William Kerr's car) against William Kerr. Dr Mathewson gave evidence at a disciplinary tribunal, with the result that William Kerr's career in Northern Ireland came to an end. It is a sad fact not only that William Kerr was able to evade the consequences of the disciplinary hearing by relocating to England, but that once in England there was not a single GP who displayed the fortitude of Dr Mathewson in pursuing any one of the many complaints against William Kerr to the logical conclusion of any form of disciplinary

Chapter 23
GPs who did not pass on the complaints

Introduction

23.1 The most frequent recipients of disclosures of abuse by patients among healthcare professionals were GPs. GPs, with whom patients were likely to have had a long professional relationship, were in many senses the obvious people to turn to. Similarly, a local surgery was likely to represent a less intimidating location and, significantly, an environment that was removed from the consultants' "domain" in the hospital.

23.2 It is thus of considerable concern that, with a few notable exceptions, which we considered in more detail in the previous chapter, the vast majority of GPs who were recipients of concerns (which ranged from poorly expressed and unspecified refusals to see a particular consultant to unambiguous disclosures of serious sexual abuse) failed to take any positive steps to ensure that these complaints were investigated and adjudicated upon.

23.3 Linda Bigwood wrote in her original written complaint about William Kerr that it was so "well known" to GPs in Harrogate that William Kerr was abusing female patients that some would no longer refer female patients to him. This was a comment that, as stated elsewhere in the Report, we consider to have been well founded – some GPs were doing exactly as she described.

23.4 In this chapter we bring together the stories of those GPs, and GP practices, who either suspected or were directly informed that something was amiss in the consultant psychiatric services provided by William Kerr and Michael Haslam, and yet failed to take any action. Many of the GP responses have already been set out as part of the detailed patients' accounts, earlier in the Report. However, the importance of the response of GPs cannot be overstated. They were the first port of call for the majority of the patients. The greatest failure of the GPs was that, for many patients, they were also the last port of call. Patients who received no encouragement from their GPs when they first voiced tentative expressions of concern generally then withdrew from any further attempt at making a formal complaint. In this chapter we have drawn together the most striking accounts of those GPs and their surgeries who, sometimes for understandable reasons, failed to pass on complaints.

Dr L H Moss & Partners – Kings Road, Harrogate

23.5 A significant number of GPs practised from this surgery – they include Drs Crouch, Crawfurd-Porter, Sweeney, Moss, Brennan, Baker and Givans.

23.6 The first evidence of any complaint to this surgery appears to be that relating to Patient A8. In a letter to the Secretary of the Leeds Regional Board (dated 20 March 1972), she refers not only to sexual advances by William Kerr but also to the fact that Dr Crawfurd-Porter had sought to persuade a fellow alleged victim of William Kerr, Patient A5, that no sexual assault had occurred. Assuming that to be correct, it would follow that by March 1972 Dr Crawfurd-Porter would have been aware of concerns about William Kerr.

23.7 At around the same period (the early 1970s) Patient A10 informed Dr Crawfurd-Porter that she would not go back to see William Kerr again after her initial consultation. Although there is nothing to suggest that she explained to him why this was the case, here was further evidence of a female patient being unhappy with the psychiatrist to whom she had been referred.

23.8 There is evidence of yet another complaint having been made to the same surgery in the latter part of 1972. In or about September/October 1972, Patient A9 was referred to William Kerr by her GP – believed to be either Dr Crouch or Dr Givans – suffering from depression and anxiety relating to her marriage. Patient A9 alleges that during her consultations with William Kerr, he made suggestions of a sexual nature and took hold of her hand and placed it on his penis. After her fourth consultation, she made a complaint to a GP at the surgery (although it is unclear whether this was Dr Crouch, Dr Givans or possibly Dr Crawfurd-Porter). She suggests that the GP "shrugged off the complaint", saying that it would not be appropriate to make a formal complaint and that if she did, she would not be believed.

23.9 In 1975, a complaint is said to have been made to Dr Crouch by Patient A13. She was first referred to William Kerr by Dr Crouch on 29 January 1975, suffering from postnatal depression. During the summer of 1975, William Kerr made a domiciliary visit, during the course of which he is said to have put his hand on her breast, attempted to force his knee between her legs, and tried to make her go upstairs. Following this incident, she states that she went to report the matter to Dr Crouch, who she says responded that as she was on medication she might have imagined it. Dr Crouch denies that any such complaint was made. However, in 1980, when in need of further psychiatric help, Patient A13 was referred by Dr Givans not to William Kerr, who had treated her in the past, but to Dr Bromham. According to Patient A13, this was due to her refusal to see William Kerr again.

23.10 We have set out a detailed analysis of the alleged disclosure to Dr Crouch in the section of the Report dealing with Patient A13's account. However, we repeat below our conclusions.

23.11 Patient A13's account highlights the difficulties surrounding the issue of believing patients. She herself recognised the difficulty and states that at the time of the alleged assaults she felt:

> "Who is going to believe me, a young lady who is on a long list of medication who has just come out of a psychiatric hospital, or a doctor of his high standing at the time."

23.12 The difficulty faced by a GP when confronted with an allegation of sexual misconduct made by a patient with mental health problems is also illustrated by Patient A13's evidence. She acknowledged that her behaviour was "not normal" and, while criticism can be levelled at a GP for failing to believe her, Patient A13 accepted that even her own husband did not believe her account of abuse by William Kerr.

23.13 However, there are a number of factors that lead us to conclude that Dr Crouch must have been aware in the 1970s and 1980s of at least some concerns regarding William Kerr's behaviour towards female patients. The senior partner, Dr Moss, admitted to the Inquiry that he considered William Kerr to be suspect. According to Dr Moss,

Dr Crawfurd-Porter (another partner) had mentioned on two occasions William Kerr's "unorthodox" practices and another (unidentified) partner had been present at this disclosure. In such circumstances, where at least three partners seem to have been aware of rumours, the Inquiry considers it likely that all the partners would have discussed the matter, even if informally, and have been aware of some level of concern. The Inquiry has also taken into account the fact that a further patient, Patient A29, similarly claims that she saw Dr Crouch following alleged abuse by William Kerr.

23.14 In 1978, difficulties arose in relation to yet another patient of Dr Crawfurd-Porter who had been treated by William Kerr. On 18 June 1978, Patient A19 was admitted to Harrogate District Hospital after taking an overdose. She was later transferred to Clifton Hospital. During an inpatient consultation, William Kerr is alleged to have sexually assaulted her. Subsequently, her solicitor, Mr Reah, telephoned Harrogate District Hospital and insisted that she be transferred to another doctor, which she was (to Michael Haslam). Her husband is said to have raised this matter with Dr Crawfurd-Porter (a family friend). Dr Crawford-Porter's alleged reaction was that she was fantasising, and flippantly dismissed Patient A19's real distress.

23.15 As Dr Crawfurd-Porter is deceased we have been prevented from obtaining his version of events. However, we are satisfied that he was well aware of William Kerr's activities, even before Patient A19's complaint arose. He had allegedly received specific disclosures from Patient A8, Patient A5, Patient A10 and possibly Patient A9, and at least one of his partners (Dr Moss) recalls Dr Crawfurd-Porter referring to William Kerr's "unorthodox" practices.

23.16 The next relevant incident of which there is evidence occurred in 1982. Patient A29 was re-referred to see William Kerr on 23 October 1981. (She had previously been referred to him in 1977.) During an outpatient consultation, William Kerr is alleged to have indecently assaulted her. She told Dr Crouch that in the future she did not wish to be seen either by William Kerr or by Dr Bromham, although she did not specify the reason why. Dr Crouch confirms that on 16 March 1982 Patient A29 told him that she was not happy with the treatment she had received from William Kerr.

23.17 Thus by 1982 there had potentially (assuming all the reported disclosures to be accurate) been at least seven patients who had voiced concerns relating to William Kerr to GPs at the Kings Road Surgery, Harrogate (Patient A5, Patient A8, Patient A9, Patient A10, Patient A13, Patient A19 and Patient A29). Despite the number of patients concerned, all within a relatively short timescale, no action was taken. As stated elsewhere in this Report, we have the advantage of hindsight and an overview that would not have been apparent to the individual GPs busy seeing their own lists of patients. However, the account of the Kings Road practice, perhaps more than any other of the GPs' surgeries we have considered, demonstrates the need to have some means of recording complaints/concerns and making sure that such matters are discussed at regular and minuted partnership meetings. Had there been such a system, one would hope that the partnership would have felt sufficiently concerned at least to inform the LMC, the District or the Region of the allegations that were being made, so that a decision could have been made at a more senior level as to whether an investigation was warranted. At the very least, a system of recording complaints would have assisted any inquiry in the future.

23.18 In addition to the patients who are said to have made the complaints set out above, there are a number of other women who were patients at the Kings Road surgery and who suggested many years later (generally in response to the police inquiry) that they were sexually assaulted by William Kerr. The relevant individuals are Patient A4 (who is said to have informed Matron Farnsworth of an assault on her in August 1968), Patient A58, Patient A57, Patient A62 and Patient A63. While it may be that these patients would not have been minded to make any disclosures to their GP at the time, had there been an investigation of patient views in response to the concerns already expressed, allegations from these women or others might have come to light at an earlier stage.

Leeds Road Surgery, Harrogate

23.19 The GPs understood to have practised from these premises include Drs Jones, Chave-Cox, Foggitt and Scatchard.

23.20 In the summer of 1972, Patient A11 was admitted to hospital after taking an overdose following the break-up of a relationship. After she was discharged she saw her GP, Dr Patricia Jones, who referred her to William Kerr. Patient A11 states that during her consultations with him, William Kerr made her feel very uncomfortable and tried to kiss her and put his arm around her. After her consultations came to an end, she continued to see Dr Jones and asked her whether there had been any complaints about William Kerr – she believes that she must have told Dr Jones what had happened with William Kerr. According to Patient A11, Dr Jones believed her but thought that if a complaint was made, William Kerr was more likely to be believed than a patient.

23.21 Patient A50 was referred to William Kerr by her GP, Dr Chave-Cox. She was first seen by William Kerr on 16 June 1983 and she states that a sexual assault took place in August or September 1983. In May 1987, Patient A50 registered with a different GP, Dr Iddon, at The Health Centre, Knaresborough. It is not in dispute that in the course of visits to see Dr Iddon Patient A50 made numerous statements to the effect that William Kerr had, during her consultations with him, insisted that she engage in sexual contact. However, Patient A50 has also indicated that Dr Chave-Cox was aware of what happened to her in relation to William Kerr. It is not clear when or how Dr Chave-Cox is said to have acquired this knowledge.

23.22 Also in or about 1983, Patient A44 was referred to William Kerr by her GP, Dr Foggitt. Patient A44 states that she told Dr Foggitt, prior to his retirement in 1996, that she had been sexually abused by William Kerr. Dr Foggitt accepts that this may have been the case and believes that he may have had a discussion about it with his partners, Drs Chave-Cox, Scatchard and Jones. Dr Jones, in her police statement, recalls a discussion with Dr Foggitt about a number of patients having made allegations relating to William Kerr. Dr Scatchard recalls a discussion in the late 1970s or early 1980s during the course of a business meeting at the practice, to the effect that it was alleged by a female patient that William Kerr had exposed himself to her. Dr Scatchard believes that he was told of the allegation solely as a matter of courtesy and he is unaware of any action having been taken.

23.23 We repeat here the conclusions we came to in considering Patient A11's account earlier in this Report:

• Given the content of Dr Jones' police statement in 1997, combined with the evidence of Dr Scatchard and Dr Foggitt, both of whom had some recollection of a partners' meeting where it seems likely there was discussion of a patient complaining about William Kerr exposing himself, we find that Dr Jones and her fellow partners (including Dr Foggitt and Dr Scatchard) were collectively aware of a number of allegations concerning William Kerr's conduct towards female patients. Despite the knowledge that concerns had been raised by more than one patient, as a surgery and as individuals they failed to take any steps to report these concerns to the hospital authorities or the Regional Health Authority, which employed William Kerr.

23.24 Unlike the surgery at Kings Road, it appears that the Leeds Road Surgery in Harrogate did have in place some more formal system of partners' meetings where concerns raised by a patient about a consultant would be discussed. However, the system seems to stop there and it does not appear that minutes were taken or records kept of the concerns such that any pattern would become apparent. Neither does there appear to have been any follow-up or real consideration of whether the surgery should take any action in relation to the concerns raised.

23.25 The Leeds Road Surgery is also notable because not only was it the recipient of concerns about William Kerr, but Dr Foggitt, one of its partners, was also the recipient of a very specific complaint by Patient B1 concerning Michael Haslam. Patient B1 was a patient of Michael Haslam from 1972 to 1974 and states that she was involved in a sexual relationship with him at the same time. Her account is that she made a complaint to Dr Foggitt about Michael Haslam's conduct but that he did not know what to do about it. Dr Foggitt did, however, take the step of referring Patient B1 to an out-of-region psychiatrist, Dr Clarkson, alluding in his referral to "some kind of sexual allegation" against Michael Haslam.

23.26 Again, we repeat our conclusions as set out in our account of Patient B1's story:

- We consider it regrettable that both Dr Foggitt and Dr Clarkson, well aware of the allegation that Michael Haslam had behaved in a sexually inappropriate way towards Patient B1 (a current, and vulnerable, patient), did nothing to alert the responsible authorities to the potential risk of danger to other patients. Dr Foggitt's evidence-free conclusion (in 1974) that this was a "one-off", and that Michael Haslam had merely been "foolish", echoes down the years. Had Dr Foggitt made some kind of report and had Dr Clarkson made some kind of report, then subsequent expressions of concern might have been taken more seriously. We do not find that there was a deliberate cover-up between Dr Foggitt and Dr Clarkson. However, their individual and combined inaction does give the unfortunate impression of doctors sticking together – or, as Patient B1 put it, "doctors closing ranks".

The Surgery, East Parade, Harrogate

23.27 Dr Pamela Reed (née Heatley) practised from these premises, as did Dr Henderson.

23.28 There are a number of patients who were registered at this surgery and allege that they were sexually assaulted by William Kerr but did not make a contemporaneous complaint. They are Patient A16, Patient A27, Patient A49 and Patient A51 (all patients of Dr Reed). However, a complaint was made to Dr Reed by Patient A31. She was referred to William Kerr by Dr Reed in 1981 because of her anorexia. In the course of a domiciliary visit, William Kerr is said to have forced her to hold his penis. A couple of years later, in around 1983, Patient A31 claims that she informed Dr Reed of what had happened. Dr Reed is said to have responded by asking her whether she wished to report it. Patient A31's answer was that she did not, as she did not think that she would be believed. Dr Reed, however, had no recollection of any such disclosure.

23.29 We have concluded (see details under the section on Patient A31) that some disclosure was made to Dr Reed. Again, we repeat our comments that appear elsewhere in this Report:

- Proceeding on the assumption that some form of complaint was made to the GP in about 1983/84, this is a further example of a doctor either failing to take forward an expression of concern or a complaint on grounds of the lack of the patient's consent. Or, and perhaps more appropriately, it provides an example of a failure to listen and at least make some record, somewhere, so that if and when there was an investigation – as for example in 1983/84 following the Linda Bigwood allegations – then there would be some material from which a wider and more accurate picture could be drawn. Then, when former patients were perhaps more willing and able to give formal statements, at least the treating GPs would have had some record of who those patients were.

23.30 Unlike the two other Harrogate surgeries discussed above, the East Parade surgery was not the recipient of as many alleged disclosures. As such, even had there been a system of recording complaints, a "pattern" would not have been spotted unless there had been good communication not only between partners within a surgery but between surgeries working in the same area. As we have repeatedly stressed throughout this Report, a lack of communication was one of the key factors in the inordinate delay between the earliest allegations of abuse and the police investigation in 1997.

The Health Centre, Knaresborough Road, Harrogate

23.31 It appears that the following GPs practised from this surgery: Drs Tyler, Iddon, Moore, Thornton, Oliver, Wade, Rushton, Plowman, Goldsborough and Bennie. Again, there are a significant number of patients from this surgery who state that they were assaulted by William Kerr, of whom a number are said to have made complaints.

23.32 Patient A54, later to become a patient of Dr Thornton, was seen by William Kerr in relation to a termination in 1972/73. She complains that, during a consultation with William Kerr, he talked about sex and exposed his penis.

23.33 A patient of Dr Michael Moore was Patient A21, who was referred in 1978 to see William Kerr in connection with problems that she had with alcohol abuse. She states that, during a period of admission to Clifton Hospital, William Kerr exposed himself to her and tried to force her to perform oral sex. When she reported the matter to a GP (who is not identified), he seemed to be aware of what she was talking about and said that another person had complained. He is said to have told Patient A21 that if she wished to pursue a complaint, she would have to be prepared to go to court. However, Dr Moore has no recollection of any complaint from Patient A21 and we have not been able to conclude that any detailed disclosure was made, save possibly hints at inappropriate behaviour. (Dr Moore does, however, accept that he received an express complaint of sexual misconduct by William Kerr from Patient A1 over 10 years earlier, in 1965.)

23.34   Patient A22 was referred to William Kerr in 1974 due to depression, and again in 1979 following the death of her husband. The referral in 1979 was made by Dr Wade, and it was to him that she complained of William Kerr's behaviour, which centred on inappropriate comments and over-familiar behaviour during domiciliary visits. On receiving the complaint, Dr Wade is said to have indicated that he was aware of such behaviour, due to previous complaints. Dr Wade has accepted that Patient A22 told him of William Kerr's "unwelcome and unprofessional advances to her". This complaint was made in March 1979. In April 1979, Dr Wade spoke to Michael Haslam about the concerns that had been raised by Patient A22 in relation to William Kerr. We deal with Dr Wade's story in more detail in Chapter 22, as he was the sole example (to the Inquiry's knowledge) of a GP who took active steps to forward a complaint about William Kerr "up the line", even though his attempts came to nothing.

23.35   Patient A32 was also a patient at the Knaresborough Road surgery. Her GP in 1972 was Dr Rushton and she subsequently became a patient of Dr Plowman. Patient A32 says that she told Dr Plowman in 1983 that William Kerr had tried to engage in sexual activity with her. While Dr Plowman is unable to recall any specific complaint relating to Patient A32, she does accept that she was aware in the 1980s that William Kerr had "an eye for the ladies". She was also aware of her partner, Dr Wade, taking his concerns in relation to Patient A22 to Michael Haslam. It is therefore clear that not only did Dr Wade take his concerns about William Kerr to Michael Haslam, but he also informed his colleagues.

23.36   Patient A50 became a patient of Dr Iddon in May 1987. She made complaints over a number of years to Dr Iddon about her treatment by William Kerr, culminating in a letter to him dated 31 December 1991. Dr Iddon accepts that complaints were made to him and that the complaints were consistent. Dr Iddon's evidence was that he had no suspicions regarding William Kerr prior to Patient A50's disclosure. As Dr Iddon was in the same surgery as Dr Wade, who had forwarded a complaint about William Kerr, this shows a worrying lack of communication between partners (although Dr Plowman was aware).

23.37 The Knaresborough Road surgery held the unique accolade of being the only surgery where a partner (Dr Wade) had taken positive steps to forward a complaint about William Kerr (reporting the matter to Michael Haslam, in his role as a senior psychiatric consultant). It also appears from Dr Plowman's evidence that Dr Wade took at least some steps to inform at least some of his partners of the concerns about William Kerr. It is perhaps all the more worrying, then, that this surgery continued to refer female patients to William Kerr and failed to follow up either individually (through Dr Wade), or as a practice, the outcome of the complaint by Patient A22 when it was evident that William Kerr continued to practise, apparently without any investigation having been made or any restrictions imposed.

Park Street Surgery, Ripon

23.38 Dr Patricia Livingstone, Dr Angus Livingstone and Drs Webb, Hill, Fletcher and Dixon worked at these premises.

23.39 In the late 1970s, Patient A23 was referred by Dr Patricia Livingstone to see William Kerr following a nervous breakdown. When she was seen by William Kerr, he is said to have suggested to her that she should find herself a lover and asked her what she would do if he were naked. While she apparently reported this to Dr Patricia Livingstone, her impression was that she was not believed. There is a reference in her GP notes for 6 December 1979 to her having had a "fraught time" with William Kerr, and Dr Livingstone referred Patient A23 to Dr Rugg instead.

23.40 Dr Patricia Livingstone's evidence to the Inquiry was that the fact that William Kerr asked questions relating to sex would not have caused concern, as this might have been part of a legitimate history-taking. As noted elsewhere in this Report, this is demonstrative of the particular problem regarding consultations with psychiatrists where sexual matters may be of relevance. This both places the caring consultant in a potentially vulnerable position and leaves them open to misinterpretation, but also provides a "cover" for the unscrupulous psychiatrist to shift the subject inappropriately towards sexual matters.

23.41 A further complaint is linked to Dr Angus Livingstone (husband of Dr Patricia Livingstone), who suggests that, in or about 1983, a patient complained to him that shortly after an appointment at Ripon Hospital, William Kerr had come round to her house unannounced and uninvited. Dr Angus Livingstone suggested that she might make a complaint but she declined to do so. Dr Angus Livingstone also suggests that over the years a number of patients complained about questions of a sexual nature being asked of them by William Kerr.

23.42 A further patient of the Park Street Surgery, Patient A70, was referred to William Kerr in 1984/85 suffering from nervous exhaustion. Her GP was Dr Hill. She was admitted to Clifton Hospital but discharged herself after three days. During that time, she complains that William Kerr asked her to lie naked on a bed and only discussed sex with her. While she made no complaint about her treatment, the date of her referral shows that even after at least two complaints were made by patients at Park Street, other women were still referred by GPs at the practice to see William Kerr.

23.43 The same point arises in relation to Patient A71, who was referred to see William Kerr by Dr Patricia Livingstone in 1986 following the breakdown of a relationship. During her consultation with William Kerr, he allegedly made frequent references to sex and made her feel very uncomfortable. She apparently did not go back to see William Kerr after her first appointment – while she made a second appointment, she did not keep it. It is not clear whether or not Dr Patricia Livingstone was aware of the second cancelled appointment or made any efforts to follow up the referral or to establish why it had not been completed by Patient A71.

23.44 The existence of a husband/wife team in this practice makes it almost inconceivable that complaints about a consultant who asked excessive questions about sexual matters would not have been discussed, even if only informally, between the partners, at least between Dr Patricia and Dr Angus Livingstone. However, perhaps due to the lack of any "hard evidence" or any detailed or explicit complaint of sexual abuse, the matter was not raised outside of the surgery.

North House Surgery, North Street, Ripon

23.45 The following GPs worked at this surgery: Drs Bennett, Brown, Keyworth, Snape, Jeary, McDowall and Anning. There are a number of patients of William Kerr who are connected with the surgery.

23.46 Dr Brown suggests that in the mid-1970s, Dr Keyworth mentioned a patient who had made a comment relating to William Kerr's inappropriate behaviour towards female patients and asked whether there were any other doctors at the surgery who had received similar concerns. A similar comment is attributed to Dr Bennett at a surgery meeting that was said to have taken place in 1988.

23.47 Patient A40 was referred to William Kerr by Dr Bennett in or around 1987. She states that she was sexually assaulted by William Kerr on a number of occasions during domiciliary visits and appointments at Ripon and Harrogate. She told her GP on 14 July 1988 that things were "not going well. Didn't want to see William Kerr any more." She suggests that Dr Bennett's response was to the effect that there had been a number of patients who were not happy with William Kerr and that there had been complaints about him. Given the timing of her comments to Dr Bennett, it is likely that Patient A40 was the patient to whom he referred in the surgery meeting in 1988.

23.48 Patient A67 was a patient of Dr Brown. She was referred to William Kerr in 1971 for reasons relating to the after-effects of treatment for Hodgkin's disease. William Kerr is alleged to have exposed himself to her. There is no record of Patient A67 having made any complaint to her GP. Another patient of Dr Brown, Patient A56, also claimed she was abused by William Kerr in 1978, although again there is no record of any complaint being made by her.

23.49 Patient A15 was a patient of Dr Jeary. She was referred to Bootham Park Hospital in July 1977 and was admitted. On 3 August 1977, she told Dr Jeary that she was unhappy with the fact that she had been asked a substantial number of questions relating to sex. She was then referred to see William Kerr in September 1977. She states that she was sexually assaulted by William Kerr during the course of a subsequent consultation. She did not inform Dr Jeary of this, but did inform him that she was unhappy with the sex-related questioning that she had received from William Kerr. Dr Jeary's response was that William Kerr needed to ask such questions. When she had further problems in 1981, Patient A15 objected to Dr Jeary referring her to see William Kerr. She was therefore sent to see Dr Bromham.

23.50 There is again evidence of concerns having been raised within a surgery (apparently at a partners' meeting) relating to William Kerr, but with no apparent effect on referrals of female patients to him and no action being taken. It is of course particularly notable in the case of Park Street Surgery that referrals to William Kerr continued because it was Park Street Surgery that referred Patient A40, who, as a jury found, was sexually assaulted by William Kerr in the late 1980s.

Picks Lane Practice, Thirsk

23.51 Finally in this chapter dealing with the attitudes of GPs and their surgeries, we move away from concerns about William Kerr to a surgery in Thirsk where concerns were instead focused upon Michael Haslam's conduct towards female patients.

23.52 The partners in this surgery in the 1980s were Drs Donald, Harrison and Thiede (the senior partner).

23.53 It was in the mid-1980s that Patient B4 (then in her late 20s) alleged to Dr Donald that she was having a sexual relationship with Michael Haslam (then in his mid-50s) while he was her treating psychiatrist.

23.54 Dr Donald's statement to the Inquiry sets out his recollection:

> "On one occasion Patient B4 mentioned to me that she had had sexual intercourse with her consultant psychiatrist, Dr Michael Haslam. At that time I was aware that Dr Haslam was treating her. It was my understanding that sexual intercourse took place in a bed away from the clinic.

> "While mentioning the event, Patient B4 did not appear to be particularly distressed about the incident and she jokingly mentioned Dr Haslam's toupee. I believed from Patient B4's comments that the sexual intercourse had been consensual and had no adverse effect upon her health. I asked Patient B4 at that time whether she wanted me to take any further action. She stated she did not.

> *"At that time I discussed this matter with my [now deceased] senior partner, Dr Derek Thiede, in the surgery, who was of the opinion that it was most likely that Patient B4 had made these matters up from his previous knowledge of her. I however was not of this opinion and believed what Patient B4 had told me."*

23.55 Dr Harrison's police statement sets out a recollection similar to that of Dr Donald:

> *"Patient B4 told me she was having a sexual relationship with her consultant psychiatrist, Doctor Michael Haslam. She was quite matter-of-fact about what she told me and I cannot remember much more about this but I have an impression that they met at a hotel. I cannot remember our exact conversation but I was shocked by what she told me.*
>
> *"I did believe what Patient B4 was saying to me and I was so disgusted by what I heard that I later spoke to my senior partner, Dr Thiede, about this and also with Dr McCllellan, a doctor from another Thirsk surgery. However, my conversation did not result in any action being taken."*

23.56 It may be worth noting here that the perception, at least of Dr Donald, that Patient B4's alleged sexual relationship with her consulting psychiatrist (whether true or not) caused her no adverse effect must be open to question: it is known that Patient B4 went on to make disclosures of a similar nature to two psychologists (Marion Anderson and Mark McFeteridge) and that in the view of Dr Timperley, a consultant psychiatrist who subsequently treated her: "Her [subsequent] psychotic breakdown related to the fact that as a patient of Dr Haslam there had been [alleged] sexual intercourse on a number of occasions."

23.57 As set out elsewhere in this Report, it was both the inaction and the attitude of the partners in the Picks Lane Practice that was to so shock Dr Simpson. In 1987, Dr Simpson commenced work as a consultant psychiatrist at Northallerton NHS Trust and undertook to visit some of the GP practices in his area. On his visit to the Picks Lane Practice he was informed that the GPs were pleased at his appointment as they could "now refer young women to a psychiatrist. Dr Haslam, they informed me, had sex with female patients." The impression Dr Simpson gained of the GPs' attitude was: "This was not illegal and there was nothing they could do about this."

23.58 Dr Simpson considered that he was under a moral duty to report what he had been told, and after discussing the matter with Dr Richardson, a colleague and consultant psychiatrist in York, he informed Dr Wintersgill of what he had been told. It was shortly after this, and after a number of other complaints (as documented elsewhere), that Michael Haslam retired from his NHS Consultant post.

23.59 We pause here to repeat that the attitude of the partners at the Picks Lane surgery does not appear to have been an isolated response. Indeed, the evidence of Dr Givans was that the attitude "it's not illegal, we can do nothing" would have been the view of the majority of the GPs at that time. We consider the attitude of healthcare professionals to sexual relationships between doctor and patient further in Chapter 29.

Conclusion

23.60 We repeat here the fact that the Inquiry was greatly assisted by the cooperation we received from North Yorkshire GPs involved in this Inquiry. We also wish to emphasise that the evidence surrounding many of the disclosures to GPs is inevitably based on recollections of events that happened many years ago. In some cases where GPs have no recollection of disclosures it may well be that either none was made, or the complaint was only in the most oblique form, such that a busy GP might understandably not have discerned the seriousness of the allegation.

23.61 However, the above account illustrates the opportunities that were missed to document concerns and raise queries at an earlier stage, when an investigation could have been conducted – one that would have been fairer to all, both to William Kerr and Michael Haslam and to their patients. We accept that all the GPs were in a situation where there was no proof of wrongdoing by William Kerr (or by Michael Haslam) and they may understandably have felt concerned about raising a concern on what may have (without the overview available to the Inquiry) seemed an isolated and unsubstantiated incident. However, in the case of at least some of the GP practices, there were sufficient complaints and concerns being raised to have activated a positive response. We find as a fact that Linda Bigwood was right in her claim that the concerns about William Kerr were so well known that some GPs were changing their referral practice. Concerns that were sufficiently strong to change referral practices should have been communicated to William Kerr's employers or the GMC. Had this information (regarding changed referral practices) been independently communicated to the District or Regional Health Authority by one or more surgeries, it is difficult to conceive that there would not have been a more positive response to the written complaint of Linda Bigwood. Investigations would then have been conducted by (at the latest) the early 1980s, not – as was in fact the case – 1997, when the police became involved.

23.62 The GP community must therefore stand with those in nursing and hospital management in recognising their part in the delay in bringing William Kerr and Michael Haslam to account for the offences that they were ultimately proved to have committed.

Section Five
Barriers to making complaints

Chapter 24
Introduction – understanding the issues

Introduction

24.1   In earlier sections of this Report, when considering the individual cases of former patients, we have described attempts to raise concerns or complaints, and identified cases where no contemporaneous complaints were raised at all. We have described instances where the complaint was not treated with the seriousness it deserved. We ascribe a variety of reasons to this. We have referred to individuals who could, and in some cases should, have acted with more rigour and more professionalism to protect existing and future patients. We here attempt to draw together some of the themes which have emerged from the evidence presented to the Inquiry.

24.2   We identify some general topics and issues raised in the course of the Inquiry, or flowing from the many factual stories outlined earlier. We are particularly keen to examine why concerns or complaints were not raised at or near the time of the alleged incident and, when raised, why on so many occasions those concerns or complaints were not given the attention they deserved. In other words, what went wrong?

24.3   The answer to that simple and straightforward question is inevitably complex – and we accept that any over-generalised answer carries the risk of unhelpful over-simplification. This is a particular danger where there are so many stories, by so many former patients, involving two psychiatrists, and a host of other "players" – consultants, psychologists, GPs, nurses, social workers, NHS managers etc – and all of this taking place over a lengthy period of time when the NHS itself was going through major changes.

24.4   It is inevitable, against that background, that any attempt at a general answer will miss some of the factors, or blur the lines. However, unless an overview is attempted, a different and false impression might remain – that there are no general lessons to be learned, that if warning signs were not noted, warning bells not heard, concerns or complaints not properly considered and responded to, the failings were merely the errors of some individuals. And, in turn, these individuals were usually extremely busy professionals, doing their best in an imperfect world. That would be an incorrect overall impression.

24.5   It is true that individuals failed to respond adequately, failed to listen, or failed to understand the significance of what they were being told – and failed to recognise the evidence of potential risk of harm not only to the patient raising the concern or complaint, but to the wider patient population, particularly the unknown number of young to middle-aged female patients who continued to be referred to William Kerr and Michael Haslam during the 1970s and 1980s.

24.6   But those individual failings – if any lessons are to be learned from this whole sorry saga – must be understood in context. We are satisfied that there were cultural factors in place during this period which made it easier, more acceptable, for those who heard the concerns or complaints not to listen – either at all, or with sufficient sympathy and understanding, and with sufficient determination to do anything of value with what they heard.

24.7   Therefore, a main reason for setting out some overall issues in this section of the Report is to enable the current decision makers, those who are responsible for the modern culture of the NHS, to ensure that lessons are learned – that contributory factors are considered, and every effort is made to ensure that problems identified no longer exist, or are rapidly eradicated.

24.8   Here we again acknowledge the limitations of the private inquiry process, and the limits of our own knowledge and industry. Although we all have our own, and occasionally overlapping, areas of expertise, and we have received enormous assistance from independent experts, representatives and contributors during the Inquiry process, we accept that we cannot do justice in this Report to broad and ever-changing topics such as "confidentiality", or "the discipline and regulation of doctors". However, we are at least confident that these are topics that must be addressed – if only so the debate can be continued elsewhere, informed, we trust, by the lessons learned from the stories told in this Report, the experiences of other recent inquiries, and the experiences in other countries faced with similar problems.

What went wrong?

24.9 We conclude that the overall picture is one of failure, or missed opportunities, over a number of years. The first serious investigation into William Kerr's practice was in 1997, almost 10 years after he had left the NHS. In relation to Michael Haslam, the Manzoor Inquiry was in 1998, again almost 10 years after he left the North Yorkshire NHS. Even then, the reasons for the 1997/1998 investigations seem to owe little to planning or monitoring. Rather, the decision to launch the Manzoor Inquiry was influenced by a variety of factors – perhaps not random, but certainly not concerted or coordinated. These factors include:

a. a police investigation;

b. new brooms – Professor Donaldson and Dr Cresswell in particular – taking a very serious view of the allegations;

c. a possible shift in culture;

d. one complaining patient had "a journalistic background and threatened to make her complaint public";

e. concerns about media involvement – there was an article in *The Guardian* published on 17 June 1997 "Consultant Accused of 20 Years of Abuse". Articles to similar effect appeared in the local newspapers, including the *Yorkshire Post* on 16 June 1997; and

f. a feeling that if something (and they were not sure what) wasn't done then they would be open to criticism for inaction.

24.10 Even with those factors in mind, there does not appear to be any sound reason why some form of investigation – with or without police involvement – could not have been carried out in the 1980s. When the Manzoor Inquiry was set up, it only heard evidence for two days and within two months was able to produce a report, together with a list of recommendations. The members of the Manzoor Inquiry were struck by the considerable similarity between the four complaints. It is our view that a similar reaction would have been reached in the early 1980s – a reaction that would probably have prompted a wider investigation.

24.11 We have carefully considered whether the allegations we have heard from former patients, and the response from the NHS, was a "one-off" situation, or possibly a "North Yorkshire phenomenon", or, as one witness described it to us, just a local and isolated "horror story". The situation as described to us in evidence was certainly exceptional in that the allegations of sexualised behaviour related to two of the three consultants responsible for the delivery of mental health services in North Yorkshire. If there had just been one allegedly errant consultant, then (if it was established, or accepted, that there was some substance to the allegations) he may have been influenced by colleagues to change or moderate his behaviour when patients were referred. But where two consultants were involved with similar allegations, it became much more problematic for medical colleagues to intervene.

24.12 Failure to react and investigate has emerged as a common theme in recent reports. The Shipman Inquiry Report has reached a similar conclusion in relation to the ability of Family Practitioner Committees to monitor GPs.

24.13 The following is taken from paragraph 4.1 of the Clifford Ayling report[1]:

"It was not until 1998 that complaints about Ayling were investigated and taken seriously. From 1971 until 1998, we have identified a number of missed opportunities when concerns and complaints about Ayling might have been acted on."

24.14 And from the Richard Neale report[2]:

"The inability of [Richard Neale's] employers to provide sufficient control and monitoring procedures only made matters worse."

24.15 So a common theme through the conclusions of these, and other, investigations[3] could be characterised as too little monitoring, with too loose control leading to a freedom for the clinicians in question to deal with some of their patients in an allegedly damaging and unacceptable way.

---

1 *Committee of Inquiry Independent Investigation into how the NHS handled allegations about the conduct of Clifford Ayling*, Cm 6298, 2004

2 *Committee of Inquiry Independent Investigation into how the NHS handled allegations about the conduct of Richard Neale*, Cm 6315, 2004

3 Such as the CHI investigation into the practice of Peter Green

24.16 The answer, therefore, to the question "What went wrong?" posed earlier is a complex combination of individual failings *and* system failures, operating in the culture that prevailed where mentally unwell patients were regularly, if not routinely, disbelieved, and where doctors were almost automatically believed. Rumour and gossip were ignored, and allegedly sexual relationships, even between a consultant psychiatrist and his female patients, were tolerated or ignored. The detail of the factors which combined to make up that culture is addressed below in the remaining chapters of this section.

Awareness, predisposition and knowledge

24.17 In summary, what is the overall lesson? What is still to be learned and improved, when the culture is so different (and we accept that it is), and there have been so many dramatic changes and improvements – particularly in relation to complaints handling, the regulation of doctors, and the positive encouragement of identification of inadequate professional performance? Complaints systems are complicated and daunting, even disempowering.

24.18 We conclude that the overall lesson is that there is a continuing and worrying lack of education or training, and a lack of knowledge or information. We accept that knowledge alone will not prevent doctors or other medical professionals sexually assaulting or seducing (or attempting to seduce) their existing, and recently former, patients. We must accept that such behaviour happens – and happens far more often than perhaps realised (see Chapter 30). However, what education and knowledge can do is to make it far more difficult for such offenders to go undetected. If, as we strongly believe to be the correct position, such behaviour should not be tolerated in our society, then education and knowledge are essential. We have identified the following areas, posed as questions, where we consider it to be of fundamental importance that there are clear answers, based on reliable information, so that doctors, other healthcare professionals, and the public, know what is and what is not permitted:

- What sexualised behaviour by medical professionals with, or towards, their existing or former patients (or health service users) is not tolerated or permitted:

  – as a matter of criminal law;

– as a matter of professional regulation; and

– as a matter of contractual (employment) obligation?

- What rights do patients (or health service users) have to raise concerns and/or complaints in respect of allegations of sexualised behaviour by a healthcare professional?

- What are the duties or obligations imposed on GPs, nurses, social workers, NHS management etc – as a matter of contract, and/or professional regulation, on receipt of any information – whether by positive disclosure or otherwise – of such allegedly sexualised behaviour?

- What rights do healthcare professionals have – as a matter of contract, or professional regulation – when they are the subject of allegations of sexualised behaviour with an existing, or former patient (or health service user)?

- When, and in what manner, should an allegation or suspicion of sexualised behaviour which could, if true, be a crime, be brought to the attention of the police?

- What information which relates to an allegation or suspicion of sexualised behaviour by a healthcare professional should be recorded in written and/or electronic form, and where and for how long should such information be retained?

- What rights do the providers of such stored and retained information (the patient or health service user) or the subject of such stored or retained information (the doctor or other healthcare professional) have in relation to:

  – access to the information;

  – correction or withdrawal of such information; and

  – destruction of such information?

- What information, and in what form, should be provided to patients or other health service users as to their rights (and obligations, if any) in relation to allegedly sexualised behaviour (or other boundary transgressions) by doctors or other healthcare professionals?

24.19 This is not intended to be an exhaustive list, but is at least a minimum set of topic headings to be addressed by the Department of Health. We consider it important, indeed of vital importance, that professional training – at all levels, and including continuing professional development – includes clear and compulsory education and training on, at least:

- the importance of identifying and maintaining professional boundaries;

- awareness of boundary transgressions (actual or imminent) by the healthcare professional, or a colleague;

- sexualised behaviour as criminal conduct, as unethical conduct;

- current local and national complaints systems;

- the correct response to expressions of concern, the making of complaints, or any other disclosures of sexualised behaviour or other significant boundary transgressions, raised by patients or health service users;

- what to do, and what not to do, if a patient (or former patient) or health service user discloses allegations of sexualised behaviour or other significant boundary transgressions by a doctor, psychologist, NHS manager, or other healthcare professional, but declines to make or take any active part in a formal complaint;

- following from the preceding point, how to deal with anonymous complaints; and

- the requirements of, and limitations on, patient confidentiality.

24.20 We address the topic of education and training in greater detail in Chapter 36.

24.21 We agree with the submissions made to us on behalf of the local NHS authorities, that there is a need for clear and comprehensive central government guidance on these and other issues, so that there is uniformity of high standards within the NHS throughout the country. We see absolutely no reason why there should be different local standards on such general problems as boundary transgressions and sexualised behaviour. It is also clear to us that the guidance should be prepared with some urgency – we hope within 12 months of the publication of this Report – on two vitally important "front-line" responses:

- The way in which records should be made and thereafter kept in respect of healthcare professionals (particularly those involved in mental healthcare) where there is an allegation (whether or not by way of formal complaint, and whether or not formally resolved) of sexualised behaviour, or other significant boundary transgression. We have referred to this in more detail in Chapter 32.

- The way in which NHS Trust staff and management should respond to the disclosure of, or the making of specific allegations of, sexualised behaviour (including, but not limited to, sexual assault). We have referred to this in more detail in Chapter 34.

24.22   We accept, in relation to this second topic for early central government guidance that, whatever the prevalence of sexualised behaviour, disclosures or allegations direct or indirect are relatively few and far between. It may be that the very "novelty" of the allegations contributed to the apparent inability of some recipients to respond. We were struck, in the course of the Inquiry, by the consistent failure of health service professionals simply "knowing what to do". Many recipients of disclosures saw barriers, saw problems; few saw the way forward, how to help the patient, how to respond. Readily accessible, and digestible, guidance is urgently required – for healthcare professionals, for patients, for former patients, and for all health service users.

24.23   All allegations of sexual abuse made against staff should be viewed with an open mind, taken seriously, and investigated appropriately.

24.24   All staff, no matter how junior, should be encouraged to report any inappropriate sexual behaviour they observe between a member of staff and patient without the fear of retaliation and personal repercussions. Turning a "blind eye" to observed or known abuse is unacceptable.

Responding to disclosure: a practical toolkit

24.25   We again agree with submissions made to us by the local NHS authorities, that "there is a minefield to negotiate" – in particular, what to do if the person disclosing sexualised behaviour, notwithstanding every support and encouragement, refuses to report the matter as a formal complaint to be actioned by the Trust, the GMC or the police, or to cooperate in any proceedings. In those, and similar, situations we are satisfied that what is required is something more concrete than generalised statements. What is needed is guidance that provides real practical assistance to those who are in receipt of disclosures – from patients who may be, who are likely to be, confused, distressed and embarrassed, not only seeking help to pursue a complaint, but seeking and in need of care and support. We were provided, by Selby and York Primary Care Trust, with a suggested set of issues to be addressed in a specific policy and supporting toolkit. In the following two paragraphs, we gratefully reproduce that document, with our own comments and concerns included (without separate identification), as at least a starting point for the production of suitable guidance – devised at national level, after close consultation with other professions, and with social services and the police.

24.26 Whenever a serious incident is alleged to have occurred and is reported or disclosed – either as an expression of concern or as a complaint from a patient or carer, or raised as a concern from a member of staff – the course of action open to managers and the decisions they face are essentially the same. They are:

- whether to investigate;

- whether to suspend staff;

- whether to inform the police, and/or other services;

- whether to inform the professional regulator (if any) of the healthcare professional concerned;

- whether to convene a panel post investigation; and

- whether to discipline.

The decisions may involve one or more of the above.

24.27 However, although this unrefined, or generally applicable, process may be appropriate for issues of poor performance (clinical or otherwise), it does not take into account the particular aspects of serious incidents which involve allegations of sexualised behaviour. Such allegations call for the same broad choice of decisions, but also involve additional difficulties such as:

- requests for anonymity;

- patient confidentiality;

- uncorroborated allegations;

- variable quality of information;

- enhanced levels of patient (and/or carer) distress; and

- criminality and forensic evidence.

24.28 All of the above are enhanced in situations where the person making the allegation or disclosure is mentally unwell (where questions of mental capacity may also arise), and where the serious incident is said to have occurred some time in the past – perhaps in the distant past. In particular, we are satisfied that there will be a need for trained care and support to be offered to psychiatric patients who raise such concerns or complaints.

24.29 Our view is that the Department of Health should develop and publish a specific policy, and supporting toolkit, to guide NHS managers in their handling of allegations or disclosure of sexualised behaviour (however, and by whoever, raised or otherwise brought to their notice). The specific policy and practice guidance should address the various issues and difficulties set out in this Report and include examples of good practice, an extended range of outcomes that could be applied, where guidance and assistance can readily be provided, guidance on record making and keeping, and include a range of preventative measures (for example, specific accessible information for patients on what they should and should not expect, and who they can speak to for confidential advice and assistance).

24.30 When such guidance is produced, it is inevitable that questions of additional, new funding will arise to support at least the following actions:

- the publication and dissemination of the guidance (which should be publicly available);

- the training of NHS managers in the application and operation of the sexualised behaviour policy and toolkit;

- the training of NHS managers in the need to provide specialised care and support for psychiatric patients who raise concerns and complaints of sexualised, or other abusive, behaviour by healthcare professionals;

- the publication and dissemination of patient information (leaflets and (possibly) posters); and

- the setting up, or supporting, of voluntary advocacy and advice services (independent of the NHS) to offer advice and assistance to patients and former patients (particularly those who are mentally unwell, or who are otherwise vulnerable). Our view is that such services should be funded centrally, and not made subject to local budgetary constraints.

24.31 All of what we have said so far in this chapter, and indeed throughout the Report, has focused on professional staff – on healthcare professionals, who are likely to be regulated by the GMC, NMC, or other self-regulatory organisations. We have not addressed, at all, the position of staff who are not in some way professionally trained and professionally regulated. We are informed that healthcare, particularly mental healthcare within the NHS, is increasingly provided by staff who are not professionally qualified, or subject to the standards of professional regulation. If this is indeed the situation – and we have seen examples in the areas of therapy – it raises an issue of real concern. We are of the view that standards of behaviour – including, but not limited to, boundary transgressions and all forms of sexualised behaviour – be drawn up nationally, and incorporated into the contracts of employment of those staff, or contracts of engagement for any self-employed persons providing mental health services within the NHS.

Accordingly, we RECOMMEND:

1. **the Department of Health should develop and publish a specific policy, with practical guidance on implementation, to guide NHS managers in their handling of allegations or disclosure of sexualised behaviour. The policy should address the various issues and difficulties set out above and include examples of good practice, as well as the extended range of options for action that could be applied; where advice and assistance can readily be provided; guidance on record-making and keeping. The guidance should also include a range of preventative measures (for example, specific accessible information for patients on what they should and should not expect in consultations, and whom they can speak to for confidential advice and assistance);**

2. in relation to disclosures of alleged abuse, voluntary advocacy and advice services (independent of the NHS) should be supported by central public funding to offer advice and assistance to patients and former patients (particularly those who are mentally unwell, or who are otherwise vulnerable); and

3. that all Trusts should develop, within their Code of Behaviour,[4] guidance to reduce the likelihood of sexualised behaviour, and it should be incorporated into the contracts of employment of those staff, or contracts of engagement for all other persons providing mental health services within the NHS.

---

4 See *Creating a Patient-led NHS – Delivering the NHS Improvement Plan*, March 2005.

Chapter 25
External factors

Introduction

25.1   In this chapter of the Report we identify a number of causal or contributing factors which are likely to have made the expression of concerns and complaints by patients more difficult, and may have contributed to the failure to address the concerns and complaints raised at, or near, the time of the alleged sexualised behaviour. We here focus on the background, external factors against which the expressions of concern, the disclosures of alleged wrongdoing, fell to be considered. These external factors describe, at least in part, the culture of the NHS and (in a generalised way) doctors and others working within it. They may help readers of this Report to understand the context in which recipients of disclosures of alleged wrongdoing operated.

25.2   As we repeatedly say in this Report there have been many and significant changes since the days when William Kerr and Michael Haslam were practising psychiatry in North Yorkshire. But without an understanding of the background at the time it is more difficult to understand the particular patient-centred factors that inhibited the raising or pursuit of their concerns (such as "believability", "credibility", "embarrassment and guilt", "publicity", etc, addressed in Chapter 26.)

NHS structures

25.3   The prevailing structure at the time has been outlined elsewhere. The charts found at the end of Chapter 5 map the NHS structure over a period that included four major re-organisations. In general there were three tiers of management: Hospital, District and Region. At intervals there were also Area Health Authorities.

Re-organisation

25.4   Re-organisation frequently led to a change in key personnel and to the loss of organisational memory and continuity that has significance when both the consultants' careers spanned 25–30 years.

25.5   Frequent change of personnel strengthened the need for good systems of documentation. However, the Inquiry found substantial shortcomings in the way the personal employment records of William Kerr and Michael Haslam were maintained; this made it far more difficult to link unresolved complaints about them over long periods of time, let alone enable a pattern of alleged behaviour to be considered.

25.6   There were separate systems for complaints about doctors not necessarily linked to the main employment file. The Inquiry heard about this from the evidence of Dr Green and Dr Donald, and also from the Regional and District legal adviser Hugh Chapman.

25.7   No file of complaints or concerns was built up at Regional level over the relevant period, so there was no opportunity to identify whether a pattern was emerging. There was no clarity over what issues could or should be taken to the Region. No protocols were in place. There was clear and obvious, but unresolved, dislocation. While consultant contracts were held by the Regional Health Authority, there was little prospect for action by Districts. The combination of failure to inform and communicate, and a sense of local level powerlessness, created yet another obstacle to the prevention of abuse.

25.8   We have also referred elsewhere in this Report to the negative effect of Circular HM(61)112. The view was consistently expressed that it left consultants untouchable and unmanageable. The only real wider communication seems to have been informal discussions between doctors who exchanged concerns with each other, but where no record of those concerns was ever made.

25.9   This "system" we were told, was designed to avoid potential and unfair damage to the reputation and career of medical professionals, but served also to screen from view the nature and number of complaints and reports about the two doctors.

25.10 The storage and destruction of critical records as part of the re-organisation process is another contributing factor, particularly once William Kerr and Michael Haslam had retired. The consequence was a loss of potentially important evidence for subsequent inquiries and investigations. There is a need for the NHS to review its guidance and practice in this regard and to implement clear standards about storage and maintenance of records in the future.

25.11 The Inquiry heard evidence that the loss of confidence in the system of record keeping was such that one doctor kept his own notes separately away from NHS premises. That should never have been necessary at the end of the 20th century in the NHS.

Professional management

25.12 Complaints about doctors were mainly investigated by doctors, particularly with regard to issues that related to disciplinary matters. However, in the period between the deletion of the medical superintendent post and the appointment (mid-1990s) of medical directors in Trusts, we were informed there was no one at a hospital level in overall charge of doctors.

Consensus management

25.13 There was no single person in charge of the hospital, but rather a small number of senior professionals corporately responsible for the overall management of the hospital. Although the intention was to enable a balance of factors to be taken into account in decision making, it offered great scope for those who wished to influence or break the rules to do so without obvious sanction. This lack of cohesion was further exacerbated by the fact that each tier of management within the NHS had its own medical, nursing, financial and administrative leadership. As the structure chart at the end of Chapter 5 clearly shows, there was no single person ultimately in charge of an NHS hospital until 1986. Furthermore, until 1992 there was nothing in the structure which enabled the NHS to line manage consultants.

25.14 A consequence of this was that staff were managed within professions, with complaints being addressed by different people from those who were investigating other aspects of the same complaint; there was no overview and management of the whole. These structures were not patient-centred but professionally focused.

We believe this was a key factor in the Patient A17 case, where the concern was raised by Linda Bigwood. The investigation resulted in a focus on the handling of complaints by nursing management rather than the main issues: the alleged sexual misconduct of William Kerr and his one-to-one meeting with the patient. In relation to the Patient A17 disclosure, the Inquiry heard evidence of the complaint being passed from staff nurse through the nursing hierarchy to nursing officer, moving on from the senior nursing officer across to the sector administrator to district administrator and then to regional administrator. Efforts were focused on communicating up the line rather than attending to, and resolving, the issue at source.

25.15   In addition to consensus management, the lack of multi-disciplinary team working and decision making also led to a system developing that was not readily open to challenge. A direct consequence of professionals working in isolation was that the alleged behaviour of the kind described to us was undetected at the time or, when raised, not investigated.

Employment of consultants by Regional Health Authorities

25.16   Non-teaching hospitals' consultants were employed by the Regional Health Authorities, and their contracts of employment were managed at a great distance from their practice. Consultants had negotiated their employment status at the foundation of the NHS – a position we were informed they jealousy guarded. Counsel for the local NHS authorities described this historical background to the situation as the price the government paid to obtain the consultants' cooperation in the establishment of the NHS in the 1940s. It remained a significant and fundamental flaw in the system, only relatively recently corrected.

25.17   One consequence of this arrangement was the requirement to transfer information across complex interfaces. The Regional Medical Officer, or those dealing with complaints on his behalf, were involved in steering the complaint or disciplinary issue by liaising with local services. The flaw in the process was the assumption that these senior regional officers, remote as they were from services, would hear about the complaints in the first place.

25.18   The processes relied on the maintenance of good relationships and effective communication as well as good record keeping.

25.19   It was possible for complaints which related to the alleged misbehaviour of consultants to be investigated by district managers, with the District Medical Officer playing a critical role – as witnessed in the Patient A17 story, where Dr Wintersgill undertook this task.

25.20   However, we have received evidence of many instances where this was not the case; lack of clarity in management areas of responsibility resulted in complaints neither being logged nor successfully passed on; one manager decided that the case was not worth pursuing because it was predicted or expected that the "next tier up" would not robustly pursue the complaint. This was the case in relation to Mr Ingham, Dr Green and others and was reinforced by evidence to the Inquiry of very poor documentation of complaints, to which we refer elsewhere in this Report.

Accountability of consultants was unclear

25.21   There was a prevailing belief that consultants were accountable only to themselves for all clinical matters; the notion of accountability to their manager in the district and regional structures was very tangential and not accepted by most consultants. This resulted from the fact that the issue of autonomy had been fudged when consultants first opted into the NHS when it was established.

25.22   Most consultants' relationships with their employers during the period 1965–88 would have been on appointment, with any other employment matters largely maintained through correspondence, the notion of regular appraisal and review with the consultant's manager having only been introduced in the 1990s and becoming standard practice in the last five years.

The prevailing culture of the medical community

25.23   An answer to the central question "Why were concerns not raised, why were concerns not investigated?" requires an understanding of the culture that prevailed in the North Yorkshire NHS medical community in the 1970s and 1980s (possibly before, and possibly later).

25.24   Given the range of services spread across the UK, it is unlikely that there was the same culture across all NHS services during 1965–88 (see Chapter 5). Even within a local area such as North Yorkshire, the culture of each organisation and to some degree departments within hospitals was different. There were some issues that reflect broadly the prevailing culture in mental health services at the time; others were more specific to the location (rural Yorkshire) and the existence of Victorian psychiatric hospitals. Over this time mental health services were developing and becoming more community orientated. New outpatient and inpatient facilities were developing in district general hospitals and in local communities.

25.25 Organisational culture has been the focus of long-standing theoretical debate and analysis. In brief terms it can be understood to be the artefacts, behaviours and beliefs that operate and are accepted as the norm within an organisation – ie it is the sum of "how we do things around here".

25.26 The issue of culture is a significant factor in understanding the context of the NHS mental health services in North Yorkshire as well as the feelings, beliefs and consequent behaviours of the patients in relation to this Inquiry. Those of the mental health professionals and the NHS managers are dealt with elsewhere in this Report. As already mentioned, one major factor which created a barrier to patients complaining was the perceived and actual power of doctors. In the hierarchy of NHS practice over the period the 1970s to the 1990s the consultant doctor was the most revered and autonomous practitioner within the system. This is how one practitioner described his view of the prevailing culture when he arrived in North Yorkshire in 1989:

> *"On my arrival … in 1989 I felt the culture was that nothing would be done if there were concerns about a consultant's behaviour. At best the consultant would be asked to go elsewhere and matters would be swept under the carpet."*

25.27 In reviewing the evidence and looking specifically at services provided by Clifton Hospital and associated community services, we have identified a number of factors that contributed to the culture of the mental health services in North Yorkshire.

25.28 There are many facets to that culture relevant to the Inquiry. We have proceeded on the basis that medical practitioners were generally wholly professional, extremely competent and caring, and that patient welfare was of paramount concern. We take that as read. But there is more to culture. After careful consideration of the evidence produced to the Inquiry, we conclude that there were aspects of the culture which made investigation of concerns or complaints less likely to be successful, and more likely to deter women patients from raising concerns or complaints at all. We identify the following topics, some of which are further developed under separate headings in this chapter. Others are considered in other chapters.

- It was a male dominated profession, in which there was tolerance among some of its members of at least "consensual" sexual relationships between practitioners and patients.

- Male senior partners of general practices set the tone – and that tone was, at least in some practices, unsupportive of complaints made by women patients.

- Hospital consultants (particularly in psychiatry) were accorded enhanced status – they were treated, and expected to be treated, as local "gods", deserving respect and obedience.

- Consultants appointed to hospital posts (in the practice area of psychiatry) were likely to occupy those posts for 20–30 years, and would become so much a part of the local establishment as almost to be immune from criticism.

- The starting position for considering mentally unwell women patients who raised concerns, or made allegations (in relation to male medical practitioners), was disbelief.

- Complaining about a fellow medical practitioner was actively discouraged, and was considered to be unprofessional.

- Junior doctors depended on consultants for good references and career advancement.

- GPs and hospital doctors operated in different domains with separate accountabilities and inadequate ways of communicating across the sectors in matters other than patients' treatment.

- Patient confidentiality was elevated to a position such that it actively prevented any action or reaction to accounts given by patients who did not want to activate or pursue a formal complaint.

Male-dominated profession and networks

25.29 One GP described the situation as follows:

> *"My impressions at the time were of an old boy network,*
> *allowing difficult issues sometimes to be covered up or ignored."*

25.30 In the period 1965–88 nearly all the consultants were male. Women were not only the exception but also not usually part of the establishment. This factor is relevant in the context of our Report, where all the patients who gave evidence to the Inquiry were female and the alleged abuse was sexual in nature. In this regard it is true that the medical profession at the time did not differ in its composition from many other walks of life. Most professional networks were male dominated (except nursing). For example, lawyers, accountants and engineers rarely exhibited a high percentage of women in positions of seniority.

25.31 The Inquiry heard evidence from women GPs. Although their references to the social networks were peripheral, we received the strong impression that they were even more out of the loop in terms of gossip and informal information.

25.32 It is therefore interesting to note that patients did not disclose more to their female GPs, and nor did the female GPs pursue concerns or complaints more assiduously. There is a range of inferences that might be drawn from this observation; however, the pertinent one here may be that there is a re-inforcement of the view expressed by one patient that disclosure would have been no easier even if she had been able to see a woman GP. One cannot therefore conclude that the availability of female GPs would necessarily have made disclosure any more likely or any easier for the women in question.

Tolerance of sexualised behaviour

25.33 Chapters 21 to 23 described instances where apparent boundary violation in respect of the two psychiatrists had been disclosed by patients and "overlooked" by GPs. It took the arrival of a new consultant psychiatrist, Dr Simpson, to challenge the status quo.

25.34 This cultural feature (acquiescence) was present not only within general practice but also in general hospital settings, and particularly in Clifton Hospital. In the latter, we heard evidence of staff gossiping openly about allegations of inappropriate offers made towards patients by both doctors, and to staff by William Kerr.

Major influence of senior partners in GP practice

25.35 The GPs who gave evidence made a significant contribution to our understanding of the nature and functioning of general practices in North Yorkshire. All practices had senior partners; these doctors had invested in the practice, were seen as the more experienced practitioners and were regarded by newer doctors as the source of advice and wisdom. In several cases we heard of their advice being sought with regard to disclosures by patients along the lines of "I would talk to my senior partner at the time and I would be guided by him".

25.36 The evidence we heard suggested that it was with these senior partners that at least some potential investigations or reporting floundered. It is not difficult to understand the position that a junior GP would be in, having received advice not to put anything on the patient's file. There is particular importance to this point in a relatively small and stable community like North Yorkshire, where health professionals and their families lived and worked together. Given this setting it seems likely that young GPs would find it even more difficult to go against the advice of their seniors – or even find another doctor to whom they could safely turn for a second opinion. In the event this proved a substantial barrier to the early raising of questions about the practices of William Kerr and Michael Haslam.

Status of consultants and patronage of junior doctors

25.37 Junior doctors were reliant on consultants for references to progress their careers. This made it very difficult for them to raise concerns or complaints about their consultant as it might have led to harm to their own advancement within the profession. This hesitation or reluctance to act seems to have been unrelated to the reliability or evidential strength of the disclosure of alleged sexualised behaviour.

25.38 The status of consultants was a real issue described by witnesses, including former patients, staff from other professions (particularly nursing staff), managers and general practitioners. Consultants were – and often still are – different from, and considered to be superior to, everyone else in a hospital. Staff within the NHS system, including those in general hospital and mental health settings (matrons, CPNs),

GPs as well as those in the allied social care and therapeutic services (social workers, counsellors etc) gave evidence to the Inquiry of their view that consultants were "untouchable". For at least one witness, the position of William Kerr reached a level of "fear".

> Q. You have spoken of the impact of William Kerr on staff and patients, that they were petrified of him, I think is the word that you have used in your statement that you have provided to us. At what level did that fear end, in terms of the hierarchy within the hospital?
>
> A. It certainly affected the sister in charge of the ward. When I started on Ash Tree House, the sister was actually off sick. There was myself, there was also another deputy. From the other deputy and down there was a definite fear of William Kerr.

25.39 For junior doctors there was the added disincentive to complain or criticise, since as Dr Mortimer and Dr Simpson made clear, their future progress and career depended on getting good references and reports from their consultant.

25.40 We are not convinced that the position has fundamentally changed and it is important not to confuse personal development with changes to the system. One witness gave evidence as follows:

> Q. What would you do today if faced with the identical complaint?
>
> A. I think if I were faced with a similar situation, I think I would, first of all, contact the consultant, the doctor involved. I would want to know what happened from his point of view.
>
> Q. That would be the first avenue?
>
> A. Yes. Because I would feel more empowered in myself to confront a consultant.
>
> Q. Is that because of the experience you have gained as a GP or because the culture is very different, because obviously now you have been in practice for many years?
>
> A. I think because of the confidence which I have developed over the years, I would not feel threatened by a consultant or subordinate to a consultant. I would want to – I would challenge him.

Q. That is a confidence that you have gained because you have been a GP for over 20 years now?

A. And because I am older and I have been around for longer, yes.

Q. As far as you are concerned, the young doctor in the same position as you found yourself in the early 1980s, finding himself in that same position in 2004, might well be subject to the same advice and options that were open to you in the 1980s?

A. I would hope that the senior partner would give rather more positive advice.

And from another witness:

Q. Hopefully this respect would be maintained, but perhaps another aspect of the relationship is the power balance that existed between GPs and consultants. Would you say that there was an imbalance in power between the position of a general practitioner and the position of a consultant?

A. Yes, very definitely. Again, this was encouraged – this attitude was encouraged in our student days.

Q. An obvious follow-up question to that is: no doubt that imbalance would be another factor which would prevent you from taking concerns forward?

A. Yes.

25.41 This belief also appears to have been accepted by District and Regional managers. In evidence, we were told that managing a consultant at District level had to be done by negotiation, as their contracts were held by Region. A general shortage of psychiatric consultants meant that the incentives that could be used to secure their cooperation were limited: "They could pretty much do what they liked."

25.42 There was in addition evidence to the Inquiry from administrators at both District and Region of a sense of powerlessness and fear of challenging consultants. This was compounded by the reality that psychiatric specialists were in short supply, while the demand for psychiatric services was substantial. GPs in particular were concerned that the withdrawal of a psychiatrist as a result of a complaint would leave the area without any psychiatric provision. The result was a general reluctance to pursue complaints – particularly given the lack of confidence in the ability of the system to deal with such complaints.

25.43 Many consultants, but by no means all, were very happy with that state of affairs. It meant that they could pursue their careers without interference, and were generally deferred to by everyone in the hospital.

25.44 All professional relationships were developed in this context: junior doctors were conscious that their next job largely depended on what their current superiors wrote about them; nurses believed that consultants could affect their careers; administrators knew they had no power over consultants and, significantly, consultants also understood this to be the case. The culture was underpinned by the structures in place.

25.45 In relation to the position of consultants, one senior manager put the position as follows when referring to the reason why there was no direct contact with other patients:

> "It is a failure of systems. It also has to do with the culture. The whole culture at the time was of consultants who were above suspicion, and how would anybody dare to move into such things as writing to patients."

Length of time that consultants were in post

25.46 The Inquiry heard from several witnesses that although there had been vacancies for psychiatrists, in general consultants were often in the same post over many years. (This was the case with William Kerr and latterly Michael Haslam.) There developed the sense that such consultants, employed by and at arm's length from the Region, were a law unto themselves and became immune from criticism. The implication of what we heard was that even if there was some disquiet, consultants were unlikely to be challenged.

Autonomous working

25.47 The Inquiry has received factual information about the NHS which helpfully describes the structure, and also the relationships of the junior doctors to these long-standing consultants. Although this changed over the period covered by the Inquiry, our attention was repeatedly drawn to the power of the consultants to work autonomously. This was accepted common practice, and afforded the opportunity for a doctor to see a patient without monitoring or control by other professionals. As a consequence, we were told, the irregular timing of some appointments – late in the evening, late on Fridays or on Saturday mornings – was never picked up. There was no suspicion, no warning bells, even when the particular consultants were the subject of consistent gossip and rumour.

Disbelief of psychiatric patients

25.48   The issue of believing patients is dealt with more fully in Chapter 27 of this Report. However, it is a matter of such significance as to be noted here. The Inquiry heard evidence from a range of professional staff who accepted that the culture within the hospitals reinforced the then widely held view that mental health patients were not to be believed. Some doctors and nurses stand out as having approached their patients' expression of concern or complaint in relation to alleged sexualised behaviour with an open mind. However, their evidence illustrated how difficult it was to ensure that a full and balanced process of investigation was undertaken. This was confirmed by the evidence of those patients who did complain.

Disincentive to criticise colleagues

25.49   The Inquiry heard from both hospital doctors and GPs how reluctant they were to criticise their colleagues. This reluctance was attributed to the fact that:

- before any complaint was advanced, there had to be "hard" evidence;

- before any complaint was advanced, the patient had to be prepared to give evidence – probably in public;

- the complaint had to be supported by evidence that was likely to be proved to a criminal standard;

- GPs had no power over hospital consultants;

- disclosure by one doctor could ruin the other doctor's career;

- it was generally "bad form" to report on a professional colleague; and

- from the GPs' perspective, the LMC was not intended for such purposes and the GMC was too slow and bureaucratic.

25.50 All these factors were latent if not always articulated and were indicative of a culture in which some healthcare professionals were too passive for too long.

Dislocation of GPs and hospital

25.51 The Inquiry has also heard from several GPs of the separation of function and activity between their work and that of the hospital consultants. This has been in part attributed to the differing purposes of the services, centrally including the fact that the role of the general practitioner was and is to provide a "whole person" service to their patients. GPs described a situation where, having decided that specialist treatment was required, they referred their patients to the hospital psychiatric services. From that point onwards, the evidence to the Inquiry indicates that there was generally only a minimal grasp of (and sometimes scant professional curiosity about) what treatment the patients might receive and little or no enquiry as to their progress beyond perusal of the formal letters and reports that emanated from Kerr and Haslam. A measure of how distant the GPs felt from the hospital system is illustrated by their surprise at psychiatrist Dr Simpson's visit to practices on his arrival in Ripon. This was clearly beyond any contact that they could have imagined by a hospital consultant.

25.52 One implication of this for patients was that they viewed themselves as having entered a separate system – and one with which the GP had little or no contact. We heard repeatedly of the lack of follow-up by GPs to the hospital referral of a patient and of a failure by the GP to pick up on hints and suggested leads that the patient timidly and tentatively offered.

25.53 To emphasise the separation of domains Dr Givans (Medical Secretary and Chief Officer, of the North Yorkshire Local Medical Committee) told us:

"Totally different complaints procedures applied to GPs and hospital doctors between 1961 and 1988. The procedures for GPs and hospital doctors which had evolved over many years were totally different in their mode of operation and most doctors working in one discipline had little or no knowledge of the manner in which the complaints procedure operated for their colleagues in the other discipline ... Neither scheme was designed nor to my knowledge operated to allow complaints by one doctor of another."

25.54 Dr Givans also told us:

"During the period covered by the Inquiry ... there was no formal procedure to enable a GP to deal with a complaint made by a patient, carer or relative about a doctor employed by the hospital authority or other NHS body."

25.55 Assuming those descriptions to be correct the absence of a "formal procedure" seems to have had the consequential effect (at least in North Yorkshire) that GPs were incapable of dealing with such complaints at all. This poverty of response, and reliance on a lack of systems, was striking – and disappointing.

Intimidating procedures

25.56 We address the detail of the complaints system in Chapter 34 and Annex 5 of this Report. Here we mention evidence to the Inquiry suggesting that the process itself was intimidating. Dr Givans told us:

"Although Community Health Councils (CHCs) were helpful and supportive to patients with complaints, the system in place from 1961 to 1988 was not 'user friendly' towards patients with complaints of a very personal and perhaps embarrassing nature.

"Whilst such a patient might have been willing to confine in their GP, who they knew and trusted, the prospect of discussing intimate details with a stranger at the CHC or a manager at a hospital was very daunting for many and prevented them taking their complaints further.

"Also many patients had a perception that if they complained to the hospital they might be prejudicing themselves in respect of future treatment at that hospital. That situation has left many patients with legitimate complaints, feeling dissatisfied and in some cases angry with their GP. Unfortunately the culture during the period covered by the Inquiry was such that normally a GP at that time did not have the ability to do more than advise the patient how to proceed."

25.57 This summary was subscribed to by many other local GPs who gave evidence to the Inquiry.

25.58 We accept that the complaints procedures were not "user friendly", and no doubt intimidating to patients. As already noted, there were no formal complaints systems within the NHS that allowed a doctor to complain about another doctor.

25.59 What we do not accept is that such limitations in the formal complaints structures provided a reason or excuse for a GP to disregard an apparently legitimate concern raised by a vulnerable, mentally disordered patient, in relation to the very consultant to whom the GP had referred the patient for care and treatment. The culture at the time may well have been doctor-centred, rather than patient-centred, and there may well have been serious problems with the complaints procedures, but we cannot accept, using Dr Givans' words, that "the culture during the period" produced a result that a GP at the time (normally or otherwise) "did not have the ability to do more than advise the patient how to proceed".

25.60 We have found nothing in the culture that produced any lack of "ability" to do more, anything positively to prevent a GP from doing nothing more than advising a patient how to make a complaint. A GP, presented with information of alleged sexual wrongdoing by a consultant, knowing of the deficiencies in the formal complaints system, had the ability to speak to colleagues, to speak to the Regional Medical Officer, to take any other steps to ensure that the cause for concern was discussed and, if necessary, removed. In our view, this was not a case of lack of ability, but rather a lack of will.

Libel

25.61 Then, and we suspect now, there was a real concern that disclosures by patients in relation to other professionals (particularly powerful consultants) could not be passed on when there was no convincing and compelling evidence. In the absence of such evidence, and a willing and believable complainant, there was fear that the GP (or other recipient) would find himself or herself sued for libel. As noted elsewhere, that real concern has percolated into this Inquiry.

Lack of governance processes

25.62 The NHS at the time was wholly reliant on patients raising concerns via the complaints system. There were no other formal mechanisms for raising concerns as we see today in incident-reporting systems and whistle-blowing policies and analysing data to plot themes and trends regularly. These processes enable patients and staff to raise concerns at an earlier stage in the modern NHS.

25.63 The whole complaints system during the time covered by our Report was predicated on having a patient willing and able to raise a complaint and then have the tenacity to stick with the whole process to its conclusion. Patients were not always willing or able to progress complaints. The result was that no action was taken to address the concerns, even though they were known about by patients and staff. As far as we could see, it was an "all or nothing" system – if there was no actively pursued complaint, nothing would be done or could be done.

25.64 The complaints mechanism on its own was a blunt instrument and is now only one critical component of the battery of governance processes in place in the modern NHS to bring matters of concern quickly to the fore and to enable prompt action to be taken to redress them.

25.65 The NHS at the time was a closed system not wanting to listen and learn from mistakes. GP Dr Moroney's evidence (see Chapter 22) sums up what it felt like at the time trying to raise a concern in the system.

Supervision

25.66 Supervision of clinical work takes place in formal and informal settings. It is built into day-to-day working in a number of ways. These include:

- operational policies that clearly identify working practices such as regular multi-disciplinary decision making, referral assessment and review meetings;

- in vivo, on-the-job learning, from peers or someone more experienced or more skilled, through skill mix and case load management through education, audit and development;

- policies outlining professional standards that specify how individual clinical work will be supervised;

- the core skills of any clinical professional of self-reflection and the ability to monitor and understand his or her own feelings and actions through the therapeutic relationship (opportunities to enable this to happen should be built into day-to-day working practices, as well as being accessible though regular clinical supervision).

25.67 Through this rich mix of supervisory activity there is now opportunity for practitioners to raise issues and concerns that they have about their own or others' practice.

25.68 We can conclude from the evidence we heard that supervisory opportunities for consultants working at Clifton Hospital were limited – probably non-existent. Supervision requires the individuals themselves to identify the need for it, and we have no evidence that either William Kerr or Michael Haslam did access regular supervision. There was certainly no evidence of a culture in place that supported or encouraged such activity.

25.69 The Inquiry heard of academic meetings taking place; however, not all consultants would be required to attend these meetings. (We did hear evidence that some GPs attended Michael Haslam's presentation of an academic seminar in Kirlian photography.)

25.70 Clinical audit was considered to be one of the ways for consultants to review practice among peers. The Inquiry heard little evidence that there was much, if any, effective auditing taking place in North Yorkshire at the relevant times – at least in relation to psychiatry.

25.71 However, we here note that Dr Bromham gave evidence that she used to attend medical audit meetings regularly, chaired by her fellow consultant Dr Rugg. The date of the meetings is unclear, but the involvement of Dr Rugg suggests that it was towards the end of William Kerr's career.

25.72 Regular and systematic supervision underpins effective clinical practice. The Inquiry believes that this should apply to all mental health professionals, including consultant psychiatrists. The Inquiry heard from the National Institute for Mental Health in England (NIMHE) of a recent pilot project focusing on supervision of consultant psychiatrists. This, alongside other models, should be considered as a matter of urgency.

25.73 There was limited clinical supervision taking place of some CPNs, but others contrasted the lack of opportunity available at that time with the range of opportunities available now.

25.74 During the 1970s and 1980s, as community services were developing, they were organised by profession. The community nursing service worked separately to consultants' workload, occasionally coming together for supervision. Consultants managed the medical referrals with their junior medical team. This way of working presented opportunity for lone working.

25.75 Modern multi-disciplinary practice is now well established. Psychiatrists, nurses, psychologists, occupational therapists and, more recently, social workers are integrated team members. Modern practice requires referral to the team and not to the individual practitioner – this mitigates against cherry-picking particular patients, as it is a team decision as to who picks up the referral.

25.76 There was evidence that both William Kerr and Michael Haslam used to see younger or vulnerable women at the end of the day, particularly the Friday afternoon clinic. Team process brings together members of a multi-disciplinary team to discuss and agree referrals and how assessments will be done, and by whom. The team meets once these are complete to identify the care or treatment plan. This increases the likelihood of evidence-based therapies being offered. Working as part of a team reduces risk but does not eliminate it; lone working can become counter-productive. Since 1991 the Care Programme Approach (CPA) identifies that each patient should have a written copy of their care plan, that they should have a signed copy of it. CPA reviews are the opportunity for the full multi-disciplinary team to have an understanding of all the patients being seen by the team.

25.77 Our general conclusion is that there is a need to examine and develop processes for ensuring communications between NHS organisations (primary, secondary, etc) to support progress made on improving structures and policies.

25.78 While responsibility for consultants is now firmly with Medical Directors and Chief Executives of Trusts and provider organisations, there is a need to remain alert to the opening up of new gaps in the transfer of information (about complaints concerns) between health and social care organisations, including NHS Care Trusts and private and voluntary providers: between NHS and other publicly funded organisations, such as the police, probation and housing providers.

25.79 There is also a need to develop a culture of staff across all services in which they accept that their loyalty to colleagues (peers or more senior staff) is not paramount but secondary to the duty of care to patients and service users.

25.80 The external factors identified in the evidence to the Inquiry and summarised in this chapter provide some of the context within which individual actions and inaction are to be understood.

25.81 We were left with the clear impression that these pre-existing cultural factors made it far more difficult for the disclosures made by former patients (of allegations of sexualised behaviour by their consultant psychiatrists) to be received and seriously considered. Indeed, the opposite was the case. In the main, there was an unsympathetic consideration: the recipients did not encourage further explanation or further detail, and appeared reluctant to offer the necessary care and support which would have enabled such sensitive concerns to be ventilated.

Chapter 26
Why patients did not complain

Introduction

26.1   We have tried in the course of the Inquiry to explore the reasons why concerns were not raised by patients, and, when concerns were raised, why they either were not pursued or were simply blocked by recipients of the information. We turn now to focus on those who did not raise their concerns at or near the time.

26.2   Obviously the former patients of William Kerr and Michael Haslam do not stand alone in being reluctant to complain where they are likely to deal with, or even be treated by, the persons who are the subject of their concerns. What is particular to their case is the lack of power, the fear and feeling of powerlessness – described in greater detail later in this chapter. In addition, as psychiatric patients they made clear to the Inquiry that they were well aware of the stigma attached to mental illness; this not only further disempowered them, but also exacerbated their concerns about complaining. We address this topic more specifically in Chapter 27.

26.3   A possible answer, and no doubt the answer favoured by William Kerr and Michael Haslam, is that the reason concerns were not raised at the time (or at least before the 1997 police investigation) is that there was no basis for any complaint – the alleged sexualised relationships, the alleged sexual assaults, did not happen.

26.4   However, as we have already noted, there is reason to believe that at least some complaints were factually true – the convictions of William Kerr and Michael Haslam are proof of wrongdoing to a criminal standard. In relation to the other incidents, the Inquiry knows that there were complaints made and that there were concerns expressed at the time. It does not follow, of course, that convictions for some offences of sexual assault mean that either William Kerr or Michael Haslam committed other offences against other women – they are both entitled to the benefit of the presumption of innocence in relation to any allegation of criminality. And a similar approach must also apply to allegations of conduct such as a consensual sexual relationship with a patient which, if true, may not be a criminal offence but may form the basis for disciplinary or regulatory proceedings. However, even if inadmissible in a criminal trial (or in GMC disciplinary proceedings), it is inevitable that the existence of the convictions does lend some support to the account given by other former patients. The jury in the William Kerr Trial of the Facts found that six charges had not been proved to a criminal standard. It does not follow that in relation to the other charges, or to the concerns and complaints not put before the jury, that "it did not happen". It is to be regretted that the truth of the many allegations directed at both William Kerr and Michael Haslam have not been, and will not be, tested. But, on any sensible view, the approach that "it did not happen" and that that is why concerns were not raised at the time, is unconvincing as a complete explanation. In any event, many concerns and complaints were raised – with doctors, nurses, friends and relatives – well before the 1997 police investigation.

26.5   What is clear is that if concerns and complaints raised at or nearer the time had been more carefully and fully investigated, then the truth or falsity of the allegations could have been resolved. What the Inquiry can do, in accordance with the Terms of Reference, is to record the concerns and complaints of which it has been made aware, and to note that the allegations made against William Kerr are strikingly similar to each other; and, additionally, that while the allegations made against Michael Haslam are different from those made against William Kerr, the allegations against Michael Haslam are also similar to each other.

26.6   The number of former patients who have now come forward to express their concerns and complaints greatly exceeds the number of patients who raised any concern or complaint at the time. For William Kerr this was 29, and for Michael Haslam a further two. In relation to Michael Haslam, the last complaint raised was in September 2004, shortly before the Inquiry closed the evidence-gathering stage of the investigation. This patient's concerns relate to the early 1970s, when she was an inpatient at Clifton Hospital.

26.7   Why should there be such a mismatch in number between complaints made at the time and those now made in total? Michael Haslam (William Kerr was, through ill health, unable to express his views to us) would have the Inquiry accept that the answer is opportunism and greed: that former patients have come forward to express concerns only in anticipation of cash payments. We do not consider this to be the case. In any society there may of course be people who are so motivated; however, our clear impression is that the former patients have come forward with considerable reluctance. They are more strongly motivated by a desire to ensure that those who they allege are responsible for what happened to them are called properly to account and that future patients should not be subject to abuse. The absence of expectation of financial reward, in terms of compensation, is emphasised by the fact that several women have come forward to give evidence, and have attended many if not all of the oral hearings, long after their claims for compensation in civil proceedings have been settled.

26.8   The Inquiry has been in existence for some considerable time. There have been fits and starts, and many delays referred to earlier in this Report. We have been deeply impressed by the commitment of the former patients, particularly those who have taken the time to attend the oral hearings.

26.9   So, if the mismatch is not explained by the expectation of financial reward, what is the explanation for patients not coming forward sooner? We suggest that the following paragraphs may provide some of the reasons why former patients who did not express concerns or complaints at the time have now come forward.

26.10   What we say in these paragraphs also has some application to the former patients who did raise their concerns and complaints at, or closer to, the time of the alleged sexualised behaviour. The barriers to making complaints may go some way to understanding why the allegations by these former patients were not pursued, were discontinued, or were not developed in any detail. Indeed some of the evidence to support these conclusions came from former patients who did raise their concerns at the time.

Patients' perceptions

Fear of the doctor's reaction

26.11 A number of former patients have told the Inquiry that they were mindful of how they would be treated by the doctor once he knew that they had made a complaint alleging some form of sexualised behaviour. For some this was a double bind, as they had made the doctor the object of their hopes – he was for them often the only one who could help. If he let them go, they were finally lost. Others were frightened that the doctor might take action against them – withdrawing their medication, taking steps that could lead to the removal of their children into care – that would be devastating for them. Many of them were simply fearful that the reaction would be strongly negative, without being able necessarily to articulate how that negativity might manifest itself – they were just wary.

Passage of time

26.12 For some former patients, the passage of time has had no real effect. They have described to us their alleged experiences from many years ago as if it was the very recent past. But for others, the passage of time has made it far easier for them to speak now. One key factor, at least for some of the former patients, is that both William Kerr and Michael Haslam are now retired and not in positions of power, and can no longer have any impact or influence. Of course, when looking at this point, it must be understood that many, indeed most, of the women are simply in better mental health than they were when under the care of either William Kerr or Michael Haslam. They are mentally stronger and more able to speak out.

26.13 It is also simply easier now to express concerns and make complaints. We address the topic in more detail elsewhere in the Report, but merely note here that the Inquiry and the local NHS, at least in relation to these two consultants, is looking at the expression of concerns and complaints not only with the benefit of hindsight, but also in a different time, when the attitude to complaints and complaining has changed considerably.

Being alone

26.14 This can be understood in a number of ways. Some former patients believed that each of them thought that they were the only patient who, so they allege, was having a sexual relationship with one or other of the consultants, or was being sexually abused by one or other of the consultants. As a result of the publicity, or as a result of the trawl of former patients in the late 1990s, they have discovered that they were not alone in raising such concerns. Some have clearly found support in the company of others who have similar stories to tell of alleged sexualised behaviour.

Prevailing culture and ethos regarding complaints

26.15 By this we mean the external factors, the barriers to complaining, referred to above. The culture at the time, which at least in part was unsympathetic to such disclosures, provided its own inhibition.

Fear, guilt and embarrassment

26.16 We have grouped these factors together because there is a considerable degree of overlap. It is to be noted that these factors appear to apply whether or not the alleged sexualised behaviour was said to be consensual/voluntary, or forced.

26.17 The following ingredients have been suggested to the Inquiry. We agree with them all, and include them here with some small additions or comments.

Fear

Patients expressed fear of:

- Being disbelieved – by the doctor or nurse to whom the disclosure is made, and/or by friends and family;

- Being criticised and possibly rejected by family, partner or spouse;

- Being branded a trouble maker – with the risk of further problems within the health service, and outside;

- Losing treatment, or of receiving inferior treatment;

- Suffering a deterioration in mental health (a strong reason for family members persuading former patients not to take concerns forward);

- Doctors generally;

- Being detained under the Mental Health Act, of being locked up, or otherwise being subjected to treatment imposed against their will, such as medication or ECT;

- Losing their children;

- The complaints process (being questioned, challenged, etc, with the medical profession sticking together);

- The criminal process (being seen by the police, giving evidence, going to Court, public exposure);

- Losing their jobs (this is particularly, but not only, relevant to former patients who were health service employees);

- Disgracing the doctor and harming his family (sometimes).

26.18 The concern in relation to fear is illustrated by the following examples from the evidence received by the Inquiry:

> *"The reason I haven't told anyone up until now is that I was too frightened to. This is because I am still a psychiatric patient and I don't think I will be believed … The reason I am talking now is because I saw a newspaper article stating that Dr Haslam is now in prison because of sexual abuse. So, I feel safe from him and safe to talk about him."*

> *"He just kept referring to his hospital. Why did he keep referring to his hospital? Why did I need to know [it was] his hospital? I took it as a threat…I was frightened to death; no other word for it." (Patient A67)*

> *"I just did not feel I could talk about it. I was worried there would be repercussions. I was working with the authority, in the authority, I did not want to get branded a troublemaker, so I just kept it to myself …" (Patient AB)*

> *"[A]t first [William Kerr] said he had ways and means of putting us in hospital. To me, that meant sectioning me. Having been in hospital before, I did not want that to happen. He just kept on about this. So I had to conform to what he had asked us to do, because I was so frightened of going back into hospital." (Patient A68)*

26.19 When one patient allegedly threatened to report William Kerr for his behaviour, her fear was apparent by his response:

> *"He just laughed, and he said he would remove my children. He said if I told anybody I would never see my children again." (Patient A61)*

Guilt

26.20 Patients expressed feelings of guilt arising from doubts about how their own behaviour may have contributed to the alleged assaults. Examples of self-questioning were:

- Have I led him on? (An inclination to blame themselves rather than believe that their doctor was capable of exploiting or harming them.)

- Did I want this to happen?

- Am I to blame?

26.21 Guilt was a constant concern for the former patients, illustrated by the following single example from evidence given in the oral hearings:

> *"I wondered whether it was me – as you do dress yourself up to look as smart as you can – I suppose in a sense I probably blamed myself." (Patient A67)*

Embarrassment

26.22 Evidence from patients included honest assessments of their own embarrassment at finding themselves in this position. Consequently, their responses were:

- a strong reluctance to talk about such matters;

- belief that the sexual behaviour was part of the treatment, and then realising that it was not;

- a sense of being flattered by the attention, that it made them feel special; and

- a form of denial which meant that they did not want to be asked about what happened.

26.23 The effect of this shame and embarrassment was encapsulated in the oral evidence of one patient:

> *"I was so ashamed and embarrassed, partly because of my upbringing, my parents' attitude towards such things, and it rubbed off on me as a teenager. I was just so embarrassed, I could not have told anyone."*

26.24 We are in no doubt that these perceptions, whether singly or together, left patients feeling unable or unwilling to pursue complaints or concerns through the appropriate channels. There is no doubt, as far as the Inquiry is concerned, that this added to the frustration and sense of isolation that many have told us they felt. It simply added to the strain and tension they already felt and compounded their sense of helplessness. They deserved better.

Chapter 27
The impact of mental illness

Introduction

27.1   Making a complaint is difficult for anyone. It requires concentration and confidence. Doing this while suffering from a mental illness was even more difficult for patients.

27.2   Approximately 90 per cent of mental illness is initially dealt with in primary care.[1] Patients are referred by their GP to consultant psychiatrists only if the GP believes specialist opinion and treatment are required. Although the thresholds for referral to mental health services have changed over the years, by definition all the women referred were ill and seeking support and treatment for their condition from a specialist.

27.3   From the evidence we heard, there were several patients who were described as being simply too ill to be able to take on the bureaucracy of the complaints system. This is graphically described by Patient B1 and her husband, as well as by Patient B3 and Patient B5 and others.

27.4   For these patients, the passage of time enabled them to come forward, although, due to the lack of contemporaneous statements, there is often no evidence available to sustain their accounts, and some loss of memory is inevitably an issue. (We here make a recommendation that the time limits for making a complaint should be relaxed, and that anyone should be able to advance a complaint, if in the interests of patient safety it is right to do so.)

27.5   It is therefore even more important to ensure that patients' concerns are recorded at the time, even if they are not personally wanting to progress the complaint contemporaneously. The cut-off time in

---

1   *Mental Illness in the Community*, D Goldberg and P Huxley (1980), London: Tavistock.

current procedures of two years should be extended in these circumstances.

We therefore RECOMMEND, regarding mental health services, the NHS should review the cut-off period for registering a complaint, as well as the criteria for initiating an investigation of an old complaint and the procedures to be applied.

27.6   The very nature of the power imbalance already described is a feature in relation to vulnerability.

27.7   It is often difficult to conduct a fair investigation of any allegations relating to sexualised behaviour. When the complainant has a mental disorder matters become even more complex. It is therefore vital that a proper investigation is conducted and documented.

27.8   Those undertaking investigations within the NHS are often inexperienced junior managers whose knowledge base is poor or non-existent about complex matters such as the impact of mental disorder on witness credibility. This situation must end as soon as practically possible.

Mental disorder

27.9   In these paragraphs we refer to various forms of mental disorder. We have tried to be inclusive but here note that there has been no attempt by us to categorise the psychiatric condition of the former patients of William Kerr or Michael Haslam who have come forward to give evidence to the Inquiry. In the main, referral for consultant treatment appears to have been on the basis of a diagnosis of a depressive or anxiety-related condition, with some examples of personality disorder.

27.10   In cases of mental illness, perceptions, cognitions, emotions, judgement and self-control may be adversely affected, and this may result in misleading information being provided during an interview. Breakdown in "reality monitoring" is an important symptom of mental illness, and when present it impairs the patient's ability to differentiate facts from fantasy. In some circumstances this can result in people believing that they have committed crimes of which they are totally innocent or falsely reporting a crime. Breakdown in reality monitoring does not require the presence of mental illness. It occurs in everyday life in relation to the memory of thoughts, feelings and events (eg it is common for people not to be able to differentiate between what they have intended to do and what they have in fact done). However, mental illness makes the breakdown in reality monitoring more extensive and frequent.

27.11   Delusions and hallucinations which commonly accompany major mental illness are often the way in which people try to make sense of events and their internal experiences. This may, on occasions, result in people misinterpreting events and the intentions of others, although mental illness does not appear to be associated with heightened suggestibility.

27.12   We were advised by Professor Gudjonsson that depressive illness does cause some people to ruminate and implicate themselves falsely in criminal activity as a way of relieving strong feelings of free-floating guilt. It is important to note the research finding that neither electroconvulsive therapy (ECT) nor depression significantly affected the patients' susceptibility to give in to leading questions or interrogative pressure.

27.13   Personality disorder is an important psychiatric diagnosis in connection with a number of cases of disputed confessions since the case of Judith Ward. Personality disorder may represent an important psychological vulnerability among some witnesses and suspects. They appear to have an enhanced tendency to confabulate their memory and recall and more readily make false confessions.

27.14   There are, of course, several different types of personality disorder (eg schizoid, avoidant, antisocial, narcissistic, paranoid and borderline), and each has different structures and styles of personality. As far as "borderline" personality disorder is concerned, it is mainly characterised by affective instability (ie marked shift in mood) and high impulsivity. There is no research evidence to show that people with borderline personality disorders are more likely to be unreliable in their descriptions of events than people with other types of personality disorder.

The effects of drugs

27.15 Many former patients were concerned about the level of prescribed medication they had been taking while under the care of William Kerr or Michael Haslam.

27.16 Professor Gudjonsson provided to the Inquiry useful information on the impact of substance use on witness credibility. This will be of interest not only to former patients but also to the NHS staff who are grappling with these issues, often without a firm evidence base.

27.17 The effect of prescribed medication on the validity and completeness of answers during questioning, or on the reporting of sexual assault, has not been specifically studied. In his review of the literature, Michael Lader describes the effects of drugs on the behaviour of potential witnesses and differentiates between different types of drugs:

- drugs prescribed to treat psychiatric disorders – these include tranquillisers, sleeping tablets, antidepressants and antipsychotic drugs;

- drugs used to treat neurological disorders that have psychological side-effects (eg anticonvulsants and antiparkinsonian drugs);

- illicit drugs, which are used by drug addicts in non-medical contexts (eg cannabis, LSD, heroin, cocaine, amphetamines, magic mushrooms and ecstasy);

- alcohol, which has sedative effects similar to that of tranquillisers.

27.18 The focus of Professor Gudjonsson's advice to the Inquiry was principally on the use of prescribed medication on the valid reporting of sexual assault.

27.19 Again, according to Michael Lader, the main drug-induced states that are relevant to testimony are sedation, disinhibition, paradoxical reactions, and alterations in concentration, memory and learning. Paradoxical reactions refer to reactions which are opposite to those normally expected from the drug. For example, increased anxiety, anger and violent outbursts sometimes accompany alcohol intoxication. Tranquillisers and other sedatives, except at the lowest doses, will impair cognitive functions, such as concentration, memory and learning. In highly anxious persons these cognitive functions are often already impaired due to the high level of anxiety, and a low to moderate dose of a sedative may reduce the level of anxiety to the extent that cognitive functions are improved. At high doses it is likely that the anxiety-relieving properties of the drug will not outweigh its direct depressant effects, thus leaving the person's cognitive impairment no better than it was, or even exacerbating it.

27.20   The other problem with some sedatives is that at a high dose they can produce a major memory distortion, including fantasy and false memory, but this only seems to occur if the drug is given intravenously. For example, there has been a discussion on how some women heavily sedated with benzodiazepines, given intravenously, report false allegations of sexual assault. The study involved 41 incidents where women reported fantasies during sedation. Of those, 27 (66 per cent) contained sexual elements, including allegations of sexual assault. Seven of the 41 cases led to litigation against the anaesthetist. All the women were certain of the authenticity of their accusations and their experiences were apparently vividly recalled. In many of these cases the assault could not have happened (eg others were present at the time, or the assault as stated was not physically possible). Most happened during dental procedures, followed by oral endoscopy and induction of anaesthesia. A relationship has been found between the dosage of drug administered and frequency of complaints. The main implication of this paper is that fantasies of sexual nature do occur during heavy sedation with benzodiazepines, given intravenously, albeit infrequently.

27.21   There is no evidence that oral medication, even at high dosages, results in sexual fantasies or false reporting of sexual assault.

Contamination

27.22   Contamination in memory due to post-event information interference commonly occurs in everyday life. Over time memory deteriorates and subsequent discussions with others, including other victims, family, friends and the police, can all potentially interfere with the memory consolidation and retrieval process. Reading about the case in the media may also contaminate memory.

27.23   In order to assess the reliability of historical sexual abuse allegations, and possible contamination, it is important to examine carefully the process whereby the allegations came to be made, commencing with the first claim, and finding out how each person was interviewed, how often, who the interviewer was, and how the interviews were recorded.

27.24 We recognise that "trawling" for evidence (ie making unsolicited approaches to former residents or patients from institutions) in sexual abuse cases can be a hazardous procedure, and may generate false allegations. This difficulty with "trawling" was recognised in a recent report by the House of Commons Select Committee on Home Affairs (HC 836-I and HC 836-II; 31 October 2002). However, as our focus in this Inquiry has been in relation to how a concern or complaint was handled, rather than with the substance of the complaint itself, for our Inquiry it was unnecessary for us to attempt to resolve or comment further on this issue.

27.25 We do, however, make these observations. First, although there is such a danger, there is no evidence to suggest that there was here any generation of false allegations – either as a result of the investigation in 1997, or as a result of our own attempts to seek information. As noted repeatedly, the matter of truth or falsehood in relation to the disclosures has simply not been an issue. Second, although the danger exists – and indeed other issues arise, such as creating a risk of causing disturbance and distress to recipients of trawl letters – the alternative, of no trawl, or an incomplete investigation, also causes difficulties. These difficulties were addressed at the time of the 1997 investigation, and a decision made. So long as the danger of false allegations is recognised, and due caution applied, we do not see anything wrong in principle with inquiries being made of other, potentially affected, former patients. Such investigations must be very carefully managed and handled, and systems put in place to protect against the risks mentioned above – including, but not limited to, the offer of counselling services for any former patients who do make contact as a result of letters written, or other invitations to come forward.

Impact of being a psychiatric patient

27.26 As far as the patients who gave evidence to the Inquiry are concerned, their side of the story needs to be viewed in the context in which they occurred. There is, therefore, a deliberate overlap of information and evidence with that contained in Chapters 25 and 26. Factors impacting on patients included the following.

Breach of trust and problems with boundaries

27.27 The alleged sexualised behaviour is said to have occurred in the context of a trusting and professional relationship between the doctor and his patient. This doctor–patient trust would have been breached once the doctors concerned initiated inappropriate sexual behaviour.

27.28 Sexual abuse carried out in the context of an apparently innocent physical examination may not initially be perceived as inappropriate. The patient may have complete faith in the doctor's integrity and accept behaviours that would in other contexts be construed as inappropriate, devious and offensive. Where there are unclear and undefined boundaries, there can be little doubt that they can be exploited by a doctor for the purpose of grooming for sexual gratification.

Imbalance and abuse of power

27.29 For all the former patients who have made disclosures of alleged sexualised behaviour, there was a hierarchy and imbalance in terms of power. As a professional group within our society, doctors have high status and are a source of influence. This was probably even more so in the 1970s and the 1980s. Within that professional group, as noted elsewhere in the Report, consultants had even higher status, and were even more influential. Where patients are seeing their consultant doctor because of psychological or psychiatric problems, then they are particularly vulnerable to exploitation, because they are in need of help, and are dependent on the doctor for improving their mental condition. This dependency could make them particularly susceptible to agreeing, in good faith, to a doctor's suggestions and requests, even if unexpected and perceived as peculiar or inappropriate. We are advised that their dependency may even extend to their going back to a doctor even if that doctor has repeatedly sexually abused them. The imbalance of power, in the case of a psychiatric patient, is also reflected in the doctor's ability to influence the patient's continued and future care in situations where the psychiatrist's words are likely to be believed rather than those of the patient.

Reluctance to make complaints

27.30 Even in present times where some of the inhibitions on complaining have fallen away, the imbalance of power and the inherent dependency on the doctor for continued and future care are likely to cause many patients to find it very difficult to make a formal complaint against their doctor. This position is likely to be exacerbated in the case of psychiatric patents. It follows, again particularly in the case of psychiatric patients, that there is a need to view delayed allegations in the context in which they occur, rather than immediately viewing them with scepticism and disbelief.

Feelings of guilt and shame

27.31 In general terms, the evidence to the Inquiry suggests that patients who are sexually abused by their doctor may experience strong feelings of both guilt and shame for allowing themselves to be used in this way. They may even partly blame themselves for what happened, particularly in the context of a depressive illness. Feelings of shame generally inhibit people from disclosing their participation in the offences of others.

Complacency of other staff

27.32 Other mental health staff may be complacent where there has been a suspicion of, or a complaint about, an improper relationship between a doctor and a patient and may not make a complaint or report because of a tacit acceptance of the status and power of senior staff (eg consultants).

27.33 Overall, the evidence to the Inquiry of both former patients and hospital staff highlighted the lack of energy and drive that being ill brings with it. These former patients, whether actually abused or not, had very limited physical and emotional strength; they were often in no position to "fight back" against what they say had happened to them, or to take any form of complaint forward. While this was rightly recognised by some of their medical carers, few were able to convert that recognition into the care and support needed in such circumstances, or (where appropriate) take up the cudgels on the patients' behalf.

Patients and culture

27.34   There was an expressed view among patients that in a situation where it was one person's word against the other's the doctor would be more likely to be heard or believed. The assumed credibility of the doctor trumped most things.

27.35   In the course of the evidence to the Inquiry, we heard from a number of former patients who presumed that their consultant was so senior that no one would be able to challenge him. They were described as being "like gods". For example, one patient told us:

> "Well if I'm getting told by my GP that he is entitled to ask those questions, how can I say that he assaulted me, because who would believe me?"

27.36   As Dr Jeremy Holmes advised us in his description of the imbalance in the power relationship, patients:

> "...who have been subject to sexual exploitation as children are more prone to such exploitation in adult life, especially when placed in a 'child-like' situation in which there is inequality of power, as is often the case between psychiatrist and patient. Those feelings can be used for good or ill, and psychiatrists must be aware of the temptations they represent and be especially careful with their patient's feelings (just as a surgeon will handle the sensitive tissues of a patient's body with extreme care and respect)."

27.37   Some former patients feared retribution or detention. It was clear to them that the consultants were in an immensely powerful position and they, in contrast, were powerless to help themselves. There was a real danger that complaining would only make matters worse for them.

27.38   Many patients thought it was not even worth raising the complaint at this time because of this perception. Patients were also reluctant to voice criticisms of their consultant – some from a, perhaps to some, surprising sense of loyalty. This respect for the professional status of a medical practitioner is illustrative of the power of the culture in framing the behaviour of individuals.

27.39 There was also considerable evidence to the Inquiry, corroborated by their GPs, that patients were told that they would have to make written statements to the police. We were told, "There really was not a system for GPs to complain about hospital consultants officially without the patient's back-up. It would be just hearsay ...", and that no investigations could take place unless a formal statement was made. This belief generated enormous anxiety – quite understandably. Patients and those responsible for their care were concerned that undertaking the formal complaint-making process would be detrimental to the patient's mental health and well-being. The consequence was in several cases a decision not to make a formal complaint – and in some cases to withdraw a complaint that had already been made. The requirements of the complaints process were effectively interpreted to silence the concerns. All that was left was another source for the prevailing gossip and rumour (see Chapter 33).

27.40 This conclusion was added to by the evidence to the Inquiry of several doctors who articulated how impossible it was for them to believe that a medical professional could and would harm a patient. Dr Wade told us:

> *"It was just incomprehensible that someone should behave in that way and one would never have imagined that this behaviour would have been from a professional colleague."*

27.41 The point in the previous paragraph requires emphasis. It is an important factor – less so now, as so many scandals have emerged, but it was in the 1970s and 1980s – and was a real impediment to any form of constructive action. It also formed one of the background features to the next paragraph.

27.42 Finally, but most significantly, there is the issue of believing patients. Throughout the course of oral evidence to the Inquiry, we heard patient after patient describe their belief that they would not be believed (see below). Again, the truth of their allegations is not being confirmed or denied; merely that opportunities that should have been taken to explore or even merely register the complaint were not taken.

27.43 This willingness to disbelieve patients sits discordantly with the research evidence on believing patients presented to the Inquiry.

Doctors and other healthcare professionals accused of sexually exploitative behaviour would have the world believe that the complainant is fabricating or imagining the event. Research carried out as long ago as the 1980s would suggest that recipients of concerns and complaints, and those given the task of investigation, should be very reluctant to treat the expressions of concern at anything other than face value.

> *"Over the past 14 or so years, our experience with more than 1,000 cases of sexual exploitation has yielded only a few in which, we believe, misleading or false information was presented by a complainant or someone assisting the complainant. Such cases have increased in number in recent years but still they are comparatively rare. In reviewing malpractice claims against psychologists, Cummings and Sobel (1985) state:*
>
>> *An interesting statistic is that of all the sexual malpractice cases that have been filed, only one person has been exonerated."*[2]

Believing and disbelieving patients

27.44 The starting point for this section of the Report must be to state the obvious: that patients who are referred to a psychiatrist come as very vulnerable people, ill or in psychological distress and in need of treatment and support.

27.45 We were advised that "Psychiatric patients are by definition often themselves psychologically vulnerable and many – especially those suffering from personality disorders – have been sexually abused as children by unscrupulous care-givers." We believe this fact merits restating in order to highlight the witnesses' accounts in their oral evidence. Many patient witnesses and their doctors made clear that these patients were very unwell. They therefore had only limited ability – if any – to cope with the demands of a making and pursuing a complaint and its possible consequences on their personal lives. Illustrative of this is the evidence of several GPs and psychiatrists who felt their patients were too vulnerable to take up or pursue complaints at the time.

2 Schoener, Milgrom et al (1989): *Psychotherapists' Sexual Involvement with Clients: Intervention and Prevention* (USA).

27.46 In addition, there was the risk of disbelief. The Inquiry heard evidence from a number of witnesses which clearly showed that patients who made contemporaneous complaints were not believed.

27.47 Patient after patient has referred to this point. Below are samples of the evidence the Inquiry has received.

> *"I think he probably thought I was a neurotic woman (which I was) and I was making this whole thing up."*

> *"I sensed, and I knew that he – he either did not believe me or he did not want to hear me."*

> *"I mean, in the state I was in, no-one was going to probably believe what I said anyway … the stigma about seeing a psychiatrist, people think you are loopy and that is it, so you just keep shtum."*

> *"Well, either I would not be believed or it was just a closed shop … the doctors all stick together."*

> *"I thought: well, who can you talk to? Who can you tell? Nobody seems to believe you."*

27.48 The concerns expressed by patients that they would not be believed was not unreasonable – certainly in the 1970s and 1980s. The Inquiry received information from GPs and mental health professionals that clearly confirmed this perspective in some but not all cases. In some cases, professionals said that although they did believe the patient, they did not take a record of the allegation or support the patient to take forward the complaint or feel that it was their responsibility to progress the concern on their behalf.

> *"The culture at that time was that psychiatric patients should not be believed due to their mental state."* (Professor Ann Mortimer, junior assistant to William Kerr in 1983)

27.49 A patient also gave evidence of the predisposition of staff to disbelieve what she was saying:

> *"… my expectation was that I would not be believed. I wanted to be believed … I do not think it ever at that stage entered my mind that anybody would believe me enough to take anything further to a complaint."*

27.50 Others took an entirely different view. For example, when Michael Haslam was giving oral evidence to the Inquiry, it was put to him that there was a culture within the York psychiatric community to the effect that those who made allegations were not to be believed if the patients had mental health problems. His response was as follows:

> *"I think it is rubbish on the part of those people who have said it. I think it is something which, if they said it elsewhere, would be actionable."*

27.51 We prefer the recollection above of Professor Mortimer. Whether or not patients were actually disbelieved because they were suffering from a mental disorder, it is clear that that was the patients' perception. That must have been known to the medical and administrative staff and it is unfortunate that greater efforts were not made to reassure patients, and to encourage them to say what they wanted to say, without fear that the exercise would be pointless, and without the risk of reprisal or at least instant disbelief.

27.52 This situation was not unique to Clifton Hospital; however, it does reflect a culture of disempowerment, and there was evidence from nurses and junior doctors of a culture of disbelief, epitomised by the responses of Sister Pauline Brown and Ann Tiplady. Nevertheless, there was also evidence from a number of staff, for example Steve Brooks and Andy Cattell, which showed that they did not routinely doubt patients' accounts and tried to raise complaints on their behalf.

27.53 Patients with mental illness may sometimes be assumed to be less reliable than other people in terms of giving accounts of themselves. An expert witness to the Inquiry, Dr Gwen Adshead, stated that there is no evidence base to support this generalised assumption.

> *"Patients, like other members of the public, may give true accounts, misleading accounts, mistaken accounts and malicious accounts of events. The fact that the person has a mental illness does not make any one of these accounts more likely.*

"When it comes to making accusations of assaults or abuse, it is theoretically possible that patients with paranoid illnesses may misinterpret a psychiatrist's actions or speech as a threat; and it is true that patients with paranoid delusions about other people may act on them. It is also true that patients with some kinds of personality disorder may form distorted or deluded emotional attachments to their doctors or therapists, and if these are not reciprocated then patients may become angry with their doctors and complain about them. The situation is particularly complicated because patients with borderline personality disorder in particular may form complex and highly emotionally charged attachments to their psychiatrists, and are more likely than other patients to be involved in sexually exploitative relationships with professionals. This is probably because experiences of childhood abuse increase the risk of developing borderline personality disorder in adulthood."

Witness credibility

27.54 Professor Gudjonsson, an expert witness to the Inquiry, identifies the basis for evaluating the credibility of witnesses. Witness credibility refers to the extent to which the account given by the witnesses is judged to be believable. It has two main components: a *motivational* component and an *ability* component.

27.55 Witness credibility is a very important issue for mental health service users, clinicians and managers. Historically the lack of credibility of a witness has been used to undermine a service user's perspective. As noted earlier in this Report, Professor Gudjonsson's work is therefore important to increase understanding in this area where historically the evidence base of those investigating complaints has been patchy or non-existent. What follows is a distillation of his evidence.

27.56 There may be a number of reasons why witnesses may be motivated to give an incomplete or untruthful version of events. These are usually for some personal gain and can include feelings of revenge, need for notoriety, financial gain, protecting someone else, eagerness to please, and fear of disclosure of sensitive or incriminating material.

27.57 The cognitive side of credibility refers to the ability of the person to give a complete, accurate and valid (reliable) account of events. Memory is an active and distortion-prone process which consists of three main stages: *acquisition* (the perception and encoding of the original event), *retention* (the period of time between the observed event and the reporting of the event), and *retrieval* (bringing back the memory into conscious awareness).

27.58   A number of *contextual* factors (eg stress at the time of the event and during retrieval, environmental conditions, interview style) and *personal* factors (eg abilities, personality, mental state, past experiences, beliefs) can influence the completeness and accuracy of the recollection at each of these three stages. When accusations are made, false accounts given by witnesses (including alleged victims of crime and suspects) may result from a false belief and a false memory. The term "memory distrust syndrome" (MDS) was introduced to explain this condition in relation to suspects. Professor Gudjonsson defined MDS to us as follows:

> *"A condition where people develop profound distrust of their memory recollections, as a result of which they are particularly susceptible to relying on external cues and suggestions."*

27.59   MDS is associated with two kinds of distinct conditions. One is where, for example, at the beginning of a police interview suspects have no clear recollection of what they were doing at the time the alleged offence was committed and have come to believe that they must have committed the offence.

27.60   The other is where suspects who at the beginning of the police interview have a clear recollection of not having committed the alleged offence gradually begin to distrust their own recollections and beliefs because of the subtle manipulative influences of the interrogator.

27.61   Although the conceptual framework for the operation of MDS was developed in the context of suspect interviews, it can be legitimately applied more broadly to include the conditions and interviewing of other witnesses.

27.62   Professor Gudjonsson uses the notion of the "ground truth":

- Are there known facts?

- Is there internal consistency across a statement?

- Is there consistency across the witnesses?

- Is there consistency across statements given at different times to the same person or to different people?

- Is there consistency with other people's statements?

27.63   The "ground truth" refers to the factual accuracies and truthfulness of the accusations (ie the clearly established facts). In cases of accusations of historical sexual abuse, there is typically a lack of supporting evidence to corroborate the accusations. Sexual abuse is typically carried out in private and without witnesses. In some cases there may have been forensic evidence available at the time of the assault, but this is compromised by delayed reporting. In the absence of forensic evidence, factors needed to establish the ground truth include:

- documented information available from the material time (ie the time of the alleged assault) – this includes circumstantial evidence relating to the accused and the accuser (eg were they alone at the time?), relevant medical records;

- the internal consistency of the account given by the witness;

- consistency of the witness's statement when given at different times to the same person or when given to different people;

- the consistency of the witness's account with those of other informants.

27.64   We have here referred to the expert evidence to the Inquiry of Dr Adshead and Professor Gudjonsson. From this evidence, and from detailed factual material provided by witnesses to the Inquiry, we are satisfied that it is wrong, and positively dangerous in terms of patient safety, to disregard disclosures by mentally ill patients of sexualised behaviour by their doctor (or other healthcare professionals) on the basis that these patients are ill – whatever the diagnosis. At all times it must be borne in mind by recipients of such disclosures, however expressed and whether or not framed as some form of "concern" or "complaint", that:

- even apparently caring, professional, respected and popular doctors can (and, on occasions, do) sexually abuse their patients;

- even patients with paranoid delusions, severe personality disorders or other psychiatric conditions may be the victims of sexual abuse by their doctors;

- patients, like other members of the public, may give true accounts, misleading accounts, mistaken accounts or malicious accounts of events, but the fact that a patient has a mental illness does not make any one of these types of account more or less likely;

- in relation to disclosures of inappropriate sexualised behaviour by doctors (or other healthcare professionals), supporting (or non-supporting) material may be vitally important (eg photographs, letters, unusual meetings or appointments, even prior gossip and rumour, etc). A response of immediate, and ill-informed, disbelief of the patient before any detailed investigation is carried out simply because the patient has a mental illness is discriminatory and wrong.

27.65 We trust that this and similar Reports may help in informing and educating NHS management – at local and at national levels. NHS policy and the evidence presented to the Inquiry make it clear that in dealing with disclosures of sexualised behaviour made by mentally ill patients (or patients with a history of psychiatric treatment), mental health professionals must proceed with an open mind; actions that are predicated on disbelieving the patient are wholly unacceptable.

Conclusions

27.66 Mental disorders do sometimes adversely affect the reliability of accounts given by patients, and the credibility of psychiatric patients is sometimes brought into question. The specific vulnerabilities of people with mental disorders depend on a host of factors, including the nature and degree of their current mental health problems, their mental state at the time of the alleged sexual abuse, their personality, their medication, and contextual factors (eg their current circumstances). In cases of major mental illness (eg schizophrenia) there may be problems due to breakdown in reality monitoring (the ability to distinguish facts from fantasy) and impaired judgement and self-control, resulting on occasion in patients making false allegations of sexual abuse against staff or other patients.

27.67 Serious problems do sometimes arise in cases of personality disorder where patients are more prone to deception, manipulative behaviour, and disregard for the consequences of their behaviour. There are of course several different types of personality disorder; each has different structures and styles of personality, which may adversely affect the reliability of patients' accounts and their credibility as witnesses. Antisocial personality disorder seems potentially the most problematic.

27.68 As far as the Inquiry is concerned, depressive illness appeared to be the primary diagnosis of the majority of the complainants. The main implication of this is not that they were likely to make unreliable informants concerning the allegations against William Kerr and Michael Haslam; rather, the concern is that they would have been vulnerable to exploitation and feelings of self-blame, making it more difficult for them to report the abuse to others at the time.

27.69 It is therefore fundamentally important that each case is considered on its own merits. It should not be assumed that persons with mental illness or personality disorder are inherently unreliable as a consequence of their disorder.

27.70 There is no evidence that psychotropic medication, prescribed at the time of the alleged sexual assault or during the reporting of it, is likely to undermine the credibility of the complaints or the reliability of the patient's version of events. A high dosage of benzodiazepines can produce a major memory distortion, including fantasy and false memory, but this only seems to occur if the drug is given intravenously. An audit undertaken by the Inquiry of the prescribing practice of the two doctors revealed no unusual pattern and suggested that it was consistent with prescribing patterns for the period.

We therefore RECOMMEND that protocols should be established to ensure that psychiatric patients who raise concerns or complaints in relation to allegations of abuse are not treated in ways that are less favourable than the treatment advised for vulnerable or intimidated witnesses within the framework of *Achieving Best Evidence* (Action For Justice, 2002). Such psychiatric patients should be treated with care, consideration and integrity.

Because medical procedures that require benzodiazepines to be given intravenously (eg oral endoscopy and induction of anaesthesia) are potentially high risk in terms of false sexual fantasies and allegations, these should always be chaperoned (see Chapter 31, Chaperones).

Chapter 28
Patient confidentiality

Introduction

28.1 The subject of patient confidentiality has arisen throughout the Inquiry. In particular, as already noted elsewhere, it has been referred to as the reason why disclosures by patients of alleged sexualised behaviour by William Kerr and Michael Haslam were not passed on by the recipients of that information to others – such as hospital administrators. It was also used by Michael Haslam (we have no knowledge of the views of William Kerr on this topic) as a reason why he, in a sexual relationship with one of his patients (or with a former patient), could not disclose that fact without the express permission of the patient herself.

28.2 It is necessary, therefore, to have some understanding of the principle of confidentiality, before considering its significance within the William Kerr and Michael Haslam stories, and how it may have impeded effective action and investigation.

The principle

28.3 It is clear that patients have a right to expect that information about them will be held in confidence by their doctors. There is both a strong private and a public interest in patient confidentiality being maintained.

28.4 The principles of patient confidentiality, relevant to our Inquiry, can be shortly stated:

> *"Patients have a right to expect that information about them will be held in confidence by their doctors. Confidentiality is central to trust between doctors and patients. Without assurances about confidentiality, patients may be reluctant to give doctors the information they need in order to provide good care.*

"Personal information may be disclosed in the public interest, without the patient's consent, and in exceptional cases where patients have withheld consent, where the benefits to an individual or to society of the disclosure outweigh the public and the patient's interest in keeping the information confidential. In all cases where you consider disclosing information without consent from the patient, you must weigh the possible harm (both to the patient, and the overall trust between doctors and patients) against the benefits which are likely to arise from the release of information. (General Medical Council, Confidentiality: Protecting and Providing Information, *April 2004)*

"Disclosure of personal information without consent may be justified in the public interest where failure to do so may expose the patient or others to risk of death or serious harm. Where the patient or others are exposed to a risk so serious that it outweighs the patient's privacy interest, you should seek consent to disclosure where practicable. If it is not practicable to seek consent, you should disclose information promptly to an appropriate person or authority. You should generally inform the patient before disclosing the information. If you seek consent and the patient withholds it you should consider the reasons for this, if any are provided by the patient. If you remain of the view that disclosure is necessary to protect a third party from death or serious harm, you should disclose information promptly to an appropriate person or authority. Such situations arise, for example, where a disclosure may assist in the prevention, detection or prosecution of a serious crime, especially crimes against the person, such as abuse of children." (Ibid)

"The right to privacy that confidentiality protects is an essential element of human rights, but it is not absolute and may be countered when the rights of others to be protected from harm are jeopardised in a serious way. When rights such as these collide, a balance must be struck between the importance of maintaining confidentiality and the harms that could be avoided if confidentiality was breached." – (BMA, Medical Ethics Today, *2004)*

28.5 As these summaries make clear, the principle of patient confidentiality is not an absolute. It probably never was. Even the Hippocratic Oath only commands doctors thus:

> *"Whatever, in connection with my professional practice, I see or hear, in the life of men,* which ought not to be spoken of abroad, *I will not divulge, as reckoning that all such should be kept secret."* [1] *(emphasis added)*

28.6 From that extract from the Oath it can be seen that the prohibition on divulging confidential patient information is not absolute. What ought and ought not to be "spoken of abroad" may change over the years, but it is difficult to draw from Hippocrates a justification which allows serious wrongdoing by a fellow doctor, disclosed by a patient, to remain undisclosed because (a) the patient had consented to the sexual relationship, or (b) the patient refused to cooperate in, or even give her consent to, any further use of the information. Of course, for the recipient of such information, there will be very difficult decisions to make, balancing the needs of the patient with the needs of society more generally. There are bound to be occasions (although they are difficult to envisage) when the recipient doctor could reasonably and properly conclude that any use of the information received would be, or could be, so harmful to the interests of the patient that any public interest is outweighed. But even in those circumstances, some (private) use of the information will be appropriate; for example (taken from the GP evidence to the Inquiry), the GP may use the information to provide the reason for not referring other vulnerable women patients to that consultant.

28.7 The principle of patient confidentiality was, and still remains, protected not only by professional regulation, but also by the duty of confidence recognised under the common law. In other words

---

1 There are various accepted English translations of this part of the Oath. For example:

"Things I may see or hear in the course of the treatment or even outside of treatment regarding the life of human beings, things which one should never divulge outside, I will keep to myself, holding such things shameful to be spoken."

And:

"What I may see or hear in the course of the treatment or even outside of the treatment in regard to the life of men, which on no account one must spread abroad, I will keep to myself, holding such things shameful to be spoken about."

And:

"Whatever, in connection with my professional practice or not, in connection with it, I see or hear, in the life of men, which ought not to be spoken of abroad, I will not divulge, as reckoning that all such should be kept secret."

In 1948, the World Medical Association in Geneva produced a shorter and simpler form, without the limitation:

"I will respect the secrets which are confided in me, even after the patient has died."

a breach of the duty of confidentiality can be the subject of legal action. Those protections are now supported by statutes – such as the Data Protection Act, the Human Rights Act, and the Health and Social Care Act. Perhaps the most important recent statute is the Human Rights Act, which incorporates into UK law the European Convention of Human Rights. Article 8 of that Convention protects private life, including confidential information. Again, that protection is not absolute, and may be overridden where the public interest so requires.

28.8 Patient confidentiality is a complex and currently controversial issue, as the NHS moves towards a fully computerised patient database. It is unnecessary to examine the principle of patient confidentiality in great detail. This Inquiry is only concerned with certain aspects:

1. Is the principle absolute?

2. Does it prevent a GP (or other medical professional) disclosing to appropriate recipients information which may reveal serious wrongdoing by others, and/or serious risk of harm to others?

28.9 The answer to those, and related, questions is "no" – and has been the same for many years, including most if not all of the period covered by this Inquiry. For example, taking the latter part of that period, *The Values of Psychotherapy* by Holmes and Lindley, first published in 1979, was arguing that even in the field of psychotherapy confidentiality can be breached where there is a benefit to the greater good in doing so.

28.10 In 1980, the Code of Ethics from the BMA required confidentiality except "(c) where there is an overriding public interest, eg real likelihood of serious future offence such as murder or arson". That exception was directed to the action of the patient, that is, the patient who might burn or kill. What of the patient as victim? Taking the subject of this Inquiry, what of the patient who claims to have been sexually assaulted by a consultant psychiatrist? A patient who discloses to her GP but asks that it not be taken further? We suggest that the answer is not completely clear – but it is not obvious that the GP is *bound* to keep such information away from other partners, or colleagues, or from health service authorities who may have been able to investigate, or make use of the information. Nobody would seriously criticise Linda Bigwood for passing on Patient A17's disclosure to Sister Tiplady.

28.11 The situation in the late 1970s and early 1980s (at least in relation to an answer to the question above) is probably reflected in the following:

> *"Where the patient is the victim of a crime eg assault, rape etc. the patient is normally only too willing to report the matter or to permit the doctor to do so. But disclosure should not normally be made against the wishes of the patient… Again the duty of the doctor is to treat his patient and to advise and guide the patient himself to make any necessary or desirable disclosure … There may, however, be a risk of repetition of a serious offence eg murder, manslaughter, criminal assault, poisoning. The doctor has a duty to the public as well as to a particular patient."* [2]

28.12 Consent should usually, we would hope almost always, be obtained before a doctor (or other medical professional) uses or discloses personal health information. But occasionally, even where it is not possible to obtain consent, information may be disclosed – with strict safeguards, and to the minimum necessary to achieve the purpose of protecting patient safety.

28.13 We accept that there is some uncertainty as to the circumstances when, in the absence of consent, a healthcare professional (in particular a doctor) can lawfully and ethically disclose to another information received in confidence from a patient. It should not require litigation to resolve those uncertainties. The issue is presently being addressed by the Royal College of Psychiatrists. But this seems to be a perfect area for the Council for Healthcare Regulatory Excellence to ensure (using its powers under sections 26 and 27 of the National Health Service Reform and Healthcare Professions Act 2002) that there is the adoption of a common and uniform position, for all regulated medical professionals and for their patients.

Confidentiality and the Inquiry

28.14 We were struck by the evidence to the Inquiry that it is only those who did nothing, or not enough, who relied on patient confidentiality to justify their lack of action. (We consider the position of Michael Haslam separately later in this chapter.) Others had no difficulty in making relevant use of the information, even if there was not considered sufficient material in the absence of an able and willing complainant to launch complaint proceedings.

---

2 "The Duty of the Doctor to Respect the Confidence of the Patient" *Med Sci Law* (1980), Vol 20, No 1.

28.15   We found examples in the evidence before us of confusion in relation to the ethical position, of positive reliance on patient confidentiality as the reason or excuse for inaction. We have little doubt that some doctors did consider the alleged actions of Michael Haslam, as reported to them, to have been unethical (if found to be true), but relied on the proposition that that information itself was in some way protected by a duty of confidentiality to justify or excuse their inaction. As noted above, we do not accept that confidentiality should ever be used as a reason for not taking further a disclosure of conduct that has clear potential to harm that patient or other patients. We do not accept that patient confidentiality should ever be used to justify inaction in the sorts of cases covered by evidence to this Inquiry.

28.16   Witnesses to the Inquiry have sought to persuade us that standards have changed over the years, and that actions and inactions must be judged against the standards and expectations of the time. For example, Marion Anderson, a consultant clinical psychologist, told us "patient confidentiality had a very different meaning then [referring to the 1970s] to what it has now, now that we have computers and notes have to be accessible to patients".

28.17   We have attempted at all times to ensure that our approach is fair and our judgments and conclusions reached against the correct ethical and legal background – meaning the correct legal and ethical background at the time. There may well have been changes in the approach to confidential patient information, particularly where there is commercial use.[3] It is also clear that the culture of protecting patient confidentiality was perhaps more entrenched in the 1970s than it is today. However, we are not satisfied that there have been significant and effective changes when it comes to the disclosure (or at least some use) of information from a patient, given and received in confidence, but which reveals the kind of risk of harm to other patients being considered by this Inquiry.

28.18   For example, in 1990 the court concluded that a doctor could not be prevented, by injunction, from disclosing information received from a patient in confidence which revealed a real risk of serious harm to others.[4] However, that decision did not create new ethical standards, but merely confirmed the existing limits of the principle of patient confidentiality.

---

3   See *R v. Department of Health, ex parte Source Informatics Ltd* [2000].

4   See *W. v. Egdell* [1990].

28.19 What is clear, perhaps beyond argument, is that the disclosure by a mentally disordered patient of a sexual relationship with their consultant psychiatrist did not require the patient's consent before that information could be acted on – in some way. (The "acting on" may have been anonymised – at least at the outset.) We are satisfied that this was the position during the main period covered by this Inquiry – from the mid- and late 1970s to the end of the 1980s. We are satisfied that this is the position now. That situation does not change:

- if the patient expressly tells the recipient doctor (for example, her GP, or another consultant) that she does not consent to the information being used;

- if the patient says that the sexual relationship was consensual; or

- if the patient tells the recipient that the information is given "in confidence".

28.20 For a medical practitioner to keep such information entirely to himself or herself on the basis of patient confidentiality is, we conclude, a perversion of that principle, and would inevitably lead to medical practitioners knowingly exposing their other patients to a risk of repeat conduct. This is the position whether or not the sexual relationship is said to be consensual or not consensual, and whatever the nature of the crossing of sexual boundaries. Where the disclosure refers to a non-consensual sexual contact – to sexual assault – it is perhaps even more inexcusable (if there are levels of responsibility) for the recipient of the information to do nothing. This conclusion proceeds on the basis, which existed in many of the stories considered in the course of the Inquiry, that the recipient either believes the disclosure or has no reason to disbelieve it. We accept that a disbelieved story, assuming there is some sensible basis for that disbelief, is without value. The medical practitioner in receipt of such information has no reason to doubt the safety of other patients.

28.21 Of course the position is difficult where, for example, the patient has made a disclosure of a sexual relationship with, or sexual assault by, another doctor but refuses to give consent for that information to be used in any way. But the fact that there are difficulties, and judgments to be made – for example, as to whether there is a real risk of harm to the patient which outbalances the potential gain by revealing the information – does not mean that it is the principle itself which prevents disclosure.

28.22 So far, we have been looking at the principle of patient confidentiality – as an ethical and legal construct. But there are elementary practical considerations to consider. For example, there may be a real disadvantage in the relaxation of the strict rigours of patient confidentiality. As one contributor to the Part 2 seminars said:

> *"Patients may be put off from disclosing if they cannot be sure that the information will be kept entirely confidential. There should be somewhere, such as an advocacy service, where patients can talk in absolute confidence because it is better for the Health Service to know about 'low level noise', or matters such as innuendo and gossip derived from conversation, even if little can be done about it, than not to know at all."*

28.23 Although we have some sympathy for this view, and there is clear value in the provision of such services, if "absolute confidence" is interpreted as meaning that all the information stops with the recipient, then the health service does not receive any "noise", low level or at all. If the information disclosed is of the kind referred to in the course of this Inquiry, then even advocacy services may be able to say to their clients, "Your anonymity will be protected unless you agree to it being waived"; but for the protection of others some, anonymised, onward disclosure may have to be made. The content of that onward disclosure should be explained – it could be as short as:

> *"It has been disclosed that Dr X sexually assaulted a patient. The patient has not presently agreed to be named, and has not presently agreed to any further details being disclosed."*

28.24 If the patient cannot be persuaded to reveal her identity, the concern will remain anonymised. But, even that disclosure may be vital in revealing a cluster of complaints, or a pattern of behaviour – information which would cause the employing Trust to consider monitoring the professional under suspicion, or carrying out an investigation, or making contact with the police.

28.25 We agree with the views expressed at a Part 2 seminar that at the early stage of disclosure of abuse the identity of the patient is not critical – what is critical is "getting the concern onto the agenda", "ensuring that the concern gets to the right place". It is fundamental for recipients of such information to keep well in mind that, whatever the patient may think, the abusive behaviour is unlikely to be a one-off – even if the sexualised behaviour is described as consensual. As one witness said in the seminar:

> *"A feature of every one of the scandals looked at [by the witnesses' organisation] over the past 10 years is that patients felt for a long time that there is no one else suffering as they had, so it's a question of how to get around the isolation."*

28.26 We consider the question of the response to gossip and rumour in more detail in Chapter 33.

28.27 Our conclusion is that the principle of patient confidentiality is of limited relevance to this Inquiry and the recommendations it must make. Patient confidentiality exists to protect patients, but there can be occasions when it becomes a cloak or screen behind which doctors seek to hide – not to protect their patient, but rather to protect themselves. As one contributor to the Part 2 seminars said:

> *"Confidentiality and the Data Protection Act can be used as a wall behind which to hide from sharing information."*

28.28 However, we entirely recognise that there are different views in relation to patient confidentiality, different views of what is, and what is not, a valid reason for breaking patient confidence. And different views as to when, and to what extent, patient confidentiality should be compromised. The dilemmas raised are well summarised in the following exchanges with a medical witness who was not involved at the time of the patient disclosures. She was asked about contact with the police, a topic covered elsewhere in this Report.

> *Q. When do you feel that the police should be involved? It is another very difficult area.*

> *A. It is, and it partly depends on obviously the wishes of the woman herself, because if she does not want the police to be informed, then you cannot call the police.*

Q. What if the woman does not want to pursue the complaint at all, but there are many complaints? What do you do then? Should the police be involved or not?

A. I think that is very difficult, because I think – there are issues for the NHS and protecting patients, where you might think about overriding confidentiality, but I think in terms of approaching the police, the confidentiality and the trust that the patient has in you, having given you the information, becomes quite difficult to override. Certainly by now, contemporaneously, dealing with the woman in the situation who said to me – who had shared something with me and said to me, absolutely explicitly, she did not want me to share that information with the police, in terms of an historical incident, then I would not share it with the police.

Q. What would you do with the information, in terms of patient safety?

A. In terms of dealing with it within the NHS, then obviously I would deal with it within the NHS, by approaching the consultant and not saying who had made the allegation at this stage, but saying that an allegation had been made and it is very serious and we need to go through it, and then go through a whole process of talking to other staff and so on, all of which is difficult and has to be done sensitively because some allegations will be unfounded but the majority will not, and that is the balance.

28.29 Whether or not there is or has been confusion in the past, whether during the period covered by this Inquiry or more recently, every effort must now be taken – by all concerned – to ensure that there is now clear and firm guidance for future action.

28.30 As noted above, we have reached clear views on this topic. We accept that there are differing views and a degree of confusion in relation to when patient confidentiality can be breached. For that reason, we have recommended at the end of this chapter that the Secretary of State should commission research and arrange for the publication of clear and authoritative advice.

Disclosure within a therapeutic consultation

28.31   A barrier that was frequently identified by witnesses to the Inquiry was the dilemma of how to respond to disclosures of abuse or complaints that were raised during a one-to-one consultation. The response to such disclosures varied widely in the 1970s and 1980s and begs the question whether this practice has changed significantly in the modern day.

28.32   In relation to evidence before the Inquiry, the counsellor Julie Levine confirms that she did not report a disclosure arising within a therapeutic consultation. Neither did Marion Anderson, a consultant psychologist. We can only assume that this was judged to be in the patient's best interests at the time. However, their decisions lacked the wider perspective of considering the potential risk to other patients. Their explanation demonstrated the supremacy of patient confidentiality among professionals at that time. They were not the only practitioners who held this perspective.

28.33   Jim Maxwell (a psychiatric nurse) had a different dilemma. He made a judgment relating to the fragile states of the patient and the potential impact that progressing a disclosure would have had on her at the time.

28.34   The ethical basis has always been there. However, an emphasis on wider patient safety and minimising risk by learning from "near misses" has meant that patient safety is much more in the forefront of clinicians' minds when considering issues relating to confidentiality.

28.35   Guidance defining the role of a Caldicott Guardian[5] emerged in all NHS organisations in 1999. A Board Director, usually the Medical or Nursing Director, oversees and approves (or turns down) requests for confidential clinical information to be shared on a need-to-know basis. This means information is shared on an exceptional rather than routine basis and usually for reasons of protecting the welfare and safety of the individual patient or other person in imminent danger.

28.36   Ethical considerations may be similar then as now, but practice has certainly changed. Lessons from child abuse inquiries and inquiries following homicides by mentally ill patients have led to a climate of

5 HSC 1999/012 Caldicott Guardians.

formal information-sharing protocols between agencies such as NHS organisations, social services, police and probation. This sort of "joined-up" work across agencies was unheard of in the period 1970–88.

28.37 Also of significance is the Data Protection Act (1998), which allows patients access to their clinical records. This was unusual during the period in question.

28.38 It is likely that similar situations still exist today. However, modern-day practitioners have not only a clear duty towards the individual patient, but also a wider duty to protect the safety of other NHS patients. Disclosure of abuse by any individual towards another must always be taken seriously. It is a very skilful job to ensure that disclosure is managed in a sensitive way so the patient does not feel exposed and their confidentiality compromised; obtaining consent from the patient to disclose information remains a primary objective.

28.39 The Inquiry heard evidence from a witness still in practice who described how the boundaries of confidentiality are now more carefully explained to patients, including in the initial assessment. A careful explanation is given by the clinician that disclosures and conversations between them will be shared within the multi-disciplinary team. It is also made clear that if patients say anything that potentially compromises their own safety or that of others then the normal rules of confidentiality will not be followed. Disclosure to other relevant parties such as senior clinicians and managers and other agencies can occur on a need-to-know basis. In all this, the Caldicott Guardian of patient information in NHS organisations plays an important role.

28.40 Confidentiality policies and information-sharing protocols in NHS organisations have been developed since the publication of Caldicott guidance. The development of protocols for the sharing of information between social care and the NHS as described above make it clear when it is important to share information on a "need-to-know basis". These policies are not new.

We RECOMMEND that Trusts' confidentiality policies should include a section on disclosure within therapeutic interactions in psychiatric practice and should be supported by inter-agency information-sharing policies to be used in all cases of patient abuse.

28.41 During the seminars in Part 2 of the Inquiry, we heard evidence from the police and social care agencies. A widespread view was that the NHS often carried out their own investigations without considering the relevance of sharing information at an early stage.

28.42 Under the NHS Reform and Healthcare Professions Act 2002, information relating to mentally ill patients should be considered at the earliest stages of investigation. We heard evidence that the NHS was and still can be slow at recognising whether a criminal, as well as disciplinary, offence has been committed. In addition, NHS organisations have been widely known to wait until the outcome of a disciplinary hearing is determined before handing over to the police.

28.43 In some cases the opposite can apply. For example, if the CPS find insufficient evidence to prosecute, or a court case results in an acquittal, the individual may still be required to face disciplinary investigations and hearings within the NHS.

28.44 Social care representatives at the York seminar used the term "do not trample on the grass". Social services staff accused of serious allegations of abuse commonly face a police investigation immediately. In the light of expertise and experience of other services, it seems clear that the NHS staff need to have adequate expertise or agree to jointly interview witnesses with the police, to reduce the number of interviews patient witnesses face.

The Inquiry believes that conducting investigations is an important specialist role and therefore we RECOMMEND that dedicated staff should be properly trained to carry out the investigations. This relates closely to the recommendations we make at the end of Chapter 33 regarding investigations generally.

Confidentiality and psychoanalysis

28.45   It may be said that in the practice of psychoanalysis different considerations apply. We accept that there is a question of judgment, and the judgment decision may be different, but the fundamentals should remain the same – at least for registered medical practitioners who are also psychoanalysts.[6]

28.46   We accept, of course, that confidentiality in psychoanalysis is paramount, above and beyond the normal doctor–patient confidentiality, and even greater than that between psychiatrist and patient (although psychiatrists can also be psychoanalysts). The reason for this is the nature of the psychoanalytic method, which "is to explore – and by doing so, to modify – the emotional factors, both conscious and unconscious, that influence thought and behaviour". The nature of psychoanalysis is such that the patient is encouraged to reveal not only inner thoughts but also dreams and fantasies in order to facilitate the therapeutic process. To understand the patient and the way his mind works, the psychoanalyst will ask the patient to say whatever comes into his mind; this encourages uncensored irrational thought. Patients are invited not just to be themselves and reveal intimate secrets, but at times to reveal their worst characteristics.

28.47   Confidentiality therefore goes to the very heart of the psychoanalytic process.

> *"This surpasses the importance of confidentiality in other areas of clinical practice, whether applied by physicians, surgeons, or psychiatrists."*[7]

28.48   What then of abuse, of risk to others? As with medical confidentiality more generally we are here considering situations where the recipient of the information either believes it to be true or proceeds on the basis that the disclosed information may be true.

---

6 However, according to the British Psychoanalytical Society approximately 70 per cent of psychoanalysts do not hold a medical qualification.

7 BICL, *Comparative Confidentiality in Psychoanalysis.* Occasional Paper number 5, page 2.

28.49 The present guidance in relation to psychoanalysts is as follows:

> *"[Where] a doctor believes that a patient may be the victim of physical or sexual abuse and the patient is not capable of giving or withholding consent to disclosure, the patient's medical interests are paramount and may require the doctor to disclose information to an appropriate person or authority."*[8]

28.50 What the guidance does not address is the situation where the patient is capable of giving or withholding consent, and the abuser is in a position where other patients may be at risk. In other words, the same position as faced by practitioners in our Inquiry. It seems to us that the answer to that question does not depend on whether or not the doctor to whom disclosure is made is treating the patient as psychoanalyst, or as psychiatrist, or as general physician.

28.51 Of course, we accept as fundamental that a psychoanalyst has to manage his relationship of trust with his or her patient, and that the psychoanalyst may choose not to pass on the information to others who could act on it. We do not suggest that the psychoanalyst is compelled to disclose (unless so compelled by rules of membership of the GMC).

28.52 We are not suggesting the imposition of a duty. However, we see nothing in the practice of the qualified psychoanalyst to prevent further disclosure in order to protect the patient from abuse, or to protect other patients of the alleged abuser who may be at risk.

Is psychoanalysis different?

28.53 We therefore ask the question: "Does psychoanalysis require special consideration and, if so, when?" Although not experts, the Inquiry believes that in the interests of patient safety psychoanalysts should be working under the same codes of behaviour and duty to report alleged current risk associated with abuse as any other practitioner.

28.54 The Inquiry recognises the complexity of maintaining confidentiality and trust but this should not be seen as a barrier to appropriate reporting.

---

8 BIICL, *Comparative Confidentiality in Psychoanalysis*. Occasional Paper number 5, page 27.

Michael Haslam and patient confidentiality

28.55 Michael Haslam was a senior consultant, he taught medical students, he no doubt set the ethical tone and standard in the hospitals where he worked, and more generally in the medical community in North Yorkshire. In his written evidence to the Inquiry, in the submissions made to the Inquiry on his behalf by his solicitor, and in his oral evidence, the protection of patient confidentiality was his mantra. The following are two samples of that oral evidence:

> *Q. That is really why I was asking you whether it would be your view that you would have been tolerant of sexual relationships between clinicians and patients, as long as the patient did not want to complain?*
>
> *A. I am not sure that I would use the word 'tolerant', I think what I would do, and what I did do in fact, if information such as that came to me, would be to ask the patient, if I were the person to whom it was addressed, ask them what they were, as it were, telling me for – in other words, I would discuss it, what they wanted, if anything to do about it. I would explain the procedures for complaining if they felt like complaining. But I would probably – well, in the one case I am thinking of, with the patient's permission, mention it to the professional concerned.*
>
> *Q. Again, I was trying to deal with the situation where the patient does not want to articulate or voice any complaint.*
>
> *A. No, I would not.*
>
> *Q. You would not do anything with it?*
>
> *A. No.*
>
> *Q. That is why I used the word 'tolerant'. You would allow such relationships to occur or continue as long as the patient did not want to make a complaint?*
>
> *A. I am not in any position to allow or not allow a relationship between two other people.*

Q. You would not take any step in respect of that relationship, other than in circumstances where the patient said they wanted to complain?

A. That is correct.

Q. Do you think that was a view held uniquely by you?

A. No.

Q. Or whether that was the widespread view within the York medical community in the 1970s and 1980s?

A. It was the view throughout medicine, throughout the church, I presume throughout solicitors, that you do not pass on information given to you in confidence by a client, without their permission.

Q. Can I ask you about a slightly different topic, which is one you have touched on already, the question of patient confidentiality, which you have indicated is a powerful feature which would prevent any disclosure of a relationship if you came to learn of one. There would presumably be cases, would there not, where there would be a wider duty which overrode the narrow duty of patient confidentiality?

A. Like if you learn somebody committed a murder?

Q. That would be at the extreme end of the scale, yes.

A. What should a doctor – this is an ethical thing, is it not, I do not think it is one you and I can answer, but what should a doctor, a lawyer or a priest do if he comes to learn that the patient or the client that he has been seeing has committed a murder, let us say? What should he do? The priest I think would say he should do nothing. The social worker should say, I should report it to my senior. What should a doctor do? It is rhetorical.

Q. It is not a purely rhetorical question, it is a question I am putting to you in order to try to understand how you fitted into the culture that prevailed in York in the 1970s and 1980s. I am just trying to establish with you the point at which you think the requirements of patient confidentiality are overridden by a duty to the wider patient population. We can take it from your earlier example that a consensual relationship is not one which would lead to you breaching the requirements of patient confidentiality?

A. Correct.

Q. If you had a case of inappropriate physical touching between clinician and patient, so a form of sexual assault at the lower end of the scale, would that require the patient confidentiality to be breached?

A. Well, I must come back to what I said at the beginning, and that is that the doctor or the priest or the lawyer can say to this client, 'Is there anything you want me to do about it?' You can say to the client, 'This is a matter which I think ought to be aired, reported, whatever' – you are still under a duty of confidentiality.

Q. Patient confidentiality is clearly at the heart of your concerns. I want to just make sure that I understood your position. If you had information in relation to a fellow consultant from a patient, but the patient would not permit you to launch a complaint, is it your evidence that even if there was now a risk to patient safety in relation to that consultant, you would do nothing because you would be breaching some form of understanding of patient confidentiality?

A. I would not quite put it like that. But if the patient did not give me permission I would not reveal, full stop.

28.56 That approach seems to have been demonstrated when Michael Haslam did receive information in relation to an expression of concern. We related in detail in Chapter 22 the story of Dr Wade bringing his concerns to Michael Haslam over William Kerr's alleged behaviour with Patient A22. Michael Haslam's expressed view to the Inquiry was that despite Dr Wade's description of the circumstances that led to Patient A22 refusing to see William Kerr again – she alleged he had assaulted and propositioned her – he did not regard it as his role "to make judgments about another" colleague and took no action to progress Patient A22 and Dr Wade's complaint. As we said before, if Michael Haslam had acted on the information he had received, William Kerr would, in all probability, have been investigated in 1979. Michael Haslam's view, in his evidence to us, was that he did not regard it as his responsibility that the matter was not taken further.

28.57   If that was the response of a senior consultant, and we here leave to one side and disregard the possibility that Michael Haslam's decision not to progress the complaint was for entirely different and more sinister reasons, then perhaps it is not surprising that other, more junior medical practitioners, adopted a similar position.

28.58   Returning to Michael Haslam's oral evidence to the Inquiry, it is interesting to see how he used the concept of patient confidentiality to protect his own position, not that, or just that, of the former patient. The Inquiry had received information alleging that he had had a long-standing sexual relationship with a patient – Patient B4. When this allegation was put to Michael Haslam, so that the Panel could better understand the adequacy of the response by Marion Anderson (a clinical psychologist who had been told of the relationship), his reaction was that he could not reveal his role, his part in the relationship, because to do so would breach his duty of confidence (described by his legal representative as "absolute, except with very narrow exceptions") owed to the former patient.

28.59   The exchange is set out below:

> Q. The next matter I want to deal with is a discussion or confrontation between yourself and Marion Anderson which related to Patient B4. You have said that you were slightly cynically amused by Marion Anderson, and reading between the lines, as I understand it, she is living in a glasshouse and is throwing stones?
>
> A. That was what I suggested, yes.
>
> Q. I have read that correctly?
>
> A. Yes.

Q. Do you accept that she did confront you about what she understood to be a relationship between yourself and Patient B4?

A. Yes.

Q. She confronted you with an allegation that you had gone with this individual Patient B4 for a weekend in Scotland?

A. That is what she alleged.

Q. That lady was in an advanced state of pregnancy?

A. Yes.

Q. She also alleged – you tell me what she alleged, beyond what I have put to you already.

A. With the qualification, I am afraid, as I have said before –

Q. The qualification is?

A. I have no evidence that this lady has any desire for these matters to be raised.

28.60 Michael Haslam took exactly the same line when questioned in relation to another former patient – Patient B11 – with whom he admits to having had a sexual relationship. Michael Haslam's admission of the sexual relationship was on the basis that she was not his patient at the time. He said this:

> *"As she did decide not to proceed, if you like, with this complaint and as she was a patient of mine, I do not see it as appropriate that I should discuss her case without her written permission. Now, having said that, there are certain parts of this letter that I can, as it were, agree or disagree with. But you take my point: I do not think, in view of the fact that she withdrew or did not proceed, and in view of the fact that she did have a professional relationship with me, that I should be discussing her case without her written permission. That is what I am saying."*

28.61 In his written evidence to the Inquiry, Michael Haslam said this:

> *"Were I to have had a physical relationship with a client I should not breach the confidentiality of that relationship without the approval of the woman involved any more than I would any other matter."*

28.62 Although, as repeatedly made clear, the Inquiry was not concerned with the truth of the allegations or disclosures made in relation to any sexual contact between Michael Haslam and his former patients, it becomes possible and reasonable to draw conclusions from the evidence given in relation to how sexual relations with patients were treated, and how the principle of patient confidentiality fits into that picture. Michael Haslam's self-protective position appears to be – using patient confidentiality as his shield – that he could not say whether or not he had had an affair with a patient because to do so would in some unexplained way put him in breach of patient confidentiality, unless and until the former patient gave him permission to speak. Applying that same approach, he could not even reveal to the Inquiry what was alleged to him by Marion Anderson – see "I have no evidence that this lady has any desire for these matters to be raised" referred to above.

28.63 Michael Haslam's position, therefore, seems to be that if there is a consensual sexual relationship between a consultant psychiatrist and (1) an existing patient or (2) a recently former patient, then the consultant cannot be asked about it because any answer would breach the duty of confidentiality owed to the patient.

28.64 There seems to be no difference in Michael Haslam's mind between the necessary confidentiality in relation to treatment given to a patient and a confidentiality that he applies to his own personal behaviour with a patient outside the category of treatment. In our view, in the latter case there is no principle of confidentiality for a clinician here at all: it is merely a fiction to protect his own allegedly unethical behaviour.

Conclusion

28.65 The important topic of patient confidentiality is clearly difficult, but we are concerned that any lack of clarity may lead to yet further barriers to the disclosure and subsequent investigation of allegations of sexualised behaviour by healthcare professionals.

28.66 Some confusion seems to us to continue to prevail (perhaps not in the extreme form contended by Michael Haslam) even at a time when there is a positive obligation to "whistle blow" or otherwise disclose evidence of poor or dangerous behaviour by fellow practitioners.

28.67 Therefore, we RECOMMEND that The Secretary of State, within 12 months of the publication of this Report, should commission and publish guidance and issue advice and instruction (preferably in consultation with the professional regulatory bodies and healthcare colleges) as to the meaning and limitations of patient confidentiality in mental health settings. Such guidance should be kept under regular review.

The Kerr/Haslam Inquiry

Volume 2 of 2

**Presented to Parliament by
the Secretary of State for Health
by Command of Her Majesty**

July 2005

Cm 6640 – II

£97.50

Contents

Section Seven: New developments that need monitoring

Section Eight: Some answers

Section Six
Problematic activities

Chapter 29
Sexualised behaviour and the psychiatrist/patient relationship

Introduction

29.1   Throughout the Inquiry, we have taken patient safety as our touchstone: "The safety of patients must be a paramount consideration in determining the way forward for the NHS."[1] That approach must also inform the consideration of misconduct, in all its guises, and an understanding of the impact of sexualised behaviour and other intimate relationships (whether or not intentionally abusive) between doctor and patient.

29.2   The topic of sexualised behaviour, and professional boundary violations more generally, is a complex area. Whilst the regulation of some activities and attitudes seem to the Inquiry to be relatively straightforward, there are other areas that need further exploration. The sensitive nature of the subject, the reluctance towards open discussion, and the absence of a consensual lexicon with which to describe the acts and behaviour at issue have all contributed to the difficulties faced by all concerned. We found that there is considerable ignorance, confusion and anxiety at all levels in relation to sexual feelings, and sexualised behaviour, involving psychiatrists and their patients. This state of affairs leaves already vulnerable patients in a yet more vulnerable position. There is a real need for open and informed discussion of this topic, and consideration of the issues it raises, if already vulnerable patients are not to be rendered yet more vulnerable. Furthermore, it seems to us imperative that lessons are learned from the evidence placed before this Inquiry, and in particular from the experiences of the former patients.

29.3   The Inquiry heard some evidence on the ethical issues raised by this topic from witnesses during Part 1 of its investigation. However, the main input was during Part 2, in reports, presentations, and from the

1 Bristol Royal Infirmary Inquiry.

discussion during the four days of seminars. We are extremely grateful to all who contributed, and we have derived enormous benefit from the submissions and representations received on this issue. We have read and considered a broad range of written material. However, we recognise the limitations of our knowledge and experience, and do not profess expertise as ethicists. Our primary role here is to bring together and distil the information available to us, to express our own views where appropriate, and make recommendations intended to bring progress, clarity and certainty.

29.4 The subject of sexualised behaviour has been discussed and debated over a number of years in relation to psychiatrists, in relation to clinicians, and more generally in relation to all medical practitioners responsible for patient care. The submissions to the Inquiry have covered all doctors registered with the GMC, other health and related social care professionals, as well as others connected closely to them. Although we will consider and comment on the wider picture identified in those submissions, this part of the Report concentrates on sexual relationships between psychiatrists and their patients (both existing and former). We consider, if only briefly, sexualised behaviour which is correctly described as criminal conduct, and also sexualised behaviour which is unlikely to be so described. Into this latter category falls sexual contact which is truly consensual.

29.5 The main emphasis in the Report, as with the evidence to the Inquiry, is sexualised behaviour between a male psychiatrist and a female patient (or former patient). However, insofar as there are lessons to be learned, recommendations made, and subsequent action taken (whether in guidance, codes of ethics, or legislation) it must be accepted that equal treatment should be extended to inappropriate sexual behaviour irrespective of gender. Sexualised behaviour between female psychiatrists and their patients, we are advised, does occur but is a small minority of all cases, as does female doctors/male patients relationships. We accept that same-sex abuse needs to be considered in similar ways to opposite-sex abuse; that any protective measures (such as chaperoning for physical examination) need to consider same-sex as well as opposite-sex professional–patient relationships. Further, any informed debate must also recognise that sexual orientation is not always clear, and that uncertainty or ambivalence may be relevant to same-sex abuse by mental health professionals.

29.6 That said, on research information available to us, a profile of the likely sexual abuser is as follows:

> *"The typical offender is a male, in middle age, who will be well trained and well established in his profession (which reduces the chance of his being questioned). Many are repeat offenders, using the same modus operandi in each case. He will have a powerful personality, almost to the point of being intimidating, yet capable and charming in other ways. There could be an aura of vulnerability or an abrasive and arrogant confidence, which may be only apparent to those who know him closely. In reality, he will be no different to any other serial womaniser, whose contempt for dependence in others is a projection of his own fear of rejection. Care and control are intertwined for these doctors, who may persuade their patients that sexual contact is an extension of professional care, or necessary to cure their sexual problems. Such doctors may present the relationship as a form of 'rescue' of the patient from their predicaments."*

29.7 Within the expression "typical offender" is, of course, a variety of individual characteristics – ranging from the psychotic to the psychopathic with the careless somewhere in between. The careless psychiatrist takes no care to notice the gradual slide from one exploitation to another, whereas the predatory psychiatrist uses the milder forms to test if more major transgressions will be tolerated. Evidence to the Inquiry suggests, at least in relation to doctors/therapists who cross the line into sexual abuse of their patients, that of the various typologies, the predatory psychopaths probably form the largest group. That class was described to us as follows:

"They resemble other sexual offenders, except they are less likely to have used violence. They are ruthless, without remorse or empathy for their victims and are the most frankly exploitative, not only in sexual matters but also in other domains, such as finance or work. They are the most difficult to rehabilitate because of their level of denial of the offending; they typically fail to comply with disciplinary or regulatory bodies, and prolong any legal process with one appeal after another. They are often superficially charming, despite an aura of arrogance, and a careful scrutiny of their employment record and interpersonal skills will reveal difficulties dating back since training days. By the time those records are being examined, usually there will be a trail of victims behind. Typically such abusers target the most vulnerable, and avoid patients who seem more robust, in order to maintain control. The end point for many of these professionals is criminal conviction and expulsion from the profession."

29.8 As we say at the outset, this is a complex area. But it is an area where problems must be identified, and solutions found. Patient safety demands nothing less.

Psychosexual medicine/psychosexual therapy

29.9 This part of the Report is devoted to sexual contact that is abusive – be it with current or former patients. It is not here intended to address, or in any way criticise, the role of clinicians and therapists in the practice of what is now generally known as psychosexual medicine. We have no reason to doubt the utility of such treatment, and no evidence to cast any doubt on the competence and integrity of practitioners. Later in this chapter we refer to the code of ethics of one organisation, the British Association for Sexual and Relationship Therapy (BASRT). However, it is to be noted that that organisation is but one of several. For example, we are informed that there are many GPs who are trained by, and are members of, the Institute of Psychosexual Medicine (IPM) – but not members of, or regulated by, BASRT. BASRT have set out some clear principles including the view that a sexual relationship with a patient is never acceptable.

29.10 The field of psychosexual medicine is diverse. The Inquiry heard evidence that psychosexual practitioners are not confined to the specialties of psychiatry and mental health. They can also be genito-urinary specialists, communicable disease clinicians and surgeons.

A significant proportion of psychosexual therapists are lay therapists or come from non-medical health professional backgrounds.

29.11   There is a surprising lack of formal regulation for psychosexual therapists. This should be an important issue for the Health Professionals Council to regulate when they come to consider the calibre of practitioner who should be permitted to operate as a psychosexual therapist.

29.12   Psychosexual medicine or psychosexual therapy can provide an opportunity for the sexualisation of the relationship between patient and practitioner. In the practice of psychosexual medicine there is obvious scope for, perhaps a need for, intimate physical examination.

29.13   However, although some former patients refer to Michael Haslam treating them for what can be described as psychosexual problems, it is to be noted that the allegations relate also to his general psychiatric practice. Psychosexual work was only part of his practice. In relation to William Kerr all, or almost all, of the former patients who have made allegations of sexualised behaviour were his general psychiatric patients.

29.14   There is no evidence to the Inquiry to cause us to express any general concern in relation to the practice of psychosexual medicine. However, we believe that it is an area of clinical practice where there is need for close, detailed and consistent regulation. We do not see any justification for a proliferation of semi-regulatory organisations. In our opinion consistency, at least within the NHS, can be achieved by ensuring that psychosexual medical services are only commissioned from suitably qualified and registered practitioners who are members of, and bound by, the professional standards of a recognised regulatory organisation – and preferably an organisation in turn overseen by the Council for Healthcare Regulatory Excellence (CHRE). Although this is a matter for the NHS, our view is that it would be preferable to have only one such regulatory organisation recognised.

What contact, or behaviour, are we considering?

The special relationship between doctor and patient

29.15 The relationship between a doctor and patient is special and conditions attach to it that do not apply in other relationships. The BMA have described that understanding in clear terms and we reproduce their view in full.

> *"The search for balance*
>
> *Patients consult doctors for a variety of health and related social purposes. This contact is somehow perceived as special. It gives doctors privileged access to anxious or sick people, to their bodies, their stories, their families, and their secrets. It requires special moral safeguards. The responsibilities that doctors owe are therefore perceived to be of a different order to the responsibilities of other service providers to their clients. This is partly because these encounters concern the very stuff of life. Although much regular contact between doctors and their patients is about relatively mundane matters, medicine also deals with the most intimate and basic aspects of survival. 'Medicine means life and death, deliverance and despair, hope and fright, mystery and mechanics. It is a microscope trained upon life's fundamentals.' For such reasons, the relationship between doctors and patients is seen as particularly important and doctors are continually urged to improve their understanding of the patient's perspective."*

Criminal law

29.16 We begin with an area of common agreement. Where the sexualised behaviour amounts to a breach of the criminal law, then that is entirely unacceptable and must lead, in addition to any criminal sanction, to close consideration of the clinician's right to continue to practise medicine.

29.17 There are now, and have been at least since the 1950s, criminal offences that particularly focus on mentally disordered patients, and vulnerable adults. For example, the Mental Health Act 1959 at section 128 provided (in summary) that it was a separate criminal offence for a man who is "an officer on the staff of or is otherwise employed in, or is one of the managers of, a hospital or mental nursing home" to have unlawful sexual intercourse with a female patient. This offence was not repealed by the Mental Health Act 1983, which provided for additional offences in relation to the ill-treatment of mentally disordered persons.

29.18 The Sexual Offences Act 2003 repealed section 128 of the Mental Health Act 1959, and created criminal offences in relation to persons with mental disorder (broadly defined), particularly, but not only, where the mental disorder impedes choice. The Act describes a sexual assault as:

> *"When one person (A) intentionally touches another person (B), when the touching is sexual, and B does not consent to the touching, and A does not reasonably believe that B consents."*

29.19 "Sexual" is then defined as follows:

> *" ...penetration, touching or any other activity is sexual if a reasonable person would consider that:*
>
> *(a) whatever its circumstances or any person's purpose in relation to it, it is because of its nature sexual, or*
>
> *(b) because of its nature it may be sexual and because of its circumstances or the purpose of any person in relation to it (or both) it is sexual."*

29.20 The Sexual Offences Act 2003 has particular significance when considering "care relationships" (see sections 38–41). In addition the Act addresses some of the problems arising from the power imbalance – not only in care relationships – but also in relation to the doctor–patient relationships, and particular concerns raised by former patients in this Inquiry. Former patients were deeply concerned about being detained under sections of the Mental Health Act if they complained about William Kerr or Michael Haslam; they were concerned about the cessation of treatment, and about the content of the treatment. If it is accepted that these concerns, when correctly analysed, reflect a response to varieties of threats, inducements and deceptions, then it is to be noted that Sections 34 to 37 of the Sexual Offences Act 2003 create specific criminal offences to cover such conduct.

29.21 There is now in place a sufficiently comprehensive framework of criminal offences, carrying very severe penalties for those in breach. Our concern is not, therefore, in relation to the existence of appropriately protective laws, but rather to the lack of awareness of those provisions, and the lack of clear, consistent and standardised guidance about the way healthcare Trusts should respond to the raising of concerns (whether or not in the form of complaint) that include allegations of conduct which, if proved, would amount to criminal acts by the Trusts' medical staff.

29.22 Health Trusts, health professionals, patients and voluntary sector organisations should be made aware of the terms of the Sexual Offences Act 2003.[2] If voluntary sector organisations, particularly those concerned with patient advocacy, are to make any substantial contribution in this particularly difficult area, then it is also clear to us that they must receive adequate public funding.

29.23 The Mental Health Bill 2004, at clause 280 (as with the Mental Health Act 1983), prohibits ill-treatment or wilful neglect of a mentally disordered patient in a hospital or care home.

29.24 The sexual assault or rape of one person by another is a crime – it is no less a crime where the alleged perpetrator is a doctor, and the alleged victim his or her patient.

29.25 Where a complaint is made which reveals an allegation of criminal conduct, such as sexual assault by a psychiatrist on a patient, we consider there would have to be very good reason why immediate contact was not made with the local police force (the officer, or officers, responsible for the investigation of the abuse of vulnerable adults), and other relevant agencies. Failure to do this, preferably of course with the patient's consent, may lead to a failure to make adequate investigation, including forensic examination.[3] We have recommended elsewhere in this Report that guidance on the handling of complaints made in relation to vulnerable adults should ensure that this topic is adequately and clearly addressed (see Chapter 34).

29.26 As already noted, we are here focusing on the psychiatrist/patient relationship where allegations of criminal sexual assault have been raised. In those circumstances, consideration should be given to

---

2 A helpful starting point from the preparation of health service-specific information is *Protecting the Public from Sexual Crime*, published by the Home Office in April 2004.

3 We were impressed by the Metropolitan Police initiative titled "Project Sapphire Strategy", dedicated to the investigation of serious sexual assaults and improving victim care.

following any locally implemented Adult Protection Procedures for Vulnerable Adults, and designed to provide a supporting framework for the protection of vulnerable adults where a disclosure or a suspicion of abuse is raised in whatever setting. Former patients who gave evidence to the Inquiry may all now be well and free of the symptoms that drove them to seek psychiatric help and support but, at the time of the alleged sexual abuse, almost all (if not all) could correctly be described as vulnerable.

29.27   We are pleased to see that a Protection of Vulnerable Adults (PoVA) policy is currently being developed to assist all agencies in public, private and voluntary sectors in North Yorkshire and the City of York who are involved in working with vulnerable adults who may be at risk of abuse, to respond effectively and appropriately. "Abuse" is defined in the emerging policy to include "sexual abuse – including rape and sexual assault or sexual acts to which the vulnerable person has not consented, or could not consent, or was pressured into consenting". It is unclear as to whether or not the emerging policy could extend to offer protection to women who raise concerns in the future, which are similar to the concerns raised by William Kerr and Michael Haslam's former patients.

29.28   Some of the former patients who have given oral evidence to the Inquiry are unlikely to fall within the category of "vulnerable adult" as defined in legislation, and in the "No Secrets" document. This is a difficult and delicate area, and we are anxious to avoid any encouragement of changes in existing practice that could lead to the yet further stigmatising of patients who are accessing mental health services. However, based on the evidence produced to our Inquiry, it may be time to reconsider the definition of "vulnerable adult" so future patients who are referred to psychiatrists are automatically afforded a similar level and degree of protection.

Non-criminal sexualised behaviour

29.29   Having considered the criminal aspects of sexual behaviour, we now turn to deal with those matters that may fall short of that standard but which nevertheless have no place in the psychiatrist/patient relationship.

29.30   The issue of abuse, in a sexual context, is not confined to sexual assault as defined in the Sexual Offences Act 2003. It covers a whole range of boundary transgressions. Indeed, without an understanding of the importance of boundaries, and the place of sexual boundaries within that wider picture, there is likely to be a distorted understanding of what is, and what is not, acceptable.

29.31 Further, a breach of sexual boundaries is not limited to a physical assault – the focus must be not only on actions, but also on words and behaviour designed or intended to arouse, or gratify, sexual impulses and desires. A breach of sexual boundaries is present in any conduct – any intimate, sexualised or sexualising behaviour – that could reasonably be interpreted as sexually inappropriate or unprofessional. Further, sexual conduct between doctor and patient which is said to be consensual, or even which is consensual, can be abusive and harmful to the patient. This is particularly so where the medical professional is acting, or even has acted, as the patient's therapist. Further examples of sexualised behaviour which are not physical assaults are described in later paragraphs of this chapter.

29.32 POPAN has recently carried out research for the CHRE – *A Comparison of UK Regulators' Guidance on Professional Boundaries*. The research also refers to lessons to be learned from healthcare regulation in Australia, Canada, New Zealand and the United States of America. The publication of that research makes it unnecessary for us to set out in great detail reference to those sources, save where there is specific reference to the topics covered by the Inquiry.

29.33 We are concerned that there is an absence of clear guidance on sexualised behaviour common to all healthcare professionals who are likely to provide care and treatment to vulnerable adults – including, central to our Inquiry, persons suffering or believed to be suffering from mental disorder. We will return to the issue of guidance later in this chapter, but here draw attention to definitions of "sexual impropriety", "sexual transgressions", and "sexual violation" taken from the recent (August 2004) guidance of the Medical Council of New Zealand – *Sexual Boundaries in the Doctor–Patient Relationship*:

> **Sexual impropriety** *means any behaviours, such as gestures or expressions, that are sexually demeaning to a patient, or that demonstrate a lack of respect for the patient's privacy. Such behaviours include, but not exclusively:*

- examining the patient intimately without his or her consent;

- conducting an intimate examination of a patient in the presence of students or other parties without the patient consenting to the presence of the students;

- making inappropriate comments about, or to, the patient, such as making sexual comments about a patient's body or underclothing;

- making sexualised or sexually-demeaning comments to a patient;

- making comments about sexual performance during an examination or consultation (except where pertinent to professional issues of sexual function or dysfunction);

- making irrelevant comments about or ridiculing a patient's sexual orientation;

- requesting details of sexual history or sexual preferences not relevant to the type of consultation;

- any conversation regarding the sexual problems, preferences or fantasies of the doctor.

Sexual transgression *includes any inappropriate touching of a patient that is of a sexual nature, short of sexual violation, including but not exclusively:*

- manual internal examination without gloves;

- touching breasts or genitals, except for the purpose of appropriate physical examination or treatment;

- touching breasts or genitals when the patient has refused or withdrawn consent for the examination or treatment;

- inappropriate touching of other parts of the body which may also be construed as sexual transgression;

- propositioning a patient.

Sexual violation *in the doctor–patient relationship means a doctor having sexual intercourse with a patient (whether or not contact is initiated by the patient), masturbation, clitoral, penile or rectal stimulation or other forms of genital or other sexual connection (including where drugs or services are exchanged for sexual favours)."*

29.34 Some assistance may also be derived – at least when considering definitions – from the guidance in other jurisdictions. For example, and we emphasise only by way of example, see the following extract from the University of Manitoba (dated 2002):

> *"College Policy on Sexual Misconduct in the Physician/Patient Relationship*
>
> *Sexual misconduct is a spectrum encompassing the whole range of inappropriate physician–patient interactions of a sexual nature, including but not limited to:*

- any behaviour, gesture or expression that is sexualised, seductive or sexually demeaning to a patient;

- inappropriate comments about or to the patient including:

  - sexual comments about the patient's body or clothing;

  - comments about the patient's sexual orientation;

  - comments about the patient's sexual performance, unless the patient consultation is for the purpose of addressing issues of sexual function or dysfunction and the comments are relevant to the management of the patient's problems;

- initiation by the physician of conversation regarding the sexual problems, preferences or fantasies of the patient, unless the patient consultation is for the purpose of addressing such issues and the comments are relevant to the management of the patient's problems;

- initiation by the physician of conversation regarding the sexual problems, preferences or fantasies of the physician;

- requesting details of sexual history or preference unless this is relevant to the patient consultation;

- suggestions of sexual involvement and/or sexual or romantic contact between the physician and the patient;

- inappropriate examinations, including:

  - examination of the breasts, genitals or anus without appropriate patient consent;

  - examination, touching or massaging of the breasts, genitals or anus when the procedure is not standard and not justifiable;

- performing a pelvic examination, an anal-rectal examination or examination of the external genitalia without wearing gloves;

- inappropriate body contact, including hugging of a sexual nature and kissing;

- dating;

- sex and any conduct with a patient that is sexual or may be reasonably interpreted as sexual;

- a failure on the part of the physician to show reasonable sensitivity for a patient's need for privacy/territoriality.

This list is not exhaustive."

29.35 There are, inevitably, some difficulties with the definitions set out above, particularly where the psychiatric care and treatment involves discussion of sexual problems, or where there is a clinical need for intimate examinations. However, those difficulties should not be an impediment to the production of clear and precise guidelines for general application in the United Kingdom.

29.36 When considering boundary violations it should be borne in mind that not only is the innocent hug, or sexual innuendo, capable of quickly turning into more sinister violations of a sexual nature, but that the boundary violation/transgression can itself (without more) be harmful. There is research to suggest that when harm is being considered, the sexually provocative statement, or tentative fondling, can be as damaging to the patient as sexual intercourse. That research appears to be consistent with the evidence to the Inquiry – the first serious, and abusive, step across the doctor–patient divide remained vivid in the recall of patients decades after the event.

29.37 The importance of the production and distribution of clear definitions and guidelines cannot be overemphasised. We accept, of course, that codes of ethics, however proscriptive, will not deter the determined offender. However, the absence of clear definitions impacts not only on the gathering of useful and reliable statistical information on prevalence, but also tends to discourage understanding of what conduct is, or is not, acceptable. As noted above, the nature of the subject, and the lack of an agreed vocabulary with which to describe it, may have hindered clarity of thought and response.

When unacceptable boundary transgressions are clearly identified it may make it less easy for health service professionals who receive disclosures of sexualised or other inappropriate behaviour to discount the information, or tolerate the alleged conduct of their colleagues. Further, clear (and available) definitions and guidelines may serve the purpose of informing a patient (and the patient's family) as to what is, and what is not, acceptable behaviour.

29.38 The definitions can be as basic as covering topics such as "What is a professional boundary?", "What is sexualised behaviour?", and "What is sexual exploitation?". The answers may be obvious to some, perhaps to the many; however, based on the evidence to the Inquiry, they are not obvious to all. It is important to understand, as we set out above by reference to the guidance from other jurisdictions, that consideration is also given to behaviours which are the precursors to sexual contact, so that behaviour which may feel, or be interpreted as, sexual is also addressed. We do not here attempt a complete list of such preparatory behaviour, but the minimum requirements for a checklist would include:

- telling jokes, stories, which have a sexual theme or content;

- ogling;

- discussing the doctor/therapist's private, and in particular, his/her sexual life;

- giving the patient/client "special" status – such as scheduling after hours' appointments, making appointments for unusual meeting places, using the patient/client as a confidant, sharing secrets, or giving the therapeutic sessions a secret element etc; and

- involving the patient in extended text, or e-mail, exchanges.

Is sexual contact always harmful to the patient?

29.39 Sexual assault – whatever the level of violence – is always harmful to the patient, and that harm may persist for years, possibly for a lifetime.

29.40 But what of so-called consensual sexual contact and consensual sexual relationships? What of other boundary transgressions? The recent advice from the Medical Council of New Zealand, referred to above, says this:

"A breach of sexual boundaries in the doctor–patient relationship has been proved to be harmful to patients and may cause emotional and/or physical harm to both the patient and the doctor."

29.41 In relation to truly *consensual* sexual relationships between a doctor and a patient, we accept that academic opinion is not all one way on the topic of harm. As recently as February 2005, it was being argued that interpersonal relationships between doctors and patients (when considering the question of harm) are no different from other interpersonal relationships. The authors said this:

"There is no evidence to suggest that harm following a failed relationship with a health professional is any different to that resulting from the break-up of a relationship with a non-health professional.

"We would like to stimulate debate on how doctors and therapists should handle sexual feelings towards patients and whether there is adequate cause for the injunction prohibiting any sexual relationships with patients and for its enforcement by ethical and disciplinary bodies. We look forward to a social climate where the doctor, when experiencing a feeling of personal affinity with a patient, is encouraged to reflect on it so as to identify restricting factors and possible consequences. Patients may not understand the ethics or the potential harm involved in a doctor–patient social or sexual relationship, but the doctor should."

29.42 The comments so far under this heading have focused on the doctor–patient relationship in general terms. However, patients with mental health problems are uniquely vulnerable to exploitation by others because their mental conditions make it difficult for them to protect themselves or protest on their own behalf. Furthermore, patients with both mental health problems, and sexual problems, may feel a sense of shame at their conditions, and be reluctant to have those problems exposed in any formal complaints or investigative procedure. Finally, patients may blame themselves for sexualised behaviour by their treating psychiatrists (or other therapists), especially if they have seen themselves as willing participants. The significance of the patient/psychiatrist relationship must not be underestimated. Taking, for example, the argument in the previous paragraph, in relation to the impact of a "failed relationship" with a psychiatrist, the evidence to the Inquiry strongly suggests that there is real harm to the patient, and harm significantly different from that resulting from the break-up of a relationship with a non-health professional.

29.43 The practice of psychiatry is further complicated by the inherent power differential between the treater and the treated. The stigma of mental illness, and the tradition of medical confidentiality, means the entire interaction between patient and therapist is shrouded in secrecy. We are advised that clear parallels can be drawn with incestuous relationships where secrecy is enforced, often by threats – of abandonment or bringing shame on the family. As with children, patients with mental health problems can effectively be silenced by simple reinforcement of the belief that no one would believe them. The patient then is torn between the prospect of losing a therapist/lover and acquiescence to ongoing abuse.

29.44 Against that background, it is hardly surprising that sexual contact, sexualised behaviour, in the patient/psychiatrist relationship is very likely to be harmful; the parallels with child abuse, and with incest, are obvious and disturbing. Furthermore, the effects are likely to be long-term and directly and provably counter-therapeutic. The very nature of the caring, curative role of the psychiatrist proceeds on the basis that the professional, who is entrusted with the vulnerable patient's care, will not use that professional relationship for personal (whether or not sexual) gain.

29.45 Clearly there is scope for further research on this topic, but from the experience of the former patients who presented evidence to the Inquiry, from our own research and from advice received from expert witnesses to the Inquiry, it is our conclusion that detrimental effects are commonplace, perhaps the norm. Some estimates are that 90% of complainants suffer long-term adverse effects. A recent survey of UK psychologists found that 93.6% of those surveyed felt that sexual contact between patients and therapist cannot be beneficial. So far as we are aware, there is no research to date examining the psychiatrist's or the patient's perception of the effects of milder forms of boundary violations, such as excessive self-disclosure or flirtation with patients in active treatment. Perhaps the most reliable conclusion is that the level of impact can vary according to the patient, and the circumstances, but there is very likely to be adverse impact, even if the relationship could correctly be described at the time as "consensual".

29.46 The identified detrimental effects, types of harm, include:

- anxiety problems;

- anger/rage;

- grief;

- loss of self-esteem;

- emotional liability;

- more regression;

- distrust of self and perceptions of reality;

- depression;

- hospitalisation;

- increased suicide attempts or other self-harm;

- increased social isolation;

- shame and a sense of responsibility for the abuse;

- marital and relationship breakdown;

- a loss of trust in the therapeutic process making it more difficult for the complainant to receive assistance of benefit from subsequent therapy.

29.47 As with other aspects of this difficult, sensitive and controversial issue, we believe there is an urgent need for debate and research and for the early production of clear guidelines and disciplinary procedures for mental health service professionals in relation to sexual contact with patients.

The reason for the close regulation of sexualised behaviour by psychiatrists

29.48 Perhaps the previous paragraphs provide the reason. We are convinced that this is an area where protection of the vulnerable patient must be paramount. Clinical autonomy has to be a secondary consideration.

29.49 Perhaps the most compelling argument against psychiatrist–patient sexual intimacy is the power imbalance between therapist and patient, which arguably renders any sexual contact exploitative. We accept that this power differential arises from the training, expertise and social status of the psychiatrist, versus the vulnerability of patients resulting from needs which they are unable to meet themselves, and because of which they seek therapy. There can be little doubt that even when the patient requests or initiates sexual contact, it is the duty of the treating professional to resist such advances in order to protect the patient.

29.50 We have received helpful advice from an independent expert, Dr Jeremy Holmes, addressing the ethical basis for the regulation of inappropriate contact between psychiatrist and his/her patient. The advice also touches on the position during the period when William Kerr and Michael Haslam were practising psychiatry in the NHS. We set out that advice in full:

> *"Health professional/patient boundary setting in psychiatric practice*
>
> *"1. The ethical principles which govern medical practice fall into four categories: beneficence (acting in the patient's best interests), autonomy (respecting the patient's freedom of choice), non-maleficence (avoiding harm), and justice (equal problems treated equally).*
>
> *"2. Sexual contact between doctor – or any health professional – and patient violates all four principles. Despite occasional short-term gratification and flattery it is never in the patient's long-term best interests. It produces both immediate and long-term harm: shame, confusion, depression, a feeling of being used rather than respected, and deterioration in psychological difficulties. It is frequently experienced as rape. Even when apparently consensual, it breaches autonomy since often patients feel they have no alternative but to comply with the abuser's wishes, and it perpetuates unhealthy dependency. It is inequitable since it is a 'service' (if that is how perpetrating doctors attempt to deceive themselves and their victims into thinking it is ethical) that is offered only to a selected few, rather than to all patients irrespective of gender, age, and 'attractiveness'.*

"3. Ethical – including sexual – violation can occur in any branch of medicine, and be perpetrated by any healthcare professional. However certain client groups, professions and clinical situations are particularly likely to foster such malpractice.

"4. Psychiatrists and their patients are one such group. Psychiatrists have considerable power over their patients. In the past their support was needed in cases of abortion. They play a principal role in detaining patients against their wishes. In the prolonged and psychologically intimate contact which comprises psychiatric treatment, whether psychotherapeutic, or using physical methods such as pharmacotherapy and ECT, they come to assume a major importance in the patient's psyche. Psychiatric patients are by definition often themselves psychologically vulnerable, and many – especially those suffering from personality disorders – have been sexually abused as children by unscrupulous care-givers. Their social supports are often flimsy, so that when harm is done to them they may have no one to turn to, and be especially prone to shame and self-blame.

"5. The opportunity for unethical practice is also enhanced in psychiatry since therapist and patient traditionally – and appropriately – meet for extended periods in conditions of unchaperoned privacy, not infrequently in the patient's home. This applies to many other mental health professionals in addition to psychiatrists – psychologists, community nurses for example. However there is a tradition in medicine in which consultants have until recently been seen as more or less 'above the law', which can increase the likelihood of violation.

"6. The term 'boundary' refers, in relation to patient and healthcare worker, to a) the distinction between a professional and 'personal' relationship and b) to the physical boundary, which exists, or should exist, between them.

"7. The practice of medicine necessarily involves transgressing boundaries which in other contexts are inviolable. Surgeons inflict wounds on their patients; gynaecologists perform vaginal examinations; physicians rectal examinations. These boundaries are 'policed' by special arrangements which include informed consent, and the presence of chaperones.

"8. Social boundaries are also subject to regulation and it is considered good practice for doctors not to form social relationships with their patients, or if (say in small communities) they do, to keep a strict separation between social and professional matters. Good professional practice requires their doctors to put their concerns to one side and to concentrate solely on the needs of the patients. Social intercourse is necessarily a two-way process which contravenes this principle.

"9. Sexual contact between psychiatrist and patient is never under any circumstances ethically acceptable and always constitutes an abuse of that relationship. This principle was no less true in the 1960s and 1970s as it is today.

"10. Physical contact between patient and psychiatrist should in general be kept to a minimum and stay within conventional limits – for example shaking hands at the start and end of sessions. A possible exception is light physical touching between a psychiatrist and an elderly distressed patient, but this must be used judiciously and preferably when there is a third party present. Physical examination of the psychiatric patient as part of a general medical 'workup' is rarely necessary in an outpatient setting, but should always be performed with a chaperone present.

"11. It is not the job of a psychiatrist to substitute for what is lacking in patients' lives but, rather, to enhance their autonomy and therefore the capacity to find what they need in the 'outside world'. A patient may appear to be in 'need' of, or even occasionally ask for, a hug or a kiss in a psychiatric context. This is almost never justified, and to give one constitutes the beginning of the 'slippery slope' which often ends in sexual exploitation. If such contact does innocently occur there should always be a third party present.

"12. The 'slippery slope' is also enhanced by a range of actions on the part of the healthcare professional. These include the wearing of informal dress, use of first names, self-revelation (eg owning up to marital difficulties), accepting and giving of gifts, and meeting at unconventional times and places (eg 'after hours' or in a café). While in themselves none of these constitutes violation – and can be termed 'boundary crossings', rather than violations – they all make such violation more likely. They should therefore always be carried out judiciously if at all, and with the knowledge and consent of the patient herself, and supervision by other members of the healthcare team.

"13. In the 1960–80s, these kinds of boundary crossings were most likely to be perpetrated by intrusive or frankly abusive psychiatrists. In the modern mental health context other professions – community psychiatric nurses who undertake home visits or psychologists who offer 'desensitisation in vivo' treatments – are more likely to run the risk of starting down the 'slippery slope'. However, their practice is in general more subject to supervision and regulation than was that of psychiatrists.

"14. It is the case that people who have been subject to sexual exploitation as children are more prone to such exploitation in adult life, especially when placed in a 'child-like' situation in which there is inequality of power, as is often the case between psychiatrist and patient. The very intimacy of that relationship can stir up powerful child-like feelings that belong to the past rather than the present (so-called 'transference'). Those feelings can be used for good or ill, and psychiatrists must be aware of the temptations they represent and be especially careful with their patient's feelings, (just as a surgeon will handle the sensitive tissues of a patient's body with extreme care and respect). The best safeguard against exploitation in this situation is regular supervision of the psychiatrist's work – however senior he or she may be – by colleagues.

"15. Sexually exploited patients invariably have low self-esteem – that is what has taken them to a psychiatrist in the first place. When they are sexually abused, that reinforces their low self-esteem in a specific way – they feel that maltreatment is what they deserve.

"16. Some patients suffering from psychotic disorders may incorporate sexual abuse into their delusional system, and feel that it is 'ordained', or has some special significance. This too provides an excellent 'justification' for the exploiting professional.

"17. Stigmatisation of psychiatric illness is widespread, including among mental health professionals. Thus their testimony may be invalidated as 'the ravings of a lunatic'. This too may be a repetition of past difficulties when sexually abused children's attempts at disclosure are dismissed by care-givers as 'evil fantasies'.

"18. Specific literature and good practice guidance in these areas only began to appear in the late 1980s. However the 'Hippocratic principles', which include not harming patients or abusing power or forming sexual relationships, are age-old and every doctor will have been aware of them.

"A number of 'fringe' therapies originating in the west coast of the USA which encouraged the discarding of inhibitions were in vogue in the 1960s and 1970s. However these have never formed the mainstream of acceptable psychiatric practice. The citing of these constitutes the kind of special pleading which perpetrators frequently use to justify their abusive actions to their victims, the outside world, and sometimes to themselves."

29.51 We recognise however that there is a balance to be struck here that does not always occur commonly with other branches of the medical profession. The consultant psychiatrist will need, in the difficult area of sexual feelings and reactions, to exhibit professional compassion which should not fall over into personal sympathy.

Sexual history-taking in psychiatric practice

29.52 The understandable difficulty facing some of the former patients was how to raise with their GP the fact that William Kerr in particular asked them very probing questions about their sex lives often at their first appointment.

29.53 Additionally, GPs giving evidence had a clear expectation that probing some detail about a patient's sexual history was an important part of the assessment.

29.54 However, had more open questions been asked by the GPs, then perhaps it may have been realised that the sort of detail patients were allegedly being asked to reveal was beyond what might reasonably be expected.

29.55 Dr Holmes told us:

> "The first meeting or meetings with any psychiatric patient, irrespective of diagnosis, are usually seen as a general assessment. Here the patient's current problems, medical and psychiatric history, family history, drug history etc. are considered and recorded. Included in this is the psychosexual history. Taking a sexual history is no less relevant than it might be to check a blood pressure in a patient presenting with an in-growing toenail (ie doctors are trained to think about the whole patient and not simply to concentrate on one isolated aspect). Thus it would be part of routine history-taking to ask when a person had their first sexual encounter, and to hear about their major relationships from adolescence until the present. Any history of sexual abuse is nowadays routinely enquired about, although this might have been missed in the 1970s.

> "In the specific instance of depression, there is often a diminution of appetite, including the libido. It is legitimate to ask depressed patients a question such as 'have you lost interest in sex recently?' However, the extent to which the sexual area is questioned must always be modulated by relevance and tact. The interviewer should guard against prurience, and only move from general questions to specific questions (such as frequency of sexual contact or extent of sexual pleasure) if it seems relevant and the patient is willing to talk about these topics. The aim is to get an overall impression of the patient's developmental history as it pertains to the symptoms. 'Have you ever experienced any sexual difficulties?' would be an acceptable question for most patients, whatever their presenting problem. Few psychiatrists today or in the 1970s or 1980s would ask about masturbation and certainly not at the initial interview."

29.56 If not currently the practice, we hope and expect that today's GPs would:

- explain to patients who they refer to a consultant psychiatrist the likely nature of the inquiry (including the asking, where appropriate, of questions relating to sexual well-being); and

- be responsive and supportive if such patients raise concerns about the level or content of such questioning. Such patient information may be an early indicator of abuse.

Nature of treatment and length of therapeutic relationship

29.57 Developing an in-depth understanding of the individual patient's thoughts, feelings and behaviours within their familial and social context is a core component of assessment, diagnosis and care and treatment of mental illness and the journey to recovery. The therapeutic relationship that a practitioner forms with the individual is critical to facilitate this. The importance of holding therapeutic boundaries whilst understanding and reflecting upon the impact the patient has on the practitioner also provides important information of relevance to assessment and treatment.

29.58 Most serious and enduring mental illness such as bipolar disorder and schizophrenia are lifelong conditions, as a result of which practitioners can be caring and treating for considerable periods of time. Most long-term professional relationships greatly benefit patients. However, it is also noteworthy that mental health professionals and general practitioners have more colleagues who are referred to professional bodies for inappropriate relationships/misconduct with patients.

We RECOMMEND that the NHS should convene an expert group to consider what boundaries need to be set between patients and mental health staff who have been in long-term therapeutic relationships, and how those boundaries are to be respected in terms of guidelines for the behaviour of health service professionals, and the provision of safeguards for patients.

Advice and guidance from healthcare regulators

Advice on sexualised behaviour

29.59 Although, as noted below, the issue of doctor–patient sexual contact can be traced back over many centuries, in the UK at least, sexual contact with patients has only relatively recently, if at all, been explicitly addressed and prohibited by organisations representing mental health professionals.

29.60 We have read and considered the current advice and guidance given to psychiatrists from the main healthcare regulator, the GMC, and also from the Royal College of Psychiatrists (RCPsych) and the Royal College of General Practitioners (RCGP), in order to see how they categorise the proscribed behaviour. (We have also considered, but do not here refer to, the codes of conduct from other regulators of healthcare professionals who are likely to be involved as therapists, such as the British Psychological Society, the UK Council for Psychotherapists, and the British Association for Counselling and Psychotherapy)

29.61 The GMC provides, in *Good Medical Practice* – 2001 (paragraph 20):

> *"You must not use your professional position to establish or pursue* a sexual or improper emotional relationship *with a patient or someone close to them" (emphasis added).*

29.62 The Royal College of Psychiatrists advises its members as follows:

> *"The psychiatrist will respect patients' privacy and dignity… be mindful of the vulnerability of some patients to exploitation within the therapeutic relationship"*

and

> *"Good practice in psychotherapy will include …paying particular attention to boundaries, time and place, and being sensitive to the psychological implications of transgressing boundaries eg through touch or self-revelation"* – Good Psychiatric Practice (Second Edition) *2004.*

> *"Physical contact may be perceived as an appropriate comfort in some situations and as an assault in others. What matters is the meaning of the doctor's behaviour for the patient, not the innocence of the doctor's intentions."*

and

*"Relationships of sexual intimacy between doctor and patient are
totally unacceptable"* – Vulnerable Patients, Vulnerable Doctors –
2002, Key Issues 15 and 16 (see also case vignettes 1 and 5).

29.63 The advice from the Royal College of General Practitioners is to
similar effect. *Good Medical Practice for General Practitioners* – 2002,
adds very little to the guidance from the GMC merely saying, at
pages 22 and 24:

*"This position of trust [as a GP] must never cross the boundary
between friendship and intimacy, especially during clinical
consultations, and when you see patients or their close relatives
in vulnerable situations such as marital breakdown or following
bereavement";*

and

*"The unacceptable GP has inappropriate financial or personal
relationships with patients."*

29.64 In addition to the above, the BMA's handbook on ethics and law
Medical Ethics Today, 2004 Edition, at pages 55 to 57 gives more
specific guidance under the headings "managing personal
relationships" and "abusive behaviour".

29.65 The handbook quotes the GMC advice above from *Good Medical
Practice* and adds:

"Managing personal relationships

*"Doctors also sometimes ask for advice on how to handle a
situation in which they feel attracted to a patient or the close
relative of a patient and therefore need to ask that person to
transfer to another doctor before it is clear whether or not a
personal relationship is likely to grow. It can seem very
presumptuous to ask patients to transfer, but this is advisable
at an early stage if a personal relationship is intended.*

"Abusive behaviour by doctors

*"Questions of misconduct can arise in any situation where there
is an imbalance of power.*

And

"Patients are often accustomed to following their doctor's instructions in relation to physical examinations, for example, even if they themselves feel unsure about the necessity for them. Patients are, therefore, often initially reluctant to question their doctor's behaviour, even when it is inappropriate.

"The BMA and the GMC strongly condemn any inappropriate contact between doctors and patients. Situations in which there is an imbalance of power, sufficient to vitiate consent or where the patient has impaired competence, are covered by the law on consent. Doctors who abuse or exploit patients are liable to disciplinary action by the GMC as well as prosecution under the criminal law. They are likely to be struck off the medical register if it is shown that they have used their position to establish an improper relationship with a patient or a patient's close relative. Health professionals who have grounds to suspect that a colleague is abusing or exploiting patients should take steps to have the matter properly investigated. Some circumstances invariably give cause for particular concern. Among the most obvious examples are patients who are consulting a psychiatrist for emotional difficulties *(emphasis added) or visiting a GP after a loss or bereavement. In such circumstances, even if doctors and patients do not themselves perceive it as such, a personal relationship will inevitably be seen as potentially exploitative and a cause for disciplinary proceedings."*

29.66 The Inquiry has asked the Department of Health to set out in written form, what advice and guidance it has given over the years on the topic of sexual relationships between medical professionals working in, or for, the National Health Service, and patients – whether existing or former. The somewhat surprising answer we received was short, and as follows:

"There has been no guidance on these matters issued by the Department [of Health]."

Advice on boundary transgressions

29.67 The emphasis in the professional guidance is on sexual *misconduct*, on sexualised behaviour, manifested in physical contact; however, it is not exclusively so directed. As we have tried to emphasise, it is important at all times to keep in mind that the real concern (and often the prelude to *physical* sexual abuse) is a failure by the medical professional to recognise and adhere to the proper boundaries which exist, and must be maintained, between clinician and patient. At this preliminary stage there is scope for manipulation, grooming and control of the potential patient victim, behaviour that may only hint at a sexual dimension, but serves to build an emotional dependency. It is this exploitation of emotional need and converting it to sexual advantage that perhaps founds much of psychiatrist/patient abuse. In the context of the relationship between the particularly vulnerable patient and the psychiatrist, awareness of boundaries becomes even more problematic. In that relationship we accept that additional complications arise from "transference" issues. (The concept of "transference" (and "counter-transference") is complicated, appearing as a consequence or production of the psychiatrist/patient relationship, and itself featuring within therapy, such as transference-focused psychotherapy. It is not possible to address the concept in any detail in this Report. We are advised that transference remains a theoretical concept, and it is often hard to specify in a particular case whether it is occurring or not.) However, the risks arising from transference (or its mishandling) and any possible consequences places a higher burden on the psychiatrist. It may serve to explain, but it cannot be used to excuse, abusive behaviour. Indeed, our view is that a failure to understand and protect against the known risks of transference could of itself be prima facie evidence of a breach of the requirements of expected professional competence.

29.68 Although there is some material in the guidance from the GMC, the RCPsych and the RCGP which covers boundary transgressions, it is opaque and generalised – see, for example, the references to *"improper emotional relationship"*, or *"the boundary between friendship and intimacy"* mentioned in the preceding paragraphs of this Report. Even the advice in the BMA handbook *Medical Ethics Today* fails to provide the firm and clear guidance patients are entitled to expect.

29.69 As already mentioned, there is some recent and helpful research in relation to Guidance on Professional Boundaries. The findings reveal that overall "the study found very little specific and detailed guidance by the nine UK healthcare regulators concerning professional boundaries and the prevention of exploitation of patients or clients". Also, the study found "Almost no guidance issued on domiciliary practice".

29.70 In the submissions to the Inquiry, after the Part 2 seminars, POPAN emphasised their concern that the use of terminology is inconsistent and that, perhaps following from the first concern, the collection and retention of data is similarly difficult. (POPAN noted that the nine UK healthcare regulators use different terminology to describe Serious Boundary Violations (SBVs).)

29.71 We are entirely satisfied that professionals and patients need more detailed assistance from the NHS (either directly or through the regulatory bodies, particularly the GMC, RCPsych and RCGP) so that medical practitioners and their patients may be better informed as to what is, and what is not acceptable, and why. Clearly there is also an issue here for the private and voluntary sector providers to address.

29.72 The dearth of guidance on sexualised behaviour, and boundary transgressions identified by POPAN (and consistent with the evidence to the Inquiry) has also to be linked with problems of accessibility. We were informed repeatedly that complaints systems were too complicated, that it was difficult to find information that was comprehensive without undertaking a time-consuming, and off-putting, paper trail exercise. In Part 2 of the Inquiry, we were provided with extremely helpful documentation from a London NHS Trust specialising in the treatment of mentally disordered patients. We were impressed by the commitment of that Trust to "responding quickly, openly and sensitively to complainants". We were also impressed by that Trust's positive involvement of its staff in the disclosure of inappropriate behaviour. We were informed that the NHS Trusts in North Yorkshire now operate procedures to a similar, if not even higher, standard.

29.73 However, even for that London NHS Trust, problems became apparent when considering sexual relationships with former patients. The following is an extract from the Trust's policy document – *Potentially Exploitative Staff Relationships at Work*:

> *"Staff/Patient Relationships*
>
> *...Relationships which develop between a member of staff and a patient,* even after discharge, *may be unacceptable and in breach of both Trust policy and professional codes of conduct. In particular, this will include* sexual, *financial or emotional* relationships of an exploitative nature*" (emphasis added)*.

29.74 The policy requires the member of staff to self-report. However, a reasonably detailed trawl of the readily available documentation at the Trust failed to reveal:

a. What is a sexual relationship of an exploitative nature?

b. What sexual relationships, after discharge, are unacceptable?

c. What sexual relationships, after discharge, are in breach of Trust policy?

d. What sexual relationships, after discharge, are in breach of professional codes of conduct?

29.75 As also discovered in the POPAN study referred to above, in the formulation of that necessary new guidance there is much helpful writing and advice on the topic – from Canada, the USA, Australia and New Zealand.

29.76 We are not satisfied that there is clear guidance – particularly from the professional regulatory bodies – setting out what conduct is prohibited, and what conduct (whether believed to be true, or reasonably suspected of being true) triggers an obligation on a doctor (or other medical professional) to share the concern and notify the GMC, and/or take other action. So far as we are aware, there is no specific advice regarding sexual contact with discharged (or former) patients in any of the guidance documents for psychiatrists in the UK.

29.77 There is an urgent need for the United Kingdom to have clear guidance.

We therefore RECOMMEND that detailed, and readily accessible, guidance should be developed for medical professionals. The guidance should be framed in terms that address conduct which will not be tolerated and which is likely to lead to disciplinary action. Such guidance, if not provided at a professional regulatory level, should be supplemented by the NHS at an employment level.

We are concerned that such guidance is not already in place.

Social outings

29.78 Therapeutic activity is a vital component of assessment treatment and rehabilitation programmes in mental healthcare aiding recovery. Therapeutic activities are most often undertaken by occupational therapists, mental health nurses, psychologists, social workers, technical instructors and care assistants, and also includes other professionals such as teachers, artists, art and drama therapists, to name but a few. Therapeutic activity takes place in all settings including people's homes, outpatient departments, day settings and inpatient units. A great deal of therapeutic activity takes place outside of NHS settings and forms a legitimate part of a patient's care plan. Activities such as accompanying a patient shopping, or supporting a patient to undertake activities such as swimming or going to the cinema, is commonplace in mental healthcare. All these activities are legitimate as long as they are an agreed and documented part of the patient's care plan.

29.79 Opportunities to engage and interact enable the mental health worker to assess and understand how the individual is coping and to identify any thoughts, feelings or behaviours which may be significant to recovery or deterioration. It is well recognised that it is unusual for consultant psychiatrists to be undertaking therapeutic activities with individual patients. Where doing so the above criteria must apply.

29.80 NHS Trusts particularly need to recognise the potential for workers to fall "down the slippery slope" perhaps unwittingly. (See paragraph 88 in this chapter.)

We RECOMMEND that policies should be developed that enable health workers to feel able to disclose feelings of sexual attraction at the earliest stage possible without the automatic risk of disciplinary proceedings. Colleagues must also feel able to discuss openly and report concerns about the development of attraction/overly familiar relationships with patients. These policies should include all grade levels, including consultant.

29.81   Any professional seeking out individuals or particular groups of patients to socialise with, attend conferences or undertake research, needs to do so having gained support and endorsement of this activity from colleagues and with relevant endorsement in line with clinical governance.

The current patient and the former patient

Introduction

29.82   The difference, if any, between sexual contact between a psychiatrist and his current patient and sexual contact with a former patient is relevant not only to an understanding of the concerns and complaints in relation to Michael Haslam (more so than in relation to William Kerr), but also to a wider consideration of the guidance and advice given to practitioners – and information (or the lack of it) given to patients.

29.83   The poles of opinion are readily identifiable – absolute prohibition of all sexual contact between psychiatrists and their patients (whenever treated), and absolute freedom of men and women (who do not lack capacity) to determine with whom they will have a consensual sexual relationship. But is there a difference between the position of the existing or current patient, and the former patient? Again, we are of the clear opinion that this thorny topic must be addressed, and clear guidance given. It is beyond the scope of this Inquiry for us to express views on doctors more generally, but in relation to *psychiatrists* engaged in any form of therapy with their vulnerable patients we can see clear and compelling arguments (developed below) to support a conclusion that there is a need for an enforceable Code of Ethics which make it plain that sexualised behaviour with existing, *and former*, patients is prohibited. In relation to the latter category, the prohibition could either be for the duration of the psychiatrist's professional life, or for some fixed period of time after there has been a clearly identifiable ending of the doctor–patient relationship. (For a period of delay to be of any value, so as to avoid the risk of "grooming", the period must be quite lengthy – in some jurisdictions, the period is two years.) An alternative, less prescriptive approach would be for sexual relationships between psychiatrists and their former patients to be permitted but only if "approved" by an identified person or body. We find this approach particularly difficult to formulate into any form of coherent ethical rule.

29.84 More generally, in relation to sexual relations between doctors and their former patients, the arguments are far more evenly balanced. On the one hand, there is the risk of harm to the former patient together with the opportunity for "grooming" during the professional relationship, on the other hand, the fundamental right of doctors and their former patients (as individuals) to enjoy their private life without restriction and inappropriate interference from the State.

The current patient

29.85 We start from the position that a sexual or improper emotional relationship between a doctor and a current patient is prohibited by all codes of ethics set up by medical professional bodies – in the UK and, as far as we have discovered, around the world.

29.86 This has been the position since ancient times –

The Oath

By Hippocrates – 400 BC

"I SWEAR, … that, according to my ability and judgment, I will keep this Oath and this stipulation… I will follow that system of regimen which, according to my ability and judgment, I consider for the benefit of my patients, and abstain from whatever is deleterious and mischievous… With purity and with holiness I will pass my life and practice my Art… Into whatever houses I enter, I will go into them for the benefit of the sick, and will abstain from every voluntary act of mischief and corruption; and, further from the seduction of females or males, of freemen and slaves… While I continue to keep this Oath unviolated, may it be granted to me to enjoy life and the practice of the art, respected by all men, in all times! But should I trespass and violate this Oath, may the reverse be my lot!"

29.87 The following extract from a 1964 decision of the Judicial Committee of the Privy Council reflects the position in the UK – then and now:

> *"One of the most fundamental duties of a medical adviser, recognised for as long as the profession has been in existence, is that a doctor must never permit his professional relationship with a patient to deteriorate into an association which would be described by responsible medical opinion as improper... Sexual intercourse with a patient has always been regarded as a most serious breach of the proper relationship between doctor and patient."*

29.88 In other jurisdictions, the position is the same. In the *American Psychiatric Association, Ethics Primer*, published in 2001, Peter B. Gruenberg M.D. picks up from the passage from the Hippocratic Oath and says:

> *"Whether Hippocrates was aware of transference or counter-transference is unknown. He was, however, keenly aware that a sexual relationship was incompatible with the trust that was necessary for a physician to inspire. Various other portions of the Hippocratic oath have been discarded (eg, cutting for the stone), but this particular item has remained and is the one admonition that all physicians and almost all laypersons recognize.*

> *"Thus, for the past 2,500 years, sexual activity with a patient has been forbidden by our own oath. It was not until 1973 that the American Psychiatric Association first published* The Principles of Medical Ethics With Annotations Especially Applicable to Psychiatry, *which included the phrase: 'Sex with a current patient is unethical. Sex with a former patient is almost always unethical' (American Psychiatric Association 1973, p. 4).*

> *"In 1993, the American Psychiatric Association Board of Trustees approved a revision of that annotation. In all iterations of the Principles published since then, the statement is now absolutely unequivocal and reads, 'Sexual activity with a current or former patient is unethical' (American Psychiatric Association 2001, Section 2, Annotation 1).*

> *"But it is more complicated than that. Sexual activity with the mother (or father) of a child patient is similarly unethical. This would apply to close relatives and care-givers of patients as well.*

"The overarching principle is that we must have only one kind of relationship with a patient – that is, a doctor–patient relationship. Dual relationships are fraught with danger for patients and for ourselves.

"Further, we understand that it would be impossible for a patient to give informed consent to such a relationship because of unconscious transferences that are bound to occur. Sexual involvement, then, is an exploitation of a patient's primitive feelings, and thus an exploitation of the patient.

The Slippery Slope

"In a large majority of cases involving sexual contact with patients and that are brought to ethics committees,[4] a familiar pattern emerges. The sexual activity does not occur in a vacuum. Sex does not happen in an unguarded moment of mutual passion. There are hints and precursors.

"Often, we hear of seemingly innocuous boundary crossings. A cup of coffee together. A ride home. A hug. A squeeze of the hand. A longer hug. A kiss on the cheek. A kiss elsewhere. A shared scheme involving the psychiatrist. Any one of these boundary crossings could be, in and of itself, innocent enough. But when they become part of a pattern, one must become alarmed. As some of these behaviours occur, there is a shift away from the exclusive professional relationship toward a dual relationship that might include the professional relationship as well as a social or romantic relationship."[5]

29.89 In Part 1 of Annex 4 we include extracts from the advice and guidance, to similar effect, provided in Canada. Advice from Australia and New Zealand is also considered, and summarised, in the POPAN study referred to earlier. Part 2 of Annex 4 contains similar extracts, but relating to former patients.

The former patient

29.90 None of the UK documents/statements referred to so far in this Report address the position of former patients, or the ethical position

---

4 In the USA these committees have a disciplinary function.

5 It has been suggested to us that "consensual" sexual relationships between clinicians and patients were not officially disapproved within the USA until 1986. At least in relation to psychiatrists it would appear that an ethical prohibition went back to 1973, if not earlier, in some parts of the USA.

when the intimate relationship has ended, and the former patient again becomes an existing patient.

29.91   There seems to be remarkably little guidance on this topic from the GMC, or from the Colleges, but we are clear from the evidence to the Inquiry that former patients may still be harmed by having a relationship with a former practitioner, even where they have been transferred to another practitioner. We accept, of course, that the degree and duration of harm depends on the nature of the care provided, and the potential the practitioner has to exploit the trust, knowledge and dependence that may have developed during the professional relationship.

29.92   In their research in relation to current guidance and advice from UK healthcare regulators, the authors of the POPAN study found that only the Nursing and Midwifery Council, the General Chiropractic Council and the General Osteopathic Council (all as at late 2004, early 2005) had anything to say on this topic.

29.93   The BMA has no working definition of the terms "patient" and "former patient". We have been informed that the BMA's Psychiatry Subcommittee has not yet considered this issue "in the necessary detail".

29.94   The same position appears to apply for the Royal College of Psychiatrists (see below).

29.95   It would appear to be the position, therefore, that there is no published guidance from the main regulators for psychiatrists, or others engaged in psychotherapy. We find this absence of guidance – clearly written and readily accessible by practitioners and by patients – extremely disturbing.

29.96   We find little comfort in the GMC's position that its views on the topic can be gleaned from decisions of its disciplinary committees.

29.97   The current position of the GMC can be taken from various sources. In his oral evidence to the Inquiry, Finlay Scott (Chief Executive and Registrar of the GMC) said this in relation to the position of the former patient:

Q. You are clear about the GMC's position, but it is perhaps difficult to identify when that position kicks in. The position the GMC adopts is that you are supposed to cease the professional relationship?

A. That is correct. If I can try to explain it in my words, the inference that can be clearly drawn from the Professional Conduct Committee cases is that you should not engage in a sexual relationship with a patient. It follows from that, and this has been made explicit, that doctors have the opportunity, if they feel themselves attracted to a patient, to end the professional relationship, allow a period to elapse and then, if it is appropriate, they can begin the personal relationship. That is a rather boiled-down version of what can be inferred from the cases before the Professional Conduct Committee.

Q. You end the relationship, there is then a cooling-off period?

A. That is correct.

Q. Following which, it is open to you to resume a personal relationship?

A. Yes.

Q. Although presumably not a professional relationship?

A. That is correct.

Q. The point at which that obligation to end the professional relationship kicks in should be immediately the doctor can see a problem on the horizon, or at some other time? The reason I ask, it is quite difficult to apply that in practice.

A. I think it is probably quite difficult to go much beyond what I have said in my own words, not presenting this as a carefully drafted GMC view. The point at which the doctor is contemplating developing a personal relationship with a patient, then he should bring the professional relationship to an end.

Q. Somebody who has been your patient does not remain off-limits once the cooling-off period has expired?

A. No. Indeed, a defence advanced before the Professional Conduct Committee in particular cases has been just that; that there had been a professional relationship but it had ended. Consequently, the doctor was free to begin a personal relationship. The concept of a cooling-off period has been recognised in the defences advanced and I think probably in the defences accepted, but I would not want to be drawn into defining exactly what that might have been in practice."

29.98 In written evidence to the Inquiry, the GMC subsequently said this:

"Ending a professional relationship if a personal relationship is to follow.

"The GMC has not issued advice to doctors on ending professional relationships if a personal relationship is to follow. It is arguably implicit in our guidance, which warns doctors against using their professional position to establish or pursue a sexual or improper emotional relationship with a patient or someone close to them.

"If a doctor wishes to establish a personal relationship with a patient, the appropriate gap between ending the professional relationship and beginning a personal relationship would depend on the circumstances, including the length and nature of the doctor–patient relationship and the mental and physical health of the patient. We are planning to review this area of our guidance in 2005, drawing on guidance issued by other regulators around the world, and taking into account any recommendations by this Inquiry."

29.99 We are not convinced that the "arguably implicit" advice is clear enough, or strong enough.

29.100 The latest information received from the GMC[6] is that "the issues around the definition of current and former patients are complex", and that "the simple answer [to our query] is that the GMC has no working definition of these terms, and the guidance it provides, at present, does not directly consider the circumstances in which

---

6 As at end of April 2005.

relationships with former patients may, or may not, be acceptable". The explanation for that position, was as follows:

> *"The GMC would wish to be cautious about defining these terms. The relationship between consultants and patients does not follow a single model, but varies according to the role the consultant is fulfilling. In psychiatry, consultants may have a number of roles, which will involve direct and indirect contact with patients, including:*
>
> a. *providing treatment and care;*
>
> b. *delegating care to more junior doctors in a team;*
>
> c. *providing medical care/advice within a multidisciplinary team where patient's need for medical services may be intermittent;*
>
> d. *having management responsibility for clinical services for a patient, for example when acting as medical or clinical director in a trust;*
>
> e. *providing inpatient care (but not community care) to patients who have recurrent acute episodes of illness.*
>
> *"In many cases whether a patient can be regarded as a 'current' patient of the doctor – or had been a patient of that doctor at all – would be open to debate.*
>
> *"The GMC would also question the practical value of such definitions in considering complaints about doctors. They take the view that doctors and former patients need sufficient time to ensure that emotions and desires have not been founded on the clinical relationships, or influenced by the inequalities inherent in doctor/patient relationships. How long before such issues become clear will vary according to the circumstances, and in some cases, because of the patient's mental or physical condition, will never be appropriate. The important issues will remain the extent to which a doctor exploited his or her professional contact with and knowledge of a patient to develop or continue a sexual or emotional relationship, and the vulnerability of the patient."*

29.101 Aside from the rights and wrongs of this approach to doctors in general, the position of the psychiatrist, particularly in light of the power to recommend hospital admission and treatment under the Mental Health Act against the patient's will, requires special consideration. Particular problems may arise. In many cases the psychiatrist is responsible for patients living in a particular catchment area. If the former patient (with whom the psychiatrist had a sexual relationship) becomes acutely ill again, it may be the same psychiatrist who is called to treat him or her in an emergency. The involvement of another colleague at that, emergency, stage would be difficult and (we are advised) could lead to undesirable or possibly dangerous delays. This consideration may also apply to any GP who is approved under Section 12 of the Mental Health Act "as having special experience in the diagnosis or treatment of mental disorder". In these circumstances, at least, the concept of the "former patient" is unclear. In such a case, with the potential for further professional contact, it may never be possible to rule out the future resurrection of the psychiatrist–patient relationship.

29.102 Our attention was drawn by the GMC to recent decisions on this topic.

> "In the case of Dr Nwabueze in 1999, the PCC erased the doctor from the register following a finding that he had, among other things, formed an improper relationship with a vulnerable patient. The sexual relationship had taken place more than a year after the patient had ceased to be registered as his patient.

> "In 2002, on appeal, the Judicial Committee stated that, while they did not suggest that such conduct could not under any circumstances have a bearing on a practitioner's conduct as a medical practitioner, there was no evidence to suggest that the alleged act was improper from a professional point of view and thus relevant to the charge of serious professional misconduct. The finding in relation to that head of charge was quashed.

> "In the case of Dr Wentzel in 2003, the doctor was erased from the register for establishing a sexual relationship with a psychiatric inpatient for who he was responsible, and for re-establishing the relationship after he ceased any involvement in her care, having been told by his employers to have no further contact with her. The PCC stated:

"'…You have told the Committee that in March 1999 when you re-established your relationship with Ms X, you thought that you were not acting inappropriately as Ms X was no longer under your direct care. The fact that you were not directly responsible for the care of Ms X does not absolve you from your professional obligations. You knew that Ms X was a particularly vulnerable individual who had past relationship problems which had led her to receiving psychiatric treatment. Furthermore, you knew that she was still receiving care from the Trust in which you were employed…'

"On appeal in 2004, the Judicial Committee upheld the PCC's decision."

29.103 In the case of Dr Nwabueze, the Privy Council did not refer to, or look for, some form of "cooling-off period", but took a much clearer line – saying, in effect, that sex with a former patient was not serious professional misconduct, unless the contrary could be shown. The charges against Dr Nwabueze contained, as Charge 4, an allegation that he had sexual intercourse with Mrs D more than a year after the professional relationship was at an end and Mrs D had ceased to be registered as a patient at the surgery.

29.104 The judgment of the Privy Council contains the following (from pages 20 to 22):

"The relevance of Head 4

"Head 4 of the charge alleged that on 26 December 1995 [a year after Mrs D had ceased to be his patient, and registered with the surgery] the appellant had sexual intercourse with Mrs D in his consulting room at the surgery. Conspicuous by its absence was any mention in this head of the reasons why this was being alleged against the appellant as an act of serious professional misconduct. Some explanation was needed because the narrative in that head of charge, which said nothing about any doctor-patient relationship at the time of the alleged act of intercourse, was equally consistent with its having nothing whatever to do with the appellant's conduct of his profession as a medical practitioner.

*"A charge or part of a charge which contains an allegation
which has no bearing on the practitioner's conduct as a medical
practitioner is irrelevant to a charge that he is guilty of serious
professional misconduct. As such it is objectionable on grounds
of law, and it should be deleted from the Notice of Inquiry.*

*"Their Lordships do not wish to be taken as suggesting that the
conduct which was alleged in head 4 could not under any
circumstances have a bearing on a practitioner's conduct as a
medical practitioner. But what was lacking in this case, once head
3 had been amended in the light of the evidence that Mrs D had
ceased to be a patient more than a year previously, was any
explanation to show that there were any circumstances which
would have entitled the Committee to hold that this alleged act of
intercourse was improper from the professional point of view and
thus relevant to the charge of serious professional misconduct."*

29.105 From that decision, and from the oral and written evidence of the
GMC to the Inquiry, it would appear that either there is no clear
position, or at least there is no present consideration of the special
position of the treating psychiatrist.

29.106 In Chapter 35, we address and consider the GMC's very recent
reaction to a doctor's admitted sexual relationship with a recently
former patient.

29.107 We note, in passing, that the 2004 edition of *Indicative Sanctions
Guidance for the Professional Conduct Committee*, supplied to us
by the GMC, does not address the position of former patients at all
under the heading "Sexual Misconduct":

*"This encompasses a wide range of conduct from criminal
convictions for sexual assault, sexual abuse of children
(including child pornography) to sexual misconduct with
patients, colleagues or patients' relatives. The misconduct is
particularly serious however, where there is an abuse of the
special position of trust, which a doctor occupies, or where a
doctor has been required to register as a sex offender. The risk to
patients is important. In such cases erasure has therefore been
judged the appropriate sanction."* [7]

---

[7] The value and importance of these "Indicative Sanctions" has recently been recognised by the Courts – see, for
example, R (Bevan) v. GMC [2005].

29.108 We understand that the GMC is currently considering the issue of sexual relations with former patients as "some doctors are unclear about how to behave responsibly when they are faced with dilemmas about professional and personal relationships". We encourage them in that endeavour. However, as with all issues of sexualised behaviour,[8] we also hope that any guidance produced and issued will not merely fall into the less-than-helpful category "aspirational", but will truly provide – for doctors, for healthcare managers, and for patients – clear guidance identifying the standards a doctor must achieve, conduct he/she must not engage in if he/she is to avoid criticism or action on registration under the Fitness to Practise procedures.

29.109 The Royal College of Psychiatry has recognised its deficiencies in this area, telling us that in its review of *Vulnerable Patients, Vulnerable Doctors* – "A particular point requiring further discussion is whether sexual relationships should be disapproved, not just between psychiatrists and current patients, but also with former patients". We hope that, after so many years of apparent inaction, the discussion will soon be converted into clear (and preferably enforceable) guidance.

29.110 The discussion within the Royal College of Psychiatrists, and no doubt its process of consultation with interested bodies, will inevitably consider the concepts of "transference" and "counter-transference". As noted above, this is not the place to consider these concepts in depth, although we observe that they are at least capable of producing more confusion than clarification. The use of terms – jargon – such as "transference" may also frustrate the process of regulation, even of investigation. A patient says "He tried to seduce me", or similar. The psychiatrist says "it's transference". Also, the use of "transference" and "counter-transference" tends to obscure the significance of "attraction" – where a patient is sexually attracted to his/her psychiatrist, and/or the psychiatrist is sexually attracted to his/her patient.

29.111 In bringing together the disparate pieces of information referred to above, the current, ethical advice to psychiatrists appears to be as follows: when an intimate relationship emerges, the treatment should be terminated, and the patient referred on to another psychiatrist.

---

8 See The Report of the Inquiry into Clifford Ayling, 2.27.

Then, after an intermediate "cooling-off" period (or a "reasonable period of time"), the psychiatrist is free to engage in a sexual relationship with his/her now former patient. Such advice must, we assume, proceed on the basis (if patient safety and welfare is the central concern) that such sexual relationships are likely to be "harm free".

29.112 But we conclude that such guidance could reasonably be seen as producing, indeed encouraging, a very unsatisfactory and tragic state of affairs for the following reasons:

- The psychiatrist is effectively using the professional relationship to develop and invest in a personal relationship.

- The patient is being deprived of his/her psychiatrist.

- The next psychiatrist is not (from the evidence to the Inquiry) concerned to address the issues for his/her new patient arising from (i) the transference/counter-transference/attraction, or (ii) the impending or actual sexual relationship with the former psychiatrist, and its possible long-term consequences.

- For the reasons set out above, the psychiatrist may be called on in an emergency to treat the one-time patient.

29.113 There are, therefore, grounds for concluding that the mismanagement by the first psychiatrist of the emerging personal relationship is itself professional misconduct.

29.114 Mental health professionals engaged in a professional therapeutic relationship (whether psychiatrists, nurses or other healthcare workers) who pursue *or even allow* a sexual relationship to develop with a patient (current, or recently former) can be seen as taking advantage of an inherent power imbalance in the relationship. This is likely to be so, even if the patient/client was a "consenting" participant at the time.

29.115 A 1991 survey concluded that harm to patients occurred in 80% of the cases in which therapists engaged in sex with a patient after termination of therapy.[9] A 1988 researcher found the women she interviewed whose therapists had waited until after termination to become sexually involved with them, experienced similar levels

---

9 We conclude that these, and other, studies that refer to "therapists" can be applied to psychiatrists.

and types of harm to those patients whose therapists had sexual contact with them during therapy. The decision-making ability of discharged patients may continue to be compromised, either because of their presenting problems, or because of residual transference difficulties. It is at least arguable, therefore, that post-termination relationships between psychiatrists (or other therapists) and their patients can never be equal since the therapist must always remain available for the patient to re-enter therapy if necessary, and/or the power imbalance created by the initial psychiatrist/patient relationship can never be restored.

29.116 On any view, there is here an urgent need for guidance, for education and training – for an overall reappraisal of sexual relationships between psychiatrists and their former patients.

29.117 In May 1989, coincidentally within weeks of Michael Haslam's transfer from NHS to private practice, Thomas G. Gutheil M.D., writing in the *American Journal of Psychiatry*, said this:

> "A surprisingly and regrettably large number of psychiatrists appear to believe, quite incorrectly, that sex with a patient is acceptable as long as therapy has been terminated first… This is clearly false. The therapist who stops treatment on June 30 and has sex with the patient on July 1 is clearly violating the fiduciary relationship just as egregiously as if the sex had occurred on June 29.

> "Audiences at risk management seminars occasionally ask, 'How long after therapy is over may one date a patient?' The only unassailable answer, in my opinion, is Never. This restraint represents the only infallible approach to liability prevention in this unclear area.

> "Regrettably, desirable clarity about sexual behaviour may be lost by even experienced clinicians."

29.118 A year earlier, Professor Coleman writing in the *Oklahoma Law Review*, said this:

> *"A more far-reaching problem may be posed by sexual relationships between psychiatrists and former patients... Although the failure to deal with the problem may be understandable [because there seems to be no single solution], it is unacceptable. To determine whether, and under what circumstances, a sexual relationship between a psychiatrist and his former patient should be permissible, it is necessary to first explore why such behaviour with a current patient is prohibited. If the same potential for exploitation and harm that exists when a psychiatrist engages in sexual activity with a current patient, does not exist when he engages in a similar relationship with a former patient, then an absolute prohibition against sexual activity with former patients would be unnecessary. Nevertheless, objective and flexible criteria should be established for determining when such a relationship may be commenced."*

29.119 We accept that there are very serious obstacles in the way of a complete prohibition on sexual contact between doctors and their former patients. As well as obstacles such as problems of enforcement, the existence of guaranteed right to private life under Article 8 of the European Convention on Human Rights (ECHR), there are also other very serious objections. A complete prohibition would unfairly, perhaps irrationally, penalise the doctor who forms a sexual relationship with a patient who ceased to be a patient many years ago, or a patient who was on the list but never treated, or a former patient who was treated (perhaps even quite recently) for a very minor injury or other medical condition. For those, and many similar situations, there seems to be no justification for a total prohibition. Even an enforced "cooling-off period" could be seen as disproportionate, even unfair and absurd.

29.120 But, in relation to the treating psychiatrist, the position can reasonably be seen as very different. Although it may be argued that to prohibit all sexual contact between psychiatrists and patients, particularly former patients, is inconsistent with the promotion of equality between doctor and patient, and thus infantilises, and discriminates against, the patient, we doubt whether that argument can prevail in light of the earlier significant power imbalance.

29.121 In this area of medicine, perhaps only in this area, we do not presently see any sound basis for relaxing the professional prohibition on patient/doctor sexual relationships when the therapeutic relationship has been terminated.

29.122 What is *unacceptable* (to use Professor Coleman's word from almost 20 years ago) is for this problem area to remain unresolved. Clear criteria must now be established, and published, for determining if and when a sexual relationship between a psychiatrist and his/her former patient may be commenced.

Michael Haslam's view of sexual contact with patients

29.123 We do not know what William Kerr would say on this subject – he is too unwell to comment. We have, however, read and heard Michael Haslam's views on the topic of sexual contact with patients. They contrast starkly with the general principles outlined at the start of this chapter. In 1992, when still seeing private patients at the Harrogate Clinic, he wrote (in his capacity as Chairman of the Society of Clinical Psychiatrists) to the British Medical Journal. This letter was written long before the investigation into William Kerr's activities, or his own. According to his oral evidence to the Inquiry, the letter was sent with the agreement of the Committee of the Society of Clinical Psychiatrists. We here produce the entire letter, so that readers of this Report can better understand Michael Haslam's openly expressed views – views, no doubt, shared with or known to colleagues and friends in Yorkshire:

> *20 July 1992*
> *The Editor*
> British Medical Journal
>
> *Dear Sir*
>
> *I refer to your leading article "Sexual Contact between Doctors and Patients" of the 13th June 1992 recently brought to my attention. Up and coming young doctors with little experience of the real world tend to see life in pictures of black and white with little knowledge or sympathy for the grey. When such opinions, however, are given the credence of the leading article in the* British Medical Journal, *people may be inclined to take them too seriously for theirs and society's good.*

Let us take a little less biased view of the facts of life as portrayed. Drs Fahy and Fisher advise their older colleagues rather as if talking about a child abuse case. It is not always the patient who is the victim, if indeed victim there be, when two adults become physical in their expression of interest in each other, but often the doctor is actually the victim. Our two friends somewhat twist the figures to fit their argument, but all doctors who find themselves in this situation are villains, children of the devil who should be locked up, they state that for the patient the overwhelming evidence is that sexual contact with the doctor is seriously harmful. If one reads the two articles that they quote as evidence for this comment, one finds that it is not quite as quoted. Those who choose to break discretion and talk to others about such a contact are likely to be those who are dissatisfied with it. Even in this group, however, 13% stated that it had been beneficial.

Juggling with such figures is rather like the attempts to show associations with alcohol and traffic accidents, there are lies, damn lies and statistics.

The surveys quoted in paragraph two show that something like ten percent of doctors had had sexual contact with a patient (or put another way, 10% of patients perhaps had had sexual contact with the doctor). The vast majority of these, however, cannot have found the experience harmful since it is a considerably smaller number where any kind of complaint is ever made. No doubt the vast majority of us would accept that to have sexual contact with a patient is a pretty risky and foolish business in view of the attitude of the General Medical Council, and the enjoyment which the press always has in giving publicity to such activities when it discovers them. Nevertheless, to suggest in the 1990s that two adults who form a relationship do not know what they are doing and are not capable of saying no, whether they be doctor or patient is absurd. For this reason therefore the advice given by Fahy and Fisher would appear to be extremely dangerous if not immoral.

I am aware in my own work of some 20 liaisons between colleagues and patients and I would not dream of reporting such cases to any official body, knowing the type of biased crucifixion which that will subsequently entail for them. Apart from anything else I would often be in breach of trust to such an individual were I to do so in terms of medical confidentiality. I would have thought that any doctor who reported such information to any sort of authority without the permission of the parties concerned would be in breach of his medical ethics to the extent that the General Medical Council should reasonably see fit to bring down the weight of its approbrium upon them.

The examples set by some of our colleagues in the United States in this area as in so many areas of human activity is hardly one which I would suggest we should feel we need to emulate (paragraph 8 of your leader). Drs Fahy and Fisher suggest that "once cases do come to light there should be help and compensation for the victim". Are they referring here to the innocent doctor seduced by a lustful female patient, or is the patient always to be seen as victim? The whole concept is frankly nonsense and the advice is naive and untenable. While Drs Fahy and Fisher are entitled to their young opinions, one would hope that the British Medical Journal *would not take the views of these two young psychiatrists as representing adult British medical opinion on so delicate a subject.*

What one certainly can agree with in their leader is the final two paragraphs. The whole subject is so wrapped with taboo and unrealistic attitudes that education of the undergraduate and some lectures in medical ethics are long overdue. As a student I cannot remember a single one. Perhaps if the press took less of an unhealthy voyeuristic interest in such matters, not only with regard to doctors and sex but also to such matters as the Royal Family, and many other areas where they intrude, then these matters could be dealt with more sensibly and the realities of existence could be recognised for what they are. The sky is not going to fall in!

Yours sincerely
Dr M T Haslam

Chairman
Society of Clinical Psychiatrists

29.124 The contrast could not be more stark – in that letter, intended for publication, Michael Haslam appears to be expressing approval of sexual contact between doctor and patient. We find his comment "The vast majority of these [ie patients who had had sexual contact with their doctors] however cannot have found the experience harmful since it is a considerably smaller number where any kind of complaint is ever made" nothing short of astonishing – whether written in 1992, 1972 or 2002. Michael Haslam seems there to be equating "complaint" with "harm" – no kind of complaint from a patient, no harm to the patient. And sexual contact by a doctor (even sexual contact by a consultant psychiatrist with responsibility for the care of the patient) merely "a pretty risky and foolish business in view of the attitude of the General Medical Council".

29.125 We sought Michael Haslam's comments on and response to that letter, asking him in particular whether or not he adheres to those views. When giving oral evidence to the Inquiry, he sought to explain the views there set out (written, apparently, with the permission of the Committee of the Society of Clinical Psychiatrists – see above) as being somewhat "tongue-in-cheek".

> Q. You were saying, certainly as far as some patients were concerned, there was a benefit to the relationship or may have been a benefit to the relationship between themselves and the clinician? Did I understand you correctly to be saying that?
>
> A. Yes. May I say about this article, the background –
>
> Q. I will deal with the article in a moment, and perhaps that will be the appropriate time for you to say what you want to say about it. But I am just dealing –
>
> A. Yes, insofar as we have gone, that is correct.
>
> Q. We are there in this position: that if a clinician embarks on a physical or sexual relationship with a client, with a patient, there is a possibility that there may be benefit to the patient. This is your thesis. I am not, as it were, buying into it, but I am putting it to you.
>
> A. We will come on to this. Clearly, if you read the whole letter, I was saying that tongue in cheek, but still.

Q. It is important to try to establish it, for reasons which will become obvious in a moment. What I am trying to establish is whether your position would be that there are some relationships which may be beneficial to a patient, ie physical or sexual relationships with a clinician which may be beneficial to a patient?

A. I think it is not beyond the bounds of possibility, although if anybody were to be proposing it, I would warn them off it, personally. I warned myself off it.

29.126 In specific reference to the content of the letter, Michael Haslam said this:

"That is my letter. That is the article by Fahy and Fisher. I do not remember this, but I do not have it. The point I was making, Tom Fahy had the presumption, if I may say so, to write this article in the BMJ in June 1992, where he quoted a number of figures and drew a number of inappropriate conclusions, and I wrote, as I say, somewhat tongue-in-cheek, to point out that the figures that he presented and the conclusions that he came to were not valid. This was an argument between two professionals on the competence or otherwise of Dr Fahy's article. That was the purpose of my writing it. I was not expressing any particular view, I was merely expressing the point that if you are seriously quoting these figures then the conclusion he was coming to was wrong. That was the point of my writing it because, as with a lot of other things such as alcoholism and crashes in cars, you have statistics, statistics and damned lies, whatever the phrase is, and his conclusions were wrong. Therefore I wrote this article – I wrote this letter to the BMJ..."

29.127 We do not accept that the letter was written, or intended to be, "tongue-in-cheek". We also reject the argument, advanced in the letter, that not infrequently it is the doctor, rather than the patient (described by Michael Haslam as the "lustful female patient"), who is victim. The power imbalance undermines the argument completely. The doctor is surrounded by the paraphernalia of his or her professional calling. It is the patient, particularly the psychiatric patient, who is in a real sense at the mercy of the doctor – not the other way around.

29.128 Further, the evidence to the Inquiry convinces us that there is no basis for the assertion that patients do not complain because they are "satisfied" by the sexual relationship. We are absolutely clear that what stops patients complaining, as already summarised, are the pressures arising from fear, shame, disgust, worry about the implications for their own relationships, the expectation that they will not be believed, the consequences of their own mental illness, and concern that the complaints system will cause them additional distress and harm.

29.129 In the letter, Michael Haslam again sets out his specious argument that doctors who themselves have sex with their patients, or who are aware of other doctors having sex with their patients, should not "break discretion", or act in "breach of trust", by reporting the matter. We have addressed the issue of confidentiality elsewhere in this Report (see Chapter 28). We reject his argument in its entirety.

29.130 It is of course true that it is not just the victims of sexual abuse who need help. Doctors who are perpetrators also need help as well as professional regulation and discipline, and possibly punishment. We accept that it is likely that many of them are themselves unhappy or depressed, or carrying the same problems as other members of the community. The doctor may be emotionally or sexually vulnerable himself or herself, may be lonely, may be in a troubled relationship, a life crisis or ill. Some of them will have been abused as children. Others may be more sociopathic or psychopathic – by which we mean lacking in remorse or moral sensibility. It is this category which is likely to be more calculating and/or opportunistic, using a position of power to obtain sexual gratification. We do not suggest that William Kerr or Michael Haslam necessarily fall into any of these categories.

Michael Haslam and the former patient

29.131 We now deal with Michael Haslam's view – as expressed explicitly in his evidence and also shown in other evidence to the Inquiry – as regards relationships with former patients.

29.132 The conduct of William Kerr and of Michael Haslam, which we know not to be unique within the NHS, reveals the danger of allowing any relaxation of total prohibition on sexual relationships between psychiatrists and their former patients. There is no doubt on the evidence to the Inquiry that there was talk, there was speculation and rumour, and there were complaints by or on behalf of patients – in relation to both consultant psychiatrists. There may have been a conspiracy of silence, but perhaps more likely there was acceptance that some blurring of the lines would not be the subject of criticism – William Kerr was "a bit of a ladies' man" and a "bit of a flirt", and may meet the occasional patient in his car for "treatment". In relation to William Kerr it was "nudge, nudge", "wink, wink", or even the blind eye of indifference, perhaps mute acceptance of what went on. The position in relation to Michael Haslam was more difficult. Perhaps the administrators and other medical professionals were dazzled, or even distracted, by the innovation of his psychosexual centre. But even in relation to his practice, there was gossip, there was rumour, and there were expressions of concern and complaints, but little reaction.

29.133 We consider it important to keep in mind at all times the applicable and accepted standards at the time when the alleged misconduct took place. Both William Kerr and Michael Haslam could find comfort in the evidence to the Inquiry from their professional body, the Royal College of Psychiatrists:

> "Complaints: *There was not a formal complaining system within the College in this period, whether from patients or from other professionals. General issues brought to the attention of staff or officers would have been redirected to the employer, the service or the GMC. The Mental Health Act of 1983 established a specific remit for a Commission to look at the complaints of detained patients.*

> "Psychosexual therapies: *The archives hold very little reference to psychosexual therapies. Clinics were often held in conjunction with other services, such as urology, family planning or gynaecology. Training courses were not provided by the College, although some consideration was given to this in 1981 in conjunction with the Royal College of Obstetricians and Gynaecologists. Some knowledge of psychosexual problems and treatment was expected in the membership examination. The issue of chaperonage was not especially emphasised and it is likely from anecdotal evidence in the 1970s and 1980s, with general lessening of formality and resource pressures, that the possibility and awareness of advisability of chaperone use for intimate and other physical examinations decreased across medical practice including psychiatry. Nevertheless, physical examination, which could include 'intimate' examinations was considered to be an important part of general psychiatric initial and emergency assessment.*

"During the 1970s the British Association for Sexual and Relationship Therapy was established, which involved psychiatrists, although there was not a formal relationship with the College. It developed its own Code of Ethics."

29.134 But it is not necessary or appropriate in this Report to consider whether or not there was in fact professional misconduct. That issue has become academic following the voluntary erasures from the GMC register of both men. However, the stories remain relevant.

29.135 The professional relationship between a consultant psychiatrist to whom a patient is referred, and the relationship between a GP in that same position seems to us to be different. A GP has a number of patients who "belong" to the practice. A patient referred to a psychiatrist, in contrast, is likely to be in a professional relationship which is shorter term, and may or may not be interrupted.

29.136 In this context we turn to consider the admitted sexual relationship between Michael Haslam and his former Patient B11. It is this relationship which would have formed a central part of the GMC case against Michael Haslam, which was discontinued in 1999 when he was invited to take, and took, Voluntary Erasure from the Register. Michael Haslam insists that his sexual relationship with Patient B11 did not take place when she was his patient, and the chronology of that relationship is set out in Chapter 5 of this Report.

29.137 But whether or not Patient B11 was strictly a patient at one time and not at another, the blurring of lines and the blurring of relationships is clearly illustrated. Patient B11 was referred by her GP to Michael Haslam as a patient in 1986, he had a sexual relationship with her from sometime in 1987 (probably by, at the latest, May 1987). The sexual relationship (even on his own account) lasted for "about a year" (the correspondence suggests that this may be an underestimate). Michael Haslam was again treating Patient B11 in mid 1989 (now privately), and continued to treat her until at least 1991. Michael Haslam insists that he is not to be criticised because Patient B11 was under the care of others at the time of the sexual relationship. One sentence in his letter dated to her then GP in January 1991 is instructive, and is relevant today:

"There are one or two problems here which perhaps need clarifying. She has been under myself of course since the original referral in 1986 intermittently, but did see sometime last year my colleague Dr X after she had had a brief trip to the District Hospital and in 1989 had had one or two appointments with Dr Y…"

29.138 As noted above, it is in the nature of the role of a consultant – whether in psychiatry or in other medical disciplines – that the meetings and treatments are irregular and intermittent. A patient may see a consultant once, or over a number of visits, regularly or irregularly, in one year, and not the next, and so on. We cannot see any safe or reliable way in which a consultant (particularly in psychiatry, where there is an extended professional relationship) can terminate and/or suspend treatment while a sexual affair takes place, and then return to the task of advising the patient, prescribing medication and/or providing other treatment. Patient B11 was referred to Michael Haslam because, in the professional judgment of her GP, she was in need of expert and independent consultant psychiatric diagnosis, advice, care and treatment. She was not referred for sex with her consultant. However, for Michael Haslam this relationship was merely a private matter for the former patient, himself, and his wife.

29.139 Merely a private matter? We profoundly disagree, and find Michael Haslam's approach to the ethical aspects of a relationship with a former patient unacceptable. How was this vulnerable former patient (if she ever was truly a "former patient") to relate to Michael Haslam after the affair was over, and she returned to the status of existing patient? Could his advice now be truly independent and impartial? This is how Michael Haslam put his approach to sexual relations with former patients, in his letter to the Inquiry in June 2004:

"...If a romantic and therefore professionally inappropriate element enters into a relationship with a client, then it is normal practice to discontinue the professional contact and refer on – to a colleague – if appropriate and explain to the client why. This is sensible advice. I give it to my students. We are all human and these things sometimes happen. If someone with whom one has a romantic liaison has been in the past in a professional relationship (eg a nurse or doctor marrying an ex-patient; a lawyer, social worker, teacher becoming physically friendly, with similar) then this might interest that individual's professional body, but romantic relations being by their nature consensual, are frankly in my view the business of the two individuals concerned, their spouses if they have any, and their maker. Some women in later life choose to make something out of such a relationship, for financial reasons usually, or revenge (the Monica Lewinsky case was a classic). But it is not the business of a prurient press or the general public, nor I submit the business of an Inquiry looking into how complaints were handled in the last century by a long-gone health authority (and when new guidelines of handling complaints were put into force years' ago anyway) half of whom are dead. Indeed I think it is inappropriate. I shall not ask you about your affairs (if any) nor shall you ask about mine...

"Were I to have had a physical relationship with a client, I should not breach the confidentiality of that relationship without the approval of the woman involved any more than I would any other matter."

29.140 This statement by Michael Haslam, that "were I to have had a physical relationship with a client, I should not breach the confidentiality of that relationship..." also leads us on to another important linked area, that of confidentiality. We have dealt with this more fully in Chapter 28.

29.141 If that was his stance when engaged as a consultant in the North Yorkshire NHS, and a stance adopted by others, there is no wonder that concerns and complaints went unheeded. Michael Haslam's overall position in relation to so-called consensual relationships with patients or former patients seems to be as follows:

- When a sexual relationship appears to be developing, the correct course is for the consultant to stop treating the patient, refer on to another consultant, and continue with the sexual relationship. At that point the sexual relationship is not unethical or unprofessional and, as it is "a consensual relationship between two adults of the opposite sex" there is no abuse. The consultant can continue to prescribe medication for the former patient, because the former patient (now sexual partner) has become a friend and is to be treated in the same way as a family member. Of course, it would follow – if Michael Haslam's approach is to be accepted – that the doctor/consultant engaged in the sexual relationship with the former patient owes no duty to reveal it, cannot be questioned about it and, presumably, is free to return to treating the patient when the sexual relationship has ended.

- If, contrary to the self-administered advice referred to above, there is a consensual sexual relationship with an existing patient, then the doctor/consultant cannot be asked about it because any answer would breach the duty of confidentiality owed to the patient. And further, applying these bizarre rules, even if the patient has at no stage considered the relationship to be anything other that a professional one, there would be no problem with the doctor "grooming" the patient for a sexual relationship, provided, at each step of the way, there appeared to be no resistance from them.

29.142 That this self-serving position (to put it at its most favourable) could have been adopted at all by a leading consultant in North Yorkshire, or in the NHS at all, causes us extreme concern. We have assumed that it is not a view adopted widely by others then or now.

29.143 It is unfortunate that the GMC chose, in 1999, not to pursue and resolve Patient B11's complaint, if only to ensure that a clear decision was given, and precedent set to counter Michael Haslam's argument (if accepted on the facts) that a sexual relationship with a recently former patient was not serious unprofessional misconduct.

29.144 What the Patient B11 story does show us is that there is urgent need for open discussion in relation to the topic of sexualised relationships between psychiatrists and their former patients including, but not limited to, these questions:

- When does the current patient of a consultant psychiatrist become a former patient?

- Is it ever permissible for a psychiatrist to have a sexual relationship with a former patient (as defined in the previous sub-paragraph)? If so, are there any restrictions on that permission?

- If not, what are the consequences?

- If not, in particular, in what circumstances (if any) can the psychiatrist resume treatment of his erstwhile patient?

Conclusions and recommendations

29.145 The medical professional bodies (such as the GMC, the Royal College of Psychiatrists) and the Department of Health, should now act to end the opportunity for line-blurring and obfuscation enshrined in the approach of Michael Haslam, and give firm and clear advice and guidance to psychiatrists as to when, and in what circumstances, they can have intimate and/or sexual relations with their patients – existing and former. There are arguments for saying, in relation to the psychiatrist and his/her former patients, that the advice should be: "never", "after the professional relationship has been clearly and openly terminated for (say) two years", or by the drawing of some other clear line.

29.146 We accept that there are also arguments, not only based on freedom of choice of the patient and clinician, and the right to private life enshrined in Article 8 of the European Convention of Human Rights, to the effect that all sexual relationships between consenting capacitous ex-patients and their ex-clinicians are permissible. There may be arguments for drawing a distinction between areas of clinical practice (such as psychiatry and psychology), and even between different medical practitioners. It is not for us to recommend what the advice should be, save that it must be clear, and readily accessible to practitioners, to patients, and to the public. We recognise that patients with severe and enduring mental illness make complete recoveries and, thereafter, should be entitled to the same treatment, rights and privileges as any other patient. We also accept that some patients referred by GPs to consultant psychiatrists should not have been so referred and were not mentally ill, nor had common mental health problems. However, in general terms, it is perhaps the case that at least for patients using secondary mental health services there is no such thing as a truly "former patient".

29.147 What is wholly unacceptable is to frame the advice or guidance in such a way as to allow too much "interpretation" to be put on its meaning and thereby give license to a consultant to argue, as did Michael Haslam when describing his relationship with Patient B11, that he was behaving professionally and ethically.

29.148 For a psychiatrist to be permitted to move from responsible consultant to sexual partner (perhaps particularly so when preceded by the kind of sexual grooming alleged in the evidence presented to the Inquiry) merely by the bringing to an end the formal, or declared, doctor/patient relationship is, and should be, unacceptable.

29.149 There is more. When a treating psychiatrist adopts the Michael Haslam approach (the advice given over the years to his students) of ending the professional relationship so he then "passed the patient on" to a colleague when some romantic element develops, the psychiatrist is abandoning his professional responsibility to that client. He is ending the professional relationship prematurely, so that he can clear the field for a personal relationship. But it is also arguable that he has been using or abusing the professional relationship (at least in part) to further the private relationship. We cannot see any basis for a responsible and competent psychiatrist to reject a patient merely because the patient has developed affection for that treating psychiatrist (with or without a sexual element). If such transference does occur – even if there is an element of counter-transference – then the caring and competent therapist will talk it through with the patient, and address it, not merely jettison the patient.

29.150 We have referred above to "the Michael Haslam approach", but we should emphasise that the evidence to the Inquiry from the GMC itself appeared equally tolerant. Finlay Scott said this:

> *"The doctors – that is why I make the point, I do not believe this is a surprise to any doctor – are aware that they ought to take steps to put an end to a professional relationship, if they wish to develop a personal relationship with someone who is or has recently been a patient. That point has been tested many times before the Professional Conduct Committee" (emphasis added).*

29.151 The present edition of *Vulnerable Patients, Vulnerable Doctors* issued by the Royal College of Psychiatrists in April 2001, and due for review in 2006, similarly does not make the position clear when it sets out the following in its "20 Key Issues":

> *"15. Physical contact can be perceived as an appropriate comfort in some situations and as an assault in others. What matters is the meaning of the doctor's behaviour for the patient, not the innocence of the doctor's intentions.*
>
> *"16. Relationships of sexual intimacy between doctor and patient are totally unacceptable. Both patient and doctor will be protected by the use of chaperones where misinterpretation is possible."*

29.152 That advice could be interpreted by a predatory doctor as allowing him or her to indulge in increasingly intimate sexualised behaviour, enabling the doctor then to jettison the patient and embark on a sexual relationship at the point when the grooming has become successful. All attractive patients are, to this kind of practitioner, fair game, potential targets or conquests. The 2001 advice of the Royal College of Psychiatrists is to be contrasted with, for example, the *Code of Ethics and Principles of Good Practice for Members of the British Association of Sexual and Relationship Therapy* (June 2003) which says this:

> *"28. It is not acceptable for a therapist to have a sexual relationship with anyone who is or has been his or her own sexual therapy client" (emphasis added).*

29.153 This produces the unsatisfactory situation, in the UK, that it is the nature of the therapy that dictates the ethical prohibition – and membership of the particular professional Association (in addition to membership of a Royal College). But for most of the former patients whose concerns and complaints have been considered by the Inquiry, there was no sexual therapy, or at least no clinical need for any sexual therapy.

29.154 As already noted, the position in England and Wales is unclear – there is no clear guidance in relation to sex with former patients. The point has been addressed by academics. For example, in 1990:

> *"A difficult point is to decide when a patient becomes an ex-patient, and to know what the ethical implications of this change in status may be. Sexual relationships in the consulting room may be wrong, but if a doctor meets a patient ten years after the closure of the case, do the same ethical constraints apply?"*

29.155 An answer was provided by reference to the American Psychiatric Association (see above), on the basis that "the patient's potential for dependence is so great".

29.156 So what of the future generations of UK doctors and psychiatrists? In October 2004, the results of a medical student survey were published in the *Journal of Medical Ethics*. The results were surprising, to some shocking. The authors' conclusion was as follows:

> *"Where students chose the consensus pre-set answer, but provided justifications which were considered non-consensus, the commonest reasoning used was that it would be acceptable to pursue the relationship if/when the patient changed doctor/became an ex-patient. The issue of sexual relationships between doctors and former patients remains an area of debate among the medical profession. The American Psychiatric Association has stated that 'sexual activity with a former patient is unethical... with no qualifications.*

> *"The Council of Ethical and Judicial Affairs of the American Medical Association has stated 'sexual or romantic relationships with former patients are unethical if the physician uses or exploits trust, knowledge, emotions, or influence derived from the previous professional relationship'.*

"The New Zealand Medical Council adopted a zero tolerance policy of sexual relationships between doctors and their patients in 1994. Two years later, a further policy statement was released which stated that whilst complaints regarding sexual relations with former patients will be considered individually, it will be presumed to be unethical if the doctor–patient relationship involved psychotherapy, or long-term counselling and support; the patient suffered a disorder likely to impair judgement or hinder decision making; the doctor knew the patient had been sexually abused in the past; or the patient was under the age of 20 when the doctor–patient relationship ended.

"This position is currently undergoing further review. In the UK, the GMC has not produced a policy statement, but like its counterpart in New Zealand, its approach would be to consider each case individually from the standpoint of a critical outside observer (General Medical Council Standards Team, personal communication, May 2003). From a legal perspective, the Californian courts have ruled that relationships between doctors and former patients should not take place until there has been at least a two-year gap, during which there has been no contact, of any sort, between the doctor and the patient.

"In considering the ethics of sexual relationships between doctors and former patients, a recent review of the literature concluded that such relationships are almost always unethical due to the persistence of transference, the unequal power balance in the original doctor – patient relationship and the ethical implications arising from these factors with respect to the patient's autonomy and ability to consent."

29.157 The details of the convictions of both Michael Haslam and William Kerr satisfy us that these psychiatrists are correctly described as predatory. The following extract from the Clinical Psychology Forum in 1993 (the year after Michael Haslam's letter to the British Medical Journal) is worth highlighting:

"Therapists also might conduct therapy with the possibility of clients becoming lovers in mind, thus entailing adverse effects such as the following. Predatory therapists may underestimate the severity of clients' problems so that they are perceived as individuals who are normally able and entitled to form validly consensual sexual and romantic relationships with whomever they please. Alternatively, client's problems may be exaggerated or inflated in order to enhance and maintain their dependence on the therapist. The confusion, fear, resentment, loss of trust, and other negative reactions that are commonly experienced by victimised clients are likely to affect adversely the therapeutic alliances between them and their therapists. More particularly, advice that would be beneficial to clients may not be given if it might contribute to the termination of sexual activity or remove the need for further treatment. For similar reasons and to maintain the dependence and acquiescence of clients, certain problems such as unassertiveness may not be addressed adequately. Clients may not be referred to other professionals when this is necessary in case the sexual abuse is revealed to such colleagues. Likewise, potentially abusive therapists may avoid supervision or consultation with other professionals. Either the client or the therapist may terminate therapy prematurely and inappropriately in order to bring a sexual relationship to an end, or ostensibly to legitimate it because the victim is no longer a client."

29.158 It is clear from our brief examination of the currently available guidance:

- that the present guidance on sexual contact between doctor and patient, from the professional bodies, is incomplete, too generalised and to an extent contradictory; and

- that sexual, or sexualised, behaviour may not be criminal, but still offend professional standards, and amount to misconduct.

We RECOMMEND that the Secretary of State, within 12 months of the publication of this Report, should convene an expert group to develop guidance and best practice for the NHS on boundary setting, boundary transgression, sexualised behaviour, and all forms of abuse of patients, in the mental health services.[10]

We RECOMMEND that the terms of reference of the expert group should not be restricted to sexualised behaviour between psychiatrists (or other mental health care professionals) and current patients, but should also address former patients.

29.159 We note that it would be of considerable public benefit if, in relation to sexualised behaviour, there were common standards and common guidance (so far as possible) adopted and applied across the healthcare profession.

---

10 This was also the view of the Ayling Inquiry – see paragraphs 2.30 and 2.31 of the Report.

Chapter 30
Prevalence and data

Introduction

30.1 The trust that exists, or at least should exist, between a patient and their doctor is fundamental. That trust is inevitably damaged by allegations of wrongdoing – of abusive behaviour. The early restoration of trust is vital – so that all patients can be at ease when being treated and cared for, whether alone with their doctor, with others in attendance, at the hospital or at home. Trust must also be restored so that doctors, and other medical professionals, can carry out their work without unnecessary levels of intrusive regulation, and without fear that unjustified allegations and accusations will damage their reputations, or even ruin their careers. There will always be a balance between systems that, as patient safety is paramount, enable unacceptable behaviour and practice to be identified yet at the same time enable clinicians and others to do their jobs properly without *undue* regulation.

30.2 However, trust can only be restored, and the correct detail and level of regulation achieved, if the nature and the extent of the problem is understood and addressed. Reliable and detailed information on the prevalence of sexual abuse will assist, even dictate, the appropriate level of response, and if there are to be significant changes – to practices, to policies – they will need to be evidence-based. For example, referring to chaperones, it would perhaps be a waste of public money – and unnecessarily intrusive – if there were a regulatory requirement that there should be a chaperone (or support person) present for every psychiatric examination or treatment, when the evidence is that only a handful of doctors ever took improper advantage of one-to-one meetings.

Only a Yorkshire issue?

30.3 In 2003 and 2004, the Professional Conduct Committee (PCC) of the GMC heard a total of 28 cases involving allegations of inappropriate sexual contact with patients, which accounted for 10% of all new disciplinary cases before the PCC. Three-quarters of these cases culminated in a finding of serious professional misconduct. As a result of these findings, in 2004, eight doctors had their names erased from the Medical Register, which accounted for 38% of all erasures by the PCC that year. These cases are considered in more detail later in this chapter.

30.4 The Inquiry has focused on, indeed has been confined to, events in North Yorkshire. But, as pointed out by Counsel for the local NHS authorities:

> *"It would be naïve to suppose that events similar to those described during the course of the evidence could not, did not, happen in other parts of the country. The conditions, structures and culture were the same in many regions."*

30.5 Whether or not confined to North Yorkshire, some readers of this Report may be of the opinion that William Kerr and Michael Haslam are isolated examples in an otherwise safe and caring medical profession, and that, based on the decisions of the juries, we are here concerned with two rogue doctors who assaulted "only" four women, and that was a long time ago. It may even be said, indeed it is said on their behalf, that William Kerr did not do what he is accused of doing (and, after all, there was only one finding of guilt – reached in his absence), and that Michael Haslam, notwithstanding the verdicts of the jury, was completely innocent of the charges laid against him. In correspondence with the Inquiry, he, and others on his behalf, continue to protest that there has been a gross miscarriage of justice. We are informed that there is in train an application by Michael Haslam to the Criminal Cases Review Commission for a return of his case to the Court of Appeal.

30.6 Against that background, it may be said that there is no general cause for concern. The vast majority of doctors, whether working in primary or secondary care, and whatever their seniority or status, do not, and would not, engage in sexualised behaviour with patients, or even with former patients. Of course that is true, but there is good evidence to lead a reasonable person to believe that some doctors do sexually assault their patients, and some doctors do have what can be regarded as consensual sexual relationships with their existing and former patients, relationships that are likely to be harmful to the patient. There is also reason to believe that some doctors are serial offenders – making it particularly important that their abusive behaviour should be detected, and ended, as quickly and as early as possible.

30.7 There clearly are incidents of sexualised behaviour between doctor and patient, and some of these incidents result in criminal trials or lead to disciplinary hearings before the GMC (where a criminal standard continues to be applied). These cases usually end up in the media, producing anecdotal evidence of prevalence. Such anecdotal evidence does tend to show that there is a problem – at GP level and at consultant level. In addition to William Kerr and Michael Haslam, there is the case of Clifford Ayling (the subject of a related inquiry), a GP in Kent convicted in 2000 of 12 counts of indecent assault in relation to 10 female patients (although many more women joined in the civil proceedings for compensation). We also draw attention to Christopher Allison, an NHS consultant psychiatrist and psychotherapist who was sentenced by Winchester Crown Court to eight years' imprisonment in December 2002 for 10 sexual assaults and two rapes. In 2003, the sentence was increased by the Court of Appeal to a total of 10 years. In 2002, Dr Paul Vinall, a consultant gynaecologist in Yorkshire, was found guilty of two counts of indecent assault (a further 26 charges were not resolved and were left on the court file). The alleged offences covered a 20-year period. Kolathur Unni, a psychiatrist, was convicted of a sexual assault during a hypnotherapy session. Dr Peter Green, a GP, was convicted of nine counts of indecent assault on five patients. In March 2004, Dr Stephen Crosby, a GP, was convicted of seven charges of sexual assault over a 21-year period (another 14 charges were not determined).

30.8 Further examples can be found on websites of bodies such as POPAN. We have also been assisted by the research of Wendy Hesketh, as set out in her 2003 paper "Medico-Crime in the UK: An Introduction":

"Moreover, it could be argued that this acknowledgement, that medical professionals might intentionally harm, has been an unavoidable admission in the wake of the Shipman murders. Further, the proliferation of the medico-crime coming to public attention in the UK of late raises the possibility that a reluctance to discuss these matters, for fear of courting controversy, is to assist any others within that minority of medico-criminals to evade scrutiny of their actions. Continued reluctance to properly debate the problem of medico-crime might be to shy away from the potential opportunity to ensure patient safety. Lastly on this point, the problem must be discussed in order to distinguish the criminal few from the majority of law-abiding, trustworthy healthcare professionals."

30.9   The allegations made against William Kerr and Michael Haslam are not common, but they are by no means unknown. And, of even greater significance generally speaking, such allegations can be true.

An example from New Zealand

30.10   In June 2000, Dr Morgan Fahey, a 68-year-old New Zealand GP and one-time deputy mayor of the city of Christchurch who had been awarded the OBE, was convicted of 13 charges of sexual abuse of 11 patients, including sexual violation and one count of rape. The offences covered a period of 31 years. Although Dr Fahey finally pleaded guilty, for months he vehemently denied the charges. The allegations against Dr Fahey are strikingly similar to the allegations made against William Kerr and Michael Haslam (and to those made against Clifford Ayling). The difference, of course, is that Dr Fahey pleaded guilty – William Kerr was unable to stand trial (and there is only one finding of guilt on the Trial of the Facts), and Michael Haslam was convicted of three offences of sexual assault but continues to protest his innocence. The lesson to be learned from the Dr Fahey story, which has been addressed in New Zealand, is that even a GP who is a pillar of the community and an international expert in his area of medicine can at the same time be a predatory sex offender.

30.11 Later in 2000, Dr Fahey was removed from registration by the New Zealand Medical Practitioners' Disciplinary Tribunal. This is an extract from the decision:

> *"The evidential material provided disclosed that all of the charges which Dr Fahey admitted related to offending which had occurred in the context of his professional practice, and all therefore involved gross breaches of trust. The offending had been persistent, and occurred over a period of 31 years. It was submitted that Dr Fahey had become a sexual predator preying on female patients. As the sentencing judge, Hansen J, noted, a number of Dr Fahey's victims were vulnerable and he appeared to have preyed on that vulnerability.*
>
> *"In relation to one patient, Dr Fahey was charged with rape and indecent assault, which assaults occurred when she consulted him regarding her pregnancy. There were a number of charges relating to indecent assaults involving women who were required to undergo physical examinations as a part of their applications for employment with Ansett [a New Zealand airline]. These offences involved inappropriate fondling and comments of a sexual nature.*
>
> *"Earlier offences involved the use of a vibrator, digital vaginal stimulation, attempting to place female patients' hands on his penis, ejaculating on a complainant and holding and kissing another.*
>
> *"All of the offences related to female patients who went to see Dr Fahey in his capacity as a general practitioner. In many instances he sought to cover up his offending by asserting that it was legitimate medical treatment. There was a degree of premeditation present in all cases. Dr Fahey was at times threatening, aggressive, and persistent. At no time did he offer any of the complainants a chaperone. On at least one occasion Dr Fahey told the patient that it was no use telling anyone what had happened as she would never be believed."*

30.12 The scandal of Dr Fahey was relevant to the subsequent significant changes in the New Zealand approach to the regulation of boundary transgressions and sexualised behaviour. We address those developments in Chapter 25 above.

Statistics on prevalence

30.13 We have had difficulty in obtaining reliable statistics on the prevalence of sexual relationships between doctors and their patients and on incidents of non-consensual sexual assaults (including rapes). It has, therefore, been extremely difficult to reach a clear position on prevalence. The Department of Health was unable to provide any information.

30.14 We start from the position, accepted by most authors and researchers in this field, that therapist–patient sexual contact is likely to be vastly under-reported.

30.15 In the UK, there has been little research effort in respect of sexual contact between professionals and their patients. Most national published surveys relating to sexual abuse have been carried out in the USA, with only one in the UK and (so far as we are aware) none elsewhere.[1]

30.16 It is not possible to access specific information via the British criminal justice system regarding convictions of professionals for sexual offences. Although the Crown Prosecution Service does collect or report statistical data relating to sexual abuse of patients by professionals for the purpose of monitoring case throughput, resources or performance, there is no data collected on types of offenders, offence or outcomes. The Home Office collects statistical data on numbers and outcomes of sexual offences for general sexual offences such as indecent assault. It is not possible to identify offenders who are professionals, whether engaged in the health service or not.

30.17 There is no national database to which the police, or healthcare regulators, have access to establish the frequency of cases of sexual assault by doctors against patients. The following is an extract from a submission to the Inquiry:

---

1 A very recent report, based on a survey of 1,000 doctors in the Netherlands, revealed that 30 male and two female GPs admitted having had sexual contact with a patient (sexual intercourse in 24 cases).

"At present, there seems to be no official database that records crimes committed by doctors (or other health professionals) against patients. Although convicted crimes in the UK are officially recorded and reflected in published statistics, it is impossible to determine from these statistics whether crimes are committed by doctors. And, although the GMC is routinely notified by the police whenever a doctor commits a crime, the GMC does not keep a database of the numbers of doctors who commit crime against patients."

30.18 There seems to us to be a need for such data to be collected, assembled and analysed, not only as a study of prevalence but also to ensure that the public can have confidence in the activities of the medical profession.

30.19 Even if figures were available – and based on convictions or findings of professional misconduct – there is good reason to expect that the figures would not be a reliable indicator of prevalence (for some of the reasons, see the discussion in Section Five). Further, findings in criminal and disciplinary hearings will include only cases where there is a willing complainant, and in nearly all criminal cases will exclude consensual sexual relationships.

30.20 And even when patients do complain, that complaint may not be acted on, or may not lead to prosecution or to a conviction. The trial of William Kerr illustrates the problem. Our Inquiry has revealed that there are somewhere in the region of 70 women who claim to have been sexually assaulted or had consensual sexual relations with William Kerr. There has been no conviction of William Kerr, and in the Trial of the Facts only one charge was found proved, to the criminal standard of proof, by the jury. Does it follow that a statistical database would record a single assault, or should it record the number of complaints or disclosures? Or where and when should it exclude the complaints that lead to criminal charges, but the jury found William Kerr not guilty? We raise these points not to answer them, nor to suggest that all 70 complaints against William Kerr would have led to prosecution or conviction, but to highlight some of the difficulties arising in relation to prevalence.

30.21 Our Inquiry has revealed that some healthcare professionals discount information given to them by patients, to the point of inaction. It is clear to us that sexual abuse of patients, particularly vulnerable patients where mental disorder is involved, is a real problem. When patients make disclosure (direct or indirect) of abuse, they need to be taken seriously. Taking such disclosures seriously, and acting on them, should in turn lead to the development of knowledge and expertise in how to respond, how to take matters further, how to assist the patient, and how to protect others who may be at risk. Studies on prevalence may assist in this process of understanding.

30.22 There is another sound reason for the creation of a reliable, and accessible, national database covering offences (including sexual offences) by doctors on patients. The cases of Harold Shipman, Beverley Allitt and Clifford Ayling show that medical professionals can commit *multiple* serious offences against their patients – but there is little information to show if these are isolated aberrations or the tip of an unrevealed iceberg. We know that sexual assault by a healthcare professional on a patient is a very rare event – the evidence in Part 1 of our Inquiry supports that proposition. But it is also true that high-profile sensational, and sensationalised, reports of killings and sexual assaults by doctors will inevitably have had a negative impact on public trust in doctors. Reliable information, gathered and stored nationally, and made available through publicly available statistics and reports, may help to restore that trust – or, at the very least, provide a more balanced and informed picture.

30.23 We, of course, accept that allegations of sexual assault are not always true. The generally accepted position in the UK is that the figure for false allegations is about 2% – almost exactly the same as for other allegations of assault.

30.24 But, as set out above, criminal cases and disciplinary hearings are rare and, we conclude, are a poor indicator of prevalence.

30.25 Looking at the wider category of intimate and sexual contact between doctors and patients, where this is no indication of assault, international studies suggest a fairly constant figure of 3–6%. Male doctors are more likely to engage in sexual misconduct than female doctors. When studies are confined to therapists, rather than doctors more generally, the figures rise to around 7–9% of male therapists and 2–3% of female therapists admitting to sexual relationships with patients.

30.26 Most researchers have included a definition of sexual contact in their surveys, which may limit the range of sexual acts that respondents describe. However, from the available information, the sexualised behaviour that takes place between doctors and their patients includes a full range of sexualised behaviour: suggestive language or behaviour; a patient stripping to their underwear, or being naked above (female only) or below the waist; telling a sexual fantasy to a patient; erotic kissing; doctors lying on top of or underneath a patient; touching; fondling; massage; genital exposure; masturbation; oral–genital contact; hand–genital contact; anal intercourse; and vaginal intercourse.

30.27 The following is a recent brief summary of the extensive literature:

> *"However, sexual relationships between doctors and patients occur. Searight and Campbell estimated that 11% of family physicians in the USA have had sexual contact with at least one patient. Thomson and White's survey of Australian general practitioners found 32% personally knew of a colleague who had engaged in sexual contact with a patient. Lamont and Woodward's survey of Canadian gynaecologists found 10% admitted knowing of a colleague who had been sexually involved with a patient. In the same survey, 3% of male and 1% of female gynaecologists reported sexual involvement with a patient. Ovens and Permaul-Woods's survey of Canadian emergency physicians found 8.7% were aware of a colleague who had been sexually involved with a patient, or former patient, with 6.2% admitting to having sexual involvement with a former patient. In the USA, Bayer et al's nationwide survey of 1,600 doctors, from various specialties, found 4.5% of respondents admitted to dating a patient, with 3.4% admitting having sexual contact with a patient. The numbers of doctors disciplined for sexual offences with patients is considerably smaller. Donaldson's survey of 49 senior doctors over a five-year period found serious concerns raised about 6% of these doctors. Of these concerns, 14% related to sexual matters. Morrison and Wickersham's study of Californian doctors (10% of all doctors in the USA) found 0.24% of doctors receive some form of disciplinary action by the state medical board per year, and 10%*

of such offences involved inappropriate contact with patients. Dehlendorf and Wolfe's analysis of sex-related orders during the period 1981–96, drawing figures from a national database of disciplinary orders taken by state medical boards and federal agencies in the USA, found disciplinary action against physicians for sex-related offences to be increasing over time.

"In the year with the highest rate of offences, 0.02% of all US physicians were disciplined for sex-related offences.

"Psychiatrists, gynaecologists and general practitioners are significantly more likely to offend than those in other specialties. Particularly vulnerable are socially isolated, middle-aged men experiencing a mid-life crisis, who are eminent in their field. The risk of sexual misconduct increases with age by a risk ratio of 1.44 with every decade. Marital discord, loss of important relationships, and a professional crisis in the offenders' lives often are trigger factors."

30.28   The information on prevalence available to the Inquiry accords with the recent work carried out by POPAN on behalf of CHRE. That report contains the following introductory comment:

> *"POPAN statistics show that exploitation of patients by healthcare workers happens across all health disciplines and all regions of the UK. Psychological abuse by counsellors and psychotherapists is the form of abuse most commonly reported to the POPAN Helpline. Sexual abuse by GPs and sexual abuse by psychiatrists are the second and third most reported types of abuse."*

30.29   So far as we are aware, there is no survey material available from the Royal College of Psychiatrists.

30.30   Few surveys of patients (rather than of doctors or therapists) have been conducted in relation to sexual contact with medical professionals, for example their GPs or psychiatrists. We are not aware of any national surveys of patients undertaken in the UK. In a US survey of therapy clients, in the early 1990s, it was discovered that almost 7% had been sexually involved with their therapists. In a 1991 study of psychologists who had treated patients who had been sexually involved with a previous psychologist, it was found that only 12% of the patients filed complaints.

30.31 From the limited evidence available, there appears to be some discrepancy in the prevalence of doctors reported to have had sexual relations with more than one patient. It is important to note, however, the finding that doctors who have had sexual contact with one patient are at a high risk of repeating this behaviour. In a 1986 study of psychiatrists, 33% of the psychiatrists who admitted having a sexual relationship with patients had done so with more than one patient. The number of patients abused by a single doctor went up to 12. A more recent study (1996) also reports that one third of the abusive doctors described by the patients in the study were "repeat offenders".

30.32 Insofar as the 3–6% range provides any assistance, it would produce the startling statistical interpolation that, as there are around 220,000 doctors currently registered with the GMC, somewhere between approximately 6,500 and 13,000 doctors are having, or have had, a sexual relationship with one or more of their existing patients. Perhaps, based on the recent survey from the Netherlands referred to in footnote 1 above, the 3% figure should be applied in greater proportion to male doctors, and the suggested totals set out above adjusted.

30.33 The statistics discussed so far refer to intimate sexual contact in a general way, concentrating on (perhaps including only) consensual relationships. There is also some available information in relation to the narrower category of behaviour alleged to be criminal, or that amounts to serious professional misconduct. The position appears to be as follows:

a. From information provided by the GMC, there were 79 cases against doctors involving improper sexual and emotional relationships with patients considered by the disciplinary committees between 1970 and 2003. The usual charge in the early years was that the doctor "had an adulterous relationship with a married woman who was his/her patient at the time". By the 1990s, with changes to the rules, the charge usually referred to an "improper [or inappropriate] sexual and emotional relationship with a patient". Of the 20 doctors referred to during the period 1995 to 2003, seven (35%) were psychiatrists.[2]

---

2 These figures relate only to consensual sexual contact between doctors and patients. They do not refer to William Kerr and Michael Haslam (as proceedings were not taken against them), and do not include any other doctors alleged to have had sexual contact with a patient without consent.

b. Additional information from the GMC revealed that the PCC heard 28 cases in 2003/04 involving allegations against doctors of inappropriate sexual contact with patients, accounting for 10% of cases referred to the PCC (as discussed later).

c. From the Medical Protection Society (MPS), during the 10-year period 1994–2003, 345 cases of alleged sexual abuse were reported to the MPS; the majority of these cases involved GPs.

d. From 24 Strategic Health Authorities (SHAs) and 315 Trusts, there were 324 cases of alleged sexual abuse by NHS staff reported between 2002 and 2004, as discussed below in paragraph 30.49 and following.

30.34 We have been informed that the Medical Defence Union and the MPS are not able to produce any reliable data to show precise numbers, or details, other than those mentioned in paragraph 30.33 above.

30.35 The Home Office collects statistical data on numbers and outcomes of sexual offences. However, for general sexual offences, such as indecent assault, it is not possible to identify offenders who are doctors. The Crown Prosecution Service does not collect or report statistical data relating to sexual abuse of patients by doctors.

30.36 It was clear to us, before we embarked on the Inquiry's own brief survey (see below), that there is little coordinated, consistent information available in the UK regarding the phenomenon of abuse by professionals of patients. We here deliberately refer to "abuse" in its widest sense, although our focus has been confined to abuse through all forms of sexualised behaviour.

30.37 The paucity of research carried out in the UK, and the variable quality of the information available in the UK, was highlighted in submissions to the Inquiry. We were particularly struck by one observation to the effect that recent attempts to access and obtain data for research purposes in this area, including information regarding the development of codes of conduct, revealed that there is no consistent sharing or recording of such information. We have reached the same conclusion – it is simply not possible for us to provide detailed data on boundary violations (or other forms of abuse) by mental health professionals in the UK due to the lack of reliable historical information. It appears likely that little or no information was collected in the past, and that reactive ethical codes were ill-developed or non-existent until relatively recently.

30.38 Even the data that is currently collected or reported seems to us to be inconsistent and not coordinated. As arrangements presently stand, there appears to be little possibility of an effective interface between different kinds, and sources, of data without strong, government-led, initiatives. As already noted, there are various sources of data in the UK regarding sexual contact between professionals and patients, but the combination of little research and lack of detail in recording procedures results in an extremely unclear picture in respect of the phenomenon of professional–patient sexual (or other inappropriate) contact in the British mental health system. The data that is available appears to be poorly disseminated or inaccessible. Very little information exists (or if it exists, is readily accessible) regarding other kinds of sexual misconduct, such as sexual harassment, or non-sexual types of abuse.

Records from the GMC

30.39 The GMC furnished the Inquiry with all disciplinary decisions of the PCC that related to sexualised behaviour by doctors during 2003 and 2004. Of the 65 cases given to the Inquiry, 28 involved allegations of inappropriate sexual contact with patients, six involved allegations of sexualised behaviour towards colleagues, and 18 involved cases of sexualised behaviour unrelated to patients or staff. There were also 13 hearings relating to previous suspensions, conditional registrations and erasures. A summary of these cases can be found at Annex 7. All doctors have been referred to by a number, in order to preserve anonymity for both them and the patients involved.

30.40 With 10% of new complaints heard by the PCC relating to sexualised behaviour by doctors towards patients, it is clear that this is neither an infrequent nor a minor issue for the GMC. Furthermore, with 75% of such cases culminating in a finding of Serious Professional Misconduct, which must be proved to a criminal standard, it is also clear that such conduct is just as serious a concern today as it was in the 1970s and 1980s.

30.41 The question, then, is how does the GMC view such conduct today. The answer can be found in the way in which GMC categorises Serious Professional Misconduct (under the new GMC rules, this would probably now be described as a failure to meet fitness to practise standards), the sanctions imposed for such behaviour, and the duration and effect of such sanctions.

30.42 The first issue is what amounts to Serious Professional Misconduct. It appears that, for the majority of cases, any inappropriate sexual contact with a patient, whether through a consensual relationship or inappropriate intimate examinations, will amount to Serious Professional Misconduct. However, it is of concern to the Inquiry that there are cases where inappropriate sexual contact with patients has been proven, and yet this did not amount to Serious Professional Misconduct, and therefore precluded the imposition of sanctions against the doctors involved. Two cases in particular illustrate this point.

30.43 Dr 26 admitted to a sexual relationship with a vulnerable patient with a history of psychiatric problems, but, without further evidence of the circumstances or context of the relationship, the actions were not considered inappropriate. Therefore, the doctor was found not guilty of Serious Professional Misconduct.

30.44 Dr 4 was found to have entered into an inappropriate relationship with a vulnerable psychiatric patient, but this was not found to amount to Serious Professional Misconduct.

30.45 While it is outside the Terms of Reference of this Inquiry to make recommendations about GMC disciplinary procedures, we would nevertheless hope that there would be a rebuttal presumption of Serious Professional Misconduct (or failure to meet fitness to practise standards) whenever a doctor is found to have entered into a sexual relationship with a patient.

30.46 The second issue relates to sanctions imposed by the PCC for such Serious Professional Misconduct. We bring the following to the attention of the readers of this Report. Sixty-two per cent of these cases resulted in the doctor's name being erased from the Medical Register. The following are examples, from Annex 7, where the PCC concluded that erasure was not the appropriate response.

- Dr 10 carried out intimate examinations on four patients, without a chaperone being present, with little or no clinical justification, and without their full consent. These examinations were found to be inappropriate and unprofessional. A reprimand was given to the doctor involved.

- Dr 50 carried out intimate examinations on five patients, without a chaperone being present, and with little or no clinical justification Dr 50 was given a reprimand.

- Dr 51 carried out inappropriate, incompetent and indecent intimate examinations on four patients, with little or no clinical justification and without full consent. Conditional registration was imposed for 12 months.

- Dr 29 admitted to a sexual relationship with a vulnerable patient with a history of depression. His name was suspended from the Medical Register for three months.

- Dr 31 admitted to a sexual relationship with a vulnerable patient with a history of depression. Conditions were imposed on his registration for two years.

- Dr 37 admitted to a sexual relationship with a vulnerable psychiatric patient. He was suspended for 12 months.

30.47 The third issue relates to the duration of any sanctions imposed as a result of a finding of Serious Professional Misconduct in sexualised behaviour cases. The following information is again taken from Annex 7:

- Dr 2 was convicted of indecent assault of a patient and sentenced to nine months' imprisonment in July 1997. His name was restored to the Register in 2001, subject to conditions, but those conditions were lifted 13 months later.

- Dr 3 was suspended in June 2001 after making improper and inappropriate comments of a sexual nature to three patients, an inappropriate intimate examination of another patient, and sexual advances towards the relatives of another two patients. After 18 months, the suspension was lifted without conditions being imposed.

- Dr 27 was suspended in November 2003 as a result of sexual advances made towards two patients, including touching one patient's breasts outside the clinical setting and without her consent. The suspension was revoked 12 months later.

- Dr 63 was suspended for 12 months in August 2002 following inappropriate and indecent behaviour with two female patients in their own home – one of whom was a 14-year-old girl. Conditional registration was granted in August 2003, and again in December 2004.

- Dr 9 was suspended after he touched the stomach and breasts of a patient who was admitted to A&E with a bruised finger. His suspension was lifted six months later.

30.48   We emphasise that we do not know the details of the decisions, in particular the details of the mitigation advanced before the Committee by the various doctors. However, there is enough here to cause us concern. The conclusion we draw from these particular decisions is that they may betray a lack of consistency and undermine the essential establishment of public confidence in the GMC's commitment to the paramount importance of patient safety.

Records from Strategic Health Authorities and Trusts

30.49   The Inquiry contacted the 28 SHAs, and through them the 600 Trusts of England and Wales, in an attempt to discover if there are reliable figures of complaints and concerns kept at a local and regional level. The Inquiry also contacted the nine regional directors for public health, to gain an insight into the number of alert letters issued following complaints of sexualised behaviour. The product of that work is summarised at Annex 6.

Information requested

30.50   The Inquiry asked for varying levels of information from the SHAs and Trusts. On a basic level, all SHAs and Trusts were asked to provide the numbers of allegations of "sexualised behaviour" in any given year, and the type of health professional alleged to be involved, ie nurse, GP etc. Those SHAs and Trusts that could provide further information were asked to include details of the nature of the allegation, the outcome of the concern, and the length of time taken to resolve the case.

30.51 Due to time constraints, and (apparent) pressures brought about by the recent introduction of the Freedom of Information Act, it was disappointing to find that not all Trusts or SHAs could give the in-depth response they would have liked to the Inquiry's request for information.

30.52 However, the response from the SHAs and Trusts was, for the most part, very positive, with over half the Trusts submitting information. Regrettably, there were particular SHAs who were either unwilling or unable to locate the information required, stating that there were no allegations of sexualised behaviour within the catchment area of their authority. Given the relatively high numbers of allegations received by other SHAs and Trusts, and the statistical improbability of zero complaints being raised, this response gives cause for concern. Of some concern was the assertion by some clinical governance leads that, since any information they could provide was incomplete, it would be of little use to the Inquiry, and therefore should not be provided. Fortunately, the majority of SHAs did not adopt this attitude, and indeed went to great lengths to be of assistance, particularly those SHAs with experience of dealing with this, and similar, inquiries, such as the Ayling and Neale inquiries. If, as recommended below, detailed data collection is to be undertaken, we expect and assume that the various levels within NHS authorities will be an important source of information. The Department of Health needs to address this inconsistency with some urgency.

Problems in information gathering

30.53 Notwithstanding the active support and cooperation of the majority of SHAs and Trusts, there were particular difficulties in accessing records relating to "sexualised behaviour". There have been considerable structural reforms to the NHS in recent years, which have had a significant impact on organisational memory. As a result, only a minority of SHAs or Trusts reported ready access to records that go back further than 2002. This is reflected in the relatively small numbers of concerns recorded as occurring before 2002 – only 61, which amounts to less than 13% of the total number of concerns received. Not only has structural reform impacted on records and record keeping, but concerns were also raised by SHAs and Trusts that it has led to inconsistency and repeated changes in policy and implementation relating to record keeping. This response was consistent with our experience when examining record keeping and retention during the period covered by the Inquiry – little seems to have changed, at least in this area.

30.54 Indeed, SHAs and Trusts highlighted the issue of the general quality of record keeping. It was noted by a number of SHAs that there was significant variation in reporting, and those Trusts that submitted a "nil return" to their SHA gave more cause for concern than those with a significant number of allegations or complaints. Furthermore, feedback received from Trusts indicates that many do not have the systems or processes in place specifically to identify and monitor such allegations of "sexualised behaviour". As a result, there were serious concerns that, since such incidents are not always recorded centrally through the adverse incident system or any other system, the data received shows only a partial picture. As a result, many contributors acknowledged that there are undoubtedly more incidents of this nature than their systems capture.

30.55 There were wide variations in the understanding of the term "sexualised behaviour". Some Trusts, rightly in our opinion, took that to include the spoken word, such as suggestive or lewd language. Other Trusts, however, categorised intimate examinations carried out without consent as physical, rather than sexual assault. Sexual assault should be included in the category of "serious untoward incident" and, as such, automatically reported to the SHA and, possibly, to the National Patients Safety Agency. Whether there is also a wider problem of definition, record keeping, training or identification of potential misconduct is not apparent from the information received. However, it was noted by some SHAs and Trusts that the investigation and recording of such concerns is a serious problem, as it is often carried out inadequately, if at all, by staff inexperienced in such types of investigation. Again, this reinforces the impression that such allegations are being under-reported throughout the NHS.

The results – a caveat

30.56 Before considering the combined results given to the Inquiry, it is important to place some qualifications on their use and any interpretations that can be derived from them. First and foremost, the results are not the product of a formal in-depth survey; they only represent returns from just over half the Trusts and SHAs contacted. Furthermore, due to the problems encountered by those gathering the information, as set out in paragraphs 30.32 to 30.37, even where returns have been submitted there is apparent under-reporting.

30.57 Notwithstanding this caveat, it was important for the Inquiry to gain some overview of the extent of allegations and concerns being lodged within the NHS, in order to put the Report and recommendations in context. In order to gain a national overview, we have increased the sample figures proportionately using a rudimentary calculation, ie where information has been submitted by only half the Trusts in England and Wales, the results have been doubled in order to get an approximation of the nationwide picture.

The results – some observations

30.58 The full breakdown of the results can be found at Annex 6, but some of the findings need to be considered here. The Inquiry received notification of an average of 205 allegations of sexualised behaviour per year across England and Wales for the years 2002–04.

30.59 Of those 205 allegations: 18% involved GPs; 15% involved doctors, SHOs and consultants; and 31% involved nurses. Given that nurses account for over 60% of the professionally qualified clinical staff employed by the NHS, it is not surprising that they represent the greatest proportion of complaints or assertions. GPs, consultants and other doctors account for only 18% of the professionally qualified clinical staff, but received a disproportionate number of complaints, accounting for 33% of allegations of sexualised behaviour. These figures were in line with data received from the National Clinical Assessment Authority, which also demonstrated a disproportionate number of concerns being raised about surgeons and psychiatrists – but only in relation to clinical performance issues.

30.60 One of the most striking figures, however, relates to the outcomes of investigations. A large proportion of allegations – 26.5% – either have no evidence to support them or are not upheld. We recognise a difficulty here: if the police investigation reveals absolutely no grounds for the complaint, it is problematic for any health authority to do other than conclude its investigation. That is not to say that, just because the *criminal* burden of proof is not reached, there are no grounds for investigation.

30.61 What was unexpected was that an even greater proportion of sexual allegations lead to disciplinary action, dismissal or a criminal conviction: 33%. If that figure is translated into the number of reported cases nationwide, this would amount to 67 cases of sexual abuse every year. This figure represents only those cases that have been effectively recorded and investigated. If, as has been indicated to the Inquiry, there is significant under-reporting of such cases, it is apparent that sexual abuse is a serious issue across the NHS.

30.62 Also of concern to the Inquiry was the finding that 9% of investigations are not followed through to conclusion because the staff member either resigns, moves to a different area, or leaves the NHS altogether. This is perhaps symptomatic of a failing of clinical governance, where responsibility is too readily influenced by other factors not relevant to patient safety. The result is that patients may remain at risk, particularly if the reason for not pursuing the investigation is because the staff member has moved to a different area. In that respect, the failure to complete investigations at a local level is leading to a failure to protect patients on a regional or national level.

30.63 But even where full investigations are followed through to conclusion, inadequate reporting or sharing of information (between Trusts, the private and voluntary sector, temporary staffing agencies or locums and SHAs) leads to further opportunities for the possible abuse of patients. In a number of cases highlighted to the Inquiry, healthcare workers were able to move from one Trust to another, with allegations and formal complaints on their employment record coming to light only after further abuses. Indeed, without any centralised records or monitoring of such allegations, investigations and outcomes, the system is vulnerable to systematic abuse as predatory healthcare workers are able to move from area to area without proper supervision.

30.64 Another shortcoming of the system that has been brought to the attention of the Inquiry is that information of this nature can be divided between a number of departments, and would therefore not necessarily be passed on to clinical governance. It is possible that a line manager would handle a complaint locally, and might not include the human resources team in that investigation, which would undermine any attempts at effective record keeping or inter-agency sharing of information.

Structural problems

30.65 One of the causes of such unstructured record keeping and information sharing is the fractured system of clinical governance. The system at present has four different interfaces in relation to governance of the whole system, working on the individual Trust/Primary Care Trust (PCT) provider level, Trust to PCT commissioner, and Trust/PCT to SHA. In addition, directors of public health are linked to eight Government Offices nationally. They do not have any line management relationship with SHAs. It is difficult for this arrangement to function as a unified incidents or record keeping system. Thus SHAs will only hear of such incidents (which may include complaints within their area) if they have not been resolved at the Trust level, using the "serious untoward incident" process. Indeed, the majority of SHAs that responded to our request were surprised at the numbers of such incidents within their area of which they had no prior knowledge. It is difficult to imagine how effective clinical governance can be carried out at the SHA level when they are unaware of such important patient safety and clinical governance issues in their area, particularly given the observation, in paragraph 30.55 above, that certain SHAs are actively avoiding knowledge of such occurrences.

30.66 At Government Office level, the regional directors can issue alert letters[3] where there are grave concerns regarding the behaviour of particular healthcare workers. Such letters are designed to cover a potential risk situation until the relevant regulatory body has time to consider the matter fully. However, we noted an unexplained mismatch between the use of such letters and the investigations of sexualised behaviour.

30.67 Another issue regarding structural problems is the use of external agencies and staff. Where outside agencies have been used, and concerns about their staff raised, it has often been left to that outside agency to conduct the investigation, or the Trust has simply asked that the agency staff involved are not sent to the same hospital. While this may satisfy the Trust's immediate duty to protect those patients within its area, it does little to protect those outside its area. As such, we regard this as a practice requiring reconsideration.

---

3 Such letters are designed to stop or restrict the person working within the NHS without pertinent information being shared across organisations.

Other clinical issues

30.68 Trusts and SHAs also reported to the Inquiry that concerns of sexualised behaviour often coincided with other clinical issues. When such a matter was reported, it was rarely a single issue. So, for example, if there were poor clinical performance, there would often be health and/or conduct issues that may have been reported previously. This was said to be true of minor cases as well as of the more serious cases, and some Trusts felt that the system was failing to intervene early enough, when many of the healthcare workers could be "rehabilitated". This would support the conclusion that even "minor" patient–staff boundary transgressions must be dealt with effectively, to prevent such transgressions escalating to more serious offences.

Duration of complaints process

30.69 Another result, which is of some concern, is the length of time it takes for a complaint to be resolved, the average duration being just over seven months. This increases to eight months where the police conduct an investigation, and 17 months for GMC involvement or where the staff member is dismissed. Some individual cases brought to the attention of the Inquiry took as long as four years to be resolved. It is difficult to draw conclusions from these figures without knowing the full details of the individual cases, and, while it is not always appropriate to set targets for complaints resolution, it appears clear that 17 months is too long to await an outcome. If the full disciplinary process that is required for dismissal is taking longer than the criminal process, this raises some concerns over the efficiency of the NHS complaints system.

The National Clinical Assessment Service

30.70 As of July 2005, the National Clinical Assessment Service (previously the National Clinical Assessment Authority) had dealt with over 2,000 requests for advice, which, according to NCAS, represented 2% of the active medical and dental workforce in the NHS. These requests for advice related to doctors and dentists about whom such serious concerns had been raised that the hospital or PCT was prompted to contact NCAS for advice or assessment. NCAS handled 704 such requests during 2004/05. Of these, about one third of the trusts require further support in handling the case, which can require specialist input over a period of months. Around 10% of the doctors about whom NCAS is contacted will require a full clinical performance assessment. Upwards of 80% of NHS organisations have contacted NCAS for advice at least once since April 2001. In 2004/05, NCAS was used by about two thirds of all NHS Trusts. These referrals come from NHS employers only and relate to clinical performance issues. NCAS does not take referrals from patients or the public, and does not collect specific data relating to incidents of sexual misconduct.

Conclusion and recommendations

30.71 The statistical evidence suggests that sexual contact not infrequently occurs in the context of medical staff–patient relationships.

30.72 There is no doubt that professional bodies and mental health organisations must confront the reality and prevalence of the sexual abuse of patients and develop appropriate procedures and patient support.

30.73 If the prevalence of patient abuse is to be reduced, it appears that the first stage is to systematically collect reliable prevalence data. We are also of the clear opinion that information, when collected, should not merely be grouped under a heading such as "healthcare professionals", but also categorised so that numbers, and even trends, can be identified for doctors (including by specialism), nurses, etc, so that professional regulatory bodies can take appropriate reactive and proactive steps. At Annex 8 is a draft document that could (if accepted) form the basis for areas of information to be included in a local and national data collection initiative.

30.74 We see no reason why the Department of Health, responsible for the health of the nation, should not undertake that task – or at least provide the framework within which data collection and possibly research can be carried out – and coordinate the various sources of information (such as those referred to above) into a single, national resource. If the exercise is to be of any long-term value, there should be a carefully formulated protocol to require collation and collection of material on at least an annual basis. It is only by that process that informed consideration can be given to the comparison of numbers and trends (if any) within and between healthcare professions, so that necessary policy decisions can be made and the impact of such decisions monitored effectively.

Accordingly, we RECOMMEND that there should be detailed research carried out and published by the Department of Health to show the prevalence of sexual assaults, sexual contact or other sexualised behaviour, between doctors and existing and/or former patients – particularly in the field of mental health.

Further, we RECOMMEND that the Department of Health should urgently investigate and report upon the need for a coordinated method of mandatory data collection and mandatory recording in relation to the area of abuse of patients by mental health care professionals.

30.75   The duty to report incidents of sexualised behaviour should apply to all NHS organisations and to other organisations caring for any NHS patients in the independent and voluntary sector, and should include all temporary staffing agencies who work in the NHS.

30.76   The NHS will need to ensure that the mechanisms for reporting incidents of alleged abuse are clearly understood in all NHS organisations and are reported by PCTs and Trusts to SHAs and regional directors of public health (so far as alert letters are concerned) in a consistent way.

Chapter 31
Chaperones

Introduction

31.1 We have been invited to consider the use of a human chaperone (or support person) as a monitoring and control measure – for the protection of both patients and clinicians.

31.2 Our attention has also been drawn to technical developments allowing for the use of video recording techniques – known as "virtual chaperones". This is a topic that requires careful study and, if pursued, closely controlled and monitored trialling. We address virtual chaperones later in this chapter.

31.3 It is important for everyone to know what the chaperoning policy is and how it impacts upon doctors and their patients in any given setting. We note that this was also the view of the members of the Ayling Inquiry Panel, who made recommendations covering this area with which we broadly agree.[1]

31.4 At the outset we observe that there are limitations on the value of a chaperone in circumstances where the clinician is intent on engaging in sexualised behaviour with his/her patients. A chaperone, human

---

1 *"We recommend that no family member or friend of a patient should be expected to undertake any formal chaperoning role. The presence of a chaperone during a clinical examination and treatment must be the clearly expressed choice of a patient. Chaperoning should not be undertaken by other than trained staff: the use of untrained administrative staff as chaperones in a GP surgery, for example, is not acceptable. However, the patient must have the right to decline any chaperone offered if they so wish.*

"Beyond these immediate and practical points, there is a need for each NHS Trust to determine its chaperoning policy, make this explicit to patients and resource it accordingly. This must include accredited training for the role and an identified managerial lead with responsibility for the implementation of the policy. We recognise that, for primary care, developing and resourcing a chaperoning policy will have to take into account issues such as one-to-one consultations in the patient's home and the capacity of individual practices to meet the requirements of the agreed policy.

Finally, reported breaches of the chaperoning policy should be formally investigated through each Trust's risk management and clinical governance arrangements and treated, if determined as deliberate, as a disciplinary matter."

or virtual, cannot be present on all occasions, in every room of the hospital, in every room of the GP's practice, at every consultation, at every domiciliary visit, or, taking an allegation in relation to William Kerr, in his car, or, taking an allegation in relation to Michael Haslam, on "outings" away from the hospital setting.

31.5 Unlike the Ayling Inquiry, we are here focusing only on mental health services. We consider it important to separate out situations when, as a matter of course and as a matter of obligation, a chaperone should be offered, and situations where we would not expect this to happen – unless the particular circumstances require special treatment.

31.6 We would expect a human chaperone to be offered and provided in any situation where, within mental health services, it is known or anticipated that there will be any form of intimate physical examination or any form of intrusive physical treatment (this is developed further below).

31.7 In contrast, we would not expect a human chaperone to be offered or available in what can best be described as normal psychiatric treatment and consultation – including, but not limited to, one-to-one meetings between a male psychiatrist (or other mental health service professional) and his female patient. We consider that such a requirement goes too far, based on the evidence we have heard. It would be an unrealistic goal and a poor use of public funds to require a chaperone to be present at all other consultations for psychiatric patients. Further, such a requirement would carry a risk of intrusion into, and interference with, the therapeutic relationship. We accept that there is a real need to preserve the environment of privacy and confidentiality that exists, and should exist, in the psychiatrist/patient relationship. As noted elsewhere, there may be a need for confidentiality to be relaxed where there is evidence of abuse – but it does not follow that chaperones should be introduced as a matter of routine. There will be occasions and situations where the offer and provision of a human chaperone is sensible and advisable, even where no intimate examination by the psychiatrist is contemplated and no physical treatment offered. For example, and it is only an example, the patient may be particularly vulnerable, with a history of abuse, calling for special measures to provide that patient with a sense of security and protection.

31.8 The fact that a chaperone is not offered or provided should not, of course, be treated as an invitation for the mental health service professional to engage in any form of boundary transgression or inappropriate behaviour. But we consider that the risk of such behaviour is better addressed, and more likely to be reduced, by improved education and training, and by clinical governance and management supervision.

The experience of the former patients

31.9 It may assist in any research into the use of chaperones – human or virtual – if the alleged experiences of the former patients of William Kerr and Michael Haslam are considered as test examples. If what they say is true, how would the offer and provision of a human or virtual chaperone have reduced the risk of the abuse occurring? Looking at the issue from the other direction, how would the offer and provision of a human or virtual chaperone have protected the doctor from the risk of a false allegation being believed and acted upon?

31.10 In looking at the experience of the former patients, it is also clear (as already noted) that some of the allegations refer to places where the provision of a chaperone may be considered impracticable – the home, the doctor's car, or any place not properly described as a consulting room or similar. Further, the provision or offer of a chaperone has no impact on contact by the psychiatrist *after* and away from the therapeutic meeting.

31.11 Where, however, the examination is in a consulting room – or similar – and is known to involve any form of intimate examination, there is little doubt that the presence of a chaperone – or at least the recorded offer of a chaperone – does have value, and may serve to limit the potential for abusive behaviour, or assist in the resolution of allegations that an assault took place at a particular time and place when a chaperone (human or virtual) was present. But with a one-to-one consultation with a psychiatrist, when there is no expectation that there will be a physical examination, the need to offer a chaperone seems to us unnecessary and even likely to interfere with the therapeutic process.

31.12 On balance, therefore, we are not satisfied that the risk of sexualised behaviour by a consultant psychiatrist (although this may be subject to the outcome of any studies on prevalence) could justify the disturbance and cost arising from the constant availability of trained chaperones.

31.13 We do not see any basis, on the evidence to the Inquiry, for making the provision of human chaperones compulsory.

31.14 Many former patients clearly expressed a need to know what to expect when attending for a consultation with a mental health professional. They identified that, had the consultation been explained in outline form through an information leaflet sent with their appointment, they would have known what to expect. This seems to us to be a widely held concern, and worthy of serious consideration.

When a human chaperone should be offered

31.15 Given our Terms of Reference, we focus here exclusively on the role and conduct of mental health professionals.

31.16 In our view, the key areas of concern are in relation to patients who are receiving psychiatric treatment where a physical examination by a psychiatrist is required, where there is risk of a loss of consciousness or where the treatment includes any kind of physical therapy by a psychiatrist. In those situations, we believe there may be a potential risk – of both misunderstanding and/or boundary violations. Where it is known or expected that there will be an intimate examination by a psychiatrist, we would expect there to be a trained chaperone offered. Based on the evidence to the Inquiry, this is particularly the case where the psychiatrist is male and the patient female.

31.17 A patient has the right to refuse to accept the offer of a chaperone. We would expect to see any refusal by the patient of such an offer recorded in writing. There may be circumstances where the psychiatrist could reasonably refuse to see the patient without the attendance of a chaperone, for example where the patient has a known history of making demonstrably false allegations against healthcare professionals, or a clear history of perpetrating sexual abuse.

31.18 Applied to the facts established by our Inquiry, we would expect to see the use or offer of a trained chaperone where there is any intimate examination, of the breasts, genital or rectal areas, as a precursor to psycho-sexual therapy – assuming that it is accepted, professionally, that such a physical examination can be carried out by a psychiatrist.

31.19 Where a chaperone should be offered, failure to offer should be seen as unacceptable behaviour, and the non-availability of a chaperone no excuse. We would not expect a support person, such as a relative or friend of the patient, to be an acceptable substitute for a trained chaperone.

31.20 If it is accepted that a chaperone should be offered, then we would expect that trained chaperones will be available so that a proper offer can be made. This is not an area (if there are any areas) where a token offer is acceptable.

31.21 We repeat – we would not expect (as any form of requirement) there to be an offer of a chaperone for a normal one-to-one consultation between a patient and a consultant psychiatrist.

Virtual chaperones

31.22 Virtual technology is already beginning to prove itself in other devices, such as the virtual chaperone – which comes in many guises, from fixed cameras to a portable "black box". The virtual chaperone is likely to comprise a digital video camera and a microphone that encrypt video and audio data directly on to DVD. This provides a permanent and accurate record of events in places such as consultation rooms in general practice or outpatient clinics, or by the bedside, when a healthcare professional may be on their own with a patient. The recording can be used by the patient or healthcare professional at a later date for review, or when impartial evidence is required at an internal inquiry or court case, thus removing the fallibility of human memory. The virtual chaperone can free up hours of staff time in situations where a chaperone is needed and can help protect staff from abuse and misunderstandings in situations where they have to work on their own. Medical and nursing students have already used the virtual chaperone as a training aid to record their performance, either in examination rooms or at the bedside. Later review gives accurate feedback and an opportunity for students to improve on their performance.

31.23 We have not heard enough evidence on this evolving area of technical development to be able to make firm recommendations in relation to "virtual chaperones" in mental health settings. However, it would be regrettable in the extreme if a device intended to offer a degree of protection to the patient led to the voyeuristic abuse by the psychiatrist, or even to the sale of the product on the commercial market.

Conclusion and recommendations

31.24 The offer and provision of chaperones (human or virtual) will not prevent the abuse by mental health service professionals of their vulnerable patients. We are not convinced that compulsory or mandatory chaperones can ever do more than limit the potential for abuse, or at least limit the places and occasions when it can take place. The cost and the disturbance to the psychiatrist/patient relationship is a price worth paying only where it is known that an intimate or personal examination is intended, or some form of intrusive physical treatment is required.

31.25 If there is to be the offer and provision of a chaperone (human or virtual), then we believe it is important for everyone to know what the relevant NHS chaperoning policy is and how it impacts upon psychiatrists (and other mental health service professionals) and their patients in any given setting. Human chaperones should be trained.

31.26 Local NHS Primary Care Trusts and any settings in which NHS patients are cared for should have clear and published policies and arrangements for the offer and use of chaperones. These policies should be based on, and consistent with, national policies and should be monitored through the usual process of inspection and review.

31.27 Only a patient with capacity should have the right to decline an offer of a chaperone. If an offer of a chaperone is declined by a patient with capacity, this should clearly be recorded in the patient's notes.

31.28 Reported breaches of the applicable chaperoning policy should be formally investigated through each Trust's risk management and clinical governance arrangements and treated, if determined as deliberate, as a disciplinary matter.

31.29 Responding to former patients' requests to know what to expect from a consultation:

We therefore RECOMMEND that mental health services should provide routine information to patients attending appointments on what to expect from a consultation with a mental health professional. This should apply to consultations in all settings, including home visits.

31.30 In the light of the recommendations of the Ayling Inquiry, we confine our recommendation to mental health services.

We therefore RECOMMEND that, where physical contact forms part of the consultation, or where there is a risk of loss of consciousness, there should be a national policy and implementation guidelines to safeguard patients and staff and support the maintenance of appropriate boundaries.

Chapter 32
Record keeping

Introduction

32.1   The topic of record keeping arises in the Inquiry in several ways:

- inaccurate medical notes/documents and how to challenge them;

- the obligation to make notes and keep a written record;

- the retention of records of untoward incidents – in this Inquiry, that can be restricted to the retention of concerns and complaints in relation to allegations of sexual abuse; and

- the destruction of records.

32.2   While all four issues touch on matters that concern the Inquiry, their resolution is not essential to our conclusions or recommendations to the Secretary of State for Health. However, in light of the strong views expressed by some former patients, we have included some comments on record keeping. We have no doubt that the obligation to make contemporaneous and accurate notes is key to a number of potentially problematical areas.

32.3   We note with agreement and approval the conclusions of the Ayling Inquiry on this point. A particularly relevant observation they make regarding the lack of adequate written contemporaneous records, and one that resonates strongly in our Inquiry in its consequential effect, is: "In consequence, a number of opportunities to take more decisive and long-term action were missed."

32.4   These topics deserve closer and much more detailed scrutiny. The pool of data from which we are able to draw conclusions and make some recommendations is limited. We have no doubt that across the NHS there is sufficient, probably substantial, material on which to base a full and accurate analysis of the whole area of record keeping. We recognise that there are resource issues to be considered both in financial and workforce terms. We all have heard anecdotally of the time that nurses and doctors spend filling in forms and the consequential loss of time that can be spent "on the front-line services" for which they essentially are trained. But the consequence of not keeping full and accurate records, and thereby not retaining information, can be dramatic in terms of subsequent lack of action. We accept the need for balance but are sure that a full and analytical examination of the issue of record keeping will be a positive and beneficial activity that has important results in the longer term for patient safety and clinical accountability.

Inaccurate medical notes/documents

32.5   A theme of the evidence from the former patients was the allegation that both William Kerr and Michael Haslam would alter a patient's records to suit their own ends, or, if not expressly alter the records, write self-serving letters and make self-serving entries on to the record so as to protect themselves and/or paint the patient (who may complain) in an unfavourable light. On one occasion, it was alleged, a letter was written to a patient's GP describing how a recent appointment had been followed up by a telephone call in which the patient was said to be feeling much better. It is said that the telephone call had never taken place. The visit on the preceding day had ended with the patient leaving after an alleged sexual assault and indicating that she was not going to return. If this is right, then the false record can only have been created to afford some defence if it were subsequently suggested that anything untoward had occurred during the appointment (along the lines of "It cannot be true; if it were, then surely the patient would not have engaged in a civilised conversation with me the following day..."). There were many other examples, raised by many patients.

32.6   The concerns have led the former patients to invite us to make recommendations which may result in changes in practice and in the law.

32.7   We regret that it has not been possible for us to determine whether or not the medical records, letters, etc, were accurate or false. We have our suspicions about some documents, but, proceeding on the assumption that William Kerr and Michael Haslam would both contend that all records were accurate, all entries reflected what actually took place and all letters were entirely truthful, we could resolve any conflict only by investigating the truth of the underlying allegations of sexualised behaviour and sexual assault – which, for reasons already explained, we were unable to do. We did consider and examine some original records to see if we would be assisted by expert forensic evidence, but we concluded that there was no clear-cut example of the possible alteration of records to justify such assistance.

32.8   We regret that this factual area of concern must, therefore, remain unresolved.

32.9   There have, in any event, been substantial changes in the law relating to a patient's right to have access to his/her medical records under the Access to Health Records Act 1990 and the Data Protection Act 1998. These statutes, in part originating from EU law and fundamental human freedoms guaranteed by the European Convention on Human Rights (ECHR), have led to the publication of Department of Health documents such as the *NHS Openness Code 1995* and the *Model Publication Schemes for Strategic Health Authorities and Primary Care Trusts* in 2003. Most, if not all, NHS health authorities now have their own detailed codes and policies explaining how medical records can be accessed, and by whom. If those laws and policies had been in place in the 1970s and 1980s, then perhaps some of the former patients' concerns would have been addressed – although, we accept, not all.

32.10   The Inquiry believes that future records management standards should include the requirement to ensure that robust tracer systems are in place. There should be one set of multi-professional records stored in a designated place for the correct period (20–25 years).

32.11   It is impossible to legislate against deliberate falsification of health records – as it is where there is any human input. Doctors and other healthcare professionals must be trusted to make accurate records and write accurate letters. Failure to do so will, no doubt, have severe disciplinary consequences.

32.12   A particular concern of the former patients is that there should be a right for a patient to call for the correction of inaccurate information in medical records. Of course, errors do occur in medical records – caused by all the pressures of working in a high-stress environment, inattention caused by tiredness, distractions, simple carelessness, etc.

The right to call for corrections of factual inaccuracy – and it must be limited to factual inaccuracy, rather than a mere difference of medical opinion – may be of value. But, in the case of alleged deliberate falsification or the addition of self-serving information, we can also see the administrative and organisational downsides, such as – and we here mention only one concern – who is to decide that the information is inaccurate where there is doubt or conflict.

32.13 The present NHS position on correction of inaccurate health records is that clear factual inaccuracies can be corrected, but unaccepted professional opinions cannot. Application can be made to the Information Commissioner in cases of disputes that have not been resolved under the local NHS complaints procedure.

32.14 We here set out the former patients' suggested recommendations – but only so that they can be considered when the existing regime is reviewed.

- Patients should be provided with copies of correspondence sent to and from their GPs. We are advised that this now happens through the Letters to Patients initiative (as outlined in the NHS Plan).

- Where it is proposed that a domiciliary visit is to be made, then that fact must be included in the referral letter and in any letter of appointment that emanates from the consultant in question. As we understand it, the latter probably occurs already.

32.15 In light of our inability to investigate the truth of the former patients' concerns relating to the alleged fabrication of their healthcare records, we are unable to make any recommendations.

We therefore RECOMMEND that the NHS should review current records management practice and ensure that a robust set of systems and practices are uniformly applied across the service.

The obligation to make notes and keep a written record

32.16 The evidence to the Inquiry revealed that there was confusion as to when, how, and where to keep the record when there was disclosure of sexualised behaviour. This confusion extended across the board – within GP practices and within NHS management at all levels, also including related organisations/agencies such as social services. It was abundantly clear to us that there was no universally applied system for the recording of complaints and/or disclosures.

32.17 As to the maintenance of records, we heard disturbing accounts of haphazard and highly individual methods of maintaining "personal" or "private" records of complaints. In almost every case, those records would have perished when the record maker moved on, because the information had not been shared with any other members of the health service. Note taking should be simple and straightforward – it is, or at least should be, elementary that notes are made as near to contemporaneously as possible, and signed and dated. There does not seem to us to be any justification for a person employed by the NHS (at whatever level) to make "private" notes relating to patient treatment or patient matters more generally.

32.18 For GP practices, the evidence suggests that – in general terms – in the 1970s and 1980s there was no accepted practice. Occasionally, but only occasionally, it would be the patient who decided – requesting that nothing should be written down. But, more often, it was the GP's decision not to make any entry into the medical record – or make any note at all, anywhere. The explanations advanced for not making an entry included the following:

- The patient did not want it recorded.

- The GP was not sure if it was true.

- It might lead to repercussions for, or even from, the consultant.

32.19 Even where an entry was made in the medical notes, it would be so cryptic as to be of little value. An example that illustrates this is Dr Wade and Patient A22. There, it was accepted by Dr Wade that his patient had made a disclosure to him of intrusive sexualised behaviour by William Kerr. The disclosure was sufficiently clear and detailed to enable him to pass on the concern to Michael Haslam. Even if it is accepted that Patient A22 did not want a detailed record to be entered in her medical notes because of concerns that William Kerr might use the evidence against her, it is unfortunate that Dr Wade made no written record that there had been any disclosure at all of sexual impropriety but added only the neutral and slightly cryptic comment "rational and still coping". Other GPs would make a private note, kept separate from the medical notes, but this was random – and the note could not be retrieved. A concern, perhaps understandable, was that the information would be seen by prying eyes – by the practice secretary, receptionist or cleaner. We say understandable, but this is no excuse for not setting up or providing a system (a safe, for example?) where notes that are considered particularly sensitive could be kept. The overall impression is of a slapdash, ill-thought-out, confused and inadequate response, indicating that the matter was considered to be relatively unimportant.

32.20 Turning to the position with social workers, Margaret Jones made an interesting observation about note keeping. This is taken from her oral evidence to the Inquiry:

> *A. I did not even write anything. We kept our own social work notes. And because this to me was so important, I did not even write notes about it. We never, of course – I think I should make this clear – social workers never ever wrote in the medical notes. They were nothing to do with us. We kept our own case notes.*
>
> *Q. Some might say that the fact that it was so important would have pushed you in the direction of recording it rather than not recording it.*
>
> *A. No, because I was worried that it could get back. I mean, I trusted our secretaries absolutely, but who was to say, with a rather tasty titbit like Dr Haslam sexually abusing a patient, that it could not have got out somehow. And I just did not want him to be in any way forewarned.*
>
> *Q. Forewarned that there was a complaint?*
>
> *A. That there was a complaint.*
>
> *Q. So it was not to do with a concern about, as it were, tittle-tattle – I know it was much more serious than that – or gossip being spread amongst hospital staff, it was about keeping information from Michael Haslam?*
>
> *A. Also, though, keeping the patient's confidentiality. It had not been easy for her coming and talking about this.*

*Q. There was no, in your mind, secure place where you could
have kept any record of what had happened?*

*A. I did not think I would forget. But it was unusual, I admit,
not to write things down. But I am pretty certain – all our notes
that were left at Clifton Hospital have long since been destroyed,
but I do not think I did write this up.*

32.21 Whether for the best of motives (avoiding any unsavoury detail
appearing on a patient record) or the worst (a concerted cover-up),
a failure to make a record leaves a "gap" in a patient's history.

32.22 We accept the submission made on behalf of some of the former
patients that proper note taking is necessary for a number of reasons:

- The expressed belief that the clinician to whom a disclosure had
been made would somehow always be available to explain or
assist a disclosing patient and that there was in consequence no
need to consign a complaint to paper is misconceived. As we have
seen, particularly in the case of mentally disordered patients, it
may be a long time before they are well enough to articulate fully
their concerns, or be strong enough to give evidence in criminal or
disciplinary proceedings. The reliability of their accounts may well
be more readily accepted if there is a record of a
contemporaneous, or near-contemporaneous, disclosure.

- A failure to record a complaint may result in that patient being
referred back to a doctor against whom a complaint has been
made. If the complaint had substance, then there is potential for
further abuse; if not, then it is likely that the doctor–patient
relationship has broken down. In neither situation would a further
referral be advantageous. As the personnel in GP practices
changes, any clinician who has future responsibility for the care
of the patient will need a full picture in order to ensure that any
referral or treatment provided is appropriate.

- The proper noting of complaints is the touchstone and foundation
of a proper complaints procedure. In a process before any panel
of inquiry (NHS or GMC) that may well conclude with disciplinary
action being taken, it would be wrong to rely only upon an oral
recollection of disclosure, perhaps made years before.

- The very fact of noting a complaint indicates that it has been taken seriously and should serve to give a patient confidence that the doctor to whom a disclosure has been made is taking it seriously.

32.23   We do not underestimate the importance of patient confidentiality. What of the right of patients to dictate what goes into, or does not go into, their medical records? We question whether there is such a "right" – the record, although containing confidential information, is surely the NHS Trust's, not the patient's. The fact that the patient has rights of access to those records under current legislation does not obviously undermine this analysis. However, where it is known that a patient may insist that the disclosure of any alleged sexual or other abuse should not go into the "normal" medical records, then there is scope for investigating whether all GP practices and hospitals should have in place a standard procedure for recording and retaining such disclosures elsewhere.

32.24   Our concern here is that the NHS should consider how to stop unresolved issues or suspicions of malpractice from "disappearing" – especially in times of reorganisation or restructuring of services.

32.25   Former patients of William Kerr and Michael Haslam invited us to include the following as part of our recommendations:

> *"Where any disclosure or complaint is made to a doctor or nurse, then it must, subject to the exception below, be noted in three separate places. In each place the record will be updated to reflect the progress of the complaint and any action that has been taken. Firstly, on the personnel file of the clinician against whom the complaint has been made; secondly, in the patient's own medical records; thirdly, in a log held by the hospital or GP practice where the complaint/incident was received. It is only in this way that complaints/incidents can be properly tracked regardless of the movements of either clinician or patient. The one exception to the above procedure arises where the subject matter of the complaint is so sensitive that it would be prejudicial to record it in the patient's own notes. Thought should be given to the maintenance of a specific log in each practice where such complaints could be recorded rather than in the patient notes. Thought should also be given to asking a patient to initial or sign a note of complaint. Where a patient refuses to sign the note, then the practitioner should record the reasons behind the refusal."*

32.26 We consider that that level of detail is not appropriate for a recommendation in this area, and would prefer the matter to be left more open. Accordingly:

We RECOMMEND that, within 12 months of publication of this Report, the Department of Health should issue guidance as to how and where any disclosure or complaint of abuse by another healthcare professional made to a doctor or nurse should be recorded (if at all) in the patient's medical records and elsewhere.

Storage and destruction of records

32.27 We have already outlined that few contemporaneous records of complaints have survived. Complaints records during the 1970s and 1980s were kept as separate paper-based systems in administrators' filing cabinets, at all the administrative levels operating within the NHS at the time.

32.28 Constant reorganisation of the NHS and the movement of senior managers as a consequence have contributed to the loss and unwitting destruction of documents that, if retained and brought together, may have revealed patterns or trends. Patterns of similar complaints have eventually been established through a comprehensive review of documents available to the Inquiry. It is relevant to ask whether this pattern may have been established much earlier on within the NHS in North Yorkshire if there had been clear standards maintained by all on the storage of complaints records, particularly unresolved, unproven complaints. In the electronic age this should be easier. However, electronic complaints systems within the NHS today are often stand-alone systems, some, though not all, linked to incident reporting systems. These are not presently linked to either electronic patient or staff records.

32.29 While clear standards relating to the retention of patients' clinical records exist and are monitored through external assessment, such as controls assurance and the clinical negligence scheme for Trusts, it would appear that no such standards apply to the storage or destruction of complaints or incident information, or of staff records once the individual is no longer employed in the organisation. If they do exist, they are not widely known about. It has not come up as a topic already addressed within the NHS.

32.30 Records management strategies and standards have been developed in Trusts as a result of controls assurance assessments. Future standards must ensure that there is clear guidance on the storage and destruction of complaints and incident information and consider how that links to patient and staff records.

32.31 Unproven allegations may need to be retained for a defined period, with relevant parties aware of where or how this information is being kept and for what purpose.

Collection and interpretation of information

32.32 It is clear that there was little systematic collection of data or a culture of interpreting trends and using information as a routine part of clinical practice, governance and management of individuals or services.

32.33 This situation has been transformed and, through the use of computerised information, NHS organisations are now able to monitor trends in relation to complaints, look at a range of data relating to the individual practice of consultants through appraisal, and use information to safely manage the system. In the case of William Kerr and Michael Haslam, in addition to monitoring trends in complaints and incidents over time, it would also have been beneficial to monitor both out-of-hours visits – both domiciliary visits and outpatient appointments. Had such simple information been gathered, then the behaviour of the doctors may have been detected.

32.34 NHS organisations today need to satisfy themselves that all these eventualities are covered in routine data capture.

The retention of records

32.35 This topic is linked to the topic of storage and destruction and is to be considered in the context of an Inquiry that has been conducted against the background of many of the documents that would have assisted us having been lost.

32.36 The following submissions made on behalf of the local NHS authorities is a fair summary of the overall position in relation to lost documents, and of the caution we must exercise:

"It is inescapable that thousands of documents have been lost. The 1991 dissolution of the then Regions led to comprehensive destruction of documents at regional level. Hardly anything relevant survives (save for some documents from the legal department in late 1987/early 1988). Dr Green accepted that he had destroyed some documents when Yorkshire Region ceased to exist. Dr Turner denied destroying documents when he left his post in 1987. For whatever reason, by 1988 documents were not available at Region that recorded all previous dealings with Dr Haslam. Yorkshire, like the whole of the NHS, was 'an organisation without a memory'. Repeated reorganisations have led inevitably to the loss of files and documents.

"The difficulty for the Inquiry is that it has, in many cases, only a partial account of a sequence of events, distorted by the accident of whose documents remain, and who is alive and able to remember and comment. The panel will no doubt exercise great caution before making findings of fact where documents are missing and memories are poor, particularly when a witness believes that records were made at the time."

32.37 We were invited, again by the local NHS authorities, to conclude that "there is no evidence of any deliberate destruction or concealment of documents by any NHS personnel for the purposes of cover-up". We are satisfied that the submission is correct insofar as it extends to NHS management witnesses, such as Dr Green, and others at district and regional level. Documents were then held in an unsatisfactory way, and destroyed in an unsatisfactory way. In part, the reason the NHS was then "an organisation without a memory" was because individuals created and retained their own documents, and felt free (perhaps even obliged) to destroy those documents when they quit their posts or when there was a relevant reorganisation. This culture was recognised by senior managers giving evidence.

32.38 But, although unable to reach conclusions about which we can be confident, we are deeply suspicious about the way William Kerr, and Michael Haslam, treated the medical records of their patients, and that suspicion extends to their friends and supporters.

32.39 We heard evidence suggesting that medical records were removed from hospital care. For example, we are wholly unpersuaded by Michael Haslam's explanation as to how he came to be in possession of the original hospital records for a patient – apparently withdrawn from hospital files by, or on behalf of, William Kerr. Indeed, there is a strong suspicion that on this occasion William Kerr and Michael Haslam were working together to remove the medical records of a patient who it was believed was intending to pursue a complaint against Michael Haslam.

32.40 Another example relates to the conduct of Senior Nursing Officer Ann Tiplady, which calls for special mention. Her evidence was that she had retained a number of patient documents after leaving the NHS but that she had then destroyed them in about 2001. Her actions were of concern to the former patients for two reasons:

- firstly, that it appears she kept copies of private personal medical records; and

- secondly, that despite the fact that the criminal prosecutions were public knowledge well before 2001, she nevertheless destroyed the records without considering that they ought to have been surrendered to the police.

32.41 We share those concerns. We find it difficult to see any innocent explanation for Mrs Tiplady's removal of the records in the first place. It is to be presumed that she considered them sufficiently important to take with her, either to use in her defence or to her advantage at a later date, or for some more mundane reason. Why destroy those documents when the police inquiry and prosecution were common knowledge rather than simply hand them over to the police? The inescapable conclusion, no innocent explanation having been advanced, is that the documents would somehow have damaged her. It is regrettable in the extreme that these and other documents were not available to the police or to the Inquiry – and this was directly caused by the actions of a former NHS employee.

A national database?

32.42   As the system of specific complaints merges with systems intended to produce information from concerned professionals, it is inevitable that more and more will be known (or at least recorded somewhere) about a doctor's performance and conduct.

32.43   An example of a recent development in this rapidly changing picture is that, in early 2005, the database known as the National Reporting and Learning System (NRLS) was introduced by the National Patient Safety Agency (NPSA). That database, according to the Chief Medical Officer (CMO), aims to help the NHS understand the underlying causes of incidents and act quickly to introduce practical changes to prevent harm to patients.

32.44   Health professionals can make reports to the NPSA via two routes. The first is through their own Trust reporting systems, and onward to the NPSA via local risk management systems linked to the NPSA database. The second is directly to the NPSA by completing an electronic form on its website. Reports through this route can be shared with the Trust or sent anonymously and only to the NPSA. All names are removed before the information is stored in the database, and the NPSA is not able to investigate individual cases. This enables themes to be identified but individual cases will not be followed up. We see no reason why such a reporting system should not be extended to cover all allegations of sexualised behaviour, or other patient abuse, if these are not already included.

32.45   One of our main concerns, arising from the evidence we have read and heard, is not only that patients were not listened to, but also that there was little attempt to connect pieces of information received. There were many opportunities missed to pick up concerns and complaints about the practices of William Kerr and Michael Haslam.

32.46   We have been informed that information is not held centrally on the nature and content of individual disciplinary investigations carried out in the NHS. A database, wherever it is kept, which is confined to criminal convictions or GMC "convictions", would not address the concerns arising from our Inquiry. As noted elsewhere in this Report, the solution may be found in clinical governance, rather than merely in disciplinary or similar formal structures, but again that does not address concerns in relation to the retention of data. The lessons learned from the Soham Inquiry[1] are that information that does *not* result in a conviction may be highly relevant in decisions relating to the care of children – it is difficult to see why a similar approach should not apply to doctors (perhaps particularly psychiatrists) who are entrusted with the care of the sick and otherwise vulnerable. We note here the evidence to the Inquiry by the CMO:

> *"As part of good clinical governance arrangements, it is important that any complaint about an incident or about care provided by an NHS body is properly investigated, so that the root causes of any problems are identified, fully understood and lessons learned. Sexual misconduct, in the overwhelming majority of cases, is a repeated behaviour which is likely to have existed for some time before misconduct or even criminal allegations are made. Good and comprehensive local clinical governance arrangements are therefore of particular importance in this field."*

32.47 We agree, but without a record of the details and outcome of any such investigation (a record held nationally and capable of surviving yet another reorganisation of the health service), the information may soon be lost – or at least lost during the professional lifetime of the doctor. When, or if, concerns re-emerge in relation to that doctor – assuming that the investigation does not lead to a criminal conviction or GMC proceedings – the concerns may be seen by the new investigator as entirely new.

32.48 We join with local NHS health authorities in welcoming, and supporting, the recommendation for a national database (Shipman 5, paragraphs 27.142–9). We agree that there should be a national, central database containing information about every doctor working in the United Kingdom – not only those who work in the NHS. In our opinion, that database should be independent from, although no doubt linked to, the equivalent site operated by the GMC. It may be that the existing electronic staff record could form the basis of their record, or it may already be capable of being extended to serve this function.

32.49 In relation to the NRLS database, mentioned above, the main and obvious defect, of course, is that the information on the NRLS

---

1 *The Bichard Inquiry Report.* London: The Stationery Office, 2004.

database is anonymised – apparently *all* names are removed, including the identified doctor. That cannot be the position if existing and future patients are to be protected from a foreseeable risk of harm. The database must not only record the concern (and any outcome, or other relevant information) but also be accessible by a closely controlled group – for example, NHS employers at an identified level, the police, the Healthcare Commission, the GMC, etc.

32.50 The national database, if it is to be an effective answer to the concerns raised in this Inquiry, must be extended to cover more than just records of disciplinary action, outcomes of complaints, etc. It must cover some of the kind of concerns that have featured in this Inquiry, even if they are not given the status of formal complaints and even where there is no patient willing to be identified. It may be that the solution is that the database merely collects together, in a single file, all information about a doctor – regarding not only complaints but also appraisals, inquiries, concerns and other performance issues. In this way, "soft" information can also be recorded, and action taken at the earliest opportunity to identify difficulties and practitioners who may be struggling. Appraisals may then take place against a wider range of information, and, if suspicion of criminal conduct comes to light – either from the database, or in the course of any subsequent NHS investigation – early contact can be made with the police.

32.51 We recognise that such a database raises important, even fundamental, concerns about the storage and retention of information, and the rights of the doctor (or other healthcare professional) to whom the data relates. It is to be hoped, and indeed expected, that doctors – concerned about patient safety and the restoration of patient trust – will cooperate with and embrace such data collection. We urge all doctors to cooperate.

32.52 We see those who have responsibility for the care of mentally disordered patients as being in a special category, and at least that group of NHS staff should be prepared to accept voluntarily that unresolved concerns and complaints should remain recorded and retained. One witness to the Inquiry put it in somewhat wider terms, which we find helpful:

"I think where professionals have privilege, and doctors and other healthcare professionals have a number of privileges in terms of dealing with people who may be very vulnerable and at risk, then I think there should be perhaps different criteria applied from the normal personnel rules. If there are situations where patients and clients make allegations and those allegations cannot be fully investigated, for whatever reason, or cannot be closed, that then indeed some record does need to be kept. I think that has to be in a separate file."

32.53 For it to be an effective tool in protecting patients with mental health problems, consideration should be given to the final national database being extended to all mental health professionals – not just doctors. This is perhaps not unrealistic. We are informed that the government has already agreed to begin the setting up of a register of all those who are permitted to work with children in this country. The technical expertise is plainly available. No doubt, the government has obtained approval for this database from the Information Commissioner. We would expect that the Information Commissioner would be consulted further in relation to any database of the kind referred to above.

32.54 The setting up of any such database, and the necessary accompanying guidance, must also address (or at least have considered) employment and defamation matters. It is of course important that the guidance be clear and practical, so that there is a national understanding of what is required and consistent practice across the country in relation to the gathering and recording of information.

32.55 We here identify issues and questions, but do not attempt to resolve or answer them, which may need to be addressed when setting up such a database:

- When is a disclosure of sexualised behaviour to be regarded/treated as closed or resolved?

- Should the subject of such disclosure (the doctor or other mental healthcare professional) have a right to demand the removal of a closed or resolved disclosure?

- Should all disclosures of sexualised behaviour involving mental healthcare professionals and vulnerable adults (such as patients accessing psychiatric services) be passed on to the local police?

- If the answer to the previous question is "no", who within the NHS should make the decision not to pass on such information?

- When is a disclosure of sexualised behaviour made in relation to a mental healthcare professional to be shared on an inter-agency basis, and with what protections (if any) for the healthcare professional?

- In what way is the policy in relation to such a database to be integrated with the NHS policy concerning the abuse of vulnerable adults?

32.56   We do not here make a separate recommendation in relation to the setting up of a national database – that has already been considered in the Shipman Inquiry. Accordingly:

We RECOMMEND that a protocol should be produced and guidance issued within 12 months of the publication of this Report regarding the collection, collation and retention of data in relation to concerns and complaints covering sexualised conduct by mental health professionals – including, but not restricted to:

- **the name of the mental health professional;**

- **the details of the concern or complaint;**

- **the date of the alleged sexualised behaviour;**

- **the date of the concern or complaint;**

- **if investigated, by whom and with what outcome;**

- **if not investigated, the reason.**

Consideration should be given to the retention period of such data, stating our preference (subject to the advice of the Information Commissioner, and the terms of the Human Rights Act 1998) that such data be retained for the lifetime of the mental health professional. All NHS staff should be made aware regularly that this data is collected and retained.

Incident reporting and whistle-blowing

32.57 Current regulations contain a number of complex provisions dealing with the issue of who can complain. Their primary focus is on patients and other people who can make *complaints on their behalf.* Four main categories of people are currently able to make a complaint. The first three of these are:

- a patient;

- a representative the patient has nominated to act on their behalf;

- a suitable person with sufficient interest to act for the patient who is dead, a child or mentally or physically incapacitated.

32.58 It is for the "designated complaints manager", rather than the patient, to determine whether they fall within any of these categories. This leaves considerable discretion in the hands of complaints managers who may not be well placed to determine the exact nature of a patient's capacity or what constitutes sufficient interest.

32.59 In addition to the three categories of complainant outlined above, regulations allow a complaint to be made by any person affected by the action, omission or decision of an NHS body. This provision has the potential to encompass a much broader range of complainants. But the issue of whether or not it is intended to extend beyond challenges to commissioning decisions is not clear. If a liberal interpretation was intended, there appears to be no need to have such specific regulations relating to patients and others able to complain on their behalf.

32.60 The effect of these provisions is that the complaints system "individualises" complaints and focuses on the expression of grievances by patients' immediate families complaining on their behalf. It fails to recognise that relatives, carers and staff who have been intimately involved in the patient's care may have legitimate concerns as a result of their own experience rather than those of the patient. The tendency to focus on the patient was reinforced on several occasions in evidence to the Inquiry when patients were advised by their GP that the onus was on them to pursue their grievance by taking it to the police, the GMC, the formal complaints procedures (if any) within the hospital and, on one occasion, the particularly unhelpful advice was "tell it to a woman's magazine". It is not then surprising that complaints were few and far between.

As one GP put it to us – a view subscribed to by many other GP witnesses and noted earlier in this Report – "the prospect of discussing intimate details with a stranger at the CHC or a manager at a hospital was very daunting for many and prevented them taking their complaints further".

32.61 It is also the case that, if the onus is placed on patients to complain, many concerns about poor performance will not come to light. A number of William Kerr and Michael Haslam's patients were anxious about making a formal complaint or having someone else identify them as having concerns. In many cases they feared retribution if their identity was exposed. Instead they communicated their concerns to a member of staff in the NHS, often to their GP, and implicitly expected that that person would pursue the issues raised. In these circumstances, they were not nominating the GP or NHS staff member to act on their behalf, as anticipated by current regulations, as this would have involved exposing their identity. This is a particular issue for vulnerable patients who might not have the resources or confidence to make a complaint without the help and assistance of a champion.

32.62 A number of other members of staff became aware of concerns about William Kerr and Michael Haslam through their observation of patient behaviour and remarks made about these doctors by NHS colleagues. Nurses expressed concerns to their superiors that William Kerr had acted inappropriately with them. The focus in current regulations on patients and their representatives now fails to allow these staff to use the NHS complaints procedure. It becomes clear then that the current regulations exclude many people from making a complaint, who might be in possession of valuable information about poor performance, unless they have permission to act as the patient's representative. These include: members of staff; relatives, friends, or carers (who may have attended to the patient in hospital or are responsible for nursing care when the patient is at home); police officers; social workers; and patient interest groups concerned about a practitioner's performance across a number of NHS Trusts or sectors. In some cases, the demand for patient confidentiality would require that investigations requiring the review of a patient's notes without their express permission would be unacceptable. This is not the case in instances in which it might be possible to establish the credibility of a complaint in other ways, such as reference to clinical audit data or discussions with other staff working in the same unit.

32.63 In short, the current regulations are unduly restrictive about who can complain. They focus on a direct connection with the matters being complained about rather than issues of patient safety more generally. The procedure is initiated by those with a certain status rather than by those with certain information.

32.64 Adopting a more liberal definition of who can complain to the NHS would have a number of advantages. In particular, it would provide a single avenue through which concerns can be channelled and managed – it would focus attention on the message, rather than on the identity of the messenger. It would also provide a route for concerns needing further investigation before a view can be taken on whether a referral to another agency – such as the National Clinical Assessment Service (NCAS), the police, or the GMC – is appropriate. This is, however, undoubtedly less daunting and threatening than a direct referral to such bodies which may require more evidence before a prima facie case of poor performance can be established. (We make this observation however, with the caveat that very early contact with, and the involvement of, the local police liaison officer may be essential – particularly where the disclosure suggests any form of recent sexual assault.)

32.65 There are a number of ways in which NHS staff could facilitate issues being raised in the complaints procedure. Firstly, staff could provide those who have concerns with information about the NHS complaints procedure. Secondly, where it is clear that more support is needed, the members of staff could help the person frame their complaint or write it down for them. Thirdly, a member of staff could make a complaint on behalf of a service user. Finally, where the service user is reluctant to have the details of their case aired, the NHS staff member could consider whether or not it is in the interests of patient safety generally to air the concern themselves. The last option may involve the member of staff discussing the matter with colleagues or superiors and accessing additional data on performance. It may also involve some use of anonymised information – at least at the outset of any investigation.

We RECOMMEND that the current regulations relating to complaints procedures should be amended to enable any person with a concern about the safety and effectiveness of the NHS to be allowed more readily to use the NHS complaints procedure. Further, the time limit applicable from the incidents complained of and the complaint being made should be relaxed.

Patient safety within the modern NHS

32.66 Following the well-established example of the airline industry, the NHS identified patient safety as the Number 1 priority. "Organisation with a Memory", launched in 2000, identified the importance of recording, analysing and learning from adverse healthcare events.

32.67 Following the establishment of the National Patient Safety Agency (NPSA) in July 2001, the NPSA established a common standard regarding a risk management process to be used throughout the NHS.

32.68 Risk management systems have been introduced as the key process to make patient care safer. This includes the reporting and analysis of incidents, scoring of the level of risk using a Risk Matrix, a clinical review of the incident and most importantly the learning of lessons.

Descriptions and definitions

Patient safety incident

32.69 The concept of a patient safety incident is an important one, as it could apply to a complaint made by a patient or an incident reported by a member of staff. Included in this description would be any unintended or intended incident which could have led or did lead to harm for one or more than one patient receiving NHS funded care. Incidents reported should include those defined by patients' carers, as well as staff.

Sources of patient safety incidents

32.70 Customer service research identifies one in eight incidents result in a *formal* complaint being made. Complaints in most companies, public or private, are seen as valuable sources of feedback/information upon which to improve services. However, if one in eight are the "tip of the iceberg" as suggested through research, reliable reporting of incidents by staff may result in an issue being addressed and risk reduced before a complaint is forthcoming.

32.71 The NHS today has well-established risk management systems. These are subject to regular external inspection for Trusts via WILLIS, the Risk Pooling Scheme and the Clinical Negligence Scheme.

32.72 Risk management is one of the seven elements of clinical governance and risk and safety continues to be one of the seven domains in the recently published *Standards for Better Health (2005), The New Healthcare Independent Regulators.*

32.73 The culture within every team, service and NHS organisation remains the vital ingredient determining whether or not there is a proactive approach towards reporting concerns and reducing risk and learning lessons.

32.74 Through their clinical governance arrangements, NHS organisations have to ensure that cultures are open and honest – reporting, analysing and learning. This is a considerable task requiring ongoing commitment and resources for continuous team and organisational development and improvement.

32.75 NHS organisations or organisations providing NHS funded care are also required to have policies in place for patients and staff to report concerns anonymously. This may be necessary because of illness or the fear of the loss of a service by a patient or fear of incrimination in relation to a member of staff.

32.76 Currently there is a facility for an anonymous concern to be reported through Incident Reporting Systems, for which there is a log. There is no such facility for recording an anonymous complaint, which may therefore result in an opportunity being missed.

Whistle-blowing

32.77 Colleagues reporting concerns about fellow colleagues has become much more widely accepted resulting from the shocking Bristol Royal Infirmary Inquiry and from the multiple deaths of vulnerable older patients in the case of Harold Shipman. The possibility that a committed professional could either intentionally or unintentionally harm patients is now more widely understood by the public, patients and professionals. There are signs that professional loyalty as previously understood is no longer an acceptable barrier to protecting patient safety.

32.78 However, although there is greater awareness across the NHS, actually raising a concern as a patient or healthcare worker is another matter. The patient giving the individual professional the "benefit of the doubt", or the professional "turning a blind eye" to something untoward, still occurs in the modern NHS despite the existence of whistle-blowing policies which have been introduced as mandatory in all Trusts since 1999.[2]

32.79 Trusts' whistle-blowing policies identify examples where an employee making a disclosure must have *reasonable belief* that any of the following offences are likely to have been committed:

- A criminal offence is, has or is likely to be committed.

- A failure to comply with a legal obligation.

- A miscarriage of justice is occurring/likely to occur.

- Improper use of public funds.

- Endangering the health and safety of individuals.

- Damage to the environment.

- Malpractice or ill-treatment of a patient by a member of staff.

- Breach of standing financial instructions.

- Showing undue favour over a contractual matter to a job applicant.

- The concealment of any of the above.

32.80 Anyone raising a concern must therefore have a "reasonable belief", if they are entitled to be protected by the Trust.

---

2 Health Service Circular HSC1999/198: *Whistle-blowing in the NHS* was issued on 27 August 1999 (www.dh.gov.uk/assetRoot/04/01/21/38/04012138.pdf), as a result of the Public Interest Disclosure Act 1998 coming into force. The HSC states that every NHS Trust and Health Authority should have in place policies and procedures which comply with the Act. A policy pack *Whistle-blowing in the NHS* was issued to all NHS employers in July 2003 to help organisations successfully introduce whistle-blowing policies:
www.dh.gov.uk/PublicationsAndStatistics/Publications/PublicationsPolicyAndGuidance/PublicationsPolicyAndGuidance
Article/fs/en?CONTENT_ID=4050442&chk=OlSxEd

32.81 What is a "reasonable belief"? Whistle-blowers should have an honest and reasonable basis for suspecting that malpractice has occurred or is likely to occur; that they honestly and reasonably believe the information to be true and any allegation contained within it is substantially true; and that the allegation has not been made for personal gain. If an employee makes a disclosure in good faith, yet the disclosure is not confirmed by an investigation, then no action will be taken against them. If an investigation reveals the disclosure was made for malicious reasons, the individual may be subject to disciplinary procedures. Whistle-blowing policies outline clearly the procedure for reporting a concern, including ensuring the anonymity of the whistle-blower.

32.82 Although the list of offences in paragraph 79 includes reference to criminal offences, and to "ill-treatment of a patient", we would prefer to see specific identification of "sexualised behaviour" and abuse of patients. It is, in our opinion, too important a topic to be presumed to be included.

32.83 During our Inquiry, it was revealed that some courageous individuals spoke out and raised their concerns. Some did so being new into their jobs and not steeped in the culture of "the way we do things around here". One such person was, for example, Dr Simpson, a new consultant psychiatrist who identified potential abuse that was being experienced by patients. This doctor was able to raise concerns and suffered no detriment to his position. Others, such as Linda Bigwood, were not so fortunate.

32.84 Working side-by-side, staff are in a position to identify abnormal behaviour by their colleagues. Enabling staff to feel able to raise these concerns constructively, so that something is done and they (as the whistle-blower) are not victimised either by the individual they raise concerns about or the wider staff team, remains a challenge in the modern day NHS. Staff side organisations have an invaluable contribution to make and staff managers will require more training to effectively implement these policies.

32.85 It is one thing for a policy to be put in place and quite another to establish a culture that supports, enables and encourages staff to raise their concerns. Whistle-blowing in small teams, such as group practices and geographically isolated areas, presents particular challenges.

32.86 Creating an easier, safer way for staff to do this without fear of victimisation is fundamental, and is one of the basic aspects of an organisation's culture that must be operating effectively. This will result in issues being dealt with earlier and potentially with less severe consequences. If these systems are in place, alongside a fully functioning incident-reporting complaints system, audit and staff supervisory system, then organisations today will have greater capacity to listen and learn than those in place during the period under scrutiny in our Inquiry.

The Inquiry seeks assurance that whistle-blowing policies in place adhere to best practice and we therefore RECOMMEND that the Department of Health should review the effectiveness of whistle-blowing policies and initiatives within NHS-funded organisations.

32.87 Having heard all the evidence, the Inquiry also believes it is important for Trusts to have clear policies on disclosing personal relationships and consider the impact these can have on care delivery.

Sharing information with other agencies

32.88 Timing and understanding of other agencies' responsibilities is very important. NHS organisations are required to have jointly-approved Protection of Vulnerable Adults (PoVA) policies with social services and the police. The NHS should assure itself that such policies are in place, applied in practice, and regularly monitored and reviewed.

32.89 Sharing information with Vulnerable Adults Officers in both social services and police about alleged abuse sooner rather than later, will ensure adequate support for the victim/complainant and appropriate investigation of the complaint.

32.90 Involvement of the police in investigations will result in a record of any allegations made, the Inquiry understands, remaining on the individual's police record and would be identified through Criminal Record Bureau checks. This clearly has implications for future employment of staff, particularly where there have been disproved complaints made against them.

32.91 During the regional seminar in Part 2 of the Inquiry, we heard from Neil Thewsey of North Yorkshire Police who made the following points:

- Consider use of access to existing PoVA database of employees – a national staff record database.

- Write guidance for clinicians about what to report and how – based on experience of guidance of child protection reporting.

- Encouragement/guidance of professionals to report incidents to police – provide criteria, checklist or similar for so doing.

- Use expertise acquired through child protection work (those already trained and experience) in

  - interviewing, taking notes, ensuring the integrity of evidence which may be used in a later criminal process, and;

  - the use of telephone/internet helplines, poster campaigns and advocacy projects.

- Learn from and emulate the model used by police in establishing a "Sexual Assault Centre" which can hear and record evidence without reporting it to the police, but does ensure appropriate evidence available if a prosecution does eventually take place.

32.92 The Inquiry was grateful to receive this advice and fully supports the objectives, set out above, of using experience and good practice to ensure that record keeping facilitates the exposure of previous concerns and activities. Only by keeping a full and relevant record will NHS employers and managers be confident that patients are not at risk from the actions of individuals, in relation to whom there are serious concerns that they may endanger patient safety.

Chapter 33
Dealing with rumour: hearing the warning bells

Introduction

33.1   Gossip and rumour are difficult topics, but topics that need to be addressed. What we have already said, in Chapter 28, in relation to confidentiality is relevant. But here, we are not looking at precise, first hand, information – whether provided by the patient, or by doctors, or by members of NHS staff, but at information which may be unreliable, may be exaggerated, may be simply wrong, but may be an indicator of concerns in relation to a particular individual.

The value of gossip and rumour

33.2   We are fully aware of the dangers and limitations of gossip and rumour,[1] but in any social or professional organisation it exists, and may have some value. We take the following, simple, example from the evidence received by the Inquiry. A GP hears from a colleague that a consultant to whom the GP refers has a reputation for having sexual relations with his patients – a rumour, just gossip. The GP does nothing with that information – why should he/she do anything? A patient of the GP then discloses to the GP that she is having a sexual relationship with that consultant, or he has propositioned her, or the consultant has behaved improperly towards her, or he has even sexually assaulted her. What was merely gossip and rumour for the GP is now apparently supported by the account of the patient. The GP, otherwise reluctant to take the patient's disclosure seriously (for whatever reason) may then react completely differently, and proceed on the basis that that patient may be, even probably is, telling the truth. The following extract from the evidence of Dr Wade to the Inquiry provides an illustration of this process:

---

1   "From Rumour's tongues, they bring smooth comforts false, worse than true wrongs." William Shakespeare Henry IV, Part 2.

A. [William Kerr's] medical expertise we regarded as being good. But he did have a reputation of potentially flirting with some patients, and this was only a rumour… Certainly, until I had the complaint presented to me in 1979, I assumed that it was purely a flirtatious thing that he indulged himself in and nothing more serious than that.

Q. Presumably that was an understanding – "understanding" is perhaps too strong a word – but that was something of which all your partners were aware, not simply yourself?

A. I presume so, yes… I think it was inevitable that the tittle-tattle was repeated in the common room, yes.

Q. Taking that a stage further, some information the Inquiry has received has been to the effect that that reputation impacted upon the referral practices of GPs, in that some GPs might be reluctant to refer female patients to him. Were you aware of that sort of feeling?

A. Yes. This, I think, was evidenced in the way that I tried to dissuade Patient A22 from choosing Dr Kerr for a consultation… Looking back, I was aware that I tried to be selective in the type of patient that I referred.

Q. You would have done so in the knowledge of his reputation as being somebody who might try it on with a female patient?

A. Yes. What I had to do was to weigh up the option of the benefit that the patient would obtain by the consultation with him as opposed to not having a consultation, or some considerable delay and therefore exposing the patient to potential risk.

Q. It sounds almost like a risk analysis, weighing up the risk of being subject to flirtatious behaviour on the one hand against the speed of treatment on the other?

A. It was indeed, yes… it was the real horns of a dilemma.

Q. You remained on the horns of that dilemma for a number of years, by the sound of it?

A. Yes, indeed.

> *Q. As far as you are aware, that was equally the case with others... who practised at the health centre coming from other surgeries?*
>
> *A. And other Harrogate surgeries and Knaresborough surgeries, yes.*
>
> *Q. You must have had real concerns on those occasions where that dilemma took you in the direction of sending a patient to see him.*
>
> *A. Indeed... But I think that possibly a prime reason for this was that there was no protocol with which to deal with such a hideous happening... But so far as I am aware, we had no recourse other than to refer to the consultant that we were allotted in the health district.*

33.3   From the evidence we have received, there may also be an important link between a doctor's understanding of patient confidentiality and gossip/rumour – in the 1970s and 1980s, and even today. The way the link works seems to be as follows – a patient informs her GP that she is having, or has had, a consensual sexual relationship with her consultant psychiatrist; she does not allege sexual assault, or the commission of a crime; the patient insists that the information is kept confidential, and her involvement must not be identified (nothing must appear in the notes etc); the GP is very concerned with what he hears, but is confused as to what he can, or should do, the information being received in confidence; he does not want to refer other, potential target, patients to the consultant psychiatrist, and feels he has to do something with the information (although protecting the identity of the patient); he tells his partners that he has concerns about the sexual behaviour of the consultant psychiatrist, but cannot give any details. A rumour is born. Of course we do not ignore the need to proceed with caution – the patient may after all have heard the same rumour and may have been influenced by it.

33.4   A further "soft information" point was made to us by a patient advocacy organisation concerned about the barriers to changing clinical teams, arising from the growing sectorisation in the provision and delivery of mental health services. It is not a reference to gossip or rumour, but rather to actions – but the analogy is clear. The submission was as follows:

"The presence of such barriers to changing clinical teams increases people's vulnerability to abuse by psychiatrists, CPNs and others in the team. The ability to change clinical teams more easily would not only enable the patient to escape abusive clinicians, it would give a direct way for managers to notice areas of concern, whether or not this relates to abuse. For example, if large numbers of people were leaving one clinical team but not others it would indicate that there is some problem within that team that may need addressing."

33.5 We share common ground again here with the Ayling Inquiry Report, which pointed up the importance of clinicians monitoring the reasons why patients moved – in Ayling's case from his GP practice – to another clinician.

33.6 Gossip and rumour can provide the background against which subsequent action or inaction can be considered and tested. Indeed the detection of abuse may depend on response to rumour or gossip. The approach of an institution to such "soft" information as gossip, rumour, innuendo, informal soundings, expressions of concern etc, may also be relevant to how that institution sees its responsibilities within society. In Chapter 35 below, we consider the discipline and regulation of doctors; in Chapter 34 we address the issue of complaints handling. A shortcoming of the present system, in terms of discipline and complaints handling is that they both tend to operate on the basis that the issue being raised is solely about a possibly aberrant member of a healthcare profession, rather than about team failures or management failings, or even failings in the systems themselves. What inevitably happens, without a patient-focused approach (and by this, we mean patients generally rather than the individual patient who is the source of the complaint – if there is a complaint), is that the single issue is addressed (or not), dealt with, and then put away, and often forgotten. There is little or no "collective memory" – merely an unrelated, uncollated, collection of separate events. That may be an adequate response where the concern is performance based, or where the concern relates to delays in the delivery of care and treatment etc, but it is completely inadequate where there may be a risk to the wider patient community, a risk of positive harm by an undetected abusive professional. A narrow approach has the effect, unintended no doubt, of disregarding the NHS's wider responsibilities as employer and as provider of high-class, safe healthcare. But if there is a change of attitude, a change of culture – which we, and other Inquiries before us, advocate – then the handling of complaints, discipline, and related functions, fall within the wider and more forward looking agenda of clinical governance. If that approach is taken, then the staff and management of the NHS would be required (and would naturally) investigate all concerns about services and individuals, not just complaints by (or on behalf of) particular patients. Such investigations may not be formalised, probably often would not be formalised, but they would all have some form of outcome – new information, a new way of looking at an existing problem, identification of a new problem, confirmation of a concern etc – which should be of benefit to the organisation, and, if acted upon, of benefit to the patient and NHS staff population.

33.7   We have noted with agreement the research by M Rosenthal quoted in the Ayling Report at page 122:

> *"Problems can go on for a very long time. Other GPs may be suspicious but they don't want to delve too deeply because if they know too much, they will have to take action. So the problem may go on for a very long time. It has to be absolutely catastrophic and threatening patient harm for someone to interfere."*

33.8   A response to rumour and gossip can then be seen as a response by a listening organisation, by an NHS keen to know why that gossip (assuming it to be a wide currency, and relevant to the members of staff performance or dealings with patients) is circulating. It is accepted, as is clearly the case based on the evidence we have heard, that vulnerable patients, patients with low self-esteem, patients who may consider themselves responsible for what has happened to them, and who may be fearful of the consequences of speaking out, will often be reluctant to complain.

33.9   Psychiatric patients (whatever the severity of their mental disorder) are likely to be stigmatised, and likely to be the subject of some degree of discrimination – direct or indirect. But it cannot follow that they should not have a voice – that what they are able to communicate should not be listened to. Their concerns may come out as a word, as a worry, as something said in an informal context, even out of context. But it is those pieces of information that may well form the basis of the gossip, and rumours – the so-called "hidden fire which produces the smoke". If the gossip is rife, if the rumours are repeated, and they are focused on one or more healthcare professionals, and if the NHS places the safety of patients above other considerations, such as professional loyalty, then there must be some response to such information – the early warning bells must be listened to.

33.10 All of what we say in this chapter, indeed in the Report, is intended to focus on the *prevention* of sexual abuse of psychiatric (and other vulnerable) patients. The aim must be to reduce the risk factors we have seen. Within institutions, those risk factors are now relatively well understood. The following have been suggested to us:

- isolation;

- the inability to complain by non-capacitous, non-verbal, patients;

- poor physical layout;

- poor staffing;

- hostility to "whistle-blowing" even if officially encouraged and even required;

- poor attention to warning signs;

- tolerated bullying;

- tolerated rude and insensitive behaviour; and

- tolerated "attitude" problems.

33.11 But the problem of sexual abuse is not, has probably never been, confined to the institution, but occurs wherever there is opportunity – in the home, in outpatient meetings, within the community.

33.12 An adequate response to rumour and gossip must be seen, therefore, as but one step in the prevention of future wrong or poor behaviour – here, the possible sexual abuse of patients.

33.13 If rumour or gossip, or sufficient intensity or subject matter, comes to the attention of NHS management, then we do not see any reason why there should not be some response – by investigation, by interviewing, by meeting (and making a note of the meeting) the healthcare professional concerned (the subject of the rumour). If there is a cultural shift, if patient safety is the focus, and information-sharing truly encouraged, required, and welcomed, then it is inevitable that "soft" information will surface. In turn, doctors and other healthcare professionals, within this more open, less self-protective, culture will know that they may be the subject of the gossip and rumour that disclosure will throw up – they will then expect, and should be educated to expect, that they may be questioned as part of the entirely proper enquiry to ensure that there is no cause for concern. If there is no truth to the rumour, the investigation will produce nothing – but better safe than sorry. If, however, there is truth in the rumour – and it betrays some underlying problem in the doctor-patient relationships, the inquiry may produce more information, or at least may put the healthcare professional on notice that concerns have been expressed, and subsequent behaviour may (we emphasise may) be self-regulated. What the NHS cannot do is deny the existence of rumour and gossip, or deny – in some "we are above that kind of thing" manner – that it may have value. As the former patients put to us, and we accept:

> *"There should be in place a reporting and investigation system that stops short of requiring a form of complaint but is triggered by notification of a concern or 'rumour' even if a patient has not provided written evidence."*

33.14 We go further, and see value in the preparation of a policy and supporting guidance, that addresses gossip/rumour even if there is no identified patient at all.

33.15 Of course, because a consultant (William Kerr) has a reputation as a "ladies man" it does not follow, at all, that he assaults his female patients, or even has so-called consensual affairs with them. A married doctor can be a flirt with other members of staff, in a work or social context, without any concern that he/she is in any way acting in an unprofessional manner with patients. He may even be just that – a flirt. Because it is rumoured that "all is not well" in the practice of a consultant (Michael Haslam), and the rumours relate to sexual impropriety, it does not follow that he sexually assaults his patients, or actually behaves with any impropriety. But, when specific allegations are made, that background is surely relevant to the reaction of the recipient of the information who is also aware of the rumours? This is particularly so where the rumours and gossip only apply to that consultant, or to those two consultants as was the case in North Yorkshire for most of the time covered by the Inquiry.

We agree with the submission made on behalf of the local health authorities that the article by Sir Liam Donaldson, published in the BMJ on 14 May 1994, provides some support for this approach when he said:

> "... almost all the names of doctors that eventually arose formally were already known to me through this informal network as people who had been giving rise to concern over a period of time."

33.16 We recognise however that gossip and rumour must always be treated with caution. For example, Michael Haslam set up and ran a psychosexual clinic. It was hugely popular and had long waiting lists. Ray Wilk, then Director of Nursing Services (mental illness), described it as the "jewel in the crown" at Clifton Hospital. This suggested to the administrators that it was a worthwhile service. It was considered to be "forward-thinking". It may be that rumours about Michael Haslam were not taken particularly seriously because it was assumed they arose out of the fact that he ran the psychosexual clinic.

33.17 The "informal network" exists, in any institution, not just within the NHS. It is, and becomes, an important source of information – often more reliable than the "formal network" where information is very carefully recorded, so as not to cause offence, so as not to invite a reaction from the subject matter.

33.18 One witness to the Inquiry, Dr Patricia Cresswell (who was a member of the Manzoor Inquiry) told us that one of her concerns was that senior management had not done enough to keep themselves informed of the feelings "on the shop floor", stating that the junior staff who gave evidence to the Manzoor Inquiry said that "a lot of people were aware of the allegations against Dr Haslam and of rumours about him". Her own views (expressed in 2004) on the position today are relevant to discussion of rumours:

"Finally, I would like to say that I think it would be very difficult for a consultant such as Dr Kerr or Dr Haslam to engage in such systematic abuse of their patients within the NHS now. That is not to say things are perfect. I am concerned that there is still a significant knowledge gap between management knowledge and the knowledge of staff on the ground. I think that management today are better informed than they were in Dr Haslam's time, but I still do not think that they are as close to the ground as they would perhaps like to think they are. I am still not sure whether junior staff would feel able to go to senior staff about what were essentially rumours about the practice of doctors or consultants. I am not sure how such openness can be achieved, but would like to think that there was some way that management and more junior staff could be kept in closer touch."

33.19 Should gossip and rumour be recorded, and if so in what circumstances, where, by whom, and for how long? In Chapter 32 we set out our views of the sharing of information, suggesting that there is scope for a national depository, or database. However, we have concluded that hearing mere gossip, mere rumour (whether received by word of mouth, or in writing) should not (without anything more) be a trigger for a duty to report. We accept that a balance must be struck between patient safety and protection of a medical professional's, or indeed anyone's, reputation. A requirement to record gossip and rumour would go too far, perhaps far too far, in terms of a balanced approach to the problems identified in this Report.

The problem of malicious gossip and rumour

33.20 It would be naïve, however, to proceed on the basis that gossip and rumour are irrelevant. It would also be dangerous and unfair for a decision maker to act solely on such a fragile and unsupported basis – unfair to the medical professional, and unfair to patients who may be deprived of services, care and assistance of the medical professional. Any employment action, or disciplinary process, based solely on gossip or rumour would be wrong and dangerous, and would lead to challenges by the affected employee. Dangerous because gossip and rumour may be inaccurate, may have originated from a malicious or jealous source, may even relate to an entirely different individual.

The evidence

33.21 It was said to us by Counsel for some of the former patients that one of the hardest issues the Inquiry has to grapple with is the actual state of awareness within North Yorkshire of the problems posed by William Kerr and Michael Haslam. We agree with that statement. Fortunately, in our Report, we do not consider it necessary to resolve every single question of who knew what, and when they knew it. We have not heard from all GPs, all consultants, all social workers, all hospital staff, who worked with or for William Kerr or Michael Haslam during the 1960s to the 1980s. We have heard from many witnesses, most of whose professed ignorance of any rumours, even any gossip, in relation to either consultant, we accept. The representatives for the local health authorities produced a very detailed and impressive 88 page schedule setting out in helpful detail from the evidence to the Inquiry in "who knew what and when" format, references to the many witnesses (over 150) who had been asked about rumours, gossip etc. From that schedule, the submission was made that only just over 30 had heard either low-level, or more serious rumours in relation to William Kerr, and just under 30 for Michael Haslam. In relation to what the schedule refers to as "serious rumour" (rather than more generalised "chit-chat", and innuendo), the figures are four for William Kerr and 15 for Michael Haslam.

33.22 We accept that the evidence to the Inquiry does not show that here was a medical community, where all (or even the vast majority) knew of rumours or all shared gossip that these consultants were engaged in sexualised behaviour with their patients. We would have been astonished 1) if that had been the case, and 2) if it had been the case, that the witnesses would have told us so.

33.23 What we do find, however, is that it is likely that many members of the medical community did know that there was something seriously wrong in relation to the practices of both consultants – and by this we mean something far more concrete than "he's a bit of a ladies man", or "he is a flirt". It was generalised gossip, fuelled and informed by disclosures, expressions of concern, actual complaints, some of which (and we emphasise only some of which) we have heard. Further, as noted elsewhere in this Report and touched on below, we detected a worrying degree of tolerance of a consensual sexual relationship between doctor and patient, which may have blurred the overall picture. We have referred before to the false premise "it is not illegal, therefore we can do nothing".

33.24 We do not go so far as to accept the submissions made on behalf of some of the former patients:

- "that knowledge of allegations was relatively widespread as early as 1970 onwards"; and

- "there were perhaps one or two isolated instances where GPs and GP practices were not 'in the loop' but in all probability most GPs were aware of a least some degree of suspicion hanging over both men".

33.25 However, we do fully accept other points made on behalf of the former patients:

- "The disclosure and allegations were sensational and the communities were close"; and

- "Many of the witnesses who heard disclosures relayed them to other gatherings of GPs or heard the stories passed round the wards".

33.26 Broadly we agree with the part of the submissions made on behalf of the local health authorities that the correct factual conclusion is *"many people knew a little, some knew a lot"*, adding that many (rather than the "most" suggested) knew nothing. We take on board the health authorities' submission, that we should guard against extrapolating too much from limited information:

> *"Because evidence has been given, understandably, by those who did know something, the impression given is that most people knew something. That is not supported by an analysis of all the statements. Furthermore, the statements represent a tiny fraction of the people working in the relevant mental health services at the time. Again no doubt the Inquiry will guard against extrapolating too much from limited information."*

33.27 There is another danger, not mentioned in that passage. When the topic is as amorphous as gossip and rumour, it is to be borne in mind that there may be difficulties in separating out the gossip and rumours which predated the departures of William Kerr and Michael Haslam, and the gossip and rumour which started to circulate, or was picked up, after 1988/89, or even after 1997 when the news of the allegations first broke out into the public arena. This is particularly the case in relation to Michael Haslam, who left the NHS under odd circumstances in early 1989, and there was bound to be gossip based on the reason for his departure (or what was believed to be the reason).

33.28 But even taking account of the dangers, and avoiding inappropriate extrapolation, we are satisfied there were enough people who knew enough, to have done far more, if necessary, to protect the safety of existing and future patients by bringing their concerns to the attention of senior NHS management, possibly even outside the Region.

33.29 The content and prevalence of the rumour in relation to the practices of William Kerr and Michael Haslam is very difficult to pin down, or to date. One witness, Carmel Duff, gave a very worrying picture of the general level of understanding in relation to Clifton Hospital. She said that the team gave her the very clear impression that when she was describing Patient A50's alleged experiences of sexualised behaviour at the hands of William Kerr, she was disclosing to them nothing they did not already know. They were also aware that others had tried before to do something, but nothing had happened and, especially as William Kerr had already retired, nothing was likely to happen again.

33.30 That was 1994 – some years' after William Kerr's retirement, but three years' before the general investigation in 1997. It is entirely consistent with the evidence of Dr Givans – to the effect that he was aware "in the early 1990s" that there were rumours (emanating from other GPs) to the effect that William Kerr had been having sex with his patients. Dr Givans' oral evidence on this topic was odd. He told us that these rumours suddenly, from nowhere, arose in the early 1990s for the first time, and this was "definitely after William Kerr had retired". But he also told us that the rumours pre-dated the specific disclosure to him by Dr Osmond of Patient A37's story who alleged rape by William Kerr. We doubt the accuracy of Dr Givans' recollection on this topic. It is far more likely, based on other evidence we have heard and bearing in mind Dr Givans' position as Secretary of the North Yorkshire LMC, that he has mis-remembered the date of his knowledge. We strongly suspect that Dr Givans, and many other local GPs, were well aware of the gossip and rumour relating to

William Kerr's alleged behaviour, some time before his retirement – we suspect by the late 1970s or early 1980s.

33.31 Dr Clarkson's written evidence to the Inquiry concerned Michael Haslam and went back, so it would appear, to the mid 1970s and early 1980s:

> "I can recall rumours about Dr Haslam to the effect that he engaged in inappropriate sexual behaviour with his female patients. I cannot recall when I gained this knowledge or where from. I can simply say that I recall that there was tacit agreement within the psychiatric consultant community that things were not right with Dr Haslam's practice."

33.32 In his oral evidence to the Inquiry, Dr Clarkson accepted that he was aware of the rumours in relation to Michael Haslam's behaviour before he heard from Dr Foggitt – rumours which he described as follows: "The general opinion was that Haslam's behaviour with patients was less than appropriate". In other words, there was rumour and gossip – picked up by Dr Clarkson – as early as 1974, only four years into Michael Haslam's career in North Yorkshire. But Dr Clarkson did not pass on his concerns (to Dr Kennedy) for approximately six years, and it was a further eight years before anything of substance was done (but, as we have seen, even then there was no investigation). The position may have been very different if, in the 1970s or very early 1980s, there had been an inquiry or some more proactive response to the concerns that Michael Haslam's behaviour was "less than appropriate".

33.33 Another example from the evidence to the Inquiry serves to illustrate the point. Dr Rugg was a trainee psychiatrist at Bootham Park Hospital from 1973 to 1975. (He later returned to York as a consultant psychiatrist in 1982, taking over the responsibility for Michael Haslam's Harrogate patients.) Dr Rugg told us, in his written statement and confirmed in oral evidence, of gossip/rumour he heard at Bootham Park during that early period. In essence, the allegation was that "a female librarian had seen Dr Haslam as a patient, and there had been sexual contact during her consultations with Dr Haslam". No further details were provided, and Dr Rugg was "given the sense that no physical force had been employed but rather that there was coercion of the patient". Dr Rugg confirmed to us that he was shocked by the information, that he expressed the view at the time "that Dr Haslam's behaviour was not standard practice", but took no further action. Shortly after going into private practice in 1975, Dr Rugg received further information, further "gossip", being told by another GP in the practice "that he would not refer patients to Dr Haslam", because a female patient had been the recipient of a "flippant comment" that she should have an affair, "the inference being that Dr Haslam would be an ideal candidate".

33.34   On their own, these two stories could be seen as perhaps not very significant (others may take a very different approach), but linked to the information held by Dr Foggitt and Dr Clarkson, at about the same time, they raise real concerns – on any sensible view of the reliability of the information. The two stories heard by Dr Rugg may link in with the descriptions in Section 3 of the Report where we tell the Michael Haslam story in greater detail, or to the disclosures in the Linda Bigwood dossier – they may not. They are likely to have been picked up if any investigation, even on a superficial level, had been undertaken in the mid to late 1970s.

33.35   How does tolerance of sexual behaviour, already mentioned, impact on rumour/gossip? The Inquiry has devoted much time and effort in attempting to identify and understand the prevalent cultural aspects of the medical community in North Yorkshire in the 1970s and 1980s. We accept that there is unlikely to be a clear answer, one that applies to all GP practices, in all areas, during these two decades. But, and based on such examples as the Patient B4 and Patient A17 stories, we are satisfied that there was a degree of acceptance of alleged sexual contact between doctor and patient, and a failure to recognise the possible dangers (for the patient concerned and for other patients) of that alleged breach of professional boundaries. But that tolerance – even if not widespread, even if confined to Harrogate, or to Thirsk and Northallerton – was based on *knowledge* of the alleged existence of the sexual relationship(s). It was that tolerance, and that knowledge, which would lead to a GP such as Dr Crawfurd-Porter (even allowing for his larger than life character and reputation as a raconteur) being able to share with colleagues his view that William Kerr was involved in "unorthodox goings-on" with his patients (a comment confirmed to the Inquiry by Dr Moss). It is obvious to us, and we are sure would have been obvious to Dr Crawfurd-Porter's audience that these "unorthodox goings-on" were sexual. Rumour and gossip it may have been – but nevertheless, information that should have caused someone, somewhere, within the local NHS with any sense of the importance of patient safety, to have taken *some* action.

33.36 We do not accept, if this is suggested, that the gossip and rumour ended within a GP partnership – such a limitation would be wholly inconsistent with the realities of life in a fairly close medical community. The "soft" information was no doubt in circulation – in relation to both William Kerr and Michael Haslam – but the reaction from the members of the medical community in the know was likely to have been tolerance, perhaps even a degree of amusement. If there was any negative reaction, apart from those who took some action, it was limited to a feeling of unease – limited by instruction and injunction from the medical hierarchy at the time (from the GMC and from the local representative bodies) that it was a professional offence to criticise practitioner colleagues without firm, and convincing, evidence. We have here mentioned Dr Crawfurd-Porter as an example. We are satisfied that he was not alone; we treat with considerable scepticism the evidence from his former partners that they had no knowledge whatsoever of the William Kerr (or Michael Haslam) rumours during the 1970s and 1980s.

33.37 Although we have concluded that there were many members of the medical community who knew of, no doubt even helped to distribute, rumour and gossip in relation to one or other, or both consultants, we have sought not to criticise any particular individual for failing to take action on the strength of that information alone. But, taken as a whole, the picture that we have built up – and with the right enquiries others could have built up contemporaneously – is one of a general area of concern that required and should have produced some clear, positive action.

Conclusion and recommendations

33.38 This is not an area of our Inquiry where we feel able to make freestanding recommendations, confined to rumour and gossip. The local NHS authorities invited us to say at what precise point such information should be acted on, and at what stage a threshold is crossed when the recipient is not merely entitled, but obliged, to take some form of positive action.

33.39 The correct response will always be dependent on factors such as (1) the subject matter of the gossip, (2) the prevalence of the gossip, and (3) the source of the gossip. However, in an area of patient safety such as protection from sexual abuse – or abuse generally – particularly in relation to vulnerable members of our society, the early detection of incidents, and the early discovery of perpetrators may depend on or be materially assisted by a positive, and proactive response.

33.40 For that to happen there needs to be a change of culture, so that investigation is welcomed and expected by all, including but not restricted to the NHS staff member (whatever his or her seniority) who is at the centre of the rumour or gossip. In answer to the question – when should rumour, etcetera, be acted upon, and in what form should that action be taken – we can only invite further research into the fine tuning of the content of the positive obligation to inform NHS management of areas of concern. We therefore recommend that the obligation to investigate (certainly in the case of suspicion of the sexual abuse of possibly vulnerable patients) should not require a complaint from one or more named patients, or even identify a named patient. It may well be that the NCAS will be able to assist in the development of the obligation to investigate.

33.41 The NHS, as an employer of staff, will be rendered powerless in their task of protecting patients safely unless regulatory bodies also recognise the need to embrace and enforce such policy and guidance.

33.42 Accordingly:

We RECOMMEND that as a matter of some urgency the NHS should clarify the context in which NHS staff have a positive obligation to inform NHS management of concerns in relation to the suspicion of the abuse of patients.

We also RECOMMEND that policies and guidance should be drawn up to clarify the obligation to investigate (certainly in the case of suspicion of the abuse of possibly vulnerable patients) without the need for a complaint from, or one that identifies, a particular named patient.

Section Seven
New developments that need monitoring

Chapter 34
Complaints handling in the NHS

Introduction

34.1   We recognise that an institution such as the NHS is essentially driven by policies, procedures and protocols, and that NHS staff will act in accordance with – even, some might say, hide behind – them.

34.2   This chapter of the Report is, in the main, devoted to the existing NHS complaints system, and to any changes to that system we consider necessary. It considers a number of ways in which current NHS complaints procedures could be improved, and outlines the reforms that need to be implemented if the current system is to perform its key functions. Our primary focus is on the handling of complaints at service level, because the main problems highlighted by the Inquiry relate to the difficult issue of how the concerns or complaints of patients and others first come to be heard and investigated.

34.3   We proceed from the starting point that it is of course essential that a complaints system should be in place – providing an opportunity for patients and service users to raise their concerns in a fair and formalised way. The system should encompass a procedure whereby the NHS staff members who are the subjects of complaints can have a fair opportunity to protect themselves from unfounded criticisms. We accept, as do all who have taken part in the Inquiry, that there have been very significant changes to complaints procedures within the NHS – some very recent. We therefore approach this topic with some caution. It is a field well covered by recommendations in recent reports. We are loath to add yet further recommendations which may cast doubt on existing systems that have not yet had time to bed in and be fully tested. But there is an even greater reason for caution. Even a yet further improved complaints system will not, without more attention, produce answers to the following three central questions:

- What can now be done to ensure that consultant psychiatrists (or other mental health care professionals) do not behave in the ways alleged by the former patients in relation to the practices of William Kerr and Michael Haslam?

- If such alleged behaviour is repeated, what can now be done to ensure that the voices of those who raise concerns or complaints are listened to?

- If procedures are adequate, what can be done to ensure they are being used to best effect by NHS staff?

34.4   Clearly, an answer to the third question will assist in answering the second – but only if information received is processed and acted on. And that processing, and action, is likely to involve not only NHS management, but also other agencies such as the police, and regulatory bodies such as the GMC. But, as we have found throughout the Inquiry, the existence of a formal complaints system is not determinative. What is needed is a system for this kind of patient (often vulnerable, often mentally disordered), with this kind of concern (peculiarly sensitive and private) – a system that can encompass the situation where the patient, for a whole variety of reasons, is reluctant, or refuses, to make a formal complaint which may draw attention to her, her condition and her concerns.

34.5   As the former patients put it in submissions to the Inquiry, the problem at the time was not so much the lack of complaints systems – but rather that a number of factors combined to render the existing systems ineffective. Those factors were expressed as follows:

- ignorance among the staff of the proper part played by patient confidentiality. This resulted in many cases, and the safety of a substantial body of current and future patients, being jeopardised by a short-term desire to protect a single patient's confidentiality;

- ignorance of the procedures that were in fact in place. Very few of the staff or managers at any level were actually aware of the proper complaints procedures governing disclosures to them;

- opacity of the procedures that were actually adopted (whether they were proper procedures or not), together with a blurring of the chain of command, and responsibilities arising once a disclosure had been made;

- a failure to set up and follow a concerted plan of investigation following a disclosure to ensure that all possible leads were followed, all relevant witnesses were approached and all the issues raised were addressed.

34.6 We have addressed some of these issues elsewhere in the Report, but consider it important to ensure that in this area these central concerns are not lost:

- The NHS redress system (including the complaints handling sub-set of that system) must be known to NHS staff.

- The procedures must be clear, accessible and intelligible.

- There must be in place clear, readily accessible plans for any necessary follow-up when there is disclosure of allegedly abusive behaviour – even if there is no formal entry into the complaints system.

- Patient confidentiality must not form an obstacle to investigation – in particular, a member of NHS staff who is the subject of the investigation cannot be permitted to refuse to cooperate on the basis of patient confidentiality.

- In many cases, particularly where there are allegations of abuse by senior establishment figures within the NHS, the complaints procedures must provide for independent scrutiny, and probably independent resolution.

34.7 The evidence to the Inquiry shows that premature involvement with a formal complaints system can have the unintended effect of *preventing* disclosure. (We say here "unintended" but recognise that for some an intended effect, although never articulated, was to move the potential complaint away from the recipient.) We are satisfied that the same holds true today. The scenario was as follows. Patient to GP: "The consultant has behaved inappropriately." GP to patient: "Do you want to make a complaint?" or "Can I show you how to make a complaint?" Patient: "No, thank you" or "I will think about it." Inevitably, no formal complaint was made and no detailed disclosure was made to, or recorded by, the GP. The acting out of that and similar scenarios inevitably stifled the flow of information, and brought potential complaints to a premature end.

34.8 But as one observer to the Part 2 seminars put it, "If a patient describes to her GP an unusual experience at the hands of a consultant, she has some motivation for doing so." Our experience from considering the evidence to the Inquiry is that, in disclosing to GPs, patients were doing much more than seeking assistance from the GP as to the mechanics of making a formal complaint; they were, to summarise their own evidence, looking for help and support in dealing with the alleged abuse. That would apply with equal force to the partial, tentative or even detailed disclosures made in hospitals, or made to social workers or to others.

34.9 Strict reliance on, or adherence to, complaints systems was advanced by Counsel for the local NHS authorities as an explanation, at least in part, for the responses to disclosures made in the 1970s and 1980s. There is certainly some truth in what she said and because we suspect that a very similar attitude is likely to prevail today – at least in part – we set the submission out in detail:

> *"It goes without saying that in order to invoke the complaints procedure there needed to be a complaint. This occurred in only a small number of the cases with which the panel is concerned. Even where there was a complaint, when it was subsequently withdrawn events ground to a halt. As a matter of fact, in none of the cases with which the panel is concerned did the complaints procedure ever run its full course. Progress was halted long before that.*

> *"Where hospital administrators or District administrators were dealing with serious complaints or concerns they were, on one view, operating the complaints procedure. In reality though given that all these complaints would have led, if proved, to dismissal, the disciplinary procedure would have to be invoked. They were powerless to invoke it. What they did therefore had a dual purpose, so that information gathered at local level could be passed to Region for use there.*

> *"Linda Bigwood's complaint was treated by the District Nursing Officer, Mr Corbett, as a grievance, which invoked yet another procedure.*

"It might be said that in every case as soon as an allegation was made it should have been passed to Region to be dealt with. The hierarchy for communication would therefore have been patient to nurse to line manager to senior nursing officer to district nursing officer to district medical officer to regional medical officer and back again. Hardly an efficient or speedy means of communication, and the result of a cumbersome unworkable structure."

34.10 We do not accept that such reliance on systems excused the failure to be more responsive, to be more proactive – simply to listen and hear. But we do accept – as noted elsewhere in the Report – that it is an attitude that was, and may still be, prevalent within the NHS. We do accept, and do not in any way criticise, that policies and procedures are important and should be adhered to. We also accept that there is a close, inevitable link between a complaints policy (and the outcome of a complaint) and a disciplinary policy.

34.11 But a complaints system and a disciplinary policy do not form the complete picture. The fact that the Region found it particularly difficult to discipline, suspend or dismiss consultants in the 1970s and 1980s did not mean that nothing could be done about disclosures of sexual abuse. The fact that NHS complaints systems in the 1970s and 1980s were cumbersome and "almost as unappealing to a victim/survivor of assault as the criminal process" did not mean that nothing could be done about disclosures of sexual abuse.

34.12 We re-emphasise these points now for the following two reasons:

- First, any complaints system, no matter how improved, is and can only ever be *a part* of the response to disclosure of abuse. It should not be seen as anything more than a part.

- Second, and coupled to the first, even with the best complaints system and the best disciplinary procedures in place, it is necessary for the NHS to receive and respond to the patient's disclosure, to their expressions of concern, *without* insisting that the complaint route, or the disciplinary route, must be followed before the patient is listened to, or at all.

34.13 Returning to the question of the interrelationship of disciplinary and other processes, a shortcoming of the current system is that where a complaint is made about the performance of an individual doctor, the current disciplinary procedure is used in a way that suggests that the issue is solely about an aberrant member of a healthcare profession rather than a team or systems failure. This narrow approach side-steps the wider responsibilities of the NHS, both as an employer and as a provider of high-quality, integrated healthcare services. All complaints processes should be integrated with the wider clinical governance agenda. This would ensure a broader approach that identifies the shortcomings of wider clinical systems, including those that fall to particular individuals (managers and clinicians), and furthermore identifies all the appropriate actions required to secure safe services for the future. Such an approach, which requires the NHS to investigate all concerns about services and individuals (not just complaints by patients) and to act on the outcomes at various levels (organisational, team and individual), would ensure that the NHS takes responsibility both as an employer and organisationally.

34.14 What we are looking to see in place is a system – uniform, clear, practicable and accessible (and as independent as possible) – that responds to expressions of concern, to disclosures of possible abusive behaviour, that allows patients' voices to be heard without, necessarily, the need for the patient to engage with a formal complaints system, and where at least some form of action can be taken (for example monitoring of a doctor's practice, noting concerns, undertaking appropriate levels of investigation, etc). The formal complaints system, to which this chapter is devoted, will then form but one aspect of a complete NHS response and redress system.

34.15 That complaints system must also link into any NHS disciplinary system – as suggested elsewhere this should be a common disciplinary system, with the same (civil) standard of proof for all staff, no matter how senior or eminent. As noted by the local NHS authorities after the Part 2 seminars, "Without an effective method for disciplining doctors, the [Inquiry's] recommendations will be limited in their effect." Although linked in the sense that information discovered during the complaints procedure may be highly relevant to the disciplinary procedures, we accept that each procedure is distinct, and performs a different role.

34.16 When it comes to the formulation, implementation and operation of complaints policies, reporting protocols or disciplinary procedures directed at an issue such as sexual abuse of vulnerable (or any) patients, we see no value whatsoever in *local*, Trust-based variations. This is an area where there should be national standards of excellence, below which local systems cannot go. This is even more important with the expansion of patient choice and increasing volumes of services delivered via the private and voluntary sector. Taking but one example, there should be a national standard/policy addressing the obligation of healthcare professionals to communicate concerns (even if not supported by clear evidence) in relation to the suspicion of sexual abuse of vulnerable patients. It would then be for the locally based Trusts/organisations to determine, if considered necessary, the appropriate communication routes.

34.17 In the Part 2 seminar phase, we were provided with a number of documents relating to the Complaints Policy and Procedure for South London and Maudsley NHS Trust. The complaints system in North Yorkshire is very similar to the Maudsley model. However, we have not seen all versions for all Trusts. There may be better versions. It is unacceptable for there to be different, and lower, standards in this most sensitive of areas – yet another example of a postcode lottery.

34.18 Accordingly,

We RECOMMEND that the NHS should, jointly with the appropriate National Standards bodies, produce a standardised complaints system to be implemented in all Trusts/organisations providing services to NHS patients.[1]

34.19 Finally, by way of introduction, we emphasise that we are here concentrating on an NHS complaints system that is capable of responding to concerns and complaints of abusive, sexualised behaviour. Inevitably our comments, and our recommendations, will apply to the wider area of grievance handling.

Reforms

34.20 The NHS complaints procedure has been the subject of a number of reforms in the last decade that have improved it in a range of ways. These include: the replacement of profession-led Independent

---

1 This may be similar to the published guidance on consent.

Professional Review panels in hospitals by panels chaired by lay members; the extension to clinical matters of the Health Service Commissioner's investigatory powers; the bringing together of secondary care and primary care complaints procedures; and the abolition of the role of convener. In these ways the procedure has become more transparent, streamlined and consumer-focused. As the procedures have again become the subject of discussion in the context of the findings of this Inquiry it is important to remember these positive developments.

34.21 However, there are still significant improvements to be made. As the structure of the procedure has become clearer, the importance of ensuring that there is an organisational culture supporting it at all levels of the NHS needs to become a priority. Most information about dissatisfaction, complaints and poor performance is actually held by relatively low-status workers in the NHS who need to be better recognised and supported. As the various experiments in NHS regulation come to fruition in the wake of the Bristol Inquiry, it is essential to ensure that the network of organisations and procedures receiving information about poor performance are coordinated in ways which allow bigger pictures to emerge. Finally, those who set up and administer NHS complaints systems need to be wholly satisfied that procedures which work well for articulate and able patients are equally accessible and welcoming for vulnerable and disadvantaged service users – such as the former patients of William Kerr and Michael Haslam.

We RECOMMEND that themes and trends arising from the data of complaints, incidents, and patient and carer feedback should be analysed on a regular basis. This should form part of clinical governance and be used to give early warning of emerging patterns of risk behaviour, in the interests of patient safety.

General concerns about NHS complaints systems

34.22 We proceed on the basis that the Council for Healthcare Regulatory Excellence (CHRE) has broadly got it right in its listing of the essential principles of good practice in handling complaints or allegations. The following set of principles was adopted by the CHRE in March 2005:

> *"A complaints process should be:*
>
> - *consumer-focused;*
>
> - *accessible;*
>
> - *transparent and open to scrutiny;*
>
> - *having clear criteria for decisions that would enable consistency;*
>
> - *independent;*
>
> - *fair to complainant and professional;*
>
> - *timely;*
>
> - *inquisitorial – a desire to find out what 'went wrong';*
>
> - *used to stimulate improvement (through feedback from complaints)."*

34.23 In the course of the Inquiry, particularly during the Part 2 seminars, we were told of continuing areas of concern all of which combine to make the present system, even as reformed, inaccessible and difficult.

34.24 For example, a repeated concern was that the complaints systems are too complex, that there are too many entrance points and too many variations and deviations. One submission was as follows:

> *"We were concerned by the great diversity in the way in which complaints are handled. Also apparent was the number of avenues a patient may choose when making a complaint. This seemed to us to be very confusing to the public."*

34.25 Another contributor said:

> *"The route of access to complaints systems of the NHS is fairly opaque even to health professionals, partly because of the frequent changes of organisational structure and also of the 'complaints systems' themselves."*

34.26 Another area of concern is the role of independent advocacy. Contributors to the Inquiry expressed the view, which we share, that the opportunity to access such independent advice, and an independent voice, is of considerable importance if complaints systems are to work and be understood by patients. If that is accepted, then it must follow that such independent advocacy services must be adequately funded (on a long-term basis), and delivered as part of a coherent, national strategy.

34.27 A final general concern is that greater information should be available to patients – not only to identify how to access complaints systems, but also to assist them in understanding that they, as patients of the NHS, can express concerns (anonymously if necessary) *without* making a formal complaint. And, if the concern results in an investigation, they can still play a part in that investigation – again, without it being a formal complainant.

34.28 One of the most important lessons to take away from the findings of this Inquiry is that systems have their limitations. We are informed that the standard to be reached when making a formal complaint in the hospital sector during the 1980s was the most liberal ever enshrined in NHS complaints procedures. Guidance to hospitals issued during this period also made much of the need to be sensitive to complainants' needs and, where necessary, for staff to record a complaint for them. All hospitals were required to have designated complaints staff whose responses to complaints were signed off by the Chief Executive. Despite this, we have found that over this period a pattern emerged in which complainants were automatically disbelieved and their concerns were commonly dismissed without investigation.

34.29 It is clear that the issues which need to be addressed are not just about how the NHS introduces better procedures, but how the NHS introduces and reinforces commitment to the ideals underpinning those procedures. Fundamentally, there needs to be a shift in NHS culture so that those who work within the system place the safety of patients above other considerations, such as professional loyalty, and that those who act appropriately are properly supported. Procedures need to focus on resolution of patient complaints rather than on responding within a targeted time limit.

34.30   The NHS complaints procedure occupies a unique role in NHS regulatory systems and clinical governance.

34.31   First of all, complaints are fuelled by patients and service users rather than NHS staff. This Report and others like it provide a salutary reminder that when internal systems of clinical governance fail or the staff operating them are complacent, it is the tenacity of individuals outside the system which can prompt the revelation of poor and unacceptable performance.

34.32   Second, an important value of the NHS complaints procedure is that the threshold necessary to prompt investigation is not as high as a referral to the GMC, a police investigation or disciplinary proceedings. This particular feature means that more than any other regulatory or redress system the complaints procedure is well placed to detect concerns about treatment and behaviour which need to be flagged up for future reference, as well as those which need to be instantly acted on or dismissed. However, as we have made clear, and will again make clear, where the concerns relate to abusive, sexualised behaviour the NHS complaints system must be flexible enough to ensure that there is cross-agency communication at an early stage.

34.33   Within these contexts this chapter focuses on the following questions which still need to be answered if the NHS complaints procedure is to fulfil its potential.

- To what extent have attempts to introduce a key set of principles for the management of complaints in the primary and secondary care sectors been undermined by the introduction of special regulations relating to Foundation Trusts?

- Do the current regulations place too many restrictions on who can complain?

- Is there a need for patient champions?

- How successful are NHS complaints procedures in encouraging complaints from vulnerable and disadvantaged groups?

- How can the training and status of complaints managers be improved?

- Who should conduct the first investigation of a complaint?

- What constitutes good practice in investigating complaints?

34.34 The remainder of this chapter considers each of these issues in turn.

Key principles to guide all complaint handling

34.35 Patients and service users who wish to make a complaint about healthcare continue to be faced with a confusing array of grievance procedures which vary according to the following factors:

- whether they are receiving private care or have their care funded by the NHS;

- the type of healthcare practitioner they are complaining about;

- whether their complaint concerns allegations of criminal behaviour;

- the remedy they seek to obtain; and

- the stage their grievance has reached in any given procedure.

34.36 On the whole these distinctions have come about for a range of historical reasons to do with the contractual status of general practitioners, which was negotiated at the inception of the NHS, and the fact that professional regulatory bodies, such as the GMC, took responsibility for maintaining registers of competent practitioners prior to the foundation of the NHS.

34.37 In recent years important attempts have been made to establish sets of key principles according to which all complaints should be investigated and responses made. The setting up of the Citizens' Charter Unit Complaints Task Force was a particularly good example of an attempt to draw on good practice across the private and public sector in the formulation of core standards. Within the NHS, the Wilson Committee argued in 1994 that the array of procedures was confusing to service users and this led to the merger in 1996 of NHS complaints procedures relating to primary and secondary care. This meant that for the first time all complaints to NHS providers were to be handled according to the same guiding principles. It was only where a complainant wanted to pursue a criminal investigation or have a practitioner "struck off" that the systems differed.

34.38   The expansion of the remit of the Health Service Commissioner to both clinical and non-clinical complaints further simplified procedures from the patients' perspective, as did the transfer of arrangements for the second stage of the complaints procedure in both the primary and secondary care sectors to the newly created Healthcare Commission. In addition the National Health Service (Complaints) Regulations 2004 require that where NHS Trusts or Primary Care Trusts (PCTs) make arrangements for an independent provider to deliver services on their behalf, they are under an obligation to ensure that the provider has in place the same arrangements for the handling of complaints as they have. In other words, NHS complaints procedures follow NHS money into the private sector.

34.39   Notwithstanding these improvements and moves towards a more accessible system, we received submissions from service user representatives, from a Member of Parliament, and from others, that the concern remains that the existing complaints procedures are confused and daunting. As one organisation put it:

> "Many people are currently wholly excluded from the NHS complaints system because of its complexity – often these are the most vulnerable, including the elderly and the bereaved… and those who have significant difficulty in getting their complaints heard or taken seriously, particularly those who have mental health problems."

34.40   There is also particular concern within the NHS that new regulations which came into force in July 2004 undermine this shift towards a simplification of procedures and the unification of the principles which govern complaints handling. There is potential for this trend to develop further as a consequence of the patient choice agenda. Most recently, NHS Foundation Trusts have been excluded from the first stage of the current complaints procedures detailed in the July 2004 regulations. These regulations:

- anticipate that Foundation Trusts might have a different form of complaint procedure in place (regulation 15a), or indeed none at all (regulation 15b);

- restrict the referral of complaints from Foundation Trusts to the Healthcare Commission to those where a complaint has been made by a patient, or the complaint is reasonably connected with the provision of healthcare or other services to patients provided by or for the Foundation Trust. This differs from the provisions relating to referral from NHS Trusts or PCTs (regulation 8), which also allow referral by any person affected by or likely to be affected by the action, omission or decision of the NHS body which is the subject of the complaint. In the context of the present Report the latter provision may be of particular use to individuals or groups who wish to challenge the failure of a Trust to act on allegations made about a practitioner;

- introduce a less than transparent procedure whereby the Healthcare Commission has to refer certain complaints to the Independent Regulator;

- do not, in contrast to the regulations relating to NHS bodies, require Foundation Trusts to prepare an annual report on complaints handling for circulation.

34.41 We are informed that these aspects of the regulations were not included in the draft version circulated for comment among NHS bodies, with the result that there was no opportunity for them to comment on this last-minute change to policy. Moreover, the fact that the current Government (as at the date of drafting this Report) aims to give Foundation status to all Trusts by 2008 undermines all current attempts to improve the NHS procedures. Efforts to simplify complaint making for patients and to determine the core principles against which a complaints procedure should be judged are now in serious danger of being circumvented.

34.42 Sexualised behaviour by psychiatrists (or other mental health care professionals) is unlikely to be confined to areas of the NHS which exclude Foundation Trusts. We see every reason for improved national standards, practices and procedures to apply throughout the NHS, for the protection of *all* patients.

34.43 Accordingly, all NHS patients should be entitled to the benefits of the same standard of response in relation to complaint handling, monitoring and reporting as NHS Trusts and PCTs, wherever they are or have been treated, in NHS Trusts, PCTs or Foundation Trusts.

34.44 The principles steering the formulation of the NHS complaints procedure should give priority to arrangements which focus on the needs of the patients rather than those which reflect the complex structure of an ever-changing NHS. Procedures should focus on making complaining as easy as possible for those whose care is being funded from the public purse regardless of the status of the organisation delivering their care.

Patient champions

34.45 Our findings in earlier chapters of the Report disclose a culture in which some NHS staff, and GPs, sought to distance themselves from complaints rather than helping their patients pursue them. This is despite the fact that GPs in particular act as advisers and agents of patients when negotiating pathways through the NHS during the therapeutic relationship. What many of the patients involved in this Inquiry needed was a "champion" to help them through the task of getting their concerns heard and, if necessary, aired formally. Linda Bigwood was able to provide a limited degree of support, but her proactive stance has been shown by the evidence to be exceptional. It has been made clear from the evidence we have heard from some former NHS staff that the idea of championing a patient in the expression of a grievance has been undermined by a professional culture in which such altruistic behaviour is considered inappropriate, even worthy of criticism. It is to be noted with regret that currently there is not even an obligation on staff who receive complaints to inform their complaints manager that a complaint has been made to them.

34.46 The situation is further complicated when more than one organisation is involved in patient care. It is logical to suggest that NHS staff should be under the same obligation to report concerns about patient safety regardless of whether the NHS body involved is their employer. However, current regulations limit the obligation of staff to reacting only to complaints that relate to the Trust for which they work. This undoubtedly restricts organisational learning across the NHS and ignores the fact that a number of different organisations may be involved in one treatment programme. It is not improbable that a patient will be referred across NHS "borders", and there may be quite complex referral routes for a single patient.

34.47 The introduction of Patient Advice and Liaison Service (PALS) means that complaints and concerns should now receive more sympathetic treatment. But it is undoubtedly the case that concerned patients will continue to approach those with whom they have an existing relationship. This is particularly the case where the patient has a therapeutic relationship with an NHS professional who is directly involved in the referral of patients to other professionals. Patients have a right to expect that the primary concern of all NHS staff should be patient safety and that they, the patient, are not alone in wanting to expose poor practice or inadequate performance.

34.48 It is clear that during some of the period under review there were very different expectations of doctors as regards patients' safety. It was the case for some time, for instance, that doctors were advised that it was unethical for them to criticise the performance of a fellow professional "unless they were in possession of strong evidence to support their accusations, and they were advised that hearsay was not acceptable". This approach to poor performance has changed. The formal position of the GMC had altered by the early 1990s. Moreover, regulations relating to complaints have for some time anticipated that complainants may need the support of a member of staff in framing a complaint or recording an oral complaint. Despite this, the evidence submitted to this Inquiry – particularly in the course of Part 2 – demonstrated that there continues to be reluctance on the part of healthcare workers to identify safety issues involving a colleague.

34.49 Many staff to whom patients made their worries known did not know where to channel the grievance. There were particular obstacles where concerns about someone operating in the secondary care sector were made to those working in primary care. The existence of different systems of complaint in these two sectors and a lack of understanding of how other sectors managed complaints provided barriers to the flow of information between the primary and secondary care sectors which inhibited the maintenance and regulation of patient safety. It is clear from this that staff need to have a good working knowledge of how complaints are handled across the NHS rather than just within their own sector so that they can allocate grievances to the most appropriate channel.

34.50 But, perhaps most significantly, there was also a reluctance or reticence among NHS staff to raise concerns about patient safety which address broader and much more difficult issues about the prevailing culture in the NHS in relation to dissatisfaction and complaints. Evidence to the Inquiry suggests that that attitude persists in the NHS. If staff are to be empowered to act as patient champions or raise legitimate concerns about performance, they have to work in an environment where complaints are seen as important and taken seriously at all levels. This involves a real commitment on the part of senior managers, clinicians and educators to devote resources to changing the expectations of staff. The Chief Medical Officer has already signalled that there should be a "duty of candour" on the part of NHS staff to report breaches of patient safety to their employers and to the patients involved.

34.51 In closing this section, it is clear and to be noted that a negative attitude towards complaints is in part encouraged by the way statistics on complaints are presented in the public domain. An increase in recorded complaints is not necessarily a bad thing. It could signal improvements in recording practices or a more proactive approach to the searching out of dissatisfied patients. But using these data to compile "league tables" can lead to the inaccurate impression that those Trusts with a proactive approach to complaints are the most problematic; this impression is not necessarily corrected by the less publicised views and reports of organisations such as the Healthcare Commission which can draw attention to good practice in encouraging complaints. These positive views do not counter the impact (or at least the perceived and anticipated impact) of the adverse publicity which may surround league tables in the local press, if a hospital has many more complaints than its counterparts elsewhere, thus providing a disincentive to being proactive in complaint handling.

We RECOMMEND that information about the NHS complaints procedure and its relationship to other forms of regulation and clinical governance should be explained to all staff during their induction process and form a core part of continuing professional development programmes. This should include advice and training on how to deal with distressed and angry patients who want to make a complaint.

We also RECOMMEND that frontline staff who receive complaints about issues that compromise patient safety – whether or not in the confines of a therapeutic disclosure – should be under an express obligation to report that matter to a complaints manager (in or beyond their own organisation), whether or not they work for the organisation named in the complaint.

Supporting vulnerable and disadvantaged groups

Introduction

34.52 An understanding of this topic is vital, if there are to be significant improvements. The patients of William Kerr and Michael Haslam were vulnerable people, suffering from a range of symptoms including anxiety, depression, agoraphobia and alcoholism. In addition, a number were also young. A significant number of these patients said they feared retribution and recrimination. We also heard evidence indicating that staff, especially nurses who expressed concern about William Kerr's practice, were disbelieved and feared recrimination themselves if they pursued their complaints. The former patients' sense of vulnerability was exacerbated by the fact that, in a number of cases where they made their worries known, they received little support, or their criticisms were deflected or quickly rejected. In several cases, their expressions of concern were either dismissed outright, or the onus was put and left on them to pursue the matter further. Inevitably, rather than travel this difficult path alone, in most instances this led to them dropping the matter. The summary of the former patients' experiences is provided in the following extract from written submissions made on their behalf:

> *"The patients who gave evidence to the Inquiry had in many cases undergone an ordeal that extended over several levels:*
>
> *(i)   first, the initial abuse at the hands of a psychiatrist who they believed held over them the power to deprive them of their liberty with no effective right of appeal;*
>
> *(ii) second, where disclosures were made some patients were subject to threats both from the psychiatrists against whom complaints had been levelled and/or from other staff;*

> *(iii) third, many who did disclose were simply disbelieved. That disbelief was reflected either in a simple failure to advance the case at all; or in the worst cases by cynical and off hand comments which had the clear effect of humiliating a patient and thereby destroying any resolve to take the matter further;*
>
> *(iv) fourth, others who did disclose had the impression that some members of the profession did believe them but regardless of that belief the complaint could not or would not be advanced in any event because the system itself would not support them. That realisation that there was a systemic failure, that the abuse might be repeated and that there was nothing they could do was often as frightening as the original abuse;*
>
> *(v) fifth and finally, when the investigation became public and witnesses appeared in the criminal trials, they were subjected to lines of cross-examination which though perfectly permissible in the criminal context served to humiliate and ridicule those who disclosed."*

34.53 The current regulations make no specific reference to the needs of vulnerable or disadvantaged groups, although this is an issue that the Department of Health has been sensitive to in the past. We were informed that evidence from empirical studies indicates that most potential and actual dissatisfaction with medical services goes unvoiced and that only a minority of those who are dissatisfied voice a grievance. In part this relates to issues of power. The relationships between professionals and patients, as well as the relationships between doctors and other staff, suffer from information asymmetry. Patients in particular are much more dependent on healthcare professionals than professionals in the public health system are on them. The well-being and even life of people who are ill are doubly vulnerable and in the hands of the health professionals.

34.54 Research suggests that dissatisfaction about clinical care is the product of a complex interaction between patients' perceptions, expectations, history of care and emotional state. As we have seen in this Inquiry, these problems are further exacerbated when those seeking to make a complaint have problems in establishing their credibility because of the type of care they are receiving.

34.55 Therefore those in that position when they raise concerns or complaints will need further professional support to ensure the issues concerning them are handled appropriately. Had an external mental health advocacy support organisation, for example, been available at the time to the former patients of William Kerr and Michael Haslam, their ability to raise the issues on behalf of disadvantaged patients might well have led to actions and investigations being undertaken at the appropriate time and not, as we have had to do, an investigation of the issues some 20 years after the events.

34.56 A corollary of that is that those investigating issues properly raised must themselves possess the necessary skills and experience to deal with them. This would include being of sufficient authority or standing to overcome barriers or resistance within the system itself. Only when an awareness of the particular difficulties faced by patients undergoing psychiatric care is raised throughout the NHS will the situation improve. The right to dignity and the maintenance of boundaries, and recognition of the susceptibility of psychiatric patients to possible abuse, should be cornerstones in ensuring that patient safety and good patient care are delivered. These things cannot be left to chance, and guidance must be prepared to ensure that those standards are fully met throughout the NHS.

The introduction of PALS

34.57 Although they have only been created recently, there is considerable support for the view that PALS officers have the potential to provide support to these vulnerable groups and that this task should be identified as a top priority for them. Given the difficulties that the vulnerable face in making complaints, PALS officers have the potential to act as the patient's champion by asking difficult questions and gathering relevant information for them. Many NHS users hesitate to frame their grievance as a complaint because of the confrontational connotations this implies. PALS officers could be well placed in PCTs and Trusts to provide a bridge between concerns, grumbles, complaints and other clinical governance initiatives by pursuing issues that service users feel unable or disinclined to follow up themselves. They have considerable potential to form a key link in clinical governance networks.

34.58 However, it is important to recognise that dealing with complaints from vulnerable groups can be time-consuming and involves additional skills and resources such as counselling and advocacy support. Moreover, we were advised that there is evidence that at present PALS officers do not have access to the resources they need in order to fulfil their promise and that they often have to perform a number of roles within PCTs and Trusts to do with the representation of patient views and participation. This impedes their ability to focus on the vulnerable. Although practice varies throughout the country, there are also indications that many PALS officers suffer from the same low status and isolation as complaints officers.

34.59 An additional concern about the effectiveness of the PALS system relates to our finding that in some Trusts the role of PALS officer has been merged with that of complaints officer. Given the fact that PALS officers were created to fulfil the task of supporting patients previously undertaken by independent Community Health Councils, it seems highly inappropriate that the function of assisting patients in voicing a grievance has, in some instances, been merged with the role of responding to these very complaints. Moreover, the association of the complaints manager with formal complaints detracts from the expectation that PALS officers would be much better placed to use informal processes and negotiation to resolve concerns.

The introduction of ICAS

34.60 The findings of recent inquiries into poor performance and systemic failure over time all point to the significance of independent advice and guidance for complainants when clinical governance systems fail to identify patient safety problems. While the introduction of PALS has considerable potential, these officers are not independent of the organisation being criticised in complaints and their credibility as patient champions will always be perceived as compromised as a result.

34.61 It is difficult to comment at length on the success of the new Independent Complaints Advocacy Service (ICAS) as the system is still bedding down and the current contractual arrangements remain temporary. But, while there is some evidence of excellence and good practice, we are advised that widespread concerns exist. The lack of long-term contracts for the current providers means that there is a disincentive for those bodies to invest in planning, restructuring or organisational learning. As with complaints staff, there is also a recognised need for training, as providers have varying knowledge of the NHS, complaints procedures and dispute resolution in general.

34.62 Former patients have clearly identified the need for an independent, non-judgmental support person to guide them when they have concerns or "when things seem to go wrong". They say they need "a safe place to talk" and to make a complaint, and we affirm the importance of such a place. There is a useful parallel to be drawn here with the prison visitor system.

We recognise that in the main PALS will remain a "sign-posting" service. In the light of this, we RECOMMEND that health and social care commissions should resource independent mental health advocacy as a priority.

The status of NHS complaints staff

34.63 It follows from what has been set out above in relation to the culture of the NHS that if complaints staff are to be effective in investigating and addressing complaints and drawing attention to systemic failings or concerns about poor performance they must have authority and status within the NHS. However, a number of studies have demonstrated that NHS complaints staff have little status and occupy low grades. This lack of authority within the NHS is often exacerbated by the fact that complaints staff may not always have direct access to more senior staff who are in a better position to raise concerns about performance. This could have an adverse effect on their ability and inclination to refer safety issues outside their immediate department. It is as a result of these concerns that the Shipman Report (volume 5) recommended that senior complaints staff be drawn from middle management.

34.64 It is equally important that complaints departments should be placed in a position which makes exchange and review of information with others interested in clinical governance as easy and efficient as possible. Concerns have been raised that where complaints staff work alongside claims or risk managers defensive attitudes to complaints are more likely to prevail. This tendency would probably be avoided by locating complaints staff within quality management departments, but this can also serve to provide an unnatural barrier between the two groups of staff concerned with providing redress. The findings of this Inquiry – as well of those of other recent inquiries with similar terms of reference – suggest that it is essential for all individuals with responsibility for investigating and overseeing staff activity to be part of a clinical governance network in which information about poor and possible poor performance is shared on a routine basis.

34.65 It is undoubtedly the case that it is much easier to envisage a clinical governance network in the secondary care sector because the organisation employing a complaints manager is likely to be large. In the primary care sector, GP practices and PCTs are very small in comparison and individuals are much more likely to perform less specialised tasks. In response to concerns about status and independence, the Shipman Inquiry recommended that PCTs be given additional responsibilities in relation to Trusts. In the sections which follow, we take those recommendations further. But for present purposes it is important to stress and appreciate the validity of the Shipman Inquiry's observation that there is unlikely to be sufficient expertise in complaint handling within any single PCT.

Training of complaints staff

34.66 Some important work has been undertaken in this field which policy makers could draw upon. A pilot scheme aimed at delivering regional training to staff in the primary care sector was launched in the early 1990s and a resource pack produced as a result. More recently, the NHS University has accredited a course aimed at complaint handlers in the NHS, Birmingham University's Health Service Management Centre has launched a course on complaints and the Healthcare Commission has developed its own three-day training programme for the chairs of independent panels. Experience of these courses has suggested that a training programme should include such issues as: regulatory structures in the health and social care sectors; clinical governance; the NHS complaints procedures; the psychology of complaints; communication and conflict resolution skills; investigation techniques and the evaluation of evidence; and the ethical responsibilities of complaint handlers.

34.67 Adequate training of staff is one of the most important issues facing the NHS organisations in their attempts to improve complaint handling. The need to enhance training will be even more urgent if the proposals relating to triage and investigation of complaints are accepted. In future, complaints managers across sectors will need to be mature, experienced and confident and to have an ability to analyse, appraise and respond to complex data and situations.

34.68 We believe that the interests of the patients and staff in the NHS lie in ensuring that the most vulnerable patients have effective support, enabling them to raise concerns and make complaints.

34.69 In order to achieve this **we RECOMMEND**:

that PALS and complaints staff should be actively linked into a clinical governance and information sharing network with regular access to data on performance issues drawn from such things as claims, patient satisfaction surveys, audit and peer review;

that PALS and complaints staff should have direct access to a line manager at board level and to senior medical staff and that they should be appointed at middle management level;

that the roles of complaints officer and PALS officer should be distinct;

that the Department of Health should introduce permanent arrangements for the provision of independent advice for mental health patients;

that the Department of Health should be responsible for ensuring a standardised training programme for PALS and NHS complaints staff.

Who should conduct the first investigation?

34.70 Since an NHS complaints procedure was first introduced there has been continual discussion about the value of formality, and very different approaches have traditionally been pursued in the primary and secondary care sectors.

34.71 Prior to 1996 the emphasis in the hospital sector was on a relatively informal first-stage procedure and little existed by way of an "appeal" system as regards complaints about clinical care, save for an Independent Professional Review which was staffed and managed by the medical profession, with no lay involvement. In the primary care sector a rudimentary informal stage existed in the form of referral to conciliation, but the main focus was on complaints that were capable of being referred to the Medical Service Committee, a tribunal overseen by the Council on Tribunals. Extensive criticism of both the lack of a formal investigation in the hospital sector and the lack of informal attempts at resolution in the primary care sector led to the merger of the systems in 1996. From that date there came into existence a single system which allowed for an informal first stage in which the provider being criticised was allowed to respond to the allegation and a formal second stage in which complaints could be referred to a quasi-independent panel. These panels have since been replaced by independent panels centrally appointed by the Healthcare Commission.

34.72 The circumstances which have led to the setting up of this Inquiry and the Shipman, Neale and Ayling Inquiries are unusual. There is a danger in reforming the existing NHS complaints procedure in response to such non-typical cases if this were to make it less effective in dealing with the majority of cases that are pursued through it. At the same time, the failures in service delivery exposed by these inquiries represent a salutary reminder of the need to ensure that systems are able to provide an appropriate response to grievances in the most serious cases. In particular they have drawn attention to the need for statements relating to serious allegations to be taken, records to be made and investigations to take place. This would not only be in the interests of responding to individual complainants but would also lay an audit trail so that patterns over time could also be traced.

34.73 The issue concerning the remainder of this section is: when should an independent investigation take place?

34.74 The first stage of the current complaints procedure does not involve an independent investigation. Where the complaint relates to care, its purpose is to give the healthcare provider the opportunity to look into the concerns raised, address them and in doing so either agree that the care has been substandard or reject the validity of the complaint. It is not until there is a rejection or partial rejection of the complaint made that there is a dispute between the parties, because until that point it is possible that the provider will agree with the complainant. This stage of the procedure provides an opportunity for speedy and effective resolution. It also satisfies the requirement that NHS staff, most of whom provide a high standard of care, be given the opportunity to put their assessment of the complaint across.

34.75 It is this initial stage, when the provider is first alerted to a concern or possible mishap, that the Chief Medical Officer has examined in his report *Making Amends* (2003). In that report, he is clearly of the opinion that NHS staff should be allowed the opportunity and given the responsibility to provide explanations, apologies and redress at that stage if appropriate without interfering with the right of the patient concerned to pursue a complaint or medical negligence claim. One of the most important aspects of the NHS Redress Scheme he proposes in the report is that data on adverse events and circumstances would be fed directly into clinical governance programmes. His scheme is ambitious and involves a considerable change in approach to mishap, but there is no doubt that it would be to the benefit of complainants to receive a speedy and appropriate response at this stage and of benefit to the NHS to receive timely and detailed information on the causes and after-effects of mistakes and poor performance. However, the detail of the scheme has yet to be worked out, and a number of outstanding issues have yet to be addressed.

34.76 There are undoubtedly a large number of cases in which informal resolution at the first stage of the procedure works well, although we doubt its appropriateness where the allegation is of sexualised or other abusive behaviour. The problem is that when too much discretion is left to local providers there is no way of knowing how well it is working, and the benefits of informal resolution can also be used to mask abuses of the system. This is one of the main criticisms directed at the first-stage handling of complaints in the primary care sector, where GP practices are under no obligation to report the complaints they receive to their PCT. In a similar vein there is no responsibility on the part of GP practices or hospital complaints managers to consider the broader implications of individual complaints. NHS bodies are required to prepare an annual report for their board but the content is limited to the number of complaints received, their subject matter and summaries of how they were handled; the outcome of any investigation; and a list of those complaints referred to the Healthcare Commission in which its recommendations were not acted on. While this information could lead to important discussion of trends and quality implications at board level, it occurs fairly late in the process, and it does not require complaints managers to identify whether patient safety issues arose from the complaints or to flag up potential problems for the future. Neither does it require them to assess whether a referral to the police, a regulatory body or a disciplinary body was considered.

The overall picture which emerges from this analysis of existing arrangements is that there is too little too late. If this is the case, when *should* a formal investigation and review of the implications of complaints take place?

34.77   Before an investigation starts in relation to a serious matter relating to patient safety, consideration should always be given to the following:

- Should the clinician continue their normal work, but under supervision?

- Should there be particular restrictions on their practice? In the case of William Kerr and Michael Haslam, this could have led to restrictions on their practice of seeing female patients (particularly seeing them alone).

- Is the risk so high that the clinician should be restricted in all matters of clinical practice, or be excluded from the Trust until the investigations are completed?

34.78   We believe that concerns and complaints relating to allegations of abuse raised by mental health patients must be investigated effectively.

We therefore RECOMMEND that those who are given the task of responding and initiating any investigation should themselves be adequately trained, equipped with the necessary skills to carry matters forward, and of such seniority as to ensure that barriers and resistance are overcome.

34.79   Consideration of this issue is particularly complex in the context of primary care, where doctors are much more independent of regulatory regimes than those in the hospital sector. According to the current regulations formal complaints about hospital staff are automatically referred to the designated complaints officer for investigation. The fact that hospitals are commonly much larger organisations than GP practices means that some distance automatically exists between the person or department complained about and the manager responsible for looking into the complaint and providing a response. By way of contrast the current procedure allows formal complaints about GPs to be directed to a complaints manager in the practice of the GP complained about. It follows that the complaints manager and GP complained about are likely to be well known to each other.

34.80   The issue of when a formal investigation and review of the complaint should take place in the primary care sector was considered in some detail by the Shipman Inquiry. It was the opinion of Dame Janet Smith that complainants should be given the option of sending their complaint either to the GP practice concerned or to the PCT responsible for the practice and that this position also reflected current government thinking on the issue. Either way, it was suggested that all complaints made directly to the GP practice should be reported to the local PCT shortly after receipt. The purpose of this recommendation was twofold. It would give PCTs an overview of all complaints received within their jurisdiction. This would allow them to look out for trends and to flag up potential risks to patient safety at an early stage. It would also allow them to assess whether complaints received by local practices involved patient safety or quality issues. Where they did, it was the recommendation of the Shipman Inquiry that PCTs be allowed to "call in" these complaints to be investigated by the PCT. The effect of this scheme was to limit GP handling of complaints to those which involved "private grievances" and to exclude GPs from handling complaints which involved "clinical governance" issues.

34.81   These proposals have considerable merit. In particular they address concerns about the need to fast-track issues involving patient safety raised by the Public Law Project in its evaluation of the 1996 NHS complaints procedure. They also provide a safeguard against complacency and defensiveness by removing the investigation of complaints one step away from those directly involved or closely connected to people complained about. They also raise a number of additional issues which were not fully considered in the report of the Shipman Inquiry:

1. The key distinction made between private grievances and clinical governance complaints serves to create a dual complaints system at the first stage of the procedure. While satisfying the clinical governance role of complaints procedures, creating a dual system threatens to undermine the redress function, which requires that all service users have a right to call NHS staff and service providers to account whatever the nature of their grievance. The bifurcation of the system could lead to concerns that it was only

complaints that contained information of use to the NHS which warranted independent investigation. This impression is reinforced by the expectation in the Shipman Inquiry Report that the majority of cases involving "private grievances" could be resolved at service level by referral to conciliation and that few of these complaints would reach the Healthcare Commission.

2. The distinction between private grievances and clinical governance concerns would be much harder to make in practice than is anticipated in the Shipman Report, which gives few illustrations of the type of cases which might fall under the respective headings. There is an indication that private grievances are those which raise discrete and minor concerns. Would a complaint about a surgery seen to be dusty on a recent visit be dismissed as a private grievance because it is discrete and minor, or could this be seen as flagging up more generic issues about standards of cleanliness? Could a complaint about a doctor being rude be seen as a discrete example of a professional under stress, or could it be a case of a doctor who is not prepared to listen to their patients? The answers to these dilemmas might depend on the frequency with which complaints of this nature were directed at particular practitioners, but those wanting to make complaints about these issues might be discouraged by the initial reaction of the PCT that complaints of this nature had been directed to the investigatory route designated for minor concerns.

3. The distinction between "private grievances" and "clinical governance issues" may be positively unhelpful when considering boundary transgressions and sexualised behaviour. If we are right in our approach to such conduct, and that there is a "slippery slope" element, and "private grievance" which suggests the existing or possible abuse of a patient (particularly a psychiatric patient) then this is never a minor matter. If such a system is to exist, then the place of "boundary transgressions" within the system must be clearly identified and spelt out. Alternatively, the approach could be taken that all such alleged conduct always engages "clinical governance".

4. It is often not until a full investigation is carried out that NHS staff can be confident that the full range of issues has been aired by the complainant. Research suggests that dissatisfied service users tend to complain about things they are familiar with, such as "housekeeping" issues relating to food or cleanliness, but when

pressed they often have concerns about clinical care which they feel less confident about expressing. In part this is explained by the fact, highlighted in the Shipman Report, that service users do not have clear standards against which to judge the more technical aspects of care and are often not in receipt of all the relevant information about a condition or treatment programme. It is also the case that complainants vary in their ability to express themselves clearly in writing. As it is only the minority of complaints managers who have the inclination or resources to follow up a written complaint with a discussion, these underlying concerns are often missed when too much reliance is placed on the letter of complaint.

34.82 For these reasons, there is sense in taking the logic of the Shipman Inquiry approach one stage further and ensuring that all complaints about primary care are directed to the PCT which oversees the activity of the GP practice concerned, or at the very least copied to the PCT. There are a number of reasons for this:

1. PCTs are expected to establish good working relationships with GP practices in their jurisdiction, but there is clearly a degree of separation between these two organisations which is more akin to the situation in the secondary care sector. As a result, requiring that all formal complaints about GPs be directed to the local PCT would mean that complainants were treated in a like way regardless of where the person they were complaining of worked in the NHS. This accords with the principle that procedures should focus on the needs of those using them rather than those operating them.

2. Referring all complaints to PCTs would avoid the bifurcation of the system mentioned above and place responsibility for identifying the issues raised by a complaint and the implications of the allegations made in the hands of one local body.

3. These arrangements bear some similarity to those in place in the primary care sector prior to the introduction of the 1996 reforms. While the formality of the Medical Service Committee hearings was widely criticised by consumer groups it is the case that FHSA staff who dealt with complaints built up a valuable profile of problem GPs in their area over time.

We RECOMMEND:

that the revised regulations should require that all formal complaints should be directed to designated complaints managers in PCTs and NHS Trusts;

that formal complaints should be interpreted as any matter that the complainants would like to be treated as formal.

The process of investigation

34.83 If the most appropriate response is to be made to complaints and maximum use is to be made of information gleaned from them the investigation of complaints needs to be genuine, thorough and fair. A strong message to emerge from our Inquiry and others is that little can be done to progress consideration of whether there is a prima facie case of poor performance (or criminal behaviour) unless a thorough investigation is conducted as soon as possible by someone with status, authority and a reasonable level of independence. The function of complaints managers at this stage of the process is twofold. They must satisfy complainants that their concerns are being taken seriously and remain alert to issues of patient safety, systemic error and poor performance. A reformed complaints procedure would be well placed to perform this function. We have referred here also to criminal behaviour, and repeat that a thorough investigation by an NHS complaints manager, no matter how senior, no matter how competent, may not be appropriate if there is at least a real possibility that it will be followed some time later by a police investigation covering the same, or very similar, ground. In the case of suspected criminal behaviour, the local police force is obviously better suited to forensic investigation, the taking of witness statements, and probably even dealing with the alleged victim. In any area such as this, there must be close cooperation between agencies if the kinds of delay that occurred in the instant cases are to be avoided in the future. What is, or is not, criminal behaviour must of course now fall to be considered under recent sexual offences legislation, and under the Mental Health Act.

34.84 Regulations currently require that the complaints manager sends a copy of the complaint and their acknowledgement to any person identified as the subject of the complaint and investigates the complaint as they see fit. At present there is no obligation on them to raise issues about the wider implications of the complaint. Revised guidance to complaints managers could usefully identify a number of key tasks to be performed in the process of investigating complaints.

Clarification of issues raised by the complainant

34.85 For reasons specified above there are very good reasons why a complaints manager should use the receipt of a formal complaint as a prompt to explore a complainant's concerns. Indeed this should be seen as an essential pre-requisite to investigating the matter with staff. There are a number of instances of good practice in the sector which could usefully be used as standards in the investigation process. Follow-up phone calls, meetings in the complainant's home and confirmation of the issues to be investigated prior to contacting staff have all been shown to be highly effective in the management of complaints, though unfortunately (so we are informed) they remain uncommon approaches.

Identification of additional clinical governance issues

34.86 Taking the lead from the complainant about issues to be investigated is a logical first step in the investigation process and one which is more likely to lead to an appropriate response and complainant satisfaction. But, it may also be the case that the complaints manager identifies broader issues arising from the complaint that the complainant is not in a position to identify or has no interest in. It is in the interests of rigour in the investigation process and the objectives of clinical governance more generally that where necessary complaints managers be empowered to add issues to those raised by the complainant. In some cases these will guide the investigation of certain aspects of the complaint. In other instances it might be more appropriate for the complaints manager to refer the issues to another member of the clinical governance network.

Collection of information relating to a complaint

34.87 Evidence submitted to this Inquiry illustrated that it would have been of considerable use for formal statements and notes to have been made about the alleged behaviour of William Kerr and Michael Haslam. The failure of staff to make or keep records of the concerns raised and responses of staff undoubtedly hampered the ability of the NHS to identify patterns of behaviour over time. For this reason it is considered essential that effective records of investigations be kept by complaints managers. Further, the chronology of our Inquiry reveals that there may be a need for such records to be kept – at least in a readily identifiable centre – for many years.

Participation of staff

34.88 The current regulations are also silent on the issue of whether or not NHS staff have an obligation to comply with the requests of the complaints manager or a more general duty of candour, of the type recommended by the Chief Medical Officer. These are matters which may be covered in the professional codes of conduct, but these codes differ between professions and not all staff are subject to regulation by such associations. Indeed it is not until a complaint reaches the Health Service Commissioner that formal rights to require information to be produced are written into NHS complaints procedures.

Outcome of the investigation

34.89 Once the investigation is complete it should be the job of the complaints manager to consider whether credible responses have been given to each of the concerns raised in the course of investigation. Although this may be a relatively straightforward process in relation to performance concerns, disclosures and allegations which refer to sexualised behaviour, to sexual assault or to consensual sexual relationships are far more difficult to categorise in this way. If the truth of the disclosures or allegations cannot be readily resolved – and we accept that this may not be the case – complaints manager will soon find themselves in some difficulties. There must, therefore, be protocols in place, toolkits, etc, which can be followed so that the concern is not merely left unresolved, or delayed, as "too difficult" – a response with which the former patients of William Kerr and Michael Haslam are very familiar. There must be a resolution – within the Trust, within the NHS – either with the cooperation of other agencies, or (if there is no question of crime) by the complaints manager (or more senior manager) setting up an appropriate form of investigation, or (probably with the agreement of the patient) by referring the matter to the Healthcare Commission for independent investigation, and where appropriate informing the appropriate professional regulator.

Responses to complaints

34.90 Letters of response should make complainants confident that a thorough investigation of their concerns has been undertaken.

Current regulations require that written responses to the complaint summarise the nature and substance of the complaint, describe the investigation conducted and summarise its conclusions. No mention is made of redress, but it is clearly good practice to offer this where appropriate in the form of an apology or compensation. The latter is not provided for in current regulations, but the fact that the Health Service Commissioner and Chief Medical Officer have been critical of this stance suggests that this is a matter which needs to be reconsidered. In all instances changes made to policy or practice as a result of the complaint should be highlighted, regardless of whether the particular complaint was found to be justified.

Consideration of whether further action is necessary

34.91 Research suggests that, even when they are dissatisfied with the response, it is a minority of complainants who choose to pursue their complaint beyond the first stage of the procedure. This has a number of implications for those concerned with issues of clinical governance. In particular it suggests that it should be the duty of NHS staff to pursue outstanding clinical governance issues where the complainant chooses not to. This is commensurate with their role as guardians of patient safety. In comparison with the responses of the Healthcare Commission, there is no obligation on complaints managers involved in stage one of the procedure to recommend what action will be taken and by whom to resolve the complaint or identify whether any other action is necessary (see regulation 19(1)).

34.92 In the majority of cases it is likely that investigation will raise few issues relating to serious concerns about patient safety. However, the cases considered by this Inquiry suggest that it is nonetheless important to address the issue on a routine basis as this serves to clarify the status of the complaint at the end of the investigation process and can serve as a marker for future investigations on related issues. There is compelling evidence to suggest that on the completion of an investigation (or, in many cases, at the outset of the investigation – see above) complaints officers should be under an obligation to consider whether there is sufficient evidence or concern about patient safety to:

- refer the case to the police;

- refer the complaint to the GMC or another professional body responsible for regulating standards in the professions;

- refer a practitioner to the NCAA;

- refer the matter to the Healthcare Commission for independent investigation;

- recommend the issue of an alert letter under HSC(97)36.

34.93 Alternatively, there may be insufficient evidence or concern to refer the matter to one of these bodies but sufficient concern to warrant extra vigilance, a review of policy or clinical protocols, or referral of the issue to the clinical audit committee or board for further discussion. In the case of disclosures or allegations which, if true, would amount to criminal behaviour, we find it difficult to describe circumstances where complaints managers could arrogate to themselves the decision as to whether or not there was sufficient evidence: that is a matter for the police. Of course, if the police – looking to a criminal trial and a criminal burden and standard of proof – are not satisfied that there is sufficient evidence, it does not follow that the Trust (or regulatory body) is thereby relieved of its obligation to attempt to resolve the complaint, or take any necessary action to ensure that patient safety is protected. There may be a need to discipline the doctor, there may even be a perceived need to dismiss the doctor. If a doctor is accused of sexual abuse, and a criminal standard is not applied (on the basis of the latest successor to HC(90)9), then it may still be possible to remove the doctor from employment with the Trust on the basis of complaints (particularly if there is more than one patient complaint) without the right to cross-examine the patients, and where the complainants are anonymised (see the decision in Ramsey v. Walkers Snack Foods Ltd [2004] LRLR 754). Of course, any employer faced with the task of balancing patient safety and the "fair procedure" employment rights of a staff member would have to ensure that there are sound reasons for depriving the staff member of the opportunity to challenge the allegations made against them. We are not here in any way intending to advise employing Trusts, or other health service employers – they must continue to take their own advice.

34.94 The importance of addressing whether complaints should be referred to other avenues for further investigation was an issue which was also given full consideration by the Shipman Inquiry, which identified the process as a form of "triage". Their suggestion that in some instances there may be sufficient evidence available to refer a complaint to one of the alternative channels identified here when the complaint is first received is strongly supported. In line with the recommendations of that report, it is also suggested that the bar on having a complaint investigated where a complainant has stated in writing that they intend to take legal proceedings should be lifted as it is not in the interests of patient safety for full investigation of a grievance to be delayed by the issuing of proceedings.

We RECOMMEND:

that current regulations should be amended to ensure that it is the duty of complaints officers to investigate complaints in a speedy, efficient *and effective* manner;

that current regulations should be amended to require complaints managers to consider the implications for clinical governance and patient safety of all complaints received. Where a clinical governance issue arises this should be reported to the relevant line manager and to the board;

that current regulations should be amended, and suitable guidance prepared, to allow and ensure that complaints managers consider the reference of any complaint received which, if true, would disclose the commission of a crime, to the local police force;

that current regulations should be amended to require complaints managers to take statements from all those staff involved in the investigation of the complaint;

that guidance issued under the regulations should clarify what constitutes a full and rigorous investigation, most notably that complaints officers be placed under a duty to raise additional issues for investigation;

that all NHS staff should be placed under an obligation to cooperate with investigations carried out by complaints managers;

that, where possible, the NHS should give clear advice and guidance on employment protocols following allegations of abuse;

that chief executives acting on the advice of their complaints managers should be given the authority to refer a complaint to the Healthcare Commission for further consideration; and

that complainants should be allowed to pursue litigation at the same time as a complaint is being investigated.

Clinical governance and plotting trends

34.95 If complaints are to be used to plot trends across specialties, sectors and the careers of individual practitioners, it is vital that data on complaints are recorded and used intelligently. Despite recommendations from various committees and inquiries (NHSE, 1994; Cabinet Office, 1995; Health Committee, 1999; Department of Health, 2000), all of which called for rigorous systems for recording and analysing adverse events, complaints and claims, integrated systems remain poorly developed. Yet, in terms of clinical governance, recording and monitoring the incidence and type of these phenomena is vital.

34.96 Hilary Scott's evidence to the Neale Inquiry provided an accurate statement of the data which are currently available on complaints across England and Wales. It is particularly encouraging to learn that the returns to the Department of Health are routinely checked for significant changes. What is less clear is the extent to which the identification of a trend prompts further detailed investigation or a referral to the Healthcare Commission in its audit role. It remains clear that national data are only of use if approaches to complaint handling and recording are consistent across the country. If the number of complaints in a given area was relatively high or there were sudden or dramatic changes, these data could prompt a more rigorous investigation. Sensibly, they would contribute to profiles of Trusts which might be used by the Healthcare Commission to determine whether further investigation of practices was necessary as part of routine audit procedures. We have touched on these matters when looking at issues of prevalence (see Chapter 30).

34.97 At service level, researchers have found limited recording and monitoring of complaints, with the result that it is highly likely that official statistics submitted to the Department of Health under-report instances of expressed dissatisfaction. In the absence of central guidance on the recording of complaints, there appear to be different systems in use. Perhaps most importantly, categories for recording complaints are often too broad to help in the identification of trends, and arrangements for reporting and acting on investigations are insufficiently systematic and rigorous. Clearly, the issue of how complaints and claims can promote organisational learning is an area where policy has still to be developed.

34.98 No matter how improved the complaints systems may be – and we are satisfied that there have been enormous improvements at every level – they are still "systems", operated by people dealing with other people. If vulnerable psychiatric patients are not to be marginalised, not discriminated against, then those who are likely to be recipients of the disclosure must be better equipped to respond appropriately. By that, we do not mean that every GP, every nurse, every social worker, every police officer, must be trained specifically to handle such expressions of concern, such disclosures, such complaints, but we do mean that likely recipients must be educated and trained to know what to do if the patient is particularly vulnerable, particularly in need of expert support. For example, that would involve early contact with local services expert in this area – this may be the police, or social services or voluntary organisations. What is important is that the local GP, nurse, etc should know who to involve, and when to involve them.

We RECOMMEND:

that the Department of Health should convene a working party to consider what information it is necessary to record about complaints in order for them to be of use in clinical governance, and the circumstances and form in which it is appropriate to record suspicions; and

that, in line with the recommendations of the Shipman Inquiry, a centralised database capable of recording a range of information about the performance of individual doctors should be set up.

Chapter 35
Employment, discipline and regulation of doctors

Introduction

35.1 In previous chapters of the Report, we have referred to the employment and disciplining of doctors, and to the role of the GMC in the handling of complaints in relation to both William Kerr and Michael Haslam.

35.2 We here bring together some of the concerns expressed during the course of the Inquiry, and our responses. We emphasise that our main focus is on one branch of medicine: psychiatry; and within that branch, one profession: doctors. However, there are clearly read-across lessons to be learned – mental health care involves care and treatment by doctors, nurses, social workers, psychologists and occupational therapists. This care and treatment, although involving inpatient and outpatient contact, is increasingly based in less formalised settings, such as day and community resource centres, or in patients' homes.

35.3 Our firm view is that the regulation and discipline of mental healthcare professionals affects and is affected by the culture of the provision of healthcare services in England and Wales. We have addressed the topic of culture in some detail elsewhere in the Report, and only make four introductory comments here:

1. In relation to the role of the GMC it is to be noted that, despite the expressions of concern or complaints over a number of years, not one such concern or complaint found its way into the GMC's offices before 1997 (for William Kerr) and 1996 (for Michael Haslam). Why this should have been the position is not entirely clear. But one suggested explanation stands out: healthcare professionals, at the time, approached the potential involvement of the GMC on the basis that there was no point in passing on disclosures to the GMC because, in the absence of firm and convincing evidence (in the form of written, sworn statements

from complainants and their witnesses) they would not investigate. This attitude to the role of the GMC formed a barrier to the effective raising of concerns. It will also have served to underline the sense of powerlessness referred to by some of the professional witnesses who gave evidence to the Inquiry.

2. In relation to the Regional Health Authorities as the employer of consultants such as William Kerr and Michael Haslam, there were formidable barriers to controlling practices, or taking any form of effective disciplinary action. Again, the evidence to the Inquiry suggests that nothing short of an admission by the consultant, or clear and compelling written evidence, would suffice before any direct action would be taken.

3. The only alternative seems to have been a protracted, negotiated, early retirement approach to the removal of poorly practising consultants. What was striking to us was the absence of any proactive approach to the investigation of concerns or complaints.

4. From the Royal College of Psychiatrists, there was little evidence produced to the Inquiry of any detailed guidance, or any attempt at action against consultants such as William Kerr or Michael Haslam during the 1970s, 1980s and into the 1990s. This may be because the Royal College did not know of any concerns or complaints; it may be because it was not proactive enough – or maybe not proactive at all. We recognise, however, that there was an impediment to action. We have been informed by the President of the Royal College, in written evidence to the Inquiry, that from 1961 to 1988 (years covering almost all of William Kerr's and Michael Haslam's periods of NHS practice) "the focus was primarily educational rather than regulatory, with a power 'to encourage and promote amongst its members and others working in allied and related sciences and disciplines the achievement and maintenance of the highest possible standards of professional competence and practice'". There were disciplinary procedures, but they were rarely used. Any such procedures were not invoked in relation to either consultant until after Michael Haslam's criminal conviction in 2003 (and that was four years after his retirement from practice and voluntary erasure from the Register).[1]

---

1 We have been informed that other psychiatrists had their membership revoked by the College, but again – consistent with the College's approach in Michael Haslam's case – only after another body (usually the GMC) had decided they were guilty of serious professional misconduct, and had taken their own disciplinary steps, such as erasure from that body's register. The removal of membership from the College could, therefore, be seen as merely a removal of membership privileges and a mark of disapproval. It is difficult to see any element of public safety protection in such a removal.

Employment and discipline of consultants within the NHS

Employment

35.4   In order to understand the environment in which the matters addressed by evidence to the Inquiry took place, it is necessary to know something of the employment regime in relation to doctors (particularly consultants) in the NHS over the relevant period. In this chapter we set out a brief overview. It is necessarily incomplete, and does not attempt to cover the full procedures back to the 1960s. It is also not possible in this Report to set out, and comment on, the employment and disciplinary position of other NHS employees. We do, however, note one difference of importance in relation to the disciplinary process – namely (until this year) the differing standards of proof in consultant and other healthcare worker investigations.

35.5   Since the inception of the NHS in 1948, a large number of Acts and statutory regulations have been passed or approved by Parliament in an attempt to modernise, rectify and amend existing policy and practices regarding the employment of hospital doctors.

35.6   The appointment of a doctor to a consultant post in the NHS required the successful candidate to have full registration with the General Medical Council and to have been interviewed by a properly constituted Advisory Appointments Committee. It was the responsibility of the Advisory Appointments Committee to ensure that the applicant had the necessary qualifications and experience to be appointed to the post. The recommendation of the Advisory Appointments Committee required approval by the appropriate Regional Health Authority which at this time held the contracts for all non-teaching hospital consultants. This was the position by the early 1980s. From 1 January 1997 applicants for consultant appointments had to be on the specialist register of the GMC.

35.7   Consultants were appointed to part-time, maximum part-time or full-time posts. For part-time and maximum part-time appointments consultants were allowed to undertake private work. Before 1979 full-time consultants working in the NHS could not undertake any paid private work, but this restriction was changed later that same year. From this date consultants appointed to full-time posts could undertake a limited amount of private practice – gross income from private practice should not exceed 10% of their gross salary. If consultants wished to undertake more private practice, they could move on to a maximum part-time contract and have their NHS salary reduced by 1/11th. The new consultant contract, which was accepted by the British Medical Association, has introduced a new approach to managing the relationship between private practice and NHS commitments. It provides a new set of contractual rules to prevent conflict of interest between the NHS and private work.

35.8 The new NHS consultant contract that was agreed with the medical profession is now the sole contract for all consultants appointed from 31 October 2003. Consultants in post prior to 31 October 2003 have the option to change to the new contract.

35.9 By the early to mid-1980s, when action in relation to William Kerr or Michael Haslam might have been considered, the regulations in force for the appointment of consultants were contained in SI 1982 No 276: *The National Health Service (Appointment of Consultants) Regulations 1982.* At this time the responsibility for the appointment of hospital consultants was that of the appropriate Regional Health Authority; where the appointee's contract covered work in hospitals in more than one Region then the Region with the maximum number of sessions took responsibility for the appointment process.

Taking up references

35.10 We have been informed of the improvements made to NHS employment practice in recent years, much of which is now embedded in mainstream human resources practice. However, there remains some further work to be done in relation to the routine and systematic application of these practices to the employment of junior doctors and consultant psychiatrists. The evidence to the Inquiry indicated that, at least in the late 1980s, there may have been uncertainties in relation to the correct source for references.

35.11 We are satisfied that the system for on-going employment checks of staff is now in place as a result of the requirement to "CRB check"[2] all new employees (as well as regular follow-up checks) as a result of the implementation of Bichard Inquiry recommendations.

35.12 We feel it is significant to note that the position is now that any complaint by a patient brought to the attention of the police will be recorded on the NHS staff CRB record, whether proven, unproven

2 CRB – Criminal Records Bureau.

or disproved. In the latter two instances this could clearly have a substantial impact upon a practitioner's practice, despite the fact that nothing had been proved (to any standard) against them.

35.13 From a patient's perspective, however, it provides another layer of protection by enabling an independent record to be kept of the fact that an allegation has been brought to the attention of the police.

35.14 The question of references also brings into focus the existence of a responsibility to share concerns, even between regulators and professional bodies – such as between a NHS Trust, the GMC and the Royal College of Psychiatrists.

35.15 It is arguable that there may already be a duty at law, obliging one regulator charged with duties of public protection to share relevant information with another public authority (here, such as an NHS Trust). The basis for the duty is the public interest, and would be subject to caveats based on confidentiality, data protection, and Article 8 of the ECHR. As there may be some uncertainty as to the scope of the duty to share, and it may impact on the content of reference, and any other requests for information, we believe that the obligation should be spelt out and:

We RECOMMEND that regulatory bodies (with responsibility for the regulation and discipline of psychiatrists and other mental healthcare professionals) and the Department of Health should be under a clear duty, in the public interest, to share information about disciplinary investigations or other related proceedings. This duty should extend to information known to the regulatory bodies and the Department of Health relating to disciplinary investigations and related proceedings, even if conducted outside the United Kingdom. Consideration should be given to the collection and retention of all information relevant to patient safety, including unsubstantiated complaints, unproven allegations and informal concerns.

We also RECOMMEND that the Department of Health should clearly state what information can be included in relation to electronic staff records relating to complaints, proven/ unproven incidents, disciplinary investigations and findings. Such a record should be established in standard form and, once established, should move with the individual to reduce the risk of staff evading detection of past misdemeanours. The Department of Health should consider whether or not, and if so how and in what circumstances, any such information should be transferable between the NHS and the private sector.

Supervision

35.16 The lack of clinical supervision of consultants evident in the 1970s and 1980s remains an area where there has been little progress even today. Chapter 25, paragraph 67, highlights the importance of regular and systematic supervision to underpin effective clinical practice. This has been adopted across all mental health professions but has yet to be applied systematically to the practice of consultant psychiatrists.

35.17 In Part 2 of the Inquiry we heard from consultants in practice today highlighting the gap and the need to consider more formal arrangements for consultant practitioners. We also heard evidence from NIMHE of a recent pilot project focusing on supervision for consultant psychiatrists.

We therefore RECOMMEND that the Department of Health in association with the National Institute for Mental Health in England (NIMHE) and the Royal College of Psychiatrists should publish guidance in relation to clinical supervision of consultant and career grade psychiatrists.

Appraisal and managing performance[3]

35.18 The Neale Report concluded that between the early 1960s and the early 1990s, the NHS's procedures for dealing with poorly performing doctors (someone whose competence, conduct or behaviour poses a potential risk to patient safety or to the effective running of a clinical team) remained more or less unchanged. If it was considered necessary to act, then the disciplinary procedures were used. It was

---

3 A more complete summary can be found in the Fifth Report of the Shipman Inquiry, Chapter 12.

not until during the 1990s that the NHS addressed this issue and procedures were introduced that enabled problems in a doctor's practice to be picked up much earlier and objectively assessed, and in the majority of cases it was possible to take a rehabilitative approach.

35.19 In 2000 the Department of Health published *An Organisation with a Memory*. The intention, according to the document, was to examine the instances of individual failures, and system failures and to contrast them with instances of positive outcomes to enable lessons to be learnt, and good practice to be recognised.

35.20 A report published by the Chief Medical Officer's expert group, *Supporting Doctors, Protecting Patients*, set out a new approach to the way poor clinical performance in the NHS should be dealt with. The report identified four key areas that needed to be addressed. They were:

- unified mechanisms for reporting and analysis when things go wrong;

- a more open culture, in which errors or service failures can be reported and discussed;

- mechanisms for ensuring that, where lessons are identified, the necessary changes are put into practice; and

- a much wider appreciation of the value of the system approach in preventing, analysing and learning from errors.

35.21 The report set out 10 key recommendations – which were all accepted by the Government for implementation as part of *The NHS Plan: A Plan for Investment: A Plan for Reform.*

35.22 The present position is that if it is not possible to resolve the concerns at local level then the National Clinical Assessment Service (previously the National Clinical Assessment Authority) can be called upon to assist. The NCAA (as it was called then) was created in 2001. Its role is to help the NHS deal in a more consistent way with poorly performing doctors. It advises employers of systematic ways of handling problems and offering assessments of the doctor. It helps find the most suitable way for the employer to deal with the problem, offering alternatives to the disciplinary route where appropriate. It is to be borne in mind that the NCAS is only concerned with doctors, and not with other health service professionals.

35.23 Recent reforms made by the GMC include the introduction of appraisal and revalidation for doctors, which it is intended will form an important part of a wider clinical governance infrastructure. Annual appraisal was introduced for NHS consultants in April 2001 following a recommendation in the document referred to above, *Supporting Doctors, Protecting Patients*. Appraisal for other groups of NHS doctors, including locum doctors, has now been introduced. The aim of NHS appraisal is to allow doctors to reflect upon and discuss their activities with a suitably qualified and trained appraiser, with a view to addressing areas for improvement. Evidence brought to the appraisal process will include positive feedback and praise, as well as complaints received and how they were responded to. The outcome of the appraisal process is an agreed and achievable personal development plan, which is kept under review between appraisal meetings.

35.24 NHS doctors will be able to submit information generated by the appraisal process as evidence for revalidation of their GMC licence to practise, which is likely to be introduced during 2005.[4] All doctors will need periodically to satisfy the GMC that they have kept up to date and are fit to practise medicine and will be expected to provide satisfactory evidence that they have continued to satisfy the requirements of Good Medical Practice and kept their knowledge and their practice up to date.

Discipline

35.25 In the period covered by this Report, particularly the early to mid–1980s, disciplinary procedures for hospital medical and dental staff were based on national guidance dating from the 1961 circular HM(61)112: *Disciplinary Proceedings in Cases Relating to Hospital Medical and Dental Staff*. In this guidance a distinction was made between "personal" and "professional" misconduct.

35.26 If the misconduct was judged to be 'personal' then it could be dealt with under internal disciplinary procedures that the employer used

---

4 There has been some delay following the Shipman Inquiry's Fifth Report, and the Review announced by the Department of Health. According to an announcement by the GMC, the Review has led to the postponement of the intended launch of licensing and revalidation from April 2005.

for any grade of staff. If the misconduct was judged to be "professional" then the employer had to follow a special procedure. In effect this procedure provided protection for a doctor against dismissal other than on the most serious grounds.

35.27   The provisions of the above circular remained in place until 1990 when further guidance was issued in circular HC(90)9, *Disciplinary Procedures in Cases Relating to Senior Medical and Dental Staff.* The essential ingredients of the HM(61)112 procedure were retained, though time limits were set for the various steps in the process.

35.28   Two new procedures were introduced:

- Professional Review Machinery: whereby a professional panel reviewed the conduct of hospital consultants who were alleged to have failed repeatedly to honour their contractual commitments;

- Intermediate Procedure, for dealing with cases of professional misconduct and professional incompetence which warranted disciplinary action short of dismissal.

HC(90)9

35.29   HC(90)9 made changes to the appeal process, which was set out in the "Terms and Conditions of Service of Hospital Medical and Dental Staff". These rights were not to apply to doctors dismissed for personal misconduct, but doctors were given a right of appeal if they felt their contract had been unfairly terminated on the sole ground of personal misconduct where this misconduct could not be fairly described as personal misconduct.

35.30   From the time of its issue difficulties were experienced with the procedures set out in HC(90)9. These included the length of time it could take to deal with a disciplinary matter, from nine months to four years, during which time the doctor concerned could be suspended on full pay. Under the guidance a doctor could appeal matters of procedure as well as the substantive decision.

35.31   The practical effect of the HC(90)9 procedures generated considerable concern over a long period of time, not only among employing authorities but also among representatives of the medical and dental professions. After considerable discussions, negotiations took place to agree a revised procedure.

35.32 In September 2003 a statement of principles was issued jointly by the Department of Health and the BMA's Central Consultants and Specialists Committee. The framework replaced all the previous guidance on discipline, suspensions and the "Three Wise Men" procedures.

35.33 Included in the 11 principles were the statements that:

- the focus was to be on helping doctors and dentists to keep up to date and to practise safely, while not punishing them for any problems with clinical performance; and

- the framework would focus on matters of clinical performance and capability – all issues of conduct were to be dealt with under local Trust procedures.

35.34 In December 2003 the Department of Health issued circular HSC 2003/12, which set out a new framework that replaced existing guidance on the suspension of doctors and dentists in the NHS in England. The document contained the "Restriction of Practice and Exclusion from Work Directions", which came into force on 5 January 2004. This required NHS bodies to make changes in their procedures to bring them into line with the principles of the framework.

35.35 The framework related to:

- the initial handling and investigation of concerns about the conduct and performance of doctors or dentists employed in the NHS; and

- the actions to be considered in protecting the public, such as restrictions on practice or exclusion from work.

35.36 The framework was developed jointly by the Department of Health, the NHS Confederation, the BMA and the British Dental Association, and constituted the first two parts of a wider national framework for handling concerns about the conduct and performance of medical and dental employees. It followed disquiet relating to the way in which complaints about, and disciplinary action against, doctors and dentists had been handled in the NHS – including particularly the use of suspension in such cases. We heard a considerable amount of evidence to suggest that the concern and disquiet were well founded.

35.37 NHS Trusts and Primary Care Trusts (PCTs) were required to notify Strategic Health Authorities of the action they had taken to comply with the framework by 1 April 2004. Strategic Health Authorities were required to provide a report on local implementation of the framework to the Secretary of State by 30 September 2004.

Personal or professional misconduct

35.38 Returning to the period covered by our Inquiry, we here draw particular attention to the chilling effect of the legal advice likely to have been tendered to Region and to District by legal officers such as Hugh Chapman (legal adviser to Yorkshire Region Health Authority from 1974 to 1989) in relation to the use of HM(61)112. His evidence may be relevant to the approach of healthcare administrators, as recently as 2004, to the use and application of HC(90)9.

35.39 Mr Chapman told us in his oral evidence that there was "no enthusiasm" throughout the Region for proceedings to be started against consultants under the terms of circular HM(61)112 – later HC(90)9. He told us of a general feeling of depression that arose whenever such action was contemplated because all involved felt that the procedures demanded by HM(61)112 were not suitable for successful proceedings to be likely. Unless the consultant left his position voluntarily, retired or moved out of the Region, attempts at removal were time consuming and difficult.

35.40 Until very recently HC(90)9 was the document still governing disciplinary procedures for the type of matters, concerns or complaints which arose in relation to William Kerr and Michael Haslam. We were informed that, at least in North Yorkshire, such allegations would fall within "professional conduct", rather than "personal conduct". In relation to personal conduct allegations, HC(90)9 made it clear that "the position of doctors and dentists was no different from that of other NHS staff". However, in relation to "professional conduct" the full, complex, time-extended and expensive procedures set out in Annex B to HC(90)9 applied. The timetable alone is an indicator of what was involved. Because of concerns at the length of some hearings the circular fixed a time limit of 32 weeks from the Chairman deciding that there was a prima facie case to the report going to the health authority. It was then up to the health authority to determine what their response should be to that report. As noted above, the overall procedure could take years to be completed.

35.41 We were also told at the York Part 2 seminar in December 2004 that administrators understood that if there was an HC(90)9 investigation, the standard of proof required for a successful action was the criminal standard.

35.42 So it would appear that Hugh Chapman's concerns – set out above – were still relevant as recently as 2004. There was still the same negative effect on investigations. Investigations which should have been carried out may still not have been carried out because it was considered, at a local level, not to be worth the time and effort unless there was very clear evidence, or an admission. That was, and still may be, unlikely when the patients were vulnerable psychiatric patients and the allegation was of sexual assault, or consensual sexual relations, with no independent witnesses. It therefore seems that in relation to disciplinary procedures, consultant psychiatrists were in the same privileged position in 2004 as they had been in 1961, and throughout the period covered by this Inquiry. We see no reason why doctors should have been treated differently from other healthcare professionals when concerns or complaints of sexual abuse were raised (whether or not such allegations were correctly categorised as "personal conduct" or "professional conduct").

35.43 That categorisation of, and distinction between, "personal conduct" and "professional conduct" seemed to us to have been a central problem with HC(90)9 – a central problem we consider was known to all involved (at whatever level) long before William Kerr and Michael Haslam left the NHS in the late 1980s.

35.44 Furthermore, we are not aware of cases where a distinction was drawn between personal and professional conduct, when the alleged sexual behaviour was with a former patient.

35.45 The reasons for this recent practice are not entirely clear. It would have been possible for Trusts to incorporate policy directions on doctor–patient boundary transgressions (including sexualised behaviour) into the conditions of employment of any consultants employed by the Trust, but the conjecture was that this was rarely, if ever, done. Without such employment-based identification of what was or what was not "personal conduct", the Trust had to rely on the standards of the GMC or possibly the Royal Colleges. In those circumstances, it would be difficult to say that the alleged behaviour did not fall within the category of "professional".

35.46   Boundary crossing (particularly sexualised behaviour) became yet more complicated and the division between "personal" and "professional" misconduct more confused when the allegation corresponded with a possible criminal charge – sexual assault or rape. Criminal behaviour could properly be said to lie within "personal misconduct", but it is also separately reportable to the GMC (as well as to the police).

35.47   We therefore surmise that where there was an admission, or irrefutable evidence, there would not have been recourse to HC(90)9. It would be unnecessary. Either the police would take over (if the alleged conduct was criminal) or the doctor involved would quickly have resigned. But in this Inquiry we have been considering situations where the doctors have denied almost all of the allegations made (and denied all allegations of sexualised behaviour with existing patients). In cases such as these, the practice seems to have been that alleged behaviour, no matter how outrageous, arising from the exercise of medical or dental skills, would have been categorised as professional conduct (or misconduct). This then entailed engaging the whole rigour of HC(90)9, including a requirement that the allegation be proved to the criminal standard. It remained a lengthy, expensive and exhausting procedure. As noted above, we were informed, at the Part 2 seminars in York, that:

> "Disciplinary procedures for medical staff follow HC(90)9, at least while a replacement is agreed as part of the national negotiation of consultants' contracts. It is currently almost impossible to take an unsubstantiated allegation of professional misconduct against medical staff through a disciplinary route that is currently under the auspices of HC(90)9."

35.48   By "unsubstantiated" we understood the contributor to the seminar to be referring to allegations where there was no admission, no other evidence which (in the opinion of the administrator) would be proved to the criminal standard.

35.49   The consequence was serious. The continuing use of HC(90)9 rendered it extremely difficult for health service employers to discipline clinical staff in a timely and effective manner. It may also have led to the situation (if a criminal standard was applied) that a male consultant psychiatrist could remain in post – treating female patients – even though the investigation had concluded it was more likely than not (the civil standard) that the sexual misbehaviour occurred; this was justified on the ground that the proof of misbehaviour could not be proved "to a criminal standard" so that they were sure.

35.50 But in relation to a nurse, or social worker, such considerations would not have arisen. Other healthcare professionals employed in the same institution, or organisation, did not share this same privileged position – nor did social workers. We can see no justification for the proposition that allegations of sexual misconduct in relation to those non-doctor professionals are to be treated as requiring less cogent evidence to support them than the same allegations if made in relation to doctors.

35.51 In relation to these workers, employment procedures did not require proof to a criminal standard. As one witness to the Inquiry said:

> *"Abuse is abuse, so I don't see why there should be any difference."*

35.52 We do not see any basis for drawing that distinction. It cannot sensibly be based on the fact that patients confide in their doctors or there is a duty of confidence or otherwise. Nor can the distinction be justified because there is a shortage of doctors – particularly of psychiatrists.

35.53 Submissions on this topic from the local health authorities included the following:

> *"The panel should recommend that the standard of proof in disciplinary procedures should be the same for all staff – ie balance of probabilities. It is the same in all other employment contexts including eg social work where allegations of sexual abuse are made by children or vulnerable adults. It is the same in the civil courts where the matters alleged are criminal offences (See all litigation in respect of sexual abuse in children's homes, civil actions for rape, Children Act proceedings). The law is helpfully reviewed in Re H (minors) (Sexual Abuse: Standard of Proof) [1996] AC 563. Where the allegation is of a serious criminal offence probability is, rightly, not easily established."*

35.54 Furthermore, there does not appear to us to be any good reason in principle why a doctor (no matter how eminent or experienced) who is accused of abuse in any of its manifestations should not, if the allegation is prima facie credible, be subject to the ordinary disciplinary procedures which apply to all other employees within the NHS.

35.55 If doctors are treated in the same way as other NHS employees, there may be less reluctance to investigate, less reluctance to act on the type of concerns or complaints referred to in this Report.

The new disciplinary framework

35.56 However, we are pleased to note that our concerns over this practice that extended over decades in the NHS have recently been overtaken by events. Between the end date for evidence and submissions to our Inquiry, and the submission of our Report to the Secretary of State for Health, the Department of Health published, in March 2005, a new national disciplinary framework focusing on matters of clinical performance and capability. The framework deals with the initial handling of concerns about performance or conduct, and the actions to be taken in response to such concerns. Local conduct procedures will apply to those cases which relate to the conduct of a doctor.

35.57 As we have outlined earlier, the first two elements of this framework were published in December 2003 (HSC 2003/12) and covered:

- action when a concern arises; and

- restriction of practice and exclusion of practitioners from work.

35.58 The complete document, *Maintaining High Professional Standards in the Modern NHS*, was published in March 2005, further covering:

- conduct hearings and dismissal;

- procedures for dealing with issues of capability; and

- handling concerns about a practitioner's health.

35.59 The new framework procedures abolish the distinction between professional and personal misconduct, and doctors are now to be treated under the same local procedure – which we note must be "fair and reasonable" – as any other member of the NHS staff. We commend this approach and recommend that the NCAA, which is charged with the responsibility to ensure implementation is managed universally and smoothly, continue to work closely with NHS authorities to create a fair and transparently just set of practical procedures.

35.60 Having spelt out the problems that HC(90)9 created and maintained, we are gratified to see that the new procedure issued in March 2005 removes the distinctions above that caused so many difficulties. We note that all NHS bodies have to implement the framework by June 2005.

35.61 One area of disquiet remains in relation to Foundation Trusts, which are only "advised" to follow the framework. We note that Monitor[5] is involved and believe that, where the procedures contained in the framework are not followed by Foundation Trusts, then they should be individually called to account for their failure to do so. We do not see any justification, where patient safety is involved, for any part of the NHS applying a different standard, or making the investigation and disciplining of allegedly abusive staff more difficult.

Accordingly, we RECOMMEND that any deviation from acceptable practice in mental health services should be identified by the relevant statutory regulatory body and, where appropriate, by Monitor, and a standard, fair and transparent set of rules governing conduct of all mental health NHS staff in all NHS bodies and Foundation Trusts be quickly established.

---

5 Monitor is a non-departmental public body established under the Health and Social Care (Community Health and Standards) Act 2003. It is responsible for authorising, monitoring and regulating NHS Foundation Trusts.

35.62 We do not want to leave the subject of employment and discipline without referring to, and emphasising, our concerns in relation to those healthcare professionals (statistically likely to be an unfortunate few) who are wrongly accused of sexual assault, or sexualised behaviour, or other similar forms of abuse. The implementation and application of the new discipline and employment procedures (when operated) should be monitored to ensure that all appropriate protections are in place for the accused employee, as well as for the patient, or former patient, raising the concern or complaint.

35.63 This becomes particularly important where, as in the accounts of the former patients of William Kerr and Michael Haslam, the person making the disclosure is believed by the recipient of the information, but the patient refuses to allow her (and it is usually a woman) identity to be disclosed. In those circumstances – proceeding on the basis that patients or former patients making such disclosures need to be supported in making and pursuing a complaint and in withholding their identity – then consideration should be given to the following approach. Where a disclosure is made – particularly in the case of a psychiatric patient – but the patient is unwilling to allow a complaint to go forward in their name, a record could be made (with sufficient detail to be of later value) and retained, and, if a further disclosure is received (or complaint made) the original discloser should be asked again if they are willing to provide evidence.

35.64 For this process to operate in a fair and efficient way, the healthcare professional may have to be (probably will have to be) informed of the situation (although the identity of the first patient may not have to be disclosed) and careful detailed protocols would have to be in place across the NHS. We touch on this topic elsewhere in the Report (see Chapter 32 on record keeping and Chapter 28 on confidentiality).

The General Medical Council

General

35.65 It is no part of our task to examine in detail, and comment on, the workings of the GMC. The Terms of Reference, and the source of our jurisdiction as a Panel of Inquiry appointed under Section 2 of the National Health Act 1977, do not allow us to make recommendations to the Secretary of State to reform the GMC, or indeed on any recommendations expressly directed at any other non-governmental body, such as the Royal College of Psychiatrists. However, the GMC's response when complaints were made in relation to both doctors has been of some importance in our inquiries – complaints, we acknowledge, that were first made to the GMC in the late 1990s. We have addressed those matters in earlier chapters, and made observations where appropriate. Further, we have received considerable assistance from the GMC in terms of documentation, written submissions and oral evidence – extending some way beyond the GMC's response to and dealings with William Kerr and Michael Haslam. In those circumstances, and acting within the limitations of our Terms of Reference, we remain of the opinion that it is valuable, perhaps essential, at least to pose the question whether the former patients of William Kerr and Michael Haslam can now be satisfied and reassured that the current disciplinary procedures and practices of the GMC are such as to ensure that alleged sexual misconduct by doctors providing mental healthcare services is properly and promptly investigated and addressed. Put another way: does the GMC now have not only the means, but also the will to exercise its statutory functions so as to play its part in ensuring (insofar as it is able) this story of repeated missed opportunities to investigate widespread allegations will not be repeated?

35.66 The reason this question is important is that the role of the GMC, as overall regulator of registered doctors in the UK, clearly assumed central importance for witnesses who gave evidence to the Inquiry – witnesses who responded (or failed to respond) to concerns or complaints. A theme that emerged, developed below, was that doctors and health service administrators did not act in response to disclosures, did not feel they could act, because the GMC would not be interested. As already noted, that local attitude to the GMC seemed to us to form an important barrier to the effective handling of concerns or complaints.

35.67 When considering the response of the GMC to the complaints made against William Kerr and Michael Haslam in the late 1990s, we heard concerns about the attitude of the GMC – about the culture of that organisation. We here repeat one comment made by a medical witness:

> *"Most of my involvement in trying to make things happen has related to my dealings with the GMC. I have found the GMC to be opaque and uninterested."* [6]

---

6 We have altered the word "disinterested" to "uninterested", the witness's obvious intended meaning.

35.68 He added:

> *"I would like to believe that in the future the GMC will take complaints seriously, as I do not believe they did so here."*

35.69 We have therefore closely considered the present position within the GMC. This has been made possible through the full cooperation of the GMC with our Inquiry.

35.70 Our first observation is that there have been considerable changes to the practices and procedures of the GMC since the 1970s and 1980s, and even since the late 1990s. For example, prior to August 2000 the GMC had limited powers to impose interim suspension or interim conditions – and the exercise of that power depended on a prior decision to refer the doctor to the Professional Conduct Committee. In turn this required that particulars of the allegations be given to the doctor, and that there was a realistic prospect of establishing serious professional misconduct at the Professional Conduct Committee. As then, and now, a criminal standard of proof in relation to the facts alleged was applied, the term "realistic prospects" must have made effective action very difficult.

35.71 Further, we note that there is an increasing level of transparency at the GMC which perhaps did not exist at all during the 1970s and 1980s, or even into the 1990s.

35.72 Until recently, the position within the GMC was straightforward – if there was no complainant willing to give evidence (in relation to allegations such as those made against William Kerr and Michael Haslam) then there would be no finding of serious professional misconduct, and no power to take action in relation to the doctor's registration. If the complainant would not, herself, take the matter further the GMC would take the view that the allegation could not be proved, and therefore the case would be closed without further action.

35.73 We were told by the GMC that the current practice is different. Finlay Scott, Chief Executive and Registrar, said this:

> "We recognise that the GMC is simply part of a much wider regulatory framework. Our fitness to practise functions now focus far more in case handling terms on the need to protect patients and maintain the public's confidence in the medical profession. We seek to engage the doctor's employer, and any other relevant NHS organisations (eg NCAA) at an early stage. Provided the complainant agrees, we now disclose the complaint to the doctor and his employer shortly after receipt. This enables us to enter into a dialogue regarding the best method of handling the complaint and/or whether there may be wider causes for concern about the doctor's fitness to practise. Therefore if a complainant was unwilling to proceed with a complaint under our procedures, for example because she is not prepared to go through the ordeal of a formal hearing, we will actively explore with the employer or other relevant organisation whether they would be better placed to take the matter forward."

35.74 This is clearly a considerable improvement on the earlier position, but it reveals a continuing need for consistency of approach and action. We will return to this topic below, when considering the position of the Royal College of Psychiatrists, but it seems to us that if there is to be sharing of information, there must also be common enforceable standards when it comes to determining what conduct is, and what conduct is not, acceptable. For example, the following questions arise:

- If the alleged conduct is not criminal – because there is said to be a consensual sexual relationship with an existing or former patient with capacity – is the NHS employer applying the same ethical standard as the GMC, the BMA and the Royal College of Psychiatrists judging that conduct? Which in turn leads to the question:

- Is there in fact a discernible common ethical standard within the GMC, the BMA and the Royal College of Psychiatrists, in relation to all forms of sexual relationships between psychiatrists and not only existing but also former patients?

- If the alleged conduct is criminal, what does the GMC do? Does it make contact with the local police? It seems to us that it should. And, if not already identified, there should be a readily identifiable liaison officer, or other personnel, to effect the free flow of relevant information.

- If there is contact with the local police, is there more than mere "hand-over"? Are systems and arrangements in place to ensure that there is continuing liaison between agencies and employers? Who ensures that there is continuing, and follow-up, protection of public safety?

- What systems are in place to deal with patients, or former patients, who are presently too unwell to give evidence or follow up their concerns and complaints? It seems to us that there should be common standards throughout the NHS (and preferably within the GMC) so that information is retained, and concerns or complaints can be re-activated when, or if, the complainant recovers to the extent of being willing and able to give evidence (perhaps with suitable protections, as now provided for in Rule 36 of the Fitness to Practise Rules, 2004). That this should be the position is apparent from the stories of the many women who have given evidence to the Inquiry – they simply got better, and became strong enough to give evidence, years after the alleged event. If the original file is closed, if contemporaneous documents are lost or destroyed (as starkly revealed in the course of our Inquiry), such vulnerable patients are disadvantaged, and other patients who may be assaulted or otherwise adversely affected are not protected.

35.75 In the light of the recent publication of the Fifth Report of the Shipman Inquiry,[7] it is unnecessary to burden this Report with fuller, detailed reference to the practices and procedures of the GMC. We therefore refer the reader to Chapters 15 to 19 of that report.

Recent decisions of the GMC

35.76 At the request of the Inquiry, the GMC helpfully provided us with examples of recent decisions of the Professional Conduct Committee (PCC) (and subsequent appeal decisions of the High Court and Privy Council). This information was later supplemented by a complete list of decisions of the PCC relating to allegations of sexualised behaviour. That fuller list is identified in Chapter 30 of this Report, in relation to prevalence.

---

7 Cm 6394, presented to Parliament in December 2004.

35.77 It is difficult to draw any firm conclusions from that material, but we do accept that there has been a change of attitude, or at least of emphasis in the role, of the GMC.

35.78 One (now well-known) decision was not referred to in the materials originally supplied to the Inquiry by the GMC, but was drawn to our attention. This decision causes us concern, and is relevant to an understanding of whether or not the GMC, in 2005, has the ability and the will to provide clear protection for vulnerable psychiatric patients. We will also refer in detail to a second recent decision of the GMC.

35.79 The first decision relates to a hearing in October 2003 – the detail which follows is in the public domain. Dr R was charged by the GMC as follows (set out, as amended, and with the record of the doctor's admissions and the conclusions of the PCC):

> *"That, being registered under the Medical Act,*
>
> 1. *At the material times you were working as a General Practitioner at the King Street and University Medical Service in Lancaster; Admitted and found proved*
>
> 2. *Between February and April 2002 you were involved in*
>
>   a. *an emotional relationship, Admitted and found proved*
>
>   b. *a sexual relationship, Admitted and found proved with a patient of the practice who you had treated, namely Mrs A;*
>
> 3. *Mrs A had a history of psychiatric problems; Admitted and found proved*
>
> 4. *Your actions as described above were:*
>
>   a) *inappropriate, Found not proved*
>
>   b) *an abuse of the doctor-patient relationship, Found not proved*
>
>   c) *not in the best interests of your patient, Found not proved*
>
>   d) *likely to bring the medical profession into disrepute; Found not proved*

> *5. At a meeting with your partner, Dr B, on 28 April 2002, and with your partners, Dr B and Dr C, on 29 April 2002, you admitted the relationship as particularised in paragraphs 1 and 2 above; Admitted and found proved."*

35.80 There was, therefore, an *admission* of a sexual relationship with an existing patient of the practice, who had been treated by the doctor, and who had a history of psychiatric problems. But, despite that admission, and in a profession where sex with a patient is said to be a very serious matter going to the root of the doctor/patient relationship, the PCC found that it had not been proved that the relationship was:

a) inappropriate;

b) an abuse of the doctor-patient relationship;

c) not in the best interests of the patient;

d) likely to bring the medical profession into disrepute.

35.81 Therefore, the PCC concluded, the doctor was not guilty of serious professional misconduct. The imposition of penalty did not arise.

35.82 This seems to us to be a surprising decision – and, so it would appear, this view was shared by the Council for Healthcare Regulatory Excellence (see below).

35.83 We are concerned that it may have been reached, at least in part, by the PCC (acting, of course, in complete good faith) applying the *criminal* standard of proof, not merely to the question of whether or not the facts had been proved, but also to the question of whether or not the doctor was guilty of serious professional misconduct. (The only facts presented to the PCC, additional to those admitted by the doctor as set out in the charge, were that both the doctor and Mrs A were married; that the doctor had been treating the patient since November 2001; that the relationship was ended by him when he told his wife and partners; and that the partners then suspended the doctor and made a statutory declaration to the GMC.)

35.84 The brief reasons for the decision were given by the Chairman to the Committee:

> "*The only information provided to us is that contained within the charge itself. We have received no evidence as to the circumstances or context of any relationship with Mrs A, nor of any treatment you provided to her. The Committee are entitled to draw logical conclusions from such facts as are admitted. However, the Committee are acutely aware of the dangers of making unsupported assumptions to fill the void resulting from a lack of evidence and we have therefore not done so. Having in mind that the standard of proof required is that we should be sure, the Committee have determined that such facts as have been found proved are insufficient to support a finding of serious professional misconduct. We have accordingly recorded a finding that you are not guilty of serious professional misconduct. That concludes the case.*"

35.85 The Council for Healthcare Regulatory Excellence (CHRE) referred the decision of the PCC to court under section 29 of the National Health Service Reform and Healthcare Professions Act 2002, seeking also to introduce new evidence (not put before the PCC) which would "fill the void" referred to in the decision of the PCC.

35.86 In 2004, the Court of Appeal ruled that there was power under the 2002 Act for such a case (where there had been an acquittal) to be referred to the court.[8] During the course of 2005, the merits of the appeal under section 29 will be determined. It would of course be inappropriate for us to comment on, or predict, the outcome of that appeal. We do not seek to do so. Our concern arising from the decision, which may or may not be shared by the CHRE, is that the PCC's approach to its task when considering the case against Dr R may (and we emphasise the word "may") reflect a continuation of the cultural problems identified elsewhere in this Report.

35.87 If the main disciplinary body of the medical profession is serious in its stance that sexualised behaviour between a doctor and their patient (certainly an existing patient) will be interpreted as serious professional misconduct (whatever the penalty subsequently imposed), then it must show that to be the case in its decisions.

---

8 Decision of the Court of Appeal, 20 October 2004 [2004] EWCA Civ 1356.

Whether or not Dr R was aware of the severity of Mrs A's psychiatric history (the reference to "serious" was deleted from Charge 3) should not go to guilt or innocence, but may, of course be extremely relevant to what disciplinary action is then taken.

35.88 Mr Finlay Scott gave evidence on the topic of the criminal standard of proof to the Inquiry. He described to us the consultations that the GMC had undertaken and the conclusions they had reached. He essentially described their view on the standard now expected to be that they must be "sure".[9] He described a sliding scale of the standard to be met, with the more serious allegations requiring proof at the top of the scale. A less serious matter could be settled on the balance of probability.

35.89 As noted above, the decision in in the case of Dr R may have been reached by reliance on the criminal standard of proof which the GMC applies in the fact finding part of the disciplinary process (or perhaps of a misunderstanding of that standard of proof when the facts have been admitted). We are of course well aware that some standard of proof, and some burden of proof, must be applied in disciplinary matters, but we are concerned that application of the criminal standard (so that the PCC is "sure") may have the effect of deterring investigation and resolution of allegations of sexual misconduct.

35.90 It provides little comfort to the former patients of William Kerr and Michael Haslam to know that doctors can continue to practise without censure if, on a balance of probabilities, there is reason to conclude that they did have a sexual relationship with an existing patient. There may be occasions – for example when the disciplinary offence charged is also a criminal offence – when the investigating committee considers that a standard close to, or even the same as, the criminal standard should be applied. However, we remain unconvinced. In any event we do not see why it is obvious that such

---

9 *Indicative Sanctions Guidance: Fitness to Practise Regulations of the GMC*: "46. Where it is making a finding of disputed facts, the panel must be sure of its decision. The issue of whether the practitioner's fitness to practise is impaired, and the imposition of a sanction, or warning, are matters of professional judgement. The panel must be sure that any proposed action (whether to close the case with or without a warning, or to impose a sanction on the doctor's registration) is sufficient to protect patients and the public interest, failing which it must consider taking action against the practitioner's registration or imposing a more severe sanction, as appropriate." Whatever the wording, the word "sure" seems to us to connote a criminal standard of proof – we see little, if any, difference between "so that you are sure" and "satisfied beyond reasonable doubt".

a standard should always be applied, or should be applied at all in relation to charges of a disciplinary nature which do not have a criminal law equivalent (such as a consensual sexual relationship with an existing patient). We note at this point the evidence to the Inquiry by Mr Finlay Scott for the GMC, to the effect that the standard of proof makes little or no difference to the outcome of disciplinary charges:

> *"Sir Donald Irvine – and of all presidents of the GMC, he is perhaps the one on record as having most visibly tried to modernise the GMC and make it evident that we act in the interests of patients and not the profession. He is on record as saying that actually the debate around the standard of proof in relation to facts is not really material; that very, very rarely would it switch from the "to be sure" test to the balance of probability. In his experience, over a long period on the Professional Conduct Committee, very rarely would it have made any difference; it is not a material factor."* [10]

35.91 We would prefer to see that assertion tested by some form of independent investigation. Such an investigation should be led by the Secretary of State so that it is the Department of Health, as the body primarily responsible for the NHS, that can itself be satisfied that patient safety is not impaired.

35.92 This is particularly so now that the Government has changed the standard of proof in relation to the discipline of doctors, in the employment context. [11]

35.93 That first recent decision we considered related to an admitted sexual relationship with an existing patient. The second decision we draw attention to is a 2004 decision of the GMC not to pursue disciplinary proceedings in relation to a doctor (a psychiatrist) where there was

---

10 We note, in passing, that the distinction between the criminal standard of proof (applied in GMC proceedings in the UK) and the civil standard of proof (applied in the equivalent proceedings in, for example, Australia) was considered to be crucial in the decision of the Privy Council in *Dr Leonard Marinovich v. General Medical Council* [2002] UKPC 36, at paragraph 24 – another "massaging psychiatrist" case.

11 There is much recent case-law on this topic. For other healthcare regulators, such as for pharmacists, the Health Professionals Council and the General Optical Society, the civil standard is applied. Unless the criminal standard is enshrined in the rules, or in statute, we would anticipate that, as a matter of law, the courts would now generally favour a civil standard of proof. It is beyond the scope of this Inquiry to go further.

an admission of a sexual relationship with a woman who had *recently* been a patient.

35.94 In that case, completed in July 2004, the GMC decided not to continue with disciplinary proceedings against a consultant psychiatrist who had been dismissed from his employment with an NHS Trust following an independent internal inquiry panel (held in accordance with disciplinary procedures modelled on HC(90)9[12]) which had concluded that, among other allegations of misconduct:

> *"the psychiatrist had embarked on a sexual relationship with a married woman shortly after he had finished treating her."*

35.95 That finding of the internal inquiry panel was not surprising, as the psychiatrist had admitted the sexual relationship – which began "two months or less" after her treatment by the psychiatrist was brought to an end.

35.96 The psychiatrist's appeal to an Employment Tribunal was dismissed – in 2003. Further, and the central reason for mentioning this case at all, as already noted, the psychiatrist had admitted the sexual relationship with his former patient. The finding by the independent review panel in relation to the sexual relationship has parallels with Michael Haslam and Patient B11 referred to earlier. What follows is taken from paragraphs 47 and 50 of the decision of the Employment Tribunal but confined to the allegation concerning the relationship with the former patient.

> *"47. Turning to the Panel's finding regarding Complainant 3 ("C3") there were six charges: … forming an inappropriate and improper emotional and physical relationship with a patient soon after treatment.*

---

12 The proceedings of the inquiry panel are a model of the problems involved in such a procedure – for example, the hearings took place over a period of 10 days, stretching over five months. Hugh Chapman's evidence to our Inquiry may have been affected by his experience of that HC(90)9 inquiry – he was the Chair.

50. ... In relation to the inappropriate physical and emotional relationship between the Applicant [the psychiatrist] and C3 the Panel found no evidence that he was contemplating any further connection with her when he discharged her on 20 May 1999. The Panel accepted that it was C3 who made the telephone call shortly after 20 May which led to the affair. C3's evidence was that the affair started on 26 or 27 May when they spent three hours together alone at the Applicant's house or flat drinking wine with crisps. She was not clear when intercourse began but certainly before the end of June. The Applicant's evidence was that intercourse did not begin until the end of July. The Applicant referred to advice which he said he had received from 'The Medical Defence Union' [MDU] possibly about 6 July in relation to the lapse of time which was appropriate before an affair could begin with an ex-patient. He told the Panel that the advice was: "Well, six weeks is a bit close. However, if the person realises they cannot be your patient again then I don't think you could be criticised." The Panel delayed its findings in an attempt to get some firm evidence from the MDU regarding the advice which the Applicant had received. It was not clear to the Panel whether the Applicant had asked the MDU regarding the period within which it was possible to socialise with a former patient or the period in which it was possible to conduct an affair with a former patient. The Panel assumed that the MDU did not tell the Applicant that within a few weeks of his ending psychiatric treatment of a vulnerable female patient it would be acceptable to begin and continue a sexual relationship with her. The Panel found the complaint proved that the Applicant was guilty of professional misconduct in commencing and forming an inappropriate and improper physical and emotional relationship soon after the termination of her treatment. The Panel made this finding whether the relationship began at the end of June or the end of July [in other words, whether the sexual relationship began at the time asserted by the former patient or by the doctor]."

35.97 From exchanges with the GMC, it is clear that the main reason for the decision to discontinue disciplinary proceedings in relation to the admitted sexual relationship with the former patient was that the main witness in the case (the former patient) had indicated that she was unwilling to assist the Inquiry. In those circumstances, without the presence of the main witness, the PPC concluded, "it would be difficult to prove a charge of serious professional misconduct".

35.98 Some features of this case, as finally disposed of by the GMC disciplinary process, merit mention when we consider our recommendations:

- The undisputed facts show that, as recently as 1999, a consultant psychiatrist could have one-to-one contact with his young female patients. Not everything is team working.

- Chaperones, whether human or virtual, would have been irrelevant.

- A representative of a medical defence organisation may have advised the doctor, in 1999, that a sexual relationship between a psychiatrist and his former patient was ethically and professionally permissible within a few weeks of the cessation of the professional relationship.

- According to the finding of the independent investigation panel, the doctor had claimed that the advice received was as follows: "Well, six weeks is a bit close. However, if the person realises they cannot be your patient again then I don't think you could be criticised".[13]

13   This advice appears to be broadly consistent with the position of the GMC. In evidence to the Inquiry, Finlay Scott said this –. referring in general terms to the doctor/patient relationship (rather than to any particular features which may arise from the psychiatrist/patient relationship):

Q. The position the GMC adopts is that you are supposed to cease the professional relationship?

A. That is correct. If I can try to explain it in my words, the inference that can be clearly drawn from the Professional Conduct Committee cases is that you should not engage in a sexual relationship with a patient. It follows from that, and this has been made explicit, that doctors have the opportunity, if they feel themselves attracted to a patient, to end the professional relationship, allow a period to elapse and then, if it is appropriate, they can begin the personal relationship. That is a rather boiled-down version of what can be inferred from the cases before the Professional Conduct Committee.

Q. You end the relationship, there is then a cooling-off period?

A. That is correct.

Q. Following which, it is open to you to resume a personal relationship?

A. Yes.

Q. Although presumably not a professional relationship?

A. That is correct.

Q. The point at which that obligation to end the professional relationship kicks in should be, what, immediately the doctor can see a problem on the horizon? The reason I ask, it is quite difficult to apply that in practice.

A. I think it is probably quite difficult to go much beyond what I have said in my own words, not presenting this as a carefully drafted GMC view. The point at which the doctor is contemplating developing a personal relationship with a patient, then he should bring the professional relationship to an end.

Q. Somebody who has been your patient does not remain off limits once the cooling-off period has expired?

A. No. Indeed, a defence advanced before the Professional Conduct Committee in particular cases has been just that: that there had been a professional relationship but it had ended. Consequently, the doctor was free to begin a personal relationship. The concept of a cooling-off period has been recognised in the defences advanced and I think probably in the defences accepted, but I would not want to be drawn into defining exactly what that might have been in practice.

Q. It would be unfair of me to try to examine exactly the point at which that obligation arises, but one thing does follow from the answer you have given: that a former patient, with whom a relationship has not developed during the relationship, is also not off limits?

A. That is correct.

35.99 Our concerns in relation to the developments in, and outcome of, the disciplinary complaints against this psychiatrist were put to the GMC. Further, we asked if the handling and outcome of this case would be different under the 2004 Rules (referred to below). We received a full and helpful response, which we can summarise as follows:

- In March 2003 the case was referred by the PPC to the PCC.

- By the late summer of 2003, it had become clear that the psychiatrist's three former patients were not prepared to give evidence.

- Independent counsel and solicitors advised the GMC that it would not be possible to pursue the complaints without the oral evidence of the former patients.

- After an adjournment, and in the absence of further information, the referral was cancelled by the PPC under the then Rule 19 procedure in June 2004.

- The admission by the psychiatrist of a sexual relationship with his recently former patient appears to have been overlooked by the GMC, its committees and its advisers.

- Under the 2004 procedures, the case would have been dealt with differently, but the outcome would have been the same – presuming the legal advice on the effect of the absence of oral evidence from former patients to be the same.

35.100 In the light of that response, it would be inappropriate for us (within the limits of our Terms of Reference) to make further comment on the case. However, what the decision does serve to do is highlight the "current" patient/"former" patient dividing line, as recently as 2004. As noted earlier in this Report, the issue of sexual relationships between psychiatrists and their former patients seems to us to be an unresolved question requiring urgent attention, not only by the GMC and the Royal College of Psychiatrists, but also by the Secretary of State. The question is straightforward: "Is a doctor, particularly a psychiatrist, permitted by the rules of his profession to have a sexual relationship with a former patient – and if so, what if any limitations are there on that permission?" The public, and psychiatrists, are entitled to a clear answer.

35.101 We address the issue of sexualised behaviour and the psychiatrist/patient relationship, covering both current and former patients, in Chapter 29.

New GMC rules

35.102 As already mentioned, the law governing the way in which the GMC handles complaints about doctors changed on 1 November 2004 – with amendments to the Medical Act 1983, and the introduction of The General Medical Council (Fitness to Practise) Rules (SI 2004 No. 2608). These comprehensive new rules concerning "fitness to practise" also take into account the handling of the former GMC offence of "serious professional misconduct".

35.103 In summary, the changes affect the way in which the GMC investigates complaints prior to deciding whether to refer a case for adjudication and the way in which cases will then be dealt with at the adjudication stage. According to the GMC, the changes are the result of a lengthy review and subsequent consultation and are designed to improve the way in which the GMC deals with complaints by making the processes simpler and more streamlined than those currently in operation.

35.104 Under the new procedures, complaints about doctors will no longer follow separate streams for health, performance and conduct. Instead, the GMC will be looking at the doctor's fitness to practise in the round.

35.105 Greater levels of investigation into complaints at the initial stages of procedures will take place and the current screening and Preliminary Proceedings Committee stages have been abolished. There is instead a single investigation stage, at the end of which the decision to refer a case to adjudication will be taken by members of staff, who are known as Case Examiners. According to the GMC, Case Examiners have been appointed by the GMC following a rigorous recruitment process to undertake this role. All decisions are taken by two Case Examiners, one medical and one lay. Where the Case Examiners do not agree, then the matter is decided upon by the Investigation Committee (a statutory committee of the GMC).

35.106 We are informed by the GMC that they can only take action if the doctor's behaviour calls into question whether the doctor should continue to be registered, because of "impaired fitness to practise".

35.107 Under the heading "impaired fitness to practise", the GMC can take formal action if the doctor has:

- behaved badly or inappropriately;

- not done their job properly;

- a criminal conviction or caution in the British Isles or elsewhere;

- been found guilty by another regulatory body, whether in the British Isles or overseas; or

- their fitness to practise impaired due to physical or mental ill health.

35.108 A finding of "impairment of fitness to practise", as with serious professional misconduct, does not necessarily lead to erasure from the Register (there are a range of responses, or penalties). Our concern, however, is that there does not appear to be a mechanism in place (national and standardised) to pick up the (to some) less serious acts, the less serious boundary transgressions which may be indicators of a wider problem (see references to the "slippery slope", Chapter 29). Perhaps this could be remedied, at least in the field of psychiatry, by providing that a category of "impaired fitness to practise" would include "serious or persistent failure to comply with the requirements of the Code of Ethics" of the Royal College of Psychiatrists, if and when such a code is introduced and made compulsory (see below). Alternatively, the GMC may be given power to issue a warning where there has been a significant departure from the standards set out in *Good Medical Practice* (GMP) or a performance assessment has highlighted a significant cause for concern. (See, for a suggestion of a way forward, the Indicative Sanctions Guidance S2-1 covering the position where there is found to be significant departure from GMP or other guidance, but a conclusion reached that there is no impairment to practise.)

35.109 We have posed this suggestion in a very tentative form. We recognise that a "non-compliance" approach – that is, non-compliance with a Code of Ethics within a particular branch of medicine – may require a radical rethink of regulation, and may, at least in the short term, cause practical difficulties.

35.110 The reason we raise it at all is our concern that there should be clear, articulated and enforceable standards for psychiatrists. Not only examples of good practice – what the good practitioner should do – but also what the practitioner should not do. There should be clear guidelines and clear prohibitions, non-compliance with which will lead to action, possibly to censure. We wish to see, as outlined elsewhere in this Report, a Code of Practice for psychiatrists which states what conduct will not be tolerated, and the professional consequences that are likely to follow. How those standards are to be enforced is, in the end, a matter for the regulators – assuming that regulation and professional discipline remains with the GMC. There are of course many models. We raise the possibility of a specialised Code of Practice as but one aspect of such regulation.

35.111 Some guidance, some prohibitions, will apply to all practitioners, whatever the discipline – sexualised behaviour, abuse of patients, is such an area. Other areas of practice, and we are satisfied that psychiatry is one of them, may require more specialised guidance in order to be clear and helpful – particularly in relation to the maintenance of professional boundaries.

35.112 As noted at the outset of this section, we are satisfied that there is much to be encouraged and optimistic about in relation to changes within the GMC, of attitude and culture as well as of systems. Some of the more recent changes are still bedding in, but we here draw attention to recent decisions that support our optimistic outlook. At the end of last year in a fitness to practise hearing, a doctor admitted to forming an inappropriate physical relationship with a patient who had a medical history of anxiety and depression. The patient was subsequently admitted to a psychiatric unit. In order to protect patients and the public interest, the doctor's name was removed from the Register. The panel commented, referring to GMP:

> *"Patients must be able to trust their doctors with their lives and well-being. All patients are entitled to good standards of practice and care from their doctors and an essential element is the observance of professional ethical obligations."*

And:

> "Doctors must not allow their personal relationships to undermine the trust which patients place in doctors. In particular, doctors must not use their professional position to establish or pursue a sexual or improper emotional relationship with a patient."

35.113 A month earlier, in a case involving a doctor who had been convicted of seven counts of indecent assault, the Fitness to Practise Panel commented:

> "The offences of which you have been convicted are a clear breach of the fundamental principles of good medical practice. An offence of this type undermines public confidence in, and damages the reputation of, the medical profession. Patients place their trust in doctors and have a legitimate expectation that they will act in their best interests. Your patients placed their trust in you as their general practitioner to act appropriately and professionally. You repeatedly and blatantly abused that trust. The Panel considers that you have acted in a totally disgraceful manner."

35.114 We find further comfort in the recent decision relating to Dr Stephen Humphreys (6 June 2005), where the GMC Fitness to Practise Panel emphasised the importance of trust (in a case concerning the viewing of indecent images of children) and recognised the different role of the criminal court process and public protection achieved by strict regulation. The Panel said this:

> "The Panel find that all indecent images of children are images of abuse. Anyone who views such material helps to perpetuate a cycle of the exploitation of children. Whilst the courts properly distinguish between degrees of seriousness, the Panel considers any proven or admitted allegation against a registered medical practitioner to be a matter of grave concern because it involves such a fundamental breach of the public's trust in doctors. This trust is fundamental to the doctor/patient relationship."

Conclusions on the GMC

35.115 The position of the GMC can be considered in general terms, and in relation to particular concerns that have been raised.

35.116 First, the general. It is clear to us that there have been considerable changes, and changes for the better, within the GMC over recent years. At this time of even closer governmental and public scrutiny we hope that any necessary additional changes will also be made, but perhaps more importantly that the GMC's central role in the delivery of healthcare in the UK will be clarified and identified. We agree, as submitted to us on behalf of the former patients and as accepted by the GMC itself, that even as recently as the end of the 1990s, that role had not been properly understood.

35.117 Those who now have the task of considering the future of the GMC should at least be aware of the submissions made to us in relation to the handling of the complaints concerning the practice of Michael Haslam, complaints raised not only by patients but by local doctors. The patients described the GMC's then response and conduct as follows:

> "A show of support for patients which amounted to nothing less than a concerted and determined decision not to investigate what were by then universally well-known accounts of Haslam's abuse; a steadfast refusal to respond to those who had made complaints in the past; complete disregard for the safety of patients. Those patients who thought that doctors would stick together and cover for one another could scarcely have guessed that if and when a doctor did take the complaint forward then it would be treated in such an off-hand manner by the very authority charged with regulation of the medical profession."

35.118 Those patient concerns raise questions about cultural issues within the GMC. There was at least a perception of "siding with the doctor", not only in relation to the resolution of complaints, but in relation to the very process of investigating and handling complaints. We have very briefly addressed some of the former patients' concerns more particularly when considering the handling of the investigation of Michael Haslam (see Chapter 19). On consideration of the evidence, we do not accept the criticism set out above, that in relation to the GMC there was "a concerted and determined decision not to investigate". As it is not within our remit to investigate, in depth, the role of the GMC we have not attempted to resolve these concerns more fully. However, we are entirely satisfied that the wider concerns are genuinely held and should be brought to the attention of the Secretary of State, and the GMC, in this public document.

35.119 Second, turning to the particular. Recognising that we are unable to make recommendations which impact on the workings of the GMC, we merely note that we can see sound and sensible arguments for a fundamental reconsideration of the desirability and applicability of the criminal standard of proof in any part of the disciplinary proceedings of the GMC. In the Fifth Report of the Shipman Inquiry[14] – where recommendations relating to the operation of the GMC were within the terms of reference – Dame Janet Smith concluded that "it is arguable that the criminal standard of proof is appropriate in a case where the allegations of misconduct amount to a criminal offence" (see paragraphs 25.297 and 27.256 and Recommendation 81). We accept that it is arguable, at least from the doctor's perspective; it is perhaps always arguable from the perspective of the affected professional, whatever the profession. However, if attention is focused on the public interest, on the interests of the patients, it is perhaps more difficult for that argument to be presented with any confidence when considering the special role that doctors perform in our society. They have a unique opportunity, and a peculiar ability, not only to help and cure, but also to harm those who are in their care. The essential question for the regulators (and government) to consider – in the context of our Inquiry – is as follows:

---

14 Cm 6394,. December 2004.

> *"Is it in the public interest for a doctor to be allowed continuing unrestricted access to the care and treatment of patients when a professional regulatory body, in a fair and reasonable process, has concluded that the doctor has probably sexually assaulted one of more of his existing or former patients."*

35.120 Further, on the particular, we would wish to see an acceptance by the regulating bodies that any proven sexual contact between mental healthcare professionals and an existing patient is automatically treated as amounting to serious professional misconduct, or conduct which amounts to a heavy presumption that the fitness of the mental healthcare professional to practise is impaired. In relation to former patients, we would hope to see the early development of clear, standardised and firm guidance – at least addressing the duties and responsibilities of psychiatrists, or any doctor, in relation to their former patients.

35.121 Finally, we encourage the GMC to give full support to doctors who find themselves in the unfortunate position of having to report concerns in relation to the practice of colleagues.

The Royal College of Psychiatrists

Standards

35.122 The Royal College seems to have been first sufficiently aware of sexual exploitation of patients to make some form of public announcement in 1989. In that year, there was a published statement from the Public Policy Committee referring, somewhat cryptically, to "sexual exploitation of weaker or less able patients by those capable of wielding more power". This statement was described two years later as "useful", and when read with *Thinking the Unthinkable* (Brown and Craft, 1989) prompted Dr Fiona Subotsky[15] to write:

> *" ... it is clear that there are major training needs for staff in this area and that enabling women patients to speak more effectively, perhaps with an advocacy service, would be an advantage".*

---

15 *British Journal of Psychiatry* (1991) Dr Subotsky is the current Treasurer of the Royal College.

35.123 In passing, that paper begins with the following quotations from 1883:

> *"Except as occasional consultants, the less men doctors have to do with female lunatics the better."*

35.124 There is now an increasing number of women psychiatrists. This can only be to the benefit of the patient population. We are advised that research consistently shows that women are more concerned with the ethics of boundary violations than are men.

35.125 In 2002, the Royal College published *Vulnerable Patients, Vulnerable Doctors*, referred to elsewhere in this Report. This is clearly an important document, and is a major step forward in terms of guidance. We are pleased to have been informed, after the Part 2 seminars, that this document will be reviewed "to make the College's views even clearer as necessary", and that a working party is considering the revision of another Royal College policy document, *Sexual Abuse and Harassment in Psychiatric Settings*. We cannot emphasise too strongly that material of this nature should be contained in "living documents" which are updated and revised on a continuing basis so as to reflect current thinking, experience and learning.

35.126 There has been a call in the course of our Inquiry for the Royal College to produce and publish a Code of Ethics – including clear guidance amounting if possible to instruction on what is, and what is not, acceptable in the psychiatrist/patient relationship. One contributor put it is as follows:

> *"The Royal College of Psychiatrists as yet does not have any code of ethics or a code of practice. This remains a black hole in terms of ethical guidance for the concerned physician or the patient."*

35.127 Whether or not this is a "black hole" is for the profession and the Royal College to decide. The present position – as with psychiatric associations in other countries, such as the USA and Canada – is that the Royal College annotates and makes specific additions to the GMC's GMP to set out principles of medical ethics especially applicable to psychiatry. To an extent, therefore, the Royal College does have a Code of Ethics, grafted onto the GMC's document. However, there may be a weakness in this arrangement: it may fail to highlight sufficiently the different context in which psychiatrists operate. Of course, as medical practitioners, psychiatrists have community of experience with the rest of the medical profession, but the differences are crucial in considering the issues to which this Report is directed. We believe psychiatrists would be particularly assisted by a dedicated document (incorporated by reference perhaps into GMP) addressing the particular ethical challenges of their specialty. We thus interpret the "call" here referred to as a request for a separate, readily accessible document that, as we have said before, clearly sets out not only the "do's" but also the "don'ts" of psychiatric practice.

35.128 It is outside our Terms of Reference, and our jurisdiction more generally, to make any recommendations affecting the Royal College. However, based on what we have heard and read in the course of this Inquiry, we add our support to that call. The production by the Royal College of a clear and comprehensive Code of Ethics addressing the particular obligations of psychiatrists would be of considerable benefit.

Discipline

35.129 The Royal College is a membership organisation, and it is not compulsory to be a subscribing member for employment as a psychiatrist. We consider that situation to be regrettable (at least within the NHS), particularly in the light of the fact that it is only the GMC which can effectively discipline registered doctors, and only the Royal College which can effectively draft and set standards particularly applicable to psychiatrists – whether or not crystallised into a published Code of Practice.

35.130 Since the days of William Kerr and Michael Haslam, the Royal College has reviewed and changed its disciplinary procedures. Earlier in this chapter we referred to evidence we had received covering the period 1961 to 1988, that "the focus [of the Royal College] was primarily educational rather than regulatory". The position today has not really changed – indeed, in "The College's Disciplinary Procedures: Suggestions for Change – March 2004" it is expressly stated, "The Royal College of Psychiatrists is not a regulatory body".

35.131 The suggestions for change make it abundantly clear that the Royal College does not see any direct regulatory role nor any direct, disciplinary role. It states:

> *"All complaints about psychiatrists are dealt with by the GMC or by employing authorities or in some instances the civil courts"*

and this is followed by the suggestion that the existing byelaw "Acting in a dishonourable or unprofessional manner or in a way calculated to bring discredit to the College" be deleted and replaced by a complaints system available to College members and the general public. However, when examined, the proposed complaints procedure is very narrowly drawn, and would not allow any investigation into the kind of concerns or complaints with which this Inquiry has been concerned:

> *"The College's complaints procedure will only apply to incidents which have occurred during the course of College business or whilst a member, trainee or associate is acting as a representative of the College or in some other College capacity. All other complaints will be redirected to the relevant body."*

35.132 We are advised that the Royal College has now clarified its disciplinary role, and it has been decided that the existing byelaw "acting in a dishonourable or professional manner" etc should be retained.

35.133 However, the Royal College (understandably) is not equipped to undertake large-scale investigations, and must therefore leave the main role to the GMC, and to the employers, supported by the NCAA.

35.134 We are advised that the Royal College retains power to terminate membership, but usually only does so after erasure by the GMC. A power to suspend is being produced. The Royal College's main function, therefore, will continue to be educational. We are advised that the clarification of standards remains an important part of that educational function.

35.135 It follows that the general public cannot look to the Royal College for any real assistance in the pursuit of concerns or complaints in relation to sexualised behaviour. It therefore becomes even more important for the GMC (or some other body) to take full responsibility for setting, maintaining and enforcing clear standards in relation to boundary crossing, including but not limited to sexual and other intimate relationships with existing and former patients.

35.136 As suggested above, a possible way forward would be that non-compliance with a professional body's Code of Practice in relation to the crossing of patient/doctor boundaries should (if it does not already do so) and of itself amount to such a shortfall in standards that disciplinary proceedings can be taken – even if there is no criminal offence, no assault. In other words, the proof before the GMC of a breach by a member psychiatrist of the Royal College of Psychiatrists' Code of Ethics (if published) would amount to evidence of serious professional misconduct, or evidence of doubt as to the psychiatrist's fitness to practise. This does not appear to us to be the present position. There are a number of mechanisms that may be used to achieve the same end point, and we believe that the indispensable foundation for progress in this area is clear standards (including clear prohibitions), with a clear outcome for breach.

Conclusions and recommendations

35.137 From the above it may reasonably be concluded that there has been a lack of cohesion and clarity when it comes to the employment discipline and regulation of doctors. We leave to one side the investigation and prosecution of criminal offences, where we expect and recommend that there be close and early liaison between local healthcare employers, national regulators and local police.

35.138 We repeat, as already noted, that there have been significant changes and improvements, particularly within the GMC, and (very recently) in relation to disciplinary procedures for doctors employed within the NHS, since the days when William Kerr and Michael Haslam were consultants in North Yorkshire. But, in relation to discipline and regulation, there still seems to be too much scope for local variation, local discretion and, thereby, both local and central inaction. It does not seem to us to be right or sensible for there to be any risk that standards in relation to the subject of our Inquiry should be set differently, investigated differently or responded to differently, in different parts of the country. Conduct that is improper and unprofessional and would result in suspension or dismissal in one NHS hospital, or in one NHS PCT, should be treated in exactly the same way in any other similar institution or environment. Patients are entitled to nothing less. A postcode lottery in relation to this of all topics is simply unacceptable.

35.139 Such an approach is consistent with developments within the NHS, and the interlocking regulatory bodies responsible for the setting and maintaining of common standards: the National Institute for Clinical Excellence (NICE, established in 1999); the National Patient Safety Agency (NPSA, established in 2001); the National Clinical Assessment Service (NCAS, established in 2001[16]); the Commission for Healthcare Audit and Inspection (CHAI, established in 2004 – now known as the Healthcare Commission); and the Council for Regulation of Healthcare Professionals (CRHP, now the CHRE, established in 2003).[17]

35.140 If harmonisation of standards and approach is the correct way forward, and we believe that it is, then it must follow that at least in relation to the possible abuse of patients the same burden and standard of proof for the finding of the facts must apply – at the local employment and investigation level, and at the national regulatory level.

35.141 What we wish to see is a clearer, more effective, more transparent system. It is not for us to comment in this Report on the broader NHS – save where directly relevant to our Terms of Reference. However, we are able to offer some suggestions and recommendations in relation to the NHS employment of psychiatrists. For the reasons set out above, it seems to us highly desirable that all psychiatrists employed within the NHS should be regulated by the same national standards – and that those standards should be enforceable, at a national level (by a body such as the GMC), as well as by the local employing body. If patient safety and welfare is, as we believe it to be, the correct touchstone, then the most straightforward solution seems to be as follows:

16 Called NCAA at the time of its establishment in 2001.

17 Recent developments within the NHS are summarised in Chapter 6 and Annex 1 of *The Independent Investigation into how the NHS Handled Allegations about the Conduct of Clifford Ayling*, Cm 6298 (2004).

- All psychiatrists employed by the NHS must be, and must remain, members of the Royal College of Psychiatrists. It may be necessary for there to be different levels of membership – accessible by examination – but it is to be presumed that doctor/patient boundary violation standards would be common to all members, at all levels. (We are advised that there are already a variety of possibilities of association with the Royal College, so that all types of psychiatrist can "belong".) Perhaps an association, or a similar level of membership, can be encouraged by NHS Trusts requiring, as extra quality control, that all professional staff belong to a named professional association. For psychiatrists that would be the GMC and the Royal College.

- If (as will be the case) psychiatrists from other Member States within the European Community are employed within the NHS, we would expect them to comply with the same standards – at least in relation to doctor/patient boundaries as set by the Royal College. Doctors from other Member States must already be registered with the GMC if they are to be employed by the NHS – if the doctor has acquired a recognised qualification granted in a Member State of the EC, they are entitled to full automatic registration. We see no reason why the same, or a similar, approach cannot be taken to membership of the Royal College.

- It is only by this, or some similar, system that patients throughout the UK can be satisfied that they are being treated by psychiatrists who are subject to the same, high, ethical standards, and that a breach of those standards could lead to appropriate, national, consequences.

35.142 As we have emphasised throughout the Report, we are concerned to see an end to patient abuse, particularly – based on evidence to the Inquiry and the convictions of William Kerr and Michael Haslam – an end to abuse categorised as sexual assault or sexualised behaviour. Such an outcome is not possible; but an end to preventable abuse may be achievable.

35.143 Our considered view is that the likelihood of achieving such an outcome would be greatly increased by recognition of the true nature and extent of the problem itself, prompted by the careful collection of data to show the true position (see Chapter 30), and particularly by a standardisation of the approach to such abuse (covering current and former patients) within the NHS and by the various professional regulatory and disciplinary bodies. We believe that there is no sensible basis for different definitions, different procedures, different standards of proof in relation to the facts alleged. These differences are dangerous when they arise, in such a widespread, national, area of concern.

35.144 All professionals involved in the delivery of mental health services covered by the Mental Health Act, whether psychiatrists, psychologists, nurses or approved social workers, etc, are subject to the guidance in the Mental Health Act Code of Practice. There is, therefore, already some commonality. There is no reason why psychiatric patients, the users of mental health services throughout the UK, should not expect the same standards of behaviour, and the same approach to investigation, discipline and regulation, if they raise concerns or complaints – wherever they are treated, and whoever within the NHS is alleged to be at fault.

35.145 So how can a consistency of approach be achieved? The present move by the Government is towards standardisation, and the inclusion under "best practice" regulation of an increasing number of professions and specialties. The CHRE is a statutory overarching body, covering all of the UK, and it is separate from Government. It was established to promote best practice and consistency in the regulation of healthcare professionals by the following nine regulatory bodies:

- General Medical Council
- General Dental Council
- General Optical Council
- General Osteopathic Council
- General Chiropractic Council
- Health Professions Council
- Nursing and Midwifery Council

- Royal Pharmaceutical Society of Great Britain

- Pharmaceutical Society of Northern Ireland.

35.146 Of course, not all of these regulatory bodies operate within mental health services. The significance for us of this framework is that it at least provides an opportunity for consistency of regulation. Some matters are immutable – abuse of patients, whether sexualised or otherwise, must be one of them. All NHS patients should know, without having to go to the trouble of making a comparative study, that they are safe from abuse while in the care of any healthcare professional – be it a doctor, dentist, nurse, osteopath or chiropractor.

35.147 This consistency of regulation should allow the CRHE to ensure, by using its existing powers or if necessary by the receipt of additional powers, that:

- the same core ethical standards in relation to abuse of patients is applied by all professional regulators;

- the same approach to patient confidentiality is applied (see Chapter 27, paragraph 13); and

- the same standard of proof and core procedural rules are applied (and our clear preference is that where patient safety is concerned, the generally applicable standard should be the civil standard).

35.148 We are satisfied that the impact of the Government's plans and investment in health services has dramatically altered the landscape of the NHS. At an organisational and structural level, it is almost unrecognisable as the NHS in which William Kerr and Michael Haslam practised. The emphases on patient safety, remedial action for poor clinical performance, closer scrutiny of untoward events and empowering patients in the management of services are greatly welcomed.[18]

35.149 However, for individual patients unfortunate enough to encounter an abusive doctor, we cannot be satisfied that those improved systems are yet fully developed, or imbedded into the culture of the NHS, so as to ensure that concerns and complaints are heeded, and if heeded at all, promptly acted on and fully investigated. Improvements at an organisational and structural level are of little value if they do not deliver, at potential victim level, adequate and effective protections.

---

18 This conclusion is in similar terms to the conclusion of the Clifford Ayling Committee of Inquiry – Cm 6298 at paragraph 6.109.

Accordingly, we RECOMMEND that the Secretary of State should invite the Council for Healthcare Regulatory Excellence (CHRE) to consider (with a grant of additional powers if necessary), in relation to the regulation of healthcare professionals, the application of common standards, practices and procedures so that patient safety can more effectively be protected.

Section Eight
Some answers

Chapter 36
Response to concerns

Introduction

36.1 In this Report we have explored in some detail the disclosures made by former patients, and the response to those disclosures, at all levels of the NHS.

36.2 It is abundantly clear that opportunities were missed, and that there was no meaningful investigation, of any kind, into the alleged activities of William Kerr and Michael Haslam until the Manzoor Inquiry in 1998 – and then only in relation to Michael Haslam. But if an investigation was possible in 1998, why not in 1988, why not in 1983? There appeared to be quite widespread knowledge and discussions about inappropriate behaviour that was, or might have been, going on. And all the discussion appeared to be focused on, and only on, William Kerr and Michael Haslam. So far in this Report we have identified some obstacles to any investigation – some cultural, such as an acceptance of consensual sexual relationships between doctors and patients, some structural, such as the consultants' contracts being held by the Region not the District; a reluctance by individuals to become involved; and over-respect for consultants and their elevated status.

36.3 In earlier chapters of the Report we have also highlighted areas of concern to the Inquiry and made a series of recommendations which, if followed, will assist in reducing the risk of psychiatrist/patient sexual behaviour, and ensure (so far as it can be) that the experiences alleged by the former patients of William Kerr and Michael Haslam are not repeated.

36.4 There is more that can be done, particularly in the areas of education and training. We now turn to consider these additional areas, and what additional measures can be taken.

36.5   As in other areas of the Report, we are here particularly concerned to focus on the situation where there is no formal complaint made to a recipient within the NHS. We have addressed the complaints system in an earlier chapter. Here we focus on the situation where, although there may not be a formal complaint at the time, proper investigation could lead to an expression of concern being converted into a formal complaint or other action.

36.6   In all this, the underlying principle to be applied is that of improving and ensuring patient safety and the development of comprehensive risk management systems with the NHS organisations. These are already subject to external validation. In addition, we are aware that reports of the most serious incidents across NHS Trusts are already reported into a national database run by the National Patient Safety Agency (NPSA). This is a necessary process in ensuring patient safety across NHS services.

Two questions

36.7   A constant concern arising in the Inquiry is how the NHS should handle general rumours without there being a specific complaint attached to a specific patient who is prepared to come forward – where (as with William Kerr and Michael Haslam) there was general noise but little more. We were informed that, by the time of the Manzoor Inquiry, changes were beginning to take place, and these have been rolling forward ever since. There has been an evolution of processes. What, in particular, has changed is the emergence of a consultant appraisal process, supported by medical directors and clinical directors aware of the practice of the consultants for whom they are managerially responsible. Prior to that, in the NHS, there was no real managerial hierarchy for consultants – a consultant was a consultant, and that was it.

36.8   But a managerial hierarchy, supported or underpinned by employment contracts, is only part of the answer. We accept – and have addressed in an earlier chapter – that where there is a willing complainant and a fair and responsive complaints system, disclosures can readily be converted into investigations, and investigations into conclusions, and conclusions into disciplinary processes. But that is not the central issue here – what if there is no willing complainant?

36.9 Two separate questions arise: the first requires us to investigate what support is offered to the patient who raises the issue, even if it does not become a formal complaint; the second is to question what the response should be to the information received. Put simply, it is the difference between handling of the patient and the handling of the information from the patient – connected but separate issues.

36.10 It is unacceptable that the disclosing patient should suffer any additional harm from that very process of revealing to the NHS the potential risk of harm to other patients. We accept that regrettably this was indeed the outcome for some of the patients who disclosed their concerns in relation to the practices of William Kerr and Michael Haslam.

Support for the disclosing patient

36.11 The patient must be appropriately supported; in particular, the patient must be offered and given early access (if required) to free independent counselling and/or advocacy services. It may be that the patient would then feel empowered through that support to take the issue forward through a formal process.

36.12 However, it must be accepted by the NHS that for some patients – particularly vulnerable patients who may be suffering from mental disorder – "taking the issue forward" is simply not going to happen, certainly not in the short term. Such patients, even in 2005, perceive themselves to be, and indeed often are, stigmatised by a diagnosis of mental disorder. It is very difficult for them to feel that they will be listened to. They may continue to feel that they are disempowered, and labelled and that their concerns (however expressed) will not be taken seriously.

36.13 We readily accept that the processes are now much improved in terms of offering support to people. But we also emphasise that the initial contact with the first member of staff who hears the allegation or expression of concern is of central importance. If that initial member of staff, that nurse, that GP, that social worker, is not able to direct the person to the appropriate support and advice (assuming that they are not able to give it themselves), then the opportunity is lost.

36.14 One important aspect of caring for the disclosing patient, is offering immediate support and a sympathetic hearing. Former patients have told us repeatedly that it was at the very earliest stages – when they felt vulnerable, used and dirty – that they needed to be listened to. Too often, they were immediately disbelieved – not after an investigation – but immediately, there and then, as the story was being told. And we emphasise that almost without exception the accounts we have heard – first or second hand – were not intrinsically unbelievable, or incredible, not so outrageous as to be rejected out of hand (unless on the wholly self-defensive basis that "doctors do not do that kind of thing!"). We therefore regret that there was a strong element in the reaction and response of some, that the disclosing patient was immediately disbelieved, simply because they were, or were considered to be, mentally ill.

36.15 Patients who gave evidence also made clear to the Inquiry how acutely they feared the loss of care and support that might follow a complaint. Patients described themselves as relieved to have found help (through psychiatric treatment) for their condition; the last thing they wanted was to have that support withdrawn. The Inquiry is aware from evidence given that in some cases – and by default – the effort to attend to the complaint rendered the patient's need for care and support less of a priority. This cannot be right and requires substantial remediation by professional staff and managers.

36.16 Our view of this fits well with the initiative of March 2000, when the government issued *No Secrets* as part of its development of adult protection procedures.[1] *No Secrets* is statutory guidance issued under section 7 of the Local Authority Social Services Act 1970, and provides the framework for inter-agency collaboration on the development and implementation of policy and procedures for the protection of adults. We are encouraged to see that the advice found in *No Secrets* is being developed and implemented across the country – although we were told that, nationally, the picture is "patchy".[2] The county and city councils of North Yorkshire and City of York have produced revised multi-agency policy and procedures for the Protection of Vulnerable Adults (POVA) (still in draft, but revised in April 2004). When read with the statutory obligation to act on any

1 DH (2000) *No Secrets*.

2 We have been provided with, and have considered, the *Adult Protection Policy and Procedures* prepared jointly by the London Borough of Southwark and the Metropolitan Police.

suspicion or evidence of abuse or neglect under the Public Interest Disclosure Act 1988, and to pass on concerns to a responsible person/agency, there is real cause for optimism that, at least in this area, the lessons of the past have been learned and it is far more likely that patients will be better protected.

36.17   In the context of caring for patients, we were particularly impressed by the following from the North Yorkshire and City of York policy, under the heading "Disclosure of Abuse, Dos and Don'ts":

> "If you are in a situation where someone starts to disclose abuse to you
>
> DO
>
> - *stay calm and try not to show shock*
> - *LISTEN carefully rather than question directly*
> - *be sympathetic*
> - *be aware of the possibility that medical evidence might be needed*
> - *tell the person that:*
>   - *they did right to tell you*
>   - *you are treating this information seriously*
>   - *it was not their fault*
>   - *you must discuss with an appropriate manager*
>   - *if they wish, contact will be made with the police or social services*
>   - *in certain circumstances the police and social services will be contacted without their consent, but that their wishes will be made clear throughout*
> - *report to your manager*
> - *write down as soon as possible as far as you are able, what was said by the person disclosing*
> - *ensure that information is noted in the case file*

DON'T

- *press the person for more details*

- *promise to keep "secrets". Explain that the information will be kept confidential, ie information will only be passed to those people who have a need to know*

- *make promises that you cannot keep*

- *be judgemental (eg why didn't you run away)*

- *pass on information to anyone who doesn't have a need to know ie do not gossip."*

36.18 We are satisfied that if that simple procedure had been followed when the former patients of William Kerr and Michael Haslam were attempting to tell their stories, there would have been a very different outcome. We have no difficulty with the "do not gossip" instruction. In a well-ordered, well-managed NHS organisation, dissemination of gossip should not be an accepted form of response to disclosures of the abuse of patients. In a poorly run or inadequately managed institution, gossip may be a key outlet acting as a substitute for an effective response to information.

36.19 We accept that there are difficulties with the *No Secrets* policy, not least in the definitions of "vulnerable person" and "abuse", which may exclude some of the former patients, and some of the incidents of which they complain. The definition of "vulnerable person" is fixed by *No Secrets* and is in turn taken from the 1997 Consultation Paper *Who Decides?*:

> *"A person aged 18 years or over who is or may be in need of community care services by reason of mental or other disability, age or illness; and who is or may be unable to take care of him or herself, or unable to protect him or herself against significant harm or exploitation."*

36.20 The definition of abuse, particularly sexual abuse, may exclude some of the allegations of so-called "consensual" sexual relationships with the consultants.

36.21 The Adult Protection Procedures, of which *No Secrets* forms a part, is well known to, and operated by, social services throughout the country. Following one of the Part 2 seminars we received a submission expressing surprise that some of the attending NHS staff appeared not to be aware of these procedures. The explanation offered was that the NHS does not take the lead on Adult Protection, and therefore NHS staff (including here GPs) feel reluctant to hand over responsibility for investigation to another organisation. As the observer said:

> *"This sort of thinking allows the needs of the organisation to supersede the needs of the abused individual."*

36.22 The same contributor also expressed concerns that Health Service employees are, by a policy decision, excluded from the PoVA lists. If this is so, and we express no views, then clearly there is a need to reconsider that policy decision in the light of the factual conclusions expressed in this, and similar, inquiries.

36.23 Finally, concern was expressed by another contributor that in some areas the title Adult Protection Officer is merely being added to a pre-existing post, whereas in others, resources have been found to create a properly trained, equipped and staffed Adult Protection Unit. The intended protection will be illusory if Adult Protection is not taken seriously, if officers are not properly trained and afforded adequate standing and status, and units are not properly funded and staffed. How seriously an NHS organisation or institution takes Adult Protection may well be an indicator of its approach to patient safety more generally.

36.24 However, even with these reservations, the policy forms a useful basis for further advice and guidance – specifically if adapted to address the kind of issues identified in this Report. We make no separate and specific recommendations in relation to the concerns expressed as set out above, but expect they will be picked up on any review of the operation and implementation of the *No Secrets* policy (or "In Safe Hands" in Wales). We do however consider that the policy should be revisited, or a new and similar policy created, to meet the needs of patients such as those who gave evidence to the Inquiry.

36.25 Accordingly:

We RECOMMEND that within 12 months of the publication of this Report the Department of Health should develop and publish national advice and guidance to Primary and Secondary Healthcare Trusts addressing the disclosure, by patients or other service users, of sexual, or other, abuse with particular emphasis on users of mental health services.

Responding to information

36.26 The second question. If the individual patient feels too vulnerable or disturbed to take a formal complaints route, how can the NHS as an organisation respond to and act on the information, even if an allegation is withdrawn?

36.27 We accept that the most difficult position is where the former patient (a user of mental health services), having made a disclosure, then withdraws the allegation. If there has been a credible disclosure, properly investigated, properly documented, and the patient says – to the satisfaction of the investigator – "I got it wrong", or "I must have misinterpreted", or "It didn't happen", then we accept that there is little the NHS can do. We expect that such a situation is less likely to occur if the patient who discloses is treated and cared for in the way we have described earlier in this chapter, but we accept that it will nevertheless happen. If, however, there are question marks over the withdrawal (such as happened with Patient A17) – for example, because of the fluctuations of the patient's mental disorder – then a more careful response is necessary.

36.28 In either event, we would hope that there will be adequate records of the original disclosure – records which will be retained in case (a) there are repeat allegations, or (b) the initial discloser wishes to re-open the allegation (and has a convincing reason for her change of position).

36.29 But if there is no withdrawal, merely a discontinuance of any complaint – and this was the position for some of the disclosing patients considered by the Inquiry – then we see no reason why the NHS should ignore and fail to use the information received. The information is not merely gossip or rumour – see Chapter 33 – but far more concrete than that. The present structures, perhaps suitably adapted, involving medical directors, nurse directors, and applying clinical governance processes, will come into play. It might not currently be possible to take the allegation forward as a named person complaining, but there may be sufficient information (even if anonymised) to raise issues or concerns, so that a suitable investigation is undertaken, which includes speaking with the healthcare professionals involved, looking at their practice and then deciding how to take the matter further. At the very least, the carrying out of an investigation may act as a deterrent to the future activities of the person identified, and possibly of others not yet known about.

36.30 We accept that there is a difficult balance to be maintained in relation to fairness – to the patient and to the staff member concerned. An allegation cannot be allowed to turn into any form of witch-hunt. But we are firmly of the opinion that there must be some response – some investigation – in order for the NHS to be satisfied that every reasonable step has been taken to protect patient safety.

36.31 However information is obtained (assuming it is given some credence by the recipient) and even if the information does not lead to the engagement of formal complaint procedures, to criminal prosecution, or to disciplinary proceedings, it may be valuable when considering performance and appraisal. Such information may also lead to the employing Trust contacting the relevant regulatory body (eg the National Clinical Assessment Service) for assistance where the disclosure relates to the performance of a doctor (or dentist). Merely because (based on the scenario set out above) the concerns could not be classed as "substantiated" for the purposes of current NCAS procedures for practice assessment, it does not follow that the information received may not have value by linking up with other information held by the NCAS in relation to that practitioner. Such contact could therefore be a valuable step in relation to improving patient safety. This is particularly so if it is accepted that there should be a central repository of "adverse incident" information in relation to doctors or other mental healthcare professionals. As noted elsewhere in this Report, the existence of such a national repository, with access being permitted by employers, regulatory bodies, the police etc, may help to prevent the failure to match up similar information which is so starkly revealed by the facts we have been considering. The central lesson is that "several streams of information can lead to the identification of concerns".[3]

---

3 NCAA (now the NCAS, managed by the NPSA) – External Education Strategy Toolkit.

The Wade/Haslam story

36.32 It may assist at this point to re-visit the Dr Wade story referred to in Chapter 22. Dr Wade, it is to be recalled, received a disclosure of alleged sexualised behaviour from Patient A22. He passed on that concern to Michael Haslam, as a senior colleague of the named doctor said to have been involved, William Kerr. Michael Haslam did nothing with that information – the disclosure took place in 1979. The processing, such as it was, of Patient A22's disclosure was on the basis that Patient A22 did not want to be involved in any formal complaint.

36.33 What should happen in today's NHS if that same scenario were repeated? The senior consultant receiving the disclosure from the GP should, at least, do the following:

- Make a careful, and full, written note of the disclosure.

- Pass on the note, as a record of the disclosure, to the Chief Executive of the Trust (or to the Medical or Clinical Director).

- Offer care and support to the GP, and, if appropriate, to the disclosing patient.

- Consider his professional duty of care and his duty (if engaged) to pass on the information to the relevant organisations including the GMC. The GMC's guidance currently advises that a doctor has a duty to "act quickly to protect patients from risk if you have good reason to believe that you or a colleague may not be fit to practise".

36.34 The receiving Chief Executive (or Medical or Clinical Director), on receipt of the written report, should consider one or more of the following options:

- Whether or not to investigate the identified psychiatrist's practice, and if so, how.

- Whether or not to offer further support and/or care to the patient and her GP.

- Whether or not to interview the identified psychiatrist, and the patient (if willing).

- Whether or not to contact the GMC or other agencies such as the police (after speaking to the GP and/or the patient).

- Whether to contact the NCAS.

- Whether or not to change the identified psychiatrist so that they are no longer the patient's consultant.

- Whether or not to restrict the practice or exclude the psychiatrist from clinical work (or all commitments) during any investigation.

36.35 If the alleged conduct is criminal, at what point do the police become involved? It seems to us that there should be consistency across the NHS, and when the allegation relates to a vulnerable adult, very early contact and liaison with the local police should take place – along the same lines as alleged conduct in relation to vulnerable children. (See also the Adult Protection Procedures, and Protection of Vulnerable Adult lists, referred to in Chapter 34 of this Report – noting that, at present, the NHS itself is excluded from the PoVA system.)

36.36 Contact with the police should involve far more than mere "over to you" notification. It is important that local policies and protocols are in place (consistent with national standards) so that police involvement is integrated into patient protection. For example, early reporting to the police may have the consequence that all other, Trust-based, investigation is frozen because of overlapping roles, and the risk of contaminating the evidence (witness and forensic). But if reporting to the police is a form of "entrance strategy", then there must also be an "exit strategy" in place, addressing issues such as:

- If there is a prosecution, what happens in relation to the Trust?

- If there is a prosecution, but no conviction, what happens in relation to the Trust and its internal investigations?

- If there is a decision not to prosecute, what happens?

36.37 These issues require, in particular, reference to the use of evidence and perhaps to the terms of any decision not to prosecute.

36.38 Trusts should be concerned, and should revisit their policies, if the above steps are not expected to be taken. Further, the policies should be clear and readily accessible, and specifically brought to the attention of all NHS mental health staff.

Education, training and practice

Introduction

36.39 There are limitations on the impact of education and training. We doubt that it is wholly possible to train doctors to be virtuous, to train them not to abuse the patients in their care. However, there is a most valuable role for education and training. First, it may assist in focusing attention on ethical issues, and on the position of the patient, particularly the vulnerable patient. Secondly, it will assist in training future and existing doctors and other mental health service professionals on how to respond to disclosures made to them, and how to pass on their own concerns about the conduct, attitude and behaviour of colleagues. Although what we say here may be of more general application, we will only consider the education and training of doctors. But, before doing so, we make this general point: that all staff at all levels should be educated on the identification and preservation of proper boundaries, and the harm caused by boundary transgressions, commencing at undergraduate level through all the relevant professions. The message must be reinforced in induction training, Continuous Professional Development (CPD) and through employment contracts that specifically detail unacceptable behaviour. The message must be supported by clear and enforceable codes of conduct by NHS Trusts and by the regulatory bodies. There must be clear boundaries, clear sanctions, and no tolerance of the abuse of patients.

Education and training, generally

36.40 Before considering the ethical issues that need to be addressed, it is useful to understand how our doctors are trained (in very general terms), and how they are introduced to psychiatry.

36.41 Pre-registration education curriculum content for pre-registration education and training programmes for healthcare professionals is determined by the individual higher education institutions in the light of recommendations from the relevant regulatory bodies. In relation to some NHS staff groups, Workforce Development Confederations and professional bodies provide advice and input.

36.42 We are informed that the Department of Health did not until recently provide direction on the content of courses, as the higher education institutions are autonomous bodies and Ministers consider themselves to be precluded from intervening in their internal affairs, including curriculum content. We are not convinced that such a "hands-off" position for the NHS is appropriate – patient safety is, after all, the responsibility of the NHS Trusts, not merely of the medically trained personnel who are employed there. In the light of the experience of this, and other similar, recent inquiries, the NHS may now consider it appropriate to offer (even demand) some input into the content of medical courses – at least insofar as the course address medico-legal, and ethical matters. We have also been advised that this area is being addressed by the GMC.

36.43   A starting point may be the production by the NHS, in association with appropriate bodies, of a quality standard document addressing "Abuse of Patients" issues covering many of the topics dealt with in this Inquiry, and including training requirements and training standards, and the need for the routine clinical supervision of all NHS professionals, as a means of improving standards, increasing detection rates, and preventing abuse.

36.44   Although we consider this to be an important area, we do not make specific recommendations on it.

36.45   One of the drivers for ensuring that academic courses in medicine are fit for purpose is that graduating students will only be eligible for registration if their courses meet the recommendations of the relevant regulatory bodies – in the case of doctors, that effectively means the GMC.

36.46   This medical education provision serves those intending to be doctors, whilst separate but equivalent arrangements apply to the education and training of nurses and allied health professionals/healthcare scientists.

36.47   Postgraduate medical training covers a doctor's training after students have graduated from their initial academic studies, and trains them to achieve the required level at which they can be placed on the GMC's Specialist Register and become eligible to apply for consultant posts.

36.48   The standard-setting, curriculum and quality assurance processes for this latter period of training is the responsibility of the Specialist Training Authority of the Medical Royal Colleges for non-GP specialities, and the Joint Committee on Postgraduate Training for General Practice.

36.49 In practice, these functions are delegated by the GMC to the relevant Royal College – in relation to this Inquiry, the most relevant College is the Royal College of Psychiatrists.

Medical training and ethics

36.50 Can society be satisfied that today's NHS doctors are now adequately educated and instructed in relation to ethical issues – here, in particular, boundary transgressions, sexualised behaviour, and abuse of patients?

36.51 We start from the position, we trust uncontroversial, that adequate training and instruction in ethics is of fundamental importance. We must not only produce competent doctors, but good doctors – doctors who not only care for their patients, but doctors who do not harm their patients (existing or former). An important means of reducing the risk of the abuse of patients is the provision of appropriate education.

36.52 We have been advised that studies have revealed that for some therapy-centred professions (such as psychology and psychiatry) only a small proportion (9% in one 1986 study) felt that patient-therapist relationships had been given adequate attention during training. In the same study 55% felt that they had received no training at all on the topic. We would be interested to see if those who are today practising psychiatry, or even today's GPs, have a similar experience.

36.53 Although we are advised that there has been a gradual increase in the amount of ethics teaching both at undergraduate and postgraduate level in the UK, the lack of research and publications in this area of abuse of patients from UK practitioners is a major source of ignorance among practising doctors and therapists. It must not be thought that the lack of evidence among UK psychiatrists can be interpreted as evidence of lack of abuse.

36.54 Added to possible deficiencies in modern teaching, are the deficiencies in the guidelines referred to in earlier chapters and the lack of regulatory sanctions. As already noted, the Royal College of Psychiatrists as yet does not have any Code of Ethics or a Code of

Practice, a significant omission in terms of ethical guidance for the concerned physician or the patient. That absence of guidance must also have impacted on the content of undergraduate and postgraduate medical education. We therefore welcome the recent introduction of the National Curriculum for Medical Ethics.

36.55 However, we should not and cannot rely on the fact that even if doctors currently being educated and trained in the country's medical schools (or, now more commonly, the medical schools across the EU) do not receive an adequate level of instruction in the ethics of medical practice, that they will "pick it up as they go along", or they can be educated in later CPD (see below). There may be advice available (see, for example, *Medical Ethics Today*, the handbook on law and ethics published by the BMA), and GMC guidance and disciplinary process decisions to consider. But if high standards are not set and enforced during the process of initial education and training, there is a concern that they may never be learned.

36.56 We would expect and hope that medical school graduates will be examined on and have had a sound knowledge and understanding of medico-legal and ethical issues, including (relevant to our Inquiry) topics such as:

- patient confidentiality, its purpose and its limitations;

- boundaries between a doctor and his/her patient – what they are and why they must be maintained;

- indicators of boundary transgressions – the "slippery slope";

- sexualised behaviour (in all its forms as discussed in this Report) with existing and former patients.

36.57 This will involve, for example, training in and a clear understanding of:

- handling concerns about boundary transgressions by colleagues;

- self-reporting;

- reporting concerns – when, how and to whom;

- recording concerns;

- complaints handling – procedures and patient/colleague support.

36.58 What is required is not merely awareness of these and similar ethical issues but why they need to be addressed (that boundary transgressions almost always cause harm), how they operate in practice, and what to do if there is a suspicion that they have been breached – by the doctor, or by a colleague.

36.59 In relation to the training doctor, we trust he or she would not become qualified without a clear understanding of his or her own responsibilities in the areas covered by this Inquiry. As concluded in a 1991, Canadian, report on "Sexual Abuse of Patients" – "it is ALWAYS the [doctor's] responsibility to know what is appropriate and never to cross the line into sexual activity". If tomorrow's doctors *know* their responsibilities, they may be better equipped to respond to disclosures, concerns and complaints, indicating that other professionals may have acted unethically or unlawfully.

36.60 It is regrettable that there appears to be a continuing failure to teach our medical students to understand their fundamental ethical responsibilities. We consider it to be important that very careful thought is given to how ethical issues are taught (in medical school education and in CPD, what the topic covers and who delivers the information. If the issues are not addressed, and monitored centrally, there is a real danger that ethical training can be delivered in a way that reinforces existing (self-protective and unhelpful) attitudes, including disbelieving patients, and attitudes generally towards patients who raise complaints. We keep well in mind that Michael Haslam was responsible for teaching medical ethics. We wholeheartedly endorse and support the following:

> *"Teaching on the subject of sexual or improper relationships between doctors and patients, including relationships with former patients requires to be made explicit. Case-based teaching would fit in with the ethos of the problem-based, integrated medical curriculum [in some medical schools]. Such teaching may help reduce the number of doctors entering such relationships in the future."* [4]

36.61 We address other relevant issues later in this chapter.

---

4 "Sex and the Surgery", Goldie, Schwartz and Morrison – *J. Med Ethics,* 2004:30; 480–6.

Pre-registration medical education and psychiatry

36.62 Having established the broad academic and training framework we were keen to understand current experience of this in practice. The focus of our researches was to establish what is in the current curriculum relating to awareness of mental health and illness. The GMC 2003 document *Tomorrow's Doctors – recommendations on undergraduate medical education* provides an outline of required content. The document should be seen as being very broad and enabling, giving responsibility to each medical school to set its own curriculum. Medical schools, until recent years, were inspected by the QAA – attention being particularly on the quality of teaching and ensuring that medical schools were delivering the curriculum as set out in their plans.

36.63 Currently it is the responsibility of the GMC to monitor the content of medical schools' curricula; although there appears to be no formal hierarchy of sanctions, its views determine practice and its reports are publicly available.

36.64 One aspect of the current arrangements is that psychiatry does not necessarily figure in the curriculum of doctors in training, unless they are specifically preparing to be psychiatrists. The evidence to the Inquiry has demonstrated some of the potential shortcomings of this, with medical practitioners indicating in some cases that they did not know what their patients' psychiatric consultations might entail (and therefore could not inform and advise their patients as to what they might expect).

36.65 It is our understanding that there is no specification of the number of taught hours to be applied to each medical speciality, nor is the order and linkage that should exist between areas of the curriculum prescribed. Thus teaching about mental health and illness appears in one curriculum as part of the unit on "brain behaviour" whilst in another it is located in the section on ethics.

36.66 In addition, doctors – both in general practice and in hospital settings – informed the Inquiry that they did not know how best to deal with patients who were mentally unwell when they expressed concerns about their treatment by William Kerr and Michael Haslam. This lack of knowledge was attributed to a lack of training.

36.67 It appears that the new two-year postgraduate "Foundation" curriculum will be central in improving the situation described above, with more emphasis on mental health and illness – a development that is welcomed in the light of the Inquiry findings.

36.68 We also received evidence of an increased emphasis in the undergraduate and postgraduate curriculum on mental health, as a result of pressure from educator-doctors and from primary care.

36.69 A significant aspect of the education system for doctors that the Inquiry was also keen to understand, is the extent to which mental health and well-being is academically examined, since there is a recognition by health professionals and educators alike, that student attention is more focused in relation to those subjects on which they are examined – a fact of life which we understand and accept. There appears to be a wide variety of practice between medical schools in this regard, which may warrant some attention.

36.70 One example of current practice provided to us was a London medical school where the teaching about mental health examination is in years 3 and 4 and forms part of the assessment of medical students. We regard this curriculum practice as a useful contribution to improving doctors' expertise and therefore the "patient experience" of those with mental health difficulties. We point out, however, that given what we have heard from GPs in particular, it is important to ensure that new generations of doctors develop the skills required for effective patient consultations and the taking of medical histories from patients with mental health conditions.

36.71 In the course of the Inquiry a recurring theme that has engaged us is that of believing patients. In this regard, we have had written and oral evidence of historical failures of procedures that were in place to deal with concerns and complaints, with some of these being attributable to patients not being believed. The Inquiry heard the oral evidence of medical practitioners in both primary and secondary care, which demonstrated to our satisfaction that in the course of their medical training little or no attention had been given to the special needs of patients with mental health difficulties nor had the issue of health professionals stereotyping patients with mental health problems as being delusional and/or untruthful been addressed.

36.72 We were therefore encouraged to be told that many medical schools now give students the opportunity to practise their skills in "listening to patients and communication skills" – beyond the history-taking – using experienced actors in simulated patient consultations. This is a positive step in ensuring that communications between doctors and patients are always regarded as an important part of medical practice. It may be worth noting here that, however skilled actors are, there may well be a role for former mental health patients in helping doctors in training to understand the difficulties and feelings raised for mental health patients in the NHS, particularly the barriers to raising concerns and making complaints – a perspective that we have attempted to address in Section 5 of this Report, when considering the barriers to making complaints.

36.73 Despite the incidence of some good curricula and teaching, evidence to the Inquiry suggests that there is too little attention paid within the existing curricula of most medical schools, to the question of communicating with patients suffering from mental health problems. We regard this as a central issue that requires attention within the curriculum and as part of a doctor's CPD.

Mental health training and GPs

36.74 Statistics show that 90% of mental health matters are initially addressed within general practice, the focus being neurotic and depressive conditions, with the psychotic and other mental illnesses being more frequently referred to psychiatrists in hospital settings. It is therefore appropriate – and current practice – that the learning requirements of GPs include psychiatry. The two-year postgraduate rotation of posts undertaken by students in years 4 and 5 commonly includes – but is not required to include – six months in psychiatry. In addition, in the last year of GP training, which takes place in a GP practice, teaching about mental health and illness is carried out by GPs working as trainers in their own practice. This teaching and learning is based on "what comes through the door" in patient consultations and what is picked up in tutorial sessions with the GP trainer.

36.75 GPs are also given video-based training, which may help to pick up any interpersonal and interviewing failings.

36.76 The Inquiry is not in a position to understand in full the advantages and limitations of the arrangement. However:

We RECOMMEND that the GP curriculum should be reviewed to ensure that sufficient focus is given to the needs, treatment and care of patients experiencing mental health problems and illnesses and that all GPs should have some exposure to psychiatry.

Mental health training and hospital doctors

36.77 The Inquiry heard evidence of the difficulty facing psychiatrists working in hospitals, with patients referred to them on a regular basis who might more appropriately be treated and supported within primary care.

36.78 Our interest is to encourage the NHS and its staff to ensure that the most effective approaches to the treatment and support of patients with mental health problems are uniformly available across the service, in the interests of improving the patient experience for those living with mental illness.

36.79 Another feature of curriculum planning by higher education institutions appears to be substantial variation with regard to teaching of, or references to, the role and uses of talking therapies. We do not seek to make judgements of curricula content in this regard, but do wish to draw attention to those areas which – in the light of evidence to the Inquiry – appear to have been neglected in the past. We are of the view that this area should be included in the training programme of future doctors.

36.80 We are, however, aware of the recent developments arising from the Modernising Medical Practice initiative. There is clearly more on the subject of psychiatry within the programme of the new "Foundation years", which it is hoped will give appropriate attention to understanding all aspects of the health needs of patients with mental health problems.

We therefore RECOMMEND that mental health issues should be part of the Nursing and Midwifery Council (NMC) Foundation Year 2.

36.81 Recording of mental health issues on a patient's notes – or elsewhere – may or may not be covered in the teaching about making patient notes. There is some guidance on this in the *Duties of a Doctor*. It seems clear to us that this is an area warranting attention (if not currently adequately addressed) as part of the training of GPs, given (a) the evidence received from patients about the distress that this issue has caused them; and (b) given also the evidence offered by GPs which indicates a large variation in their understanding and actions in dealing with this matter.

Training on receiving concerns and complaints, and voicing concerns about colleagues and other professionals (medical or otherwise)

36.82 If, as outlined earlier in this chapter (and elsewhere in the Report), the initial response to a disclosure of abuse is correctly identified as being critically important (whether or not expressed as a formal complaint), then this issue should immediately link into training, continuing education and development, and to the prevailing culture of the NHS. There is no value in a system of patient protection if those who have day-to-day contact with patients are (1) unaware of the system's existence, and/or (2) untrained in its practical application.

36.83 If NHS staff are too focused on formal complaints systems, and disciplinary procedures, then it is inevitable that valuable information will be lost.

36.84 We are keen to ensure that the importance of training and education in relation to patient safety, in all its forms, is brought to the fore. Not only so that doctors and other healthcare professionals are fully aware of the issues relating to maintaining professional boundaries (with particular emphasis on not engaging in sexualised, and other abusive behaviour), but also that they are taught about (and continue to receive information and instruction in relation to):

- obligations to share concerns;

- how to handle and manage patient disclosures;

- how to access, or direct patients towards, counselling and other voluntary and independent support services;

- how to access NHS complaints systems; and

- how and when to operate multi-agency procedures.

36.85 The Inquiry received a great deal of evidence from the former patients about how doctors responded to them when they complained or raised concerns about their alleged treatment by William Kerr or Michael Haslam. Chapters 6–21 of this Report cover this matter in detail and demonstrate the shortcomings of medical practitioners in this regard. Information received about the content of current postgraduate education and training indicates that the areas covered include how to respond to patients; critical incident analysis and how to respond to it – including dealing with patient complaints. In our view the NHS should reaffirm its commitment to the maintenance of patient safety (and to quality healthcare) by ensuring that any annual appraisal should include (if it does not already include) a section about managing a patient complaint, or any disclosure by or on behalf of a patient of allegedly abusive behaviour.

36.86 What appears to be missing in the education and training process is how to manage complaints about colleagues and fellow professionals appropriately. In view of the evidence received by the Inquiry and the intention of the NHS to avoid future mistreatment and abuse of patients, it will be necessary to ensure that this serious gap in training provision has been comprehensively addressed.

Investigation of concerns

36.87 We turn, finally, when considering information received, to focus more specifically on the important topic of investigation – investigation prompted by the expression of concerns, however and from whoever received. We have touched on this subject in Chapter 35 when considering the role of investigation when a complaint has been made.

36.88 The lesson that stands out from the information received in Part 1 of the Inquiry is that the local NHS management in place during the 1970s and 1980s were unable to, or incapable of, carrying out an effective investigation. It may be that there were structural problems, it may be that they were simply following the then procedures, it may be that there were personnel problems – it may be that it was a combination of these and other factors. We have set out our conclusions elsewhere in the Report. What is important is that it must not be allowed to happen again. To that observation we add a question, for consideration by NHS Trust managers:

> *"If a patient alleges (in confidence) that she had been engaged in a sexual relationship with a consultant psychiatrist employed by the Trust, do you now have in place clear and simply-written guidance to explain (1) how that information should be handled and responded to, and (2) how an investigation into the issues raised by that information would be conducted and managed?"*

36.89 That question can be reformulated and represented in many ways. The central issue is as follows – is the Trust ready and equipped to respond? The absence of a clear, straightforward and readily accessible answer should cause immediate concern to the Trust's management.

36.90 It is not possible, or appropriate, for us to attempt to formulate an investigation policy. Fortunately, and in any event, much has already been done by the NCAS (now, from 1 April 2005, managed by the National Patient Safety Agency) in its comprehensive and detailed Toolkit launched in November 2004. But, as already note, the activities of the NCAS are confined to doctors and dentists. We do not see any reason why its remit should not be extended, or its developed models should not be adopted (and possibly adapted) by the NHS Trusts themselves, or by other organisations responsible for patient safety.

36.91 "Investigation" (and "investigating") is defined in the Toolkit as follows:

> *"In everyday usage, 'investigating' means a careful search for the truth. In the context of managing individual clinical performance, it can help to distinguish investigation from analysis and assessment. Investigation identifies what happened and how, while analysis and assessment uncover why it happened and suggest what might stop it happening again. However, the scope of 'investigation' may also depend on whether informal or formal processes are being used. An informal investigation may well look at 'why?' as well as 'what?', even though a formal investigation should confine itself to 'what?' and leave separate decision-making processes to work out what to do next and whether there were mitigating circumstances.*

> *"In this section we are generally using 'investigating' in a broad sense, to include a search for explanations as well as facts."*

36.92 We agree with that approach. What is important is that a system is in place so that an investigation is triggered by the kind of information we are here considering – disclosure of, or serious rumour/gossip in relation to, sexualised behaviour by a healthcare professional, particularly in the area of mental health.

36.93 We would prefer to see the detailed content of that investigation determined by the NCAS – informed by recent Inquiry Reports. This will mean that the Toolkit will need to be updated, or a section created, to concentrate on this kind of disclosure in relation to sexualised behaviour. The updated version, if it is to serve a useful purpose, will have to address at least the following issues:

- Who is to be responsible for conducting the investigation?

- When are the police to be involved, and who makes that decision?

- What to do if the police are involved, but decide not to launch a prosecution?

- When is the GMC, or other appropriate regulatory body, to be contacted – and, if so, with what consequences for the investigation?[5]

- What to do if the alleged sexualised contact is said to have been consensual?

- What to do if at the time of the alleged sexualised behaviour, the doctor/patient relationship had ended?

- When, in what circumstances, and by whom (if at all), other patients (other potential victims) will be contacted as part of the investigation?

- What records are to be retained of the investigation, by whom, and for how long?

36.94 From submissions received from the NCAS we note that it is their expectation that NHS Trusts carry out a full and detailed root cause analysis when a serious incident arises so that all contributory factors are identified. We are not convinced that such an approach is

5 The following is taken from the NCAS's website – "Referring to the GMC is always an option for the NHS, if there is immediate and serious danger for patients. But there are also cases where there is a need for development training, or a change of role or other management intervention to help the practitioner overcome performance difficulties. The NCAS's aim is to help the NHS deal with these less serious cases and keep practitioners in employment, using a consistent framework of assessment and action planning."

appropriate where the disclosure alleges sexualised behaviour. We do, however, wholly endorse the NCAS approach to investigation:

> *"Open and Fair,[6] open for staff and patients to speak up, open for staff to tell patients/carers when an incident occurs and fairness in handling for both staff and patients."*

36.95 When the NCAS considers investigations in relation to allegations of sexualised behaviour, it may perhaps keep in mind not only the experiences of the former patients of William Kerr and Michael Haslam, but also the following views of the Health Service Ombudsman arising from the investigation into the response of NHS Trusts where there had been allegations of sexual misconduct:

> *"Areas of concern expressed by the Ombudsman about NHS incident investigations*
>
> *"There are undoubtedly complexities in incident investigation, and our cases illustrate the fact that it can be difficult to distinguish between recent and distant experiences, delusions or inaccurate memories and real events, and distress associated with memories that are associated with abuse. However, these problems should not preclude thorough and objective investigation. In fact, the clinical context behoves mental health services to investigate with particular rigour.*
>
> *"A recurrent theme of cases has been the lack of appropriate investigation. This is unfair on staff and clients. The focus on simply disproving allegations leaves the staff member and Trust open to later allegations. Typically, staff witnesses are interviewed, but not patients. Reporting to the police is erratic and evidence is often not preserved. In one case past police involvement was cited as meaning that the Trust did not have to answer a complaint. Patients may then face further difficulties in pursuing their complaint because the police do not think their evidence will stand up."*

---

6 This term also refers to the NCAS policy statement – *Being Open – Communicating patient safety incidents with their patients and their carers.*

36.96 Accordingly:

We RECOMMEND that early consideration should be given to extending the remit of the National Clinical Assessment Service (NCAS) to cover other healthcare professionals, particularly those providing care and treatment in mental health services.

Continuous Professional Development

36.97 If the patient experience is to improve, education and professional development in these crucial areas must include not only those who are currently training to be doctors but also existing cohorts of doctors working in the NHS mental health service.

36.98 CPD is of central importance in the areas covered by this Inquiry. Standards change, society's expectations change, ethical requirements change, legal requirements change, and complaints procedures change. Those changes are of little value if they are not known to, and responded to by, the current generation of doctors. We received an impression (and it could be no more than that) from medical witnesses to the Inquiry that there was resistance to change and, of even greater concern, a resistance to information about change. CPD is only of value if the content is actually considered by doctors, and *actually* absorbed by them, and passed on and incorporated into the GP practices for which they are responsible. The same considerations apply to hospital doctors. For that reason, at least in relation to ethics training, we would expect to see increasing emphasis on attending refresher courses, rather than on mere reading requirements.

36.99 We also observe that although there have been substantial changes in society's needs and expectations of its doctors, it is clear to us that some doctors themselves have neither taken the opportunity for professional development nor kept in touch with those developments and changes. Inevitably, therefore, there are currently in the NHS doctors who were educated and qualified 10 years ago or more, who may not be adequately trained in the approach to the central issues pertinent to this Inquiry, such as confidentiality, maintenance of boundaries, the raising of concerns or complaints, management of complaints from staff or patients, and inter-agency working.

36.100 The areas of professional development in relation to mental health patients highlighted by evidence to the Inquiry included, but are not limited to:

- raising concerns/complaints in general practice, in community settings and in hospitals;

- ethical standards in relation to boundary maintenance;

- ethical standards in relation to sexualised behaviour with current and former patients;

- issues relating to the definition of a "former" patient;

- the understanding of treatments for mental disorders;

- the understanding of "transference" and "counter-transference";

- keeping mental health patient records in hospital;

- keeping mental health patient records in general practice, PCTs, etc;

- incident reporting systems;

- dealing with/storing of confidential information;

- dealing with concerns/complaints when the patient is very distressed/unable to cope;

- dealing with concerns/complaints made by vulnerable patients (including but not limited to patients receiving mental health services).

36.101 While some doctors in hospitals or general practice may make a point of ensuring that they address these as part of their personal professional development, there has been no systematic requirement for doctors do so.

36.102 With regard to the free movement of professionals across the EU, there is an urgent need for discussions and examination of the issues between jurisdictions to ensure that as far as possible standards and requirements in this regard are uniformly applied. If not, then it is to be expected that stringent CPD requirements will assist in remedying any perceived differences or deficiencies. However, we observe, we have not received any information to indicate that EU-trained doctors are in any way inadequately trained or instructed in the ethical areas covered by this Inquiry. Indeed, it is just as likely that the UK has lessons to learn.

36.103 The special payment to GPs for attendance on accredited CPD courses no longer exists; the debate about the benefits and disadvantages of this is a source of lively debate. If the absence of special payments is a real disincentive, then reintroduction should be considered.

36.104 We are aware of and appreciate the appraisal website that requires all doctors within a PCT to log their CPD activities on it; this information forms part of the annual appraisal process. As part of this log doctors are expected to identify their patients' unmet needs and their own educational needs.

36.105 GP practices are expected by their PCT to undertake critical incident reviews, but these are not quality-controlled reviews.

36.106 The importance of continuous updating and extension of skills, knowledge and experience is recognised as being an important part of professional life. Given the significant proportion of the population that will experience mental health problems in their lifetime, we take the view that CPD for all doctors should include mental health, including (but by no means limited to) those topics mentioned above.

36.107 In the area of handling the possible abuse of vulnerable adults, it is clear that cross-agency working is of increasing importance, whether with social services, the police or other public service agencies.

We therefore RECOMMEND that the NHS should review the curriculum content – at all education and training levels – to ensure that medical practitioners are able to undertake appropriate cross-sector working (including within NHS ie primary/secondary boundary) as part of their practice.

We RECOMMEND that those responsible for developing the curricula for education programmes of healthcare professionals should ensure that:

1) information about and discussion of the ethical responsibilities of healthcare professionals to bring poor performance to light is given due weight; and

2) students are made aware of: forms of regulation and clinical governance operating in the NHS and the ethos which underpins them; the relationship between the different systems; and how they can be accessed.

We RECOMMEND that professional training includes: compulsory education and training on the maintenance of professional boundaries, awareness of boundary transgressions, sexualised behaviour as unethical conduct, response to expressions of concerns and complaints, complaints systems, what to do if a complaint is made but the person making the complaint declines to take an active part in a formal complaint, as well as the requirements of, and limitations on, patient confidentiality.

Chapter 37
Concluding remarks

Conclusion

37.1 At the beginning of this Report, we posed these questions:

a. How could it be that the voices of the patients, and former patients, of William Kerr and Michael Haslam were not heard?

b. Why were so many opportunities missed?

c. As formulated by Counsel for the health authorities, "At the heart of this Inquiry is the question – How could it happen?"

37.2 With the enormous benefit of hindsight, with a mass of written and oral information, and with the advantage of an overview, we can see that the answers are, as one might expect, to be found in a combination of factors – some human, some organisational. There is no single cause. In the course of the Report, we have identified some individuals who, in our opinion, are open to criticism. We have also identified areas of concern where we consider changes made so far are inadequate, and accordingly we have made recommendations – brought together in the Executive Summary.

37.3 We accept as broadly correct the following summary from the submissions made on behalf of the health authorities:

"The reason why a consultant was able to continue in practice and assault his patients … was a mixture of a flawed structure, poor procedures, systems failures, individual and collective failures in an institution that was created at a time when to most, if not all, people the idea that patients might need protection from doctors was unthinkable."

37.4 With different emphasis on "individual and collective failures", this summary broadly accords with the submissions made on behalf of the former patients of both William Kerr and Michael Haslam. That concentration on individual failure is exemplified in the following extract from closing submissions to the Inquiry made by Counsel for those patients:

> "'System failure' is a relatively modern expression ... But, and I speak here on behalf of all the patients – I would not wish for the focus of any blame to be shifted from those individuals on to a system where it is truly the fault of the individuals that this conduct continued unabated.

> "[Witnesses to the Inquiry] agreed that they believed the patients had been abused – very seriously abused; they believed that criminal assaults were being carried out; they knew Dr Kerr's and Dr Haslam's reputations as well, and then they carried on referring.

> "Those, for the main part, we do not say are system failures, they are personality failures and they are failures which can be righted or corrected, if attention is paid in the first place to instruction and to awareness in the medical community of the burden that necessarily flows from administering health care. Doctors, GPs, nurses, counsellors, all assume obligations when they undertake that course of training. When they wish to practise, they assume a burden to look after precisely the sorts of patients that sit behind me today, precisely the sorts of patients who had the courage to disclose and were then so short-changed by individuals, not by the system – the system worked in 1966 [a reference to Northern Ireland], the system could have worked if individual doctors, GPs, had taken extra steps."

37.5 We take the reference to the system working in 1966 as meaning that it led to a complaint being followed up to the level where action could be taken on it. In terms of what actually happened, of course, William Kerr was simply moved on to another jurisdiction, with the opportunities for further alleged activities that harmed and degraded further patients.

37.6 We recognise that it is a complex notion for an institution to hold that patients (or service users) of the mental health service are by definition "outsiders" to the institution, and to the NHS. Many of the patients who gave evidence to the Inquiry have drawn attention to aspects of a "them and us" culture – they referred to doctors closing ranks, to not being believed because it was their word against the word of a doctor, to the power of consultants. Those comments could apply to many branches of the health service; being a mental health patient adds a further level of stress and vulnerability. The patients who gave evidence to us were being asked to recall events between 15 and 30 years ago. At that time they were, in the main, young vulnerable women who had been referred for consultant care and treatment when mental disorder carried even more of a stigma than it does now – women in need of therapeutic support, looking for help to put their lives back on some form of even keel.

37.7   The overall position is the same now as it was then: all staff in an institution and in the NHS generally have an obligation to recognise this imbalance of power, to keep in mind how it must feel to the outsider (the patient) to engage with this apparently close-knit society.

37.8   The NHS itself has changed in many ways, and there are new models of mental healthcare. The national service framework for mental health set new horizons for mental health care. Significantly, new investment has been put into community mental health teams such as crisis resolution and home treatment teams, assertive outreach teams and early intervention teams, in addition to the more traditional community mental health teams.

37.9   The majority of patient contacts are now undertaken within patients' homes. The full multi-disciplinary team primarily involves mental health nurses, social workers, occupational therapists, psychologists and health and social care assistants, working with a consultant psychiatrist and junior medical staff.

37.10   Multi-disciplinary teamworking in itself involves a process of review with team colleagues and includes the patient. These team processes are important in providing valuable opportunities for shared decision making and supervision. The mechanisms themselves are important in helping the key worker maintain clear professional boundaries.

37.11   But, whatever the improvements, whatever the "models of mental health care", it must be accepted that patient abuse will continue. The abuse itself may develop into different forms, or have different beginnings. Already there are concerns that the new technologies may lead to new problems. Mobile phone numbers of patients are being used in some services to remind them to turn up for appointments. We are aware that this could lead to further exploitation of vulnerable patients. There are already concerns relating to the use of cameras within mobile phones. Whatever the detail, however abuse begins or boundaries are crossed, psychiatric patients will need to be able to raise their concerns and, where necessary, make complaints.

37.12 The potential barriers to complaining, to expressing concerns without encountering a formal and intimidating complaints system, are enormous. We list them elsewhere in the Report. We conclude that the onus must be on all healthcare and administrative staff within the NHS (at least within mental health services), whatever their position:

   a. to acquire the predisposition/first response that a concern expressed by a patient should be taken at face value;

   b. actively to encourage people who tentatively signal concerns to articulate them;

   c. to follow through those concerns with the diligence and the importance that they deserve.

37.13 We understand that this is no mean task, when much of the work that hard-pressed NHS mental health staff undertake is incident-led and life-critical. However, if cultural change is to be achieved, this will be a key aspect of it. This view informs the matters addressed below.

37.14 Much of the focus of the evidence and submissions presented by the local NHS authorities was on systems. We accept that the complaints system nationally and locally, and the system for the discipline of consultants, were antiquated and inadequate. It may well be that "the system was so bankrupt that it required me and my colleagues to leave on the loose, a man who I firmly believed was abusing his patients" – based on the evidence of a senior NHS witness.

37.15 The focus was on the need for a willing and cooperative complainant – the mantra was "No complainant, no complaint". One piece of oral evidence epitomises this approach:

   "Because it was not a complaint by a patient [referring to the Linda Bigwood dossier], *I would not have treated it as a complaint. I would say that there was no complaint from the patient."*

37.16 We regret that such a rigid, procedures-based, approach contributed to the failure to act, the failure to investigate, indeed the failure to respond. A rigid adherence to systems – particularly in a culture where consultants are exalted and psychiatric patients routinely disbelieved – does not begin to address the complexity of the issues raised in an allegation of sexual contact between patient and doctor. What if the patient is too frightened to complain? What if they do not have the capacity to complain? What if they say that they are having sex with the consultant psychiatrist but they have been told that it is – and believe it to be – part of the treatment? What if they say it is consensual? What if there has been a disclosure, believed by the recipient, but the patient then retracts? It seems clear that even today there is the risk that a "No complainant, no complaint" approach persists – not least of all because it provides the easiest, least effort, response.

37.17 The absence of a complaint by a complainant willing and able to give evidence – in a GMC hearing, in a criminal trial, or in disciplinary proceedings – does not seem to us to be an adequate reason for not investigating at all. We agree with the observations of Sir Liam Donaldson (then the Regional General Manager and Director of Public Health) given in his oral evidence on 1 September 2004:

> *"There was nothing to stop anyone, at any point, designing an investigation to establish the facts and get them into a report which could then be the basis for people to consider."*

Later adding:

> *"... even though the initial investigation may only be sitting in an armchair talking to half a dozen people that you trust to really say, look, is there anything in this?"*

37.18 In an area such as this it is not an adequate investigation, for any person working in the NHS, merely:

a. to receive a disclosure of sexual misconduct (whether framed as a concern, as a complaint, or simply as something told to a nurse or GP etc);

b. to speak to the consultant concerned, ask him if there is any truth in the allegation and, on hearing the denial, do nothing more.

37.19 We accept that there have been important and major changes to the NHS complaints system – operated both locally and nationally. However, the system remains, in our opinion, far too complicated and intimidating for some patients, and we have addressed our concerns in Chapter 34 and elsewhere. But a formalised complaints system, though no doubt very protective of the doctor or nurse about whom the complaint is made, does not always address the kind of disclosures referred to in the evidence – disclosures that are likely to be far more common among the mentally disordered patient group. In our view, a healthy NHS and a healthy regulatory system for healthcare workers should be able to provide an approach and a supporting mechanism (if needed) that focuses on patient care, and provides a solution to the following forms of disclosure by a psychiatric patient:

    a. "I have been sexually propositioned by Doctor A, but I do not want to complain."

    b. "I do not want to make a fuss, or get anybody into trouble, but I think you should know that Doctor A has sexually assaulted me."

    c. "I would otherwise complain of the consultant's actions, but I am worried about what will then happen as regards my future treatment, so I prefer to remain silent."

37.20 If the system is unable to address these (and similar) forms of disclosure, then information that may well be credible, which will allow doctors and other healthcare practitioners to be held to account, and which may well be of value in the prevention of a risk of foreseeable harm to other patients, will be lost – or will be so isolated as to be worthless. We recognise that there are difficulties in developing such a system, but to give sole and undue weight to legal advice regarding the likelihood of concerns/complaints being proved – to a criminal or even to a civil standard of proof – may well protect the institution and its employees, but may also result in a regrettable failure to protect other patients.

37.21 In relation to psychiatric patients (perhaps more so than in other areas of medical practice), we believe that one of the main components of any answer to the questions posed at the beginning of this chapter is that there has been a failure by the "system" to cater for or fully understand the position of such victims of abuse. Without such understanding, any complaints system is almost bound to fail them. Psychiatric patients were, and are, in a peculiarly vulnerable position:

- By definition, they suffer from mental health problems.

- By reason of those mental health problems, they may struggle to articulate and maintain expressions of concern and complaint.

- By definition, they will have limited resilience and stamina and may be instinctively reluctant to use their limited resources to pursue a complaint or concern. Their main priority is likely to be focusing on recovery, on suppression of symptoms, simply on "getting better".

- By reason of those mental health problems, they are less likely (unless adequately supported) to be able to stand up to the rigours of formal processes of investigation and complaint resolution.

- By reason of their mental health problems, they are more likely to be distressed and confused, which makes taking down statements or recording information particularly difficult (even by experienced and trained listeners).

- By reason of the stigma that attached and still attaches to those problems, they are vulnerable to the consequences of complaints being aired and subject to the prejudices of others disinclined to believe what they say.

- They may also feel vulnerable to retribution by the person against whom the complaint is made. There is a fundamental imbalance of power that makes the consequences of a failed complaint almost too awful for the victim to contemplate.

- They are unlikely to speak out because of a reluctance to share their concerns and complaints with close family or friends for fear of being disbelieved, because they feel shame or because they fear being blamed/found wanting.

- They feel guilty that they are in some way responsible for what has happened.

- They are unsure whether the activities might really be a legitimate part of their treatment.

- They are not entirely able to convince themselves that they have the right to articulate their complaints against a professional who they assume is trying to help them.

37.22 If psychiatric patients with these characteristics, all of which contribute to a real loss of empowerment, are put into a culture where sexual contact may be accepted by some, where disclosures are instinctively disbelieved, where the tools for addressing issues raised are blunt and ineffective, then a situation exists where abuse can take place, and go unchecked, for years – even for decades.

37.23 The present system is much improved, and witness after witness told us that what happened to these former patients, in terms of anyone listening and responding to their concerns and complaints, could not happen now. The systems have changed, and we accept that some of the more entrenched aspects of the self-protective culture have disappeared.

37.24 The opportunities for abuse are now much reduced: there is teamworking, consultant psychiatrists do not generally make domiciliary visits alone, the large hospitals with remote buildings have been demolished, and "fringe" treatments such as CO_2 therapy and massage by a male consultant psychiatrist on a female patient would be regulated and questioned. There were more, similar, comforting words from representatives of the NHS, and from the GMC. However, there is no cause for complacency.

37.25 Change of culture is at the heart of real change. Whatever the systems in place, if those who operate them at all levels are not focused on patient safety, then other factors, other pressures, will prevail.

37.26 It is at this point that we mention – almost at the end of the Report – a particular reason for optimism in relation to North Yorkshire. The area has had more than its fair share of medical care based scandals – it has clearly learned some very painful lessons. However, our additional cause for optimism is based on the response by existing and former NHS staff to our Inquiry. We are pleased to record that present and former members of the NHS staff, represented by Kate Thirlwall QC, all provided statements and, when called, came to the Inquiry. There has been no question of any need for the exercise of powers of compulsion. The detailed statements they supplied provided the Inquiry with information, much of which we could not otherwise have obtained; information that we accept was used, quite properly, to make witnesses feel very uncomfortable indeed. We take the fact that they came willingly and participated willingly, that they embraced the Inquiry and participated in it so effectively, as a clear indicator that attitudes have changed, at least in North Yorkshire, and that there has been a cultural shift in the right direction.

37.27 We accept, therefore, and as we have noted in other parts of this Report, that there have been significant cultural changes, and that it would be less easy for a consultant psychiatrist to act as it is alleged William Kerr and Michael Haslam did. But experience, information on prevalence, and common sense, tell us that cases like those of William Kerr and Michael Haslam cannot be seen as unlikely to recur. Furthermore, we are not entirely reassured by the references to new ways of working, since they also contain the potential for would-be abusers to develop new ways of perpetrating and concealing abuse of patients – for example, as a result of "informal" rehabilitation work with patients in social, community settings. The opportunities for abuse of the mentally disordered and vulnerable adult during domiciliary visits does not appear to have been addressed by the NHS, or by healthcare regulators.

37.28 During the course of the Part 2 seminars in York, we explored with local NHS representatives the *current* approach to dealing with sexualised behaviour by a medical professional with a patient. We did not investigate the circumstances of the incident in question in any detail, and as it did not concern either William Kerr or Michael Haslam, as an event, it falls outside our terms of reference. However, as an illustration of cause for continuing concern, we consider it worthy of mention. We were told about a healthcare professional (an unqualified nurse) who disclosed to colleagues that they were having a sexual relationship with a patient. The response of colleagues was to tell them to stop the relationship. The matter was only reported to management when it became clear that the relationship had not stopped. Management did not appear to be critical of this inadequate process. The inevitable inference we draw is that if the prohibited sexual relationship had stopped there would have been no reporting, and management would have no knowledge of the matter. Consequently, if the same healthcare professional engaged in another sexual relationship with another patient at another hospital and the same pattern was repeated, again nothing would be known by management and nothing would be done. We are bound to question how much more likely this is to occur if the healthcare professional is a still powerful consultant.

37.29 Looking to the future, systems and the healthcare managers who maintain and monitor those systems must be alert to protect vulnerable psychiatric patients from physical abuse – from sexual exploitation by *all* healthcare professionals, not just for example predatory psychiatric consultants. And this protection must extend to include inpatients, outpatients, and patients (or service users) cared for in the community. We mentioned earlier in this chapter the new models of mental health care in the NHS; as with much of modern life, nothing stays the same. However – and this must not be overlooked – any new systems must not only be centred on patient safety (all witnesses to the Inquiry seemed to be in agreement with that proposition), but must also recognise that healthcare professionals and other staff have rights too. These include the right to fair treatment and the right not to be disadvantaged by malicious and untruthful allegations. We do not underestimate the difficulties in achieving the correct balance.

37.30 Have all of the concerns identified by this Inquiry been addressed? We fear not. Our investigation covered a period of over 30 years – when NHS and social services staff and GPs were just as dedicated as they are now. There may have been recent wake-up calls – recognised in this and several other Inquiries. But the tendency of institutions to develop a culture of accepting, or denying the existence of, the unacceptable has not fundamentally changed. Insufficient safeguards are in place to ensure that healthcare professionals have neither the desire nor the opportunity to sexually abuse vulnerable patients. Investigating a complaint is time-consuming and a distraction from other responsibilities, and, at the end of the day, allegations may not be proven. So, why bother? Investigating a complaint may cause personal and professional discomfort or awkwardness with colleagues; in addition, it may put career progression at risk. When a disclosure is investigated, there may still be (as with Deputy Sister Bigwood) a tendency to focus on the messenger, rather than on the message. These and other explanations show how resistance to action can set in. Even today we believe that it could still take tenacity and courage to get a complaint dealt with properly. If the complaint is not a clear one from a coherent, rational and willing complainant, the recipient may still succumb to the temptation to take the "easy" course and do nothing, or merely file a record of the incident. Mental health staff who raise concerns, or act as the conduit for concerns, may themselves be unjustly (and perhaps inadvertently) penalised for so doing.

37.31 Individuals with the attitudes and responses reflected in some of the evidence given to the Inquiry create a culture that is infectious and leave a legacy that cannot be changed overnight. Neither can such staff – who may be competent in other ways – be instantly replaced. Because of, and perhaps even despite, the above, the systems and the culture of the NHS (and of leading healthcare regulators such as the GMC) must continue to change and develop to make patient safety, particularly the safety of vulnerable psychiatric patients, of central importance and a focus of its development planning and implementation.

37.32 In summary, then, we are of the view that much has been achieved in developing an understanding of:

- the requirements of a patient-focused service; and

- the risks of an obstructive or inherently resistant culture developing in a large organisation like the NHS.

37.33 Nevertheless, we conclude that substantial risks remain that patients and staff who raise concerns or complaints will not be heard, and we are not persuaded that their concerns will even now, in 2005, be speedily and appropriately addressed.

Annexes

Annex 1
Chronology of key events: William Kerr

Date	Key event
8 Oct 1925	William Kerr born.
1964	Complaint of alleged sexual assault brought against William Kerr while he was practising in Northern Ireland.
6 Jan 1965	William Kerr commenced employment at Clifton Hospital, York.
1965	Patient A1 complained to Dr Moore, GP in Harrogate, about sexual suggestions made by William Kerr.
1965	Patient A2 is said (by a friend, Patient A22) to have informed Dr Rushton that William Kerr "tried it on" and "touched her bottom".
13 Feb 1967	William Kerr was appointed consultant in psychiatry at Clifton Hospital.
1968	Patient A4, a student nurse at Harrogate General Hospital, reported to the hospital Matron that William Kerr had behaved inappropriately towards her.
1969	William Kerr appointed Deputy Medical Superintendent of Clifton Hospital.
1970	Patient A10 informed her GP, Dr Theo Crawfurd-Porter, that William Kerr had allegedly exposed himself to her. Dr Crawfurd-Porter's response was "My God, the fool!", and no action was taken to progress the complaint.
1971	Patient A6, a student nurse at Harrogate General Hospital, reported to Home Sister and Hospital Matron an allegation that William Kerr had allegedly sexually assaulted her during two consultations at the student nurses' accommodation.
1971	Patient A7, an inpatient, alleged to Sister Atkins (deceased) of Clifton Hospital that she had had a sexual relationship with William Kerr while he was treating her.
1972	Patient A9, outpatient, complained to her GP (at Dr Moss & Partners, Kings Rd) of inappropriate sexual advances and indecent assault by William Kerr during domiciliary visits.
1972	Patient A11, outpatient, complained to Dr P Jones, GP at Leeds Road Surgery, Harrogate, about sexual suggestions made by William Kerr during consultations. At a partners' meeting the issue of this allegation, and others, was discussed. No further action was taken by the GPs.
20 Mar 1972	Patient A8, a former patient of William Kerr at the time, wrote a letter to the Secretary of the LRHB to complain about William Kerr's inappropriate behaviour during a consultation in late 1969 and alleged sexual assaults on another patient, Patient A5.
6 Oct 1973	Patient A8 wrote to the Health Service Commissioner to complain about William Kerr's behaviour.

Date	Key event
10 Nov 1973	Patient A8 wrote to Sir Alan Marre, Health Service Commissioner, repeating the above complaints. The response, dated 20 Nov 1973, stated that the complaints were outside the Commission's jurisdiction and should be pursued through the DHSS.
30 Nov 1973	Patient A8's mother wrote to Sir Alan stating that the HA was aware of Patient A8's allegations and asked whether the Commissioner would investigate the HA's conduct. No response was received.
Oct 1975	Patient A13 reported to Dr Crouch, GP at Dr Moss & Partners, allegations of inappropriate sexual conduct by William Kerr during a domiciliary visit.
1976	Patient A14 alleged to Sister Wearing at Clifton Hospital that she had been indecently assaulted by William Kerr.
1978	Patient A15 hinted to her GP, Dr Jeary, about a concern regarding William Kerr, but made no explicit disclosure.
1978	Patient A16 objected to her GP, Dr Jeary, referring a family member to William Kerr (due to her past experiences in 1972).
1978	Patient A17, inpatient, allegedly disclosed to Nurse Busby, at Clifton Hospital, a sexual relationship with William Kerr. Nurse Busby allegedly told Patient A17 to "keep quiet".
11 Mar 1978	Patient A18, outpatient, told Dr Day, GP at Park Parade Surgery, Harrogate, that she did not want to see William Kerr at her home. She alleged, to the Inquiry (but not Dr Day), that William Kerr had indecently assaulted her.
Jun 1978	Patient A19, inpatient, alleged that sexual intercourse with William Kerr occurred on a number of occasions within Clifton Hospital. She told a friend about the allegations. The friend informed Patient A19's husband, who approached a solicitor for advice. The solicitor contacted the Harrogate District Hospital and Patient A19 was transferred from William Kerr's care to the care of Michael Haslam.
28 Mar 1979	Patient A22, outpatient, alleged to Dr Wade, GP of Eastgate Surgery, Knaresborough, that she was indecently assaulted during a domiciliary visit. Patient A22 also spoke to the police. Dr Wade referred Patient A22's complaint to Michael Haslam.
1979	Patient A23 complained to her GP, Dr Rosemary Livingstone, that William Kerr talked too much about sex. Some time later, in 1983, Dr Angus Livingstone (husband of Dr Rosemary Livingstone) received a complaint from a patient that William Kerr had made an unannounced visit to her home.
Mar/Apr 1979	Patient A26, inpatient at Clifton Hospital, reported to Thomas English, psychiatric nurse, allegations of inappropriate propositions being made to her by William Kerr. Mr English spoke to his supervisor, Sister Pauline Brown. Sister Brown alerted William Kerr to the allegations and was told by William Kerr that the allegations were malicious.
Early 1980s	Patient A19 spoke to Marion Anderson about her allegations against William Kerr.
1981	Patient A27 was being treated by a private psychotherapist, and disclosed her allegations against William Kerr in respect of treatment that she had undergone in 1972.
1981	Patient A28 alleged that William Kerr would touch her and masturbate during domiciliary visits. Her belief is that she informed her former GP, Dr Witcher, although the doctor denied this.
1982	Patient A17, inpatient, allegedly disclosed to Sister Wearing that she had been involved in a sexual relationship with William Kerr.

Date	Key event
Early/mid Jun 1983	Patient A17 allegedly disclosed to her GP, Dr Margaret Smith, an allegation that she had had a sexual relationship with William Kerr. Dr Smith's alleged response was that Patient A17 should sell her story to a women's magazine.
Jun 1983	Patient A17, admitted as inpatient at Clifton Hospital on 6 June 1983, disclosed to Deputy Sister Linda Bigwood that she had been involved in a consensual sexual relationship with William Kerr while she was his patient between 1973 and 1975. The relationship involved consultations at Dragon Parade, where sexual intercourse would take place. Deputy Sister Bigwood referred the disclosure to her supervisor, John Monk-Steel, Nursing Officer, who passed it to his superior, Anne Tiplady, Nursing Officer. The SHO, Dr Mortimer, was advised of the allegation, as was William Kerr.
Jun 1983	Deputy Sister Bigwood was transferred from Ash Tree House Ward to a geriatric ward on Rosedale Ward.
4 Jul 1983	A one-on-one meeting was arranged between Patient A17 and William Kerr. Patient A17 verbally retracted her allegation. Deputy Sister Bigwood objected to the private meeting.
18 Jul 1983	Patient A17 made her first written retraction of the allegations against William Kerr.
Jul 1983	Patient A13 revealed an allegation against William Kerr to a community worker, who passed the information on to Deputy Sister Bigwood.
1 Sep 1983	Deputy Sister Bigwood wrote a formal complaint to the District HA, detailing her grievance with the local HA's handling of her raising concerns about William Kerr after the disclosure by Patient A17. The letter also detailed wider allegations against William Kerr, including an allegation that many Harrogate GPs were aware of William Kerr's conduct with female patients and for that reason avoided referring female patients to him.
Late 1983	Patient A31 reported to Dr Reed, GP, an alleged sexual assault by William Kerr during a domiciliary visit in 1981.
Late 1983	Patient A32 disclosed to Sarah Cotterill, friend and nurse, an allegation of indecent assault during a domiciliary visit. Patient A32 also complained to Dr Plowman, GP.
3 Nov 1983	Dr Wintersgill, Specialist in Community Medicine with the YDHA, and Mr Price, consultant surgeon and member of the District Management Team, interviewed William Kerr in relation to the HA's ongoing investigation of the concerns raised by Deputy Sister Bigwood.
3 Nov 1983	Patient A17 made her second written retraction of her allegations against William Kerr.
Late Nov 1983	Dr Wintersgill referred Deputy Sister Bigwood's complaint to Dr Turner, Regional Medical Officer.
1 Dec 1983	Dr Turner declined to take any action, on the basis of the written retraction by Patient A17.
Dec 1983	Mr Chapman, YRHA Legal Adviser, gave an advice that independent investigations should be undertaken by the YRHA into: • the local HA's handling of the Bigwood complaint; and • Patient A17's retraction, to ensure it was not obtained under duress.
Dec 1983	Mr Raymond Wilk, Director of Nursing Services (Mental Illness), York, conducted an investigation, at the direction of Mr Corbett, into the local HA's handling of the Bigwood complaint.
12 Jan 1984	Dr Wintersgill and Miss Armitage, Senior Nursing Officer, interviewed Patient A17 in relation to the allegations made against William Kerr.

Date	Key event
15 Feb 1984	Mr Wilk published a report on his investigation. The report detailed a number of errors by the nursing and administrative staff in handling both the allegations made by Patient A17 and the concerns raised by Deputy Sister Bigwood. It described the local HA's investigation as "shallow". Mr Wilk concluded that the staff should be counselled on the errors. No investigation of William Kerr's conduct was undertaken.
1984	Patient A19 complained to Mr Stephen Cook, CPN, of an alleged sexual relationship with William Kerr.
5 Apr 1984	Mr Corbett, District Nursing Officer, wrote to Deputy Sister Bigwood's union, COHSE, to advise that the investigations in relation to handling of the Bigwood complaint were finalised.
11 Apr 1984	Dr Wintersgill wrote to William Kerr to advise that the investigation into the handling of the Bigwood complaint was finalised and apologising for "… *any anxieties that this unfortunate occurrence may have caused.*"
Mar 1985	Deputy Sister Bigwood wrote a further complaint to the HA, again raising concerns about William Kerr.
10 Jun 1985	Meeting convened by COHSE to discuss the outstanding matters raised by Deputy Sister Bigwood in her Mar 1985 summary. In attendance were: Deputy Sister Bigwood, Mr C Brace, Branch Chairman of COHSE, Mr Whyte, Branch Secretary of COHSE, Mr Wilk, Director of Nursing Services (Mental Illness) and Mr Ingham, District General Manager.
29 Jul 1985	Mr Ingham wrote to Deputy Sister Bigwood addressing the matters raised in the 10 Jun 1985 meeting. In the letter Mr Ingham asserted that *"the relationship between a Consultant Psychiatrist and a patient is such that it is possible for a consultant to decide to see a patient alone, even when a complaint of this nature has been made."* William Kerr had been consulted by Dr Green on the drafting of the letter and had approved the final form of the letter before it was sent.
30 Jul 1985	Patient A37 informed her GP, Dr Nixon, that she had had sexual intercourse with her psychiatrist. Dr Nixon entered the allegation in the notes and advised Patient A37 to report the matter to the appropriate authorities.
14 Oct 1985	COHSE replied to the letter from Mr Ingham, advising that the response was *unsatisfactory*.
4 Aug 1986	Patient A37 telephoned George Wood of YHA to ask how to lodge a complaint against a psychiatrist at Clifton Hospital. She claimed that she had had a sexual relationship with the consultant. No further action was taken by Patient A37 or the YHA.
1987	Patient A38 informed a nurse, Colin Smith, that William Kerr had made inappropriate sexual advances to her. However, she did not want to take the matter further and the nurse did not report the complaint.
Summer 1987	William Kerr allegedly indecently assaulted Patient A40, outpatient, at Ripon Hospital. In the Trial of the Facts before Judge Meyerson QC at Leeds Crown Court in late 2000, the jury found the facts relating to this allegation as being proved, and as a consequence William Kerr was placed upon the Sex Offenders Register.
9 Sep 1987	William Kerr wrote to the YRHA to give notice of his intention to retire from the NHS, with effect from 10 Sep 1988.

Date	Key event
17 Sep 1987	COHSE wrote to Mr Stokes, Regional General Manager, revisiting the issues of the handling of the Bigwood complaint and enclosing a further letter from Deputy Sister Bigwood, dated 22 Sep 1987, which repeated the previous detail and noted matters that had not been satisfactorily addressed by Mr Ingham. The letter also made mention of allegations against Michael Haslam.
22 Sep 1987	Dr Green wrote to William Kerr to acknowledge receipt of the notice letter and to make note of Dr Green's gratitude for the *"valuable contribution"* William Kerr had made to the Yorkshire Region.
3 Dec 1987	Dr Green sought Mr Chapman's advice in relation to what course the YRHA should take in replying to COHSE's letter dated 17 Sep 1987. Dr Green's note indicated that the RMO, Prof Haward, was already aware of the allegations against William Kerr and Michael Haslam. The note requested advice as to whether the police should be involved.
15 Dec 1987	Dr Green wrote to Mr Ingham enclosing a copy of Mr Chapman's advice dated 10 Dec 1987. The advice suggested that the police should be advised of the allegations outlined in Deputy Sister Bigwood's letter of 22 Sep 1987 and that if they did not want to take the matter further then there should be further consideration given to William Kerr's position.
15 Dec 1987	Mr Ingham spoke to Sergeant Ellerker. The police said that they would require more specific complaints and names of complainants before investigating.
3 Mar 1988	Dr Green wrote to COHSE outlining that the District's investigation in relation to Sister Bigwood's complaint had been *"carefully considered"* and contained uncorroborated evidence.
27 Apr 1988	Dr Green wrote to Mr Chapman saying that he had *"little enthusiasm in the circumstances* [due to William Kerr's impending retirement in Sep 1988] *for pursuing issues that are now so dated"*.
10 Sep 1988	William Kerr retired from the NHS at age 63.
25 Feb 1997	Patient A50 went to the police to complain that William Kerr had sexually assaulted and raped her during the period 1982 to 1986. The police spoke to Patient A50's CPN, Carmel Duff, who confirmed she was the recipient of complaints about William Kerr and that "dozens" of female patients had made similar allegations.
18 Mar 1997	Police informed the HHCT executive of its intention to undertake an investigation into allegations made against William Kerr.
19 Mar 1997	Mr Graham Saunders, CE of HHCT, wrote to Sir Liam Donaldson, CMO (then Regional Director of NHS Executive, Northern and Yorkshire), to advise that a strategic group had been set up by the Trust in relation to the police investigation.
16 Jun 1997	The HA sent a standard letter to approximately 1,200 female patients treated by William Kerr between 1975 and 1985.
17 Jun 1997	Mr Barrie Fisher, CE of NYHA, wrote to all the CEs of NHS Trusts to ask for assurances that effective complaints procedures and systems for dealing with disclosures of alleged misconduct were in place.
15 Jul 1998	William Kerr was arrested and charged with 15 counts of sexual assault (including rape). He was bailed to appear in court on 10 Dec 1998.

Date	Key event
20 Nov 1998	William Kerr was charged with a further four counts of sexual assault.
	William Kerr appeared in court on 10 Dec 1998, and 7 Jan, 11 Feb and 1 Jul 1999. The matter was referred to the Stipendiary Magistrate, who, on 25 Oct 1999, committed William Kerr to the Crown Court.
	The Crown Court set a pre-trial hearing on 14 Apr 2000 to determine the question of fitness to plead.
	William Kerr appealed to the Attorney General that he was not fit to plead.
17 Apr 2000	Jury found William Kerr not fit to plead. Trial date was set commencing on 27 Nov 2000.
27 Nov 2000	Trial of the Facts commenced at Leeds Crown Court before Judge Meyerson QC.
18 Dec 2000	Jury found one charge of indecent assault against William Kerr proved and six charges not proved, and were unable to reach a decision on the remaining 12 charges.
19 Dec 2000	William Kerr was granted an absolute discharge and his name was placed upon the Sex Offenders Register for five years. The CPS decided not to seek a rehearing of the matters upon which the jury were not able to reach a decision.

Annex 2
Chronology of key events: Michael Haslam

Date	Key event
7 Feb 1934	Michael Haslam born.
1969	Michael Haslam appointed Consultant in Psychological Medicine at Clifton and Harrogate District and York Hospitals.
18 Mar 1974	Patient B1 informed Dr Foggitt, GP, of her sexual relationship with Michael Haslam.
20 Mar 1974	Dr Foggitt referred Patient B1 to Dr Clarkson and in his referral letter explained to Dr Clarkson the reason for the "out-of-region" referral to him. Patient B1 was admitted to Scalebor Park and had one consultation wherein she informed Dr Clarkson of the sexual relationship with Michael Haslam.
4 Jun 1976	Patient B2 instructed solicitors to write a letter to Mr Holroyd, District Administrator, York, to inform the District of her sexual relationship with Michael Haslam, which had commenced in Aug 1974 and continued until May 1976.
13 Jul 1976	Michael Haslam, through his MDU solicitors, wrote to Mr Holroyd denying the sexual relationship.
12 Apr 1977	Mr Inman, Regional Administrator YRHA, wrote to Mr Holroyd informing him that Patient B1 had decided to "not press" the complaint, but had refused to sign a formal withdrawal of the complaint.
1980	Dr Clarkson disclosed to Dr Kennedy, Consultant Psychiatrist at York, that he had previously taken over one of Michael Haslam's patients (Patient B1 in 1974) due to "some kind of sexual allegation".
Jan/Feb 1981	Michael Haslam indecently assaulted Patient AB on two separate occasions at an out-building in the grounds of Clifton Hospital, conduct that gave rise to guilty verdicts on counts one and two of the criminal charges Michael Haslam was convicted of at Leeds Crown Court in Dec 2003. The Court of Appeal upheld these convictions.
1 Mar 1981	Patient AB wrote to Mr Holroyd, in relation to Michael Haslam's inappropriate conduct in Jan/Feb 1981.
May/Jun 1981	Patient AB informed Margaret Jones of Michael Haslam's treatment techniques and complained about inappropriateness of massage. Margaret Jones spoke to Mr Holroyd about the concerns. Mr Holroyd interviewed Patient AB. Mr Holroyd did not contact Michael Haslam about the complaint.
11 Mar 1983	Patient B3 informed Nurse Alan Greenfield that Michael Haslam had "kissed and fondled her" in 1981. In Dec 2003 Michael Haslam was convicted of sexual assault of Patient B3. The Court of Appeal upheld this conviction.

Date	Key event
14 Mar 1984	Mr Terry Beverton, Assistant Director of Nursing Services, Clifton Hospital, interviewed Nurse Greenfield in relation to an allegation of *"inappropriate use of counselling techniques on his ward and in particular his counselling of Patient B3."* Nurse Greenfield informed Mr Beverton of Patient B3's disclosure in Mar 1983.
15 Mar 1984	Mr Beverton wrote a report of his discussions with Nurse Greenfield, including the disclosure of concerns regarding Michael Haslam. The report was passed to Mr Raymond Wilk, Director of Nursing Services (Mental Illness), York. The report recommended that Nurse Greenfield be removed from Ash Tree House Ward, immediately.
19 Mar 1984	Patient B3 disclosed to Sister Cath Little her relationship with Michael Haslam. Sister Little compiled a statement for Patient B3 and had it signed by Patient B3 and herself in the presence of two witnesses: Mr Andy Cattell, Student Nurse, and Mr Brian Cottingham, Nursing Officer.

Mr Wilk and Mr Beverton interviewed Patient B3 in relation to her statement. |
20 Mar 1984	Dr McIntosh, DMO, transferred Patient B3 to the care of Dr Kennedy at Bootham Park Hospital.
25 Mar 1984	Patient B3 and her husband wrote to Mr Wilk to withdraw their consent for the use of her statement until such time as clarification was provided to them of the *"purpose"* of the statement.
11 Apr 1984	Patient B3 instructed her solicitor to write to Dr Turner to say that she did not want the matter to proceed. Patient B3 sought to clarify that her statement had been made as part of her treatment rather than as a form of complaint.
19 Apr 1984	Dr Turner met Michael Haslam to address the closure of the Patient B3 matter.
18 Jun 1987	Patient B5 informed Dr John Moroney, GP at Monkgate Surgery, of a complaint about Michael Haslam's treatment methods. Dr Moroney telephoned Dr Kennedy.
24 Jun 1987	Dr Kennedy spoke to Michael Haslam regarding the concerns raised by Patient B5. Michael Haslam admitted that he *"sailed close to the wind, only to give comfort"*.
Jul 1987	Patient B6 informed Dr Hanslip, SHO at Clifton Hospital, that Michael Haslam had propositioned her when she saw him in York.
22 Sep 1987	Sister Bigwood wrote to the Chairman of the YRHA to raise concerns that had been disclosed to her in relation to the conduct of Michael Haslam.
Oct 1987	Dr Christopher Simpson, Consultant Psychiatrist, had a meeting with a local GP surgery in Thirsk (Dr Harrison, Dr Donald and Dr Thiede). He was advised by the GPs that they welcomed his arrival as they could recommence referral of female patients to a psychiatrist, which they had refrained from doing while Michael Haslam was in the area. Dr Simpson referred this conversation to *"senior doctors in the York Health Authority"* (Drs Richardson and Wintersgill).
1988/89	Dr Hanslip told Dr Reilly, Consultant Psychiatrist, of the disclosure by Patient B6 in Jul 1987.
Summer 1988	Patient B5 transferred to the GP practice of Dr Moran. Patient B5 informed Dr Moran of inappropriate sexual advances made by Michael Haslam.
24 Sep 1988	Mr John Hughes of Gateway Residential Services plc wrote to Michael Haslam enclosing a contract for negotiating Michael Haslam's appointment as Medical Director of the Harrogate Clinic, a private nursing home.

Date	Key event
26 Sep 1988	Patient B7 informed Mr Stephen Brooks, CPN, that Michael Haslam had sexually assaulted her in Jul 1988 at Clifton Hospital. This offence gave rise to a guilty verdict on count four of the criminal charges Michael Haslam was convicted of in Dec 2003. The Court of Appeal upheld this conviction.
27 Sep 1988	Patient B7 informed her GP, Dr Moran, of her allegations.
28 Sep 1988	Patient B7 was admitted to Bootham Park Hospital under the care of Dr Reilly. Patient B7 informed Dr Reilly of the sexual assault.
2 Oct 1988	Michael Haslam wrote to Dr Kennedy denying *"any impropriety"* and suggested to Dr Kennedy that a meeting be arranged with Patient B7 so that the matter could be discussed with her in his presence.
4 Oct 1988	Dr Green wrote to Dr Kennedy requesting statements from Dr Reilly, Dr Moran and Mr Brooks, together with the medical notes of Patient B7. Dr Kennedy spoke with Dr Haward about the complaint. Dr Kennedy advised Michael Haslam of the complaint.
12 Oct 1988	Dr Kennedy sent the statements of Dr Moran and Mr Brooks to Dr Green with Patient B7's medical notes. Dr Kennedy enclosed a memo detailing various other concerns regarding Michael Haslam that had come to his attention as far back as 1980. Dr Kennedy suggested that Michael Haslam be *"counselled to consider retirement"*.
	Dr Kennedy received a letter advertising the impending opening of the Harrogate Clinic, noting Michael Haslam in the post of Medical Director.
24 Nov 1988	Dr Green met Dr Patrick Hoyte, Michael Haslam's legal representative from the MDU, to discuss the matter.
	Dr Green wrote to Michael Haslam to invite him to attend a meeting at the RMO's office on 5 Dec 1988.
5 Dec 1988	Michael Haslam met Dr Green and Dr Haward. Michael Haslam denied all allegations of inappropriate conduct. Michael Haslam was offered two options: to resign, or to remain and undergo a disciplinary investigation by the RHA.
8 Dec 1988	Michael Haslam tendered his resignation from the NHS, to take effect on and from 1 Apr 1989. No restrictions were placed upon Michael Haslam's practice, nor was he suspended with full pay during the notice period.
8 Mar 1989	Mr Graham Saunders, Harrogate District Health Authority, wrote to Dr Kennedy to advise that Michael Haslam had been appointed Medical Director and Person in Charge of the Harrogate Clinic.
30 Mar 1989	Dr Kennedy wrote to Mr Saunders with a reference for Michael Haslam. The reference contained the following remarks: *"I have been made aware indirectly as a fellow consultant psychiatrist and later directly as a manager of the service of a series of complaints about unprofessional behaviour by Dr Haslam towards female patients … I feel I have to bring this to your attention because the number of unsubstantiated complaints of this kind is unusual. I have records of six such incidents spread over the years, three of which were in the last two years in the run-up to Dr Haslam's retirement, which he decided to take at the age of 55, after a discussion with the Regional Medical Officer."*
12 Apr 1989	Harrogate Health Authority approved the Harrogate Clinic's application for registration, with Michael Haslam appointed as Medical Director.
Aug 1989	The RHA granted an Honorary Consultancy to Michael Haslam.
Mid-1990	Michael Haslam resigned as Medical Director of the Harrogate Clinic. He remained a resident consultant.

Date	Key event
Dec 1993	Michael Haslam was appointed Medical Director of the South Durham NHS Trust. This was a non-clinical appointment.
11 Mar 1996	Dr Timperley, consultant psychiatrist in Scarborough, informed the GMC that Patient B4 had disclosed to him alleged sexual abuse of her by Michael Haslam.
23 Sep 1996	Patient B10 wrote to the GMC wishing to raise a complaint.
2 Oct 1996	GMC solicitors interviewed Dr Timperley. Dr Timperley explained that in his opinion Patient B4 was not fit to participate in the GMC investigation.
11 Oct 1996	In response to a request for further information, Patient B10 revealed to the GMC that the complaint related to Michael Haslam.
Oct 1996	As a result of the complaint by Patient B10, a patient of the Harrogate Clinic, Michael Haslam's outpatient and admission rights at the Harrogate Clinic were suspended.
29 Mar 1997	Patient B10 discontinued her complaint.
29 Apr 1997	While reviewing the matters concerning William Kerr, the Harrogate Healthcare Trust Board noted that there were concerns regarding Michael Haslam.
20 Jun 1997	Mr Barrie Fisher, CEO York Health Services Trust, and Mr George Wood, Deputy CEO, decided to set up a Serious Incident Committee to monitor the concerns relating to Michael Haslam.
9 Jul 1997	Dr Kennedy wrote to the GMC advising of allegations he had received in respect of Michael Haslam.
13 Aug 1997	Detective Chief Inspector Hunt wrote to Mr Wood advising that the police investigation into Michael Haslam, which arose from former patients contacting the police during the William Kerr trawl for witnesses, would not be proceeding due to a lack of evidence.
18 Aug 1997	The HA advised the GMC that it would be undertaking an internal investigation into Michael Haslam's conduct – the Manzoor Inquiry.
7 Oct 1997	Michael Haslam was suspended from the post of Medical Director at South Durham NHS Trust.
21 Oct 1997	Professor Liam Donaldson, Regional Director of Public Health (as he then was), issued an alert letter [HSG(97)36] about Michael Haslam to NHS executive bodies.
10 Dec 1997	Dr Richardson, consultant psychiatrist in York, wrote to the GMC describing rumours among his colleagues relating to Michael Haslam.
15 & 16 Jan 1998	The Manzoor Inquiry conducted interviews of relevant witnesses. Michael Haslam refused to answer questions when interviewed by the chairman, but did make submissions through his solicitors.
19 Jan 1998	The HA advised the GMC of its "heightened concerns" about Michael Haslam.
4 Mar 1998	The HA provided a copy of the interim Manzoor Inquiry Report to the GMC.
22 Jun 1998	The HA sent the GMC a copy of the final Manzoor Inquiry Report dated 19 May. The GMC decided that since the Report did not include dates, names of patients, or records of interviews, or permit Michael Haslam to cross-examine witnesses, the Report was not prima facie evidence to support a referral to the Preliminary Proceedings Committee (PPC).
Sep 1998	Michael Haslam was dismissed from South West Durham Mental Health NHS Trust.
21 Oct 1998	The police forwarded to the GMC all material relating to Patient B3, Patient B7 and Patient B11.

Date	Key event
11 Nov 1998	The HA forwarded further material supplementing the Manzoor Inquiry Report. The names of the patients involved in the investigation were released to the GMC.
18 Jan 1999	Michael Haslam applied to the GMC for voluntary erasure.
24 Jan 1999	The *Sunday Times* published an article with the headline, "Psychiatrists accused of serial rapes".
25 Feb 1999	The GMC referred the complaint of Patient B11 to the PPC.
1 Apr 1999	A PPC meeting decided to refer the complaint of Patient B11 to the Professional Conduct Committee (PCC) of the GMC. Michael Haslam was invited by the PPC to apply for voluntary erasure.
15 Apr 1999	The GMC granted Michael Haslam's application for voluntary erasure of his name from the GMC Register. The GMC thereafter had no jurisdiction to investigate or prosecute any disciplinary action against Michael Haslam.
Sep 1999	Michael Haslam was counselling patients at Nutrition Associates, Galtres House, Lysander Close, Clifton Moor Gate, York. He continued to counsel patients until Mar 2000.
20 Jan 2000	Michael Haslam issued proceedings for libel against Times Newspapers Ltd.
5 Sep 2002	Michael Haslam was arrested and charged with four counts of indecent assault under Section 14(1) of the Sexual Offences Act 1956 and one count of rape under Section 15(1) of the Sexual Offences Act 1956.
12 Dec 2003	A unanimous jury at Leeds Crown Court convicted Michael Haslam on four counts of indecent assault and one count of rape.
16 Dec 2003	His Honour Mr Justice Gray of Leeds Crown Court sentenced Michael Haslam to seven years' imprisonment. His Honour further ordered that Michael Haslam's name be placed upon the Sex Offenders Register.
20 May 2004	The Court of Appeal allowed Michael Haslam's appeal and quashed the conviction for rape made in Dec 2003. It upheld the convictions on the four counts of indecent assault. Accordingly Michael Haslam's sentence was reduced to three years' imprisonment.
Oct 2004	Michael Haslam discontinued his libel action in relation to an article published in the *Sunday Times* in January 1999. He further agreed to make a substantial contribution to the newspaper's legal costs.

Annex 3
Index of legislation and guidance on employment

1   RHB(51)80 Staff: conditions of service – Machinery for dealing with disciplinary cases (also called BG[51]77 and HMC[51]73)

2   HM(56)98 NHS Medical and Dental Staff – Disciplinary proceedings in cases relating to professional behaviour or competence

3   HM(60)45 Prevention of harm to patients resulting from physical or mental disability of hospital medical or dental staff

4   HM(61)112 disciplinary proceedings in cases relating to hospital medical and dental staff

5   HC(77)2 Checks on doctors' and dentists' identity and references

6   PM(81)26 Disciplinary erasure from the medical register, suspensions and extensions of suspensions of registration

7   NHS (Appointment of Consultants) Regulations 1982

8   SI 1982/276 The NHS (Appointment of Consultants) Regulations 1982

9   HC(82)10 The Appointment of Consultants and Senior Registrars

10 HC(82)13 Prevention of harm to patients resulting from physical or mental disability of hospital or community or dental staff (The "Three Wise Men" Procedure)

11 Medical Act 1983 – part V Professional conduct and fitness to practise

12 SI 1984/994 The NHS (Appointment of Consultants) Regulations 1984

13   HC(87)16 "Erasure from the medical register, suspensions of registration, impositions of conditions on registration and restoration to the medical register".

14   PM(87)7 Doctors, dentists and dental auxiliaries: registration and employment

15   EL(89)p/148 Hospital medical and dental staff – locum tenens engaged through private agencies

16   HC(90)9 Disciplinary procedures in cases relating to senior medical and dental staff

17   SI 1990/407 NHS (Appointment of Consultants) Amendment Regulations 1990

18   HC(90)19 The appointment of consultants and directors of public health

19   TEL(91)2 Appointments of consultant medical and dental staff to NHS trusts

20   HSG(91)28 Settling individual employee grievances in respect of NHS Conditions of Service

21   SI 1992/664 NHS (Service Committees and Tribunal) Regulations 1992

22   EL(92)53 Recruitment procedures – validation certificates and qualifications

23   EL(92)84 Doctors: registration and employment

24   Council Directive 93/16/EEC dated 5 April 1993 OJ L165 36:7 July 1993

25   HSG(94)49 Disciplinary procedures for hospital and community medical and hospital dental staff

26   Medical (Professional Performance) Act 1995

27   GC 3/95 Section 42 of the General Whitley Council Handbook – disciplinary and disputes procedures

28   General Medical Council. Duties of a doctor: good medical practice. London 1995

29   SI 1995/3208 The European Specialist Medical Qualifications Order 1995

30   Chief Medical Officer for England. Maintaining medical excellence. London: Department of Health, 1996 (letter to chief executives and medical directors of NHS trusts)

31   SI 1996/701 NHS (Appointment of Consultants) Regulations 1996

32   HSG(96)24 The NHS (Appointment of Consultants) Regulations 1996

33   EL(96)19 Implementation of new complaints procedure

34   Good Practice Guidance booklet that accompanied the issue of NHS (Appointment of Consultant) Regulations 1996

35   The General Medical Council. The new performance procedures: consultative document. London: GMC, 1997

36   HSG(97)36 The issue of alert letters about hospital and community medical and dental staff

37   EL(97)48 Codes of practice in hospital and community health service locum doctor appointment and employment

38   EL(97)78 The management of doctors with problems

39   A First Class Service: Quality in the new NHS December 1997

40   HSC 1999/198 – Whistleblowing and public concern at work "Toolkit" issued with HSC

41   HSC 2000/19 Appointment procedures for hospital and community medical and dental staff

42   SI 2000/1803: The Medical Act 1983 (Amendment) Order 2000 (Aug)

43   HSC 2002/011 The issue of alert letters for health professionals in England (Nov 2002)

44 HSC 2002/011 Appointment procedures for hospital and community and medical and dental staff

45 Statutory Instrument 2002 No 3135: The Medical Act 1983 (Amendment) Order 2002 (Dec)

46 Assuring the quality of medical practice January 1997

47 HSC 2002/008 Pre and post appointment checks for all persons working in the NHS in England May 2002

48 Modernisation Agency: recruitment information Nov 2002

49 Role, remit and procedures of the General Medical Council Dec 2002

50 SI 2003/1250 The General and Specialist Medical Practice (Education, Training and Qualifications) Order 2002

51 New framework for discipline and suspension: Joint statement of agreed principles

52 HSC (IS) 10 WHSC (IS) 11 Health Service Commissioner March 1974

Annex 4
Guidance issued outside the UK relating to the doctor/patient relationship

Introduction

1   This annex contains some relevant extracts from professional guidance issued in countries outside the UK. It is supplemental to, and to be read with, the material set out in Chapter 29 of the Report. The material is here reproduced to assist decision makers in the UK in understanding how the issues of doctor/patient boundary transgressions, and sexualised behaviour, have been considered in other jurisdictions. The extracts are by no means complete or comprehensive – the constraints of the overall size of the Report have also dictated heavy editing. Even within those limitations, we are confident that this comparative exercise is both useful and instructive.

2   The extracts relate to both the *current* and the *former* patient – the annex is divided accordingly. The main focus is on the doctor. However, the extracts are of more general application, where in medical practice there is opportunity for abuse.

3   The terminology used is not always familiar. There is reference to broad terms such as "counsellor" and "therapist", as well as to doctor, psychiatrist etc. Some overall assistance in the use of terminology may be obtained from the following extract from Advocateweb in the USA (http://www.advocateweb.org), accessible through the UK website of the Prevention of Professional Abuse Network (POPAN) at http://www.popan.org.uk:

> "*The terms used to discuss the issue of sexual exploitation by counsellors are often ambiguous. In order to eliminate confusion, we will use these definitions:*

"Counsellor – any psychiatrist, psychologist, nurse, psychotherapist, therapist, social worker, chemical dependency counsellor, member of the clergy or other person, whether licensed or not, who provides or claims to provide psychotherapy, counselling, assessment or mental health treatment.

"Client – any person who uses the services of a counsellor.

"Sexual exploitation – inappropriate sexual conversation, dating or suggestions of sexual involvement by the counsellor, and/or any sexual or romantic contact between client and counsellor which may include but is not limited to sexual intercourse, kissing, and/or touching breasts or genitals.

"Boundary – something that indicates or marks a limit. In a counselling relationship, a boundary is the limit that exists to keep the relationship professional in order to ensure that clients are getting their needs met. When boundaries are violated, people feel intruded upon and perhaps even confused about their own sense of self."

The current patient

4   The Canadian Psychiatric Association developed its advice between 1978 and 1992, as follows.

5   1978 –

"The practice of psychiatry rests upon the relationship between the patient and psychiatrist. This relationship is to varying degrees part of the therapeutic process and may become an intensely emotional one. Many of the ways in which a patient deals with these feelings give the psychiatrist a considerable, potential capacity for influencing the patient's decisions.

"The ethical psychiatrist will scrupulously avoid using this relationship to gratify his own emotional, financial and sexual needs. He will avoid influencing the patient in any way which does not bear directly upon the treatment goals."

6   1988 –

"Sexual contact between physician and patient, ranging from courtship behaviour to sexual intercourse, has been taboo from the earliest days of medical practice. This prohibition has served the moral values of society worldwide so that it has never been seriously questioned. Physicians found to have contravened the rule continue to be severely disciplined by their peers.

"The Canadian Psychiatric Association has addressed issues of ethical concern by reviewing the Canadian Medical Association Code of Ethics and annotating it specifically for psychiatry. Annotation number 1, entitled "Respect for the Patient," addresses the nature of the psychiatrist/patient relationship. It states that the ethical psychiatrist will scrupulously avoid using this relationship to gratify his or her emotional, financial, and sexual needs.

"Physicians enjoy a privileged relationship with patients based on trust. The power and prestige of the physician, with the right to touch and explore physically and psychologically, place him or her in an advantageous position. It cannot be accepted that physicians and patients are ever similar to any consenting adults. To maintain trust, the physician must avoid initiating or responding to any forms of sexual advances. Sexualizing the relationship is a clear breach of trust. The outcome is destructive for both, but the patient suffers the greater damage as the dependent partner in the dyad."

7   1992 –

"Sexual contact between physician and patient has long been considered unethical. The doctor is in a position of power and trust, and sexualization of the relationship is a betrayal of that trust. This is particularly true in a psychotherapeutic relationship. In psychotherapy, patients are encouraged to suspend their customary defences and reveal private thoughts and feelings in the expectation of being helped. In addition, in therapy, patients develop intense feelings towards the therapist which are a manifestation of transference, i.e., a repetition of feelings experienced in earlier important relationships. The Canadian Medical Association Code of Ethics Annotated for Psychiatrists specifically prohibits any exploitation of the patient's vulnerability within this relationship stating, 'the ethical

psychiatrist will scrupulously avoid using this relationship to gratify his own emotional, financial and sexual needs.'

"Lending support to these ethical considerations, there is clear evidence that patients can be harmed by sexual contact with their therapists. Documented harmful effects include greater difficulties with trust, poor self-concept and problems expressing anger. Patient victims may have been sexually abused as children or adults and are re-victimized by sexual contact in therapy. More seriously ill patients, those with psychoses or severe personality disorders, are harmed the most.

"Despite increasingly frequent warnings in recent years, such as those cited above, sexual exploitation of patients continues to occur. Among psychiatrists who responded to a recent US survey, 7.1% of the male psychiatrists and 3.1% of the female psychiatrists acknowledged having had sexual contact with their patients. As the authors state, 'These offenders were apparently unaware of, or willing to ignore, the clinical contraindications and ethical prohibitions.'"

8   The 2002 statement from the University of Manitoba (http://www.umanitoba.ca) setting out college policy on sexual misconduct in the physician/patient relationship is also relevant to any debate on the position of the current patient. It states:

"Current patient

"There are no circumstances in which sexual misconduct in the current physician/patient relationship is acceptable. Therefore:

"A physician must not initiate any form of sexual advance to a patient. It is the ethical responsibility of the physician to avoid using the physician/patient relationship to gratify inappropriately his/her own needs.

"A physician must not respond sexually to any form of sexual advance by a patient. It is never appropriate for a physician to attempt to meet a patient's sexual needs. Sexualizing the physician/patient relationship has no therapeutic value.

"Physician/patient sexual contact is abusive regardless of whether the physician believes that the patient consents. Patient consent is never an acceptable rationalization.

"It is the physician's responsibility to set and control appropriate boundaries in the physician/patient relationship."

9   The College of Physicians and Surgeons of Nova Scotia adopts a similar position (http://www.cpsns.ns.ca):

"Current patient

"The College recognizes there are no circumstances in which sexualized conduct in the current physician-patient relationship is acceptable. Such activity is abusive regardless of whether the physician believes he or she has consent, or uses any other rationalization to excuse the behaviour. It is the physician's responsibility never to cross the line into sexual misconduct. Sexual misconduct is a spectrum encompassing the whole range of inappropriate physician-patient interactions of a sexual nature including the following examples:

— *Voyeurism as may be expressed by inappropriate disrobing or draping practices that reflect a lack of respect for the patient's privacy.*

— *Subjecting a patient to an examination in the presence of medical students or other parties without the consent of the patient or when consent has been withdrawn.*

— *Inappropriate comments about or to the patient, including making sexual comments about the patient's body or clothing.*

— *Inappropriate comments about the patient's sexual orientation (homosexual, heterosexual or bisexual).*

— *Making comments about the patient's potential sexual performance during an examination or consultation, except when the examination or consultation is for the purpose of addressing issues of sexual function or dysfunction, and the comments are relevant to the management of that patient's problem.*

— *Requesting details of sexual history or sexual preference in any situation when this is inappropriate.*

— *Initiation by the physician of inappropriate conversation regarding the sexual problems, preferences or fantasies of the physician or patient.*

– *Failure to obtain permission for and/or inappropriate examination of breasts, genitals and anus (procedure not standard practice and not justifiable).*

– *Performing a pelvic examination, anal-rectal examination, or examination of external genitalia without wearing gloves.*

– *Inappropriate body contact, including hugging of a sexual nature and kissing.*

– *Touching or massaging breasts, genitals or anus, or any other sexualized body part for any purpose other than appropriate physical examination or treatment.*

– *Physician-patient sex, whether consented to or initiated by the patient, and any conduct with a patient that is sexual or may be reasonably interpreted as sexual. Such activities may include, but are not limited to, the physician encouraging the patient to masturbate in the physician's presence, masturbation by the physician of himself or herself or the patient, and contact between the mouth, genitals, or anus of the physician and the mouth, genitals, or anus of the patient.*

"This list is not exhaustive. Physicians should always keep in mind a patient's perception of what might constitute sexual misconduct, recognizing that this can vary widely from individual to individual. Communicating what will be done and why it is needed can help alleviate misperceptions, ensure cooperation and reduce the risk of patients perceiving procedures as inappropriate or abusive.

"Risk behaviours that can warn a physician that he or she may be in danger of crossing professional boundaries are often present. A list of potentially inappropriate behaviours is contained in Appendix A: Warning signs of risk behaviour."

The former patient

10   As before, when considering sexual relations with a current patient, we see some assistance in the ethical advice and professional guidance in other countries. For example, the current ethical advice of the American Psychiatric Association is as follows:

"A physician shall uphold the standards of professionalism, be honest in all professional interactions and strive to report physicians deficient in character or competence, or engaging in fraud or deception to appropriate entities.

"The requirement that the physician conduct himself/herself with propriety in his or her profession and in all the actions of his or her life is especially important in the case of the psychiatrist because the patient tends to model his or her behaviour after that of his or her psychiatrist by identification. Further, the necessary intensity of the treatment relationship may tend to activate sexual and other needs and fantasies on the part of both patient and psychiatrist, while weakening the objectivity necessary for control. Additionally, the inherent inequality in the doctor-patient relationship may lead to exploitation of the patient. Sexual activity with a current or former patient is unethical" *(emphasis added).*

11   In some parts of the USA, therefore, sexual activity by a psychiatrist with a former patient is unethical – without reference to the time elapsed, and without reference to the treatment or subject area.

12   For a psychologist in America, however, there is a different standard, and a two-year interval is referred to. The current (2002) advice from the American Psychological Association is as follows:

"10.05 Sexual Intimacies With Current Therapy Clients/Patients

Psychologists do not engage in sexual intimacies with current therapy clients/patients.

10.06 Sexual Intimacies With Relatives or Significant Others of Current Therapy Clients/Patients

Psychologists do not engage in sexual intimacies with individuals they know to be close relatives, guardians, or significant others of current clients/patients. Psychologists do not terminate therapy to circumvent this standard.

10.07 Therapy With Former Sexual Partners

Psychologists do not accept as therapy clients/patients persons with whom they have engaged in sexual intimacies.

10.08 Sexual Intimacies With Former Therapy Clients/Patients

> *(a) Psychologists do not engage in sexual intimacies with former clients/patients for at least two years after cessation or termination of therapy.*

> *(b) Psychologists do not engage in sexual intimacies with former clients/patients even after a two-year interval except in the most unusual circumstances. Psychologists who engage in such activity after the two years following cessation or termination of therapy and of having no sexual contact with the former client/patient bear the burden of demonstrating that there has been no exploitation, in light of all relevant factors, including (1) the amount of time that has passed since therapy terminated; (2) the nature, duration, and intensity of the therapy; (3) the circumstances of termination; (4) the client's/patient's personal history; (5) the client's/patient's current mental status; (6) the likelihood of adverse impact on the client/patient; and (7) any statements or actions made by the therapist during the course of therapy suggesting or inviting the possibility of a post-termination sexual or romantic relationship with the client/patient."*

13   In 1992, the position was slightly different; this section of the Ethics Code reads as follows:

> *"4.07 Sexual Intimacies With Former Therapy Patients*

> *a) Psychologists do not engage in sexual intimacies with a former therapy patient or client for at least two years after cessation or termination of professional services.*

> *b)* Because sexual intimacies with a former therapy patient or client are so frequently harmful to the patient or client, and because such intimacies undermine public confidence in the psychology profession and thereby deter the public's use of needed services, *psychologists do not engage in sexual intimacies with former therapy patients and clients even after a two-year interval except in the most unusual circumstances. The psychologist who engages in such activity after the two years following cessation or termination of treatment bears the burden of demonstrating that there has been no exploitation, in light*

of all relevant factors, including (1) the amount of time that has passed since therapy terminated, (2) the nature and duration of the therapy, (3) the circumstances of termination, (4) the patient's or client's personal history, (5) the patient's or client's current mental status, (6) the likelihood of adverse impact on the patient or client and others, and (7) any statements or actions made by the therapist during the course of therapy suggesting or inviting the possibility of a post-termination sexual or romantic relationship with the patient or client" (emphasis added).

The recent omission of the underlined parts of the opening sentence of paragraph 4.07(b) is relevant.

14   The position in US states varies, but the following 2002 statement from New York State is believed to be typical:

"FORMER PATIENTS – Sexual behaviour with a former patient is inappropriate when the sexual involvement results from or appears to result from the use or exploitation of the trust, knowledge or power obtained from the professional relationship. The American Psychiatric Association considers sexual behaviour by a psychiatrist with a former patient unethical."

15   In other countries, different standards apply.

16   In September 2002, the Royal Australian and New Zealand College of Psychiatrists (RANZCP) produced an important overview document – *Overpower or Empower: Boundaries in Psychiatry*. The report is currently the subject of a detailed implementation plan. At page 20 of the report, there is a passing reference to former patients:

"The RANZCP Code of Ethics clearly states that boundary transgressions are unethical. This includes situations of asking patients on a date during a professional consultation, rural practitioners asking a patient for a date because potential romantic partners are also patients, sexual harassment, using sex for therapeutic purposes, abusing physical examination procedures and a longstanding patient relationship evolving into intense lovesickness or infatuation. There is still debate about the issue of romantic involvement of psychiatrists with former patients. *The ethical guidelines also indicate that any abuse of*

therapeutic power is prohibited. However, the existence of ethical guidelines has been insufficient to prevent boundary transgressions" (emphasis added).

17 The continuation of that debate can be seen, for example, from an extract from an article written by the New Zealand Health and Disability Commissioner in August 2004:

"Medical ethics

"For over 2,000 years, it has been a fundamental tenet of medical ethics that doctors may not enter intimate sexual relationships with their patients. The Hippocratic Oath (c. 400BC) states that in their professional lives doctors must abstain from 'the seduction of females or males'. The modern rationale was articulated by Dr Robin Briant, former Chair of the Medical Council [in New Zealand], in 1994:

"The doctor–patient interaction is for the patient's benefit and there is no place in it for a sexual liaison. It would do immense harm to the quality of doctor–patient interactions generally if it were even suspected that intimate or sexual relationships may evolve from medical consultations. Only when people feel safe in a professional relationship can they entrust it with their most private emotional, psychological and physical secrets.

"The Council has taken a strong lead on sexual boundaries in the doctor–patient relationship, and its new revised statement (July 2004) reiterates its 'zero tolerance' position on doctors who breach sexual boundaries with a current patient, rejecting the view that 'changing social standards require a less stringent approach'. For former patients, the rule is 'proceed with extreme caution, and seek peer advice'. It is 'never acceptable' to end the professional relationship for the sole purpose of initiating a sexual relationship, or to become involved with a patient one has counselled.

"Judicial tolerance

"In the Wiles case (2001), District Court Judge Lee described the Council's 'zero tolerance' policy as exhibiting 'vestiges of a paternalistic attitude which sees women as childlike beings unable to think and act independently for themselves and needing protection for their own good'. The judge thought that requiring a 'clean break' before a doctor commences a sexual relationship with a patient could be resented by patients as 'unjustifiable interference with their right as mature adults to live their lives as they see fit'.

"Even though Ms Y was a current patient when sexual intimacy began, the GP's conduct was excused because there was no evidence of exploitation. He was 'genuinely in love' and, having made alternative arrangements for Ms Y's care, was free to enter a sexual relationship, without any need for a 'clean break'. Discipline was not warranted. The High Court found no error of law on appeal."

18   So far as we are aware, the latest position from New Zealand is reflected in the 2004 document from the Medical Council of New Zealand referred to in Chapter 29 of the Report – *'Sexual Boundaries in the Doctor-Patient Relationship'*, under the heading 'Sexual relationships with former patients'. We consider this advice to be so relevant, and recent, that we here set out this section in full:

"71. There are times when two people, such as a doctor and a patient who meet through a professional service, want to start a personal relationship.

"72. However, research shows that a former patient may still be harmed by having a relationship with his or her former doctor even if he or she has been transferred to another doctor. Although not definitive, the research indicates that harm is often linked to the intensity of the doctor-patient relationship. For example, the length of the professional relationship, the frequency of contact and the type of care provided.

"73. Because each doctor-patient relationship is individual, and because everyone reacts differently to circumstances, it is difficult to have clear rules on when it is or is not acceptable for a doctor to have a relationship with a former patient.

"74. Council's zero-tolerance position on sexual relationships in the doctor-patient relationship has not expanded to include doctors and former patients. The Council recognises that where a former doctor-patient relationship was very minor or temporary a total ban on any subsequent relationship is unfair and unrealistic. An example could be where a doctor treats a minor condition such as a sprained ankle in a one-off situation.

"75. The Council also recognises that in some situations a doctor has to practise and socialise within a small community. The doctor will then find it difficult to socialise with individuals who are not, or have not been, a patient at some stage. For example, rural areas or patients with a certain sexual orientation or live within a cultural community.

"76. However, there are some situations where it would never be acceptable for a doctor to have a relationship with a former patient.

When a sexual relationship is never acceptable

"77. A sexual relationship between you and a former patient is never acceptable if:

- *the doctor-patient relationship involved psychotherapy, or long-term counselling (informal or formal) or emotional support;*

- *the patient has had, or has, a condition or impairment likely to confuse his or her judgement or thinking about what he or she may want to do;*

- *the patient has been sexually abused in the past;*

- *the doctor-patient relationship is ended for the sole purpose of initiating a sexual relationship.*

"78. A sexual relationship between you and a former patient will always be regarded as unethical if it can be shown that you have used any power imbalance, knowledge or influence obtained while you were the patient's doctor.

"79. It is important that you recognise the influence you have had as the patient's doctor, and that the resulting power imbalance from the professional relationship may continue for some time after the patient stops consulting you.

"80. If you are thinking about developing a relationship with a former patient, it requires serious consideration. Make sure you consider any possible future harm to the patient before making a decision.

"Things to consider

"81. The Council strongly recommends that you make this decision in consultation with respected peers. Issues to consider include:

- *The length of the doctor-patient relationship. The longer the relationship the less appropriate a personal relationship is because the power imbalance from the doctor-patient relationship is more firmly entrenched;*

- *When did the doctor-patient relationship finish and what interaction have you had with the patient since? As discussed in sections 17-20 the power imbalance is often not immediately recognised. If the patient has only recently adopted the 'former' status sufficient time may not have passed for the emotional connection as a patient to abate;*

- *What was the context of your relationship with the former patient? Did your professional relationship include a supportive, advisory or informal counselling role? Was there formal counselling? Are there privacy issues to consider? In these circumstances, developing a relationship with a former patient is not acceptable;*

- *The type of doctor-patient relationship. Were you a family doctor and if so will you still be caring for other family members? Were you a surgeon and, if so, what impact did the surgery have on the patient, ie was it minor or life changing? Overall, what impact has your care had on the former patient?*

- *Your understanding of the dynamics of the doctor-patient relationship and your knowledge of the concept of transference. Refer to the literature to check that you fully understand the dynamics of your relationship with the former patient reference annotated bibliography;*

- *The patient's understanding about the dynamics of the doctor-patient relationship and his or her knowledge of the concept of transference. If you are considering having a relationship with a former patient, the Council expects you to tell the patient about the issues to do with possible harm from a doctor-patient relationship. It may be appropriate to help the patient get independent counselling;*

- *The circumstances surrounding ending of the doctor-patient relationship. The Council does not believe it is acceptable to end a doctor-patient relationship for the sole purpose of starting a sexual relationship;*

- *The patient's degree of vulnerability. For example, patients undergoing psychotherapy may be particularly vulnerable, as may those with certain psychological, physical or character traits.*

"82. The doctor-patient relationship is often very intense. Even though it may not be thought so by either you or your patient, by considering the above points you can more accurately assess the intensity. Remember that the more intense the doctor-patient relationship, the more likely it is you and your patient may find yourselves in a situation where feelings towards each other are more likely to become confused between professional care and personal feelings."

19   This helpful advice is given in two forms – *A Guide for Doctors*, and *A Guide for Patients*. The extracts set out above are from the former. We consider the dissemination of information to patients (health service users) to be fundamentally important, and here also reproduce an extract from the latter guide, for patients:

"A patient may want to start a personal relationship with his or her former doctor or vice versa.

"Research shows that a patient may be harmed as a result of having a relationship with his or her former doctor. Each patient-doctor relationship is individual and every person reacts differently, so it is difficult to have clear rules about when this type of relationship is not appropriate.

"There are some situations where it would never be appropriate for a doctor to have a relationship with a former patient. A sexual relationship between you and your former doctor is not appropriate if:

- *the patient-doctor relationship involved psychotherapy, or long-term counselling (informal or formal) or emotional support*

- *you have had in the past, or you now have a difficulty likely to confuse your judgment*

- *you have been sexually abused in the past.*

"A sexual relationship between you and your former doctor will always be seen as unethical if it can be shown that the doctor has used any power imbalance, knowledge or influence obtained while he or she was your doctor.

"If you are thinking of having a relationship with your former doctor, you should know about the harm that may result from a patient-doctor relationship. You may want to talk to a counsellor.

"You may also want to think about the following questions and answers.

- *How long was the patient-doctor relationship?*

"The longer the patient-doctor relationship, the more likely the power imbalance will still be there.

- *When did the patient-doctor relationship end, and what interaction have you had since?*

"Research shows that if you have only recently become a former patient you may still have a patient's emotional connection to the doctor.

- *Did the doctor's professional relationship include him or her giving you support, advice or counselling?*

"Research shows that when a patient-doctor relationship has included support, advice or counselling (formal or informal) the patient and doctor may be more likely to confuse feelings and boundaries. This is often called 'transference'. It may seem that both parties jointly agree to start the relationship, but problems develop around this later.

- *Are there privacy issues to consider?*

"Even when you are no longer in a professional relationship with the doctor, you need to remember that, as your doctor, he or she was aware of all your health information. If the doctor is still treating people you know, no information about their health should be shared with you, even if you are now in a personal relationship."

20   The position in Canada, at least at state level, is reflected in the following taken from the 2002 statement from the University of Manitoba. (The advice in Nova Scotia, referred to above, is to similar effect.) Although not suggesting a prohibition on a sexual relationship with a former patient, we consider this to be clear and helpful guidance. Additional guidance may be necessary in relation to psychiatrists or other therapists.

"Former Patient

"The dynamics of the physician/patient relationship do not necessarily end with the completion of treatment or the transfer of patient care. There is a risk of abuse of power on the part of the physician since, whether intentionally or not, he/she may use or exploit the trust, the confidential information, the emotions or the power created during the professional relationship.

"In any sexualized conduct with a former patient, the physician has a duty to ensure there is no exploitation by the physician of the power imbalance between the parties resulting from the earlier physician/patient relationship.

"It is not acceptable to terminate a physician/patient relationship with the intent of engaging in a sexual relationship. The physician's ethical obligation not to exploit the physician/patient relationship for the physician's personal advantage applies whenever a physician considers termination of the physician/patient relationship to pursue a personal relationship. The physician must recognize the risk of abuse in any such circumstance, and must realistically assess the emotional dependence of the patient. Where a physician/patient relationship is terminated with the intent of entering a personal relationship, the physician is accountable for any exploitation.

"Factors to be considered in assessing whether sexualized contact with a former patient is appropriate include but are not limited to:

- The type and duration of the therapeutic relationship.

- The physician's understanding of the dynamics of the physician/patient relationship.

- The patient's understanding of the dynamics of the physician/patient relationship.

- The physician's understanding of the boundaries involved in a physician/patient relationship.

- The patient's understanding of the boundaries involved in a physician/patient relationship.

- The circumstances surrounding the termination of the physician/patient relationship.

- The physician's knowledge of the concept of transference.

- The patient's degree of vulnerability. (For example, patients undergoing psychotherapy may be particularly vulnerable, as may be those with certain psychological, physical or character traits.)

"Given the very special nature of the psychotherapeutic relationship, it is rare for personal relationships to be established between physicians and their former psychotherapy patients in which the previous physician/patient relationship is not exploited in some way.

"A physician who is considering a personal relationship with a former patient is encouraged to:

- *act cautiously, allowing adequate time for consideration of the potentially complex issues, including:*

  - *the vulnerability of the former patient, including factors such as the maturity of the individual, whether the individual has an illness or condition likely to impair decision-making ability,*

  - *the potential for the physician to exploit the trust, knowledge and dependence that developed during the physician/patient relationship*

  - *ensure that the former patient has a good understanding of the dynamics of the physician/patient relationship and the boundaries applicable to that relationship, both through direct discussion and consultation with an independent third party,*

  - *consult with colleagues and/or the College before embarking on the relationship."*

21 Information contained in a paper from RANZCP relating specifically to boundary transgressions gives details on two important factors:

"a. Unwillingness of patients to report boundary transgressions and sexual misconduct

"The history of complainants of sexual misconduct is notable for denial by authorities and professions that such incidents occurred. This situation has improved as the consequences of sexual misconduct have become known, the community has become less tolerant of these offences and there has been encouragement to report the offenders. However, complainants do find barriers to reporting. Barriers reported include

- *A perception that the complaint won't be taken seriously.*

- *Self-blame by the patient.*

- *Fear of being discredited by being labelled as insane by their therapist.*

- *Awareness of the trauma of investigative procedures.*

- *Minimizing the effects of the offence.*

- *Ignorance about how to make a complaint.*

- *Fear of retribution from the therapist and/or an ongoing relationship with the offending doctor.*

b. Factors improving reporting rates of complainants of boundary transgressions

"There are some strategies that increase the likelihood that patients will report transgressions. Redressing the power imbalance in the therapeutic relationship and the likelihood of empowering the patient are increased by

- *Providing information that convinces patients they are not to blame.*

- *Giving patients an understanding of their options regarding the offence.*

- *Assisting the complainant in initiating action.*

- *Giving continuing support to the patient.*

- *Preparing the patient to give evidence."*

Conclusion

22   There is a wealth of available material on these topics from regulatory bodies in Australia, New Zealand, Canada, the USA, and elsewhere. We have heavily edited and restricted the extracts both in this annex and in Chapter 29.

23   We are convinced that there is much to learn from this material and from a comparative approach. We have found particularly useful, guidance from outside the UK that gives detailed descriptions of behaviour which is considered to be unacceptable, and which also gives a clear indication as to the importance of early signs of boundary transgression in identifying potential abusers and failing doctors and other healthcare professionals. On our opinion, as set out in the body of the Report, mere generalised "good doctor" statements are of little value in this difficult area. Doctors/ psychiatrists and other healthcare professionals – and their patients – must have a very clear guide as to what conduct, what behaviour, will not be tolerated, and why.

Annex 5
The NHS complaints system from the 1960s to 2004

Introduction

1   This annex deals with the largely factual description of the procedures in place in the NHS for dealing with complaints. It is not intended to be all encompassing, but provides sufficient background at both national and local level for what follows to be read in context. Those readers familiar with procedures in the NHS will be aware of the structures it describes; for those readers not so familiar, it will act as a template for considering the actions that occurred during the period covered by this Report.

2   It begins with a brief description of the procedures that were around in the 1960s and ends with those that were in place during the evidence-gathering stage of the Inquiry in 2004. It draws largely on material prepared by officials at the Department of Health; Counsel for the Health Authorities in this Inquiry; and Professor Linda Mulcahy of the School of Law at Birkbeck with material she prepared for this Inquiry and the Neale and Ayling Inquiries. We are grateful for the considerable amount of information given to us by the local NHS members and to Laura Roper of Browne Jacobson, the solicitors who trawled through the local NHS records.

3   This annex does not explore in-depth the external factors and the work of other bodies and organisations that influenced the development of the procedures. A more detailed description of that can be found in Chapter 4 of the Richard Neale Inquiry Report.

The NHS complaints system from the 1960s to 2004

4   There have been various complaints procedures put in place since the inception of the NHS, covering non-clinical complaints, clinical complaints and complaints about primary care practitioners. This annex is a summarised, factual account of the various procedures

and does not attempt to discuss their effectiveness or otherwise. A complete list (compiled from known and available records) of legislation and guidance issued by the then Ministry of Health, the Department of Health and Social Security, and most recently by the Department of Health can be found at Annex 3.

5   A project paper published by the King's Fund in 1980 (based on working papers of the Royal Commission on the NHS) refers to complaints procedures in the NHS. The following is an extract from that paper:

> "*Complaints procedures*
>
> "*The National Health Service Acts in 1946 established only one formal procedure to deal with complaints against professionals who contract to provide family practitioner services. Doctors and others working in the hospital service as salaried employees were subject to internal discipline and the Minister of Health was and is accountable to Parliament, for the actions of NHS personnel. Individual patients could sue salaried and contracted professionals through the courts, if they wished. Local health authorities had no generally established procedures but complaints against their employees could also be directed through the courts.*"

6   As far as we are aware (and as confirmed by the research undertaken relating specifically to the handling of complaints in the NHS in hospitals prior to 1966), whilst the 1946 NHS Act made clear that the relationship between hospitals and doctors was a contractual one whereby an employee could be sued for breach of contract, no formal procedures for complaints falling short of this level existed in hospitals before 1966.

Ministry of Health Guidance HM(66)15

7   The first record of any documentation issued by the Ministry of Health relating to the handling of complaints in hospitals is HM(66)15. The authorities managing hospitals may well have had their own local processes for handling complaints. However, there was no legislative basis for a hospital complaints procedure until the Hospital Complaints Procedure Act 1985.

8   HM(55)66 – reporting of accidents in hospitals – is referred to in HM(66)15. This circular required hospitals to complete a report of any accidents or other untoward occurrences to patients, staff, or any other persons on the hospital's premises. The reports were confidential and were prepared for the use of the solicitors to the Regional Hospital Board and the Hospital Management Committee or the Board of Governors in the event of a complaint being made or legal action.

HM(66)15 – Methods of dealing with complaints by patients

9   HM(66)15 was a document issued by the Ministry of Health which set out in general terms how complaints should be handled, "subject to possible variations in different types of hospital eg special arrangements may often be needed in psychiatric hospitals". The circular contained no detail as to what the "special arrangements" might be. It is assumed, given no evidence to the contrary, that this procedure covered non-clinical and clinical complaints.

10   The circular reads as if the Regional Hospital Board would be in some way involved in the handling of the complaint, but in practice it appears that whilst the Regional Hospital Board was kept informed of serious developments and issues, the complaint was handled at local level.

11   HM(66)15 enabled Hospital Management Committees (HMCs) to establish fully independent inquiries to consider complaints which could not be resolved in a more informal way. It seems clear that HMCs had powers to resolve complaints themselves, without the need to refer the matter to Region. Keeping Region informed of serious matters was a courtesy, not a requirement.

12   At the same time that HMCs were abolished the Regional Hospital Boards were replaced by Regional Health Authorities. The change in constitution does not appear to have led to more referrals of complaints to Region, although the courtesy of informing Region of particularly serious complaints for their information continued.

13   Following the procedures in the circular was not mandatory upon the NHS. HM(66)15 recommended the creation of a four-stage process involving oral/informal complaint handling by frontline staff, written/formal complaint handling by a senior member of staff within the department, referral to the Hospital Secretary, and referral to an independent inquiry or further investigation by members of the HMCs.

14   The two key principles governing the handling of complaints were the necessity for speed and the transparent handling of grievances. There were four main stages to the complaint procedure:

- The first stage was that oral complaints should initially be dealt with at service level.

- Where the grievance could not be resolved to the complainant's satisfaction the guidance required a second stage, whereby the grievance be reported to a senior member of staff in the department to which they related, who was expected to make a brief note of the complaint and circumstances. At that stage "appropriate" action should be taken and the complainant informed of the result.

- Where the grievance was still not resolved to the complainant's satisfaction, a third stage was available whereby the complaint was required to be put in writing and shown to the Secretary of the Board of Governors or HMC (or senior member of staff designated by the Secretary). Again, action was expected to be taken as appropriate (in agreement with Head(s) of department concerned) and reported to the complainant.

- Where not resolved to the complainant's satisfaction, the memorandum required that as a fourth and final stage the complaint should be reported to the Board of Governors of the HMC or an appropriate committee for decision as to further action. These management committees could do one of three things:

  - decide that no further action was necessary;

  - appoint one or more members of the authority to undertake an investigation/hearing and report back;

  - refer serious complaints to an independent inquiry chaired by an independent lawyer or other competent person from outside the hospital service.

15   If the complainant remained unhappy, this was the end of the road. It was not until 1973 that the office of the Health Service Commissioner was created.

Additional guidance issued to clarify and extend HM(66)15

Letter of 1966

16   The guidance contained in HM(66)15 was supplemented in a 'Dear Secretary' letter issued to Hospital Secretaries on 9 December 1966 which gave further guidance as to the organisation of independent inquiries which could be held at stage four of the procedure created by HM(66)15.

17   This additional advice suggested that the hearing should be in private and that intimate details contained in the report should not be widely circulated.

18   It was not anticipated that the parties would be legally represented and hospitals were encouraged to expel expectations of this kind or the suggestion that these expenses might be legally funded.

19   Finally, the letter suggested that decisions about ex gratia payments could only be made by the Minister for Health.

Letter of 1970

20   Further guidance on handling complaints was issued to Hospital Secretaries on 27 July 1970. The letter advised hospitals that they should publicise their complaints procedures. Particular emphasis was placed in this letter on the distribution of information leaflets detailing the names of those to whom letters of complaint should be sent.

21   The letter also suggested that staff should be instructed about the recording and onward transmission of suggestions and complaints which could not be settled on the spot.

Consultation about the operation of the complaints procedure

Department of Health and Social Security 1976

22   The DHSS issued a substantial draft code of practice for complaint handling and circulated it for comment in June 1976 (DHSS, 1976).

23   The protocol accepted the distinction between clinical and non-clinical complaints, but it did this by concentrating on non-clinical

complaints and avoiding the issue of how clinical complaints should be managed.

24   The draft code reflected many of the concerns of the Davies Committee, which had been the first government-sanctioned investigation of the hospital complaints procedure, chaired by Sir Michael Davies. In particular it suggested that complaints procedures should be publicised; complainants should be assisted in making complaints; complaints should be recorded; and that they should be referred to a more senior level if necessary.

25   While the principle of managerial control of complaint handling was accepted in relation to the handling of non-clinical complaints, this was not the case where complaints involving clinical judgement were concerned. Appendix Four of the draft code reproduced the guidelines drafted by the Joint Consultant's Committee (JCC) for the separate handling of clinical complaints.

26   The draft code of practice runs to 30 pages and details how complaints should be dealt with in wards and departments; by senior staff at the hospital; by the District Administrator; by the Area Health Authorities; and how matters which may involve criminal offences should be handled.

27   Interestingly, the draft code stated that if it appeared, or someone alleged, that a patient has or may have suffered injury; loss or damage to personal property; been deprived of treatment, food, comforts or any other benefit to which they were entitled; been victimised in any way or suffered any damage to his rights, property or person, the matter should be reported to the person in charge of the ward *whether or not a complaint had been made.* If a member of staff considered it inappropriate or impossible to report the matter to their superior, they could report it to the chief officer of their profession for the District or the Area.

28   The draft code added that the matters mentioned above were outside of the issues which were within the competence of a ward sister or charge nurse to investigate. Such matters should be referred by them to a member of the senior staff of the hospital who should refer such matters to the District Administrator if they consider it appropriate. The senior member of the Hospital staff should investigate such matters themselves if they chose not to refer the matter to the District

Administrator – otherwise, it was for the District Administrator to investigate such allegations. Unfortunately, this part of the draft code (like the majority of it) was never implemented.

29   The draft code also did not distinguish between written and oral complaints, going so far as to state that where a complainant had made an oral complaint they should not be asked to make a written complaint unless it was *essential* that they do so.

HN(78)39

30   The draft code was followed in 1978 with a further consultation document (HN(78)39), which took account of the comments of health authorities and other interested parties. It claimed to reflect the widespread view that the arrangements proposed were too detailed and complex, and that a simple procedure was needed. This consultation document did not deal with the handling of clinical complaints as this issue was still being considered separately in light of the Select Committee's first report.

Amendments to the procedure: HC(81)5

31   HC(81)5 introduced additional, much more detailed, guidance on complaints handling which sought to amplify but not replace the guidance contained in HM(66)15 and the Letters issued in 1966 and 1970.

32   The guidance reiterated the importance of publicising complaints procedures and went into considerably more detail than previous guidance about the importance of good communication, especially where disadvantaged groups were concerned.

33   The procedure introduced an expectation that formal complaints should be made within a year of the complainant becoming aware that they had a cause for complaint.

Formal complaints

34   The guidance placed a new emphasis on formal complaints and argued that both oral and written complaints were capable of being formal complaints. The definition of what constituted a formal complaint was fuelled by the objectives of the complainant with the distinction between formal and informal complaints resting on

whether the complainant wished to have their grievance investigated by a senior member of staff and/or required a written or oral explanation. Formal complaints were to be reported by nurses and non-medical staff to the ward sister, who in turn would report the matter to a senior officer. If medical or dental staff received a complaint they were to be referred to the consultant concerned. The memorandum recognised oral complaints as legitimate complaints but if the senior staff within the hospital could not resolve the complaint concerned, the code stated that the complainant should be told to write to the District Administrator. If the complainant was not willing or able to write to the District Administrator, staff were advised to put the complainant's complaint in writing and get them to sign it. No advice was given as to what should be done if the complainant was not willing to put their complaint in writing or sign a statement prepared for them.

35   The guidance laid down one additional governing principle which placed a new emphasis on the needs of those complained about. It required that any member of staff should be fully informed of any allegations made about them at the outset and be given the opportunity to provide an explanation. It is also required that staff should be advised of their right to seek the help and advice of their professional association or trade union before commenting on a complaint.

36   Unlike previous guidance (but in line with concerns of the Davies Committee) this circular anticipated that the senior officers asked to investigate complaints might not be able to agree a response with the senior members of staff responsible for the provision of the service involved. In these circumstances it set up an additional procedure whereby the matter could be referred to the District Management Team and then on to the health authority for consideration.

37   The guidance placed more emphasis on arranging meetings with the complainant than had previously been the case in formal procedures.

The clinical and non-clinical divide

38   The most striking feature of the guidance was that in respect of a divide between clinical and non-clinical complaints made by the JCC. The new clinical complaints procedure mirrored the procedure for stages one and two of the non-clinical complaints system, except that

it was a consultant rather than a senior officer who was empowered to coordinate the responses. However the new guidance provided a third stage of the complaints procedure for clinical complaints. This allowed for an Independent Professional Review to be set up, at the discretion of the Regional Medical Officer, and undertaken by two consultants in a relevant specialty. This procedure was reserved for complaints which were of a *substantial* nature and was said to provide an alternative to litigation and the quasi-independent inquiry structure set up in the 1966 guidance.

39   The section of the guidance dealing with clinical complaints did not refer to the possibility of disagreements about the contents of the response. Moreover consultants retained the discretion to write directly to the complainant about the clinical aspects of the complaint.

40   One of the most notable features of the clinical review procedure was that clinicians almost exclusively oversaw it. Moreover, rather than having a judicial function it was described as being in "the nature of a clinical consultation".

Application of the national guidelines in Harrogate and York 1966–82

Harrogate

41   The "internal review into policies and procedures designed to protect patients and staff" conducted by Harrogate in 1998 states that Harrogate did not have a formal complaints procedure until 1988 when they were prompted to adopt one by the Hospital Complaints (Procedure) Act 1985 (see later).

42   Between 1948 and 1974 health services in Harrogate were run by the Harrogate and Ripon Hospital Management Committee. The minutes of the HMC in 1967, 1968 and 1969 demonstrate that written complaints received by the authority were dealt with by the Secretary of the HMC in consultation with the heads of departments concerned. Only the more serious complaints would go before the full HMC. It is unclear from the minutes how much investigation was carried out by the Secretary. In most cases it is recorded that at the end of the process "the Secretary sent an appropriate letter".

43   Arthur Lister was the Group Secretary to the Harrogate and Ripon HMC between 1965 and 1969. He confirms in his statement that he

personally dealt with all written complaints which were received by the HMC, and that he also dealt with any oral complaints which could not be resolved on the spot to the complainant's satisfaction.

44   In 1974 NHS structure changed. Health services for the whole of North Yorkshire began to be run from one statutory body, the North Yorkshire Area Health Authority. Health districts, such as Harrogate Health District, were responsible for the operation or delivery of NHS services. However, as mentioned above, these health districts were not statutory organisations in their own right and were controlled from the North Yorkshire Health Authority central office at York until 1982.

45   Despite the status of health districts, it would appear that they did decide independently how to administer complaints. On 1 April 1974 the new District Management Team held its first meeting. During that meeting it was decided that the District Administrator should assume responsibility for the handling of complaints in consultation with the appropriate services and broadly in accordance with the procedures suggested in the Davies Report. It was also decided that the District Administrator should produce a report summarising the complaints he had received for the District Management Team every six months.

46   Although the Secretary of the HMC had orally reported complaints to the HMC at six-monthly intervals, Harrogate's centrally maintained written record of complaints received starts in 1974. Initially, this record was brief, recording only the complainant's name and the date the complaint was made. Over the years it developed to include details of the complaint.

47   When the HMCs were abolished in 1974 no guidance from central government was published to help authorities deal with the transition from HMC to Area Health Authorities and health districts. Harrogate therefore adopted the approach advocated by the Davies Committee. In fact, most of the measures adopted by Harrogate were later included in HC(81)5 as part of government recommended policy.

48   On 10 July 1975 the District Management Team minutes indicate that a decision was taken that in future the consultant in charge of a patient's care should be informed of any complaint made by them. Again, this was a measure which was implemented nationally as part of HC(81)5, but Harrogate's adoption of this policy indicates that as early as 1975 it was accepted practice for the consultant to have knowledge of complaints made by his patients.

49   The minutes do not specify whether consultants should have been informed of a complaint by a patient whose care they were responsible for where the complaint was against them, although given what we know about complaints handling in later times an educated guess would be that the consultant would have been informed of the complaint.

50   On 12 February 1976 the District Management Team minutes state that from then on there should be a central point for incoming letters of complaint and from where a copy could be sent to the consultant in charge of the patient's care. This suggests that from that point on, anyone making a complaint should have been directed to write to one person in particular. The District Administrator took on this role in Harrogate as is confirmed in the witness statement of Arthur Lister, the District Administrator in Harrogate at the relevant time.

51   The change in policy in 1976 and subsequent change of practice indicates an early attempt by Harrogate to establish a centralised complaints handling system similar to that which the NHS operates today. However, Harrogate was forced to change its policy on this point by the new national policy introduced in 1988. The national policy recommended that as far as possible complaints should be handled at the unit level.

52   The "internal review into policies and procedures designed to protect patients and staff" conducted by Harrogate in 1998 states that although Harrogate did not have a formal complaints procedure until 1988, from 1982 the process outlined in a memo from the District Administrator (Designate) was followed. Unfortunately, Harrogate have been unable to locate this document.

York

53 York A HMC minutes indicate that HM(66)15 was broadly followed in the York A area. (York A included Bootham Park and Naburn as well as general medicine.) The HMC in York A had four sub-committees of which the Establishment and General Purposes (EGP) sub-committee was one. The Secretary to the HMC sat on this sub-committee. During the early 1960s (and, significantly, from as early as 1964, ie two years before the national guidance was published), all complaints were reported to the EGP sub-committee on a monthly basis. The Secretary to the HMC would actually deal with the complaints, but all complaints were reported in detail to the EGP. The EGP's minutes were reviewed by the HMC during their meetings.

54 Interestingly, there was only an average of four to five complaints a month and so reporting each complaint to the EGP sub-committee in full was not time consuming. Assuming all complaints were properly recorded and reported, this suggests that during the 1960s there was not a culture of patients complaining about the NHS.

55 The full HMC would then review the EGP sub-committee minutes monthly, and so were kept informed of complaints as they were expected to under HM(66)15.

56 However, the minutes of the full HMC meeting held on 2 March 1967 outline a proposed change in the way in which the HMC handled complaints. The EGP sub-committee was to continue to consider complaints and the Secretary to the HMC was to continue to handle complaints on a day-to-day basis. The major change was that from 1967 the EGP sub-committee would only receive a report on complaints twice a year. It would only hear the detail of individual complaints if the complaint raised a particular problem which required immediate resolution.

57 The reasoning behind the shift in approach is unclear, particularly as a perusal of the subsequent complaint reports reveals that the number of complaints being made did not increase significantly, and so the motivation for the change would not appear to have been an increase in the volume of complaints.

58 Although this might be seen as a retrograde step (in terms of keeping the HMC and its sub-committees informed of complaints), the approach was still in line with HM(66)15 in that it was the Secretary of the HMC who dealt with complaints and that complaints were reported to the HMC, via its review of the EGP minutes, on a regular basis.

59 York B's HMC minutes from 1964 to 1974 reveal a more ad hoc approach to complaints handling than in York A or Harrogate. (York B comprised Clifton and its satellite hospitals only.) Certainly, the full HMC were provided with details of accidents and inquests on a monthly basis. Complaints were dealt with by the HMC, as is demonstrated by the fact that on several occasions the HMC was provided with reports of enquiries into complaints. The enquiries had clearly been conducted by members of the HMC. The resulting reports are extremely full which suggest that those complaints were fully investigated.

60 The HMC minutes do not reveal whether less serious complaints were dealt with by the Secretary of the HMC, without recourse to the full HMC.

61 Claims for compensation or complaints involving a financial element were dealt with by the Finance and General Management sub-committee, although it is not clear from the minutes whether all such claims were reported to the sub-committee or whether more minor claims were dealt with away from the sub-committee.

62 The minutes of the Medical and Allied Services sub-committee from 19 May 1969 reveal that a decision was taken that, from then on, "the Chairman or Vice-Chairman of the HMC, together with two 'liaison' members and the Superintendent Physician concerned should investigate any complaints or charges made against staff by patients". This extract appears to suggest (together with ensuing minutes) that every complaint received by a patient was investigated by a "panel".

63 To have every complaint received by the HMC investigated by such a large panel or "enquiry" seems surprising. However, this approach may reflect the type of complaints received by York B as opposed to York A and Harrogate which both had acute services within the HMC. It is clear from the minutes that the complaints received by

York B were either of a financial nature and brought by the family members of the admitted patient (and dealt with by the Finance and General Management sub-committee), or of a serious nature such as alleged physical assault, and instigated by either the patient themselves, or their family member.

64   This labour-intensive method of dealing with complaints lends support to the suggestion that HMCs at this time (1964–74) did not routinely receive large numbers of complaints. Indeed the minutes support this suggestion.

65   It is not possible to say whether York B followed HM(66)15 on its introduction in 1966, although it is clear there was a complaints policy of sorts in place both prior to and after that date. It might be said that York B exceeded the requirements of HM(66)15 by having a full "enquiry" into every complaint, when the national policy only required such an enquiry in the most serious cases.

66   The handling of complaints changed when the new structure was introduced in 1974. The minutes of the District Management Team reveal that a new approach was adopted.

67   Minutes of the York District Management Team from 9 February 1976 reveal that the team was presented with a summary of complaints received in 1975. The summary was extremely general in nature, listing only the number of complaints received and the broad categories into which the complaints fell.

68   From 1977 York kept a formal written record of complaints received. This was a more complete record than the summaries which had previously been presented to the District Management Team. Initially, it listed the complainant's name, the number allocated to the complaint, the date of receipt of the complaint, the hospital at which the complainant was treated, and stated whether the complaint was clinical or non-clinical in nature. In later years the record broadened to include the complainant's name, the number allocated to the complaint, the nature of the complaint (eg "staffing levels – maternity unit", "treatment of daughter – availability of speech therapy"), the initials of the administrator who was allocated to deal with the complaint, the date on which the complaint was received, the date on which the complaint was acknowledged, the date of any holding

reply, the date of the final reply and the date upon which the complaint file was closed.

69   The District Management Team minutes of 27 January 1975 report on the handling of a particular complaint. The minutes reveal how a serious complaint would have been handled in York at this time. Mr Holroyd, the District Administrator, reported the fact of the complaint and the action taken by that stage (he and the District Nursing Officer had met with the complainants) to the District Management Team. This suggests that the District Administrator would be the person who would receive complaints. This matches the approach taken by Harrogate at the same time.

70   The District Management Team then went on to agree that the District Administrator and the District Nursing Officer carry out a full investigation of the matter and reported back at the meeting of the District Management Team on 10 February 1975. As well as the formal investigation report, Mr Holroyd presented a list of recommendations for change resulting from the investigation.

71   This clearly shows that serious complaints were reported to the District Management Team who would then decide whether an investigation was required and who would undertake it. It is possible that the investigation undertaken by the District Administrator and the District Nursing Officer in this instance was an investigation in line with the requirements for an investigation or "enquiry" where the complainant is not satisfied with action taken by the District Administrator as set out in HM(66)15. It is also worth noting that it was possible as early as 1975 for a complaints investigation to result in real constructive change, as occurred here.

72   The content of a further minute of the meeting of the District Management Team of 20 July 1976 reveals more about how complaints were handled from 1974. The draft code of practice attached to the 1976 consultation paper was produced to the District Management Team for their comments. In assessing the new code, features of the policy then in place are outlined.

73   The minute states that the current emphasis was on the importance of all formal complaints being made in writing, with replies to virtually all complaints being sent by the District Administrator. On the other hand, the draft code sought to ensure oral complaints

were handled systematically by being recorded in a record book and by being followed up by a person not lower than the grade of ward sister.

74 The District Management Team were concerned that the requirement in the draft code to consider oral complaints would be difficult in practice and that there may be problems with interpretation in this regard. Accordingly, they agreed to submit comments to the Government on the draft code.

75 All of York's complaints were dealt with by one person, the District Administrator. Again, any good work put in place by York in establishing a system whereby one person was responsible for handling all complaints (and could therefore have an overview of complaints made) was thwarted by the national requirement to introduce written policies in line with the recommended national policy in 1988 which was that, as far as possible, complaints should be handled at the unit level.

76 Information booklets produced for patients at Clifton Hospital between 1974 and 1982 directed patients to report any complaints to their ward sister initially, who "very often" would be able to reassure the patient or sort out any worries the patient had. If the ward sister was unable to reassure the patient, she would "record them in writing and pass them on".

77 Given what we know from the District Management Team minutes from the same time period, it is to be assumed that the complaint, which would by now be in writing, would eventually reach the District Administrator who would respond to the complaint.

78 The leaflets also inform patients that they can contact the Secretary to the Area Health Authority if they would prefer. This shows that the Area Health Authority did have some responsibility for complaints handling in this time period, although the extent to which it is likely that patients availed themselves of the ability to contact the Area Health Authority is unclear.

79 The York Health District *Health Service Complaints Procedure* document, which was a locally produced document introduced in 1981, served merely to communicate the content of the new HC(81)5 national policy to staff. It does not provide guidance on how clinical

complaints should be handled, directing medical practitioners to Part III of the Circular directly and to a letter from Dr David Bolt, the Chairman of the British Medical Association's (BMA's) Central Committee for Hospital Medical Services for advice on dealing with clinical complaints.

80   Like the national policy, the local policy gives no guidance on what to do where a patient discloses a serious issue but does not want to make a complaint. Formal complaints are defined as complaints which the patient wishes to be investigated by a senior manager and upon which they expect to receive a written reply or oral explanation from the senior manager concerned. There is no definition of an informal complaint and the policy only applies to formal complaints.

81   If an informal complaint is a complaint which a patient is happy to have resolved at local level (which is what the policy implies), then there is no guidance, implied or otherwise, as to what to do when a patient does not want to complain, but where a serious matter has been disclosed.

82   Again, like the national policy, the local policy also distinguishes between a written complaint and an oral complaint. There is a requirement that oral complaints are put into writing by staff, and that the patient concerned signs the written statement or orally agrees its content. Again, there is no guidance as to how an "oral" disclosure should be taken forward if the patient does not sign off or agree orally the content of the written statement.

83   There seems to have been no guidance as to what to do when a patient withdrew a complaint.

84   The policy also requires (in line with national policy) that any member of staff involved in a complaint should be fully informed of the allegation being made against them and given an opportunity to reply. The decision as to whether complaints should be referred up to the District Administrator is left with senior management at a local level. They had to refer complaints to the District Administrator where the complainant was unsatisfied by the outcome at local level, but had discretion as to whether a complaint should be passed up to the District Administrator in other circumstances. This may explain why,

when allegations were withdrawn by patients, they never reached District level, despite the seriousness of the allegations being made.

85   On 26 September 1984 the minutes of the York Health Authority reveal that the authority agreed to the set up of a Special Professional Panel (SPP) in line with the proposals contained in a report to the board. Prior to the decision being taken, a conversation took place about the role of the SPP. The SPP was described as "an informal procedure for the examination of individuals' actions by fellow professionals with the opportunity to discuss any problems".

86   Whilst HC(82)13 introduced the requirement for each health district to have an SPP, it seems that some sort of "Three Wise Men" panel existed in York prior to this time. Raymond Marks was a member of the "Three Wise Men" from 1977 until 1985. Raymond Marks does state that in the 1980s the "informal" "Three Wise Men" procedure was formalised into an SPP. It would seem that prior to 1983, York's "Three Wise Men" were not a statutory requirement and was probably established by the consultant body as a method of regulating themselves.

87   HC(82)13 states that the panel could take any referral about any "report of incapacity of a consultant due to a physical or mental disability".

88   Raymond Marks states that when a GP reported a disclosure by one of his patients of sexual assault at the hands of Michael Haslam in 1988, he felt it was inappropriate for the SPP to deal with the referral. This does seem to accord with the national remit for the panel.

89   The description of the SPP in the York District Management Team minutes as "an informal procedure for the examination of individuals' actions by fellow professionals with the opportunity to discuss any problems" accords with the circular. It seems that it was intended to allow consultants to investigate worrying reports about other consultants with the hope of giving them a "friendly word of advice" which would steer them back onto the straight and narrow. It left the decision as to whether the matter complained of was so serious that it should be referred to a higher authority to the panel, and even gave them free rein not to refer matters up where they felt they would be able to steer the malfunctioning consultant back to better performance.

Policy reviews of the clinical complaints procedure

90   In 1983 the DHSS circulated a brief report on the operation of the clinical complaints procedure.

91   The report drew on data supplied by doctors and NHS managers (DHSS, 1983), and concluded that on the basis of this, the new trial "appeals" procedure had been a success.

92   In support of this contention, it was reported that the independent assessors appointed to review the work of colleagues had received the full cooperation of the doctors involved and had gained access to health records of patients in all cases.

HC(81)5 – Health service complaints procedure

93   HC(81)5 modified but did not replace HM(66)15. In particular, paragraph 7(iii) of HM(66)15 relating to serious complaints or incidents not resolved by the authority's officers remained in force.

94   The circular contained general information as well as an Annex (Memorandum on handling complaints) comprising three parts and two appendices:

- Part I – information for all staff in regular contact with patients.

- Part II – for senior staff investigating [non-clinical] complaints.

- Part III – detailing the procedure for investigating clinical complaints.

- Appendix 1 – suggested paragraphs for hospital booklets for patients.

- Appendix 2 – complaints that may involve criminal proceedings.

General principles underpinning complaints handling

- All complaints should be investigated thoroughly and fairly, and as quickly as circumstances permit.

- Complainants (and complained against) should be kept informed of reasons for unavoidable delay in resolving the issue.

- Any member of staff involved in a complaint should be fully informed of any allegations at the outset and given an opportunity to reply.

- Health authorities were *advised* to implement systems for monitoring complaints to identify trends etc.

Stages of the complaints procedure

95 The complainant could either raise the concerns on the spot with the member of staff or make a formal complaint (orally or in writing).

- **Part I** – non clinical complaints

  "Minor criticisms" should be dealt with on the spot by frontline staff. If not resolved or if "formal complaint" requested then:

- **Part II** – non-clinical complaints

  "Formal complaints" as requested by the complainant (either oral or written), made to *hospital* staff, were referred to, and required investigation by and response from, senior staff (oral) or District/Area Health Authority (written) – see below.

96 If the formal oral complaint was not resolved then the complaint must be made in writing to the District/Area Health Authority. The complaint was then referred to an appropriate senior member(s) of staff for investigation and report. A reply was agreed between the District Administrator and senior member(s) of staff and sent by the District Administrator (or Chairman if thought appropriate). If still not resolved, then the complaint would go to the Health Service Commissioner:

- **Part III** – clinical complaints procedure

  This was the same as for non-clinical complaints except that if the complainant renews the complaint to the District Health Authority or consultant in writing, then the consultant informs, and discusses the complaint with, the Regional Medical Officer (RMO). The RMO considers the need for further discussion with the complainant, or goes to independent professional review. Then, the complaint is reviewed – various options available – by two independent consultants ("second opinions") nominated by the JCC. They report their findings to the RMO in confidence. The District Administrator then responds to the complainant, taking advice from the RMO on clinical matters.

NOTE: it was still possible to invoke the independent inquiry procedure outlined in paragraph 7iii(b) of HC(66)15.

Services provided outside the hospital setting

97   The procedure set out in the circular only applied to services provided in hospitals. However, District Health Authorities were asked to consider applying the general principles of the complaints procedure to complaints about services provided outside the hospital setting (eg community health services).

Special Professional Panels – the "Three Wise Men" HC(82)13

98   This circular issued in 1982 advised health authorities to "request appropriate medical and dental committees to introduce procedures to help prevent harm to patients resulting from physical or mental disability, including addiction, of all medical and dental staff employed by health authorities".

99   Each District appointed a pool of four to five consultants who could sit on an SPP. A Chairman of the panel was then elected by its members. The panel then established a sub-committee of three – this became generally known as the "Three Wise Men". Any referrals regarding medical or dental staff thought to be endangering patients had to be made to the Chairman, who would then convene the "Three Wise Men" to consider the referral.

100   The "Three Wise Men" were required by HC(82)13 to take any steps necessary to investigate any referral of medical or dental staff made to them. If following a referral and investigation they were satisfied that a report had substance they were required to inform the practitioner concerned about the referral and give them an opportunity to be interviewed by the panel. If they felt "that the possibility of harm to patients [could not] be excluded by the exercise of their influence with the practitioner concerned" they should report the matter to the RMO, who would then consider the information and decide whether further action was necessary. If the clinician's fitness to practise was an issue, then a report to the General Medical Council was to be considered.

Hospital Complaints (Procedure) Act 1985 and HC(88)37

101 Further changes to the hospital complaints procedure were prompted by the Hospital Complaints (Procedure) Act 1985 which was introduced as a Private Member's Bill.

102 This legislation made it compulsory for all hospitals to put a complaints procedure in place. It took three years for guidance to be issued under the Act (HC(88)37) and, when it did appear, it served to rubberstamp the arrangements made between the DHSS and JCC in 1976 and the guidance contained in HC(81)5.

HC(88)37 – Hospital Complaints Procedure Act 1985

103 This circular contained general information on the requirements for the complaints procedure and, for the first time, Directions (secondary legislation) setting out the mandatory requirements.

104 HC(88)37 was not radically different from the earlier guidance on complaints. The main difference was that hospitals were expected to appoint a designated officer to deal with complaints. The Unit General Manager was suggested as a person who would be appropriate to undertake the task. The designated officer was to be the person to whom complaints should be addressed and was to be responsible for the investigation of all complaints other than those which were concerned with clinical judgement, serious untoward incidents, disciplinary proceedings, physical abuse of patients and criminal offences. The code stated that these matters might well be for the Unit general manager to consider but in coordination with other senior officers, such as the Regional Medical Officer or the District General Manager.

105 It is interesting to note how closely the categories which were not for consideration by the designated officer in HC(88)37 match those which could be investigated without a complaint under the 1976 draft code. However the guidance under HC(88)37 about how these issues should be handled was unclear. It is not clear who is to have ultimate responsibility for these matters and whether they can be investigated only if a complaint has been made. The implication is clearly that a "complaint" was required before action could be taken. Equally, it was not clear what "appropriate action" in relation to such serious complaints would be, although it was clear that any such action would have to be in line with local policy.

106 The code stated that the designated officer must be satisfied that any complaint was being investigated with the patient's consent, where he or she was able to give it.

107 The code stated that it was not a requirement that a complaint was made in writing. Where an oral complaint was made, a note should be made of that and a statement prepared for the patient to sign. It added that a patient's refusal to sign the statement should not delay the investigation of the complaint.

108 This does not seem to sit well with the earlier requirement that complaints could only be taken forward with the patient's consent. The reader is left confused about what to do where a patient has made a complaint and expressed a desire to take it forward, but later refuses to stand by the allegation and refuses to sign any statement.

109 Finally, the code stated that it was important that complaints from any source, patient or staff should be dealt with satisfactorily. This acknowledges the possibility of complaints by staff. The procedure did not apply to community health services but health authorities were asked to consider that the general procedure was also adopted in respect of community health services.

General principles underpinning complaints handling

110 No one should be inhibited from making valid complaints and they should be fully confident that they would be given full, proper and speedy consideration. Otherwise as per previous guidance.

111 Health authorities were required to implement monitoring arrangements to monitor trends.

Stages of the complaints procedure

Non-clinical complaints

112 Where complaints were not resolved on the spot, investigation of the complaint was undertaken by a "designated officer" who completed a report and responded to the complainant. If it was not resolved, then the complaint could go to the Health Service Ombudsman.

Clinical complaints

113 As for HC(81)5.

114 Complaints involving serious untoward incidents, disciplinary procedures, physical abuse of staff, or a possible criminal offence should be brought to the attention of the "designated officer's" senior officer so appropriate action could be taken under national or local procedures.

115 NOTE: HC(88)37 cancelled HC(81)5 but not HC(66)15. Therefore, it was still possible to invoke the independent inquiry procedure outlined in paragraph 7iii(b) of HC(66)15.

Application of the national guidance in Harrogate and York

Harrogate

116 In 1989, in direct response to the requirement to have a complaints procedure, Harrogate Health Authority published a Patients' Complaints Procedure. The procedure largely replicated national policy.

117 The position in relation to clinical complaints remained unchanged and, like York, Harrogate appended Part III of HC(81)5 to the document.

118 The guidance under the Act required a designated officer who would have responsibility for dealing with all non-clinical complaints received by the local NHS. The designated officer had responsibility for investigating all complaints which could not be resolved by discussion with the complainant. This included all "oral" and "written" complaints. The designated officer also had the responsibility of notifying the Headquarters Service Manager of all complaints in order that they could be recorded centrally. Here we see Harrogate finally returning to the stance it had previously taken in 1976.

119 Where a complaint had both clinical and non-clinical elements, the designated officer was required to get the consultant concerned to approve the letter of response that was due to be sent to the complainant.

120 Significantly, the designated officer also had responsibility for ensuring that when a complaint was made and the patient it concerned was capable and competent, the complaint was made with their knowledge and consent. This seems to have the effect of prohibiting a complaint being advanced without the patient's knowledge and consent.

121   If the complaint concerned a "serious untoward incident" or physical abuse of a patient, it had to be brought to the attention of the Unit General Manager in order that "appropriate action" could be taken. The policy states that appropriate action *may* have involved disciplinary proceedings or members of the SPP. Again, this seems to give the Unit General Manager an extremely wide discretion as to how complaints of the most serious type should be dealt with.

122   The policy also recognised the value of complaints in terms of indicating weak areas and also required the publicity of complaints procedures.

123   In 1993 Harrogate issued a *Revised Procedure for Handling Patients' Complaints* document. The policy was stated to be for implementation from 1 April 1993. The stated reason for the change in policy was that there was to be a change in management structure, and also that patients were now entitled to receive a reply to a complaint from the Chief Executive or General Manager under the Patients' Charter.

124   The memo setting out the changes in policy also provides a summary of the then existing procedure. As in 1993 there were six designated officers covering all of Harrogate's sites who handled complaints for the appropriate Unit General Manager. Robin Watson was the designated officer for complaints addressed to the Chairman or Chief Executive.

125   There were notices in the public areas of each site informing patients who the appropriate designated officer for complaints was.

126   Robin Watson oversaw the handling of complaints throughout the Trust. He registered all complaints and summarised and analysed them for the quarterly reports which were presented to the Executive Group and the Quality and Value for Money sub-committee. A similar report was also produced for the North Yorkshire Health Authority.

127   Thus in 1993 Harrogate was still acting squarely within the requirements of HC(88)37.

128   Under the revised policy, when the Chief Executive received complaints they would be passed by Robin Watson, who would pass them to the appropriate Clinical Director for investigation and reply. If there were several directorates involved in any one complaint, Robin Watson would decide which was the most appropriate directorate to deal with the complaint. Some complaints would be so serious that they would be investigated at a Trust HQ level with a reply from the Chief Executive.

129   Where complaints were mistakenly addressed to a hospital, the Director of Operational Services at that hospital would decide who should take the lead in investigating and replying to the complaint.

130   The policy also commented that verbal complaints could be accepted by any member of staff. Staff were warned not to be in any way discouraging to verbal complainants.

131   This amendment to their complaints policy shows that Harrogate was "on the ball" when it came to complaints handling. Harrogate made sensible amendments to its policy which was modelled on national policy, and did not just wait for a new national policy to be published. It is also interesting that as early as 1993 Harrogate had a designated officer who had overall responsibility for handling complaints within the Trust.

York

132   Very little documentation in relation to a York complaints policy exists from this period. York had a complaints policy in place relatively early (1981). Therefore, by the time it became compulsory for health authorities to have a complaints policy in place in 1985, York had already had a policy in place for four years.

133   Little change would have been required to York's 1981 policy to ensure it complied with the 1988 circular. As mentioned above, the major change introduced in 1988 was the requirement for "designated officers" to deal with complaints. It is possible that York maintained the status quo in relation to complaints and made the "designated officer" the person who was already dealing with complaints for them.

134 It is clear from the minutes that the authority received information about compensation claims against the authority from the District Administrator (later the General Manager), so it is likely that he was the person who coordinated complaints handling overall.

135 As little documentary evidence exists in relation to this time period, it is important when assessing the effectiveness of the procedure in place to consider the oral and written evidence of those witnesses who administered York's complaints policy during this time. Key witnesses in this regard are Stuart Ingham and Peter Kennedy.

136 Under the 1981 policy, if a complaint was made about a consultant they had to be informed of that complaint. We were told that William Kerr was permitted to amend a letter that was to be sent to Linda Bigwood in 1985 with regard to the appropriateness of a consultant psychiatrist seeing a patient alone who had made allegations against him. Again, given the content of the complaints policy, this would appear to have been the appropriate response. However, although in that sense appropriate – as noted in our Report, we consider the lack of transparency to be wholly inappropriate.

137 The preceding paragraphs set out the complaints framework against which the local NHS actions are to be considered.

138 However, there is nothing in the various complaints policies that prevented local investigation – even if there was no formal complaint, or a formal complaint was withdrawn.

139 Further, all complaints procedures are dependent on human "operators". If a recipient of a concern or complaint is reluctant to investigate, or unsympathetic to the patient, or overly sympathetic to the doctor concerned, the then-existing procedures made it easy to eliminate the complaint at an early stage, or at least discourage actual or potential complainants.

Hospital and Community Health Services and primary care practitioners – April 1996 to July 2004

- March 1996, June 1998 and October 2002 – various sets of Directions relating to the handling of complaints by NHS bodies.

- 1996 – amended Service Committee and Tribunal Regulations in relation to primary care practitioners.

- EL(96)19 – Guidance on the implementation of the NHS complaints procedure.

- Practice-based complaints procedure guidance for primary care practitioners.

140 In 1995, for the first time, the Department issued detailed guidance on how the NHS bodies and primary care practitioners should handle complaints. This expanded on the mandatory requirements set out in the Directions and Regulations. The interim guidance referred to (EL(95)121) was intended to allow the NHS to get up to speed, prior to implementation, on what the new NHS complaints procedure would look like based on progress made at the time. The procedure did not come into force until April 1996. The procedures contained the following details:

- Each Trust had to appoint a complaints manager who would have responsibility for the administration of the complaints policies in the Trust.

- All complaints made in writing to an appropriate person within a certain time limit had to be considered and dealt with under the policy. There was also a discretion granted to the Trusts to extend the time for making a complaint in certain circumstances. Complaints could still only be pursued with the consent of the patient or the person representing them. Anyone who received a complaint had to forward it to the complaints manager.

- Oral complaints could be received and acted upon but after a "preliminary consideration of the complaint". If the complainant still wished to pursue the matter, the complaint had to be put in writing. The complaint could either be put in writing by the complainant, or on behalf of the complainant if it was signed by them.

- The complaints manager had to arrange for each written complaint to be investigated and a reply sent to the complainant. Each Trust had to appoint a "convenor". The convenor role was generally met by a non-executive director of the Trust. If a complainant was dissatisfied with the results of the investigation into their complaint, they could ask the convenor to consider whether their complaint should be referred for consideration by an independent panel. The convenor could decide to convene an independent panel to consider the complaint, could ask the Trust concerned to take disciplinary action, could ask for a further investigation into the complaint at Trust level or could decree that the complaint should not be investigated further. If the convenor decided that the complaint should be referred to a panel, a panel should be convened by the Trust. The panel should produce a report into the complaint for consideration by the Trust.

General principles underpinning complaints handling

141   The key policy objectives for the complaints procedure are:

- ease of access for patients and complainants;

- a simplified procedure, with common features, for complaints about any of the services provided as part of the NHS;

- separation of complaints from disciplinary procedures;

- making it easier to extract lessons on quality from complaints to improve services for patients;

- fairness for staff and complainants alike;

- more rapid and open process;

- an approach that is honest and thorough, with the prime aim of resolving the problems and satisfying the concerns of the complainant.

142   NHS Trusts and health authorities were *required* to produce quarterly monitoring reports for their Boards to consider trends, lessons that can be learned and the need for action to improve services.

143   Complaints information should also feed into NHS organisations' clinical governance arrangements – clinical governance started in the NHS from 1998. Clinical governance puts in place mechanisms to improve the quality of clinical services throughout the NHS by providing a coherent framework for clinical quality improvement in

the NHS; building on the existing quality activity; and ensuring that quality is a central consideration for all NHS organisations.

Stages of the complaints procedure

- "Local Resolution" – covered resolution of complaints ranging from on the spot action by frontline staff to a formal response from the Chief Executive of the NHS Trust or health authority (latterly primary care trusts (PCTs);

- If not resolved then:

  - "Independent Review" – complainant can request an independent review. Decision made by "convener" (non-executive director of the relevant NHS Trust or health authority (PCTs). Three options for convener:

    - refer the complaint back for further local resolution (option to request independent review again);

    - decide that everything that can be done has been, so no further action (complainant can complain to the Health Service Commissioner);

    - establish an independent review panel to investigate the complaint, and report, including any recommendations.

- If not resolved then:

  - complain to the Health Service Ombudsman.

144   The Ombudsman's remit was extended from April 1996 to include clinical issues and complaints about primary care practitioners. NHS staff and primary care practitioners (and their staff) were also enabled to complain to the Ombudsman if they felt that they had suffered hardship or injustice through the operation of the NHS complaints procedure.

145   Complaints involving disciplinary action, referral to the relevant regulatory body, an independent inquiry under Section 84 of the NHS Act 1977, or investigation of a criminal offence should be referred to a suitable person who can take the decision whether to initiate such action. The complaint investigation should cease while the separate action is being taken except if there are issues in the complaint not subject to the separate action.

146   NOTE: NHS Trusts also have the option of instigating their own independent inquiry (there is no record of HC(66)15 ever being cancelled).

Application of the national guidance in Harrogate and York

147   Both Harrogate and York introduced new complaints policies which came into force on 1 April 1994, as they were required to. Both policies were in line with the national policy.

148   The investigation into William Kerr in 1997 prompted both Trusts to re-evaluate their complaints policies and other procedures – see Harrogate's "internal review into policies and procedures designed to protect patients and staff", and in York, the Manzoor Inquiry.

149   Both Trusts published procedures for staff to raise concerns – Harrogate in November 1998 and York in March 1999. Both policies aim to provide a mechanism by which staff can seek the advice of senior management if they are concerned about something.

NHS bodies and primary care providers – July 2004 onwards

150   We include this brief resume for completeness, as it has a relevance to any recommendations that we make in respect of complaints handling in the future:

- the National Health Service (Complaints) Regulations 2004;

- 1996 and 2004 – regulations applying to primary care practitioners;

- guidance to support the implementation of the National Health Service (Complaints) Regulations 2004; and

- practice-based complaints procedure guidance to primary care practitioners.

151   The Health and Social Care (Community Health and Standards) Act 2003 gave the Secretary of State the power to make regulations on complaints handling by the NHS in England. The National Health Service (Complaints) Regulations 2004 came into force on 30 July 2004.

152   The Complaints Regulations 2004 set out the statutory framework for the handling of complaints by NHS bodies, "local resolution", and the "independent review" of complaints by the Healthcare Commission where local resolution has been unsuccessful in resolving matters.

153   The intention had been to implement Complaints Regulations in full from 1 June 2004. However, Ministers decided on a phased implementation of the reformed NHS complaints procedure following an approach from the Shipman Inquiry. Therefore, the local resolution stage remains broadly unchanged and the Complaints Regulations simply consolidate and rationalise the various sets of Directions on complaints handling by NHS bodies issued since 1996. The Complaints Regulations do not apply to primary care practitioners other than Part III (Independent Review by the Healthcare Commission). Separate regulations issued in 1996 and in 2004 require primary care practitioners to operate a local resolution process.

154   We are advised that amended Complaints Regulations covering both primary and secondary care will be issued during 2005 once consideration has been given to the recommendations made by the Shipman Inquiry (as well as the Ayling, Neale and Kerr/Haslam Inquiries).

NHS Foundation Trusts

155   NHS Foundation Trusts are not covered by Part II of the Complaints Regulations, which deals with local resolution. They will have their own process for handling complaints, which may well differ from local resolution as part of the NHS complaints procedure. NHS Foundation Trusts are subject to the independent review stage carried out by the Healthcare Commission but only in relation to complaints by or on behalf of patients. They also come within the jurisdiction of the Health Service Ombudsman.

156   The Healthcare Commission has agreed a protocol with the Independent Regulator of NHS Foundation Trusts about the circumstances in which the Commission will refer a complaint to the Regulator where it does not fall to be considered under the Complaints Regulations.

Local resolution

157 A complaint should be made in the first instance to the NHS body or primary care practitioner providing the service. Local resolution is seen as the most effective way of resolving complaints. It aims to resolve complaints quickly and as close to the source of the complaint as possible using the most appropriate means.

158 A person can raise their concerns immediately by speaking to a member of staff (eg doctor, nurse, dentist, GP or practice manager) or someone else, eg the Patient Advice Liaison Service (PALS). They may be able to resolve matters without the need to make a more "formal" complaint.

159 However, if the person does want to continue with a complaint they can do this orally or by writing (including by e-mail) to the primary care practitioner or the NHS body concerned. The complaints manager should record a complaint made orally in writing.

160 A primary care practitioner should send a response to written complaints within 10 working days or from the chief executive of the NHS organisation concerned within 20 working days.

Independent review

161 If the complainant is not happy with the response to their complaint at local resolution, they can request an independent review by the Healthcare Commission (known in statute as the Commission for Healthcare Audit and Inspection). The Commission will assess the most appropriate way of resolving the complaint. This might include:

- referral back for further local resolution;
- no further action – the Commission believes that everything possible has been done;
- investigation by the Commission;
- referral directly to the Ombudsman;
- referral to the relevant professional regulatory body;
- referral to the Independent Regulator of NHS Foundation Trusts;
- Health Service Commissioner (Ombudsman).

162   If they are not satisfied with the response at independent review, the complainant may approach the Health Service Commissioner (Ombudsman). She is independent of both the NHS and Government. The Health Service Commissioner's (Amendment) Act 1996 widened the jurisdiction of the Ombudsman to include complaints about clinical judgement/treatment and family health services, and means that she can now look at all aspects of NHS care.

163   Section 118 of the Health and Social Care (Community Health and Standards) Act 2003 amends the Health Service Commissioners Act 1993 to allow the Ombudsman to investigate complaints of maladministration against the Healthcare Commission (among others) in relation to its role in the NHS complaints procedure. Complaints about the Commission (as a Non-Departmental Public Body) when carrying out its other roles would be considered by the Parliamentary Commissioner for Administration.

164   In March 2005, the Department of Health issued details of a new procedure contained in the document *Maintaining High Professional Standards in the Modern NHS*. The procedures are mandatory for NHS bodies generally, but advisory for Foundation Trusts. We deal with this in more detail in Chapter 34 of our Report.

Legislation and guidance issued on the NHS complaints procedures

Family Health Services – 1946 to 1996

1946   National Health Service Act 1946 [Section 42 and Schedule 7]

1948   Statutory Instrument 1948 No. 507 – The National Health Service (Service Committee and Tribunal) Regulations 1948

1950   Statutory Instrument 1950 No. 983 – The National Health Service (Service Committee and Tribunal) Amendment Regulations 1950

1953   Statutory Instrument 1953 No. 1175 – The National Health Service (Service Committee and Tribunal) Amendment Regulations 1953

1956   Statutory Instrument 1956 No. 1077 – The National Health Service (Service Committees and Tribunal) Regulations 1956

1974   Statutory Instrument 1974 No. 455 – The National Health Service (Service Committees and Tribunal) Regulations 1974

1974   Statutory Instrument 1974 No. 907 – The National Health Service (Service Committees and Tribunal) Amendment Regulations 1974

1984   HN(FP)(84)16 – Leaflet: Complaints about dentists, chemists, opticians and family doctors

1987   Statutory Instrument 1987 No. 445 – The National Health Service (Service Committees and Tribunal) Amendment Regulations 1987

1990   Statutory Instrument 1990 No. 538 – The National Health Service (Service Committees and Tribunal) Regulations 1990

1990   Statutory Instrument 1990 No. 1752 – The National Health Service (Service Committees and Tribunal) Regulations 1990

1990   FPCL190/90 – Family Health Service Complaints

1990   FPCL(90)51 – Family Health Service Complaints

1990   MISC6/90 – Family Health Services: Complaints Procedures: Notes of Guidance to the FPS Complaints Procedures

1992   Statutory Instrument 1992 No. 664 – The National Health Service (Service Committees and Tribunal) Regulations 1992

1992   HSG(92)17 – Family Health Service Complaints: Changes from 1 April 1992

1993   Statutory Instrument 1993 No. 2972 – The National Health Service (Service Committees and Tribunal) Amendment Regulations 1993

1994   Statutory Instrument 1994 No. 634 – The National Health Service (Service Committees and Tribunal) Amendment Regulations 1994

1995   Statutory Instrument 1995 No. 3091 – The National Health Service (Service Committees and Tribunal) Amendment Regulations 1995

Hospital complaints – 1966 to March 1996

1966 HM(66)15: Methods of dealing with complaints by patients

1966 9 Dec 1966: "Dear Secretary" letter – Arrangements for "Ad Hoc" Committees of Enquiry

1970 27 July 1970: "Dear Secretary" letter – Suggestions and complaints about hospitals

1976 HN(76)107: Health services complaints procedures (Consultation on Code of Practice)

1978 HN(78)39: Health services complaints procedure (Further consultation)

1981 HC(81)5: Health services complaints procedure (Clinical and non-clinical procedures)

1982 HC(82)13: Prevention of harm to a patient resulting from physical or mental disability of hospital or community medical or dental staff [the so-called "Three wise men" procedure]

1982 HN(82)16: Leaflet about hospital complaints procedures

1983: HN(83)31: Report on the operation of the clinical complaints procedure

1985: Hospital Complaints Procedure Act 1985 (reference Section 17 of the NHS Act 1977)

1986 DA(86)14: Hospital Complaints Procedure Act 1985 (Consultation document)

1988 HC(88)37: Hospital Complaints Procedure Act 1985 (Includes policy guidance and Directions)

1989 Statutory Instrument 1989 No. 1191(C.39) – The Hospital Complaints Procedure Act 1985 (Commencement) Order 1989

1990 HC(90)9: Disciplinary procedures for hospital and community medical and dental staff

1995   EL(95)121: Implementation of the new complaints procedure: Interim Guidance

Hospital and Community Health Services and primary care practitioners – April 1996 to July 2004

1996   EL(96)5: Acting on Complaints: Training for Local Resolution

1996   EL(96)19: Complaints – listening...acting...improving: Guidance on implementation of the NHS complaints procedure

1996   Directions to NHS Trusts, Health Authorities, and Special Health Authorities for Special Hospitals on Hospital Complaints Procedure

1996   Miscellaneous Directions to Health Authorities for dealing with Complaints

1996   Statutory Instrument 1996 No. 669 – The National Health Service (Functions of Health Authorities) (Complaints) Regulations 1996

1996   Statutory Instrument 1996 No. 698 – The National Health Service (Pharmaceutical Services) Amendment Regulations 1996

1996   Statutory Instrument 1996 No. 702 – The National Health Service (General Medical Services) Amendment Regulations 1996

1996   Statutory Instrument 1996 No. 703 – The National Health Service (Service Committees and Tribunal) (Amendment) Regulations 1996

1996   Statutory Instrument 1996 No. 704 – The National Health Service (General Dental Services) Amendment Regulations 1996

1996   Statutory Instrument 1996 No. 705 – The National Health Service (General Ophthalmic Services) Amendment Regulations 1996

1996   Statutory Instrument 1996 No. 706 – The National Health Service (Fund-holding Practices) Regulations 1996

1996   Complaints – listening...acting...improving: Guidance for general practitioners

1996   Complaints – listening...acting...improving: Guidance pack for general dental practitioners

1996   Complaints – listening...acting...improving: Guidance pack for optometrists

1996   Complaints – listening...acting...improving: Guidance for community pharmacists and other providers of NHS pharmaceutical services

1996   EL(96)58: New NHS Complaints Procedure: Independent Review (Training pack for independent review panel members; briefing pack for clinical assessors; profession-specific questions for clinical assessors)

1996   FHSL(96)45: Family Health Services: Additional guidance on implementation of the NHS complaints procedure – "FHS disciplinary procedures – a guide for health authorities"

1997   FHSL(97)24: Family Health Services: Additional guidance on implementation of the NHS complaints procedure and the FHS disciplinary procedures

1998   HSC1998/010: Personal liability of non-executive directors

1998   HSC1998/059: NHS complaints procedure: confidentiality

1998   Directions to Health Authorities on dealing with complaints about family health services practitioners and providers of personal medical services July 1998 [replaced Directions issued in 1996]

1998   Directions to NHS Trusts, Health Authorities and Special Health Authorities for Special Hospitals on Hospital Complaints Procedures (July 1998)

1998   Directions to Health Authorities on dealing with complaints about providers of personal dental services other than NHS trusts (October 1998)

1999   HSC1999/104: Personal liability of non-executive directors: amendment of indemnity

1999   HSC1999/193: Good practice guide for conveners

2002   Directions to Primary Care Trusts on Dealing with Complaints
        (September 2002)

2002   Directions to NHS Trusts, Health Authorities and Special Health
        Authorities for Special Hospitals on Hospital Complaints Procedures
        (Amendment) Directions 2002 (September)

2002   Directions to Health Authorities on Dealing with Complaints about
        Family Health Services Practitioners and Personal Medical Services
        (Amendment) Directions 2002 (September)

2002   Directions to Health Authorities on Dealing with Complaints about
        Providers of Personal Dental Services other than NHS Trusts
        (Amendment) Directions 2002 (September)

2002   Health Authority (Construction of References) Directions 2002
        (September) [ensured that complaints legislation applied to Strategic
        Health Authorities]

2003   The Primary Care Trusts and Strategic Health Authorities
        Implementation of Pilot Schemes (Personal Medical Services)
        Directions 2003 (April) [Article 28 and Schedule 2]

2003   Health and Social Care (Community Health and Standards) Act 2003
        [Chapter 9 – Sections 113 to 119]

2004   Statutory Instrument 2004 No. 291 – The National Health Service
        (General Medical Services Contracts) Regulations 2004 [Part 6 –
        regulations 92 to 98]

2004   Statutory Instrument 2004 No. 627 – The National Health Service
        (Personal Medical Services Agreements) Regulations 2004 [Part 6 –
        regulations 86 to 92]

2004   Statutory Instrument 2004 No. 865 – The General Medical Services
        and Personal Medical Services Transitional and Consequential
        Provisions Order 2004 [Part 3 – regulation 51, Part 4 – regulation 58]

2004   Alternative Provider Medical Services Directions 2004
        [Part 3 – Article 9]

NHS bodies and primary care providers – July 2004 onwards

2004   Statutory Instrument 2004 No. 1768 – The National Health Service
       (Complaints) Regulations 2004

2004   Guidance to support implementation of the National Health Service
       (Complaints) Regulations 2004

2005   Maintaining High Professional Standards in the Modern NHS (March)

Annex 6
Data and case studies

Prevalence results

Below is a chart showing the number of allegations of "sexualised behaviour" by NHS staff towards patients, broken down by year and staff position. These figures represent actual reports from the 310 trusts across the country that responded to the Inquiry. The final column shows how reports about each type of professional relate as a percentage to reports concerning all professional groups.

Position	1999	2000	2001	2002	2003	2004	2005	Total	% total of complaints received
Consultant (not including Psychiatrists)		1		4	1	8		14	3.5%
GP		1	2	18	18	23	6	68	17.2%
SHO/Doctor	2	4	6	3	7	18	2	42	10.6%
Nurse	1	6	8	31	31	38	9	124	31.3%
Psychiatrist		3		1	1	5		10	2.5%
Healthcare/ Nursing Assistant		4	8	9	9	32	5	67	16.9%
Dentist				2	3	3	1	9	2.3%
Staff			3	8	11	16		38	9.6%
Chaplain/Priest			1			1	1	3	0.8%
Allied health professional			1	5	6	8	1	21	5.3%
Total	3	19	29	81	87	152	25	396	–

Outcome of allegations

Below is a table showing the outcome of allegations of "sexualised behaviour" by NHS staff towards patients. These figures represent reports from trusts and SHAs that gave an in-depth response to the Inquiry's request for information. The second column shows the type of outcome as a percentage of all reports, whilst the final column indicates the type of outcome as a percentage of all resolved complaints (ie those that are not ongoing, where the outcome is yet to be determined).

Outcome	Number	% of total	% of total resolved cases
Dismissal/Disciplinary action/Conviction	63	25.4%	32.3%
Police investigation/Charges/Trial with no disciplinary action	32	12.9%	16.4%
Police investigation/Charges/Trial with outcome pending or unknown	25	10.1%	–
Advice/Training for Individual	11	4.4%	5.6%
No evidence/not upheld	52	21.0%	26.7%
Passed to governing body – GMC/NMC/ Outside agency	7	2.8%	3.6%
Complaint withdrawn or not made formal, therefore no action	13	5.2%	6.7%
Staff left/moved/retired/resigned/died before disciplinary hearing carried out	17	6.9%	8.7%
Ongoing	21	8.5%	–
Outcome unknown	7	2.8%	–
Total	248	100%	100%

Statistics from POPAN's Helpline (taken from POPAN submission)

Below is a chart showing primary reports of abuse by doctors made to
POPAN's Helpline in the period 1 October 2003 to 30 September 2004.
It does not list cases where more than one type of abuse is reported
concerning the same doctor. The third column shows how reports about
each type of professional relate as a percentage to reports concerning all
professional groups. We have not included here a breakdown of calls
concerning counsellors, psychotherapists, complementary therapists etc.
Coming from a small charity, not widely known, the figures show the
number and type of calls to the Helpline made by people who knew the
Helpline number and who chose to call it. They are not claimed as reliable
indicators of the prevalence of abuse in themselves.

Position	Number	% of total reports	Sexual	Emotional	Physical	Emotional/ discriminatory
GP	13	50%	8	2	1	1
Psychiatrist	8	30%	8	–	–	–
School doctor	1	4%	1	–	–	–
Paediatrician	1	4%	1	–	–	–
Consultant (unspecified)	1	4%	1	–	–	–
Neuro-surgeon	1	4%	–	–	1	–
Gynaecological surgeon	1	4%	–	1	–	–
All	26	100%	15	1	2	1

Annex 7
GMC PCC Cases 2003 and 2004

This annex provides a précis of the disciplinary decisions of the Professional Conduct Committee of the GMC that relate to allegations of sexualised behaviour by doctors during 2003 and 2004. All doctors have been referred to by a number, in order to preserve their anonymity and that of the patients involved.

- **Dr 1** [Jan 2003] Poor level of care in intimate examination, without chaperone. Not Guilty of Serious Professional Misconduct (SPM).

- **Dr 2** [Jan 2003] Convicted of indecent assault and sentenced to 9 months imprisonment in July 1997 for assaulting female patient. Erased from Register April 1998. Restored to Register December 2001, subject to conditions. Conditions lifted in January 2003. *"The Committee are satisfied that you have shown some insight into the behaviour which led to your erasure."*

- **Dr 3** [Jan 2003] Suspended for 12 months in June 2001 for serious professional misconduct, for making improper and inappropriate comments of a sexual nature to three patients, an inappropriate intimate examination of another patient, and sexual advances towards a relative of two patients. Continued suspension of 6 months in June 2002. Suspension lifted in Jan 2003: *"The committee have taken note of your profound expressions of regret and your assurances that you now have insight into the behaviour which led to the original finding of serious professional misconduct."*

- **Dr 4** [Feb 2003] A consultant psychiatrist, Dr 4 began an inappropriate relationship with a vulnerable psychiatric patient, which was found proved to be inappropriate, unprofessional, and an abuse of his professional position. However, it wasn't held to be SPM. No reprimand given.

- **Dr 5** [Feb 2003] Insensitive and improper intimate examination of a patient leading to a loss of dignity for the patient (not alleged as an assault). Found guilty of SPM in Feb 2002, leading to conditions being made on continued registration. Conditions revoked in Feb 2003.

- **Dr 6** [March 2003] Found to have made sexual advances towards two female colleagues, a nurse and an auditor, and along with clinical failings, was found to be guilty of SPM. Conditional registration imposed for 3 years, although all conditions related to clinical performance, and not behaviour towards female colleagues.

- **Dr 7** [March 2003] Charges relating to making or possessing indecent images of children.

- **Dr 8** [April 2003] Bound over for charge of indecent exposure – Dr 8 was in his car with adult material and masturbated in full sight of a woman and three young children. Guilty of SPM, and given the isolated nature of the incident, a strong reprimand given.

- **Dr 9** [April 2003] Rubbed the stomach, tapped the breasts, and put his arm around a patient who came to A&E with a bruised finger. Suspended for 6 months for SPM. Suspension lifted in April 2003, after the Committee was reassured by evidence from Dr 9.

- **Dr 10** [May 2003] Objected to husband/chaperone being present during an intimate examination of a patient, and required her to remove her top and bra whilst listening to her chest. Carried out an intimate examination of a second patient against her wishes, and also made inappropriate comments. Carried out examination of a third patient's breasts without clinical requirement and without chaperone. Carried out intimate examination of a fourth patient against her wishes, and made inappropriate comments to her during the examination. All these facts were found to be inappropriate, unprofessional, and without respecting the patients' wishes (ie without full consent). Found guilty of SPM, although *"The Committee accept that there is no suggestion that at any time was there any sexual or improper motive in [Dr 10's] examination of these patients"*. And *"in light of the evidence that you have remedied your past deficiencies, they find it sufficient to conclude [Dr 10's] case with a reprimand"*.

- **Dr 11** [May 2003] Convicted of three counts of indecent assault on patients, two of which were on 'vulnerable young women', and sentenced to 9 months imprisonment in Jan 2003. Found guilty of SPM, suspended, and Dr 11's name erased from the register.

- **Dr 12** [June 2003] Charges relating to making or possessing indecent images of children.

- **Dr 13** [July 2003] Found guilty of SPM after making sexual advances towards a nurse and a doctor, and acting aggressively towards other colleagues. Reprimand given.

- **Dr 14** [July 2003] Alleged to have made unwanted sexual advances towards a receptionist. None of the charges were found proved, as the standard applied by the PCC was "sure beyond doubt". Not guilty of SPM.

- **Dr 15** [July 2003] On the facts, Dr 15 told a patient's husband to leave the room before carrying out an examination on the patient, and did not offer a chaperone. Originally charged with conducting an anal examination and a breast examination that was not clinically required, but these charges were deleted after a 'rule 27 submission'. Therefore not guilty of SPM.

- **Dr 16** [July 2003] Convicted in Oct 1998 of indecent assault on a patient and given an 8-month suspended sentence. June 1999 the PCC suspended Dr 16's registration for 12 months for SPM. June 2000 (before the suspended sentence for the criminal conviction had expired), the PCC granted conditional registration for 12 months under the condition that Dr 16 was to remain under the supervision of another practitioner. The same conditions were applied in June 2001, and again in June 2002 and July 2003, despite allegations against Dr 16 being investigated by the GMC in July 2003 on a separate matter.

- **Dr 17** [July 2003] A male prison doctor in a male prison was advised about maintaining a degree of distance between himself and the inmates/patients. In Sep 1997, he again was warned against contact with patients, unscheduled visits, and intimate examinations without chaperones present, and that all intimate examinations should be passed to other doctors. These warnings were repeated again in June 1998 and again in April 2000, with added instruction that any visits to patients must be with an escorting Wing Officer, and that any further breaches would lead to a referral to the GMC. The eventual charges brought against Dr 17 were for intimate examinations carried out without clinical justification or a chaperone, and touching and massaging patients' genitals. Some of these charges were found proved, including meeting up with a patient upon his release. Guilty of SPM. Registration suspended and name erased from the Register.

- **Dr 18** [July 2003] A hospital practitioner in Psychiatry, Dr 18 attempted to pursue a sexual relationship with a vulnerable psychiatric patient. In particular, by: visiting her home address and calling her when it was not necessary for professional purposes, asking her to marry him as a second wife, giving her £10 to be his wife, saying *"Hello Mrs [Dr 18's name]"*, and culminating in an indecent assault and a weekend away where sexual intercourse took place. Found guilty of SPM, and name erased from the Register.

- **Dr 19** [Aug 2003] A Consultant Psychiatrist, Dr 19 made inappropriate advances towards a vulnerable patient in his care, by using a "relaxation technique" involving massage of arms and shoulders, and asking her out to dinner, as well as requesting her mobile number. Found guilty of SPM in Aug 2002, and had conditions placed on his registration. Conditions removed in Aug 2003 on assurances from Dr 19 that he would not repeat his behaviour.

- **Dr 20** [Aug 2003] Convicted of two counts of indecent assault on two patients in Oct 1998. In June 1999, the PCC found him guilty of SPM and had his name erased from the Register. In Dec 2000, Dr 20 applied to have his name restored to the Register, whereupon the PPC set conditions for restoration: professional competence, good character and good health. By Aug 2003, the PCC had received no further contact from Dr 20, so his name was not restored to the Register.

- **Dr 21** [Aug 2003] Found to have carried out intimate examinations on a child, who was 9 years old at the time, even though he wasn't the child's GP. He was also found to have inappropriately applied medi-wipes to the child's labia. When the child was 11, Dr 21 was found to have gone into her bedroom whilst she was sleeping, and rubbed her legs, with no medical justification. It was not found proved that Dr 21 put his hand under her knickers and rubbed her bottom. The PCC found that those actions that were found proved were not inappropriate, not indecent, and not unprofessional. The child's mother made a statement to the police, which later formed part of the evidence to the PCC. Dr 21 wrote a letter to the child's mother, which included a form of words that he urged her to use when writing to the GMC, although the PCC found that this did not amount to pressurising the mother into withdrawing the information in her witness statement to the PCC, or attempting to hinder the investigation of the PCC. Writing such a letter was not deemed inappropriate or unprofessional. The PCC concluded that Dr 21 was not guilty of SPM.

- **Dr 22** [Sep 2003] Several conduct charges, including accessing "inappropriate material" on the internet. Reprimand given.

- **Dr 23** [Sep 2003] An SHO responsible for the care of psychiatric patients, after the discharge of a vulnerable psychiatric patient, Dr 23 had an emotional and sexual relationship with the patient. Dr 23 was moved to a different hospital and told not to have contact with the patient, but was found to have continued a sexual relationship with her. Found guilty of SPM and his name was erased from the Register.

- **Dr 24** [Sep 2003] Admitted to a sexual relationship with a vulnerable patient, between 1979 and 2002. Found guilty of SPM and his name was erased from the Register.

- **Dr 25** [Oct 2003] A consultant psychiatrist, Dr 25 was alleged to have made advances on a patient, but found not proved, although Dr 25 admitted to telephoning her on a number of occasions. He was also found to have had a consultation with another patient in her car, and invited her to play badminton. Found not guilty of SPM.

- **Dr 26** [Oct 2003] Admitted to a sexual relationship with a vulnerable patient with a history of psychiatric problems. The PCC had no details other than the charge itself, and therefore had no evidence of the circumstances or the context of the relationship, nor the treatment provided. As a result, they found his actions were neither inappropriate nor an abuse of the doctor-patient relationship. Therefore not guilty of SPM.

- **Dr 27** [Nov 2003] In Nov 2002, Dr 27 was found by the PCC to have made sexual advances towards two patients, including touching one patient's breasts outside the clinical setting and without her consent. Dr 27 was suspended for 12 months, but that suspension was revoked in Nov 2003, as the PCC were impressed with Dr 27's newfound appreciation for the status of women.

- **Dr 28** [Dec 2003] Convicted of Breach of the Peace in June 2001, after inviting two women to his car and then making "suggestions" which left them in a state of distress and alarm, Dr 28 was given a warning by the PCC. Again in March 2002, Dr 28 was convicted of theft and Breach of the Peace, after stealing a colleague's keys, breaking into her room, and leaving semen on her bedding and on an item of clothing. As a result, in Dec 2002 Dr 28 was suspended from the Register for 12 months. Suspension extended for a further 3 months in Dec 2003, as Dr 28 was found to have lied in a letter to the PCC when trying to have his suspension lifted.

- **Dr 29** [Dec 2003] Admitted to a sexual relationship with a vulnerable patient with a history of depression, which began in 2002. Found guilty of SPM and his name was suspended from the Register for 3 months.

- **Dr 30** [Feb 2004] Charges relating to making or possessing indecent images of children.

- **Dr 31** [Feb 2004] Admitted to a sexual relationship with a vulnerable patient with a history of depression. Two-year conditional registration imposed: work in a group practice, with mentoring on maintaining appropriate boundaries.

- **Dr 32** [Feb 2004] Charges relating to making or possessing indecent images of children.

- **Dr 33** [March 2004] Alleged to have made sexual contact with a 14-year-old babysitter in Aug 1979. Due to the passage of time (21 years), PCC found it difficult to establish the true facts. None of the charges were proved. Not guilty of SPM.

- **Dr 34** [April 2004] Charges relating to making or possessing indecent images of children.

- **Dr 35** [April 2004] Charges relating to making or possessing indecent images of children.

- **Dr 36** [May 2004] Charges relating to making or possessing indecent images of children.

- **Dr 37** [May 2004] Admitted to a sexual relationship with a vulnerable psychiatric patient. Guilty of SPM, and suspended for 12 months (the maximum length of suspension permitted).

- **Dr 38** [May 2004] A locum psychiatrist, Dr 38 was charged with rude, bullying and inappropriate remarks towards colleagues. None of the numerous charges were found proved. Not guilty of SPM.

- **Dr 39** [June 2004] Charges relating to making or possessing indecent images of children.

- **Dr 40** [June 2004] A psychiatrist SHO, Dr 40's name was erased from the Register in April 1999, for pursuing an improper sexual relationship with a patient. Dr 40 applied to have his name restored to the Register in 2000, and 2001, but this was refused on both occasions. In Sep 2002, the PCC agreed to restore his name subject to satisfactory assessments of professional competence and good character. Name restored to the Register in June 2004.

- **Dr 41** [June 2004] Charges relating to making or possessing indecent images of children.

- **Dr 42** [June 2004] Conducted intimate examinations for Disability Allowance on two patients, both young women alone in their homes. During the examination of the first patient, Dr 42 was found to have removed her bra and knickers without her full consent, touched her breasts without her consent, and touched her buttocks and pubic area. These actions were found to be inappropriate, clinically unjustified, but not indecent. During the examination of the second patient, Dr 42 was found to have put his hands inside her clothing and felt her breasts and groin area, without her full consent, which again was found to be inappropriate, clinically unjustified, but not indecent. This second incident was conducted in this manner even though the police had interviewed Dr 42 when investigating his conduct in relation to the previous incident. The PCC found that there was no indecent intent in these examinations, and stated they were not "Intimate Examinations" as defined by the GMC's guidance. Dr 42 found guilty of SPM, and given conditional registration for 3 years – no clinical contact with patients except under the direct supervision and continuous presence of a senior registered Medical Practitioner in active clinical practice.

- **Dr 43** [June 2004] Found (despite his denials) to have had a sexual relationship with a patient over a period of 9 years. Guilty of SPM and name erased from the Register.

- **Dr 44** [July 2004] Convicted of three offences of indecent assault on female patients carried out during consultations, and sentenced to 18 months' imprisonment. Name erased from the Register.

- **Dr 45** [July 2004] Dr 45 examined Mr X for disability benefit, at his home, where Miss Y was present. Miss Y was Mr X's girlfriend, though Dr 45 denied knowing this at the time. Dr 45 admitted to leaving the room and engaging in sexual activity with Miss Y. The PCC found that the witnesses were unreliable, and that the facts were not proved "beyond all reasonable doubt". The PCC accepted Dr 45's evidence that he was an unwilling party and unaware of the true relationship between the patient and Miss Y. The PCC concluded that the engagement of sexual activity by Dr 45 was as an unwilling party and was therefore not unprofessional, not inappropriate, not an abuse of his position and not an exploitation of Miss Y's vulnerable position. Therefore not guilty of SPM.

- **Dr 46** [July 2004] Whilst a trainee GP, Dr 46 carried out inappropriate breast examinations on two patients without explaining the nature or purpose of the examinations, and therefore did not have their full informed consent. Also made inappropriate remarks during the examinations, and did not offer a chaperone. In Oct 1999, found guilty of SPM, and name erased from the Register. Applied in July 2004 to have name restored, which was granted subject to independent evidence of professional competence and good character.

- **Dr 47** [July 2004] Admitted to having a sexual relationship with a vulnerable patient with a history of depression, which continued for over 20 years, beyond his retirement in April 1998. Found guilty of SPM, and his name was erased from the Register.

- **Dr 48** [July 2004] Dr 48, an Ear, Nose and Throat specialist, examined a patient for balance problems. After finding no cause, he asked the patient to pull her trousers down and get on to an examination couch, whereupon he performed an "examination" on her groin area inside her underwear. He then asked her to remove her upper clothing and examined her breasts. At no point was a chaperone present or offered. No record was made of this examination. The PCC found that the examination was inappropriate, as it was outside the matter for which she was referred, although it was not found to be outside his remit of expertise, and the examination was apparently clinically indicated. Dr 48 was found guilty of SPM and suspended for 6 months (out of a maximum of 12).

- **Dr 49** [July 2004] Charges relating to making or possessing indecent images of children.

- **Dr 50** [July 2004] Found guilty of SPM for carrying out inappropriate intimate examinations on five different female patients, with no chaperone present, and with little or no clinical justification. Following expressions of regret and apologies, the PCC concluded that there were no perverse sexual motives in these examinations, and that Dr 50 is not a danger to patients. Guilty of SPM, but only given a reprimand.

- **Dr 51** [Sep 2004]. Found guilty of SPM in Sep 2003 after carrying out inappropriate, incompetent and indecent intimate examinations on four female patients, including touching their breasts without consent, and with no clinical justification. Conditional registration granted for 12 months: no locum posts; no private practice; a mentor to be appointed; at least 6 months supervised training in Obstetrics and Gynaecology; and a chaperone always to be present during intimate examinations. Having failed to comply with conditions, Dr 51 had similar conditions imposed on him in Sep 2004 for a further 12 months.

- **Dr 52** [Sep 2004] Prior to Feb 1999, Dr 52 acted in a 'wholly indecent and improper manner' whilst conducting physical examinations of at least two of his male patients. In Feb 1999, Dr 52 was found guilty of SPM and conditions placed on his registration for 6 months, including not carrying out intimate examinations without a chaperone present. Dr 52 breached those conditions on a number of occasions in the following 6 months, by conducting inappropriate intimate examinations without a chaperone. The PCC instructed that his name be erased from the Register in April 2000. In Sep 2004, Dr 52 applied to have his name restored, but was refused, as he had again been convicted of a dishonesty offence (theft) since his name had been erased.

- **Dr 53** [Sep 2004] Charges relating to making or possessing indecent images of children.

- **Dr 54** [Sep 2004] Charges relating to making or possessing indecent images of children.

- **Dr 55** [Sep 2004] In June 2004 Dr 55 was convicted of two counts of rape of girls aged 5 and 11, which he filmed, having administered almost lethal levels of Temazepam to sedate his victims. Sentenced to 15 years imprisonment. Guilty of SPM, and his name erased from the Register.

- **Dr 56** [Oct 2004] Dr 56 confessed to his senior partner to having affairs with an unspecified number of patients, over which he had no control, expressed concerns that he was unable to comply with the GMC's "Good Medical Practice" and stated he was fundamentally flawed and therefore permanently unfit to practise as a GP, and asked the GMC for voluntary erasure. The GMC were informed of the affairs, and refused voluntary erasure. Dr 56 was found guilty of SPM and his name was erased from the Register in Oct 2004.

- **Dr 57** [Oct 2004] Admitted to having a 14-month-long sexual relationship with a vulnerable community psychiatric patient. Found guilty of SPM, and name erased from the Register.

- **Dr 58** [Oct 2004] A Locum Psychiatrist, in Feb 2003 Dr 58 was found guilty of SPM for falling below reasonable professional standards and making sexual advances towards three nurses (with a police caution for one of them), and suspended for 12 months. Conditional registration granted in Oct 2004, to run for 18 months, including supervision and training.

- **Dr 59** [Oct 2004] Charges relating to making or possessing indecent images of children.

- **Dr 60** [Nov 2004] Charges relating to making or possessing indecent images of children.

- **Dr 61** [Nov 2004] A psychiatrist and a GP, Dr 61 embarked on a sexual relationship with a vulnerable patient with a long psychiatric history. He was called in to make an assessment of the patient for the purposes of detention under s.2 Mental Health Act. A disclosure to the ward manager lead to a confrontation with Dr 61, who admitted his involvement with the patient. Dr 61 was then refused access to the patient by the ward manager, and told to leave the premises. Dr 61 admitted his involvement with the patient to the police in an interview. Found guilty of SPM, and his name was erased from the Register.

- **Dr 62** [Nov 2004] Convicted in March 2004 of seven counts of Indecent Assault on female patients over a period of 21 years, whilst conducting intimate examinations. Sentenced to 5 years, imprisonment. Name erased form the Register.

- **Dr 63** [Dec 2004] In Aug 2002, Dr 63 was found guilty of SPM, for inappropriate and indecent behaviour with two female patients. Whilst examining a 14-year-old girl at her home, Dr 63 touched her vagina whilst her mother was out of the room, and after an examination of a second patient, he touched the breast and thigh of her mother, again in her own home. He was suspended for 12 months. In Aug 2003, having received no evidence that he had re-offended, the PCC granted conditional registration, to include 6 months of supervision, and no unsupervised home visits for 3 months, and instructed that chaperones must be present for all intimate examinations of female patients. Similar conditions were imposed in March 2004 for 12 months. In Dec 2004, it became apparent that Dr 63 had been disqualified nationally from inclusion in all Performers Lists for his conduct by his local PCT, so he could not comply with the conditions of supervised GP practice. New conditions imposed in Dec 2004 for 12 months, including prohibition against intimate examinations of female patients without a chaperone.

- **Dr 64** [Dec 2004] Found to have made unwanted sexual advances towards a nurse, including pressing his erect penis against her body on two occasions. Found guilty of SPM, and his registration was suspended for 6 months.

- **Dr 65** [Dec 2004] Charges relating to making or possessing indecent images of children.

Annex 8
Suggested areas of research and questioning for national data collection initiative (abuse of patients by NHS professionals)

1. Details of professional

Profession	Specify categories
Age	....
Gender	Male/female
Previous abuser?	Yes/no

2. Patient details:

Gender	Male/female
Age	....
Diagnosis	Specify categories
History of child abuse	Yes/no
When did abuse take place?	If yes, was it sexual/emotional/physical Before discharge/after discharge

3. Type of abuse:

- Sexual

– suggestive behaviour	Yes/no
– client stripping to underwear	Yes/no
– being naked above (female only) or below the waist	Yes/no
– therapist telling a sexual fantasy to a client	Yes/no
– erotic kissing	Yes/no
– therapist lying on top of or underneath a client	Yes/no
– touching	Yes/no
– fondling	Yes/no
– massage	Yes/no
– genital exposure	Yes/no
– masturbation	Yes/no
– oral-genital contact	Yes/no
– hand-genital contact	Yes/no
– anal intercourse	Yes/no
– vaginal intercourse	Yes/no
● Physical	Yes/no
● Financial	Yes/no

- Racial   Yes/no
- Emotional   Yes/no
- Social/dual roles   Yes/no
- Professional (eg breach of confidentiality)   Yes/no

4. Outcome of allegation   Positive/negative/unknown

5. Impact of abuse on patient

6. Duration of abuse   one sexual encounter
less than 3 months
3–11 months
1–5 years
over 5 years

Appendices

Appendix 1
The Chairman and Panel profiles

Chairman of the Inquiry: Nigel Pleming QC

The Inquiry Chairman is Nigel Pleming QC. He practises in all areas of public law and has a special interest in mental health issues.

Panel Member: Ros Alstead

Ros Alstead is the Director of Nursing at the Birmingham & Solihull Mental Health NHS Trust. At the time of appointment she was Director of Operations and Director of Nursing at South Birmingham Mental Health NHS Trust.

Panel Member: Ruth Lesirge

Ruth Lesirge is a former Chief Executive of the Mental Health Foundation. She is now a Visiting Fellow at the Centre for Charity Effectiveness, Cass Business School City University, and has an extensive freelance consultancy in the voluntary and public sectors.

Appendix 2
The Secretariat and the Legal Team

The Inquiry team has seen significant changes in staffing throughout its lifespan. The Inquiry Secretary and the Inquiry Chairman and Panel would like to thank all those staff members employed on an agency basis who have found permanent positions outside of the team and may not be mentioned below.

Everyone, however, made a valuable contribution to the work of the Inquiry and were all integral members of the team.

Secretariat

Inquiry Secretary/Communications:	Colin Phillips
Assistant Inquiry Secretary:	John Miller
Assistant Inquiry Secretary:	Kypros Menicou
Inquiry Solicitor:	Michael Fitzgerald
Deputy Solicitor:	Duncan Henderson
Commissioning Manager (Experts):	Dr Ruth Chadwick

Counsel to the Inquiry

Counsel:	Bruce Carr
Junior Counsel:	Clare Brown

Legal Team

Senior Legal Support:	Stephen Taylor
Paralegal:	Tom Brennan
Paralegal:	Karoon Akoon
Paralegal:	David Altberg

Administrative and Secretarial support

Administrator:	Emily Frost
Administrator:	Philip Otton
Personal Assistant:	Virginia Berkholz
Administrator:	Gurjeev Johal

Stage 2 – Seminars

Facilitator:	Bruce Carr
Co-ordinator:	Kypros Menicou
Rapporteur:	Kathryn Ehrich

Appendix 3
Background matters for the Inquiry

Procedures

1   In October 2002 a draft Procedures Paper was produced by the Inquiry, setting out the procedures that were to be adopted. The paper was sent to those individuals and bodies who had expressed an interest in the work of the Inquiry. The Procedures Paper detailed how the Inquiry would deal with document-gathering, requests for witness statements, the use to be made by the Inquiry of statements or other documents, and confidentiality undertakings. A copy of the Procedures Paper can be found at Appendix 6. A List of Issues was also distributed with the Procedures Paper for consultation. That document set out the issues that the Panel proposed to explore in its work. It acted as a guide for the preparation of witness statements, and more generally in connection with the Inquiry's work. A copy of the List of Issues is at Appendix 7.

Powers

2   Section 2 of the National Health Service Act 1977, under which the Inquiry was first established, does not give the Chairman the power to compel witnesses to attend the Inquiry hearings. The absence of compulsory powers had caused some difficulties to the Inquiry in obtaining documents. Understandably, those whom the Inquiry initially approached for documentation, such as the North Yorkshire Police and the GMC, were cautious about disclosing some documents to the Inquiry without the force of compulsory powers. It should also be noted that the former patients of William Kerr voiced their concern at a very early stage about the Chairman's lack of compulsory powers. They thought the Secretary of State's initial decision in this respect caused the Inquiry to lack credibility. Certainly some of the bodies approached by the Inquiry for the provision of documentation expressed some surprise at the initial lack of compulsory powers. As the document-gathering process

progressed, it became clear that, without compulsory powers, the production of certain important documents could not be guaranteed. Accordingly, once it became clear in December 2003 that, following the conclusion of Michael Haslam's trial, the Inquiry would proceed, the Chairman wrote to the Secretary of State for Health seeking additional powers under Section 84 of the National Health Service Act 1977. This Section includes powers for the Chairman to compel the production of documents and the attendance of witnesses to give evidence. On 26 January 2004 the Secretary of State indicated by letter that he thereby granted those powers to the Chairman of the Inquiry.

3   The Chairman did exercise his powers under Section 84 formally on one occasion to secure the attendance of one witness deemed important to the Inquiry who had indicated a reluctance to give evidence, and on four other occasions to facilitate the giving of evidence by those who had felt under threat from Michael Haslam's intimation of legal proceedings arising from evidence given to the Inquiry. The Chairman also exercised his powers under Section 84 formally on other occasions to facilitate the production of documents where those in possession of them had felt unable to release them to the Inquiry on a voluntary basis. As a result, the Inquiry has been able to secure access to all known relevant documents.

Documentation available to the Inquiry

4   The Inquiry was granted the benefit of useful resources provided by a number of interested parties.

5   First, mention must be made in respect of the former patients, their family members and supporters, in particular the Advocacy Network – Leeds, and their legal representatives, for the contribution of documentation and statements to assist the Inquiry's work.

6   The Inquiry also received voluminous records and documentation from the Department of Health and a variety of NHS organisations especially Selby & York PCT and Craven, Harrogate and Rural District PCT and Harrogate Healthcare NHS Trust. The trusts agreed to release a vast number of documents, greatly assisting the Inquiry's task. The Inquiry is greatly indebted to the trusts for the efforts its legal representatives assumed in collating the above material in addition to the mammoth undertaking involved in interviewing and

taking statements from all the health services' employees, both past and present.

7   The North Yorkshire and West Yorkshire Police provided the Inquiry with a large collection of information in relation to the criminal investigations and trials of both William Kerr and Michael Haslam. The Inquiry also received assistance from the Crown Prosecution Service.

8   The Inquiry also had access to documents in the possession of the *Sunday Times* newspaper regarding the libel proceedings and Michael Haslam.

9   Large volumes of material were provided by the GMC, albeit in a piecemeal fashion, and on occasions requiring the formality of a summons under the powers granted to the Chairman by the Secretary of State.

10 By way of submissions and provision of relevant studies and professional guidance, the following bodies need to be recognised for their generous contribution to the investigations of the Inquiry:

- Department of Health, Complaints and Clinical Negligence Policy Team
- British Medical Association
- Mental Health Act Commission
- Information Commissioner
- Royal College of Physicians
- Royal College of Psychiatrists
- Royal College of General Practitioners
- Institute of Psychiatry
- South London and Maudsley NHS Trust
- NHS National Clinical Assessment Authority
- NHS National Patient Safety Agency
- Complaints and Clinical Negligence Workstream
- British Confederation of Psychotherapists

- Institute for Mental Health Act Practitioners
- Royal Free and UCL Medical School
- Judy Gilley Associates
- NHS National Institute for Mental Health in England
- Healthcare Commission
- Health Service Ombudsman
- British Association for Sexual and Relationship Therapy
- Employment Tribunals, Leeds
- Institute of Risk Management
- Wendy Hesketh, University of Ulster
- Professor Linda Mulcahy, University of London
- Consumer's Association
- Metropolitan Police, Project Sapphire
- Prevention of Professional Abuse Network (POPAN)

11   Very many people, including former patients of William Kerr or Michael Haslam, healthcare professionals – especially GPs – and others, contributed their views and gave the Inquiry evidence. The Inquiry is grateful for the amount of time and effort this involved and greatly appreciates the commitment of many people to this part of their work.

Anonymity of patients

12   The Inquiry, as set out in its Procedures document, sought to maintain patient confidentiality in so far as was possible. All patients giving evidence were identified throughout the oral hearings using a letter and number, rather than their real names. This approach has been maintained in this report, although as a further precaution the code letters and numbers used differ from those used during the oral hearings.

Gathering witness statements

13   In order to structure the work in Part 1, a List of Issues was produced which reflected the Terms of Reference. The Solicitor to the Inquiry

wrote to everyone who might be able to give relevant evidence, asking them to produce a witness statement. Such requests were accompanied by a document, which set out matters arising from the Terms of Reference and the List of Issues about which it was thought the witness would be able to provide evidence. In most cases these requests were made through the legal representatives of the participants. The Inquiry is most grateful for the assistance of all who provided witness statements and acknowledges the considerable assistance of the legal representatives of those participants in obtaining witness statements and subsequently providing them to the Inquiry.

14   Witness statements received by the Inquiry were not routinely disseminated to other participants in the Inquiry. Where the maker had given permission however, statements were provided to other selected participants for clarification, confirmation or rebuttal purposes. The limit to the dissemination of witness statements was necessary to preserve patient confidentiality and also to encourage all those who had relevant evidence to give to the Inquiry to do so freely. Before any documents or witness statements were disseminated to participants and their representatives, they were first required to sign a confidentiality undertaking, which acknowledged that it was necessary to keep such material confidential and to be used solely for the purposes of the Inquiry.

Gathering documents

15   Section 2 of the National Health Service Act 1977, under which the Inquiry was established, does not give the Chairman power to require the production of documents. Accordingly, the Secretariat wrote to the relevant public bodies seeking voluntary production of all related documents. The Secretariat had the task of managing the considerable amount of documentation that was submitted in response. The documents were read and assessed by the Inquiry team.

16   For the purposes of reading and handling the documents, the relevant documents were electronically scanned and the images linked to a document management software package acquired by the Inquiry for that specific task. This facilitated speedy access to any particular document, which could then be viewed on the screen of the personal computer of the Inquiry team members.

17   With the oral hearings in mind, the Inquiry team produced a bundle of documents comprising approximately 50 lever arch files, which was circulated to the legal representatives of the two principal participants in the Inquiry; the former patients; and the health trusts. As with the witness statements, the bundle was supplied subject to the terms of the confidentiality undertaking.

18   In order to allow participants to prepare for the oral hearings, the Inquiry circulated in advance of those hearings a written Opening Summary. This document set out the factual chronology of the Kerr/Haslam story as it appeared to the Inquiry on the basis of the evidence gathered at that stage. The introduction to the Opening Summary emphasised that the document was not exhaustive. The summary included accounts of the concerns and complaints raised in relation to the practice and conduct of William Kerr and Michael Haslam. This was in accordance with paragraph 1 of the Inquiry's Terms of Reference. Once again, the Opening Summary was circulated subject to the Inquiry's confidentiality undertaking. Participants or their representatives were entitled to (and did) submit questions for consideration by Counsel to the Inquiry in relation to individual witnesses. This procedure was set out in the Inquiry's Procedures document.

Legal expenses

19   A private Inquiry such as this does not have any power to make a payment of legal costs from public funds or by any other party. However, the Secretary of State indicated to the Inquiry that if the Chairman made a recommendation that the legal costs of a participant should be met out of public funds, then it would be sympathetically considered. The Chairman made such a recommendation in respect of the costs of representation of the former patients of William Kerr and Michael Haslam, represented by Irwin Mitchell, Solicitors, Leeds. The Chairman also made recommendations in respect of the costs of representation of two other witnesses to the Inquiry and in relation to Michael Haslam. The Secretary of State accepted the recommendations in each case.

Dealing with potential criticism

20   As the Chairman made clear at the preliminary meetings in York, if it was considered necessary to criticise the way in which events, including complaints, had been handled in the past, Inquiry

procedures were designed to ensure that persons who may be affected by such criticisms would be given a proper and fair opportunity to respond. The procedures for the representation of participants and other witnesses, and the preparation of their statements, seemed to meet those requirements. However, as was also made clear at the preliminary meetings, a further step was proposed to ensure fairness.

21   The further step was that no criticism would be made of any person without ensuring that that person first had a proper opportunity to answer the criticism. Wherever it was possible to do so, the witness would be informed in writing by the Inquiry team of the nature of the potential criticism before they were called to give evidence. Where that was not possible, for example, because potential criticisms emerged at a time after oral evidence had been given, then they would be given an opportunity to respond before any report was submitted to the Secretary of State.

22   Notices of potential criticism were sent to witnesses where it appeared that they might be criticised for their conduct in relation to matters covered by the Inquiry's Terms of Reference. Each witness was given the chance to address these points during the course of their evidence. The Solicitor to the Inquiry wrote to those witnesses or their representatives after they had given their evidence to invite any further comments in writing to supplement what had been said in oral evidence.

Appendix 4
The modified form of private inquiry

1   In Section One of this Report we deal with the evolution of the Inquiry following its announcement by the Secretary of State on 13 July 2001. We explain how the private inquiry originally established by the Secretary of State evolved into a modified form of private inquiry. When settling upon the Inquiry Procedures document, which is at Appendix 6, we attempted to adopt procedures which recognised and reflected the somewhat changed nature of the Inquiry following the concessions made by the Secretary of State, and the decision of the court in the judicial review proceedings.

2   But what were the practical consequences of operating within the confines of this hybrid Inquiry? If we had been established as a public inquiry it is likely that all documents and statements received by the Inquiry would have been released to the public, perhaps on a website; and hearings would have been accessible to all. Our proceedings by contrast, required us to impose restrictions on the circulation of documents, statements and the record of the hearings held, essentially in private. Preserving patient confidentiality was paramount when considering distribution to participants in the Inquiry of material provided to us by other participants. We decided that, generally speaking, we would make available to a participant only that material which was considered necessary for that participant to contribute to the work of the Inquiry, for example for the purposes of obtaining written comment and/or rebuttal. Thus, contrary to what might have happened in the case of a public inquiry, the complete Inquiry bundle of relevant documents and witness statements was not given to each and every participant. We endeavoured to send out to participants or their legal representatives only documentation relevant to that participant. Where necessary, documents were sent in redacted form. Material supplied to participants or their legal representatives by the Inquiry was expressly subject to their confidentiality undertaking and agreement not to use this material for purposes other than the Inquiry.

Appendix 5
Terms of Reference

The overall purpose of the Inquiry is:

1   To assess the appropriateness and effectiveness of the procedures operated in the local health services –

    a. for enabling health service users to raise issues of legitimate concern relating to the conduct of health service employees;

    b. for ensuring that such complaints are effectively considered; and

    c. for ensuring that appropriate remedial action is taken in the particular case and generally; and

2   To make such recommendations as are appropriate for the revision and improvement of the procedures referred to above.

The Inquiry is asked:

1   To document and establish the nature of and chronology of the concerns or complaints raised concerning the practice and conduct of William Kerr and Michael Haslam during their time as consultant psychiatrists in the North Yorkshire mental health services (and in William Kerr's case establishing where possible details from his past practice before this).

2   To identify the procedures in place during the relevant period within the local health services to enable members of the public and other health service users to raise concerns or complaints concerning the actions and conduct of health service professionals in their professional capacity.

3   To investigate the actions that were taken for the purpose of –

    a. considering the concerns and complaints which were raised;

    b. providing remedial action in relation to them; and

c. ensuring that the opportunities for any similar future misconduct were removed.

4   To investigate cultural or organisational factors within the local health services that impeded or prevented appropriate investigation and action.

5   To assess and draw conclusions as to the effectiveness of the policies and procedures in place.

6   To make recommendations informed by this case as to improvements which should be made to the policies, and procedures that are now in place within the health service (taking into account the changes in procedures since the events in question).

7   To provide a full report on these matters to the Secretary of State for Health for publication by him.

Appendix 6
Inquiry Procedures

Introduction

1   This Procedures Paper sets out the procedures that the Inquiry proposes to adopt. It follows drafts circulated for comment in September 2002 and January 2004.

2   The Inquiry is an independent Inquiry that was set up under section 2 National Health Service Act 1977. Accordingly, its remit is to inquire into the National Health Service ("NHS") and the Department of Health in accordance with its Terms of Reference. The Inquiry intends:

a. to contribute, to the best of its abilities, to developing good and effective practice within the NHS today;

b. to conduct its investigation into how the NHS handled allegations into the performance and conduct of William Kerr and Michael Haslam in a fair manner. It will receive evidence upon good practice and procedures at the time of the events in question. It will endeavour to understand the reasons why actions were taken (or not taken). Any critical comments or findings will reflect its understanding of the practices at the time in question, and will seek to further the overall goal of fostering good practice in the NHS today;

c. to seek a thorough and full understanding of the nature and extent of these allegations and how they were handled. It will, however, balance these considerations against the practical constraints caused by the considerable lapse of time between many relevant events and now; and by the need to bring its inquiries to a close and to make recommendations promptly; and

d. to respect patient confidentiality as far as is possible consistent with the proper fulfilment of the Inquiry's Terms of Reference and to minimise distress to patients, to NHS staff (whenever employed) and other healthcare professionals, and any other witness to the Inquiry.

3   The Inquiry does not have jurisdiction under the 1977 Act to inquire into non-NHS bodies such as the General Medical Council ("GMC") or private hospitals although it is concerned with interfaces between the NHS/Department of Health and the GMC or private sector and any other relevant body

Document gathering

4   The Inquiry is asking that anyone who holds documents that are relevant to its work supply these documents to the Inquiry. Where necessary, originals will be copied, and the originals returned to their owners.

5   The Inquiry team is analysing the documents it holds in order to build up a detailed preliminary picture of events, and also to discover whether there are further documents it should see. It may therefore contact people to ask for further assistance.

List of Issues

6   The Inquiry is sending out a List of Issues with this draft Procedures Paper. That document aims to set out the issues that the Inquiry wishes to explore in its work. The List of Issues is a guide for the preparation of witness statements, and more generally in the Inquiry's work. Although it is recognised that the List of Issues is not cast in stone, it is hoped that it will not be substantially changed, and will form the basis for the Inquiry's investigation and report.

Witness statements

7   The Inquiry intends to gather much of its evidence in written form. It will therefore be inviting anyone who wishes to participate and has relevant evidence to give, who has not already done so, to supply a written statement, or make arrangements to have one prepared. This applies even if, for example, a patient has already written letters or made complaints and these have been provided to the Inquiry by another person or organisation as part of the document gathering exercise. Witnesses may supply copies of statements already prepared for other proceedings, which will be treated as their evidence to this Inquiry. If a statement has already been provided,

the Inquiry may ask for a further statement providing clarification or focusing on areas of particular concern.

8   The Inquiry Solicitor, Michael Fitzgerald, will send out requests for new, or further, written statements. Each request will indicate broadly the matters upon which the Inquiry seeks assistance; those persons (and/or their representatives) who are requested to provide such statements may also wish to look at the List of Issues and Opening Summary, when available (see below) for further guidance.

9   When it is able to do so, the Inquiry will also supply copies of documents that may assist a witness in preparing their evidence. However, before any such material is sent to a witness, he or she will be asked to sign a "Confidentiality Undertaking" (see below).

10   There are a number of ways in which a person may arrange for a statement to be provided to the Inquiry. The Inquiry Solicitor or one of his colleagues can take statements, if any witness would like the Inquiry's help in making a statement. If so, witnesses will have the opportunity to alter, add to or amend their draft statements before signing. Or the witness may wish to prepare his or her own statement. They can seek the help of a legal representative, or other representative (such as a trade union official) to do so. When he thinks it appropriate, the Inquiry Chairman, Nigel Pleming QC, will make recommendations to the Secretary of State for Health about meeting the costs of legal representation. The Chairman has already recommended legal representation at public expense for former patients, and that recommendation has been accepted by the Secretary of State.

Use of statements or other documents

11   The Inquiry is concerned with complaints that touch on very personal matters relating to the health and well being of patients in the care of William Kerr and Michael Haslam. A great number of the documents and written statements sent to the Inquiry are bound to be confidential in nature. The Inquiry will seek to respect that confidence, so far as it is able to do so.

12   But to allow the Inquiry to explore the material it receives, it must, first, be able to circulate it amongst the members of the Inquiry team, and the Inquiry Panel, for the purpose of analysis.

13   It must also be able to question other people about the witness statements and documents it has received where this is required for the purpose of seeking confirmation, clarification or rebuttal. For example, if a former patient's statement states that she made a complaint, the Inquiry needs to be able to ask those to whom she spoke, or those who had a broader responsibility for complaints-handling, about her evidence and to discover to whom the complaint was passed. The health service personnel who are asked about the complaint may also need access to the former patient's medical notes, to remind themselves of the patient and their contact with her at the time when the matter was raised. If allegations in respect of the conduct of William Kerr and Michael Haslam are raised that have not been the subject of criminal or other investigation, fairness may require that such allegations are put to them, so that the Inquiry may record their responses.

14   All these considerations may mean that a statement or a document or record needs to be referred to or disclosed to other persons (and/or to their representative), when this material forms the basis for questioning those persons or for seeking further information from them. The Inquiry will seek to ensure that the information disclosed is limited to that which the person who is being asked to comment reasonably requires to see in order to be able to respond and to assist the Inquiry.

15   Requests for such further information or comments would usually take place in writing, after the Inquiry has been sent a statement or document whose contents it needs to draw to the attention of other persons. The Inquiry might also need to ask a witness giving oral evidence to comment on other documents or witness statements during the oral hearings.

16   The Inquiry may also, subject to the "Confidentiality Undertaking" referred to below, wish to send copies of statements of witnesses or other documents to other participants (and/or their representatives) in the Inquiry, if it considers that their comments on the issues raised by such material would assist it in fulfilling its Terms of Reference. The material sent by the Inquiry may be redacted in order to preserve confidentiality.

17   The Inquiry would therefore wish all those who submit documents and witness statements to it to waive confidentiality to the limited extent necessary to allow such analysis, questioning and restricted further disclosure to other participants to be carried out. As set out below, when a statement or document is disclosed to another person, that person will be bound by a Confidentiality Undertaking in respect of the material circulated. It is also the case, of course, that if and in so far as disclosure is made by the Inquiry to persons under a more general duty of confidence – such as medical staff – that general duty will apply over and above the particular duty of confidence arising from the Confidentiality Undertaking.

18   When the Inquiry asks for a statement, it will also ask the witness whether he or she agrees to their evidence being circulated in the way outlined above. If witnesses have already sent statements or other documents, in confidence, to the Inquiry, the Inquiry will also write to them to ask for their permission to use their evidence in the way outlined above. If permission is not granted, and as a result another witness cannot be asked to comment on evidence which affects them, then fairness may dictate that the Inquiry is unable to rely upon the "non-disclosable" evidence supplied to it when making its findings. Alternatively, the Inquiry will consider making use of its powers under Section 84 National Health Service Act 1977 (see below, paragraph 28) or any other powers of disclosure it may possess, if it considers that the public interest justifies such a step.

19   When the Inquiry is in possession of material which relates to a patient, but which has not been supplied to it by the patient herself, it may need to seek the comments of others on that material. In doing so, it will seek when possible to reflect the views of the patient upon such disclosure (if known), but it will also have regard to the wider public interest in being able to carry out its investigation effectively. Again, disclosure will only be made subject to the provision by the intended recipient of a Confidentiality Undertaking as set out below.

20   In order to preserve as far as possible, patient confidentiality and to encourage all those who have relevant evidence to give to the Inquiry to do so, the Inquiry does not intend to circulate the documents and statements it has received generally to all those who are participating in the Inquiry and/or who are represented. It will, however, circulate statements and documents as set out in paragraphs 11 to 16 above, and provide an account of the information known to it in the Opening Summary (see below, paragraph 24).

Confidentiality

21   The Inquiry does not intend that any patient who gives evidence to it will be publicly identified by name; neither will they be identified by name to other participants except in circumstances such as those described in paragraph 13 above. In addition, any other witnesses who consider that their evidence (or part of it) or their names should be kept confidential and should not be disclosed to any persons who do not form part of the Inquiry team, are asked to raise their concerns with the Inquiry, as soon as possible. They are asked to outline the extent of the confidentiality they seek, and the reasons for so doing. The Panel will consider each such request on its merits, and indicate to the witness how any evidence submitted by him or by her would be treated by the Inquiry.

22   Further, all persons taking an active part in the Inquiry, including legal representatives, will be asked to sign a written "Confidentiality Undertaking". They will be asked not to disclose further any information or documents supplied to them by the Inquiry. At the end of the Inquiry, they will be asked to hand back any such documents, together with all copies, and to destroy any electronic copies made.

23   It should be recognised by all who give evidence to the Inquiry, or who take part in its investigation, that there is no legally enforceable restriction on what those present at any oral hearings held by the Inquiry can say publicly about what has occurred at those hearings. Thus, to the extent that oral evidence is given at those hearings, it may not be possible (at least for the Inquiry) to restrict the content of that evidence entering the public domain should those who were present choose to talk about it. The "Confidentiality Undertaking" does not apply to such oral evidence. It is, however, hoped by the Inquiry that the content of its private hearings will not be so disclosed. Such disclosure may undermine the Inquiry's investigation, and may cause the Inquiry to take all reasonable measures available to it, to protect the private nature of its investigation, and protect witnesses who appear to give evidence, and its procedures. However, restrictions on revealing documents or the content of documents supplied to participants and subject to the Confidentiality Undertaking would still remain effective. In order for confidentiality to be respected, it may be necessary for particular evidence to be given to the Inquiry in anonymised form or, in exceptional circumstances, given wholly in private. The Panel will approach such issues on a case-by-case basis.

Opening Summary

24 In order to allow those participating to prepare submissions and contributions to the Inquiry, the Inquiry proposes to circulate, in advance of the oral hearings, a document which will seek to summarise the evidential material before it and to identify:

a. issues which it appears to the Inquiry are not in dispute; and

b. issues which are more controversial and which are likely to be the subject of exploration in the course of oral evidence.

25 The Inquiry will call for written responses to and comments upon this Summary. This will enable it to add further relevant material, to correct any mistakes of fact, and to define or narrow the areas of dispute or which require further exploration. The document will only be provided to those who have signed the Inquiry's "Confidentiality Undertaking" in view (in particular) of its provisional status.

Attending the oral hearings

26 As stated above, the Inquiry is gathering much of its evidence in written form. As well as asking for written evidence, the Inquiry may also ask a person who has given a witness statement to give oral evidence at its hearings. It is for the Inquiry Panel to decide whom it wishes to hear from in oral hearings. The purpose of oral evidence will be:

a. the clarification of evidence that is insufficiently clear;

b. the testing of evidence where this is required; and

c. the exploration of disputes of fact or controversial issues, or matters of opinion.

27 The choice of oral witnesses may be linked to a selection of "exemplars" – that is, an illustrative range of cases, relating both to patients who raised concerns at or near the time of the incident which they say took place, and to those who did not feel able to make a complaint or raise any concerns until 1997 or afterwards.

28 The Secretary of State of Health has granted the Chairman powers under Section 84 National Health Service Act 1977. These powers enable the Chairman to issue a summons that would require a person to attend an Inquiry hearing, on a specified date, in order to give evidence, or to produce documents. The Inquiry will primarily seek to gather its evidence with the voluntary assistance and cooperation of all potential witnesses. However, it will consider making use of the powers conferred if it considers that significant evidence is being wrongly or unreasonably withheld.

29 The Inquiry will take evidence on oath. Again, the power to take evidence on oath has been conferred on it by Section 84 National Health Service Act 1977.

30 The hearings will take place privately. Attendees will include, first, those who are present in order to give oral evidence, and their legal representatives. Sympathetic consideration will be given to a request to allow a witness to be accompanied by a "supporter" such as a member of their family. Apart from this, attendance will be limited to:

a. the former patients (or, if deceased, their personal representatives) of William Kerr and Michael Haslam and their legal representatives. Arrangements may be made for carers of patients who are ill or infirm to be able to attend with the patient concerned;

b. the legal or other representatives of the local National Health Service bodies, including any legal representative of local general practitioners and the Local Medical Committee;

c. NHS healthcare staff, professionals, managers or other staff who worked with William Kerr and Michael Haslam, who may attend at the invitation or with the agreement of the Panel. Staff who are assisting the Inquiry by the provision of written or oral evidence to it will generally be welcomed, and encouraged, to attend; and

d. those other persons who request admittance, and who the Panel judge to have a sufficient and proper interest in the subject matter of the Inquiry and/or will be able to contribute to its understanding of the issues arising.

However, any permission to attend granted to members of the groups outlined above will be subject to the further considerations set out in paragraph 23 (evidence in private) and paragraph 31 (maintenance of an atmosphere that furthers the objectives of the

Inquiry). The Panel will consider any request received from William Kerr and Michael Haslam, and/or their legal representatives, to attend the oral hearings, under heading (d) above, and in the light of these further considerations.

31   The Panel will be concerned to maintain an environment in the hearings that enables open and frank discussion, that minimises distress to witnesses, to patients, health service staff and any other participants, and which helps to preserve patient confidentiality. The Inquiry will consider whether to exclude anyone whose presence could materially damage these objectives, or whose exclusion is required to further the objectives of the Inquiry. Further, the Inquiry may need to restrict the number of those who may attend the oral hearings of the Inquiry on any given day, for practical reasons relating to the size of its hearing chamber etc.

32   In order to verify individual entitlement to attend the oral hearings, those who wish to attend will be required to apply to the Inquiry in advance for a pass. The letter of application should explain the reason why it is said that the applicant is eligible to attend the hearings. If granted, the pass will be available for collection from the main reception of the Hilton Hotel, York on the morning of the hearing to be attended. There will be a requirement to provide photographic evidence of identity, such as a passport or drivers licence, before collecting a pass. During the course of the oral hearings, the application for a pass should be made to the Inquiry.

33   A list of witnesses who are intended to give oral evidence will be circulated in advance, again on a confidential basis, to legal representatives. Any request for information about the hearings by those who are not legally represented will be considered on a case-by-case basis.

Notice of matters requiring explanation

34   Before any witness gives oral evidence, the Inquiry will indicate, normally by letter, the issues or topics about which it wishes to hear further.

35   Further, if there are any matters that require explanation, because the Inquiry is concerned about the way in which events unfolded or matters were handled, the letter will indicate those areas of concern.

36   The main purpose of these letters is to assist witnesses giving oral evidence so that they know what topics will be addressed in questioning. But it is also to enable those who face possible criticism to understand the areas of concern that may be raised at the hearing. They should not be taken to indicate that the Inquiry has pre-judged matters, but are written to give all witnesses a full opportunity to consider all matters to be dealt with in oral evidence. As a result, their contents will not be disclosed to other participants. As well as giving oral evidence, witnesses may file a further statement in response, if they so choose. If so, they should aim to do so as far as possible before the date of their oral evidence, and no later than seven days before it.

37   If new matters requiring an explanation from any other witness or other participant are raised during the course of oral hearings (in particular, after a person has already given oral evidence), the Inquiry will ensure that he or she is given an opportunity to respond to the new matters. Such an opportunity may be afforded by inviting the witness to comment in writing or (at the Panel's discretion) by asking them to give further oral evidence.

Opening submissions

38   At the start of the oral hearings, the Panel may hear opening submissions by Counsel to the Inquiry that introduce the issues before the Inquiry. With the permission of the Panel, participants or their legal representatives may then also make an opening submission. These submissions should be designed to help the Panel in their task, by informing it of matters that the participants wish to see addressed. They are not an opportunity to give evidence, which will be heard later. Submissions will be time-limited, so as to enable all participants to have an equal voice in the time available.

Questions at the hearings

39   Counsel to the Inquiry will ask the witnesses questions. Participants or their legal representatives may submit written questions to Counsel or the Solicitor to the Inquiry not later than 48 hours in advance of the relevant witness giving oral evidence. Counsel will seek to ensure that the questions or issues suggested will, if relevant, be put to the witness (subject to any time constraints for hearing evidence).

40   The witness' own legal representative may ask questions of that witness at the close of the questions from Counsel to the Inquiry and from the Panel, if he or she wishes to do so, in order to clarify any evidence given during the course of the hearing. It is not envisaged that this process should take more than 15 minutes, and the Chairman may intervene to prevent further, lengthier questioning.

41   Questions put to witnesses must be related solely to matters within the Inquiry's Terms of Reference.

Circulation of transcripts of the hearing

42   The Inquiry intends to circulate copies of the transcript of the evidence taken in the oral hearings to legal representatives, strictly on condition that the transcripts are used solely for the purpose of the Inquiry (including for the purpose of seeking instructions on any aspect of the evidence given).

Closing submissions

43   Shortly after the Panel has finished hearing oral evidence from witnesses, participants in the Inquiry or, if represented, their legal representatives, may submit written submissions about the evidence that has been heard, and the inferences that may be drawn from it, to the Panel. The Inquiry is also likely to schedule a further one-day hearing after receipt of these submissions, at which each participant will have the opportunity of making oral concluding submissions to the Panel. Again, submissions will be time-limited, so as to ensure that fair use is made of the time available.

Publication

44   The Inquiry will write a report for publication in full by the Secretary of State for Health. Patient names and case histories will remain anonymous in that report, although health and social care professionals, including managers and other staff, may be named (subject to any ruling that the Panel has made on the position of any individual, see paragraph 21 above). Sometimes, in order to explain its findings, evidence will need to be referred to or extracts quoted: but the Inquiry will make every effort to ensure that this is done in such a way as not to identify any individual patient.

45   At present, the Inquiry does not anticipate a need to publish the statements submitted to the Inquiry. If, for some reason, it takes the view that it would be helpful for a particular statement to be made public, it will approach the maker of the statement for permission.

Appendix 7
List of Issues

National policy background

1   What were the relevant national policies and guidance relating to complaints-handling within the NHS from 1961 to 1988, when William Kerr or Michael Haslam were employed as psychiatrists within the NHS and thereafter up to 1997?

2   What amendments or special provisions, if any, was it recommended should be made to such policies and procedures when handling complaints or allegations made by patients who were or had been in receipt of psychiatric services?

3   What modifications have been made to those policies or guidance since 1997?

Local policy background

4   What were the relevant local policies, guidance or protocols in place relating to complaints-handling, from 1965–1988, within each of the Yorkshire NHS organisations in which William Kerr and Michael Haslam were employed as consultant psychiatrists and thereafter up to 1997?

5   What modifications have been made to those policies, guidance or protocols since 1997?

Linkages

6   What were, and are, the linkages between the national and local complaints-handling systems, and other relevant processes, including:

a. disciplinary procedures relating to healthcare professionals;

b. any systems for monitoring performance or the quality of clinical care;

c. user information or patient advocacy services?

7   What impact does each of these linkages have upon the effectiveness of the complaints-handling process and procedures?

Appointments

8   To what positions within the NHS were William Kerr and Michael Haslam appointed, from 1961–1988?

9   Were appropriate and adequate procedures adopted when each of these appointments was made?

10   To what positions were William Kerr and Michael Haslam appointed, if any, after 1988?

11   What role, if any, was played by the NHS (whether at national or local level) in relation to such appointments made after 1988?

12   Were appropriate and adequate procedures adopted in relation to any NHS involvement in any such appointments after 1988?

Complaints and concerns voiced between 1961 and 1997 (date of police request for evidence)

13   What allegations about the conduct of William Kerr and Michael Haslam were made to, or passed to:

a. health or social care professionals, or other staff, working for local National Health services; or

b. general practitioners; or

c. other health or social care professionals?

14   In respect of each allegation:

a. when was it made;

b. who made it;

c. what was the nature of the allegation made;

d. to whom was the allegation made;

e. what were the expectations of the person making the allegation: did he or she wish the matter to be treated as a complaint, and if not, what action did he or she wish to be taken;

f. what was the immediate response of the recipient of the allegation to the person who had made it?

15   In respect of each allegation, what action was taken:

a. to record the allegation;

b. to pass it to the appropriate authorities;

c. to investigate it and to establish its credibility;

d. to provide any appropriate support or assistance to the person making it;

e. to inform the person raising the concern or complaint of the action that would be taken, and to see whether this met their expectations?

16   What action was taken to deal with the substance of the allegation?

17   Were any lessons learnt from the complaint, or from the experience of investigating it?

18   What action was taken to ensure that the likelihood of similar complaints being made, in the future, was reduced?

Independent Review of allegations against Michael Haslam (Manzoor Inquiry 1997/98)

19   What led to the setting up of an Independent Review of allegations against Michael Haslam and how was it constituted?

20   What were the findings and recommendations of the Independent Review and what steps were taken to act upon them thereafter?

21   Did the Review, when considered in the light of any actions taken in response to its work, represent an appropriate and/or effective response to the allegations against Michael Haslam?

Concerns and subsequent complaints

22   Were there patients who had concerns about the professional conduct of William Kerr or Michael Haslam but who did not voice their concerns to any health or social care professionals or other responsible individuals, until the police request for evidence in 1997, or after that date?

If so:

23   Why did they not raise their concerns?

24   Were there barriers to raising concerns or complaints about healthcare services received, during the period when William Kerr and Michael Haslam were in professional practice, and if so, what were they?

25   Were there health or social care professionals, or other NHS staff, who formed the view that the conduct or practices of either William Kerr or Michael Haslam raised issues of concern, but who did not voice their concerns?

26   If so, why did they not raise these concerns?

Effectiveness

27   How effective were the policies and practices described under 1–7, and 16, at investigating the allegations, and/or resolving the complaints, described under items 10–17?

28   How effective were the policies and procedures described under 1–7, at capturing any of the concerns identified under items 19–23?

29   How effective were the policies and practices described under 1–7, and 16, at learning lessons from the information received, and at taking action to reduce the likelihood of similar future complaints?

30   Were there barriers to effective complaints handling, and if so, what were they?

Current practice

31   To what extent would the policies and procedures presently in force address or remedy any inadequacies found under 24–30?

32   If similar concerns or complaints were raised today, is it likely that they would be handled in a more or less effective manner?

33   How do current systems of clinical governance seek to learn from the experience of users of NHS healthcare services, and/or avoid the need for formal complaints to be made?

34   What examples of good practice have been identified in the course of the Inquiry, not already incorporated into present policies or practice, from which useful lessons may be learned?

Vulnerable patients

35   Are there modifications to present policies, procedures and practice on complaints handling that should be made to:

   a. safeguard the legitimate interests and needs of patients who are or have been in receipt of psychiatric services, or of any other group of vulnerable patients;

   b. safeguard the legitimate interests of professionals or other staff working with vulnerable patients; and

   c. ensure that the process of handling a complaint does not damage the therapeutic needs of a patient; or that any conflicts between treatment needs and effective complaints handling are kept to a minimum?

Recommendations

36   What recommendations can the Panel make that would strengthen or improve the complaints handling policies and procedures now in force within the NHS, in the light of its findings in these cases?

37   What recommendations can the Panel make that would strengthen or improve the ability of the NHS to learn effectively from the experience of users of NHS healthcare services?

Appendix 8
Witnesses and their legal representatives

Witness	Representatives
Certain former patients of William Kerr and Michael Haslam	Michael Mylonas, instructed by Rachelle Mahapatra of Irwin Mitchell, Solicitors
North & East Yorkshire and Northern Lincolnshire Strategic Health Authority	Kate Thirlwall QC, instructed by Nick Parsons and Louise Carney of Browne Jacobson, Solicitors
Selby & York Primary Care Trust	
Craven, Harrogate & Rural District Primary Care Trust	
Harrogate Healthcare NHS Trust	
York Hospitals NHS Trust	
Dr W Turner	Steven Ford, instructed by Laura Roper of Browne Jacobson, Solicitors
Mr R Wilk	Steven Ford, instructed by Amelia Wallington of Browne Jacobson, Solicitors
Dr W J Green and Professor R A Haward	Emma Michaels of the Medical Protection Society
Drs G A Crouch and A Day, General Practitioners	Dr I Barclay of the Medical Protection Society
Dr J Iddon, General Practitioner	Catherine Longstaff of the Medical Protection Society
Dr D Jeary, General Practitioner	Andrew Oates of the Medical Protection Society
Drs J Moroney and M Plowman, General Practitioners	Dr D J Watson of the Medical Protection Society
Drs C J Bennett, G T Foggitt*, J Henderson and D M Whitcher*, General Practitioners	Adrienne D'Arcy of Hempsons, Solicitors
Drs I G C Brown, R J Givans, M Harrison, P A Jones, N Moran, L Moss, R J Nixon, P J Reed, and M Smith, General Practitioners	Philip Gaisford, instructed by Adrienne D'Arcy of Hempsons, Solicitors
Drs J Donald, A M Livingstone and P R Livingstone, General Practitioners	Richard Partridge, instructed by Adrienne D'Arcy of Hempsons, Solicitors
Dr Alexander Osmond, General Practitioner	Peter Fitzpatrick of Howrey Simon Arnold & White, Solicitors
Dr Galal Badrawy*	Peter Fitzpatrick of Howrey Simon Arnold & White, Solicitors

Witnesses	Representatives
Linda Bigwood	Alison Callcott of Scott-Moncrieff, Harbour & Sinclair, Solicitors
Dr Beryl Bromham	Chris Horsefield and Diane Hallatt of Beachcroft Wansbroughs, Solicitors
General Medical Council	Tom Rider of Field Fisher Waterhouse, Solicitors
Michael Haslam	Philip Chapman of Mitchells, Solicitors

* Denotes a witness who provided a witness statement but was not called to give oral evidence.

Appendix 9
Lay witnesses

The Inquiry received written evidence from the following witnesses in the form of Inquiry Statements. In addition, those witnesses designated "O" also gave oral evidence to the Inquiry.

In addition to the witnesses identified below, we received written evidence from or relating to 79 former patients of William Kerr and 17 former patients of Michael Haslam. Of the total, 24 patients gave oral evidence to the Inquiry.

Witness	Position	O
Abrines, Dr Malcolm J	General Practitioner, Danes Dyke Surgery, Scarborough (1992–present)	
Adams, Dr Robert	Consultant Psychiatrist (1990–present)	
Anderson, Mrs Marion R	Clinical Psychologist, Bootham Park Hospital (1967–84) and Harrogate Hospital (1984–95)	O
Badrawy, Dr Galal A	Senior House Officer/Registrar, Naburn and Bootham Park Hospitals (1974–80)	
Baker, Professor Mark R	Medical Director, NYHA (1994–2001)	
Bennett, Dr Christopher J	General Practitioner, North House Surgery (1977–present)	O
Berry, Mr Peter	Administrator, Clifton Hospital (1948–94)	
Beverton, Mr Terry	Assistant Director in Nursing, YHA (1982/3–86)	O
Bigwood, Ms Linda	Deputy Ward Sister, Clifton Hospital (1982–84)	O
Boyes (formerly Armitage), Ms Celia	Continuing Education Officer, Clifton, Naburn and Bootham Park Hospitals (1983–85)	
Boyle, Dr Roger	Consultant Physician and Cardiologist, York District Hospital (1983–2000)	
Bradley, Mr John G	Consultant Orthopaedic and Trauma Surgeon, Scarborough and North East Yorkshire NHS Trust (1977–date); member and Chair of the "Three Wise Men" committee (1986–96)	
Bradley, Ms Pamela B	Chief Nursing Officer and Director of Acute Services, Harrogate Health Authority (1987–92)	

Witness	Position	O
Bromham, Dr Beryl M	Part-time GP assistant, Purdysburn Hospital, Belfast (1960–65); Registrar/Medical Assistant (1965–73) and Consultant Psychiatrist (1973–88), Clifton Hospital	O
Brooks, Mr Stephen [Steve] J	Community Psychiatric Nurse, YHA (1985–present)	O
Brown, Dr Ian G C	General Practitioner and Senior Partner, North House Surgery (1963–97)	O
Brown, Ms Pauline	Ward Sister, Clifton Hospital (1973–90)	O
Bulmer, Ms Elizabeth A	Community Psychiatric Nurse, Harrogate Health Authority (1985–86); Clinical Nurse Specialist, Harrogate Healthcare Trust (1986–99)	
Busby (nee Osborn), Mrs Jillian M	Night Sister/Nursing Officer/Senior Nursing Officer, Clifton Hospital (1971–90)	
Cattell, Mr Andrew [Andy]	Trainee Nurse, Clifton Hospital (1982–85)	O
Chapman, Hugh	Legal Adviser, YRHA	O
Clarkson, Dr Alan D	Consultant Psychiatrist, Scalebor Park Hospital (1971–96); Chairman of Yorkshire Psychiatric Sub-Committee (1993–96)	O
Coates, Mrs Hanora	Anaesthetic/Recovery Nurse, Norman House, Harrogate District Hospital (January–June 1986)	
Conyers, Ms Jane B	Occupational Therapist, Community Mental Health Team, Harrogate Healthcare Trust (1984–2002)	
Cook, Mr Stephen W	Community Psychiatric Nurse, Harrogate area (1982–86)	O
Cotterill (nee Jones), Mrs Sarah	Nurse, 11 Queen's Road (private clinic), Harrogate (1977–98/99)	
Cottingham, Mr Brian J	Nursing Officer, Acute Admissions Wards, Clifton and Bootham Park Hospitals (1983/4–94)	
Cresswell, Dr Patricia [Tricia] A	Consultant in Public Health Medicine, NHS Executive Northern & Yorkshire (1996–98)	O
Crouch, Dr George A [Alan]	General Practitioner and Senior Partner, Kings Road Surgery, Harrogate (1973–present)	O
Currie, Dr Simon	Consultant Neurologist, outpatient clinics at Bootham Park and Naburn Hospitals (1973–81) and Harrogate District Hospital (1980–94)	
Day, Dr Albert T	General Practitioner, Park Parade Surgery, Harrogate (1967–87)	O
Deacon, Dr Vivien	Consultant Psychiatrist, Harrogate District Hospital/Clifton Hospital (1986–98)	
Donald, Dr Jack	General Practitioner, The Lambert Medical Centre, Thirsk (1982–present)	O
Donaldson, Professor Sir Liam	Regional Director and Director of Public Health of the NHS Executive Northern & Yorkshire (1996–98); Chief Medical Officer (1998–present)	O

Witness	Position	O
Duff, Ms Carmel M	Trainee Psychiatric Nurse, Clifton Hospital and Bootham Park Hospital (1987–89); Staff Nurse; Norman House, Harrogate (1989–90); Sister, Knaresborough Hospital (1990–91); Community Psychiatric Nurse, Harrogate area (1992–2001)	O
English, Mr Thomas G	Psychiatric Nurse, Clifton Hospital (1977–79)	O
Etchells, Mr Derek	Community Psychiatric Nurse, Harrogate Health Authority (1981–82)	
Exton (formerly Spencer), Ms Kathleen M	Secretary to William Kerr, Clifton Hospital (1982–88)	
Fisher, Mr Barrie	Chief Executive, NYHA (1994–2002)	
Fitzharris, Ms Lynn	Various nursing positions, Clifton Hospital and York District Hospital (1976–78 and 1980)	
Foggitt, Dr Graham T	General Practitioner, Leeds Road Surgery, Harrogate (1966–96)	O
Foster, Mr David	Hospital Administrator, Harrogate Hospitals Unit (1983–88)	
Gallacher, Mrs Margaret	Nursing Assistant, East Parade, Harrogate (1988–94) and Briary Hospital, Harrogate (1998–2001)	
Givans, Dr Robert J [John]	General Practitioner, Kings Road Surgery, Harrogate (1969–92); Medical Secretary, North Yorkshire LMC (1984–present)	O
Greaves, Mr Gerry	Staff Nurse/Charge Nurse/Ward Manager, Clifton and Bootham Park Hospitals (1975–93)	
Green, Dr William J	Consultant in Public Health Medicine, YRHA (1987–95)	O
Hanslip, Dr Judith M	Senior House Officer for Michael Haslam (Feb–July 1987)	
Harrison, Dr Martyn T	General Practitioner, Picks Lane Surgery, Thirsk (1977–90)	O
Haslam, Michael	Consultant in Psychological Medicine, Doncaster Royal Infirmary (1967–70); Consultant Psychiatrist to the York and Harrogate Hospitals, based at Clifton Hospital (1970–89)	O
Haward, Ms Patricia	Staff Nurse/Senior Staff Nurse, Norman House and Hawthorn Day Unit, Harrogate District Hospital (1985–2003)	
Haward, Professor Robert A	Regional Medical Officer, YRHA (1986–94)	O
Healey, Ms Valerie	Occupational Therapy Worker/Staff Nurse, Whixley Hospital, Harrogate (1979–89)	
Hebblethwaite (nee Metcalf), Mrs Delia H	Administrator/Secretary, Clifton and Bootham Park Hospitals (1979–2000)	
Henderson, Dr John	General Practitioner, East Parade Surgery, Harrogate (1978–present)	O
Holbrey, Ms Judith M	Director of Corporate Development and Nursing, Harrogate Healthcare NHS Trust (1997–2000)	
Holroyd, Mr William A H [Arthur]	District Administrator, York Health District (1974–82); Regional Administrator, YRHA (1982–85)	O

Witness	Position	O
Hudson, Ms Sandra M	Patient Affairs Officer/Voluntary Services Coordinator/Senior Administrator, Clifton Hospital (1974–87); Senior Administrator, Bootham Park Hospital (1987–90)	
Iddon, Dr Jonathan N	General Practitioner, Knaresborough Road Health Centre, Harrogate (1974–present)	O
Ingham, Stuart	District Administrator, YHA (1982–85); District General Manager, YHA (1985–87)	O
Jeary, Dr Derek	General Practitioner, North House Surgery, Ripon (1996–2003)	O
Johnson, Mrs Susan	Director of Nursing (1989–91); Hospital Director (1992–97), Harrogate Clinic	
Johnston, Ms Sarah	Community Psychiatric Nurse, Harrogate Healthcare NHS Trust (1989–99); Team Manager, Knaresborough Community Health Team (1999–2001)	
Jones, Ms Margaret [Meg]	Head of Social Work, Clifton Hospital (1975–87)	O
Jones, Dr Martin A	General Practitioner, Church Lane Surgery, Boroughbridge (1993–present)	
Jones, Ms Penelope	Assistant Director of Joint Planning (with Mental Health), NYHA (1995–99/2000)	
Jones, Dr Phyllis A	General Practitioner, Leeds Road Surgery, Harrogate (1971–present)	O
Justice, Ms Janet	Care Assistant, Bootham Park Hospital (early 1970s) and Whixley Hospital (1976–79)	
Keenleside, Dr Clare L	General Practitioner, Beech House Surgery, Knaresborough (1994–present)	
Kell, Ms Hyla	Community Psychiatric Nurse, Harrogate/Knaresborough (1986–95)	
Kelly, Mr Martin	Student Nurse/Staff Nurse/Charge Nurse/Nursing Officer, Clifton Hospital (1969–92)	
Kennedy, Dr Peter F	Consultant Psychiatrist, Bootham Park and Naburn Hospitals (1980–86); Unit General Manager for Mental Health (1986–88), District General Manager (1988–92), YHA; Chief Executive, York Health Services NHS Trust (1992–99)	O
Kerr, Dr Arthur	Consultant Psychiatrist, Belfast (1960s)	
Knight, Mr Steven H	Community Psychiatric Nurse, Northallerton Health Authority (1979–87); Clinical Nurse Specialist, Harrogate Healthcare NHS Trust/ Craven, Harrogate & Rural District PCT (1987–present)	
Langford, Ms Jane A	Staff Nurse/Deputy Sister, Clifton and Naburn Hospitals (1979–85); Sister, Bootham Park Hospital (1985–90)	
Larkin, Dr Hugh	Consultant Physician, Harrogate District Hospital (1983–present)	O
Levine, Ms Julie	Private Counsellor (1979–present)	

Witness	Position	O
Lister, Mr Arthur	Group Secretary, York 'A' Hospital Management Committee (1969–74); District Administrator, Harrogate Health District (1974–82)	
Lister, Mr Peter A	Staff Nurse/Deputy Charge Nurse/Ward Manager, Clifton Hospital (1982–88), Community Psychiatric Nurse (1989–92)	
Livingstone, Dr Angus M	General Practitioner, Park Street Surgery, Ripon (1977–present)	O
Livingstone, Dr Patricia R [Rosemary]	General Practitioner, Park Street Surgery, Ripon (1979–present)	O
Logan, Ms Elizabeth M	Chief Nursing Officer, York 'A' Hospital Management Committee (1969–74); Area Nursing Officer, NYHA (1974–82)	
Loizou (nee Cooke), Dr Marilyn	Consultant Psychiatrist, Harrogate Healthcare NHS Trust (1988–present)	O
Lucas, Ms Grace J I [Jane]	Ward Sister (1981–85), Community Psychiatric Nurse (1985–present), Harrogate Health District	
Luxton, Ms Deirdre	Secretary to Michael Haslam, Clifton Hospital (1977–89)	
Mackley, Mr John S	Various nursing posts: Clifton Hospital, York District Hospital, Naburn Hospital, Scotton Banks Hospital, Knaresborough (1977–87); Unit Manager, Knaresborough Hospital (1987–88); Community Psychiatric Nurse, Harrogate (1988–91)	
Mackley (nee Ward), Mrs Veronica M	Various nursing posts: Clifton Hospital (1976, 1980–86), York District Hospital (1978–80) and Bootham Park Hospital (1987–90)	O
Marks, Mr Raymond	Consultant in Anaesthetics, YHA (1971–99) and elected member (1977–93) and Chairman (1982–93) of the "Three Wise Men" (later Special Professional Panel)	
Marshall, Dr Patricia R	General Practitioner, Birstwith area (1979–99)	
Martin (nee Bryden), Mrs Janet M	Clinical Psychologist, Clifton Hospital (1970–73) and Scarborough, Whitby and Ryedale PCT (1973–present)	
Mathewson, Dr James S Y	General Practitioner, Lisburn, Belfast (1954–90)	
Mawson, Mrs Elaine	Various medical record, administrative and management positions, currently General Manager, Harrogate District Hospital (1967–present)	
Maxwell, Mr James	Staff Nurse, Naburn Hospital (1978–81)	O
McDowall, Dr Morag S	General Practitioner, North House Surgery, Ripon (1993–present)	
McFetridge, Dr Mark	Clinical Psychologist, Scarborough & North East Yorkshire NHS Trust (1992–96)	O
McIntosh, Dr Alexander W	District Community Physician, North Yorkshire Area Health Authority (1974–82); District Medical Officer, YHA (1982–88)	O
McKechnie, Mr Ian	Community Psychiatric Nurse, Knaresborough/Harrogate (1985–87)	
Metcalfe (nee Pinder), Mrs Janet I	Secretary to William Kerr (1987–88)	

Witness	Position	O
Milner, Mr John C	Consultant in Orthopaedic and Traumatic Surgery, Harrogate Healthcare Trust (1972–2000)	
Monk-Steel, Mr John	Charge Nurse, Clifton Hospital (1976–79); Nursing Officer, Clifton Hospital (1979–84)	O
Moore (née Kid), Mrs Joyce F	Student Nurse (1974–77), Staff Nurse (1977–80), Ward Sister (1980–84), Clifton Hospital; Community Psychiatric Nurse, Craven, Harrogate & Rural District PCT (1984–present)	
Moore, Dr Michael D	General Practitioner (1965–96)	
Moore, Dr Samuel R W	Area Medical Officer, NYAHA (1974–82)	
Moore, Dr Sheila M	General Practitioner, Station Parade Surgery, Harrogate (1961–88)	
Moran, Dr Neil	General Practitioner and Senior Partner, Strensall Medical Practice, York (1975–present)	O
Morgan (previously Davey), Ms Lynne	Registered Mental Nurse, Bootham Park, Naburn and Clifton Hospitals (1969–76)	
Moroney, Dr John D	General Practitioner, Minster Health, York (1986–present)	O
Morris, Dr Marion	Registrar, Clifton Hospital (dates unknown)	
Morris, Dr Michael D	Clinical Assistant, Clifton Hospital (c.1960–86)	
Mortimer, Professor Ann M	Senior House Officer, training for consultancy in psychiatry, Clifton Hospital (1982–84)	O
Moss, Dr Leonard H	General Practitioner, King Road Surgery (1946–80)	O
Mountain, Ms Linda N	Student Nurse, Clifton Hospital (1972–75)	
Myers, Dr Kenneth W	General Practitioner, Haxby Group Practice, York (1972–present)	
Nicholson, Dr Roger	Consultant Psychiatrist, Cross Lane Hospital (1983–present), Clifton Hospital	
Nightingale, Mr Stephen	General Administrator (Operational Services), Harrogate Health Authority (1974–83)	
Nixon, Dr Ronald J	General Practitioner and Principal, Church Lane Surgery, York (1974–present)	O
O'Donahue, Ms Rachel	Secretary, Kings Road Surgery, Harrogate (1969–89)	
Osmond, Dr Alexander	General Practitioner, Church Lane Surgery, York (1968–93)	O
Owens, Mr Nicholas J	Deputy Charge Nurse, Clifton Hospital (1987–89) and Abdale House, Harrogate (1989–90/1); Community Psychiatric Nurse, Harrogate Health Authority (1990/91–present)	
Parkin, Mr Jonathan	Nurse, Harrogate Hospital (1975–84), variety of nursing management posts, Harrogate Hospital (1984–present)	

Witness	Position	O
Parsons, Mr Keith A	Unit Administrator, Clifton Hospital, and Sector Administrator for the York Psychiatric Sector (1978–84)	O
Pears, Ms Diana	Nurse, Clifton Hospital (1967–73); Sister, Scarborough (1973–77/8); Community Psychiatric Nurse, Harrogate (1977/78–97)	
Peermahomed, Dr Rafic	Locum Senior House Officer, Clifton Hospital (1968–69); Registrar in Psychiatry, Clifton Hospital (1969–70)	
Perry, Mr Andrew	Staff Nurse, Clifton Hospital (1974–94)	
Pheby, Dr Derek F H	Clinical Assistant, Harrogate District Hospital (1977–78)	O
Plowman, Dr Margaret A [Ann]	General Practitioner, Eastgate Surgery, Knaresborough (1973–2000)	O
Randal, Ms Lesley F	Trainee Nurse, YHA (1984–86), Staff Nurse (1986–92)	
Randall, Mr Kenneth	Community Psychiatric Nurse, Knaresborough Hospital/ Clifton Hospital then East Parade, Harrogate (1984–92)	
Rann, Mr Michael D	Psychiatric Nurse, Norman House Day Hospital (1985–87) and Harrogate Clinic, Harrogate (1988–99)	
Reed (nee Heatley), Dr Pamela J [Jean]	General Practitioner, East Parade Surgery, Harrogate (1967–92)	O
Reid, Ms Amanda M	Clinical Psychologist, Craven & Harrogate PCT (1991–present)	
Reid, Mr Chris S	Unit Administrator/Planning & Operational Services Manager/ General Manager, Clifton, Bootham Park and Naburn Hospitals (1984–97)	
Reilly, Dr Stephen P	Consultant Psychiatrist, Bootham Park Hospital (1987–present)	
Reiss, Dr Stefan H	Locum in Psychiatry, Clifton Hospital (1978–79)	
Richardson, Dr Gregory J R	Psychiatric Registrar, Naburn and Bootham (1975–77); Senior Registrar then Consultant Psychiatrist (1980–present)	O
Rix, Mr Keith J B	Consultant Psychiatrist/Consultant Forensic Psychiatrist, High Royds Hospital, Ilkley (1994–2000)	
Rugg, Dr Anthony J [Tony]	Consultant Psychiatrist, Clifton Hospital (1982–92) and Harrogate District Hospital (1992–present)	O
Ryan, Dr Catherine M D	Consultant Psychiatrist, Briary Unit, Harrogate (1992–present)	
Saunders, Mr Graham	District Administrator, Harrogate Health Authority (HHA) (1982–85); District Manager, HHA (1985–92); Chief Executive, Harrogate Healthcare NHS Trust (1992–2001)	O
Scatchard, Dr Michael A	General Practitioner, Leeds Road Practice, Harrogate (1971–present)	
Scott, Dr Alan K	General Practitioner, Gillygate Surgery, York (1965–2000)	
Scott, Mr Finlay	Chief Executive, General Medical Council (1994–present)	O
Seagrave, Mr Patrick	Community Psychiatric Nurse, Selby and York PCT (1995–present)	
Shewan, Mr Mike	Senior Nurse, Bootham Park, Naburn and Clifton Hospitals (1984–92)	

Witness	Position	O
Shields, Mr Colin	Community Psychiatric Nurse, Knaresborough (1981–83) and Harrogate (1983–86)	
Silver, Ms Deborah A	Student Nurse, Harrogate District Hospital	
Simmons, Dr Adrian V	Consultant Physician, Chapel Allerton Hospital (1980–99)	
Simpson, Dr Christopher J	Consultant Psychiatrist, Northallerton NHS Trust (1987–present)	O
Sims, Professor Andrew	Consultant Psychiatrist, St James's University Hospital, Leeds (1979–2000)	
Sippert, Dr Alan	Regional Psychiatrist/Assistant Senior Medical Officer, Leeds Regional Hospital Board (1963–69)	
Skinner, Mr Adrian E G	Senior Psychologist, Bootham Park Hospital (1977–85); Principal Psychologist/Consultant Psychologist/Director of Clinical Psychology, HHA (1985–present)	
Smith, Mr Colin J	Trainee Registered Mental Nurse, YHA (1976–79); Staff Nurse, YHA (1979–85); Community Psychiatric Nurse, Harrogate District Health Authority (1985–89)	O
Smith, Dr Margaret M	General Practitioner, Church Avenue Surgery, Harrogate (1969–91)	O
Smith, Dr Peter S	General Practitioner, Haxby Group Practice, York (1981–present)	
Snape, Dr Catherine J	General Practitioner, North House Surgery, Ripon (1987–98)	
Snider, Mr Kenneth A	Consultant in Public Health, NHS Executive Regional Office, Northern & Yorkshire (1997–2001)	
Spark, Mrs Vikki	Planning and Operational Services Manager, Monkgate Health Centre (1985–87); Unit General Manager, Priority Services, Harrogate Healthcare Trust (1987/88–92)	
Staines, Dr Jillian A	Trainee in General Practice, Haxby & Wigginton Health Centre, York (1982–83 and 1984–85); Senior House Officer, Clifton Hospital (February–July 1984)	
Sutton-Haigh, Ms Nicola A	Senior Staff Nurse, Abdale House, Harrogate (1991–2000)	
Sweeney, Dr Richard C	General Practitioner, Kings Road Surgery, Harrogate (1984–present)	
Thornton, Dr Timothy J	General Practitioner, Knaresborough Road Health Centre, Harrogate (1981–present)	
Timperley, Dr Malcolm R	Consultant Psychiatrist, Tees & North East Yorkshire NHS Trust (1989–present)	O
Tiplady, Mrs Anne	Senior Nursing Officer, Clifton Hospital (1980–85)	O
Townsend, Mr Graham P	Community Psychiatric Nurse, Harrogate Healthcare NHS Trust (1985–present)	
Tragheim, Ms Jennifer R	Divisional Nursing Officer, Northallerton (pre–86); Nursing Director/Chief Nursing Officer, Harrogate District (1986–89)	

Witness	Position	O
Turnbull, Ms Jean	Clinical Assistant, psychiatric clinic, Harrogate District Hospital (1979–92)	
Turner, Dr William	Regional Medical Officer, YRHA (1976–86)	O
Village, Dr Anne L	Senior House Officer, Clifton Hospital (November 1980–April 1981)	
Visick, Dr Robert H	General Practitioner, Fulford Park Surgery, York (1968–99)	
Voce, Ms Elizabeth	Sister (1981–84) and Senior Sister (1984–present), Ripon Community Hospital	
Wade, Dr John B [Barry]	General Practitioner, Eastgate Surgery, Knaresborough and Knaresborough Road Health Centre, Harrogate (1962–95)	O
Ward, Dr Jean P	Anaesthetist, Harrogate Hospital, Scotton Band and Ripon District Hospital and clinics (early 1960s–1989)	
Wearing, Mrs Barbara	Ward Sister, Clifton Hospital (1971–95)	O
Welsh, Mr Tom	Senior Nurse Manager, Harrogate Health District/Harrogate Health Authority (1981–2001)	
Whitcher, Dr David M	General Practitioner, The Tollerton Surgery, York (1980–present)	
Whitcher, Mr Michael	Staff Nurse, Bootham Park and Naburn Hospitals (1975–77); Deputy Charge Nurse, Knaresborough (1977–78); Community Psychiatric Nurse, Harrogate Health Authority (1978–83)	
Wilk, Mr Raymond	Director of Nursing (Mental Health), YHA (1982–86)	O
Wintersgill, Dr William	Specialist in Community Medicine, YDHA (1983–88)	O
Wood, Mr George	Deputy Chief Executive, York Hospitals NHS Trust (and equivalent positions) (1983–present)	
Woodcock (nee Shaw), Mrs Susan E	Clerk to the Psychiatric Surgeries, Harrogate District Hospital (1969–73)	
Woolfson, Mr Louis	Night Charge Nurse/Night Supervisor, Clifton and Bootham Park Hospitals (1975–97)	
Yates, Ms Rowena	Clinical Assistant, Clifton Hospital (1979–90)	O

Appendix 10
Commissioned experts and their reports

Expert	Report
Dr Gwen Adshead, MB, BS, MRCPsych, MA (Medical Law and Ethics), Consultant in Forensic Psychotherapy, West London Mental Health Trust	*"Sexual boundary violations in psychiatric practice: an overview. Confidentiality and disclosure of medical information"* co-written with Professor Roy McClelland *"Sexual boundary violations by doctors: Confidential Report of Advice to the Kerr/Haslam Inquiry"*, co-written with Sameer Sarkar
Dr Michael Crowe, DM (Oxon), FRCP, FRCPsych, Late Consultant Psychiatrist, South London and Maudsley NHS Trust, Late Honorary Senior Lecturer, Institute of Psychiatry (Kings College, London), now consulting at 21 Wimpole Street, London	*"Psychosexual Therapies and Sexual Abuse in Psychiatric Practice, and the Scope for Improving Safeguards for Vulnerable Patients and Mental Health Professionals"*
Dr Tanya Garrett, BA, MSc (Clinical Psychology), MSc (Psychotherapy), PhD C Psychol, AFBPsS, Chartered Clinical and Forensic Psychologist Honorary Senior Lecturer, University of Birmingham	*"Sexual contact between mental health professionals and their patients: Ethical issues, codes of conduct, research findings, typologies and recommendations for policy and procedures in the NHS and improving the safety of patients"*
Professor Gisli H. Gudjonsson, Professor of Forensic Psychology at the Institute of Psychiatry, King's College, London, and Head of the Forensic Psychology Services at the Maudsley Hospital	*"The Assessment of Allegations of Sexual Abuse in Psychiatric Practice, and the Scope of Improvements in the Handling of Concerns and Complaints"*
Dr Jeremy Holmes, MD, MRCP, FRCPsych, UKCP, Consultant Psychiatrist/Psychotherapist, Devon NHS Partnership Trust, Professor of Psychological Therapies, University of Exeter, and Psychoanalysis Unit, University College London	*"Note of Expert Advice on Aspects of Psychiatric Practice in Response to Questions from the Panel"*
Dr Michael G Jeffries, BSc, MB, ChB, DCCH, FRCGP, General Practitioner, Betws-y-Coed Practice	*"The Professional Duties and Obligations of General Practitioners in the Handling of Allegations, Concerns and Complaints Made by Patients Referred to Specialist Services"*
Professor Roy McClelland, Consultant Psychiatrist, Belfast City Hospital, Professor of Mental Health, Queen's University Belfast, Chair, Confidentiality Advisory Group, Royal College of Psychiatrists	*"Sexual boundary violations in psychiatric practice: an overview. Confidentiality and disclosure of medical information"* co-written with Dr Gwen Adshead

Expert	Report
Professor Linda Mulcahy, LLB, LLM, PhD, Anniversary Professor of Law and Society, School of Law, Birkbeck College, University of London	*"Description of the NHS Complaints procedures for Committees of Inquiry into the performance and conduct of Neale, Ayling, Kerr and Haslam"*
Sameer P. Sarkar, MD, Consultant Forensic Psychiatrist, West London Mental Health Trust	*"Sexual boundary violations by doctors: Confidential Report of Advice to the Kerr/Haslam Inquiry"*, co-written with Dr Gwen Adshead

Appendix 11
Inquiry seminars presenters and participants

Local seminars – Presenters

Seminar 1: **Handling concerns and complaints by people with mental vulnerabilities**

Presenters: David Brown – Director of Mental Health, Craven, Harrogate & Rural District PCT

Julie Finch – Head of Patient Safety & Governance, Craven, Harrogate & Rural District PCT

Seminar 2: **Disclosure and sharing of Information**

Presenters: Mrs Rachel Ingham-Jones – Associate Director of Human Resources, Selby & York PCT

Mr Gary Millard – Director of Mental Health and Social Inclusion, Selby & York PCT

Dr Jim Isherwood – Medical Director – Provider Services, Selby & York PCT

Seminar 3: **Protecting patients**

Presenters: Dr Jim Isherwood – Medical Director – Provider Services, Selby & York PCT

Mr John Brown – Associate Director of Corporate Affairs, Selby & York PCT

Seminar 4: **Psychosexual therapies and professional autonomy In psychiatric practice**

Presenters: Dr David Butler BA (Hons), Msc, DClinPsychol, AFBPS – Consultant Clinical Psychologist, Selby & York PCT

Mr Gary Millard – Director of Mental Health and Social Inclusion, Selby & York PCT

Local seminars – Participants

Martin Coyle – Coordinator, Advocacy Network, Leeds

Nick Parsons – Partner, Browne Jacobson Solicitors

Louise Carney – Browne Jacobson Solicitors

David Brown – Craven & Harrogate Rural District PCT

Geoff Griffiths – Business Relationship Manager – Commission for Social Care Inspection

Michael Mylonas – Counsel acting for Irwin Mitchell Solicitors

Kate Thirlwall QC – Counsel acting for Browne Jacobson Solicitors

Dr Robert Ashworth – Postgraduate Dean, Yorkshire Postgraduate Deanery

David Sneath – Regional Chair (Leeds), Employment Tribunals (England & Wales)

Fiona Peel – Lay Member, General Medical Council

Finlay Scott – Chief Executive, General Medical Council

Rachelle Mahapatra – Solicitor, Irwin Mitchell Solicitors

Diane Edwards – Leeds Mental Health Advocacy Group

Hilary Dyter – Advocacy Manager, Leeds Mental Health Advocacy Service

Bill Harland – Mental Health Legislation and CPA Manager, Leeds Mental Health Teaching NHS Trust

Bridget Gill – Head of Corporate Services, North & East Yorkshire & Northern Lincolnshire SHA

David Thompson – Assistant Director for Performance Improvement, North & East Yorkshire & Northern Lincolnshire SHA

Jayne Riggall – Complaints Manager, North & East Yorkshire & Northern Lincolnshire SHA

Sally Casley – Acting Head of Clinical Governance, North & East Yorkshire & Northern Lincolnshire SHA

Tanya Matilainen – Head of Patient Experience, North & East Yorkshire & Northern Lincolnshire SHA

Peter Kennedy – National Institute for Mental Health in England, Leeds Mental Health Teaching NHS Trust

Steve Shrubb – Director, North East Yorkshire and Humber, Leeds Mental Health Teaching NHS Trust

DCI Neil Thewsey – North Yorkshire Police

Dr John Givans – Medical Secretary, North Yorkshire Local Medical Committee

Di Troup – Area Services Manager, Rethink

Dr David Geddes – Medical Director, Primary Care, Selby & York PCT

Gary Hardman – Director of Nursing and Workforce Development, Selby & York PCT

Mrs Rosemary Davis – Head of Psychosexual Therapy Service, Selby & York PCT

Chris Binns – Solicitor, Switalski's Solicitors

Dr Michael Crowe – Expert Adviser to the Inquiry

National seminars – Presenters

Seminar 1: **Psychosexual therapies and professional autonomy in psychiatric practice**

Presenters: Dr Michael Crowe, DM (Oxon), FRCP, FRCPsych
Dr Sameer Sarkar
Dr Gwen Adshead

Seminar 2: **Protecting patients**

Presenters: Dr Michael Crowe, DM (Oxon), FRCP, FRCPsych
Professor Linda Mulcahy

Seminar 3: **Handling concerns and complaints by people with mental vulnerabilities**

Presenters   Professor Gisli Gudjonsson
Professor Linda Mulcahy

Seminar 4: **Disclosure and sharing of information**

Presenters: Professor Roy McClelland
Jane O'Brien

National seminars – Participants

Wendy Hesketh – Academic Lawyer

Peter Walsh – Chief Executive, Action Against Medical Accidents

The Revd John Eatock – British Association for Counselling & Psychotherapy

Corinna Furse – Chief Executive, British Association for Sexual and Relationship Therapy

Barry Gower – Vice Chair of The Ethics Committee, British Association for Sexual and Relationship Therapy

Sally Openshaw – Chair – British Association for Sexual and Relationship Therapy

Lou Corner – Chair, British Confederation of Psychotherapists

Penelope Garvey – Member, British Confederation of Psychotherapists

Mary Twynham – Member, British Confederation of Psychotherapists

Leslie Forsyth – Director of Operations (North), Commission for Public & Patient Involvement in Health

Steve Carney – Head of Complaints and Service Improvement, Commission for Social Care Inspection

Gerald O'Hagan, Deputy Regional Director – South East – Commission for Social Care Inspection

Michael Mylonas – Counsel acting for Irwin Mitchell Solicitors

Kate Thirlwall QC – Counsel acting for Browne Jacobson Solicitors

Chris Bostock – Head of NHS Complaints and Clinical Negligence Project Team, Department of Health

Liz Fleck – Head of Complaints and Clinical Negligence, Department of Health

David Sneath – Regional Chairman, Employment Tribunals (England & Wales)

Fiona Peel – Lay Member, General Medical Council

Finlay Scott – Chief Executive, General Medical Council

Dr Joan Trowell – Member, General Medical Council

Dr Judy Gilley

Gurpreet Chahil – Head of Patient Complaints, Healthcare Commission

Richard Mash – Head of Legal Services, Healthcare Commission

Trish Longdon – Deputy Parliamentary and Health Service Ombudsman

Jon Wigmore – Acting Director of Complaints Investigations, Health Service Ombudsman

Michael Wood – Health Service Ombudsman's Office

Hilary Scott – Independent Development Consultant, HSD Public Service Development

Anne Jones – Assistant Information Commissioner (Wales), Information Commissioner's Office

Yens Marsen-Luther – Chief Executive, Institute of Mental Health Act Practitioners

Rachelle Mahapatra – Solicitor, Irwin Mitchell Solicitors

Dr Iain Barclay – Head of Medical Services (Leeds), Medical Protection Society

Christopher Heginbotham – Chief Executive, Mental Health Act Commission

Steve Klein – Mental Health Act Commission

Henrietta Marriage – Head of Legal Unit, MIND

Dr Peter Old – Associate Director (Advice and Support), National Clinical Assessment Authority

Professor Alastair Scotland – Chief Executive – National Clinical Assessment Authority

Rachel Munton – Interim Programme Director NIMHE Black & Minority Ethnic Mental Health Programme and Director of Mental Health Nursing, National Institute for Mental Health in England

Susan Williams – Joint Chief Executive, National Patient Safety Agency

Chris Bostock – Head of Complaints and Clinical Negligence Team – NHS Complaints and Clinical Negligence Project

Sandy Taylor – Chief Executive, County Durham & Darlington Priority Services NHS Trust

Jacky Hayden – Postgraduate Dean, North Western Deanery

Liz McAnulty – Director of Fitness to Practise, Nursing & Midwifery Council

Rachael Kenny – Manager, Patient Advice and Liaison Service

Jonathan Coe – Chief Executive, Prevention of Professional Abuse Network

Police Inspector Heather Gay – Project Sapphire, Metropolitan Police

Dr Geoff Roberts – Director and Medical Adviser, Warrington PCT

Dr Alan Cohen – Member, Royal College of General Practitioners

Dr Iona Heath – Member, Royal College of General Practitioners

Steve Jamieson – Head of the Professional Nursing Department, Royal College of Nursing

Dr Fiona Subotsky – Senior Officer, Royal College of Psychiatrists

Dr David Roy – Medical Director, South London & Maudsley NHS Trust

Mike Bowen – Quality Assurance and Regulations Manager, United Kingdom Council for Psychotherapy

Frances Blunden – Principal Policy Adviser, Which?

Appendix 12
Other Inquiry reports referred to

"Learning from Bristol: the report of the public inquiry into children's heart surgery at the Bristol Royal Infirmary 1984–1995" Cm 5207, The Stationery Office, 18 Jun 2001

"The Shipman Inquiry – Fifth Report – Safeguarding Patients: Lessons from the Past – Proposals for the Future" Cm 6394-I, II, III, The Stationery Office, 09 Dec 2004

"Investigation into issues arising from the case of Loughborough GP Peter Green" Commission for Health Improvement, 30 Aug 2001

"The Bichard Inquiry – Report" HCP 653, The Stationery Office, 22 Jun 2004

"Committee of Inquiry Independent Investigation Into How The NHS Handled Allegations About the Conduct of Clifford Ayling" Cm 6298, The Stationery Office, 09 Sep 2004

"Committee of Inquiry to Investigate How the NHS Handled Allegations About the Performance and Conduct of Richard Neale" Cm 6315, The Stationery Office, 09 Sep 2004

Appendix 13
Expenditure of the Kerr/Haslam Inquiry: July 2001 – July 2005

Type of expenditure	2001/02[1,2] £k	2002/03 £k	2003/04 £k	2004/05 £k	2005/06 £k	Total £k
Panel[3]	–	52	29	278	54	413
Counsel	–	13	22	292	18	345
Legal fees[4]	–	–	16	257	–	273
Expert contributors	–	4	–	43	1	48
Staff	24	97	193	650	61	1,025
Premises	53	19	–	274	–	346
Information technology & telecommunications	17	27	2	521	34	601
Other administrative costs	23	24	34	75	2	158
TOTAL	117	236	296	2,390	170	3,209

These are the full provisional accounts up to the publication of the Inquiry Report. Final accounts will be prepared in due course.

NOTES

1. The financial year runs from 1 April to 31 March.
2. The Inquiry was announced in July 2001 and the Secretariat established shortly thereafter.
3. The Chairman and Panel Members were appointed on 31 January 2002.
4. Costs of the legal representation of former patients and other participants.